Searching for Equity

Sólo le pido a Dios
Que lo injusto no me sea indiferente

Searching for Equity

Conceptions of Justice and Equity in Peasant Irrigation

Rutgerd Boelens
Gloria Dávila
(editors)

Preface by Nobel peace Prize-Winner Rigoberta Menchú

1998

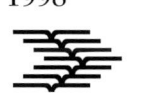

Van Gorcum

© 1998 Van Gorcum & Comp. B.V., P.O. Box 43, 9400 AA Assen, The Netherlands

ISBN 90 232 3385 9

Layout and printing by: Van Gorcum, Assen, The Netherlands

Presentation

One of the most urgent and important problems humanity will be faced with in the 21st century is the one of the availability and distribution of water. As we all know, water is vital for the natural world and human life. In this respect it is not surprising that it is often compared to life itself. However, together with the growth of the world population, the process of industrialisation, the intensification of agricultural production and the unequal expansion of the (water) consumer society, we have been witnessing the increasing scarcity of water and the contamination of this same resource in the last decades.

The growing shortage of water calls for appropriate and equitable management, to ensure that both current and future populations can live in a situation of 'sufficiency' and that not just the affluent, but the poor and oppressed, can benefit and have their rightful share.

Apart from focusing on the wider framework of (in)equity and (in)justice in society and rural development, this book highlights the use and distribution of water for irrigation purposes in peasant societies. As an illustration, it concentrates upon a central case: the Andes. Irrigation is not only a key activity for the alimentation of the world's population, it also constitutes a very important social arena where people and institutions meet to distribute the benefits and the burdens of the agricultural production process. In this daily struggle, characterised by unequal power structures, it is not uncommon to see that peasants, indigenous and poor people increasingly have to pay the costs of the growing water scarcity, and that, in addition, they carry most of the burdens.

The authors who contributed to this book come from very divergent backgrounds: sociologists, lawyers, peasant and indigenous leaders, economists, irrigation engineers, anthropologists, community workers, agronomists, and so on. Together, they offer an enormous range of expertise and academic experience from all over the world, to deal with the theme of equity and justice in peasant irrigation. They show that the questions of water demand, availability and distribution, as well as the distribution of other rights and obligations in irrigation, do not just depend on climatic and physical conditions, but are man-made. In this area, public policy, national legislation and development interventions have more than once played a role in continuing or accelerating existing processes of social differentiation. Notwithstanding its structural foundations, the actual - man-made - social injustice can and should also be counteracted by human efforts and creativity.

In this search for equity, the very diverse and rich conceptions of social justice in rural society and peasant irrigation, as well as its translation in forms of social organisation, will have to be given a prominent place. Which is exactly the aim of this book. As such, we hope and foresee that the contents of the book will make an important contribution to the urgent debate on equity, among policy makers, development institutions, peasant and indigenous organisations, scholars and students and others who are involved in the field of rural development. A debate that should not only remain academic or rhetorical, but should result in changes towards more social justice in the practice of water distribution and irrigation development in peasant societies.

Hans Simons,
Chairman of the board,
SNV

Contents

Part VIII   Andean Irrigation, Organisation and Equity

Reflections
Rutgerd Boelens & Gloria Dávila

Acknowledgements

This collective book is the fruit of a long and rich communication process involving many persons who were convinced of the importance of its central theme. To all, our true gratitude.

The authors have contributed their experiences, creativity, visions and ideals to the present book and to the very necessary and important debate about how to achieve more justice and equity in rural development in general and, specifically, in the areas of irrigation and water distribution. We would like to give them especial thanks for the work they have carried out.

We also would like to express our gratitude to the Netherlands Development Organisation (SNV), the Swiss Agency for Development and Cooperation (SDC), the Royal Dutch Embassy in Ecuador, the German Agro Action, the Interchurch Organisation for Development Cooperation (ICCO) and Wageningen Agricultural University, for their generous assistance in the publication of this book.

Many persons have helped us in the writing and editing process. For all their stimulating support we would like to thank Hans Achterhuis, Jos van Aggelen, Vicente Alvarado, Ludolf & Germen Boelens, Aeilt & Aly Boelens, Gaby Brohet, Patricia Camacho, Mariana Collaguazo, Bea Coolman, Lina Cuenca, Bernita Doornbos, Hugo van Drunen, Geert van Duinhoven, Gerda de Fauw, Trudy Freriks, Lou Franssen, Antonio Gaybor, Gerben Gerbrandy, Marjan Haitsma, Erik Heijmans, Misha Heijmans, Jan Hendriks, Luís Heredia, Lida Miranda, Cily Keizer, Piet & Ina Keun, Esther & Robert Keun, Jeroen Kroezen, Humberto Latacunga, Hugo Olazával, Rosanna Manosalvas, Peter Meier, Eric de Milliano, Peter Mollinga, Joost Oorthuizen, Isabel Palpieris, Verónica Peña, Lizette Poelstra, JanGeert vander Post, Daniel Prieto, Leida Rijnhout, Luís Rodriguez, Gladis Sarango, Noeke Ruiter, Yvonne Sluper, Lupe Valencia, Linden Vincent and Enrique Vela.

Very special thanks are due to Samuel Dubois, Patricio A. Mena Vásconez and Sara van Otterloo for the exceptional work they have performed on the translation and successive revisions of this book. Without their support the book would not be what it is.

Rutgerd Boelens & Gloria Dávila
Arnhem - Quito, July 1998

Preface

by Rigoberta Menchú Tum
Nobel Peace Prize-winner
UNESCO Goodwill Ambassador

Let us begin the preface to this valuable book by saying that we are increasingly being assaulted by the process of globalisation. As Uruguayan writer Eduardo Galeano stated during his visit to Guatemala in mid-1996, this so-called globalisation is a process that tends to perpetuate the dependence of Southern countries on those in the North. Globalisation emphasises free markets, in both domestic and international economic relationships. This free market means freedom of trading without any kind of barrier. The process intensifies day by day, putting Third World economies at an increasing disadvantage in relation to the so-called First World. It is a response to the State-intervention economic model, i.e. the benefactor State. This model has failed. It was supposed to curb the growing impoverishment of the majority of our countries' population and also solve the marked mismatches and economic crises in the economies of developed countries. But this economic model has not only increased poverty, it also failed to solve the cyclical economic crises in the First World.

The globalising process has economic impacts but also penetrates all walks of our societies and communities. Our cultures are facing an outside ideology with concepts that try to standardise values and norms, erasing our knowledge, logic, capacities, historical foundations, and the variety of our communities and organisations. This great diversity can be seen in many areas, including the field of local water management. In many indigenous communities throughout our continent, water and irrigation are indispensable for community agriculture and survival. Water is life. For many centuries, peasants and indigenous peoples have created their irrigation systems, their organisations and their working patterns in order to operate and maintain these systems collectively. A basic fundament has been, and still is, the set of agreements among families and communities to equitably distribute rights and duties within the production system. Despite the immense variety of practices and customs related to peasant irrigation, the collectivity seeks to balance benefits and burdens with social justice.

However, globalising agricultural exploitation processes are not aware of or do not recognise this reciprocity that characterises our conceptions of water and irrigation. National laws do not respect our visions either, and often impose a blanket vision of justice and organisation that is not ours. They correspond to outside logic and rules that do not achieve justice either in irrigation or in the distribution of water for other community activities. Communities, according to the rules of liberalisation, are also confronted by increasing scarcity, as water is monopolised by a few powerful players. In many modern irrigation projects and systems, the wealthy become wealthier and the poor poorer. Thus, our communities' water, land and production rationality are increasingly taken over by others.

In general, the current globalising process drags us all along with it and tends to affect especially the poor majorities, including indigenous peoples. Historically, the dependence of Southern countries, where most indigenous peoples live, makes them receivers of First World agricultural technology and inputs. The impact of these so-called modern agricultural technologies and inputs on the South is varied. Firstly, we have to take into account that technology transfer also implies culture transfer. Not only machines and materials are transferred but also norms and ideologies. Secondly, many technologies transferred from developed countries to underdeveloped ones are obsolete. Thirdly, technologies sent to us from the North are often highly predatory and polluting, with immediate and long-term consequences for the environment and natural resources. Indigenous peoples face a capitalist logic that is totally different from and opposed to their own logic. This logic has a severe impact on indigenous communities since it does not fit into their social context, it denies their cultural traditions and identity, and it does not consider the need to preserve the environment and to optimise the sustainable use of natural resources. Over-exploitation of what little land they have, by applying a short-term capitalist rationality of production, is causing the gradual abandonment of fundamental cultural values, such as the sense of community and maintaining a reciprocal relationship between humans and Nature. This last value is fundamental for maintaining an ecological balance.

This does not mean that each indigenous people's culture is or should be static, that they are not undergoing changes, or that they must remain immobile over time. The problem is that the cultural transformation, in its current expression, has negative implications from the standpoint of human survival; moreover, these changes are provoked by interests that are external not only to our own peoples' development but also to the collective interests of humanity itself.

Undeniably the new ways of working, the new logic of production and the use of so-called modern technologies have a quick positive effect, since they certainly increase the short-term productive capacity of the land. However, thinking of the future, in the long term the positive effects are dwarfed by the cumulative damage that destroys the environment, natural resources and human relationships. Gradually, the sense of community which characterises indigenous peoples is destroyed as competition and individualism are fostered.

Furthermore, the use and application of most modern technologies in Southern countries are very closely related to the agrarian structure, i.e. land and water tenure.

Modern production relationships fit into conventional capitalist modes of agricultural production, in which the *minifundio/latifundio* (peasant/plantation) relationship is fundamental. Therefore, usually the introduction of modern technologies is strongly linked to relationships exploiting farm workers who, in the case of Latin American countries and many other parts of the world, are indigenous. Moreover, after the incorporation of outside 'modern' technology, peasants and indigenous people not only often lose their own norms, reciprocal working relationships and specific knowledge about the environment and production methods; usually it also means less demand for labour, plus other social consequences that increase and deepen poverty to extreme levels. We can see daily that these processes accelerate rural-urban migration and even migration to other countries, which can be temporary or permanent. The immediate consequence is family disintegration, and the family is still the basic organisational and functional structure within peasant and indigenous communities. It expresses and gathers our community vision, despite the deep changes it has undergone during over 500 years of imposed cultural values and organisational forms foreign to American indigenous peoples.

To this family breakdown we must add the gradual loss of identity through insertion of peasants and indigenous people into another culture, abandoning their own cultural practices and values. This acculturation process can result in total assimilation into the dominant culture. Of course, this is not an irreversible tendency; but exactly because of that, it is necessary to recognise and respect our rights including the right to our culture and to recover and develop it, establishing new inter-cultural relationships based on unrestricted mutual respect.

Can a traditional technological model be compatible with modern technology? How can this be achieved? The answers are not easy, but a first step towards this goal would be to adapt modern technology to the conditions of indigenous communities. In other words, their culture, their social, economic and political settings must be considered. For example, for many years several NGO initiatives in a number of countries, including those from the North, have accompanied local efforts that promote organic agriculture, to ensure sustainable production and safeguard biodiversity, land and water. Organic agriculture, of course, is not new. It has its origins in the birth of agricultural societies and reached high levels on the American continent through a long process of development by the Aztec, Inca and, many years earlier, Mayan civilisations.

In the same way, it is fundamental to base development and improvement of irrigation systems on indigenous technologies and production modes. We know of ancient cultures, such as the Incas in the Andes, who had extensive expertise in the art of irrigating and organising. Present-day communities also have important irrigation knowledge, abilities and customs directly related to the indigenous culture, feasts, rites and community life. Reciprocal relationships and the search for equity within a solid organisation largely determine the strength of a community and its potential for its own sustainable, dignified development.

Achieving a constructive relationship between these two types of technologies calls for a technological exchange on equal footing. This way Southern countries, especially peasants and indigenous people, will be able to use modern agricultural technology according to their own needs, culture, and social, economic and political environment, with immense possibilities to improve modern technologies on the basis of their concept of sustainable development.

Finally, it is necessary to insist on one important issue. As a consequence of the globalisation process, we, indigenous people, are increasingly facing an approach to production that goes against our own. The process fosters competition and individualism in the constant search fuelling capitalism: increasing profits and over-concentration and centralisation of capital. It has deepened the scourge of inequities affecting Southern countries in favour of those in the North, placing the former in a situation of greater dependence and increasingly widening the breach between wealthy and poor people in Southern countries. Globalisation promotes predatory development that is destroying our planet and with it our possibility to reproduce as human beings. The way wealth is produced and distributed has degenerated into rapid deterioration of the environment and natural resources. The inadmissible concentration of wealth in a few centres excludes most of humankind from the benefits of scientific and technological advances and productive integration. In the world of globalisation, science and technology matter in so far as they perfect production techniques and methods in order to become more competitive. The aim is to boost productivity in order to beat the competition. In this race to get the upper hand economically, the environment and natural resources are only the means to an end: the unbridled build-up of wealth. Ecological deterioration and worsened poverty as a consequence of ever-greater concentration of riches in the coffers of the wealthy few are simply statistics jeering at Nature.

Equitable, sustainable development will remain a dream if the irrationality of the universalising economic model is not abandoned; if the ultimate goal is the individual and not the community; if the Northern countries' political, social, economic and cultural processes still feature the yearning for a greater and increasingly rapid accumulation of wealth and concentration of capital, dragging the Southern countries along with them.

This imposed development logic confronts us as indigenous peoples, and it is clear that this logic goes against our traditions, culture and identity, and we are evidently at a disadvantage. Overcoming this disadvantage is a challenge we must face, at the threshold of the 21st century. It will be necessary to sever the ties of discrimination and isolation, consequences of centuries of the racism that has characterised relationships between non-indigenous against indigenous people. This will call for technological and knowledge exchanges among different cultures and peoples. Indigenous peoples have an enormous potential to foster sustainable development with social justice. Equitable, sustainable development can be described as a process of gradual, dynamic change in communities' quality of life. The fundamental axis

and subject of development is human beings; the foundation is the process of production and distribution on the base of sufficiency and social justice. Forms of production and consumption habits should ensure environmental conservation and
recovery seeking harmony between human beings and Nature.

Equitable, sustainable development will not be viable without respect for historical
and cultural diversity as the foundation to build peoples' indispensable unity. This
will entail, as a basic element, equal rights and opportunities among men and women
of the community, while respecting our cultural values and norms. It implies unrestricted citizen participation in the exercise of genuine democracy, in collective decision-making. Such equitable, sustainable development is one of the roots of the
Peace tree and will, at the same time, guarantee a decent life for the generations of
the coming millennium.

The contents of this book, related to the search for equity and the conceptions of
social justice in peasant irrigation, are very illustrative of the potentials and abilities
of peasants and indigenous peoples in the search for sustainable development. This
alone makes it valuable.

Rigoberta Menchú Tum
Guatemala

Prologue: 'Agua'

Rutgerd Boelens

> *To the peasants and 'lackeys' of the Viseca hacienda, with whom I have shivered during chilling night-time irrigation, and danced at carnival festivals, inebriated with joy, to the rhythm of the tinya and the flute.*

This is the opening dedication of the book 'Agua', written by Peruvian anthropologist and author José María Arguedas.[1] Few people have sought to understand the roots of the Andean society with such personal conviction and commitment as he did. Arguedas wrote his books, not as an outside observer of the Andean rural world, but as a participant, living in it, and he told its stories 'from the inside', from the experiences lived by the peasants and indigenous peoples. He often lived and recounted the happenings of this world through the character of a child, Ernesto, just as he did in the story of 'Agua'. Although he was the son of white parents, he shared the world of the indigenous peasants, and spoke the Quechua tongue. Arguedas grew up among the indigenous people, in the town near a hacienda. His father was a 'rebellious' lawyer who roamed around the country to keep away from the authorities. Arguedas accompanied his father during his childhood years, and this began his longing for learning about this Andean world, for participating in the thoughts and visions of peasants, men and women.[2]

The little-known story 'Agua', or 'Water', portrays an accurate image of certain core problems of water distribution practices in the Andean irrigation reality. It touches on a wide range of themes including ethnic identity, history, indigenous world-view, migration, organisation, oppression and the peasant struggle for justice. It provides an ideal introduction and background for the present book on equity in peasant irrigation. We analyse several excerpts from 'Agua' below, in order to highlight certain issues that will receive special attention later in this book.

As Arguedas shows us, irrigation in the Andes is not located in an ahistorical context; rather, it is the result of developments in pre-Conquest, colonial and contemporary times. Irrigation water, which was the foundation of major civilisations in the Andes, has also been the motivating resource for an ongoing struggle among several stakeholders, and has often fostered the inhuman domination of the many by the few. Irrigation water in the Andes is both lifeblood and power; it can make people come to life, and it can make them suffer.

> *"San Juan is fading away", the horn-blower said. "The plaza is the heart of a town. Just look at our plaza, it's worse than the puna* [3]*"....*
> *Tayta Inti must surely want the earth to die, because he glared straight down with all his might. His rage made the world burn, and made men cry...*
> *There was no more pasture on the hillsides; only dry bushes; brown, leafless, they lent the mountain slopes a certain air of vegetation and scrub brush.*
> *"The little farms of the poor peasants of Tile, of Saño and all over, are all pale, just like that. It's because of don Braulio's bad temper. Taytacha God has nothing to do with it, my little Ernesto".*
> *"That's true. Don Braulio's maize, don Antonio's, doña Juana's is all plump, nice and green - there's even mud on the ground. And what about the peasants? Dry, bowed, withered; it hardly even sways in the wind."*

In 'Agua' the large landowner in the region of San Juan, don Braulio, appropriated all irrigation water. Once a week, he arbitrarily distributed a little to the small farmers in the four communities of San Juan. Many families depended on this water to irrigate their dry land and feed their children. This dependence, together with the uncertainty about receiving this vital resource or not, strengthened the power of the landlord, and fostered internal division and fatalism among the peasants.

> *"Water, little Ernesto. There's no water. San Juan is going to die because don Braulio gives water to some people, but he hates the others."*
> *"But don Braulio says he has made the water common for everyone, by taking it away from don Sergio, from doña Elisa, from don Pedro..."*
> *"That's a lie, boy. Now the whole month long it is for don Braulio, and the water distributors are afraid; they tremble when they think of don Braulio."*

Many families got no water, or didn't get it when they really needed it. Pantaleón, a man just back from the Coast, felt sadness and rage when he saw how the landowner oppressed the peasant families. What hurt the most was how the peasants just accepted this situation. He called people together with his horn.

> *"There's land, Pantacha, but the water is lacking. You'd better make your horn wail to get people to come."*
> *The peasant brought his horn up to his mouth, and began to play a blacksmith's tune. In the silence of the morning, the horn's voice was strong and cheerful, scattering through the little hamlet, and encouraging it... Like every Sunday, when they heard his horn playing, people began coming to the village square.*
> *Every Indian in town surrounded us. Some began to repeat the huayno in a low voice. Many women raised their voice, forming a chorus...*

The role of Pantaleón - known affectionately as Pantacha - is central in this story. He had been born in the zone and was a *comunero* like all of them. He knew the communities intimately and received great respect from them. His commitment to his people led him to fight for them, but he knew that changes must not and cannot come from outside, but must come from within.

> "*Where does don Braulio get his money? He takes it away from the comuneros; he steals the water; he takes it away right in front of our eyes, from the people, from the animals, from the Indians. Don Braulio is as hungry as a stray dog.*"
> *Bernaco sat down next to me and whispered in my ear:*
> "*This Pantacha has come back from the Coast with an attitude. He says all the big bosses are thieves.*"
> "*It must be true, Bernaco. Pantacha knows*"...
> *Pantacha looked at us, one by one; his eyes shone with tender affection.* "*Mak'tillos! Mak'tillos!*"
> *He raised his horn and began playing the huayno that the San Juan people sing when they clear out the big canal from the K'ocha reservoir.*
> *The peasants' eyes reflected the tenderness that they felt for Pantaleón; they regarded him as an elder brother...*

Travelling in other parts of the country had given him a chance to broaden his outlook. He had seen injustice elsewhere, and this led him to rethink his own ideas about equitable distribution of water in his own region, in San Juan. Water must not be distributed like alms to the peasant irrigators, it is not a matter of charity, it is a matter of *rights* and *equity*.

> ..."*on the Coast, the top-dogs take all the water, too; the small tenants who rent the land, they irrigate at the end, along with those who have two or three plots; they give them a little, as if it were alms to a beggar, and their land is thirsty year after year. However, the main bosses in Nazca have more money; any one of them could buy all of San Juan, with all its maize fields, its alfalfa fields and its livestock. They are just like gringos, all of them, tough guys, and they and their workers get their own way as if they were Taytacha, the big boss in the church.*"

As in the case of Pantaleón, in processes of development and change, outside ideas and proposals or people can often act as 'sparks' or catalysts: they confront the existing situation with a new alternative. Of course, this does not always result in beneficial changes. Sometimes the new proposal offers wonders and leaves behind only disappointment. Sometimes the proposed alternatives cannot compete with existing forces, bent on maintaining the prevailing structure of domination. This is not often taken into account by development project and programme planners. Not only the *contents* of the alternative proposal, but also the constellation of powers and the cumulative experience of the peasant community lead poor and oppressed families to decide whether to change or hold on. When all is said and done, after a few years the projects leave the site, but the peasant families remain to bear the consequences...

Pantacha spoke of rising up, of revolt, and they were afraid of that, remembering what happened to the Chaviña comuneros. In Chaviña, they tore down eight leagues of fencing that don Pedro put up on community land; they ran don Pedro off, fleeing for his life. But then the soldiers came to Chaviña and shot people right and left, their old people and their children; the only ones who escaped were those who ran off into the hills.

Depending on each case, on the power structures and room for manoeuvre to change the current situation, the peasants' logic for survival may be innovative and creative, or suffocating and paralysing. In 'Agua', the network of social relationships between the landlords and the villagers and *huasipungueros* basically reinforced acquiescence to structures of domination and inequitable distribution of vital resources. In some cases, it even led to opportunism among the dependent peasants, who would try to lean on the more powerful actors to avoid ending up in a worse situation. Don Inocencio is a clear example of this:

"Sanjuankuna!", said don Inocencio, "Don Braulio has lots of money, the hills and fields belong to him. If our cow gets onto his field, he starves it to death in his own stable; he can have us whipped, if he feels like it. Let's defend don Braulio, I say. Pantacha is just a horn player, he's not the big fish."

Another important role in the paralysing, conservative structure is played by the protégé of the powerful ones, don Vilkas. He was related to the *mistis* in town by *compadrazgo* and *compañia* arrangements, so he often acted as the large landowner's spokesperson, his *mayordomo*, controlling and overseeing his own people. Don Vilkas was an old man, and lived in a cave belonging to don Braulio. He also got land from the boss to plant his own crops; he was an Indian with privileges that the boss gave him because he helped the landlord.

Don Vilkas was respected by almost all the villagers. When they distributed water, when they divided up responsibilities for celebrations, don Vilkas always spoke up.

It would be too simple to speak of just two opposing classes in the struggle for water. In Andean communities, there are many interest groups and social relationships for survival that go to make up complex, changing networks, and give rise to contradictions and alliances among the different actors. They call for a more profound analysis of the local reality and the logic of production. To distribute water, irrigators not only consider the volume of this production factor in relation to the land to be irrigated, but also the different relationships that must be respected. Here, respect for leaders, for elders - 'taytas' - such as don Vilkas, is a key element.

Don Vilkas, as a link between the peasants and the *mistis*, and because of the respect in which he was held, was a decisive factor in the people's fatalistic outlook on irrigation water. He was very angry about Pantaleón's music and rebellious talk:

"Sanjuankuna: you are making Taytacha God angry with your dancing. When the land is dry, there is no dancing. You have to pray to our patron saint, San Juan, to send us rain"...
We turned around to look at don Vilkas: he was furious.
"What's that, tayta?", Pantacha asked him.
"The main issue is to be respectful, you horn-blowing mak'ta!."

Never before in the plaza of San Juan, had a villager spoken up against the bosses. On Sundays, they would gather in the hallway of the jail house, whining for water, and then dragging back home; whether they got an irrigation turn or not, they felt bitterness in their hearts, thinking that their poor maize fields would finally dry up completely this week. But this Sunday Pantacha shouted out boldly against the mistis. In front of don Vilkas he called the main bosses to account...
The horn-blower got up on the dividing wall in the hall; he looked every single peasant straight in the eyes, and they were afraid.
"But listen, there are so many of us, and only two or three bosses"...

The story that Arguedas presents shows that peasant conceptions about 'equity' are diverse, changing, not unilateral. He also shows us that a critical conception alone is not enough to achieve greater justice in irrigation; users also need power and, therefore, they need organisation and resources to materialise this justice.
For that reason, the dominant class was afraid of organised peasant sectors, such as the Tinkis:

"Tinkis, they are real comuneros!", exclaimed the horn-player.
Don Vilkas looked down on the Tinkis; when he saw them in the square, he would proudly raise his head, but then he would watch them until they reached the hallway; he was afraid of them, because they were united, and because their varayok', who had studied the law, did not have much respect for the mistis.

So, the issue of equity in water distribution cannot be isolated from the issue of water users' organisation, their resources, their power and their capacities. Pantacha understood this, and so did don Vilkas.

Pantacha laughed out loud, looking at don Vilkas.
"Jajayllas!" He put his horn to his lips and played the comical huayno of the wanaku-pampas:

Akakllo from the rocky fields,
noisy little birdie from the boulders;
don't tease me, akakllo.
Pretentious akakllo,
misti engineer, they call you
jajayllas akakllo!

Show me how you drill holes
jajayllas akakllo!
Show me your papers.

In this *huayno*, Pantacha pokes fun at don Vilkas, but not only at him. Why does he call him a *misti engineer*? Perhaps because the peasant communities know that engineers usually take the side of their own class, that academically-trained professionals, like lawyers, technicians, judges and other learned folks, have mostly helped the well-to-do? Perhaps because the peasant families understand that the 'pretentious engineers' have rarely tried to actually understand the peasants' own way of thinking; that, consciously or unconsciously, a technician understands the landlords' way of thinking better? It is a fact that the high-sounding speeches of the intellectual class seldom result in coherent, consistent practice in the field. Sometimes they lack the knowledge or ability to understand peasant conceptions; other times they are not open or do not wish to understand this world, which does not coincide with their own interests.

Meanwhile, the tension in 'Agua' reaches its climax. Don Pascual came to the plaza, since it was his turn to distribute the water this week.

"Sanjuankuna, ayalaykuna, tinkikuna!", cried out the voice of Pantaleoncha, "Don Pascual is going to give k'ocha water to the people who need it. This will surely make don Braulio mad; but Pascual is the one to distribute, don't you think?"
In a moment, Pascual came up to speak: "We agree with the musician Pantacha. This week, the k'ocha water is going to don Anto, to widow Juana, don Jesús, don Patricio... Don Braulio will be upset. But at least once, poor folks will get water this week... Tayta Inti makes the rain go away; k'ocha water is all we've got to irrigate; the k'ocha will fill up this time for the comuneros."

"Good work, don Pascual!"
"Don Pascual, distribute as your conscience leads!"
"Listen to your conscience, tayta!"
"Yes, your conscience!"
"Don Braulio abuses the peasants. We, the community, will demand the respect we deserve. The k'ocha water will be for the Indian folk!"
"That's true, neighbour: in our town, there are only two or three mistis, and so very many of us... They are people just like us, with eyes, a mouth, a belly. K'ocha water for the people!"
"You see? Mama-allpa, mother earth, she gives water for everyone equally."

Obviously, this was not the opinion of the boss, don Braulio, who arrived in the plaza just then, and heard what Pantaleón and don Pascual were saying. He was drunk, and had his assistants with him. The villagers, who had seemed ready to face up to the boss and stand up for their rights to equitable water distribution, got scared.

The big boss demanded to hear how the water was to be distributed:

> *Don Pascual jumped up on the table... "Monday for don Enrique, don Heracleo;*
> *Tuesday for don Anto, widow Juana, don Patricio; Wednesday for don Pedro, don*
> *Roso, don José, don Pablo; Thursday for..."*
> *The boss jerked upright as if they had whipped him across the back; his eyebrows rose*
> *like the crest of a fighting cock; and rage shot out from his eyes.*
> *"Friday for don Sak'sa, don Waman..."*
> *"Pascualcha, shut up!", shouted don Braulio...*
> *"Don Braulio, k'ocha water is for those who need it, no one owns the water!", shouted*
> *Pantacha.*
> *"Comunkuna folks first!", added don Wallpa.*
> *The boss whipped out his gun...*
> *Pantacha raised his horn up high. Like the midday sun, his gaze was burning, and*
> *raged in his eyes. He leaped onto the cursed misti... Don Braulio pulled the trigger and*
> *the horn-playing mak'ta fell, belly-down, on the stone floor.*

After Pantacha was murdered, Pascual and some peasant leaders were jailed. 'They chickened out: they forgot their courage... Like roosters from another henhouse, they just stood there, staring at the ground'. The villagers fled, 'overtaking each other, still intimidated, looking back from time to time'. Little Ernesto stayed behind, furious.

'Agua' was written in 1935 and shows part of the roots of the current situation. The peasant conceptions of equity in Andean irrigation are not simply derivations of the so-called 'pure Indian world-view': Arguedas shows the influences of colonial and postcolonial power relationships, of strict hierarchy, of the process of *mestizaje*. He shows both the perception of fatalism and the protests and rage against unfair circumstances. Arguedas wrote with the blood of his heart, to express his solidarity with and profound commitment to indigenous peasants, and his despair at outside domination and abuse of power. He was part of two separate worlds, two apparently incompatible worlds, tearing him up. Understanding, feeling and forming part of the world of the oppressed and at the same time living and being part of the world of the ones in power who denied the values of the first was too much for him. As Eduardo Galeano wrote, his feat of giving these peoples a voice was also his curse:

> He felt that everything he had was betrayal or failure, a useless tearing apart. He
> could not be an Indian, he did not want to be white, he could not stand to be both
> the contemptuous and the despised. He walked the lonely road bordering this
> abyss, between the two enemy worlds dividing his soul. Many avalanches of
> anguish came down around him, worse than any landslide of mud and stones;
> until he was crushed. (Galeano 1986)

With the vision that the future would be even worse, that the subordination of the Andean indigenous world by the white-mestizo society would destroy the peasant communities, tearing apart their culture and sapping their strength, Arguedas drew the only personal conclusion that he could: in 1969 he committed suicide.

In 'Agua', little Ernesto, or José María Arguedas himself, takes stock of what he has seen happen:

> Watching them drag Pantacha away, rage filled me until my soul overflowed. "Wikuñero allk'o dog!", I shouted after don Braulio.
> I jumped into the hall, feeling just like a man, a real man, just like Pantacha. I am sure that the soul of auki Kanrara got into my body; I couldn't stand the hugeness of my rage. I wanted to split open, bursting my chest, my veins, my eyes.

In another book about injustice and the issue of equity in the Andean countryside, "El jinete insomne" (The sleepless horseman), Peruvian author Manuel Scorza (1991), after searching for equity and recognition of communities' rights, concludes:

> " There is nothing to celebrate", said Bustillos, "We have failed. The engineer failed us.
> We have no land registration map."
> "Next time, I will hire the engineer myself".
> "That will do us no good, sir," insisted Bernardo Bustillos.
> "I have proven what I wanted to prove."
> "And what did you want to prove?"
> "I have proven that we can't prove anything! And when all people understand that it is impossible to prove a just cause, then the rage will begin. I leave you as a legacy the only thing I have: my rage."

Will it be possible, in this book, to get closer to the issues of justice and equity in irrigation? After so many failures, and the worsening of social injustice in processes of rural change and development, it is important to try. However, the issues are also extremely complex. We cannot speak of a single conception of equity in irrigation, because there are many different concepts. They even vary within peasant communities themselves, and within a single peasant irrigation system. Sometimes these ideas are complementary, and sometimes they are contradictory. But even so, it is indispensable that we investigate this diversity and draw workable, well-thought-out conclusions, because historically the pre-established recipes and blueprints applied in the field of irrigation have always tended to reinforce injustice and structures of domination. For this reason, even when viewing such diverse conceptions, an attitude of cultural relativism - as if all concepts were equally valid - is out of place. Conscious, critical, participatory analysis is of key importance.

Ecuadorian author Jorge Fernández wrote another novel entitled 'Agua', in 1936, one year after Arguedas. His book, based on an approach of social realism, describes a conflict about water between the peasants and huasipungueros of a hacienda, against the landowner and local authorities. An apparently fair distribution of water was destroyed by the wealthy. Manipulation of distribution; expropriation of water rights by legal authorities; deception by some peasant leaders; disappointment in the attorney's false efforts; this all results in a desperate fury among the peasants. In the subsequent uprising, the large landowners and authorities win the battle, but at the price of a large-scale massacre, in which both parties really lose out. Fernández (1985) concludes:

> All these lovely, fruitful fields, which are like an immense heavenly garden, are in mourning, bloodstained because of the struggle over water...
> In the end, neither the one nor the other has any place within justice.

In everyday life, peasants often show that confrontation under unequal power positions is not the only answer possible; there are various ways to give expression to peasants' resistance and the day-to-day struggle for equity. Perhaps, according to the local conditions, another way can be found, or if not, such a new pathway may be built, in order to take the opposite direction. Arguedas shows that the fundamental pre-condition for respecting different forms of equity and justice is freedom for all human beings, room for manoeuvre in order to make one's own decisions, without bonds of subordination or imposed regulations:

> *The community members from Utek'pamba are better than those from San Juan and the ones from Tinki in the puna. Proud Indians, masters of their destiny...*
> *The fields of Utek' are never melancholy; they live far away from the sky; even if the fog is black, and the storm is booming over the earth, Utek'pampa is cheerful...*
> *Utek'pampa: Indians, mistis, outsiders and others, everyone is comforted when they see it, away up there past the canyons, gazing up from the roadways!*

Arguedas - speaking through little Ernesto - concludes the story of 'Agua' with hope for change and the quest for liberty, in which equity is lodged:

> *All alone, on that parched hillside that afternoon, I cried for the villagers, for their small fields charred by the sun, for their starving animals. The tears filled my eyes; the clear sky, the plains, the blue hills all trembled; Inti, ever-larger, ever-hotter... scorched the world. I fell on the ground...*
> *And then I ran down the hill, to join forces with the organised peasants who own their fields and live in Utek'pampa.*

* * *

Almost seven decades after 'Agua', we can see that the forms of oppression and the social relationships of production and distribution have changed. However, often the results of resource distribution, as in the case of water, have not changed much. At present, public and private irrigation project efforts, and water laws, often plan water distribution on the basis of prescriptions with criteria that are supposedly 'universal and objective', but in fact are technocentric and legalistic.

Has the present-day project taken the place of the former hacienda? Are we, today's engineer, lawyer or sociologist, the new version of yesterday's *mayordomos*? Let us reflect on this.

Notes

1   The quotations from Arguedas' novel 'Agua', used in this text, are translations of parts of the Spanish edition of the novel (Arguedas 1987), published by Editorial Horizonte in Lima, Peru. Italics and bold characters are the author's own addition.
2   See, among others, Galeano (1986), Zoon (1982) and Flores Galindo (1988).
3   For Quechua and/or local words, please see the glossary below:

Glossary (Quecha/Spanish folk):

auki	=	holy hill or mountain
compadrazgo	=	'godfathership', often with an asymmetric character
compañía	=	sharecropping, a relationship exchanging production factors
comunero	=	member of an Andean indigenous and peasant community
huayno	=	a kind of traditional Andean music
huasipunguero	=	indigenous (semi) serf, bound to the hacienda by extra-economic force.
Inti	=	the sun
¡jajayllas!	=	exclamation of conceited contempt
k'ocha	=	lake
mak'ta	=	young man
mak'tillo	=	boy
mayordomo	=	foreman of the hacienda, representing the boss
misti	=	person belonging to the dominant classes, usually (although not necessarily) of mixed Spanish and native ancestry (mestizo)
puna	=	highest ecological zone of the Andean highlands
tayta (taytacha)	=	respectful term like 'sir', also used for the most influential community member, and for God.
Varayok'	=	mayor of an Andean community
!Wikuñero allk'o!	=	Vicuña-hunting dog!

(source: Arguedas 1987; and the editors).

References

Arguedas, J.M., 1987 (1935). 'Agua'. In: *Relatos completos*. Editorial Horizonte, Lima, Peru.
Fernández, J., 1985 (1936). *Agua*. Editorial El Conejo, Quito, Ecuador.
Flores Galindo, A., 1988. *Buscando un Inca*. Editorial Horizonte, Lima, Peru.
Galeano, E., 1986. *Memoria del fuego III. El siglo del viento*. Siglo Veintiuno Editores, Madrid, Spain.
Scorza, M., 1991. *El jinete insomne. (Cantar tres)*. Siglo Veintiuno Editores, Mexico City, Mexico.
Zoon, C., 1982. 'José María Arguedas: Diamanten en vuurstenen'. In: *Volkskrant* 22 -10 -1982.

About this Book

Rutgerd Boelens and Gloria Dávila

The topic

Anyone knowledgeable about rural development will have heard the stories and may have examined the critiques of many irrigation projects' impact on the issues of justice and equity. Often, large investments increase production, but at the price of accelerating social differentiation among people living in the area of influence, between water haves and have-nots. The less privileged can seldom break out of the vicious cycle of poverty, whereas the more powerful groups often can strengthen their social and economic position. Many studies have criticised major injustices within rural development, some of them analysing the unfair distribution of water resources in irrigation development. This book will make no attempt to repeat or summarise what has already been written on this topic. It is not the purpose to just question the 'Great Injustice' of unequal water tenancy and accumulation but, above all, to focus on the more subtle processes of social justice and injustice that accompany daily practice in rural development and irrigation intervention. They demonstrate that the strong clamour for 'Greater Equality' is indeed very important in the struggle for redistribution of water resources, but concurrently they show the importance of enlarging the strategic space for Diversity, characterised precisely by local differences and expressed in historical and contemporary peasant irrigation development processes. The latter is necessary in order to avoid destroying the normative foundations of endogenously generated systems, supplanting people's own rules by 'modern', supposedly universal standards; and in order to promote the creation of strong peasant systems, well-suited to people's specific circumstances and considered equitable by the users. This is about the paradox of the right to equality and the right to be different, within the field of peasant irrigation.

Although they have received little concrete attention in irrigation intervention practice, several studies have argued that users' conceptions regarding equitable distribution of rights and duties in their irrigation system are the basic building-blocks for systems that not only will be fairer but also more sustainable, more productive and better managed. However, what are these conceptions, and how can they be assessed? How are they rooted in history, in local culture, in organisational forms and processes of negotiation among different interest groups? How can we cope with the enormous diversity, contradictions and dynamic interrelationships among these con-cepts? How are these concepts linked with or opposed to the concepts of equity held by 'outside' stakeholders who intervene in the rural reality? How can peasant concepts of equity be materialised through concrete irrigation practices? How do legalistic policies and infrastructural biases in projects place hurdles in the way of creating equitable, sustainable, community-managed systems? These are some of the core questions that will be addressed in the following chapters.

To address the issue of equity in peasant irrigation, it is clearly insufficient just to analyse the distribution of irrigation water resources alone. We must also examine the distribution of other rights related to irrigation practice, as well as the distribu-tion of obligations involving peasant irrigation. Further, it is also necessary to broaden the analytical focus since there are generally other users who require the same water, but for other, non-agricultural uses. And it is necessary, moreover, not to limit the approach solely to the level of the irrigation system, since part of the causes of injustice and various potential means for change toward a more equitable situation are often lodged within the system's interaction with external actors and related to the system's position within overall social structures. Therefore, any analy-sis must be multidisciplinary - this book's authors come from a wide range of disci-plines and fields of work.

Indeed, irrigation manuals contain guidelines on how to calculate crop water requirements, how to design irrigation canals and distribution structures, how to improve irrigation efficiencies, how to distribute water 'rationally' among plots, etc. However, there are no instructions on how to address the *fundamental* problem of equity in irrigation systems. Even so, we shall not attempt to seek equitable rules with universal validity, or an allegedly generic peasant position on the issues of jus-tice and equity in community irrigation. We would like to foster and facilitate deeper, broader reflection on these issues, as a piece of the groundwork for much-needed debate and to encourage and promote location-specific discussion in all particular cases.

How this book's contents are organised

The book is divided into an introductory section, eight parts with conceptual and empirical contributions, and finally some reflections. Of these eight basic parts in the book, the last four focus on the book's central case, which is peasant irrigation in the Andes region.

Chapter contents and section sequence are structured like a funnel, from general approaches to more particular cases and analyses (see Figure 1).

general and conceptual analysis of norms and values, equity and justice

(in)equity and (in)justice in the *peasant and indigenous world:*
power structures and peasant rights

equity in *peasant irrigation:* some central themes and conceptual contributions

equity in peasant irrigation in *specific cases,* in various continents of the world

social framework for irrigation and equity in the central case: *the Andes*

equity, peasants and *policy and legislation* on irrigation in the Andes

conceptions about equity in Andean irrigation: *cases and experiences*

notes about *achieving equity* in Andean irrigation: the peasant organisation

GENERAL

ANDEAN CASE

Figure 1: Thematic structure of the book

Thematically, the book begins with an overall conceptual analysis of the issues of justice and equity, in Part 1. Issues of values and norms - imposed or self-constructed -
are addressed. Part 2 examines issues of equity and justice in the peasant and indigenous world, with its power structures, peasant advocacy processes, normative frameworks and peasants' common-law systems. Part 3 concentrates on the issues of
peasant irrigation in general. The chapters in this part present some conceptual tools
and ideas relating irrigation with the theme of equity. Part 4 also looks at concepts
of equity in irrigation, but specifically. These chapters analyse equity in concrete
cases of peasant irrigation, from various countries the world over.

The following parts 5 to 8 go more deeply into the book's core area: conceptions
regarding equity in peasant irrigation in the Andes. Accordingly, Part 5 starts with a
conceptual framework and overall backdrop for the cultural, historical, socio-geo-
graphical and socio-economic setting for irrigation in the Andes. Part 6 presents a
critical analysis of policies and laws on irrigation and water resources in several
Andean countries. During the last several years, an intensive debate has been, and is
still going on about water resource legislation in these countries. Next, Part 7 probes
the issue of equity conceptions in Andean irrigation by analysing concrete cases in
several Andean countries. Part 8 presents approaches and concepts regarding
Andean irrigation, with reflections about how to put concepts of equity and justice
into practice in specific irrigation systems. The Reflections at the end of the book are
not a conclusion summarising the preceding chapters' ideas, but rather bring
together several central themes of the book and present the editors' reflections for
further discussion.

PART I

EQUITY AND JUSTICE

Introduction

Dreams and nightmares are made of the same materials, but this nightmare claims to be the only dream we are allowed: a development model that despises life and worships things.
Can we be like them? The politicians' promise, the technocrats' raison d'être, the fantasy of the needy: the Third World will become the First World, and will be rich and cultured and happy, if it behaves itself and does as it is told, without balking or objecting. A prosperous destiny will reward the starving for their good behaviour, in the last chapter of the soap opera entitled History. *We can be like them*, according to the gigantic lighted billboard burning alongside the road leading to developing the underdeveloped, and modernising the backward.
But *what cannot be, cannot be, and anyway, it is impossible* [...] The world's precarious balance, teetering on the edge of the abyss, depends on perpetuating injustice. Many must be poor to enable a few to squander. (Eduardo Galeano, 1995, in: *Ser como ellos*, Tercer Mundo Editores, Bogota).

Pursuing dreams imposed by others, accepting *their* definition of real needs, universal knowledge and true justice, seeking to be equal with them as the maximum expression of equality, these are functional aspects for maintaining and reinforcing the existing power structures.

Discourses emerge and policies are implemented under conditions of unequal power. Out of so many varied ideas, experiences, concepts, practices, norms, identities and social relationships that exist the world over, the only ones considered as important and true are those that come from or are associated with the visions and rationalities of the most powerful groups and societies.

This is not only a subjective opinion of the controlling sectors, but an ideology and reality, most often interiorised by and shared with the groups that lack power: the mutual acceptance of this reality actively disempowers those who have the least power to start with.

Concepts about justice, equality and equity do not elude this logic. Their practical definition and implementation are often dominated by the groups, sectors, entities and societies of the powerful. More and more often, local concepts about these values - based on a specific historical background, a logic of their own, differently expressed and applied - are uprooted and cast adrift in the community. They are standardised and institutionalised according to the criteria and norms of *others*, who can thus more readily establish the rules of play, concealing their own interests and formulating policies that justify their interventions. This is reflected, for example, in the field of peasant irrigation.

If justice is grounded in equal treatment for all, and if the contents are imposed from outside, by the universal model for development and progress, by hegemonic groups or by 'the nation', what concept of equality are we talking about? What or who is the point of reference to develop the models?

Equality is always in reference to others, which leads to a question: equal to whom or to what? Equality so everyone will increasingly try to assimilate and copy those who dominate and control the production of 'knowledge'? Equality that calls for running the gamut already defined by those who colonise the truth, imagination and social reality?

Or are there other pathways that, crossing with and getting to know other diverse paths, lead to people's own concepts of equality and equity?

> I am my own foundation,
> I go beyond actual historical facts,
> to begin the cycle of my own freedom.
> (Frantz Fanon, 1970 (1952) *Peau noire, masques blancs*. Editions du Seuil, Paris).

1

Justice and Equity: a Critical Perspective

*Pat Lauderdale**

Theories on justice and equity, and guidelines for putting them into practice in the West, are often found in philosophical literature. Justice as a concept is presented as universal and transcendent rather than grounded in a social reality that has a particular historical and comparative context. Most of the dominant theories focus on what justice *should be*. They use concepts such as equity or fairness in various ways rather than studying how justice is defined by people in specific places and at particular times. These concepts increasingly are exported and imposed via hegemony (Gramsci, 1971), often through processes of cultural imperialism (Fanon, 1970). The recent claim, for example, that the world is now engaged in a battle for justice between homogenous globalization (vulgarized as McWorld) and secessionist self-determination (misrepresented as Jihad) is quite misleading.

Nozick's entitlement/libertarian view, Mill's utilitarianism, and the social contract of Rawls via Kant represent some of the more popular Western theories of justice and will be outlined below. Justice from an entitlement perspective emphasizes the importance of private property and individual freedom in reaction to the increasingly controlling role of the State. Entitlement stresses the importance of liberty and efficient economic relations - whereby liberty is posited as more crucial than equality. As a philosophical treatise on justice, this view suggests that in the interest of fairness we should place liberty ahead of equity.

While emphasizing that there should be respect for individual rights in acquisition and transfer of property, such a system of social relations has not been realized in practice. In fact, its assumptions about justice in acquisition and transfer have not only proved unworkable, they are a central part of the allegiance or entitlement for the privileged and typically reproduce or increase inequality in class and community relations. In addition, following a strict reading of this framework, most current property holdings would be unjustified because of the transgression of rights in acquisition, manifested by the appropriation of land by colonizers from indigenous peoples throughout the world. When implemented, entitlement theory has placed efficiency (e.g. violation of individual rights) before equity, and greater inequality has ensued (Frank, 1996).

Justice from a utilitarian view, following Mill, usually calls for providing the greatest utility or happiness for the greatest number, the majority. A central part of this theory demands that people treat each other equally, yet equity can be sacrificed for the greatest utility or happiness. Even more problematic is how the majority often has been defined, e.g., Aristotle's exclusion of slaves, and modern nation-states' exclusion of indigenous peoples in their native nations. The *majority* typically is defined as those who support implicitly or explicitly the Western Liberal Project or narrow meanings of rational 'man' or technological development. Yet, who is the majority in the world system? Following current standards from most international organizations, the majority of the population in the world consists of 'minorities'. Moreover, within many societies the *real minority*, i.e., those peoples treated as such, has been defined as the indigenous communities.

Rawls employs the concept of a social contract to provide a fair procedure for autonomous choices, and as the foundation for ethical principles. Rawls posits that people should make such choices without knowing the specific impact on themselves. This social contract metaphor, then, uses a veil of ignorance to correct such possible inequities. Behind this veil, people make decisions about the principles of procedurally fair resource allocations. Yet, the role of conventional planning and policy-making in implementing the contract reveals a consistent allegiance to uncritical plans of development with, once again, efficiency before equality. Planning and planners often do not serve the interests of justice because the planners or their political authorities serve their own interests at the expense of others. Rawls' just principle - inequities favoring some would be justified only if they benefited all - seems circumvented or suffocated.

The problems mentioned above can be addressed by deriving principles of justice within a particular historical and comparative context. That is, justice can be conceptualized within social relations and material conditions that are *specific and concrete*. In this context, justice can become an important idea for analyzing change, 'development,' and the use of law. Legal equality is an abstract ideal that often has been employed as a metaphor for justice. Following the Western model of liberalism, in the United States in the 18th century, for example, the individual was defined as independent and autonomous, the fundamental unit of society. Rather than viewed as subjects of queens or kings, individuals were defined as citizens of the State who were born equal and free. Yet, these definitions excluded the majority of the society. Under the declaration that all 'men' are created equal, women and slaves were ignored. Legal equality for women and slaves did not become a fact until the 20th century. Legal equality, therefore, was a metaphor that emerged from specific, historical conditions.

A naive acceptance of legal equality and justice has led to the belief that their realization is concentrated in proper State activities and that law is a politically neutral guarantee of equality and freedom. Another metaphor often equated with achieving justice is that of progress. The granting of political emancipation for women in the

1920s in the U.S. and their leadership roles in various political institutions today is viewed as a modern condition resulting from or an expression of progress. A comparative, historical examination can, once again, place such progress in context. In North America, indigenous Iroquois women chose chiefs for *centuries before* Canadian laws granted equality between men and women. The Iroquois confederacy is governed by its own laws, constitution and government. The League of the Iroquois, created some time between A.D. 1000 and 1450, under a constitution called Kaianerkowa or Great Law of Peace and ratified by the five nations which composed the Iroquois league, consisted of a council composed of delegates elected by their nation. The imposition of Western notions of formal legal equality contravened the understood assumptions of these indigenous cultures.

People organize information differently in a schematic manner and individuals will develop one particular schema instead of another for explaining what they view as reality. Certain ideas and events are identified and acted upon while others are ignored or suppressed. This brings us to the need to analyze which view of reality, of justice and of equity is used, and who are the actors that developed or imposed this view. Such an analysis requires an examination of the relationship between 'schemes of interpretation' and specific social relations. This analysis includes: (1) the social organization that enables the definers of social 'reality' to do their defining; and (2) the relationship between power and the mechanism by which information is disseminated. Power is intimately connected with knowledge. Those who generate and control knowledge are often perceived to speak the truth. '"Truth" is linked in a circular relation with systems of power which produce and sustain it, and to effects of power which it induces and which extend it - a "regime" of truth' (Foucault, 1979).

Justice, then, is a concept that is useful when we examine how it is constructed in different social and political situations and how it is used as a source of legitimation for the development and use of rules such as law (Lauderdale, 1997). The study of justice includes an analysis of the fair distribution of benefits and burdens, including rights, obligations, desserts, and needs. This approach includes analyses of public plans and policies set up to implement ideas of justice. This grounded approach attempts to mitigate the view of researchers as technicians who are unable to translate findings for the benefit of practitioners and the view of the practitioner as only placing 'Band-Aids' on problems of social justice and equity. Moreover, this study of justice differentiates between short and long term impacts of change, and the problem of well-intentioned suggestions for change that may result in unfortunate consequences. The comparative and historical analysis of theories and practices of justice is an important alternative to most of the philosophical perspectives on what justice should be.

The comparative and historical analysis of justice considers the crucial role of non-economic factors such as religious beliefs and ideology which people sometimes privilege over the goals of Western development. Liberation theology, to take just one possible example, appeared as a religious social movement in reaction to the binding ties between the elites and the Catholic Church. The ties exacerbated gross inequities, especially those of land use and ownership. By the late 1960s, the movement received worldwide attention, primarily through the publication of Gustavo Gutiérrez's *A Theology of Liberation* (Gutiérrez, 1972). The theology begins, not with theory, but with the realities of injustice experienced by the peasants and indigenous people of Latin America. It calls for individuals, communities, and corporate entities to be involved in a series of choices. The choices involve extricating oneself from serving the interests of the rulers of society in exchange for working for the marginal and oppressed of society. The goal is to establish solidarity and live and work daily with the oppressed. These people include anyone who has been dominated: the economically poor, the politically oppressed, the sexually discriminated.

From this perspective on injustice experienced, justice is seen as a structural phenomenon with the dynamics of the world market system portrayed as unjust. Such an approach seems consistent, for example, with the structural relationships in peasant societies. There is convincing evidence that most peasants maintain and practise, first and foremost, the norms of reciprocity and the right to sustenance, rather than the dynamics of a market system of profit or accumulation, even in the face of major obstacles (Scott, 1985). Working with the oppressed is interpreted as a pragmatic prescription to fight poverty and oppression and to liberate people here and now.

Some approaches to justice, therefore, stress the development of peoples and not economies, noting the conditions under which economic dependency works against community- determination and autonomy (Lauderdale and Cruit, 1993). In essence, the argument is about whether certain kinds of growth could really solve the problems at hand. Sacredness is found in the relationship between the land and the people who work it. The dominance of capital as the developing principle contradicts the ethical principle that labor must be given priority in development of an economy based upon justice. There must be an ethics of means as well as ends. The turgid scholasticism found in many ethnocentric theories of justice based on Western philosophy can profit from analyses of where perceptions of justice emerge (Oliverio, 1997).

Homogenous development proposals which are based solely on abstract and universalistic criteria have been unable to respond to indigenous peoples and peasants throughout the world who are still experiencing the full presence of injustice in the form of poverty, landlessness, dispossession, political and religious oppression, and genocide. Philosophical formulas become hollow without systematic explorations of the sources of injustice, including those within indigenous and peasant societies. These examinations include, at least: (1) the continued exposure of exploitation in labor relations; (2) an analysis of how participants are excluded from the creation of policy agendas and decision-making processes; (3) an explication of factors leading to the erosion of community solidarity and identity, and the right to sovereignty; and (4) the long-term cost to nature when it is defined in modern terms as separate and subservient to humans rather than defining both humans and the environment as nature. Of course, this work includes being aware of the conflicts within indigenous and peasant groups - there is diversity within diversity and monolithic formulas have proven disastrous.

* * *

The modern State has legitimated its control and expanded its jurisdiction by deconstructing indigenous solidarity, experiential education and family and community welfare, as it constructed national citizenship, formal education, and limited forms of government welfare for individuals. The concepts of nation-state and citizen were presented as major sources of solidarity and identity, emphasizing an abstract concept of nationalism. Formal education, especially higher education, with rigid hierarchical organization, unbridled competition, and dichotomous conceptions of students such as bad versus good, was touted typically as superior to experiential learning. The State centralized welfare amidst claims of its progressive care, yet modern forms of State welfare often have created varying levels of stigma for recipients and the State has created new and disproportionate forms of repressive punishment.

Indigenous peoples often resist State-centered development because it destroys their culture and nature. Such people are confronted with problems that developers take for granted, including free expression of language and religion, the right to live within self-determined cultures and traditions, and basic sustenance such as clean water, air, and land. For approximately thirty years, Frank (1996) has analyzed the exploitative relationships between centers (technologically developed countries and cities), and satellites (technologically underdeveloped countries and areas). Frank has shown how the indigenous people of Latin America, rather than having had development pass them by, have suffered the butt-end of capitalist development. They have been marginalized not because they occupy remote areas of the country but because they occupy the final hinterland of the last metropolis and they therefore bear upon their backs the weight of all the other satellites.

We also should be aware that no monolithic group of indigenous peoples exists per se and that struggles for equality, equity, and justice are largely particularized, responsive to specific crises and situated within a given cultural context. Individual peasants also often diverge depending on their position relative to the issue at hand, whether it be hydroelectricity, irrigation rights, land claims, or self-determination. In this regard, we come back to the difficulty with the 'McWorld vs. Jihad' characterization noted at the beginning of this chapter. Such vulgarizations imply a choice of strategies limited to assimilation or secession, and fail to acknowledge the dialectical nature of the conflict between totalization and particularism, corporate monoculture and bio-regional diversity, and abstract universalism versus indigenous identity. Despite the apparent penetration of the 'Third World' by technology, cultural capital, and the world market, it may well be that in the approaching millennium, the world will witness the triumph of wisdom over knowledge, teaching us how to live in balance with the natural environment and create sustainable communities in the true spirit of justice and equity.

Note

* I appreciate the thoughtful comments of Randall Amster, Rutgerd Boelens, and Annamarie Oliverio. Also, I want to thank Andreas Gunder Frank for bringing me into this project.

References

Fanon, Frantz. 1970. *Black Skin, White Masks*. New York: Grove Press.

Foucault, Michel. 1979. *Discipline and Punish*. New York: Vintage Books.

Frank, Andreas Gunder. 1996. The Underdevelopment of Development. pp. 17-55 in: *The Underdevelopment of Development*, edited by Sing Chew and Robert Denemark. London: Sage.

Gramsci, Antonio. 1971. *Selections from Prison Notebooks* (translated by Quentin Hoare and Geoffrey N. Smith). London: Lawrence and Wishart.

Gutiérrez, Gustavo. 1972. *Teología de la Liberación*. Salamanca, Spain: Ediciones Sígueme.

Lauderdale, Pat. 1997. Indigenous North American Jurisprudence. Forthcoming in: *The International Journal of Comparative Sociology.*

Lauderdale, Pat and Michael Cruit. 1993. *The Struggle for Control: Law, Disputes, and Deviance*. New York: NY Press.

Oliverio, Annamarie. 1997. *State of Terror*. New York: SUNY Press.

Scott, James C. 1985. *Weapons of the Weak: Everyday forms of peasant resistance*. New Haven: Yale University Press

2

Reclaiming Equality, Equity and Diversity

Annamarie Oliverio

The modern State's impact and involvement in issues concerning equality, equity and diversity cannot be underestimated. The State is the political apparatus that dominates society. From human rights to civil rights, social movements, protest groups and dissident writers have consistently appealed to the State either directly or indirectly to establish systematic and equitable laws and practices by which societies and people can live. Yet, inasmuch as the State rhetorically involves itself in such phenomena, its inherent political structure lends itself to processes of standardization but not necessarily equality; uniformity but not necessarily diversity; and institutionalization but not necessarily equity.

Equality, as it is defined and applied by the modern State, is an abstract term that has not been substantiated in reality. The State claims to abolish distinctions among people that are determined by birth, social rank, education and occupation by declaring these as non-political distinctions. It proclaims legal equality for every member of society by treating the diverse elements which compose the real life of a nation from the standpoint of the State. But the State, nonetheless, does allow the existence, development and institutionalization of social differentiation through private property, education and occupation. Far from abolishing such differences, the State exists only so far as they are presupposed (Inverarity et al., 1983).

Yet, equality has been a major demand of civil rights and peasant movements all over the world. Rights to vote, go to school and work have not resulted in an equal voice or equitable politics for all diverse groups of a society. Orwell's platitude that 'all of us are equal, but some are more equal than others,' crudely illustrates this point. Equality is not possible in a State based on hierarchy, domination, power and transcendence to a specific standard: the standard imposed by a 'western ideology' (Fanon, 1987).

Inherent to the principle of equality, then is the notion of assimilation. The State, because of the standards upon which it is based, its presuppositions, is designed to transcend symbolic elements of difference and diversity. Women, for example, as symbolic elements of patriarchy, or ethnic minorities, as symbolic elements of racism can only become 'equal' once they have assimilated and adopted the values, standards and principles of a stratified, hierarchical society. In this way the State often obscures fundamental racism and patriarchy.

State policies attempting to provide equitable solutions such as affirmative action for diverse groups are laden with similar fundamental problems as 'equality' policies. The State's provision of equity tends to focus on the integration of subordinate groups into mainstream society, rather than acknowledging their diverse conscious-ness and values. Ideal-type categories are constructed by the State, not to be used as analytical departure points for recognizing differences in social consciousness by cul-ture, subculture or regions, but as definitive definitions of diversity which when applied have the ironic consequence of denying diversity and therefore equity.

Cultural policies as they are produced in specific institutional sites including State agencies, private think tanks, universities, schools, museums, galleries, community arts centers, heritage sites, theme parks, media industries and rural and urban devel-opment projects negotiate the texts, programs and planned environments of their intended subjects. Furthermore, such policies interact with political and economic forces. Thus, representations of 'multiculturalism' or 'tolerance' are created in the image of market demands and rhetoric. In this context, the construction of equity, like that of equality, is more rhetorical than substantive in its claims of diversity and vulnerable to the same fundamental constraints of a State that privileges domination and relations of power.

It is a small wonder that globalization processes, including the expansion of vio-lence, technology, media, communications, global markets, international production of goods, immigration and tourism, usually act as if to obliterate differences between people and cultures. Differences are to be transcended. Indeed, to consider issues of diversity or resistance rather than State-defined national and international political boundaries is often viewed as inefficient, costly, naive and sometimes dangerous (Oliverio, 1997). Consider, for example, the sacred land interests as defined by var-ious indigenous groups. The State has responded to such interests by ignoring or redefining them and coopting the land under the labels of 'development' and 'progress' or by defining such claims and actions as deviant, subversive or 'terrorist.'

Rather than simply bemoan (or celebrate) such inexorable processes of Western-type uniformization and globalization, it is important to understand them. While in prison, Gramsci (1971) attempted to understand such seemingly paradoxical processes via his examination and development of the theory of hegemony. For Gramsci, hegemony is produced via the practices of 'institutions and organizations whose task it is to influence common sense' (Augelli and Murphy, 1988:24). Institutions such as education, media, and government organizations are involved in a process of generating information that appears simple and devoid of any intrinsic political problems or philosophical critiques. Teachers, for example, will often end-lessly repeat certain simplified concepts to children until those concepts become part of a common, normal, 'taken-for-granted' unquestioned understanding.

Another practice involves the creation and implementation of political policies promoting socially accepted conventions combined with different and new interpretations. Gramsci, as one example, notes numerous instances from his own Italian society of State legislation combining conventional Catholic conceptions (existing for centuries) with new Fascist programs (cf. Caldwell, 1986). A similar process can be observed in the interaction between the creation of multicultural programs within conceptions of 'traditional Euro-American values.' Thus, hegemony, according to Gramsci, while referring to a dominant ideology, does not necessarily refer to a repressive process in its infusion. Religious leaders, educators, government agents, legal and medical experts, researchers, development institutions and the media all partake in practices of disseminating and promoting certain dominant, paradigmatic interpretations of reality. And, of course, language and text as vehicles by which to communicate and disseminate information are inextricable to this process of producing hegemony.

The way in which the State sustains paradoxical relations and outcomes was also essential to Gramsci's theoretical formulation of hegemony. One of the most central and seemingly irreconcilable paradoxes that led Gramsci to develop the concept of hegemony was the unquestioned acceptance of a Fascist, elitist regime by the largely peasant Southern Italian region during the twenties and thirties. This fundamental paradox spawned a number of contributing paradoxes, some of which directly questioned Italian aestheticized representations of reality among literature, arts, theater and public, national media (Gramsci, 1966). The economic strife of the Southern Italian region, the needs as defined by the people, could not have logically predicted their allegiance to an elitist political system (cf. Augelli and Murphy, 1988; Mouffe, 1979). The Fascists made promises to 'develop' and modernize the southern Italian region while still allowing the people to maintain their Catholic traditions. Other political parties, such as the Communists, made no such promises. In other words, as was mentioned before, a policy had been developed which combined traditional, conventional values, with a new ideological proposal. Development and modernization, however, meant different things to the people and to the State ('paese reale' versus 'paese legale'), Fascist or otherwise. This difference or contradiction, between the interests and the wishes of the people on the one hand, and on the other, the implicit contents of the official program, is a fact with which Italians continue to struggle in their current political structures and practices. This paradox is readily forgotten by modern society or defined as a historical aberration rather than a structural process of domination by States.

All societies possess culturally constructed and socially organized processes for remembering and forgetting the past. Symbolic forms, including narratives and stories, express the past and relate it in complex ways to current social interests. As such, they commonly produce multiple (often conflicting) versions of the past and at particular historical moments, they may become sites of intense struggle. This would appear to be the situation in a number of modern nation-states all over the world. Various groups of people worldwide are strongly challenging State representations and definitions of their cultures and needs. And, such challenge groups are often met with hostility and violent retaliation as States aim to protect their territorial sovereignty at the expense of people's economic and political sufficiency.

Discourses of democratic participation, political correctness and the promise to preserve cultural diversity stand in stark contrast to the disparities that exist in reality. Paradoxically, the latter part of this century has produced some of the most intractible and passionate conflicts over cultural homogeneity. Even in the U.S. where the State actively denied its indigenous roots, slavery and immigrant contributions in the attempts to construct a distinctively 'American' culture, the claims made by diverse groups are increasingly undeniable as they challenge the application of a specifically Euro-American culture and values in resolving problems of rapid change, equity and justice.

At the present historical moment, the U.S., for example, may be viewed as a site of intense discursive struggle over the construction and interpretation of its national past. Groups defined as subordinate, including racial, gender, religious and issue-interest groups challenge dominant representations of history. These included on-going challenges posed by indigenous groups resurrected during the Columbus Day historical rendition and recent 'race riots' in Los Angeles reminding the public that nearly forty years after the Civil Rights movement, African Americans are still not treated equally or equitably by the State's social control agents and agencies.

Complex societies throughout the world are rich with different social groupings and diverse people. Maintaining the production of the past as a monolith is becoming increasingly difficult in States where multiple and oftentimes conflicting versions of the past exist simultaneously in place and space. Furthermore, the exportation and imposition of such monolithic representations globally produce little more than resentment, frustration, despair and strife. Processes of institutionalization preclude diverse people from attaining political and economic sufficiency, unless they transcend diversity and become part of mainstream society. Such struggles provide an index of hegemonic crisis worldwide as assimilation to unworthy standards is increasingly realized as an unworthy goal.

Despite the uncompromising nature of State institutions, their tendency to transcend differences (that happen to be part of real people), the struggle for equality and equity continues both for their potential to improve life for subordinated people and because it provides a course of action in aspiring to the realization of a just society. It is, however, essential to remember the *type* of equality and equity that *people*, not institutions, desire. Struggles concerning gender, racial, class, ethnic, indigenous and religious issues as well as issues of sexual preference, age discrimination and physical/mental challenges have dominated the rhetoric of many States and fascinated experts in social phenomena. While the initial struggles of such marginalized groups focused on achieving equality, the standard to which these groups were equalizing was paradoxically the standard which they were challenging. The political and economic sufficiency sought by diverse peoples is a strong and broad enough position to give them a voice in the decision-making that affects their cultures as well as allowing for their influence, even if only by example (See Lauderdale and Cruit on the Barukin culture, 1993).

The comments here present a more general examination of equality, equity and the processes of uniformization imposed by a Western model that denies the differences between people and does not consider the various social constructions and perceptions of what is 'fair' or 'equitable'. Let us return to and conclude with an illustration from my culture of origin. The modern Italian state is viewed as having incorporated a Western ideology in exchange for its economic recovery since World War II. One of the reasons for the acceptance of Fascism during the 1920s and 1930s in Southern Italy was the regime's promise to provide equity and equality for Southern Italians, who historically have been considered subordinate. The same promise was made after Fascism by liberal democrats. Today, political differences between the North and South appear to be diminished as both Northern and Southern Italians appear to aspire to and enjoy similarly hedonistic lifestyles. But, appearances are deceiving. The South is still plagued by the absence of one very important scarce resource and basic need which precludes Southerners from realizing or fulfilling their definition of equity. They lack water. Southern Italy has been and continues to be plagued by a lack of water. In the heat of the summer, entire water systems are looted or rerouted to irrigate corporate (in this case, big business) agricultural fields, while the people of the villages and towns turn to alternative systems of finding and using water they have known for centuries. The State's imposition of equality and equity as though it were a uniform social construction has indeed denied Italy of its diversity and diverse needs.

Concepts of equity and equality must be reclaimed from this pervasive and uniformizing attitude, which would seem to affirm that people who seek them out and fight for them simply 'would like to be the same or fit in with dominant Western conceptualizations'. No, on the contrary, they already have an identity, including definitions of equity and equality appropriate for the economic and political sufficiency of their own society.

References

Augelli, Enrico and Craig Murphy. 1988. *America's quest for supremacy and the Third World: a Gramscian analysis*. London: Pinter Publishers.

Caldwell, Leslie. 1986. Reproducers of the nation: women and the family in fascist policy. pp. 110-41 in *Rethinking Italian Fascism*, edited by David Forgacs. London: Lawrence and Wishart.

Fanon, Frantz. 1987 (1961). *Les damnés de la terre*. Paris: Decourverte.

Gramsci, Antonio. 1966. *Quaderni del carcere: letterature e vita nazionale*. Giulio Einaudi Editore.

Gramsci, Antonio. 1971. *Selections from the prison notebooks*. New York: International Publishers.

Inverarity, James M., Lauderdale, Pat and Barry C. Feld. 1983. *Law and Society*. Boston: Little, Brown and Co.

Lauderdale, Pat and Michael Cruit. 1993. *The struggle for control*. Albany: State University of New York Press.

Mouffe, Chantal. 1979. *Gramsci and Marxist theory*. Boston: Routledge and Kegan Paul.

Oliverio, Annamarie. 1997. *The State of Terror*. Albany: State University of New York Press.

3
Equity and Rule-making[1]

Rutgerd Boelens

> *The principle of equality before the law is valid for the identical and profoundly unjust for the diverse* (Rodrigo de la Cruz, 1993).

Equity is about fairness, about 'social justice', about the 'acceptability' of something. Often, it refers to people's perception of a fair relationship between certain items in an exchange situation, between rights and obligations, benefits and burdens, advantages and disadvantages.[2] Therefore, equity is directly related to rules and rule-making processes *and* to the exchange and distribution of material or immaterial resources in specific social settings. So, it is hardly surprising that several actors use the concept in their own political struggle, according to their own ideology and interests.

While local groups try to defend their equity perceptions, in order to structure their own society according to their own principles, there is a strong tendency for powerful groups or institutions to try to define these rules *for them* in order to extend their control over these groups. An important mechanism is to require these local groups to '*equalise*' themselves to the dominant groups and models and to take over their norms. In this chapter we analyse how the imposition of this would-be 'equality' - an equality according to external standards and models - leads to the denial and destruction of the diverse needs, rules and equity perceptions of local peasant communities, meanwhile promoting the interests and domination of those in power. We will argue that the currently very common concept and policy objective regarding the 'demarginalisation of peasant families' too often hides - mostly unconscious - strategies that aim to incorporate the rationalities and resources of these families into externally controlled and institutionalised development.

However, if we regard equity as a human-made, ideological construction, it means that we not only have to analyse it critically as a political purpose that can be *abused* to 'advance inequitable interests'. It may also be a tool in the struggle for *changing* existing conditions of subordination.

This chapter presents some notes related to the process of formulating and implementing the equity concept. First we briefly address the themes of equity and interests, and the relation between equity and legal justice. Next, we analyse the process of rule-making with respect to equity and justice. Subsequently we examine the functioning of an 'equalising model' and the process of institutionalising local forms of equity. Finally, we will focus on the search for recovering the vitality of local equity conceptions and equitable practices.

Equity and interests

Each culture, subculture, region, peasant community or water user association has constructed and still is constructing its local, heterogeneous conceptions of equity. However, the imposition of a certain conception about 'what is equitable' by other cultures, classes or by abstract definitions, tends to cause the loss of local values and autonomy. It denies the heterogeneous character and the peculiar practices of equity in specific situations and places, and paradoxically acts in a way to undermine equity itself. Local equity concepts are replaced increasingly by external definitions, that come to rule formal relations and local everyday life. In Mungoshi's book 'Waiting for the rain' (1989), the Old Man, when reflecting on the erosion of their values and norms, expresses this feeling with the following metaphor:

> We are playing the drums of the other, making so much noise that we cannot even hear the beating of our own hearts.

In reality, not all the processes of external re-definition of equity in peasant communities express themselves as brutal impositions. Often they are generated during the (continuous) interactions of local communities with other social entities. The hybridisation of the conceptions of equity in peasant communities can strengthen the latter, but may also undermine their existing power and knowledge.

The most powerful 'external' norms about equity are those that do not *appear* to be imposed from the 'outside'. They are the new, implicit and internalised perceptions of what people find 'normal', what is marked as 'abnormal' and about how people should behave and think. Obviously, the dominant classes and cultures are interested in 'inventing' or promoting an ideology (including its equity concepts and practices) that legitimises its oppression and intervention. Here, the construction of an *equality* concept has been important. In the following we will analyse this concept briefly in relation to the themes of legal justice and the equalising discourse.

Justice and equity

Commonly, the fundaments of national legislation proclaim the equality of all humans with regard to the law. Discrimination must be avoided, equal people have a right to equal treatment. The law should approach justice, has to provide justice, and in the positivist tradition it is even identified with justice. So, legal justice is based on the idea of equality, at least formally and rhetorically. It is supposed that this justice is or should be omnipresent, just as its regulating forces. The generality of the application of justice guarantees that everyone in society can have equal rights, opportunities and obligations. Especially in consensus based theories, the expectation is that justice, as a harmonious concept that represents universal truth or the common interests of all citizens, is reflected in the law, its legal procedures and even in its empirical outcomes. This positivist justice however, has encountered various fundamental problems.

A first assumption to review is the equality of all humans before the law. If all people are to be equal, then the basic, but hidden issue is: equal to whom? *Who must be equal to whom?* As history shows, in practice the norms and standards for this so-called equality are defined not by the dominated, but by the dominating[3]. The denial of people's intrinsic diversity and of their specific knowledge and lifestyles, in order to gain control over them with universalised rules and institutional practices led to Illich's (1972) inversion of the common saying that people are born equal:

> *People are not born equal, but made equal*

In other words, official (legal) equality is not just a rhetorical question. It is a powerful concept which in some cases is very important in emancipation processes, but in others it is related to practices promoting uniformity, among others through positivist legal justice systems that try to impose supposedly universal rules[4].

Furthermore, it is important to observe that liberal and positivist justice typically defend the very important civil and political *individual* rights, but often fail to address properly the economic, social and cultural *collective* rights. Both are complementary, however. Especially in societies with a high social differentiation, these collective rights are the only way for many social and ethnic groups to be able to sustain their rights as individuals. 'The full exercise of individual rights necessarily involves the recognition of collective rights' (Stavenhagen 1994). Other chapters in this book illustrate the importance of the recognition of collective rights in peasant irrigation, versus the individualising rules of actual water legislation in many countries.

Other problems implicit in positivist visions of justice refer to the point of the ideological contents and functioning of the law, when it is seen as an harmonic, social contract that reflects common interests which are supposed to govern society[5] (see also Boelens & Doornbos 1996). With respect to the latter, pluralist and ruling class theories, as well as the more recent structural contradictions theory (see e.g. Chambliss & Zatz 1993) seek different explanations of law and justice, its creation, implementation and reproduction or reformulation. This occurs in interaction with other normative systems, in political arenas characterised by (unequal) power structures, through struggle and negotiation.[6]

Notwithstanding these more adequate conceptual frameworks, the idea that law represents justice as a general and universal concept is still the most widespread and powerful (implicit) vision. It claims that the rules of society must be directed at the general constitution, generating and defending equality, and that law cannot be based upon particular and exceptional cases. Schaffer & Lamb (1981) showed that, in several historical societies and situations, the law and its judges had to declare what is 'right', and faced the problem that:

> General rules do not deal with particular cases.... When there is a system of legal rules (a procedural institutionalization, that is to say) its necessary generality would make the outcomes in 'individual' cases unfair, that is inequitable....

Whereas justice deals with 'rightness in general', equity in its legal essence deals with 'fairness in particular cases'. The law, because of its generality and universal statements, often is inadequate to properly address the enormously diverse social reality.

In history, some countries have recognised this fact when faced with the problem of law losing its legitimacy: justice was perceived of as being 'unfair' in many specific cases, and common-sense-equity or knowledge-of-the-world-justice offered better solutions. Common laws were called upon and in some cases this second set of principles (fairness) was institutionalised (in the Roman empire: *jus gentium*). This was not to replace the set of rightness rules (*jus civile*), but to 'complement and adapt it'. In fact, ironically, it appeared that the official law, justice, *could survive thanks to the 'fairness' and acceptability of common laws* that were incorporated: an institutionalised equity (Schaffer & Lamb 1981).

In various Andean countries we can see that 'special law' was created to deal with the agrarian questions and the legalisation of peasant communities. This special law was 'added' to the national law. It therefore not only complemented the latter and prevented its downfall for being too general (and thus useless), but it also nailed and lock up common law (see e.g. Wray 1993; Boelens & Doornbos 1996). Therefore, 'in a certain manner, the history of this special law is the one of both recognition and denial of social diversity' (Vidal 1990).

Local, dynamic perceptions of equity are made static when they are institutionalised and generalised in legal frameworks. Apparently, 'rightness' is not sufficient and not appropriate to specific situations, but the answer cannot be to simply include 'fairness' in legal justice.

> It may be *a priori* and Aristotelian that legal rules are general and individual cases are particular, hence the need to appeal from one set of rules to another. The point is, however, that the other set of rules, equity, itself becomes a system, an institution, and is to be similarly explained (Schaffer & Lamb 1981).

The institutionalisation of equity opened the way for another problem: *who* defines this equitable common-sense and who is to select the 'right' common law principle among the many that exist? Obviously, individual and institutional interests are at stake, and especially the powerful are likely to define and win the game. Below, in 'the struggle for rule-making', we will elaborate upon this theme.

Here we conclude with a first observation that the distinction between legal justice and equity may offer preliminary grounds for approaching the concept of equity as a useful social construct. In this construct equity stands for fairness not according to some general principles, but according to the conceptions of social justice of diverse localities. In our case, this refers to the conceptions that rule peasants' livelihood strategies and their social production relations. Continuous interactions occur within the community as well as with other normative and social fields: localities generate and re-establish their equity principles during the process of production and distribution, and at the same time, the equity principles structure this process. Therefore, the form and contents of these principles are dynamic. The examples in other parts of this book, e.g. the rules for production and irrigation practices in Andean communities, offer important insights in how local communities structure their livelihood according to these equity principles.

A second preliminary conclusion that can be made is the fact that the enclosure of equity in institutional frameworks, official policies and legal constructions bears great risks. Equity easily loses its proper dynamic and unfair games may be played in the name of equity. This is not to say that equity should *not* form one of the principal criteria for interactions with peasant communities. On the contrary it should, *but the question is not so much how institutions must define equitable principles and 'shape equity' for these communities, but how equity is formulated and functions in the communities themselves*. This is the starting point, not the end, for joint political action.

The struggle for rule-making

As we have seen, with respect to both 'Justice' and 'equity' the making of rules and the power to influence this process is of central importance. Therefore, this part focuses briefly upon the struggle for defining and implementing rules.

Rights have sources, such as the State, the peasant community, or mixed sources, which authorise access and defend the legitimised claims that are made by applicants to certain benefits. Because of the fact that the *legitimisation* of authority - and thus of power - is the corner stone of the rights systems, the concepts of 'law' and 'rights' cannot be seen as just neutral and apolitical social contracts between the 'authorisers' and the 'authorised'. Correas (1994b) defines law as

> a discourse with a prescriptive character, produced by those who hold the power. This power is recognised as legitimate, either by the majority of a population or by its armed forces, and organises the violence which legitimates itself precisely by the recognition of this discourse as 'law'.

The circular logic of this definition is a basic feature of discourses and the power they exercise. Foucault showed that discourses are not just thoughts and ideas expressed in words or texts, or 'propaganda', but real practices with rules and conditions, they are specific conjunctures of power and knowledge. The more the discourse is internalised by the people and accepted as true and legitimate, the stronger the influence of the prescriptions it establishes and the stronger its self-fulfilling forces, actions and effects.

The definition of Correas is essentially based upon the idea that the ruling classes define the rules[7]. However, notwithstanding the fact that this can explain to a great extent the making and implementation of law in concrete situations (e.g. in the case of peasant communities facing national law) its deterministic character should be revised. Chambliss (1993) relativises Marx' well-known statement that 'the ruling ideas are the ideas of the ruling', pointing out rightly that:

> That there are ruling-class interest and influence in vast areas of law cannot be denied. That it is the only force responsible for law creation or law implementa-tion, however, is erroneous. . . The ruling class must respond somehow to force-ful demands made by organised groups or risk losing not just the ideological legitimacy of the system but the ability to control its own destiny.

So, structural social, cultural, and ideological contradictions create conflicts and dilemmas which cannot be ignored and cause changes in the socio-legal sphere. However, the new laws respond to particular urgent and major conflicts, in stead of tackling the fundamental contradictions upon which these conflicts are based. Therefore, the resolutions reveal and create new contradictions, and new conflicts and dilemmas emerge (Chambliss & Zatz 1993). It is obvious that in this process of struggle to create and reformulate law and concepts of justice, the interest groups are not in an equal position. Although the outcomes in terms of legal change are very heterogeneous and respond to local situations and encounters, it is quite common - and not surprising - that the powerful groups see more of their interests represented in the law. So 'Justice' is not necessarily just, and although it may claim to represent 'general and universal principles of rightness', it would often be better to speak of 'particular principles of powerful interest groups who want to universalise these principles'. In the political arena groups seek to universalise their version of justice.

Notwithstanding the power expressed by the formal rules and legal justice, it is valid to relativise their direct and uni-directional impact (as is the case with the impact of equity rules). Various 'theories of justice' and 'theories of equity' exist to explain how people should distribute benefits and burdens[8]. The actual *outcomes* of these dis-tribution practices, however, may be quite different from the intended results. Plans and procedures are mediated by a process of implementation that is constituted by actors with divergent interests and contradictory opinions regarding the equitable distribution of the benefits and burdens in question. They claim, negotiate and strug-gle for 'their rights'.

Examples can be found at all levels in society. Many countries have established clear regulations for land and water tenancy reform, for example by expropriating and redistributing large estates that are underutilised. This in order to provide at least the basic conditions for human subsistence for the 'have nots'. However, in many cases the landowners maintain all of their properties, even if they simply possess 'too much' to be able to achieve an efficient, productive land and water use. Some squander and many suffer. In cases where reforms have been implemented, many land and water rights have accumulated in the hands of the relatively well-off outside the 'target group'.

Another common example: although irrigation projects typically formulate rules and schedules for distributing the water 'rationally, equitably and efficiently', most of the projects result in disproportional accumulation of water access and rights by the large farmers or by those at the head-end of the system, at the expense of the small farmers and the tail-enders.

So it is important to distinguish between conceptions and even decisions with respect to equity and justice, and the actual implementation and its outcomes. This is valid not only when we analyse the myth - but commonly practised ideal - of 'legal and social engineering', which often characterises the juridical system, public policies and/or development interventions. The discontinuity between idea or rule vs. effect is also important when trying to understand endogenous processes in peasant societies, including the interactions between peasant communities and outside agencies. Peasant *conceptions* of equity do not necessarily transform themselves into *rules* regarding equitable practice. Furthermore, actual rules may not be reflected in practical *decisions*; and finally, decisions do not automatically lead to the intended *results*.

This is even more true because rules and rights do not simply refer to the distribution of 'things' or 'qualities' as such, but to the right to act in a certain way in relation to the rights of other people. They are part of the social relationships between these people. Only when rules succeed in having an impact on existent social relationships, and thus on the actual distribution of rights and obligations between people, rules are effective (Moore, 1973)[9].

The myth of a society and social relationships that simply could be shaped by law or by public interventions, as implicit in the legal and social engineering approaches, should be dismantled. This, however, does not withdraw or deny the power these agencies (and the law) have. Although their formal objectives may not always be achieved, unconsciously and notwithstanding the sincere and conscious planning, their interests based upon class, intellectual, gender or ethnic position mostly face less obstacles in reaching their goals. Apparently, not only the formal objectives, plans and rules, but especially the power position of these actors - and the Foulcauldian 'discourse' they produce - is of central importance, which makes it necessary to analyse in more detail the power they express.

Thus, it is not sufficient to analyse formal rules and law according to the statement above of Correas, as a 'discourse produced by the ones who *hold* the power'. Besides official law as an instrument of power there are other, more powerful mechanisms that impose behaviour and so have important roles in the definition of basic norms that rule people's lives. In the light of the theme of pretended 'universal justice' and the existence of 'diverse equity' we will briefly analyse the power of the equalising and subordinating model. Here, not so much the *possession*, but rather the strategic *functioning* of power is of central importance.

Exclusion and inclusion

Historically, the power structure relations in Latin America and elsewhere have been analysed as contradictions between interest groups that did or did not *possess* power. In the case of the Andes, the colonial kings, *conquistadores* and *hacendados* were made visible and honoured - 'placed upon a pedestal' - as a result of the exploitation of the invisible masses of indigenous peoples, peasant communities and *huasipungueros*. The power of the powerful was exercised by *excluding* the subordinated classes from resources, services or social life (see e.g. Galeano 1983, 1986). This vertical and excluding power, however, did not penetrate into all areas of communal life: even the subordinated groups had their own authority in areas where the power of the dominant groups was not effective.

Nowadays the opposite occurs: not the powerful authorities and landlords, but the communities and the common people are made visible. At the same time, contrary to the vertical power, this horizontal and including power itself and the groups that benefit from it can remain invisible. The power surpasses the forces of national regulation or the State, and is not restricted to class relations only. It functions because of its presence, penetrating people and society. It is not exercised only by the State or dominant classes, but also enforced by the dominated (Foucault 1989). *Norms are the instruments of this horizontal power, they shape the model* and according to this, uniformity and equality is proclaimed.

For example, we may find it surprising that, the world over and regardless of the socio-cultural background of the region and peoples in question, irrigation technicians and development professionals often teach and introduce basically the same irrigation techniques and knowledge. This is a technology that is based on norms and standards developed in western universities and enterprises. It contains norms that share the same rationale of water scarcity and water requirements, irrigation efficiency, allocation rules, role and function of measurement structures, water application methods, commercial crops, organisational structures, and so on.

However, it is far more surprising that nobody is surprised when peasants themselves, the world over, whether they are Nepalese peasants, indigenous irrigators in the Andes or Shona farmers in Zimbabwe, *ask for this same technology*, in order to 'progress' and leaf behind their traditional 'backward' technology; in order to become like the western-oriented, '*modern*' farmers.

The standards for this equality are taken away from the diverse local communities; they are determined and spread by this disciplining equalising power, making us want to be all 'equal', that is: equal to the powerful model.

This power is exercised rather than possessed; it is not a 'privilege', acquired or preserved, of the dominant class, but the overall effect of its strategic positions - an effect that is manifested and sometimes extended by the position of those who are dominated (Foucault 1989).

So, modern power seeks for the *inclusion, rather than the exclusion* of peasants and other oppressed classes into contemporary society (Foucault 1989; Achterhuis 1988). At the same time this 'uniformity' and 'equality' makes it easy to measure people and their behaviour. They are individualised, classified and made 'cases' according to their resemblance, or not, to the model. [10]

Previously excluded groups feel the *obligation and need to participate* in this game that sets new rules for their lives, communities, irrigation systems, households, etc. Paradoxically, the less privileged social groups, who think they can take equal advantage of the universal standards, reinforce these norms, although they do not derive the expected benefit. On the contrary, it causes a continuous disappointment, social and cultural disintegration and the position of 'permanently backward people', due to the impossibility of meeting the norms for being equal.

Fanon (1982, 1984) analysed this imposed otherness in the case of the black and colonised people, whose minds and social existence are whitened by the norms of the white and dominant, but still they remain 'black' in the eyes of these colonisers. Because the latter are held up as the model, the oppressed internalise their imposed inferiority and 'blackness'. Black is not a fact, but a social creation by white, an externally determined condition. If white and its related ideology had not existed, neither would have black and the varying degrees of blackness. The imposed equalisation to the white simply would not have existed, but now it has become a powerful mechanism for oppression, enforced by oppressor and oppressed[11]. Yet, the ones who represent the equalising model, who imprint their own image on the consciousness of the others and 'require them to become equal', will not recognise and never intended to recognise these whitened colonised as 'equals'.

> The bourgeois ideology, which is a proclamation of the fundamental equality of men, succeeded in not contradicting itself, and invites inferior men to become human beings, according to the western example of the humanity that it represents. . . In spite of being fundamentally racist, it generally succeeds in hiding this racism through ever more subtle modifications; thus, maintaining its proclamation of men's extraordinary dignity. (Fanon, 1982).

Girard (1986) and Achterhuis (1988) explained the functioning of this desire to resemble the occidental, white, male, scientific values and models[12]. Galeano expressed the power mechanism as *ser como ellos* (to be like them). He describes how Simón Bolívar saw his dream broken into pieces, a dream of a Latin America creating its own models. In the words of Fanon, they had been fighting for white justice and white freedom, for an existence that is moulded in the image of the West:

Bolívar shouted at the ones in power, incapable of creation, only capable of importing ideas and commodities from Europe and the United States: 'Imitate originality!' exhorted and accused don Simón, 'Imitate originality, since you try to imitate everything!' (Galeano 1995).

So, the process of equalisation, the homogenisation of thought and the loss of authenticity are central themes in the analysis of this normalising (or discursive) power. Whereas the classical expropriation of economic surplus value from the peasants was and still is a result of traditional power; the expropriation process of the peasants' knowledge, of their logic and styles of production and of their being and imagining, is more intense; it is the result of the modern power, of 'equalising normalisation'. The two forms of power are present in contemporary society (see also Achterhuis 1988).

It is important to mention that the normalising power should not only be seen as something 'remote', solely structuring relations on a supralocal or international level (as the explanations of power in structuralist State theories use to do). This 'horizontal power' is present in everyday interactions, 'it actually manifests and reproduces or transforms itself in the workplaces, families and other organisational settings of everyday life' (Foucault, quoted in Long 1989). It is omnipresent and invades every area of social life. As such, it may be 'more present and intensive' than the traditional vertical power. In contemporary encounters of peasant communities and entities of the wider society, truth, knowledge and consciousness are reshaped (see Escobar 1995) according to the normalising model[13]. This process can be observed e.g. in many social encounters between peasant communities and State administrations or 'developmentalist' programmes that aim to 'include (demarginalise) peasants and indigenous peoples in contemporary society'.

The 'demarginalisation' of peasants

As a result, the concept of demarginalisation and the provision of equality for the peasants must be seen in another light. The legalist analysis is that peasants and indigenous people are backward (lack of schooling and literacy problems, etc.) or do not have sufficient *access* to the law and therefore to the social benefits of wider national society. The answer is to provide more legal extension (explaining the law), improve the means of communication and facilitate legal and institutional access. In the developmentalist analysis, in the same way, the causes of this marginalisation are analysed in terms of the exclusion of 'the poor', from the essential resources and services. Brenninkmeyer & Wierema (1994) describe the marginalisation as the lasting exclusion of people from (components of) social life.[14] Therefore, the objective of development co-operation is to nullify this exclusion, a process referred to as 'demarginalisation'.

However, some basic questions must be addressed. Are 'the excluded' really excluded, or are they rather included in a subordinated position within the actual power structures? In *what* must these 'excluded' be included? What exactly is the new game in which these people have to participate and equalise themselves, and who defines the rules of this game? What are the norms and standards to be achieved in this demarginalisation effort? Must they accept and internalise the external standards for equality and equity, and accordingly claim their new rights?

Of course, this is mostly not a conscious and intentional process. However, that is exactly what characterises its power. State-peasant interactions and development interventions usually have many effects that do not correspond with the formal objectives. These 'side effects' often relate to the question of equity, and may even generate scarcity instead of relieving it in peasant communities. Let us focus upon this phenomenon in the following, analysing some basic problems which arise when outside entities wish to implement and institutionalise equity in practice. This means that rules for distribution, and therefore institutions, are set up to relieve needs and scarcity.

The existence and creation of scarcity and the institutionalisation of 'equitable distribution'

Equity conceptions are directly related to the allocation of scarce resources. In situations of scarcity, normative systems, such as law or peasant customary rights, establish and implement rules for the distribution of the scarce benefits and for the related distribution of burdens and responsibilities: the question of equity becomes prominent. These normative systems of rights and obligations, or property regimes, usually differ enormously from one location to another, just as the perceptions of what is fair and unfair differ in particular situations. Bromley (1992) rightly points out that 'property regimes take on their special character by virtue of collective perceptions regarding what is scarce, and hence *possibly* worth protecting with rights, and what is valuable, and hence *certainly* worth protecting with rights'.

However, the combination of the value and scarcity of a certain resource is not just an objective 'fact' in a particular society. Values are socially determined according to the dynamic of specific local perceptions and external influences and interactions. In the same way, scarcity is socially constructed, although it may seem less obvious.

For example, in the case of irrigation, Hunt and Hunt (1976) showed that water scarcity may be created by new power structures that destroy existing balances of socially defined demands:

> Water scarcity is not a fixed condition of any place, but rather a particular relationship between supply and demand for water at a given point in time. If demand is greater than supply, then there is scarcity. [. . .] In the Tehuacán Valley, early in the colonial period, water shortages and conflict developed between villages planting traditional crops and haciendas planting sugar as a cash crop,

because haciendas took more than their 'legal' share of communal waters. This cropping pattern introduced scarcity because of the high water demands of sugar vis-à-vis traditional crops. [. . .] When such cases were taken to court, the local communities invariably lost their traditional rights, and a new allocation system favoring the haciendas was imposed from above.

Apart from the lack of resources according to certain 'absolute' or 'objective' needs, the existence of scarcity is strongly related to 'the conditions and possessions of the other' (See Girard 1986; Achterhuis 1988). These needs, which emerge as a result of comparison between human groups or individuals, are relative (this, however, does not deny the importance of these needs as perceived by the actors themselves).

Examples are numerous.
• In the case of irrigation, clear examples are those projects that provide water to the people living below the canals, thereby increasing the relative water scarcity of the community members who have their fields and homes above the canals (and sometimes destroying the existing social ties between 'above' and 'below').
• Another classical example of relative water scarcity is provided by irrigation projects which fail to pay proper attention to the tail-enders of the system: notwithstanding the fact that the water availability in an absolute sense may have been increased, the scarcity and uncertainty experienced usually increases too.
• Very common examples can be seen in those irrigation interventions which fail to recognise existing conceptions of water distribution, which are perceived as fair by the local communities. For example, local conceptions may be based on sharing water shortage among all families, while the intervention may promote or impose water distribution according to the possession of land. In these cases, usually the poorest are given less water, less inputs, less credit and more relative scarcity, just 'because they have less land'.
• Relative water scarcity also increases in cases where interventions create new needs and expectations for water (e.g. by changing crop patterns, settlement schemes, introduction of wells, etc.), but fail to support the implementation of good functioning systems and the capacity to maintain them.

Relative needs do not refer only to material resources, such as water, but, even more importantly to non-material or abstract objects, e.g. development services, specific irrigation knowledge, etc. These needs are continuously refined and renewed, thereby creating and reformulating perceptions of scarcity. Irrigators now experience a previously not perceived lack of modern knowledge and technologies and start to neglect their own. In this way, the new needs can strengthen those institutions that first promote and then provide these so-called needed services and goods[15]. These institutionalised distribution practices require critical analysis.

Institutions that are set up with the goal of achieving a more equitable distribution do not usually act in a way whereby only this objective is met. Schaffer & Lamb (1981) called it 'the irony of equity':

> Grant that equity necessitates the setting up of rules for distribution. The imple-
> mentation of equity, bringing it into action, however, also means their institu-
> tionalization. There is then the problem of access. . .
> It is the governance of institutional action by these rules and standards which
> produces the irony of equity. . . In the end, it is those procedures which come to
> dominate, and so determine outcomes. . . The procedures then are seen to pro-
> duce highly inequitable outcomes.

First, the already advantaged, who possess the social resources to deal with institutional relationships, have far more possibilities to benefit from institutionalised distribution (UNESCO, 1978). Second, the process of institutionalisation is related to
the mentioned 'creation of needs and scarcity'. It is a consequence, *inter alia*, of the
need for institutional maintenance and reproduction. In this process of institutionalisation, 'rural problems' are constructed according to the 'labels' that these institutions pre-establish. The categories or labels used, often are inadequate for understanding the reality of peasant communities. In fact, they tell more about the
labellers, their plans, objectives and visions than about the labelled themselves
(Wood 1985). However, this does not deny the power of these labels: they are *made*
reality. The same institutions that construct the scarcity perception among the
people, are the ones who are 'qualified and authorised' to solve these problems,
thereby often replacing many local forms of peasants' knowledge, practices and skills
oriented at peasants solving their own problems[16].

The history of irrigation interventions has produced some interesting and amazing
examples. Depending on the school and the national or institutional background of
the development mission or engineering team, the problems of peasant communities
and their irrigation systems are identified and formulated. Unintentionally, the prescriptions for 'curing' the irrigation practices normally correspond closely with the
vision, capacities and medicines that the intervening institution can provide. Their
implicit vision of equity is usually part of these prescriptions. In this way, outside
institutions tend to reproduce not only their products (e.g. the irrigation concepts,
techniques and methodologies), but also the *logic* and the *way* in which their clients
should make use of these products *and* they shape the clients' *perception of the need*
for these products.

The discontinuity between on the one hand the peasants' real needs and on the other
hand the institutional services is structural because of the (inevitable) process of
institutional standardisation and labelling. Peasants' needs are specific and refer to
the members of their household, class, ethnic and gender position, the particularities of the peasant community and the heterogeneous production system. However,
most institutions can only offer standard services or items, so, to some extent,
peasants' problems and roles are pre-determined to fit the institutional and
ideological framework.

Institutionalisation itself is not 'wrong'. As a general process it is inherent in human

organisation and rule-implementation. Besides, peasants themselves also institutionalise many of their rules and activities to achieve better co-ordination and more
efficiency, to obtain official recognition of their right to more self-determination, and
sometimes, to create more internal transparency. However, an important distinction
must be made between the (self-)strengthening of institutions to fulfil one's *own*
needs and the building of those institutions that seek to do this 'for others'. Even in
the case of the latter, they may be very important in the peasants' struggle for equity, and peasant organisations may identify them rightly as strategic partners. But it
must be kept in mind that the creation of institutions-for-others, unintentionally,
often responds to a process whereby power, so-called neutral services and institutional knowledge are combined to also serve institutional interests, replacing local
people's specific knowledge and needs. Regrettably, many development programmes
and projects are 'good' examples, although there are also very important exceptions.

The challenge is to find a form of action that fulfils not only 'absolute' needs in a way
that is perceived as equitable, but also suppresses the creation of 'artificial scarcity'.
This action should also avoid the process of institutionalisation that universalises
people's specific problems and solutions. The institutionalisation of equity creates a
paradox that calls for serious discussion, profound analysis and conscious practice.
A proper analysis of implicit interests and the functioning of institutional discourses
is a first step.

Heterogeneity and hybridised equity

If we want to understand equity conceptions in peasant communities and irrigation
practices or in development interventions, it is not sufficient to only analyse
distribution practices: equity in distribution is intrinsically related to the process of
production itself. We must look at the historical and dynamic social relationships that
constitute the production system, the organisation and division of labour, the forms
of property of the means of production, the logic of peasant production, their relationships with wider socio-economic systems, etc. In this process of rural production, not only the material inputs and outputs and the rights, roles, responsibilities
and obligations are produced, but simultaneously, the local conceptions of equity
themselves are created, transformed or reconfirmed.

So, as stressed by Lauderdale (Ch.1), rather than searching for general definitions
and fundamental principles of equity, we should analyse and try to understand the
enormous diversity of equity conceptions in peasant organisational forms, as well as
in our own societies and cultures; and we should analyse the ways these rules and
rights are constructed and used in practice, and the power they represent. This
makes it possible to review critically the discourses that legitimatise specific
dominant representations of equity and justice. Such a review should take into
account that not all peasant customary rights are necessarily more 'equitable' (see
also Benda Beckmann *et al.*, Ch.6), so an attitude of reifying the latter must be avoided. When different perceptions of equity conflict and oppose, the peasants' criteria

cannot escape critical analysis either. The basic question, however, is: *Who models whose concepts of equity? Who models whose future?*

A second fundamental issue is the fact that in many peasant communities and irrigation systems, the rules, rights and obligations, and the notion of equity that they carry, form the core of their production systems, organisational strength, collective action, self defence and sustainability (and as such even sustain entire regions and countries). It is therefore of crucial importance to analyse the processes and conditions that foster subordinating norms and external dependence and the ones that empower endogenous rule making (see Bolin 1994; Boelens & Doornbos 1996).

We have suggested that equitable rules do not necessarily lead to equitable practice. Neither the State, the development institutions, nor the peasant communities or the water users' organisations can expect to simply select the right rules and then wait patiently for an automatic correct follow up and the 'fair' outcomes. Thus, peasant conceptions of equity, when expressed in explicit and collective norms and rules, can be seen merely as *instruments*, as *weapons* to use in the political arena where different interest groups meet, first to fight, negotiate and formulate the rules of the game and second, whether there is a complete consensus or not, to defend the actual application of these rules.

Because of the processes of confrontation, negotiation and recreation of its contents, equity as a conceptual tool for political action does not refer to some set of static principles. In each particular situation it is created, reconfirmed and reformulated in dynamic social interactions. A major challenge for peasant communities facing renewed obstacles for self-determination in the actual crisis and subordination, is the hybridisation of equity conceptions: not through absorption into a globalising model, but through the interaction and mixing of existing forms of local equity towards various new forms, adapted to the particularities of local conditions and the new obstacles and challenges of contemporary society.
In fact, this process of hybridisation of equity it is already going on, in the processes of struggle and exchange in many particular communities, irrigation systems, peasant organisations and networks.

We have presented equity as a concept that lodges different and heterogeneous sets of localised fairness principles, contrary to the 'universal and omnipresent' rightness of justice. Justice deals with general situations, equity with specific, particular cases. This sometimes leads to important misconceptions, for example, when equity is associated with the 'individualisation' of normative reality and social action. However, *the right to be different, the right to construct one's own models and norms and respect for heterogeneity can only be achieved by collective action and mobilisation.* Furthermore, the claim for both the right to equality and the right to difference is not a contradiction but a paradox:

The search for equality in the middle of difference goes hand in hand with its contrary: the finding of difference in face of the empire of equality (Ribadeneira, 1993).

Peasants' participation or 'demarginalisation' is a much abused concept. It often refers implicitly to participation and inclusion in the model, objectives and decisions of the intervening parties. It is rarely understood as the endogenous organisation of a process of social mobilisation. It is not the people or cultures who are to be included in a globalising 'participatory development', through the assimilation of their diverse and specific equity conceptions, knowledge and skills into a framework of institutionally defined needs. No, it is their voice, their decision, their autonomously defined interests, that should be included.

Equity calls for the creation of fair access *by* peasant communities according to their own and diverse models, more than planning *equality* for them. Instead of others defining the rules for production and distribution, support to peasant communities should be directed at political action: the joint removal of obstructions to the negotiation of equitable practice. This then refers to processes where the actual rules for equity are negotiated by the very peasant families and organisations themselves.

Basically it is not a question of peasant communities *receiving* equity, but *demanding* it.

Notes

1   I am very grateful to Hans Achterhuis, Geert van Duinhoven and Erik Heijmans for their valuable comments on an earlier version of this chapter.
2   A major problem in the effort to approach the concept of equity is the fact that its contents are intrinsically heterogeneous and differ according to the interest groups which use the concept. Besides, we encounter implicit or explicit definitions of the concept in several scientific disciplines, such as law, economics and philosophy, that show great diversity and even contradictions within one and the same discipline. Moreover, these definitions may differ considerably from the various notions of 'equity' in popular language.
3   On the one hand, it must not be denied that, currently and historically, the idea of equality has provided important grounds for the struggle for liberation of oppressed peoples. On the other hand, it is this more subtle use of equality and homogenisation, however, that serves to perpetuate the subordination of the 'non-equals': all those cultures and peoples, e.g. peasants, indigenous and black peoples, *who were taught to strive for being equal* to the dominant and white classes and to accept their values, norms and visions as the maximum expression of progress and truth.
4   This is not to deny the great importance that legal justice systems can and often do have in spheres of social life, e.g. in the defence of human dignity and certain basic human rights. This, however, should not lead to the formulation of *inflexible, detailed* rules for regulating behaviour in *all* spheres and activities of the diverse society (see Boelens & Doornbos 1996).
5   Another problem with the aforementioned concept of (positivist) justice is the fact that it fails or refuses to make the distinction between the formal rules (official juridical texts) and their interpretation and application by law-users (Correas 1994a). The theoretical function of the latter is to apply and use the law, not to create it. However, in practice it can be seen that law is used and 'reformulated' in diverse manners, according to the very diverse social conditions that are encountered and the specific interests and visions of people who apply the law (see e.g.

Vidal 1990) and interact with other people subject to the law (see e.g. Benda Beckmann et al. 1989). Law is effective or not, according to the recognition of the authority of the applying actors; the resemblance of legal rules to real practical conditions and problems; and/or the power of the discourse that sustains the legal rules.

6   These theories also show that people usually apply more than one set of normative rules, and often practise a strategy of 'legal shopping' in other normative systems.

7   Although this idea is basic in Marxist tradition, others before Marx applied similar statements, e.g. Thomas Hobbes: 'Non veritas, sed auctoritas facit legem' ('Not truth, but authority defines the law'; quoted in Tromp 1990).

8   In practice, general principles may be formulated by State bureaucracies, outside institutions, social movements, peasant communities or other entities to express their formal conceptions about an equitable distribution. These principles can be specified through the determination of certain basic *criteria* and the development of corresponding *mechanisms*. The latter are operationalised by concrete *procedures* (see also Elster 1994).

9   'Most rules of law, in fact, though theoretically, universal in application, affect only a limited category of persons in a limited number of situations' (Moore 1973).

10 In the words of Foucault we might call it the 'political anatomy of peasant communities'.

11 'The rejection of Self came as a result of identification with the Other and as a result of the acceptance of the Other's image of one's 'inferior' caste' (Gendzier 1985). See also Achterhuis (1991).

12 It is necessary to distinguish between the various concepts of equality. Nowadays, it does not deal only with the question of equal distribution of scarce material resources (the subject of class struggle), but also with the equal distribution of all possible abstract themes, such as status, happiness, respect, etc. This leads to the comparison of all men to see 'if they are sufficiently equal', trying to resemble to the uniform standard, and the frustration of the ones that do not succeed in approximating the model. Apparently this concept of equality has always existed. However, Achterhuis (1988) shows that it is the result of the penetration of modern (capitalist) Western ideologies and counter-ideologies. Instead, several ancient cultures linked the concept of equality to ideas of diversity and pluriformity.

13 Consequently, the model is 'globalised' and the local regime of power and knowledge subordinated.

14 'Marginalisation is a concept that has already been used for a long time in social sciences. More specifically in the framework of development assistance it refers to a process which excludes persons from their means of livelihood' (Brenninkmeyer & Wieringa 1994).

15 The mechanisms of 'relative scarcity' make it possible that others, who have the power to impose their vision and image, come to define the needs of peasant communities, thus *creating* scarcity by expanding 'artificial needs'. The increasing expansion of so-called 'needs' through discursive practice magnifies the perceived scarcity and reinforces dependence and subordination. Or, as Illich (1972) writes, it is the creation of a 'heaven on earth that always stays just out of reach when one appears to come closer'.

16 We might compare it with a kind of Orwellian 'NewSpeak': often these institutions create a world and a vision by addressing those problems that they themselves can formulate and by asking only those questions that they themselves can answer.

References

Achterhuis, H.J., 1988. *Het Rijk van de Schaarste. Van Thomas Hobbes tot Michel Foucault*. Ambo. Baarn.

Achterhuis, H.J., 1991. *Frantz Fanon*. Kritisch Denkers Lexicon. January 1991. Samson Uitgeverij, The Netherlands.

Benda-Beckmann, F. von, A. Van Eldijk, J. Spiertz & F. Huber, 1989. 'Interfaces and janus-faces: a critical appraisal of the interface approach in development sociology from a socio-legal studies perspective'. In: Long, N. (ed.), 1989.

Boelens, R. & B. Doornbos, 1996. *Derecho consuetudinario campesino e intervención en el riego. Visiones divergentes sobre agua y derecho en los Andes*. CESA/SNV. Quito.

Bolin, I., 1994. 'Levels of autonomy in the organization of irrigation in the Highlands of Peru'. In: Mitchell & Guillet, 1994. *Irrigation at high altitudes: the social organization of water control systems in the Andes*. American Anthropological Association.

Brenninkmeyer, V. & Wieringa, 1994. 'NGO's en de financiering van economische projekten - dilemma's en beleidsprincipes'. In: *Derde Wereld*, vol.12, no. 4, 1994. Nijmegen.

Bromley, D.W. (ed.), 1992. *Making the commons work. Theory, practice and policy*. ICS, San Francisco.

Chambliss, W.J. & M.S. Zatz (eds.), 1993. *Making law. The State, the law and structural contradictions*. Indiana University Press.

Chambliss, W.J., 1993. 'On lawmaking'. In: Chambliss, W.J. & M.S. Zatz (eds.), 1993.

Correas, O., 1994a. 'La teoría general del derecho y el derecho alternativo'. In: *El Otro Derecho*, Revista del ILSA, no.15.

Correas, O., 1994b. *Introducción a la sociología jurídica*. Ediciones Coyoacán. Mexico DF.

Cruz, R. De la, 1993. 'Aportes del derecho consuetudinario a la reforma jurídico del Estado' In: Ribadeneira *et al.* (1993).

Elster, J., 1994. *Justicia Local. De qué modo las instituciones distribuyen bienes escasos y cargas necesarias (Local Justice, 1992)*. Gedisa. Madrid.

Escobar, A., 1995. *Encountering development. The making and unmaking of the Third World*. Princeton University Press. Princeton. New Jersey.

Fanon, F., 1982. *De verworpenen der aarde (Les damnés de la terre, 1961)*. Van Gennep. Amsterdam.

Fanon, F., 1984. *Zwarte huid, blanke maskers. (Peau noir, masques blancs. 1952)* Van Gennep. Amsterdam.

Foucault, M., 1989. *Discipline, straf en toezicht (Surveiller et punir, 1975)*. Historische Uitgeverij. Groningen.

Galeano, E., 1983. *De aderlating van een continent (Las venas abiertas de América Latina, 1973)*. Van Gennep. Amsterdam.

Galeano, E., 1986. *Memoria del fuego*. Tercer Mundo Editores, Bogotá.

Galeano, E., 1995. *Ser como ellos*. Tercer Mundo Editores, Bogotá.

Gandarillas, H. et al., 1992. *Dios da el agua. Qué hacen los proyectos?*. Hisbol. Cochabamba.

Gendzier, I.L., 1985. *Frantz Fanon. A critical study*. Grove Press, New York.

Girard, R., 1986. *De romantische leugen en de romaneske waarheid. (Mensonge romantique et vérité romanesque)*. Kok Angora. Kampen.

Hunt, R. & E. Hunt, 1976. *"Canal irrigation and local social organization"*. In: Current Anthropology, vol. 17, no.3, pp. 389 - 398.

Illich, I., 1972. *Deschooling Society*. Harper & Row Publishers. New York.

Long, N. (ed.), 1989. *Encounters at the interface. A perspective on social discontinuities in rural development*. Wageningse Sociologische Studies 27, Wageningen Agricultural University.

Moore, S.F., 1973. 'Law and social change: the semi-autonomous social fields as an appropriate subject of study'. Law and society Review, vol 7, no. 4, pp.719 - 746.

Mungoshi, C.., 1989. *Waiting for the rain*. Zimbabwe Publishing House. Harare.

Ribadeneira, J.C., et al., 1993. *Derecho, pueblos indígenas y reforma del Estado*. Colección Abya-Yala, vol. 2. Quito.

Schaffer, B. & G. Lamb, 1981. *Can equity be organized? Equity, development analysis and planning*. Institute of Development Studies, Sussex University. Brighton.

Stavenhagen, R., 1994. *'Indigenous rights: some conceptual problems'*. In: Indigenous Peoples. Experiences with self-government. (W.Assies & A.Hoekema, eds.), University of Amsterdam & IWGIA. Copenhagen.

Tromp, B., 1990. *Het einde van de politiek?* Dubioboeken. Academic Services. Schoonhoven.

UNESCO, 1978. *Towards a development aimed at reducing economic social inequalities*. Report of meeting on equity and development. UNESCO / IDS. Brighton. Sussex.

Vidal, A.M., 1990. *'Derecho oficial y derecho campesino en el mundo andino'*. In: Stavenhagen & Iturralde (eds.), 1990. Entre la ley y la costumbre. I.I.I. & I.I.D.H., Mexico.

Wood, G., 1985. *'The politics of development policy labelling'*. Development and Change 16 (3), pp. 347 - 373.

Wray, A., 1993. *'El problema indígena y la reforma del Estado'*. In: Ribadeneira et al. (1993).

PART II

EQUITY, POWER AND PEASANT RIGHTS

Introduction

With rules, as with the measure of redistribution to least fortunate groups, there is a fundamental error of false objectivity or instrumentality which runs through contemporary social philosophy of the just. The issue is taken to be the selection of good rules where good rules are principles and selection is a matter of nominating, verbalization or legislation. All would then, it is supposed, follow. This is to mistake the nature of rules in social action where rules are to be seen as a complex. They are in part weapons, whose only reality is their use, in part arenas or battle grounds themselves and in part forces, factors, actual presences in their own right. (Bernard Schaffer & Geoff Lamb, 1981. *Can equity be organized?* Gower, Farnborough / UNESCO, Paris).

I am not so naive as to believe that an appeal to rationality and respect towards the human being would be able to change the world. For the Black in the sugar plantations in Le Robert there is only one solution: struggle. And he will not commit himself to this struggle after a Marxist or an idealist analysis, but simply because he can see his existence only as a struggle against exploitation, misery and hunger. (Frantz Fanon, 1970 (1952), *Peau noire, masques blancs*. Editions du Seuil, Paris).

The concept of equity is closely linked to the existing power configurations. Peasants are part of these structures and feel their consequences day in day out. This is why the peasant world does not face the construction and implementation of the equity concept as a theoretical issue. To approach peasant conceptions of equity in the distribution of productive resources and understand their meanings, it is essential to focus on the social structures that surround them.

In primitive societies, producers control the means of production, including their own labor, and exchange their own labor and its products for the culturally defined equivalent goods and services of others. [. . .] Peasants, however, are rural cultivators whose surpluses are transferred to a dominant group of rulers that uses the surpluses both to underwrite its own standard of living and to distribute the remainder to groups in society that do not farm but must be fed for their specific goods and services in turn. (Eric Wolf, 1966, *Peasants*. Prentice-Hall, New Jersey).

Peasants and indigenous peoples actively try to make use of the fissures and widen their scope within the power structures, attempting to increase their control over the production process. Their strategies are based on both resistance and transformation: they struggle for the continuity of their families and their collectivities, as well as for a fundamental change in the unjust relations of distribution and exchange. In this logic of production and reproduction and, more generally, in internal and external social relationships, customary law plays a central role. It is a dynamic law that interacts with the official law and other normative systems.

Is this customary law, with its hybrid and varied expressions and its great diversity of content, a central issue for peasants and indigenous peoples in their struggle to gain more control over the production process?
Can it be included as a starting point from which to construct more equitable relations of production and distribution?

4

Peasants and Power

Jan Douwe van der Ploeg

Throughout history farmers and peasants have been struggling, all over the world, to expand their control over the agricultural production process. These struggles involve not only activities located on the farm, but also the politico-economic conditions in which farming is embedded. Although peasant or farmer struggles did and sometimes do take the form of massive, violent confrontations, they are mostly expressed in less visible but equally important processes. One of these processes of resistance is the ongoing *distancing* of farming from markets. It is actually through such a mechanism that the phenomenon of the 'family farm' was created and reproduced. And as will be outlined below, it was and is exactly through the same mechanism that concerned farmers and peasants create 'room for manoeuvre' as well as the 'line of defence' they need so desperately when confronting highly adverse politico-economic conditions and power relations. Let us first look at an illustrative case from the Netherlands, to facilitate a comparative analysis.

Hemmema

The first farm accounting available in the Netherlands goes back to the 1569-1573 period. It regards the farm of Hemmema, who managed the farm records himself. What the accounting records show, for each year under consideration as well as for the indicated period as a whole, is quite a precarious situation. Out of all the resources needed to be able to farm, a huge part was mobilised on the markets of that time. Take cattle, for fattening and milk-production. Cattle can very well be raised ('reproduced') on the farm itself. Hemmema, however, needed to buy them time and again. The same went for hay and manure. Considerable amounts of hay and manure produced on the farm were sold, and when Hemmema needed these items himself he had to purchase them again on the market. For land, labour and capital the same story could be told. Land was rented at least partly, which implied considerable costs. Labour was recruited and capital was obtained partly through loans. Hemmema's farm was, in short, highly market-dependent. The process of production was *commoditized* to a considerable degree. That is: many labour objects (such as cattle), many instruments and also part of the labour force, *entered the process of production as commodities*. Beyond mere use-values that can be applied to produce according to the autonomous insights, knowledge, experience and strategies of the concerned farmers, they have exchange-values. Through these labour objects, instruments and labour force, commodity relations penetrated into the heart of the farm's labour process. Consequently, the agricultural process of production was to be organised according to market logic.

Alarmingly, the associated monetary costs were equal if not superior to the monetary benefits obtained by selling the produced and processed items. In Hemmema's case, monetary costs were more or less 105% of the monetary benefits. This explains and illustrates the precarious situation in which Hemmema found himself. And Hemmema was relatively well-off. He owned at least part of his land. Many other farmers had to rent it completely. For them the balance was even more negative. They could only 'survive' -and the same went for Hemmema- because they controlled at least some resources: some land, some cattle, some labour, etc. ('the pure part' as the folk concept at that time went). So they could at least try to secure their families' 'reproduction'.

The high market dependence (or in other words, the high degree of commoditization) that was characteristic of farming in the 16th century, was, as far as the farmers were concerned, an absolutely non neutral phenomenon. It implied high dependence on an awkward power structure. The 'land market' was controlled by a rural aristocracy, the 'capital market' by relentless usurers. The markets for what we now call 'non-factor inputs' (e.g. cattle, hay, manure, etc.) were ruled by different urban interests, representing the emerging bourgeoisie. The high degree of commoditization implied, in daily life, a subordinate position in the arenas controlled by powerful others.

Petty Commodity Production, towards a distancing from markets

From Hemmema onwards, over the centuries, a considerable part of the daily struggles of Dutch farmers has been oriented[1] toward reducing this market dependence. Throughout our agricultural history, farmers have consciously been striving to reduce the degree of commoditization, by replacing resources mobilised through markets by resources produced and reproduced on their own farms. Quite often they have used such mechanisms as mutual co-operation and non-commoditized, socially regulated exchange to achieve this higher degree of independence. Other important mechanisms are found in increased 'technical efficiency', that is, to produce more output with the same amount of inputs or resources. The quality and quantity of labour proved decisive in this respect.

In this way the 'family farm', understood as a unit that owns and controls most if not all relevant resources on which agriculture is based, was created. Hence, the 'family farm' is not a remnant of the past, as is commonly assumed - it is the outcome of a long process of struggle and emancipation.

Slicher van Bath, the well-known agrarian historian, introduced a beautiful concept to analyse and understand this process. *Farmers' freedom*[2], according to Slicher, has a twofold content. It refers to 'freedom *from*' (e.g. freedom from usurers, merchants, etc.) and simultaneously it refers to 'freedom *to*', that is, to organise farming in line with one's own interests, insights, knowledge and strategy.

Through their struggles for farmers' freedom, Dutch farmers created a constellation that can be described with an analytical term derived from the Marxist tradition. I refer here to 'Petty Commodity Production' (PCP). Mostly we refer to farming as Simple Commodity Production (SCP)[3]. Essential to SCP is the conversion of commodities (obtained on input markets) into other commodities (to be sold on the output markets) using labour force which is non-commoditized. Applied to farming, this implies that a fundamental characteristic of the 'family farm' is the notion that labour is family labour, while other resources are mobilised on the markets.

In contrast, PCP refers to the fact that not only labour, but also a considerable part, if not all of the land, capital and the 'non-factor inputs' are owned and controlled by the farming family (or community). Not only labour but most or all relevant resources are *non-commoditized* and hence used and regulated with *non-commodity mechanisms and circuits*. Therefore, relatively autonomous and historically guaranteed reproduction is crucial.

I prefer to use the concept of PCP, more than SCP, as an analytical category to explain the position of the farmers mentioned above. In the first place, since it reflects the historical process of Dutch farmers' emancipation[4]: the 'freedom-from' was used as a 'freedom-to' that led to the *boom* of Dutch agriculture in the 1850-1950 period[5] and to a certain prosperity for Dutch farmers[6]. Secondly, because it enables us to better understand one of the fundamental features of Northwest European and especially Dutch farming: it is, so to speak, more 'peasant-like' than many agricultural systems e.g. in Latin America[7]. (This feature of hidden strength, however, for many observers remains a mystery). Thirdly: it is precisely in this historically created and consciously extended PCP, where we encounter the *room for manoeuvre* farmers need to face adverse market conditions and/or power structures.

So, on the one hand it is amazing that liberalism preaches stronger market integration for Latin American agriculture, whilst it is precisely their *distancing* from markets that explains the relative success of European farming. On the other hand, it is equally amazing that the 'left' remains unable to understand the daily struggle of farmers to achieve such relative autonomy[8].

I feel that an adequate understanding of such 'room for manoeuvre'[9] is strategic to any discussion of farmers' knowledge and particular norms governing internal relations within farming communities (e.g. 'the moral economy of the peasantry' tradition). It is also strategic for any discussion on how to link the work of NGO's and others to farming communities.

Room for manoeuvre and comunidades campesinas

The historically created 'room for manoeuvre', as entailed in PCP, differs considerably according to the different time-space locations we want to take into account. I referred earlier in this text to the Dutch experience, but not because I think that such an experience should be considered by any means as a 'blueprint' or a 'guideline' for Latin America. I simply wanted to refer to the *hidden strength* of Dutch agriculture as it has been created by farmers themselves. The more so, since the 'official story' about our history systematically neglects this crucial aspect. I further think that lack of autonomy (the lack of PCP) is one of the big problems in Latin American agriculture. But I am also convinced that, quite differently from the Dutch historical experience, in Latin America it will be especially the *comunidades indigenas* or *comunidades campesinas* that will emerge as one of the strategic mechanisms to create or extend such autonomy. During the 1970s and the early 1980s I had the privilege to be able to participate in the impressive struggles of the comunidad de Catacaos in the North of Peru. Later I lived through similar experiences. It is impossible to go into details here, and probably unnecessary as well, since most people reading this chapter will have more and probably even richer experiences than the ones I referred to. The point is that, in daily struggles (and in sometimes massive clashes with the State) the same longing for and building of *autonomy,* of 'room for manoeuvre', or of 'farmers' freedom' is omnipresent. This was already recognised by the great Peruvian socialists Mariátegui and Castro Pozo. My point is that their insights and notions should be retrieved.

Farmers' knowledge as a line of defence

Especially in a world subjected to strong trends towards liberalisation, globalisation and the dominance of international capital it is and remains important to also consider self-controlled 'room for manoeuvre' as a very important *line of defence*. This not only applies to Third World agriculture, but is equally important in Western Europe as well.

Farmer's knowledge ('art de la localité' as the beautiful French expression goes) is crucial to maintain 'room for manoeuvre' once conquered. That is: farmers' knowledge itself becomes one of the major lines of defence. I raise this point here especially since today, the 'expropriation' of farmers and peasants follows increasingly the line of replacing farmers' knowledge by so-called expert knowledge. Often, technical programmes are introduced that imply a marginalisation of farmers' knowledge, without in the end offering any better alternative[10]. Increased market dependence, increased commoditization, is quite often the only outcome[11].

Farmers *and especially peasants* are not defenceless in a globalising world dominated by awkward power relations. There are strategic lines of defence. Exploration of these lines, and especially their further strengthening, is crucial. It is also a starting point to define agendas for co-operation among scientists, NGO's, farmers and farmers' communities.

Ayuda, respeto y la misma lucha: the relevance of counterculture

One last observation I want to make here touches on one of the main topics of this book: equity and other typical 'peasant' norms. The world of peasants[12] is characterised by the need to co-operate. As it is said in Peruvian *altiplano* potato production: 'se necesita *ayuda*' (one needs help, from others). 'Ayuda' is crucial to organise potato production in the highly complex, differentiated eco-systems characterising the Andean mountains. 'Ayuda', together with other ingredients, enables the farmers to produce well, resulting in *respeto*, respect in the farmers' community for having demonstrated that one is a good farmer[13]. 'Respeto' leads, in turn, to 'ayuda'. In this way, farming is grounded in relatively autonomous, historically guaranteed reproduction. Labour force input ('ayuda') does not depend on relations governing the labour market. It depends on 'respeto'. And 'respeto' can be earned regardless of the market.

Farmers' notions of equity, co-operation, etc., are therefore nodal points in any strategy to confront the highly disrupting effects of liberalisation, globalisation and dominance of international capital. They are, so to speak, 'lines of defence' and not, as sometimes assumed, remnants of the past, echoes of a disappearing culture. Rather, they are expressions of a highly valid (and highly needed) *counterculture*. And it is not only in Latin America where the expressions of such a counterculture are to be noticed. Western European agriculture is today blossoming with many, many expressions of such a counterculture, embodying many such lines of defence.

'Que hagamos todos la misma lucha' (Let us all join in the same struggle). This is one of the most confusing and one of the most promising expressions heard in the daily turmoil of Latin American agriculture. Latin American farming is characterised by a highly complex division of labour. Some people are *golondrinas*[14], others are *estables*[15], or *eventuales*[16]. Then there are the *campesinos*, and broadening the horizon and vocabulary, there are the *precaristas* from Costa Rica, the *libres* and *arrieros* from Colombia (both in old and in new forms) and ever so many other forms and expressions from all over the continent. The interesting and promising point is that these different conditions have become very interchangeable (today a 'minifundista', tomorrow an 'estable', the day after tomorrow - after the strike - an 'eventual'). And they are also related to a common denominator ('my brother is an eventual, I am an estable, my father is...', whatever). The notion of 'Nosotros, los pobres del campo' ('We, the poor of the countryside'), increasingly emerges as one of the central counterpoints to the dividing impact of current developments. 'Hacemos todos la misma lucha' is one of the most striking outcomes of the processes of marginalisation and division. It means that it is probably only by departing from norms elaborated in peasant communities that ways forward can be constructed. And if they are to be successful, these ways must be grounded in consolidation and expansion of autonomy and 'farmers' freedom'.

Notes

1 One could even argue that this struggle is still going on. Probably it is especially manifest in periods of crisis such as the one we are currently witnessing.

2 It is important to note that the original Dutch term, 'boerenvrijheid', has a double meaning. It is associated with the freedom of *farmers*, but refers as well to the freedom to organise *farming* in the desired way.

3 In most literature, PCP is associated with the past and/or with remoteness. PCP should be typical for the peasant, whilst SCP, it is assumed, is the typical condition for the farmer. The transformation from PCP to SCP, then, is understood as being typical for the transition from a (partly) natural economy to a 'fully commoditized economy'. This assumption or representation is, I believe, basically wrong. It does not help to understand current peasant and farmer struggles, nor does it allow for the elaboration of any practical contribution to these struggles.
   Finally, it might be useful to refer to the difference between SCP and PCP, on the one hand and Capitalist Commodity Production (CCP) on the other, especially since CCP remains an important phenomenon, e.g. in South American (large-scale) agriculture. CCP is production-oriented to create surplus value. Only those commodities are produced that entail surplus value (for the benefit of the one controlling the production process). This can only be done by using labour force as a commodity, so that surplus value can be extracted from labour inputs. Hence, in CCP all resources enter the production process as commodities. In SCP the same applies with one important exception: the labour force. In PCP, not only labour, but also a range of other resources enter the production process as non-commodities.

4 Farmer unions referred, in the previous century, to this particular struggle for decommoditization as the 'struggle for the fullness of power' ['strijd voor de volheid van magt'].

5 This boom depended crucially on the quantity and quality (craftsmanship) of farm labour. With this concept I do not refer to wage-earning labourers on capitalist farms, but to the labour force of farmers and their families. As a matter of fact, employment in Dutch agriculture rose, during this period, from 300,000 to 650,000 units. Consequently, historians often refer to this period as the one of a decisive *repeasantisation*. Large farms disappeared, especially CCP farms, whilst small PCP farms blossomed. It is only after 1957, during the modernisation project, that agrarian employment in the Netherlands started to decrease.

6 Needless to say, the creation and extension of PCP throughout our agrarian history also has deeply affected the distribution of total wealth produced by farmers. They could obtain, in this way, a larger share. This evidently does not mean that this part might not be reduced again through other mechanisms. Some of these mechanisms reside within agriculture itself. See in that respect: Van der Ploeg (1995); esp. chapter 6.

7 See for a detailed, empirical analysis and discussion: Van der Ploeg (1990).
   Especially chapter 5 contains a comparative analysis that underpins this conclusion.

8 The still unresolved disputes about 'kulaks', the fear of 'kulakisation', and hence the dominance of Leninist and Stalinist views over those of the Narodniki and the 'Chayanovians' explain this historically-reproduced ignorance and incapability.

9 As far as the theoretical contours of this concept are concerned, the interested reader is referred to the work of my colleague Norman Long, who also discusses this notion in relation with the labour class. See e.g. Long (1995).

10 As José Carlos Mariátegui argued: 'change as such is not the problem, the problem is that much change doesn't bring any progress, it results simply in regression'. Already quoted agrarian historian Slicher van Bath wrote an essay, in the early 1980s, partly based on Latin American examples, under the heading: 'Not all changes bring improvements'.

11 For an empirical analysis, the reader is referred to J.D. van der Ploeg, 'Sistemas de conocimiento, metafora y campo de interacción: el caso del cultivo de la patata en el altiplano peruano', in: *Agricultura y Sociedad*, 56, julio-septiembre 1990, Madrid, pp. 167-201.

12 Again, I am using here the term 'peasants' in the broadest possible sense, including the 'peasants' of Western Europe.

13 This materialises in an interesting way: the farmers with high yields need a lot of assistance for the harvest. Many people assisting in this harvest are paid 'in kind', with part of the harvest, or with the reciprocal return of labour days. Hence the respect.
14 This is a Peruvian expression for the highly mobile work force that moves from one area to another, from e.g. rice transplanting, to cotton-picking, to sugar cane harvest, etc.
15 People having more or less secure employment in agrarian enterprises.
16 Workers being contracted on a daily basis.

References

Ploeg, J.D. van der, 1990. *Labor, Markets, and Agricultural Production*, Westview Press, Boulder.
Ploeg, J.D. van der, 1995. *Beyond Modernization*, Van Gorcum, Assen.
Long, N., 1995. Creating space for change: a perspective on the sociology of development. *Sociologia Ruralis*.

5

The Imposition of Western Values and the Peasants' Struggle for Equity

Gerrit Huizer

Introduction: inequitable distribution on a world-wide scale

During the last few years, much literature has appeared on the ecological implications of economic development, mostly related either to the future (Third Millennium) or to the past (500 years of 'world system'). Environmental movements and action groups have taken up these issues, as well as some agencies or representatives of global corporate circles such as the Club of Rome in 1972 or the Business Council for Sustainable Development in view of the 1992 United Nations Conference on Ecology and Development in Rio de Janeiro, where future relationships between humankind and the earth were discussed (Schmidheiny, 1992).

As can be seen from the relevant reports but particularly from *Global 2000*, the voluminous report presented to former president Carter in 1980 with projections about the world's ecological situation at the beginning of the Third Millennium, the 10% of the world's population living in rich Western capitalist countries will consume over 60% of the world's products, while 80% of humankind living in the so-called Third World (after Eastern Europe and Japan have also taken their relatively modest share) will be left with about 20% of all goods and services. Thus, in the year 2000, the few (10%) living in Western Europe and the USA will consume - per capita - 24 times as much as the great majority of humankind, and it is expected that this discrepancy will gradually worsen. The cultivation at extremely low remuneration of coffee, tea, bananas, sugar, cotton, fruits, flowers and so many other cheap products for the 'world market', which means the Western countries, is one visible expression of this discrepancy, which has grown over a long time, but has accelerated and doubled during the past three development decades according to the *UN Human Development Report 1992*.

Western penetration, changing local values and forms of resistance

The first centuries of encounter between indigenous and Western people and cultures were massive, shocking and disastrous for the indigenous peoples in many cases, such as the conquest of South- and Central America by the Spaniards in the 16th century, the 'pacification' of indigenous North-American peoples by the whites in the 18th and 19th century, submission of Bantu peoples in Southern Africa during the 19th and 20th centuries and the Melanesian peoples during the 20th century. In academic literature, some attention has been given to the destruction of natural, cultural and spiritual values as a result of capitalist penetration world wide. Useful efforts to analyze these issues have been made by Fanon (1961), Wolf (1982), Taussig (1980, 1987) and to some extent by eco-feminist scholars such as Mies and Shiva (1993).

With respect to the West itself, various historical studies show that the objectifying mechanistic world view promoted by the 'scientific revolution' in Western Europe was taken up by the powerful elite groups of that period to repel the particularly 'animistic' folk knowledge and popular spirituality prevailing in England and elsewhere among the 'uncultured' masses in a period of economic change and revolutionary turmoil (Berman, 1981; Merchant, 1980). As Maria Mies (1986) and Vandana Shiva (1988) show, such a process is at present being pursued on a global scale with the still further spread of Western 'developmentalism' through the 'world market' that followed several centuries of imperialist penetration.

The 'discovery' and conquest of the Americas was a crucial step in this submission leading to a decimation of the population in what Eric Wolf (1982) called 'the great dying'. As Mies (1986, p. 75) observed: 'In the same measure as European conquerors and invaders 'penetrated' these 'virgin lands', these lands and their inhabitants were 'naturalized', declared as wild, savage Nature, waiting to be exploited and tamed by the male civilizers'. This conclusion is confirmed by a carefully documented study of the influence of the Spanish conquest on the role of women in the Peruvian Andes (Silverblatt, 1987, p. 139) stating: 'For many indigenous women the theft of their lands and their bodies was a dual yoke thrust on them in the dehumanizing process of Spanish colonization'.

Silverblatt also noted how, for Latin America after the Conquest, the Inquisition started to propagate the demonization of 'animism' and Mother Earth (Pachamama) worship. In this context, local values and practices were also blamed, such as communal, equitable land use prevailing among the various indigenous societies which were subjugated. So, the change and devaluation of local values by the dominating, penetrating culture can be and often has been a very subtle process. Earlier, the same had been done in Europe in the witch trials unleashed by the publication in 1487 of *Malleus Malificarum* by Dominicans Kraemer and Sprenger with the blessing of Pope Innocentius.

Salomon (1987, pp. 148-165) found in South America that some of those who were persecuted as 'witches' or 'idolaters' were in fact leaders of indigenous resistance movements, e.g. against the levy of taxes. To mention an example, in Andagua, close to Arequipa, around 1750 the local population, led by Gregorio Taco, consistently refused to pay taxes to the Spanish rulers. Upon investigating the case, the authorities realized that the strength of Taco's leadership was related to his importance as the guardian of his family shrine of pre-Christian mummified ancestors. These were believed to be very powerful deities and worshipped in secrecy in caves where they were kept. These ancestor mummies were viewed as the real owners of the land. The Spanish ecclesiastical and judiciary authorities were divided about how to tackle this conflict. Finally, it was ended by capturing and publicly burning the mummies, leaving the local population in bitterness and 'deep consternation and melancholy' (Ibid., p. 156). The burning of the mummies was meant to also burn the cultural values that defended equitable local relations and protected the people against outside exploitation.

The dialectical relationship between Western capitalist penetration, with its destruction of values such as equitable and sustainable land use, and the resistance of the indigenous peoples against this process, has also been studied by Taussig (1980, 1987). In his meticulous analysis of the aggressive imposition of sugar plantations on a traditional peasant economy in the Cauca valley in Colombia and of tin mining among the Bolivian Aymara Indians, he shows that these processes caused a considerable increase in sorcery, witchcraft and other magical practices. The new ways of producing not for direct use but in quantities far beyond local needs, for an impersonal 'market', and also the rather inhuman ways of producing this wealth (for others) through semi-slave or minimally salaried labour, created a climate in which individualism, envy and hatred could flourish. Envy between those who 'sold their soul' to the new system of extravagant exploitation of people and nature and those who resisted. In this climate, traditional healing capacities could be used in sorcery and counter-sorcery, in witchcraft and counter-witchcraft in the service (or not) of usury, profiteering and unjust exchange. Taussig (1980) observed a close relation between the reaction to the introduction of what he calls, following Marx, 'commodity fetishism' and a growing belief in the force of the devil, similar to what occurred in the late Middle Ages, when early capitalism was emerging in Europe.

Taussig explained this growing devil-belief among the Colombian peasants in the area he studied as 'part of an egalitarian social ethic that delegitimizes those persons who gain more money and success than the rest of the social group' (Ibid., p. 15). It seemed to be a reaction of the peasants to what they saw as 'an evil and destructive way of ordering economic life' (Ibid., p. 17). This evil refers to the market-economy as well as the plantation/agribusiness form of production, things which - at present - are rather beyond questioning and accepted as neutral, natural laws of economics by Westerners, unaware of their own 'ingenuous ethnocentrism' as Taussig (1980, p. 139) points out. He also noted how local communities saw some of their most capable members trapped into the 'devilish' modernization process rather than resisting the disruption of traditional community values. At times the community tried to keep such individuals in line with its values by (the threat of) bewitching them. But in fact this bewitching and its counterforces often further enhanced the undermining of traditional solidarity. Enterprising individuals who were confronted with a 'bad conscience' problem, with illness or bad luck, could retaliate by witch-accusation and demand punishment, even the death penalty.

In conclusion, foreign penetration tried to undermine local, often equitable values, sometimes by subtle manipulation such as labelling these cultural values as 'devilish'. At the same time, local communities often tried to use forms of sorcery to defend their values as an answer to the -in their eyes devilish- outside economic and cultural exploitation. But often this only increased the erosion of their own norms and values.
As history has shown, local communities developed various other forms of resistance against the undermining of their values. One of them, that of the organized peasant struggle to demand equitable land distribution, will be outlined in the later part of this chapter. Let me first describe some of my own experiences related to local equitable values and external penetration.

Some personal field experiences

Peasant men and women are strongly aware of the possibility of an equitable, sustainable way of life and are far less simple-minded, weak or underdeveloped than Westerners may think in their readiness to 'help' (or arrogance?). I learned this during a first field experience in 1955/56 as a UNESCO-sponsored development volunteer in a small village in El Salvador (Huizer 1972, ch.2). I noticed that in the village the old holistic Maya culture had only apparently disappeared. In spite of five centuries of influence by white landlords, coffee planters and Catholic priests, there existed a kind of cosmically-rooted spirituality, equity (though not equality), togetherness and solidarity.

They also felt a strong tie with Mother Earth, the land, even though they had lost this land in the past to the local landlords. This solidarity and spirituality gave them the power to live, survive and, in spite of everything, to hope for a better future. Their patience towards their oppressors gave me a feeling that precisely in their material poverty they had a kind of inner civilization from which I could learn much. Indirectly, they showed me a reflection of the barbarity of the Western 'civilization' that had devastated theirs. It had used, rather misused, their 'Mother Earth' to produce coffee and sugar on a large scale for the world market, while their children were undernourished. They were highly distrustful of any outside intervention.

Peasant 'apathy' and distrustful non-participation in 'development' projects initiated 'top-down' proved in this and many other cases to be justified as a rationally, consciously adopted strategy of not letting themselves be exploited more than they already were. I also experienced that, under more encouraging conditions, their 'apathy' could easily transform itself into considerable effort. On the whole, peasants and particularly the women took their position much less for granted than outsiders usually thought. Moreover, peasants as well as the local elites appeared to have a good deal of awareness of the fact that 'development' had to do with creating blatant inequalities (by taking away their land) and also with gradual erosion of their natural resources. Because of the worsening, inequitable situation, elites were also quite aware of potential peasant rebelliousness and felt the need to maintain a strong military police force to keep people 'in their place'. At times, indeed, peasants came into open resistance.

During many such village experiences in different Southern countries, it often struck me that there were certain people, men and women, with a special capacity to express clearly what their peers were feeling about exploitative situations. It was possible to recognize such people as persons with *charisma*, a kind of spiritual strength and radiation rooted in (what remained of) their local culture. When crisis situations became acute and confrontation with the powerful could no longer be avoided, those with *charisma* were the crucial motivators of their peers to act against the physical and psychological power that landlords and rich farmers have over 'their' peasants.

During the mid-1960s I had another revealing practical experience of these development dilemmas in Chile, while assisting in setting up a United Nations-sponsored regional community development programme in the Punitaqui valley to the North (Huizer 1972, ch.2). In that area, a system of equitable land distribution within the local *comunidades* still prevailed, though strongly threatened by outside forces. The initial non-participation of the peasant communities and their distrust in the programme was caused by the typical state of underdevelopment of the area, where the woods and small goldmines had been depleted by Chilean entrepreneurs in the recent past.

The community development projects to be introduced were, upon closer scrutiny, clearly and expressly resented by the local population as palliatives. It was relatively easy to discover through a participatory approach, that what the people really wanted was to recover the fertile communal valley lands from those entrepreneurs and landlords who had usurped those lands in view of a planned irrigation scheme about which the elite had information. Therefore the peasants had been pushed up the deforested mountain slopes during the past decades. With the backing of a new law and through pressure from the local population, the land reform process was put in motion. In this case the State (police and local development agency employees) hesitantly backed the new reform legislation. Fear of spreading communist and socialist trade-union influence may have been a reason to appease and content the local protest movement which thus was successful but remained rather localized. However, in September 1973, eight years later, some of the outstanding community leaders in this valley were summarily executed without trial as 'communist agitators'. This happened after the Chilean State had radically changed its character due to the coup by dictator Pinochet and the army, with support from foreign interests.

The most important lesson I gradually learned in the course of many years in the villages where I worked was that 'development' is not so much a technical problem but, particularly to the local people, a political issue with considerable spiritual-cultural implications: mostly the powerful (e.g. landlords or local elite) were benefiting considerably more and often at the cost of the poor majority. Moreover, the culture of equitability had been replaced by exploitation and the 'culture of repression'.

The Latin American historical context

The colonial period brought forms of natural and social imbalance to Latin America which persist until today. The fertile valleys or coastal lowlands, cultivated by the indigenous peoples during pre-colonial civilizations in a generally equitable manner, were transformed into large estates belonging to the conquerors and their heirs. In some areas they were used for pasture, elsewhere for plantation agriculture. The indigenous peasantry was in part sent as cheap labour to the mines, in which the conquerors were most interested. Or they were driven into subsistence agriculture on mountain slopes, if they did not want to work on the estates. Once a new status quo was established by armed force, legal provisions were made to give the indigenous population minimum guarantees for survival. Regulations were issued which protected the remainder of indigenous *comunidades* from complete extinction. Many cases are known, however, where recourse to such legal protection was in vain and where the peasants had to take up arms to defend their rights against usurpations. Mostly such self-defence activities were countered by the armed forces of the landowners or the army, and smothered in blood. Sometimes they reached such proportions that region-wide protest movements developed into a kind of war, such as the movement led by the Indian leader Tupac Amaru in the Andean highlands, at the end of the eighteenth century.

After the end of the colonial epoch in Latin America at the beginning of the 19th century (following the Napoleonic wars) the local white or mestizo elites in most countries expanded their wealth and power aggressively, mainly at the expense of the remaining indigenous communities. Thus, the process of pushing back the indigenous peasant population from their communal lands towards even more remote and barren agricultural areas went on. The 1953 IL0 report on indigenous peoples stated:

> With the advent of the republican form of government, the existence of the remaining aboriginal communities was endangered by the fact that the substantive Latin American legislation, informed by the European doctrine of economic liberalism, disowned the principle of corporate ownership of land and refused to grant them legal status. This facilitated the alienation of communal land, either by purchase or by appropriation on the part of powerful landowners, with the result that many members of *comunidades* became tenants or peons on haciendas. Unfamiliar with the official language and bewildered by a money economy, the Indians parted, often unknowingly, with land and water rights which had suddenly acquired a scarcity value (ILO, 1953).

Particularly in countries with a large, concentrated indigenous population, such as Mexico, Bolivia and others, this process, called 'the rape of the villages' led to what was considered as 'internal colonialism' (Gonzalez Casanova, 1962; Stavenhagen, 1962). It also led to numerous peasant revolts to defend communally-owned village lands. One study indicated that in Bolivia between 1861 and 1944 more than 2,000 peasant rebellions or movements occurred over land problems and against imposed servitude (Antezana, 1966).

Most of these resistance movements were bloodily repressed since they were local, scattered and not organized on a large scale. Only few of these rebellions became widespread and had a considerable national impact, e.g. the peasant movement led by Zarate Willka in 1898-1899 in the Bolivian highlands, which helped a Liberal government come to power. However, in this case as well as in many others, after the change of regime, promises of justice for indigenous peasants were forgotten, leader Willka was assassinated and peasant armies were overwhelmed by the government's army (Huizer, 1972).

As a consequence of further penetration by world market demands (sugar, coffee, oil) in the first half of the twentieth century, large-scale sustained, well-organized peasant movements have emerged to retain or recover communal land. These movements were directly or indirectly related to broader political or trade-union activities.

In the case of Mexico, one of the most outstanding peasant leaders was Emiliano Zapata, who at the age of thirty was elected president of the committee of his village, Anenequilco in the State of Morelos. The committee was attempting to recover its communal lands lost to the expansion of sugar estates. After legal means proved ineffective, time and again, peasants felt they had the right to take the law into their own hands, occupied the lost lands and joined the national revolutionary movement begun in 1910 by middle-class intellectuals, who opposed dictator Porfirio Díaz.

Thanks partly to continuously organized peasant pressure in various parts of the country, ideas from Zapata's local reform programme were integrated into the Mexican Constitution (Article 27) in 1917. In spite of this official acceptance, however, effective re-distribution of land took place only in those areas where the peasants were well organized or armed for protection against the violent landlord opposition to reforms through their so-called 'white guards'. For years, Zapata resisted many attempts to frighten or to bribe him. In 1919 he was assassinated. Communal land rights (ejidos) were however part of the Constitution and remained so until they were abolished in the 1990s, in order to promote privatization and commercialization in the context of the North American Free Trade Agreement. This was an important theme of the recent Zapatista rebellion in Chiapas.

The quest for equitable land (re)distribution: some important examples

Land reform, as carried out in Chile in the late 1960s and early 1970s, was strongly supported by United Nations agencies. As several UN studies of the 1960s (see United Nations, 1968) strongly emphasized, the need for redistribution of land as promoted by peasant movements for a more equitable society, is a precondition for any other form of rural development. Historical examples were the peasant rebellion in Mexico led by Emiliano Zapata and that of the revolutionary movement led by Chinese communist peasant leader Mao Ze Dong. Both movements put the dilemma of redistributing productive assets, in order to give the poor a fair chance and share, forcefully on the global agenda. In their footsteps similar - though often less radical - land reform movements have followed. However, in most debates on rural development since the 1980s, the advantages and risks of equitable redistribution of productive assets such as land, as a beginning for effective local development, are hardly taken into account, if at all. This neglect is the more remarkable since the revolutionary redistributive development model of China has been followed - though less radically - in Japan and later in Taiwan and South Korea.

In China during the 1920s, when over half of the peasantry was landless or semi-landless and prevailing exploitative relationships had become more blatant because of corruption and regional power struggles between the so-called warlords, social movements emerged that would result in outright revolution. They promoted equitable land distribution and were inspired by Taoist values. Already before the triumph of the Chinese peasant movements, the land reform implemented in areas under their control had a strong radiating influence in some surrounding countries. In Japan semi-landless peasants, mainly tenants, had been organizing since the First World War to achieve better tenancy conditions. This movement was growing rapidly, but was seriously hindered by the Japanese military that came to power after the Manchuria incident in 1931 (Huizer, 1980). After defeat of the Japanese army in 1945, the peasant movement proved to be still alive, though many leaders had spent years in jail, and it was quickly re-activated, able to pressure for reforms in the land tenure situation. Between 1946 and 1949 almost all land property in excess of one hectare was redistributed equitably among tillers, mainly through purchase and resale. Altogether, a broad domestic market for industrial goods was created by giving the peasantry access to the means of production and helping them to further improve their situation by officially sponsored farmers' associations.

A few years later, a similar land reform was implemented in Taiwan, strongly backed by the Rural Reconstruction movement created by James Yen with US support and guidance. The Taiwanese government was, in those years, dominated by Chinese who had fled from mainland China and had no landed interests to defend in Taiwan (for an overview see: Huizer, 1980, pp. 46-63). Therefore the Government was determined to carry out reforms and found ways to deal with local landlords' opposition. One technique used to dispel such opposition was the wide dissemination of information on drastic reform measures taken in China. The moderate forms of the reform programme in Japan were pointed out in comparison. This form of publicity was reported to be highly successful. In addition, reforms were introduced in a 'gradually progressive' manner.

Later, the Syngman Rhee government in South Korea also initiated a radical land reform, under pressure from US occupation forces to counter growing rural unrest and movements sympathetic to the communist government in North Korea that had carried out reforms similar to those in China (Barraclough, 1991).

Korten's (1992) assessment of the successes of these Asian 'tigers' points out that these were due particularly to institutional foundations which included a radical redistribution of land among the mass of small and (formerly) landless farmers, and creation of member-managed rural organizations. Although, as he noted 'none of these societies had consistently democratic national administrations' (Ibid., p. 75), local power monopolies that elsewhere seriously distorted development of local economies were checked. 'In Japan, Taiwan and South Korea, government's hand was particularly strong in land reform and education', also taking 'a variety of measures to provide their own agriculture and industries with substantial protection from foreign competition' (Ibid., p. 77). As a result, the expanding domestic rural markets for industrial goods and services became the initial basis for demand-driven development of local industries, 'equity-led' rather than 'export-led' (Ibid., p.77).

Moreover land reforms in Japan, Taiwan and South-Korea were imposed and financially aided by the US. This was, as a UNRISD study (Barraclough, 1991) points out, to keep radical peasant movements in those countries from following the Chinese example and taking their fate into their own hands by abolishing semi-feudal conditions. These facts - often ignored - regarding the exemplary development successes of NICs leave the present discussion on the free market and democracy as a prerequisite (or not) for development co-operation wide open. There is no 'end of history' and it should also be observed that the equitable land redistribution in Japan, Taiwan and South Korea, was a response to the peasant revolution that had taken place in China between 1927 and 1949.

Recently, new pressures for such reforms have emerged. In addition to grassroots activities from landless and semi-landless peasants and policy statements by international rural development agencies, world-wide concern for more appropriate use of land has been expressed by those concerned with ecology and the 'common future' of all mankind. The link between environmental deterioration and large-scale commercial agriculture that has replaced more sustainable local agricultural systems is coming increasingly under scrutiny. New appeals are made to governments and enlightened elites to show the 'political will' to transcend entrenched vested interests to benefit humanity as a whole. Thus, the United Nations World Commission on Environment and Development Report (the so-called Brundtland report) stated:

In many countries where land is very unequally distributed, land reform is a basic requirement. Without it, institutional and policy changes meant to protect the resource base can actually promote inequalities by shutting the poor off from resources and by favouring those with large farms, who are better able to obtain the limited credit and services available. By leaving hundreds of millions without options, such changes can have the opposite of their intended effect, ensuring the continued violation of ecological imperatives.

Given institutional and ecological variations, a universal approach to land reform is impossible. Each country should work out its own programme of land reform to assist the land-poor and to provide a base for co-ordinated resource conservation. The redistribution of land is particularly important where large estates and vast numbers of the land-poor coexist. Crucial components include the reform of tenancy arrangements, security of tenure, and the clear recording of land rights. In agrarian reforms, the productivity of the land and, in forest areas, the protection of forests, should be a major concern (WCED, 1987, p. 141).

Grassroots pressure for equitable land use has recently become publicized again through the Zapatista movement (EZLN - Zapatista Army of National Liberation). A number of small towns in Chiapas were occupied by indigenous peasant rebel forces to demonstrate that they would no longer tolerate brutalities and land usurpations by local landlords and politicians. The rebellion, as was noted by many observers, also used modern means, such as the Internet computer network. The occupations of small towns and the consecutive massive intervention by the Mexican army were so effectively publicized world-wide, that the government had to come to a truce, so as not to lose face internationally. Negotiations have been going on since early 1994 about how atrocities by landlords and their political allies could be ended, how land could be officially allocated to the many peasants entitled to it according to the law just abolished to make place for privatization, part of the North American Free Trade agreement (NAFTA), how cultural identities could be effectively respected and how local and national elections could be organized more democratically.

From most cases of more or less equitable land redistribution, it can be seen that they generally came about as a result of considerable pressure from below and accompanying unrest. Governments that responded positively to these pressures have mostly survived and their economies have benefited from the reforms implemented. Equity in the distribution of vital resources is not merely a side issue, but a basic condition for further national development that aims to benefit the whole population. Governments which have tried to violently oppress reform movements have had to face endemic rural unrest and instability, and this will continue into the next millennium.

References

Antezana, Luis, 1966. *El Movimiento Obrero Boliviano (1935-1943)*. La Paz.
Barraclough, Solon, 1991. *An End To Hunger? The Social Origins of Food Strategies*. London: Zed Books.

Berman, Morris, 1981. *The Reenchantment of the World.* Ithaca: Cornell University Press.

Fanon, Franz, 1961. *Les damnés de la Terre.* Paris: Maspero.

Gonzalez Casanova, Pablo, 1963. Sociedad plural, colonialismo interno y desarrollo. In: *America Latina,* VI, no. 3.

Huizer, Gerrit, 1972. *The Revolutionary Potential of Peasants in Latin America.* Lexington, Mass.: Heath-Lexington Books, (Spanish version: *El Potencial Revolucionario del Campesino en America Latina,* Mexico: Siglo XXI, 1973).

Huizer, Gerrit, 1980. *Peasant Movements and their Counterforces in South-East Asia.* New Delhi: Marwah Publ.

International Labour Office (I.L.O.), 1953. Indigenous Peoples. Studies and Reports, No. 35. Geneva: ILO.

Korten, David, 1992. *Getting to the 21st Century. Voluntary Action and the Global Agenda.* New Delhi: Oxford & IBH Publ. Company.

Merchant, Carolyn, 1980. *The Death of Nature. Women, Ecology and the Scientific Revolution.* San Francisco: Harper and Row.

Mies, Maria, 1986. *Patriarchy and Accumulation of Capital on a World Scale. Women in the International Division of Labour.* London: Zed Books.

Mies, Maria and Vandana Shiva, 1993. *Ecofeminism.* Halifax, Nova Scotia: Fernwood; London: Zed Press.

Salomon, Frank, 1987. Ancestor cults and resistance to the state in Arequipa, ca. 1748-1754, in: Steve J. Stern, ed., *Resistance, Rebellion and Consciousness in the Andean Peasant World, 18th to 20th Centuries,* Madison/London: University of Wisconsin Press.

Schmidheiny, Stephan ; with the Business Council for Sustainable Development, 1992. *Changing course: a Global Business Perspective on Development and the Environment.* Cambridge, Mass. [etc.]: MIT Press.

Shiva, Vandana, 1988. *Staying Alive: Women, Ecology and Survival in India.* New Delhi: Kali for Women/London: Zed Press.

Silverblatt, Irene, 1987. *Moon, Sun and Witches. Gender Ideologies and Class in Inca and Colonial Peru.* Princeton: Princeton University Press.

Stavenhagen, Rodolfo, 1963. Clases, colonialismo y aculturación. In: *America Latina,* VI, no. 4.

Taussig, Michael, 1980. *The Devil and Commodity Fetishism in South America.* Chapel Hill. University of North Carolina Press.

Taussig, Michael, 1987. *Shamanism, Colonialism and the Wild Man. A Study in Terror and Healing.* Chicago/London: University of Chicago Press.

United Nations, 1968. Report of the World Land Reform Conference, E/4298/Rev.1. New York: United Nations Publ.

Wolf, Eric, 1982. *Europe and the Peoples Without History,* Berkeley / Los Angeles / London: University of California Press.

World Bank, 1983. 'China'. *Socialist Economic Development,* vol.3, Washington, D.C. World Bank.

World Commission on Environment and Development (WCED), 1987. *Our Common Future.* Oxford/New York: Oxford University Press, (Brundtland Report).

6

Equity and Legal Pluralism: Taking Customary Law into Account in Natural Resource Policies[1]

Franz von Benda-Beckmann, Keebet von Benda-Beckmann & Joep Spiertz

One of the most important issues in natural resource policies is the search for appropriate property regimes that could ensure a more efficient use of natural resources, sustainable resource management, and a more just or equitable distribution of access to resources as well.[2] For decades, government interventions into the natural resource laws of tribal or village populations pursued a policy that assumed that such indigenous customary legal and management systems had to be substituted by 'modern' law and resource management. This was to be achieved by creating a private law regime for property modelled on European legal systems, and by declaring large tracts of natural resources State property. The pre-existing local laws, if recognised at all, were assumed to be an obstacle on the way to economic development. Especially property regimes with strong communal characteristics were held responsible for inefficient resource exploitation. They were seen, moreover, as opposed to 'fundamental' western values, as well as constraining too strongly the individuals' opportunities for making optimal productive use of resources and the earnings from such production. These rights were also regarded as insecure, and last but not least, they could not be given as collateral for productive credit rural people were supposed to require in order to enter market production.[3] After Hardin's paper on the *Tragedy of the commons* (1968), communal property forms have also been blamed for ecologically unsustainable resource uses.[4] More recently, however, we find almost the opposite position in research and policy recommendations. Communities, community based rights, and communities' customary laws have been discovered as a positive factor in resource management. These approaches are based upon the conviction that such norms are an expression of the people's own values, and that intervention and legislation have to avoid measures that would weaken or contradict them.[5] The obvious failure of many resource rights reforms has certainly contributed to these new insights. Increasingly, therefore it has been argued that customary community based rights should get more attention and wider recognition in natural resource policies.

In both policy paradigms, customary law is a problematic notion because it is often associated with three interrelated assumptions which are independent from the negative or positive moral or pragmatic values one attributes to customary laws. First, many researchers and policy makers start from the assumption that in every society or ethnic group there exists a coherent set of norms that can be labelled customary or traditional law. These 'deeply ingrained' legal systems are supposed to govern local people's behaviour as well as their response to outside intervention. Second, all the law which is not enacted and applied by State institutions is usually seen as 'customary' law, that is based upon customary behaviour patterns that find their origin and legitimation in historical usages. Third, in the notion of customary law, law and behaviour or practices are considered to be more or less identical. The terms customary law and customary practices are often used interchangeably; often this dual meaning is in the use of the concept 'custom'.

In our contribution we want to take a critical look at these assumptions. For policies aiming at taking customary law into account that are based upon these assumptions are likely to fail. So in the first part of our paper we shall explicate our own understanding of customary law and its relations to actual social practices. In the second part we shall discuss the implications of our considerations for natural resource management policies that aim at improving equity, effectivity and sustainability of resource use.

Customary law, local law, and legal pluralism

Legal pluralism

In nearly all contemporary rural areas in third world States, one can see some form of legal pluralism with respect to the management and exploitation of natural resources.[6] Rights to political and administrative control, over resources and rights to use and transfer them, are not merely regulated by laws made by State legislatures and applied by the courts. Prior to the advent of colonising powers and the colonial States they established, local communities had their own political and economic organisations and their own laws, as well as procedures in which conflicts were managed.

In non-literate societies, these laws were unwritten and usually transmitted orally, often at public ceremonies. Many societies had also religious laws. The colonial rulers introduced their own law, primarily establishing a new political and administrative constitution of the new political entity and also creating rights over those natural resources they intended to exploit. Especially the resources that were not exploited in a sedentary fashion by local people (the infamous wastelands) were declared State domain. The more the State got involved in the control and exploitation of people, their labour and natural resources, the more indigenous legal systems were officially substituted by State law. On the other hand, the representatives of State legal systems, but also of customary or religious legal systems often constructed more or less clear spheres of validity and applicability for parts of these systems.

While such legal constructions of the validity of non-State laws may have limited influence, people's laws are still an important aspect of rural life. Though inevitably changing, and often considerably weakened as a consequence of economic and political developments, these laws continued to exist in most third world countries. That means that also today, rural people, researchers and State or project officials are not simply confronted with a single, unitary legal system but with a co-existence and complexity of legal phenomena derived from and embedded in a multiplicity of normative systems and rights.

Customary law and local law

The term 'customary law' can be, and often is, used in two meanings. The first meaning is a descriptive characterisation of rules. One speaks of customary rules because these rules have been 'accepted and used by local communities for a long time'. In the second sense, customary law refers to a system of rules which is named 'customary law'. But it should be noted that there may be more than one construction of 'customary law'. Local people are not the only actors who thus classify and label rules as belonging to a legal system. Customary law in most legal systems is also a category of which the characteristics and substantive content are defined by law makers, judges or other experts. In legal anthropological literature, therefore, it has become common to distinguish 'people's customary law' from 'lawyers' customary law'.[7]

Such co-existence usually lies at the basis of considerable legal insecurity and conflict. For the ways in which (bundles of) rights to natural resources are conceived, how the objects of such rights are defined, and the question of who rightful rights holders are is resolved, may differ in the various legal systems. Moreover, so-called customary or traditional rules of behaviour, are, and probably always have been, intermingled with norms emanating from other sources of power and authority, generated outside local communities, such as the State and government agencies, religious teachings at various levels, etc. The same holds true for the institutions involved in water management. Some are based in traditional leadership positions and councils, others, like Water Users Associations, are quite recent institutional developments in which State administrative regulation with more traditional ideas over decision making powers are amalgamated. Such rules and institutions have become known as neo-traditional, 'hybrid' (Holleman 1978), 'combined' (Fitzpatrick 1983), or 'compounded law' (F. von Benda-Beckmann 1983). Moreover, State law usually also becomes part of the legal elements used in rural communities.

The law in villages (the living law) therefore cannot simply be identified with customary law. There usually is more than only customary law in villages, and not all village law is customary. Older and newer versions of 'traditional' or 'customary' property relations may co-exist, and local village versions of customary property law may co-exist with customary law creations of State courts or legal science. Studies carried out in Nepal, Indonesia, and elsewhere as well[8] have shown that in real life, even in the most isolated villages, different kinds of customary rules co-exist. Many elements of customary law are formed by very general and abstract principles which allow many different interpretations of what they mean with respect to a concrete situation.

The use of the term 'customary law', without further qualification, thus can be very confusing because not all customary rules in the first sense need to be part of customary law in the second sense; while not all rules said to be part of customary law are in fact customary. Conventional conceptualisations of customary law do not account for the empirical lack of distinction between the various kinds of norms. So, the whole constellation of 'customary rules' that are expressed and used at the local level, appears to be far more complex and dynamic than one might expect. In order to make analytical distinctions between such multiple levels and sources of rules or law and their amalgamations in actual social processes, it has been suggested to introduce as a further analytical category the concept of local law, i.e. the locally dominant mixtures of interpretations and transformations of the surrounding universe of plural legal repertoires (Spiertz, 1992; F. and K. von Benda-Beckmann, 1991; K. von Benda-Beckmann et al., 1996).

This emphasis on the existence of local law does not mean, of course, that the notion of customary law could be replaced by the notion of local law, or that customary law would play no role of significance in rural communities. But when looking at the relationship between customary and local law, we can be faced with different situations. Many elements of local law may be customary in the sense of being based upon an assumed continuity of local legal tradition. Such rules and principles may, but need not be incorporated into the systemic category of 'customary law'. Customary law, or different constructions of customary law, is part of the legal pluralism which constitutes the environment in which local laws are generated in different localities. Depending on the context in which people interpret or otherwise deal with law, elements of customary rules may have become part of a newly developed and dynamic local law. In other situations, however, customary law (even when old fashioned and no longer regularly used) for strategic reasons may be presented as an objectified or idealised system of rules, quite irrespective of the actual local law on the ground.[9] Especially in arenas like parliament, courts and administration, but also in development projects, authoritative, objectified versions of customary law often become a powerful means of promoting or defending specific interests.

Customary law and customary practices

This leads us to the relationships between law - whether customary, local or State law - and social practices. Socio-legal studies in the field of law and behaviour have generally demonstrated that the mere existence of legal rules and principles, whether originating from government legislation, tradition or contemporary local law making, does not justify to draw direct conclusions with respect to the behaviour of people. Rules and principles only become significant in natural resource management when people - farmers, government officials, project managers, etc. - orient their behaviour towards these rules, and when this orientation thus becomes one of the factors which influences their behaviour in matters of resource management or in decision making processes. The plural legal situation complicates matters because following one rule, State law, often means contravening another, local or customary law. Therefore, in plural legal contexts we are always confronted with the question of the *relative* significance of one type of legal rules in relation to others, apart from the question which other, non-legal factors, play a role.

As was mentioned above, the perception of the dynamic character of the interrelationships between customary law and people's practices is often obscured by the assumption that customary law and customary practices would be more or less identical. The terms are often used synonymously. The frequent use of the word 'custom' which denotes both customary rules as well as customary behaviour, contributes to such ambiguity. The consequence of this is that the relationship between customary *law* and actual *behaviour* cannot be examined systematically. However, whether this hidden postulate of a general empirical congruence between rules or principles of customary law and the type of behaviour to which the rules and principles refer is correct, can only be determined by empirical research. It should be stressed that one certainly cannot simply assume such a congruence. But it would be equally misleading to assume that the rules would have no significance for behaviour when there is no congruence between rules and practices. Legal rules and principles do not only become significant if people behave according to the rules. Even when people's practices deviate from legal rules, they may function as a source of positive or negative motivation. They can also be used as a resource in social interaction: to legitimate claims to water or land in struggles over natural resources. Under certain conditions they may be the only way of justifying one's claim to rights or to participation in resource management (see Turk 1978, Moore 1978; F. von Benda-Beckmann 1983, 1989).

This is particularly so when rights are problematic or disputed, and when people negotiate rights or submit their contradictory claims to an institution with decision making authority. The way in which people use legal rules and principles becomes different then. In ordinary life and activities, rural people usually are not interested in claiming explicitly a specific legitimation for their normative rules as custom, customary law, State law, or religious law, nor do they have any interest in making scientific or legal categories. But this is different in social processes of disputing. Claims have to be justified, and this usually has to be done by reference to legal rules and principles.

We also cannot assume that there is a clear relationship between rules about rights to natural resources on the one hand, and the actual rights of individuals, groups of people or agencies on the other. We therefore need to distinguish the *legal constructions* of rights from the *actual social relationships* that connect concrete right holding individuals, groups or associations with concrete and demarcated resources.

Customary law and its definitions of rights to natural resource management do not tell us how rights are actually distributed over the population. This distinction is important. If it is not made, there is no room for looking at interrelationships between legal forms or types of property relationships and the concrete manifestations of property relationships in social and economic life. Nor can questions concerning the relationship between types of natural resource rights and their distribution be adequately dealt with systematically. For instance, whether certain types of property rights are likely to lead to concentration and accumulation of property by a few (see Berry 1988, Bruce 1988, Sugarman 1983), whether they have stronger or lesser functions for social and economic security (Chambers and Leach 1989, F. von Benda-Beckmann 1990, van de Ven 1994), or are likely to lead to more or less sustainable resource use cannot be answered. With respect to the theme of equity in water distribution, for example, equitable rules about water distribution (whether they are customary or official) do not necessarily lead to equitable practice.

Implications: How does planning benefit from research?

Taking customary law into account

In contemporary development policy it is deemed important to involve local people in the process of change and development intervention as well as take their customary institutions and laws seriously into account. However, the above considerations show us that we move in a complex field of problems and dilemmas where no easy general answers can be expected. Moreover, the expression 'to take customary rules and practices into account' itself is ambivalent. In one sense, which we call the *normative sense*, it means that such rules and practices should be recognised as *deserving validity,* as valuable elements in the overall context of water management organisation. But to take into account can also mean: seeing them as relevant factors in the multitude of factors *that together* constitute present reality, independent from the question of any normative or moral evaluation of them.

Taking customary law into account in the normative sense

Customary law is often taken to be inherently democratic, egalitarian, equitable and therefore as deserving support, while State law or government regulations are not. Since the sustainability of natural resource use has become an important issue, customary law and practice of resource management is regarded as being based upon indigenous environmental knowledge that is very sensitive to nature and to ecologically responsible resource exploitation. This may often be the case. However, it cannot be simply assumed. There is ample evidence that in local communities unequal power relationships often greatly affect the ways in which resources are distributed and managed. Upon closer inspection, it turns out that local law establishes and legitimises many differences in political power and rights over land and water resources. Unequal access to water may be a result of 'legal' unequal land distribution, which in turn is a result of rules of kinship and inheritance and local forms of social stratification. In many local societies, gender relations are systematically skewed with respect to rights to land and water (K. von Benda-Beckmann 1990-91). Such differences often have an additional basis in religious rules and categories, such as caste, but these legal elements are often not seen as forming part of customary law, and therefore are easily neglected. Yet they are very customary, and they are very significant for concrete property relations to natural resources.

Research projects on natural resource rights have shown that there is a fundamental difference between original occupants, settlers, water and land users, and late-comers. Often original settlers have stronger rights to larger parts of natural resources (see F. von Benda-Beckmann 1979, F. von Benda-Beckmann and Taale 1992). But if newcomers belong to higher and more powerful classes, they may also obtain more rights (for Nepal, see Shukla et al. 1996, K. von Benda-Beckmann, Spiertz and F. von Benda-Beckmann 1997). Research in India and Nepal has shown that women usually do not have rights to irrigation water on their own account. Widows and divorced women have difficulties obtaining, or keeping access to water, for example because they are discriminated against in rotational distribution systems of water allocation. They may get a turn to water, but only at night. Local gender inequality is further enhanced by the fact that decision-making over the maintenance of irrigation infrastructure, intimately related to access rights, is very much a male concern. And the research has shown that there may be conflicts between rights to drinking water - a female domain - and rights to irrigation water - a male domain. Moreover, in disputes and contacts with outside agencies, women are usually in a weaker position because men tend to function as the main intermediaries and brokers in the communication and interaction channels to these agencies (K. von Benda-Beckmann 1990/91).

It appears that local differences in political and economic power are crucial for our understanding of the question whether, by whom and with how much success decision making authorities, functionaries of village institutions or State courts, can be mobilised. To defend their interests, the powerless have far more difficulty in mobilising law and legal institutions, whether State institutions or other, than the powerful (Galanter 1974, K. von Benda-Beckmann 1984). When considering the normative recognition of local and customary laws and rights, one has to ask questions such as: Are 'the people', or 'the farmers' a homogeneous category? Is there social stratification? How are power positions supported by local law? Who are the social, economic and political elites? To what extent are gender differences important? This then leads to questions concerning natural resource rights, such as: Are rights to water different for different social classes? Different for men and women? Different for original occupants and newcomers? Different for people of different caste? And, very important, who profits from the existing arrangements?

Therefore the simple fact that under the legitimation of State laws that do not recognise local or customary laws, rural people are regularly oppressed and exploited economically, does not mean that local laws are democratic or equitable. A too quick and enthusiast embracing therefore may only contribute to the continuation or even reinforcement of social and economic inequalities. In some situations, and for some categories of the population (women, descendants of slaves, bonded labourers, discriminated immigrants, low caste persons), State law may be an important resource in their struggle for emancipation (see F. von Benda-Beckmann and Taale 1992). A general plea for 'community rights based development' without looking at the internal social organisation of communities and the functioning of their laws, as it is sometimes advocated (Lynch and Talbott 1995) therefore should be treated with caution.

What is to be recognised: customary law or local law?

The normative validation of local and/or customary rules, rights and principles is problematic also in another respect. When State legislators, judges, or sympathetic researchers are open to give more official recognition and sanction to non-State law, they tend to think of non-State law only in legal categories such as 'customary law' or 'practices'. By that they usually mean a normative construction of customary rights and customary practices which are only validated under the conditions that (a) such rights can be considered to be historically grown at local level, free from interference of outside agencies such as the administrative agencies of the colonial or independent State, and (b) it is sustained by actual practice. As we have explained before, these constructions capture only certain social contexts, namely the rule and decision making of the State apparatus or other specific local decision making settings. It is these dogmatic constructions which count, and not the norms and values described in ordinary people's own terms. Government legislators or judges may have little use for some 'local' law, certainly if social practices are not in accordance with these rules. They do not really wish to give the ordinary local rules validity in the dominant legal framework they are operating in. But even if they wanted to, they would find it almost impossible to incorporate such customary law. Often there is not one generally accepted local law, nor is there is a valid criterion on which to select among the existing versions of local law. Moreover, none of the existing versions may go back to ancient tradition. Finally, incorporation almost inevitably leads to change and distortion. The colonial history has shown that it is exceedingly difficult if not impossible to incorporate customary law into the State legal system without changing it in a fundamental way.

This poses another dilemma for researchers and legal advisors, who sympathise with local law, and who often are the persons who have, and want to produce the necessary evidence on customary law. If they want to make local law relevant in the court and policy contexts, they may have to adapt and thus change and distort their findings, framing them in a language which will be more readily accepted by policy makers. If not, they may risk that policy makers and judges will not find their research evidence relevant in their own framework of 'customary law' relevance. The researcher thus may be attempted to change roles from academic scholar to an advocate for customary law, and risk becoming a bad scholar; or else he remains a research scholar and risks becoming an unsuccessful advocate.[10] The decision will usually be a pragmatic and political one; social science cannot help making this choice.

Taking customary or local law into account as significant factors

But, however one may value local law and practices, they are facts of social life and have to be taken seriously in order to understand people's behaviour. In many regions around the world, normative principles attached to principles of social stratification, in combination with differences in economic wealth and political power, still largely determine access to land and water and the distribution of water and maintenance obligations.[11] Differences in land ownership determine differences in access to water. One may wish these factors were irrelevant and one may not want to take them into account in the sense of accepting or legitimating their normative validity. Yet they are a fact of local law, a factor that very likely will influence the consequences of whatever intervention is proposed.

It becomes especially important to take such explanatory factors into account in relation to policy objectives that are concerned with such values as a just, sustainable and efficient management and use of water. Research carried out, among others, in Indonesia and Nepal shows that in general farmer managed irrigation systems are more reliable and efficient than government operated systems (Lam, Lee and Ostrom, 1994). This seems to suggest that local or customary law in this realm deserves support. The example from Bali for instance (Spiertz 1991) indicates that local law may under certain conditions also guarantee equal distribution and allocation of water. But other research, for instance in Nepal, has shown that this is not necessarily the case (see F. and K. von Benda-Beckmann and Spiertz 1996). However efficiently the farmer managed systems in Nepal may function, they are notoriously malfunctioning if it comes to equal distribution. Could it be, then, that in Nepal these systems function better than agency managed systems, precisely because of the political and economic power inequalities shaped by local, or customary law? In the heat of the defence of suppressed people, it is easily forgotten that they may be as much suppressed by their own elites as by government agencies. Reliability and efficiency do not necessarily go hand in hand with equality and justice nor with sustainability. Thinking through realistic possibilities for future developments, one needs an understanding of what the role of local law and practices has been in each of these respects. A somewhat romantic picture of local affairs, assuming that if only local people were left in peace they would unfold their creative possibilities, on closer examination may turn out to represent a totally unrealistic view of the functioning of customary law with respect to the objectives of equitable access to, and distribution of natural resources combined with economic efficiency and sustainability.

This poses another dilemma which can only be solved by a *political* choice and for which social sciences do not provide a solution. Are we primarily interested in sustainable management of water, or is equal access to water as important, or even more so? How do we resolve the sometimes contradictory concerns for equity, sustainability, and economic growth? Wishing to attain all three objectives in a well-balanced way will not remove the actual constraints. The equity issue is particularly difficult because rights to water, as we have seen, are so intimately related to wider socio-political organisation. Depending on the choice we make, the kind of intervention will be different. Basically, a choice has to be made between two options: marginal improvements that leave the local socio-political constellation more or less intact, or attempting a more fundamental change in land and water distribution, which may be faced with nearly insurmountable political obstacles.

Conclusion

It may be evident that the complexity that emerges from research cannot be directly applied or fully incorporated into restatements or changes of the law by policy makers. Still, such research does provide a more adequate picture of the legal situation and the relative weight of the various legal systems at the local level. It also may provide some valuable explanatory insights into the reasons and causes which have led to the current situation. This will help forming a realistic assessment of the most likely outcomes of newly planned interventionist measures. All these are important preconditions for responsible policy making. While research does not contain clear directives for policy, and while it cannot provide guarantees for success, it allows a realistic consideration of policy alternatives and their probable intended and unintended consequences. These considerations may be pretty pessimistic ones, for they may point to necessary changes that are politically nearly impossible to achieve. But this is pessimistic only if one compares a more realistic assessment with too optimistic expectations of social science and policy making.

Notes

1   This paper is largely based upon a longer article entitled Water rights and policy. Pp. 77-99 in J. Spiertz and M. Wiber (eds.) *The role of law in natural resource management*. The Hague: VUGA, (1996).

2   See for instance McCay and Acheson 1987, Berkes 1989, Ostrom 1990, Reeve 1991, Schlager and Ostrom 1992, Vogler 1992, Bruce and Migot-Adholla 1994, Lynch and Talbott 1995.

3   For critical reviews of these assumptions, see F. von Benda-Beckmann 1989, Dove 1986, Coldham 1978, Hitchcock 1980.

4   Hardin's publication has triggered off a voluminous literature on the nature of communal resources and (un)sustainable resource use. See for instance McCay and Acheson 1987, Berkes 1989, Gibbs and Bromley 1989, Ostrom 1990, Bruce 1988, Wiber 1993.

5   See for instance Lynch and Talbott 1995 with many references. A shift from the earlier 'replacement paradigm' in land reform policies to an 'adaptation paradigm' is also propagated in Bruce and Migot-Adholla 1994.

6   There is a multitude of literature on legal pluralism, both empirically and/or conceptually and analytically oriented. See F. von Benda-Beckmann 1979, 1992, 1997; K. von Benda-Beckmann 1984. For systematic treatments of the conceptual questions, see Vanderlinden 1971, 1989, Griffiths 1986, Merry 1988.

7   See K. von Benda-Beckmann 1984, Lam 1985, F. and K. von Benda-Beckmann 1985, Woodman

1988, Spiertz and de Jong 1992, K. von Benda-Beckmann et al. 1996, F. von Benda-Beckmann and Taale 1992.

8   See for Nepal, U. Pradhan and R. Pradhan; Shukla et al. 1993; U. Pradhan 1990, 1994; Dixit 1994. For Indonesia, see Ambler 1989; Spiertz 1992; F. von Benda-Beckmann, 1989,1991, K. von Benda-Beckmann 1984. For Sri Lanka and the Philippines, see Wiber 1991, 1993; Spiertz and de Jong 1992.

9   See F. von Benda-Beckmann 1979, 1989; F. and K. von Benda-Beckmann 1985, 1991; K. von Benda-Beckmann 1984, 1990/91; Clammer 1973; Maddock 1986, Moore 1978, Snyder 1981, Spiertz 1991, Spiertz and De Jong 1992, Werbner 1980, Wiber 1991, Woodman 1988.

10 The anthropologist Ken Maddock has discussed this dilemma in a very vivid manner with respect to the land-rights question of Australian Aborigines (Maddock 1986).

11 See R. Pradhan and U. Pradhan (1996) and other contributions in Spiertz and Wiber (1996).

References

Ambler, J. (1989) *Adat and aid: Management of small-scale irrigation in West Sumatra.* Diss. Ph.D., Cornell University.

Benda-Beckmann, F. von (1979) *Property in social continuity: Continuity and change in the mainte-nance of property relationships through time in Minangkabau, West Sumatra.* The Hague: M. Nijhoff.

Benda-Beckmann, F. von (1983) Why law does not behave: Critical and constructive reflections on the social scientific perception of the social significance of law. In H. Finkler (comp.), *Proceedings of the Symposium on Folk Law and Legal Pluralism,* XIth IUAES Congress, 1983, Vancouver. Ottawa.

Benda-Beckmann, F. von (1989) Scape-goat and magic charm: Law in development theory and practice. *Journal of Legal Pluralism* 28: 129-148.

Benda-Beckmann, F. von (1990) Sago, law and food security on Ambon. Pp.157-199 in J.I.H. Bakker (ed.) *The world food crisis: Food security in comparative perspective.* Canadian Scholars' Press Inc., Toronto, Ontario, Canada.

Benda-Beckmann, F. von (1992) Introduction: Understanding agrarian law in society. Pp. 1-22 in F. von Benda-Beckmann y M. van der Velde (eds.) *Law as a resource in agrarian struggles.* Wageningen: Pudoc.

Benda-Beckmann, F. von (1995) Anthropological approaches to property law and economics. *European Journal of Law and Economics* 2:309-336.

Benda-Beckmann, F. von (1997) Citizens, strangers and indigenous peoples: Conceptual politics and legal pluralism. To appear in *Law and Anthropology* 9.

Benda-Beckmann, F. & K. von (1985) Transformation and change in Minangkabau. Pp. 235-278 in L. Thomas y F. von Benda-Beckmann (eds.), *Change and continuity in Minangkabau.* Athens: Ohio University Monographs in International Studies.

Benda-Beckmann, F. & K. von (1991) Law in society: From blindman's-buff to multilocal law. in: *Living law in the Low Countries,* Special issue of *Recht der Werkelijkheid:*119-139. Amsterdam: Vuga.

Benda-Beckmann, F. & K. von (1994) Property, politics and conflict: Ambon and Minangkabau compared. *Law and Society Review* 28:589-607.

Benda-Beckmann, F. von & T. Taale (1992) The changing laws of hospitality: Guest labourers in the political economy of rural legal pluralism. Pp. 61-87 in F. von Benda-Beckmann and M. van der Velde (eds.) *Law as a resource in agrarian struggles.* Wageningen: Pudoc.

Benda-Beckmann, F. & K. von, & H.L.J. Spiertz (1996) *Local law and customary practices in the study of water rights.* Paper presented at the workshop on Waterrights, Conflict and Policy, January 22-24, Kathmandu.

Benda-Beckmann, K. von (1984) *The broken stairways to consensus: Village justice and state courts in Minangkabau.* Dordrecht: Foris.

Benda-Beckmann, K. von (1990/1991) Development, Law and Gender-Skewing: An examination of the impact of development on the socio-legal position of Indonesian women, with special reference to Minangkabau. *Journal of Legal Pluralism* 30/31: 87-120.

Benda-Beckmann, K. von, H.L.J. Spiertz & F. von Benda-Beckmann (1997) Contesting rights to water in Nepal irrigation: A legal anthropological perspective. Forthcoming in E.H.P. Brans, E. de Haan, A. Nollkaemper and J. Rinzema (eds.) *The scarcity of water: Emerging legal and policy responses.* Environmental and Policy Series. London: Kluwer International.

Benda-Beckmann, K. von, M. De Bruijn, H. Van Dijk, G. Hesseling, B. Van Koppen & L. Res (1996) *Rechten van vrouwen op natuurlijke hulpbronnen.* Wageningen: Internationaal Agrarisch Centrum.

Berkes, F., ed. (1989) *Common property resources: Ecology and community-based sustainable development.* Londres: Belhaven Press.

Berry, S. (1988) Concentration without privatization? Some consequences of changing patterns of rural land control. Pp.53-75 in R.E. Downs and S.P. Reyna (eds.) *Land and society in contemporary Africa.* Hanover and London: University Press of New England.

Bruce, J.W. (1988) A perspective on indigenous land tenure systems and land concentration. Pp. 23-53 in Downs, R.E. and Reyna, S.P. (eds.) *Land and society in contemporary Africa.* London: University Press of New England.

Bruce, J. & S. Migot Adholla, eds. (1994) *Searching for land tenure security in Africa.* Dubuque: Kendall/Hunt.

Chambers, R. & M. Leach (1989) Trees as savings and security for the rural poor. *World Development* 17: 329-342.

Clammer, J. (1973) Colonialism and the perception of tradition in Fiji. Pp. 199-220 in T. Asad (ed.) *Anthropology and the Colonial Encounter.* Atlantic Highlands: Humanities Press.

Coldham, S. (1978) The effect of registration of title upon customary land rights in Kenya. *Journal of African Law* 22: 91-111.

Dixit, A. (1994), Water projects in Nepal: lessons from displacement and rehabilitation. Pp. 74-85 in: Dipak Gyawali and Ajaya Dixit (eds.) *The Himalaya-Ganga: Contending with interlinkages in a complex system.* Water Nepal Vol.4/1.

Dove, M. (1986) The Ideology of Agricultural Development in Indonesia. Pp.221-247 in C. McAndrews (ed.) *Central Government and Local Development in Indonesia,* Singapur: Oxford University Press.

Fitzpatrick, P. (1983) Underdevelopment and the plurality of law. Pp. 161-178 in S. Spitzer (ed.) *Research In Law and Sociology* 3.

Galanter, M. (1974) Why the 'haves' come out ahead: Speculations on the limits of legal change. *Law and Society Review* 9: 65-160.

Gibbs, C.J.N. & D.W. Bromley (1989) Institutional arrangements for management of rural resources: Common property regimes. Pp. 22-32 in F. Berkes (ed.) *Common property resources: Ecology and community-based sustainable development.* London: Belhaven Press.

Griffiths, J. (1986) What is legal pluralism? *Journal of Legal Pluralism* 24: 1-50.

Hardin, G. (1968) The tragedy of the commons. *Science* 162: 1234-1248.

Hitchcock, R.K. (1980) Tradition, social justice and land reform in Central Botswana. *Journal of African Law* 24: 1-34.

Holleman, J.F. (1978) Disparities and uncertainties in African law and judicial authority: A Rhodesian case study. *African Law Studies* 17: 1-35.

Lam, M. (1985) The imposition of Anglo-American land tenure laws on Hawaiians. *Journal of Legal Pluralism* 23: 103-128.

Lam, Wai Fung, M. Lee & E. Ostrom (1994) An institutional analysis approach: Findings from the NIIS on irrigation performance. Pp. 69-93 in J. Sowerwife et al. (eds.) *From farmers' fields and back: A synthesis of participatory information systems for irrigation and other resources.* Colombo: IIMI, and Rampur: IAAS.

Lynch, O.J. & K. Talbott (1995) *Balancing Acts: community-based forest management and national law in Asica and the Pacific.* Washington: World Resources Institute.

Maddock, K. (1986) Asking for Utopia: A study in aboriginal land rights. Pp. 240-259 in K. von Benda-Beckmann and F. Strijbosch (eds.) *Anthropology of Law in the Netherlands.* Dodrecht: Foris.

Mccay, B.J. & J.M. Acheson (eds.) (1987) *The Question of the Commons.* Tucson: University of Arizona Press.

Merry, S.E. (1988) Legal pluralism. *Law and Society Review* 22: 869-896.

Moore, S.F. (1978) *Law as process.* London: Routledge and Kegan Paul.

Ostrom, E. (1990) *Governing the commons.* Cambridge: Cambridge University Press.

Pradhan, U. (1990) *Property rights and state intervention in hill irrigation systems in Nepal.* Diss. Ph.D., Cornell University.

Pradhan, U. (1994) Farmers' water rights and their relation to data collection and management. Pp. 187-198 in J. Sowerwife et al. (eds.) *From farmers' fields and back: A synthesis of participatory information systems for irrigation and other resources.* Colombo: IIMI, and Rampur: IAAS.

Pradhan, R. & U. Pradhan (1996) Staking a claim: Law, politics and water rights in farmer managed irrigation systems in Nepal. Pp. 61-76 in J. Spiertz and M. Wiber (eds.) (1996) *The role of law in natural resource management.* The Hague: VUGA.

Reeve, A. (1991) The theory of property: Beyond private versus common property. Pp. 91-114 in D. Held (ed.) *Political theory today.* Oxford: Polity Press.

Schlager, E. & Ostrom, E. (1992) Property-rights regimes and natural resources: a conceptual analysis. *Land Economics* 68(3): 249-62.

Shukla, A.K., K.P. Gajurel, G. Shivakoti, R. Poudel, & N.Shrestha (1996), *Dynamism in water rights and arbitration on water right conflicts: cases of farmer managed irrigation systems from East Chitwan.* Paper presented at the workshop on Water rights, Conflict and Policy, January 22-24, Katmandu.

Snyder, F. (1981) Colonialism and legal form: The creation of 'customary law' in Senegal. *Journal of Legal Pluralism* 19: 49-90.

Spiertz, H.L.J. (1991) The transformation of traditional law: a tale of people's participation in irrigation management on Bali. *Landscape and Urban Planning* 20:189-196.

Spiertz H.L.J. (1992) Between cannibalism and pluralism: On the construction of legal frameworks in irrigation management in Bali and Sri Lanka. Pp. 89-109 in F. von Benda-Beckmann and M. van der Velde (eds.) *Law as a resource in agrarian struggles.* Wageningen: Pudoc.

Spiertz, H.L.J. & I.H. De Jong (1992) Traditional law and irrigation management: The case of Bethma. Pp. 185-202 in G. Diemer y J. Slabbers (eds.) *Irrigators and engineers: Essays in honour of Lucas Horst.* Amsterdam: Thesis Publishers.

Spiertz, H.L.J. & M. Wiber (eds.) (1996) *The role of law in natural resource management.* The Hague: VUGA. Special issue of *Recht der Werkelijkheid.*

Sugarman, D. (1983) Law, economy and the state in England, 1750-1914: Some major issues. Pp. 213-265 in D. Sugarman (ed.) *Legality, ideology and the state.* New York: Academic Press.

Turk, A. (1978) Law as a weapon in social conflict. Pp. 213-232 in Ch. Reasons and M.M. Rich (eds.) *The Sociology of Law: A conflict perspective.* Toronto: Butterworth.

Vanderlinden, J. (1971) Le pluralisme juridique: essai de synthèse. Pp. 19-56 in J. Gillissen (ed.) *Le pluralisme juridique.* Brussels: Université Libre de Bruxelles.

Vanderlinden, J. (1989) Return to legal pluralism. *Journal of Legal Pluralism* 28:149-157.

Ven, J. Van De (1994) Members only: Time-sharing rice fields and food security in a Sumatran valley. F. and K. von Benda-Beckmann and H. Marks (eds.) *Coping with insecurity: An 'underall' perspective on social security in the Third World.* Special issue Focaal 22/23: 85-96.

Vogler, J. (1992) Regimes and the global commons: space, atmosphere and oceans. Pp. 118-137 in A. McGrew and P. Lewis et al. *Global politics: Globalization and the nation state.* Cambridge: Polity Press.

Werbner, R.P. (1980) The quasi-judicial and the experience of the absurd: Remaking land law in North-Eastern Botswana. *Journal of African Law* 24: 131-150.

Wiber, M. (1991) Levels of Property Rights, Levels of Law: A Case Study From the Northern Philippines. *Man* 26: 469-492.

Wiber, M.G. (1993) *Politics, property and law in the Philippine uplands.* Waterloo (Canada): Wilfried Laurier University Press.

Woodman, G.R. (1988) How state courts create customary law in Ghana and Nigeria. Pp. 181-220 in B. Morse and G. Woodman (eds.) *Indigenous law and the state.* Dordrecht: Foris.

7

The Rights of Indigenous People over their Territories and Natural Resources

Xavier Mena V.

Before analysing specific themes related to productive and cultural systems of the Andean region (Parts 5 and following), we will briefly illustrate several of the problems faced by indigenous people in other regions of the American continent by means of an introductory examination of the right they have over their territories and natural resources. These territories are the land and regions ancestrally inhabited by indigenous people, such as the Amazon. The situation is different from regions that have been subject to continuous interactions and confrontations with other dominant cultures, as in the case of the Andean region, which requires a different, specific analysis.

For indigenous people the definition of *land* is very important. The definitions of soil, subsoil, natural resource, waters, etc. are not universally shared. To appreciate the ideas of indigenous people over the ownership of their territories it is important to know the legal and the indigenous conception with respect to the terms annotated. In this sense, contradictory juridical positions exist over the nature of natural resources, both renewable and non-renewable, that in most cases affect the interests of indigenous people. For the indigenous way of thinking, for example, it is inconceivable to separate soil from subsoil. This situation has created a very poignant problem, especially in territories that have been granted to indigenous people but in which States reserve the right of using underground natural resources.

It is not possible to speak of a true advance in the relationship between States and indigenous people if States do not accord them a legitimate autonomy over their territories. This problem is very characteristic of many countries that have incorporated the existence of autonomies of indigenous people into their internal legislation, but that actually delegate political authority to a State agency in order to watch over the interests of the assigned territories.

There is no doubt that pressure on indigenous territories has greatly reduced their size. The situation of indigenous people in some Latin-American countries is quite delicate, basically due to national policies that have induced massive migrations of other groups. The newcomers substantially take over indigenous territories, with the aftermath of systematic environmental and cultural destruction. Furthermore, the State-directed mobilisation of indigenous populations, to carry out infrastructure projects for national development, often creates disastrous situations for the uprooted communities. These migration policies result in invasion by settlers into indigenous territories. Even in lands already granted to indigenous people, invasions have occurred. Insecurity in the possession of land for both indigenous people and invaders is the result of a chaotic situation in the legalisation of landholding.

What follows is an analysis of six controversial juridical, social, cultural and economic points in relation to indigenous lands and natural resources:
• right over ancestrally occupied lands;
• the permanent, inalienable character of that right and respect for the special relationship between indigenous people and the land;
• forms of political authority;
• natural, coastal and subsoil resources;
• development projects that affect autonomy;
• land legalisation.

Rights over ancestrally occupied lands

A widespread characteristic in most production systems of indigenous people is the consideration of land as a basic element for the survival and conservation of their cultural identity, rather than an element of mere commercial exploitation. For indigenous people, territories that have been occupied and used as part of their permanent ethnic tradition are so firmly rooted in their culture that they consider it inconceivable for their jurisdiction to be transferred, sold or leased to a third party.

Generally, indigenous people are closely bonded to the lands they inhabit. They know their territory intimately; it is the place where they satisfy their needs, where they hunt and fish and, in some places, where they carry out agriculture and keep livestock. The relationship of these people with the natural environment, both productively and spiritually, is the basis for their subsistence and survival. Indigenous people are historically identified with their region, which has been inhabited by them for centuries, even before any European presence in the continent. Nevertheless, many people have already lost their ancestral territories or part of them, and many no longer exist as specific collectivities.

It is necessary to recognise these people's right to property and possession of lands traditionally occupied. States must arrange their legislation and take the necessary measures to guarantee the effective respect of those territories. The need to create a legal condition that determines indigenous territories as inalienable, imprescriptible and indivisible often is indispensable if we want to rescue the few existing ancestral indigenous territories.

The permanent, inalienable character of the right of property

In contrast to Western concepts of property, which have an element of financial speculation, for the indigenous culture land has a spiritual and historical value that transcends strict legal and financial affairs. Rodolfo Stavenhagen once noted the fact that
while modern nationalism has invented the concept of 'homeland', indigenous people had and have their own concepts by means of which they establish the relationship between a determined space, a specific history, a distinctive culture and a
particular world view.

Territorial rights are basic for the cultural and economic development of indigenous
people. Most of these people consider land a common good, that is, they do not conceive of property as an individual right. In this sense, property is a good with the
right to use but without the right to appropriate it. All group members are co-owners
of the territory.

In an inquiry by the Inter-American Commission on Human Rights regarding the
right to private property, its use and enjoyment, the indigenous organisations that
answered this question stated that

> generally, the sense of private property as conceived in Civil Codes is not com-
> patible with the concept and practices of collective property among indigenous
> population groups, with which the use and enjoyment of family property is guar-
> anteed. This modality must be guaranteed and respected by States when granting
> ownership of those ancestral lands and their natural resources to said indigenous
> people. The State must establish the means to return these resources to indige-
> nous populations. On the other hand, the indigenous population must have full
> right to use, enjoy and benefit from their assets, which must also be recognised
> and guaranteed by the State (In: Report of the Inter-American Commission on
> Human Rights, OAS, 1992).

The land has a value of cultural identity and can have a religious and sacred value.
From the very beginning, the land has constituted the reason for being of indigenous
people. In practically all native cultures, the relation with the land has a deep spiritual meaning; it is land with the remains of their ancestors. This has been one of the
most delicate, sensitive problems, especially when people are forced to move by reasons that States consider other priorities. Throughout history, many people have
been obliged to emigrate to other zones in which they settled or where they obtained
access to a new territory, generally of worse quality and much smaller than their original habitat. The cultural and sacred value of the land can never be compensated for
merely with another piece of land.

Forms of political authority over indigenous territories

The form of political authority over indigenous territories is a problem mainly based on the capacity of a State to organise territory. Positions maintain that territory's autonomy constricts State sovereignty by establishing autonomous zones within national territory without the State's political presence. In several countries' legislation the existence of autonomous political forms has been recognised, although the State will always be present. The position of indigenous organisations goes further when they establish that community leaders will be the only ones entrusted with the administration and political control in their territories.

In some countries, the figure of 'reservations' has appeared as a means to legalise areas to protect certain groups and indigenous people. The main object in establishing a reservation is to preserve a culture and ensure respect for the rights of a distinct human group from historical, cultural and ethnic points of view. However, the creation of reservations has caused many problems, especially when governments evacuate ethnic groups to other regions with the pretext of projects in the national interest. Among the criticisms of the reservation system is the fact that the reservation is not controlled by the indigenous group but by the State-created administrative authority. This, in most cases, denies their cultural reality and therefore, through ignorance, obstructs their own practices and rights. In this sense, a viable alternative is to let the group manage their reservation with help from the governmental entity when required.

In granting an indigenous group territorial control and autonomy, communities should have more rights to apply own laws and administer justice according to standards and procedures adopted by the community. Thus, the community will have more authority to defend their territory against any type of unjust interference. Autonomy becomes a fundamental aspect that must be agreed upon by States and indigenous people since recognition of indigenous people's ownership of their territories makes sense only if autonomy over their management is guaranteed.

Natural, coastal and subsoil resources

Indiscriminate logging, abusive extraction of natural resources and destruction of coastal mangroves by companies intervening in indigenous territories have clearly shown the urgent need to rationalise use of land and other natural resources.

The right to effective ownership, possession, use, conservation and control of surface and sub-surface renewable and non-renewable resources belonging to lands and other territories traditionally and still occupied or used by indigenous people, including plants, wildlife and water, is the right for which indigenous organisations have been fighting for decades. Nowadays, both international norms and domestic legislation recognise these rights. However, almost all legislation subordinates the subsoil to the State. Exploitation of subsoil resources mostly harmed biological and ethnic diversity. The purpose has been to impose on indigenous cultures a disjointed concept of Nature, renewable resources versus non-renewable ones, promoting recognition of ownership of some resources but not of others; or recognition of the use but not ownership; or recognition of ownership but without autonomy for management; among many other incoherences.

The extractive ideology of the subsoil, which establishes that resources are State property, extends mechanically to natural resources. This leads to absurd situations, such as recognising indigenous rights to the land but not to subsoil resources or natural resources on the land; in other words, they are abstract owners of nothing.

This same situation occurs with water-courses because, by law, rivers are State property, denying indigenous people's rights regarding rivers and lakes. This situation has generated many legal problems since the law often allows third parties to exploit fisheries and the hydrobiological wealth of water-courses found within indigenous territories.

To achieve effective results in environmental protection it is necessary to recognise the indigenous people's rights with also ecological criteria. Indigenous territories must not be seen as islands; it is of vital importance to consider the space-time dynamics of the group and the systematic relations between their territory and areas of influence in the region. Actions affecting natural resources outside the territory clearly have effects on it and viceversa. To safeguard the water system, guarantee tropical forest fisheries and water wildlife, it is necessary to protect and manage rivers all the way from their headwaters to riparian areas and flooded forests, to ensure their principal food source.

Development projects in indigenous territories that affect their autonomy

Pressure on indigenous territories has taken away large areas to develop projects of national interest or changed their land tenure condition to the civil-law concept. Indigenous territories are usually located on land rich in natural resources. State-sponsored development projects (such as dams, hydropower systems, ports, airports, new cities, highways, etc.) or projects by private enterprise (among others, tourism, wood, crops, livestock, pools, etc.) have aroused interest in land that, until a few years ago, had little commercial value. Such development projects on indigenous land generate serious conflicts of authority.

Furthermore, agrarian reform during this century in several American countries has produced different reactions and outcomes affecting indigenous cultures. In some countries they have achieved relative progress but in general, the reality of indigenous ownership of agrarian property finds itself at a profound disadvantage compared to large private holdings, and even compared to small landowners.

Productive soil is concentrated in a few hands, indigenous territories are broken, native people become migrant workers - small farmers cannot obtain capital - all these factors condemn most Latin American indigenous farmers to poverty and migration. It is no longer possible to generalise that indigenous peasants live in identifiable, compact communities. Many have abandoned their communities to look for work on large farms, plantations, mines, petroleum and large infrastructure projects, to colonise jungle and forest low lands and to emigrate to squatter settlements in large cities. This analysis reflects, above all, the reality of most indigenous people inhabiting the Andean region and Central America. Basically, in the Andean zone indigenous and peasant land property is greatly subdivided and the sense of private property is increasingly rooted, from large to small landowners. The great error of agrarian reform in several countries was to divide the land in microproperties. Furthermore, large *hacienda* owners took advantage of agrarian reform to sell large non-productive areas to the State, for distribution to indigenous communities.

This problem did not occur in the same way in Amazonian territories. The Amazon basin was not part of the European conquest's loot. Interest in these lands began only with the advent of exploitable natural resources (mines, petroleum, wood and, to a certain point, tourism). In these unexploited territories, a series of colonisation policies have resulted in thousands of colonists invading indigenous territories, causing serious conflicts, with indigenous people as the main victims.

The mobilisation of an indigenous population by the State when it considers this unavoidable in order to carry out infrastructure development projects, often produces dramatic situations for the members of that population. Usually, the ecological milieu is quite different, mobility is restricted, and nomad groups are forced to live a sedentary life. Generally, religious and cultural practices are modified, and crops are determined in advance by governmental representatives.
All international treaties agree on the right of indigenous people to remain in their territories and not to be mobilised out of their traditionally occupied ancestral lands, except under very serious, restricted circumstances.

Legalisation of land

The result of national policies fostering massive migration is seen in colonists' invasion of indigenous territories. The legal base regarding the concession of lands to indigenous people often is characterised by a chaotic situation. The legal limitations include, among others, concession models that do not establish the indigenous authorities' legal status, purposes or administrative capacity and functions. Lack of support by local powers for indigenous authorities' defence of their land, and the fact that land grants to native people entail the same limitations and attributions as those awarded to colonists, leaves them vulnerable to sale, taxation, expropriation, to extinction of ownership, etc. Another serious problem affecting indigenous people's attempts to legalise their territories is the recognition of their right to land that, however, excludes underground resources and natural resources on the surface.

If the legal status of indigenous territories is not resolved by national administrations, and furthermore, if those territories are legalised but face on-going invasion and colonisation with the above incoherences, indigenous people's subsistence will be increasingly unstable and the complete extinction of their territories and production systems will be a matter of only a few more years.

PART III

IRRIGATION AND EQUITY

Introduction

Our irrigation system will never be like the one of our neighbours. There, the engineers have done everything and peasants had no right to participate in decision-making. There, the State decides who is to irrigate, how they must irrigate, when the canal will be closed for cleaning, how much they should pay for the water and all those things. Actually, they do not have a peasant irrigation organisation and there isn't any peasant struggle either. Our system is going to be different, we are struggling for a *peasant* irrigation scheme! (Antonio Lasso, leader of the peasant and indigenous organisation of Licto, Ecuador).

Peasants around the world, who try to increase their control over the production process and to generate a more equitable distribution of irrigation benefits and burdens, know that the problem of administering and managing irrigation is not limited to only the biophysical process of watering the crops. Neither is it limited to making plans and designs, excavating ditches, lining them with concrete and organising people to take water in and out.

In irrigation, technological, organisational, legal, political, agro-productive and cultural domains interact, cross, mix up and oppose each other. These 'socio-technological constructions' are generated and re-defined in complex situations: situations in which very divergent law systems interact within a diverse institutional landscape, where the confrontation of classes, ethnic groups, genders or castes is present, all with different interests and objectives and with quite unequal starting points, powers and opportunities.

Interests related to development and use of irrigation do not just differ among the irrigators themselves but also between them and those who use the water for other purposes, between users and non-users of the same region, between users and development institutions, between users and the State, etc.

The irony of the paradox is the fact that, notwithstanding all the diverging interests, the irrigation system can only function in a sustainable manner if a foundation of consensus is laid and relationships of mutual accountability are established among the different interest groups. In the difficult environmental situations faced by peasants, the sustainable management of an irrigation system demands the intensive and permanent collaboration of many actors.

Moreover, if user-management of the system and more user-control of the production process are to be obtained, it is essential that this collaboration be founded in a distribution of rights and duties that is considered equitable by the users themselves. This is fundamental for establishing and strengthening a collectivity. Furthermore, this collectivity and its various parts also require that the irrigation system provides a positive balance between benefits generated and the resources invested, as compensation for sustaining the system.

In practice, the above mentioned paradox generates very diverse answers, from eternal conflicts, verticalist water control regimes and complete failures, to strong and sustainable organisations based on a shared normativity.

8

Collective Management and Social Construction of Peasant Irrigation Systems: a Conceptual Introduction

Rutgerd Boelens

This chapter aims to make some points about irrigation management in peasant systems - with emphasis on communal systems - and to reflect briefly on intervention practices in this field and their relation with equity issues. It begins with some general observations about peasant irrigation management and certain basic principles for water distribution. It then goes on to analyse the relationship between water rights and the creation and conservation of the normative system, the infrastructure system, and the organisational system of peasant irrigation. It analyses why peasant irrigation may be characterised as a social construct, and concludes with reflections on the social contents of irrigation technology and the development of irrigation as a negotiation process.

Peasant management of irrigation

In many regions of the world, agriculture lacks sufficient or reliable rainfall to obtain harvests that will cover rural and urban families' different needs. For this reason, irrigation systems and practices have been developed as a man-made supplement to natural precipitation.[1] On the basis of climatological and biophysical factors, peasant families or intervening institutions usually know how to define required flow rates and volumes, timing for proper water application and the necessary irrigation methods to provide a suitable water supply.

However, it is one thing for the peasant family or engineer to know when and how much water is needed to irrigate their crops, and where and how to apply the water, but quite another thing to know how to obtain and make sure of the continuous, timely arrival of this resource that is so vital for production. This does not depend only on the family, community or agency itself. It depends also on the availability of water and on agreements reached concerning use of the water among various families and various communities and institutions, all involved in the irrigation system and in the local or regional watershed area. In this broader context, water resource users are not only those families or entities with interest in irrigation but there are also groups with other interests in water. Altogether these diverse user groups determine the demand for water. Other purposes include use of water for human consumption, for livestock raising, for industry, for hydro power generation, for home-building, for tourism, and so on. Sometimes, users' interests converge, but there are often also opposing interests, especially if water is scarce and when precipitation is uncertain. When scarcity and uncertainty prevail, conflicts often arise. Water is life and people fight to gain or maintain their livelihood. Provision of the theoretically required or desired irrigation water is modified, mediated and shaped by countless factors, often social and non-plannable.

Thus, the peasant art of irrigation, plus potential institutional support for irrigated farming, are not confined to 'simply' planning optimal amounts of water and scheduling the distribution, defining methods of application and building conduction canals. These are just elements that form part of a broader perspective and have to take into consideration varying conditions, which together make up the setting of irrigation and the production process. At the level of irrigation systems or (micro-) watersheds, beyond the analysis of certain individual practices or techniques in isolation, it is above all the *management of irrigation* that merits the centre of attention. Water management is the pivotal issue that brings together and gives a background to both individual and collective irrigation knowledge, techniques, customs, rules and practices.

In systems managed by peasants, this irrigation water management is positioned within and forms part of the logic of their social environment and agricultural production systems. Irrigation management takes shape according to the production system's specific needs, conditions and power structures. Therefore, it is fundamental not to rely on general prescriptions and statements, but to understand how this management is structured in each specific place. The objectives that rural families have regarding irrigation cannot be generalised and accepted as guidelines for analysis and action, without more in-depth examination. Women may have specific problems, and therefore their interests and solutions regarding irrigation may be different from men's perceived needs. Large landowners or agribusiness entrepreneurs may pursue goals in irrigation that do not match peasant and indigenous communities' interests, etc. Consequently, concepts about equity in irrigation will also differ greatly from place to place.

These diverging interests in irrigation, even when it is a collective activity shared by peasants and/or indigenous communities, mean that one cannot assume that 'the users themselves always seek the most equitable management and distribution regarding irrigation water'. The long-standing systems often feature injustices based on class, ethnic, gender or other distinctions. In the case of new irrigation systems, where water is introduced in a local setting, a new production factor - a powerful, conflict-ridden one - is inserted into existing social relations.[2] This means that even those social relationships that were characterised by a relatively equitable and reciprocal balance may have become conflictive or oppressive after the introduction of water.

However, generalisations should not be made: in other cases, irrigation water plays an important role precisely in reinforcing social cohesion.

Many actors take part in the planning, implementation, operation and maintenance of irrigation systems; together they create, beyond the technical and production-related demand for water, a social demand. Water is the liquid that makes their plants grow, but it is also the fuel for the zone's organisational engine, the blood in the veins of the rural production system, the heart of survival and coexistence of rural families. Therefore, irrigation water is not simply *'just another element'* in peasant families' production systems (as so-called 'integrated' projects sometimes assume, when referring to the 'irrigation component'). For peasants in many areas of the world water is *one of the mainstays and fundamental pillars* of the production system. Depending on conditions, irrigation may be useful to *intensify* and *increase* agricultural production, to *ensure* it, to *diversify* it and/or to *free it from seasonal constraints*. As a result of this central characteristic of irrigation water - being one of the fundaments of coexistence - peasant management of their own system and their own reality, under their own norms and decision-making power, is one of the major challenges for peasant irrigation. This is *also* the case in systems co-managed with other institutions.

Peasant management of irrigation systems involves multiple activities including both management of the factor 'water' (identification, acquisition, allocation, distribution, applying and drainage) and management of the factor 'infrastructure' (identification, design, construction, operation, maintenance and modification). The users' organisation regulates, co-ordinates and monitors these activities, generally together with other institutional actors with whom it interacts, resulting in collective and individual actions to operate and sustain the irrigation system (see, for example, Chambers 1980; Coward 1985; Uphoff 1986). On the basis of the irrigation system's operational requirements, the organisation establishes the roles and functions, and determines users' rights and obligations. This is a continuous, iterative process which grows, matures and adapts throughout the 'life of the system', according to irrigators' experiences and institutional, biophysical and conjunctural changes, both 'internal' and 'external'. The organisation is responsible for making decisions about the above mentioned activities, and for co-ordinating the mobilisation of required resources (such as labour, money, building materials, etc.). In a process of ongoing negotiation and communication, it must also see to adequate management of conflicts among users, communities, institutions or with other systems. The difficult art of peasant irrigation management requires well-consolidated forms of organisation that will negotiate, inform and plan; co-ordinate, oversee and monitor; regulate, authorise and enforce.

Principles of water distribution[3]

Following from the argument above, when we speak of the issue of 'water distribution' in peasant irrigation, we make a conceptual separation of certain physical and social aspects of irrigation from their real-world context where such separation is not present. In peasant irrigation, the distribution of water does not only imply the distribution of a certain volume and time of water among various canals, fields or irrigators: the practical rules governing water distribution in peasant systems are wholly inserted into broader normative and productive systems, with their own history and rationality. This means that, for instance, it is generally difficult or impossible to replace a certain existing form of distribution with another 'technically more rational and efficient' one, without causing many changes in other aspects of the irrigation and production system. Thus, for example, aside from reflecting the agro-climatic and geophysical circumstances of the zone, the water distribution rules are closely related to social norms that regulate the distribution of *other* (non-irrigation) resources and benefits in peasant communities.

This also means that, when groups of irrigators, at a given point in history, begin to define and develop their own basic principles to distribute available water, they will not only take into account the criterion of technical and economic efficiency in irrigated agriculture (although this may be a major consideration). Water distribution in peasant systems has often become consolidated as the result of a lengthy process with experiments and modifications to adapt to both social relations and physical needs. For this reason, both within the direct sphere of irrigation itself and in other areas, water plays a social and technical role far beyond just 'helping make plants grow efficiently'.

This is more obvious *outside* the field of irrigation since families, according to their needs, have established multiple uses and varied purposes for water, even when using water formally labelled as 'irrigation water'.

However, also *within* irrigation practices peasants distribute water in ways that do not necessarily match with the 'technically and productively optimal' approach, since they must also consider the irrigation water's *social efficiency*. Some examples:

a). In situations where people are greatly overburdened with work, or in zones where other activities of the peasant economy are more important than irrigation, 'hurried' watering (often with large flows and short turns), accepting significant wastage, may be the solution in order to *gain efficiency in other activities* of families' economies. b).Further, in many peasant communities, irrigation water is not only the 'fuel for the productive engine', but also works as the *'oil lubricating the engine of social relationships'*. c).Similarly, to optimise the *transparency* of water distribution, to *simplify* the distribution schedules and/or improve the feasibility of *social control*, communities often consciously grant lower priority to technical efficiency than would theoretically be possible (see, for example, the cases described by Gerbrandy & Gutiérrez in Part 7). d). Besides forbidden robbery of water, many peasant systems also have *permissible water robbery*, which seems to 'break with rational water distribution' but which reflects, rather, water's social function (see e.g. Gelles, Chapter 23). e). The *sequence of irrigation turns* in certain distribution arrangements is often based not only on technical considerations, since the water's social function may be overriding, expressed in criteria such as 'first the elderly' (social security and respect), 'certain crops first' (productive and food security, see e.g. Chapter 28) or the turn schedule is made compatible with the ritual functions that must be performed along with irrigating. f). Above all, more than just the criterion of 'crop water requirements', the concrete way in which water is distributed in many peasant systems is strongly rooted in the historical process of generating and conserving *water rights*, investments made by families to gain these rights, and the rules of inheritance and exchange of rights. We will come back to this topic below.

In practice, we can see that communities apply different modes or principles of water distribution, all of which are *expressions* of the abstract notion of water rights (water allocation) in specific places and systems. As an illustration of this diversity, a list (by no means exhaustive) of some of these basic principles is outlined below, as a prelude to a more detailed analysis of the concept of 'water rights'. The principles of distribution establish the basic terms, priorities and/or operating rules regarding rightholders' access to water. Each - often applied in combination with other rules - is the key to constructing the water distribution system in a different situation, in a given (sub) culture, socio-political setting, historical period and biophysical locality. The perception of equity among user families is generally an important factor in determining these principles for water distribution:

- families receive water proportionally to the irrigation area that they possess in the system (more land means more water);[4]
- all families receive the same flow and time (the same volume of water)
  - without limits on the area they wish to irrigate, or
  - to irrigate the same pre-established area;
- all families receive enough water to 'fill the field' ('until finishing', without absolute limits on the duration of the turn, each one taking the time that is 'actually needed')
  - for the same pre-established area, or
  - without absolute limits on the area to be irrigated;
- families receive water proportionally to the irrigable area they possess, however, up to a pre-established limit (allocation 'with a top limit', to share scarcity among everyone: the 'poor' irrigate their whole land, the 'rich' irrigate a part until they reach this ceiling);
- families receive water according to their contributions or 'investments' (capital, labour, and others) during irrigation system construction;
- families receive water according to transfer agreements that they have negotiated (for example, purchase and sale of water shares; exchange of water rights for other resources, etc.);
- families receive water according to their land's location (e.g., 'upper and lower moieties', 'tail-end or head-end', etc.);
- 'open access' ('free usage' depending on water availability, which often means access according to power structures and defence capability);

- families receive water according to demand (with or without restrictions);
- 'first come, first served';
- families receive water according to the utility or usefulness that this resource offers them (for example, with compensation for those families to whom the water is less useful);[5]
- families receive water according to the size of the family unit (more members means more need);[6]
- families receive water according to their social position (for example, 'priority for the elderly'; or water access priority according to class, gender or caste);
- families receive water according to the priority granted to certain crops they grow in the irrigation system.

There are many additional rules as well as distinctive matrices of combinations among the basic principles. Further, if we combine this list of principles for receiving irrigation benefits (in this case, to obtain water) with the range of possible obligations accompanying these rights, one could imagine that this opens up a huge variety of possibilities regarding the normative model and the way of distributing water, not only in theory but also in practice. This diversity increases even more when we see that - as is usual in peasant irrigation - water rights and the associated distribution principles are connected with the family's affiliation or socio-adminis-trative status as a requirement to receive water (for example, belonging to the com-munity, the neighbourhood, the organisation, etc.).

Among the many existing combinations, a few illustrations of the variety of distrib-ution principles that fit within the combination 'water rights - obligations to work', include:

- In some systems, everyone works equally on construction (obligations) and all receive the same amount of water (rights). In others, they also work equally but they receive water according to the area of land they have; and in others, they work equally in construction, but must contribute proportionally (according to the family's land area) to maintaining the system.
- In some systems, water is received according to labour input in construction, where the amount of labour contributed (the investment) is not directly restrict-ed, and the gaining of water rights is also 'unlimited' (these may even be sold or traded when there are surplus rights, see Yoder & Martin, Chapter 13). In other systems, however, future users are obliged to contribute equally to construction in order to all have the same rights to water and to decision-making. Further, there are also systems in which everyone must work proportionally according to the land they hold, in order to be able to irrigate all of their land.

There are countless examples in peasant practice that are largely the result of com-binations of rights, obligations, and the irrigator family's status in the social setting. These modes provide the form, force and specific characteristics of each peasant irri-gation system.[7]

It is important to observe that the basic principles generally refer to characteristics related to right-holding *families,* and the allocation is also to families (and communities), even in those cases in which the characteristics of their fields are decisive.[8] By contrast, projects designed by outside agency professionals usually allocate and distribute water *to irrigated land or to irrigable areas* (see also Diemer, Chapter 9). In these designs, a distribution principle such as 'allocation according to the utility of the water' has another meaning: calculating crop water requirements (water utility according to evapotranspiration and water use efficiency) and compensating for those crops and pieces of land that need more water, without taking into account the water's social function. The technical balance among the system's agricultural and physical characteristics overrides the social balance among human users. Here we have one of the central issues around which perceptions of equity diverge.[9]

Diversity in modes and basic principles of water distribution in peasant systems contrasts with the uniformity among most systems designed by NGOs or governmental agencies, whether they are 'participatory projects' or not: each family will receive water according to the amount of land that they have, providing they pay their fees. Sometimes there is the additional condition that irrigators must participate in the water user organisation. Here, irrigation projects and irrigators' organisations are generally designed using standardised, 'proven' norms, rather than in response to the peasants' own normative systems. Let us therefore look at some features of the latter - peasant irrigation rights - and then analyse their relationship with other fundamental areas of peasant irrigation systems.

Rights in peasant irrigation

Unlike government-granted water rights, which in many countries are related to *individuals*[10], peasant water rights in community systems are granted to families *for belonging to a collectivity* and for meeting the corresponding collective obligations. Peasants in many regions of the world build their identity by being dutiful community and irrigation system members, and therefore *the rights of each individual are derived from the collective rights and duties.* And these collective rights are not uniform nation-wide, as usually is the case in official legislation, but vary from one irrigation system to the next.

It is very common to observe in peasant communities that the irrigation rights of a family depend not only on performing their obligations in the very irrigation system but also on performing the other collective tasks that are established by the community.[11] Basically, water rights are social relationships among humans and not only between the user and the water (see Chapter 3); thus, they are rooted in the other components of the peasant community's normative system. This again illustrates that water distribution - which is the concrete reflection of water rights - cannot be isolated from the rest of the social and productive relations in peasant communities, nor can it be changed or simply replaced by some other system without an in-depth analysis with the users regarding the consequences.

In the normative and organisational frameworks of a given peasant system, the contents and strictness of rules and the intensity of their enforcement are not usually constant, but change according to the agricultural season (and the precipitation that year). During dry seasons, in systems where water is short, good organisation has well-respected rules, precise social control, sufficient capacity to manage conflicts and good administration of distribution. During the rainy season, the rules are often more flexible: there is less social control and sometimes other, less demanding ways to distribute water are chosen.

Similarly, it is common for those systems that on the whole experience more water shortage to feature a more urgent need to create a tight normative system than those systems that have sufficient or abundant irrigation water.

Also, when a new irrigation system is put into practice, in the first years of use it is common for water scarcity to increase, since the infrastructure is often not yet complete when irrigation starts and an increasing amount of families and land are joining the system. At the beginning the rules can be more flexible (and people form 'bad habits'). The hard part comes when, later, they have to get used to stricter rules and less water per family.

Depending on who authorises the right, how it is organised socially, and with what regulations and powers, we can distinguish among: public property regimes (State-owned), private property regimes (individual institutions or persons), common property regimes (collective ownership) and free access situations (no regulations). See, for example, Bromley *et al.* (1992). In practice, at different levels of society, these regimes are often combined and make up complex matrices. Basically, we can distinguish among the following central *mechanisms* for obtaining water rights in peasant irrigation (see Hoogendam 1995; Boelens & Doornbos 1996). These mechanisms are based on regulations that may be rooted in one of the mentioned property regimes or come from a combination of them. In a given region, it is not unusual for several mechanisms to operate simultaneously, and it is also common to find mixtures of 'peasant' and 'governmental' mechanisms:

- *concession* of water use rights, granted by the State administration to individuals or groups of applicants;
- granting of formal or informal title over socio-territorial waters by their inhabitants (*socio-territorial entitlement*);
- agreements for *permanent transfer* of water rights from one right-holder to another such as in the case of purchase and sale, rental, inheritance, barter or gifting (alliance-building);[12]
- acquisition of rights and access to water *by force*: in many regions of the world, power groups have expropriated water by coercive force from peasants and indigenous peoples. These rights are not always backed and authorised by the State (though often they are), but it is very common for them to be institutionalised in local procedures, within prevailing power structures;

- *peasant investment* of their own resources (e.g. labour, capital, goods, intellectual or organisational inputs, or others) to build or rehabilitate irrigation infrastructure, in order to *auto-generate water rights*.

There is interaction between these mechanisms for obtaining rights; they may reinforce or oppose each other. A very common example: the mechanism of 'State concession' could oppose the mechanism of 'take-over by force', returning irrigation rights to the original right-holders (who obtained their rights, for example, by the mechanism of socio-territorial demands). In practice, however, the reverse has often been true: the mechanism of State concession has reinforced the mechanism of forcible take-over. Another common example: Many irrigation systems in conquered or colonised regions were built by peasants and/or indigenous peoples. According to the mechanism of 'rights created by peasant investment', they should have obtained water rights. However, large parts of such systems benefit large landowners, who used the mechanism of force to make the peasants work and obtain water rights themselves: a confrontation between two mechanisms.

We may consider the combination of rights and obligations in peasant irrigation as basic foundations of their self-managed systems. Before and during system construction, and during system use, irrigators develop this set of norms that guide both system creation and administration, the utilisation of water, and relations among users (Apollin & Boelens 1996). Therefore, the last mentioned mechanism (of peasant investment) is of great importance to peasant communities when managing their own irrigation systems or doing so jointly. Coward (1983, 1986) states that users, by investing, create hydraulic property, a common ownership of the system that is the factor which links irrigators and drives social action in peasant irrigation.

> Investments to create irrigation facilities always create, or rearrange property relationships with regard to those new facilities. In other words, one cannot build facilities without establishing property [...] The creation of irrigation works establishes among the creators property relations, which become the social basis for their collective action in performing various irrigation tasks. (Coward 1983).

So, excluding true peasant participation from the creation or rehabilitation of irrigation infrastructure prevents the structural process of creating or rearranging of rights and of sustainable organisation (Apollin & Boelens 1996). Further, after generating rights, users must maintain or conserve them. They do so by fulfilling their obligations within the irrigation system, which also takes the form of peasant investment. Participation in collective work, payment of dues, attendance at meetings, etc., are important obligations, both to conserve one's rights and to keep the irrigation system itself working.[13] Without these mandatory contributions by each family to the collectivity, the irrigation system is not sustainable; that is why the conservation of irrigation rights plays a key role in effective irrigation system management.[14]

In the case of the waterrights creation mechanism, we can summarise that peasant investment in construction (or rehabilitation) of the system creates rights, while peasant investment in maintenance reaffirms and re-creates them. This concept should not lead to static analytical frameworks regarding the functioning of normative systems in peasant irrigation. In each case, it is necessary to study the actual expression.

As for the *contents* of these peasant irrigation rights, a distinction may generally be made between two complementary (not separate) parts: individual and collective rights. Each irrigating family's *individual rights* involve using the water to which they are entitled and using the infrastructure that makes this usage possible. *Collective rights* involve participating in collective definition of the rules of play, i.e. the right to take part in creating, reaffirming and modifying the norms governing irrigation management: participation in decision-making about the system.

Depending on the degree of autonomy of the peasant system, this collective right is limited (shared with other institutions) or autonomous: the distinction between the two is gradual and depends on each concrete case.

Collective rights to shared or limited management generally refer to participation in decision-making about:
• the system's internal operation and administration; rules for and principles of water distribution;
• maintenance, extension or modification of the irrigation infrastructure;
• definition of contributions in labour, money and goods, as well as intellectual, organisational and ritual contributions;
• definition of (internal) penalties to apply and conflict resolution.

Collective rights to autonomous management, in addition to the decision-making rights already mentioned, include:
• the right to take part in decision-making about which families are (new) right-holders and which are not (or are no longer) and about criteria regarding transfer of one family's rights to another;
• the right to (re)formulate the irrigation constitution and so change important aspects of the normative system.
(see also Ostrom 1992; Hoogendam 1995; Boelens & Doornbos 1996; Gerbrandy & Hoogendam 1997).

Another important matter regarding analysis of the contents of peasant irrigation rules and rights is to distinguish between *rights for purposes of external identification* (rights of the group of users versus 'outside' groups and families who do not hold rights) and *rights for purposes of internal regulation* (in which the varied rights of one member of the group of right-holders are defined versus those of other members). The two forms of rights generally are complementary and may be quite different. Moreover, as Benda Beckmann *et al.* (Chapter 6) have pointed out, the formally expressed peasant or customary rights are not necessarily the same as the rights ruling actual practice (i.e. concrete social relations) of peasant irrigation.

Social norms in irrigation technology

Unity of basic elements in peasant irrigation

In peasant irrigation, the normative system offers the key foundation of the system. The basic mechanism of 'peasant investment' to obtain and maintain rights to water and to decision-making leads, in practice, to understanding a central feature of peasant irrigation, that is, the strong interdependence and firm unity among three main aspects:
- generation and reconfirmation of *rights (norms)*;
- construction and rehabilitation of the *infrastructure*;
- creation and strengthening of the *organisation*

(Boelens & Doornbos 1996; Apollin & Boelens 1996).

Rules, rights and obligations shape and are shaped by collective action and social organisation, around collective ownership of the irrigation infrastructure. Developing a peasant irrigation system presupposes an ongoing process of interaction among the three elements: peasants attempt, consciously or unconsciously, to synchronise and harmonise these main aspects.

For example, when a peasant group has identified the possibility of obtaining irrigation water from a given source, they begin defining the initial *norms* (especially preliminary rights and obligations of each participant) for water distribution. They also know that they need to (re)create a suitable *organisation* for the physical and social work to be done, and will make this organisation functional first for the process of lobbying and negotiation, later for the construction activity. At the time when the construction of *infrastructure* begins, the peasants know that they do not only generate their canals and structures, they are also generating their rights. And conversely, the irrigation infrastructure is adapted during the construction process to the agreed rights: the canal network, its layout and conduction capacity, the division facilities and so on directly reflect the norms agreed upon for water distribution. In other words, the infrastructure must enable the users to concretise their rights. (Chapter 37) When the system starts to function the organisation is adapted again, now to the need to operate and maintain the infrastructure and to oversee compliance with the established rights. The maintenance activities, at the same time reconfirm the rights, conserve the infrastructure and strengthen the organisation itself. *The interaction is continuous*, also in the later phases of the system. At each point in rehabilitating or changing the irrigation infrastructure, peasants reason on the basis of this logical framework of a dynamic unity among rights-organisation-infrastructure. If one changes, then the other elements must also change and 'harmonise' in order to enable proper functioning of the system. Seen in this light, the system is dynamic and 'living'.

By contrast, in many of the systems (co-)constructed by intervening agencies where serious problems arose in operation and management, we could observe that the lack of correspondence and synchronisation among the normative, organisational and infrastructural system was part of the root of the problem, with consequences that are often disastrous for operation and maintenance. Irrigation interventions often, unconsciously, break up this unity by establishing rigid and separated planning of infrastructure, organisation and operative and distributive norms, based only on institutional timetables.

We have seen that the heart of a peasant irrigation system is not so much the hydraulic infrastructure itself, but the ongoing *interaction between* this infrastructure system and the organisational and normative systems. Irrigation technology is an expression or materialisation of irrigation norms.[15] And when norms change, the infrastructure must also be adapted, because otherwise it will break down, be abandoned or even work against the interests of (groups of) users. Irrigation technology is a *social construct*; social and normative relationships among human actors shape the irrigation works and its organisation. At the same time, contributions to construction, rehabilitation and maintenance of this infrastructure shape the specific features of the social relationships and the normative system of these actors. Therefore, to be able to analyse the irrigation system in greater depth, it is not sufficient to examine the hydraulic system only as a set of 'technical and material elements'. Irrigation technology and techniques *contain social contents* making up the key parts for operation and for distribution mechanisms.

In practice, irrigation technology is not always designed, validated and adapted through a process respecting the interdependence and unity among the three central elements. Social construction of irrigation is not an art monopolised by users who make their own design, perhaps alongside institutions that support this dynamic process. On the contrary, internal or external imposition of interests and norms usually breaks up the above triangle logic. The *externalisation* of the irrigation design process may be and often is one of the main causes contributing to this problem. Therefore, it would be worthwhile analysing the famous 'technology transfer' that is currently an extremely powerful driver in irrigation development. To promote a better understanding of its possible consequences, let us briefly analyse the social construction of irrigation technology from the angle of outside design.

Social contents in irrigation design

In the last three decades, it has been very common to speak of transferring irrigation technology, a major issue, especially in development co-operation. However, irrigation technology (knowledge and skills[16]) is not *transferred* - as if these qualities were things that could be handed over - because the party that has the technology keeps it, and the knowledge and skills do not 'leave' the first party to become the property of others. So, it would be better to speak of *reproduction* of irrigation technologies: the idea is to reproduce knowledge and skills to generate, use and modify irrigation systems[17] (see Illich 1979; Mollinga *et al.* 1987). This reproduction may occur locally, for example from peasant to peasant, but also from one society or interest group to another.

The concept of reproducing technology shows us that irrigation technology and techniques are not neutral. Problematic effects of a certain irrigation technology do not emerge solely and simply because of the ways that humans use it (for example, 'misuse'), or because of the status of social relations in which the technology is used (e.g. inequitable distribution of properties, exploitative relationships), nor only because of existing capacities (e.g. educational level, degree of organisation) in the 'receiving' society.[18] The technology *itself* also contains norms 'included by the designer'. Therefore, it is crucial to analyse the process of designing this technology, which takes place under conditions of social interactions and institutional interests, and is guided by a network of values and norms which surround and influence the designers.

In this process of developing technology, designers include their perceptions and objectives: impacts, effects and ways of use in rural practice, that is, the 'mission' of the technology when it is put into operation. These implicit and explicit assumptions by designers regarding the use and impact of the technology include their norms in regard to organisation of the labour force, definition of roles and responsibilities (system and household management), distribution of benefits and responsibilities, etc.

Once the irrigation technology is applied, the 'directions for use' (or, in other words, the 'social requirements for usage', or the 'technology code') inserted by the designer will structure the way in which users have to work with it (see Bijker *et al.* 1987; Mollinga & Mooij 1989a, 1989b; Artifacto 1990; Boelens & Temmink 1990; Van der Ploeg 1991). The irrigation technology will reflect the norms and practices current among the production relations in the *designer's* social setting (whether the designer is a peasant, a civil or hydraulic engineer, a technical assistance agency or, in Latour's terms (1987) a network of values, norms, social interests, etc.).

In those cases in which peasants endogenously develop and design their own technologies (the 'art of the locality') in a historical, cyclical sequence of observing, analysing, evaluating and adapting, this process will reinforce their autonomy, diversity and adaptation to local circumstances (Van der Ploeg 1991). This will maintain the unity of the technical-normative-organisational systems in irrigation that we have mentioned above (see diagram 8.1.a).

However, when irrigation technology is 'transferred' - rather, reproduced - from a group or network of designers to a group of users coming from a different social framework, such as from the urban context to the countryside, from one country to another, or from one social class to another, these social requirements for usage are externalised: users are no longer the designers, and no longer include their own objectives and norms in irrigation design. They face social requirements and norms defined by other people (see diagram 8.1.b).

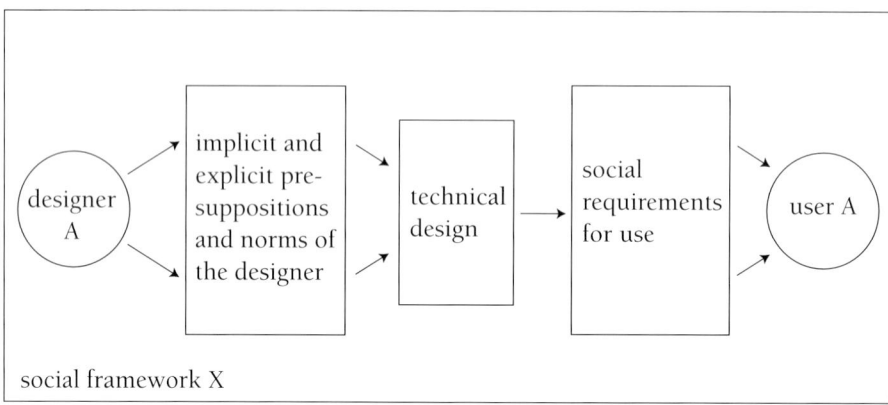

Diagram 8.1.a; Design of irrigation technology in a situation where designers and users share the norms and assumptions regarding the function, use and impact of the respective technology. In many of these situations, the users *are* the designers.

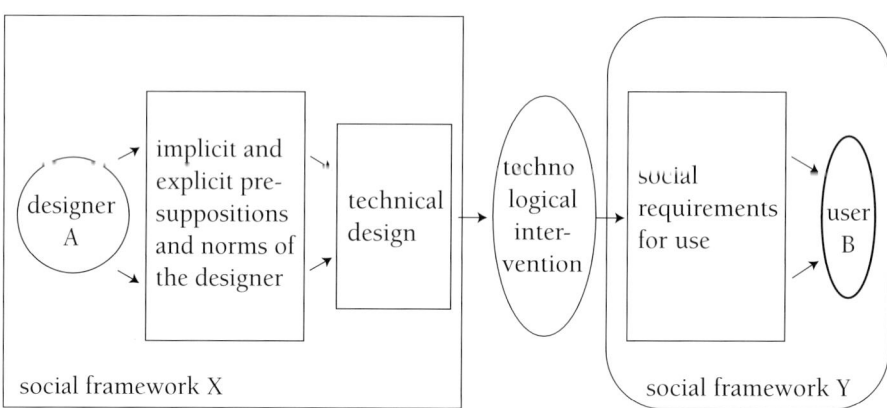

Diagram 8.1.b; Design of irrigation technology in a situation of discontinuity, in which the designers have norms and presuppositions regarding the function, use and impact of the respective technology, *different* from the ones which the users have.

Source: Based on Frouws & Van der Ploeg (1986), Artifacto (1989) and Boelens & Temmink (1990).

In the second case, to make the irrigation technology work, many of the central assumptions that the designer had regarding the use and effect of the technology must be borne out in reality. Thus, to a certain degree, the 'reality expected by the designer must be realised' if the irrigation is to operate rationally. It often becomes 'necessary' to restructure the local situation with regard to the organisation of labour, the definition of roles, the distribution of water, the division of production, etc. In practice, we can see that the outside designer's social and institutional setting often normalises irrigation technology: male domination in the design process adds in gender norms, the colonial roots of irrigation science adds cultural norms, etc. In this process, peasants' own knowledge, skills and norms, such as those involving equitable organisation of labour and equitable distribution of rights and obligations, can be (and historically have often been) expropriated. This process of expropriation is often more far-reaching than just economic expropriation: not only the means of production are expropriated but also the way and the local logical framework of production. We can speak of a process of *expropriating peasant knowledge*. Peasant considerations about equity are an important part of this knowledge. (See also Van der Ploeg 1991).

It is important to consider that it is generally not a question of reproducing - in a modified form - only the technology of one society in another. Often a *vision* is also reproduced; in this case, for example, a vision about nature and the use of natural resources, about equitable distribution among users, about property and gender relationships, etc. Within this vision, concepts such as 'rationality' in irrigation, scarcity of water, distribution of benefits and burdens, etc. play a central role. When using the technology, these abstract concepts become expressed in concrete practices.

However, we should not consider the reproduction of irrigation technology and its social norms as a deterministic, uni-directional process. The social relationships present in the designer's society and environment are not simply transplanted and reproduced in the user's society.

First, neither 'the designer' nor 'the user' are monolithic blocks with unilateral assumptions, but rather complex networks of values and norms, in each of which dynamic social interactions, divergent interests and the non-congruence of expectations and outcomes, are present.

Second, the technology designed by the dominant sectors must not be considered as an omnipotent force. Although it *seeks to structure* new social relationships in the 'receiving' society (taking as its image the characteristics and norms of the designer's dominant society) it generally cannot produce direct replication because the social norms in the technology are *mediated* by the receiving society. Peasant groups are sometimes opposed to using the technology in the way planned by the outside institutions. They also include their own interests and ideas and - sometimes against outside operating plans - build and implement systems according to their own ways of working and organising.[19] That is, the design and implementation process regarding irrigation systems does not come down to just 'technical decisions'; it is a negotiation process involving personal and institutional interests and preferences, for both technicians and peasants.

Third, because - although still on a reduced scale - attempts have increased to conduct a truly participatory or interactive design and construction process between certain support institutions and user groups, achieving an appropriate hybridisation of academic and peasant knowledge. The prerequisite condition for including peasants' own norms in irrigation technology, is to stop considering 'participation' as a project that the *peasants* have to get involved in. On the contrary, in those cases where technical and social assistance is really needed, the professionals and institutions are the ones who would have to *participate in the peasants' reality*, to accompany them in the process of critically including their own social contents in irrigation technology.

Ultimately, irrigation development obtains its concrete form, neither through 'charitable aid' (or rather, philanthropic imperialism), nor through 'harmonious autonomous peasant development', but through ongoing processes of negotiation, both internal and external. Peasant families, groups of irrigators, communities, users with alternative uses for water, private development institutions, the State and so on, all have to get together to confront and defend their interests in irrigation development. They will define their own strategies, call in the necessary resources and means to enter in the different arenas, at the local, regional or (inter) national levels, to negotiate, exert pressure and voice demands. These same arenas - formal and informal fora for interaction, discussion, conflict and sometimes consensus - are major sources of technological, normative and organisational changes in peasant irrigation (see Chapter 37). According to strategic alliances and the power that different peasant groups are able to wield jointly in these negotiations, they will be in a position to express and concretise their own viewpoints regarding equity.

It is also time to recognise that irrigation development is really not a linear process of planning, implementation and outcomes, with predictable effects. The process of change brings to the fore a set of results, both expected and unexpected, which generally lead to modifications or even breakdowns in the planning of the original 'project'. The intervention cannot and should not consider social reality as something entirely 'plannable' or 'achievable'. In the process, changes are attained through conflicts and negotiation, reflecting the commitment or imposition of the interests by the different stakeholders. Therefore, it is crucial to explicitly try to include not just the interests expressed and proposed by the 'formal negotiators', but also those from the less visible groups with interests and priorities that are often denied. Further, in these arenas, not only the peasants but also support institutions and their professionals must make their objectives and assumptions explicit, in order to make more open, more collective, more productive negotiation possible, and in order to achieve results of the irrigation design and management process which are considered to be more equitable by the users.

Notes

1   Irrigation must provide the water to maintain the necessary soil moisture. Peasant families, consciously or unconsciously, 'calculate' in their daily practice and as a result of experimentation, learning and inherited customs, the balance between the various factors related to irrigation water demand, which go to make up a complex matrix. Aside from certain 'social requirements', these factors include: effective precipitation, crop characteristics, plant growth phases, soil type and characteristics with regard to capillary movement and water retention, surface water runoff and percolation losses, sufficiency of air available to the plant, erosion control and timeliness of providing a new 'dose' of water to crops' root zone.

2   Or, to put it another way, introducing irrigation entails a change in productive forces (including irrigation technologies) and this entails a change in production relations (including relations of ownership in irrigated farming). The search for equity must then focus on both aspects: technological means of irrigated production and relationships among human beings. Both are closely related, giving irrigation its sociotechnical nature.

3   Much of this section is based on Boelens & Doornbos (1996).

4   This principle is not only applicable in peasant systems. Rather, it is the basic, conventional principle for distributing water in systems designed by outside development agencies. In such cases, it is combined with the principle of 'receiving water according to how much one pays'.

5   For example, in the Andes, the higher areas have less ecological potential to increase their production with the same amount of water (longer growing seasons); and there is also the possibility of greater crop diversity at lower altitudes (ecological levels with different climates). So, the utility of water at higher altitudes is usually less, and certain systems compensate for this by giving higher-up communities advantages such as more water, turns during day time or other compensatory measures. Another example already mentioned is the basic principle of 'filling the field', regardless of how long it takes, because water utility is different for different soil types.

6   This is a variation on the rule of dividing water among communities according to the number of families in each participating community.

7   There are also many technical possibilities (water distribution schedules and application methods) for putting each of these allocation approaches into practice, which, because of their numerous combinations, lead to an even greater diversity in peasant irrigation.

8   A common idea in many peasant and indigenous systems in the Andes is for both families *and* their plots to have water rights. See, for example, Gerbrandy (Chapter 28) and Gerbrandy & Hoogendam (1997). In these cases, in the same way, the rural household (and not only the irrigated land) is an entitlement holder.

9   Moreover, unlike design and allocation criteria in conventional projects ('allocation of water only considering the land'), some of the peasant principles mentioned make it possible to allocate water to landless families (generally the poorest people, or young people yet to start their own families). They can use their water rights on rented land; sell their rights; barter their rights or begin a reciprocal relationship with another family that has land but needs access to water (in the Andes, this practice is called 'working in company' or 'working half and half').

10 Often, official regulations establish that the irrigator receives personal rights to water, pays water fees and fines personally to the governmental (sub) agency, etc. Furthermore, this individual irrigator generally is defined as the 'head of household', which usually means a man. By contrast, many peasant societies grant rights to families and consider their rights as part of community property.

11 This refers basically to systems managed by peasants organised into communities. In large systems, however, management is often shared with other, non-peasant institutions and the rules are more solely 'water-oriented' and less 'integrated'.

12 Rental of waterrights, and the semi-permanent exchange of water use rights for the right to use other production resources are specific forms of such transfer. In the Andean case, for example, there is reciprocal exchange of scarce resources, where one family may provide the land and water, the other family may offer the labour and the seed or animal traction for ploughing,

and they will share the harvest. They share access to water, with a semi-permanent authorisation by the owner.

13 Literature on this topic often emphasises that 'peasant investment' in irrigation facilities consists fundamentally of labour contributed to the construction process and system maintenance. Although this is an essential element to create and conserve rights, there are other important factors, such as a) money (dues), b) goods (agricultural produce, local materials, instruments, machinery and others), c) intellectual inputs and organisational efforts, such as at meetings, d) operational contributions to water distribution and e), in certain peasant societies, what we called 'communal cultural investment', which is present in the communities' collective memory (for example, participation in ritual activities involving irrigation, and remembrance of the blood, sweat an tears and the casualties 'invested' in the system. See Boelens & Doornbos 1996).

14 This logic of 'peasant investment' must *also* be critically analysed, and not only in positively valued terms (such as sustainability and autonomy). In Arroyo & Boelens (1997) we have analysed the consequences for female irrigators, who are already overburdened with work, in communities with much male migration.

15 This means that both equitable norms, established by collective consensus, and oppressive, unjust norms, established under conditions of unequal power structures, may be reflected and materialised in the technology.

16 Irrigation technology is the knowledge and skill applied consciously to generate, operate, modify and conserve technical-normative-organisational systems, in order to change the dry-land agricultural production process into one in which the application of water and the water balance are controlled - in a certain way and to a certain degree. This definition implies that the generation and implementation of irrigation *technology* is not limited to *scientifically* generated technologies. There are many irrigation technologies in the world; peasant groups have created and used a wide variety of them for many centuries, with specific knowledge and skills adapted to different places and social frameworks. The irrigation system, with its facilities, techniques, organisational forms and rules for use and conservation, may be analysed as the *materialisation* of a certain irrigation technology.

17 This formal objective is often not wholly met in practice, since 'transferring' capacity to solve one's own problems, generate one's own technology and define one's own norms would run against the established powers and interests. Often efforts are limited to simply 'delivering' the capacity to *use* (and repair and maintain) irrigation systems.

18 The mistaken assumption, that '*it is not machines, tools and technologies that are to blame, but the distribution of technologies and the people who (mis) use them*', is an idea shared by the Marxist tradition and the modernisation school. Unfortunately, socialists have critiqued too little the basic characteristics and norms of productive forces (*inter alia*, technology), thinking that changing just the production relations could solve situations of exploitation (in this case, by transferring the irrigation technology from the haves to the have-nots). See Ullrich, 1984, 'Wedstrijd zonder winnaars', De Uitbuyt, Wageningen.

19 The impacts of irrigation technology do not depend only on the characteristics of the technology itself, but begin to emerge only when applied in concrete usage, under locally specific conditions (see Mollinga & Mooy 1989b). Mediation by interest groups means that no stakeholder, nor even 'top-down interventions', can impose or transmit their irrigation technologies and techniques in just a one-way direction (but they can still cause seriously harmful impacts).

References

Apollin, F. & R. Boelens, 1996. *El riego en la comunidad andina. Una construcción social.* CICDA-CESA-CAMAREN-SNV. Quito.

Arroyo, A., & R. Boelens, 1997. *Mujer campesina e intervención en el riego andino. Sistemas de riego y relaciones de género.* CAMAREN-CESA-SNV. Quito.

Artifacto, 1990. *Het sociale van het materiele.* Dept. of Irrigation and Soil and Water Conservation, Wageningen Agricultural University.

Bijker, W.E., T. P. Huges & T. Pinch (eds.), 1987. *The social construction of technological systems.* MIT Press, Cambridge Massachusetts y Londres.

Boelens, R., & G.J. Temmink, 1990. 'Irrigatie en Participatie in de Peruaanse Andes.' *Derde Wereld,* vol. 9, 90 1&2, DWC. Nijmegen.

Boelens, R., & B. Doornbos, 1996. *Derecho consuetudinario campesino e intervención en el riego. Visiones divergentes sobre agua y derecho en los Andes.* CESA-SNV. Quito

Boelens, R. & J. Noordholland de Jong, 1997. *Hacia una visión integral del riego andino.* Módulo de capacitación, No.1, CAMAREN. Quito.

Bromley, D.W. (ed.), 1992. *Making the commons work.Theory, practice and policy.* ICS Press, San Francisco.

Chambers, R., 1980. 'Basic concepts in the organization of irrigation'. In: *Irrigation and agricultural development in Asia: perspectives from the social sciences.* Ed. E.W, Coward Jr., Cornell University Press. Ithaca N.Y.

Coward, E.W., 1983. *Property in action. Alternatives for irrigation investment.* Document prepared for the workshop on Water Management and Policy, University of Khon Kaen, Thailand. Khon Kaen.

Coward, E.W., 1985. 'Technical and social change in currently irrigated regions: rules, roles and rehabilitation'. In: *Putting people first: sociological variables in rural development.* Ed. M.M. Cernea, Oxford University Press. Oxford.

Coward, E.W., 1986. 'State and locality in Asian irrigation development. The property factor'. In: *Irrigation management in developing countries: current issues and approaches.* Eds. Nobe & Sampath. ISARD, Studies in Water Policy and Management no.9, pp. 491 - 508.

Frouws, J. & J.D. Van der Ploeg, 1986. *Agrarische Ontwikkelingssociologie.* Unpublished document, Department of Sociology, Wageningen Agricultural University.

Gerbrandy, G. & P. Hoogendam, 1997. *La diversidad en los derechos al agua en el riego andino de Bolivia.* International Congress of Americanists, July 1997. Quito.

Hoogendam, P., 1995. *Derechos sobre el agua: propiedad pública, propiedad privada e infraestructura de riego.* Seminar on Irrigation Management Transfer, Riobamba, November 1995. Quito

Illich, I., 1979 (1973). *Tools for Conviviality.* Fontana / Collins. Glasgow.

Latour, B., 1987. *Science in action: how to follow scientists and engineers through society.* Open University Milton Keynes.

Mollinga, P. et al.., 1987. *"Wetenschap, technologie en Derde Wereld".* Revoluon vol.12. Nijmegen.

Mollinga, P. & J. Mooy, 1989a. *"Technologieontwikkeling als driehoeksverhouding".* Revoluon vol.13, nr. 2, Nijmegen.

Mollinga, P. & J. Mooy, 1989b. *Cracking the code. Towards a conceptualization of the social contents of technical artefacts.* Technology Policy Group, Occasional Paper no. 18, Open University Milton Keynes.

Ploeg, J.D. Van der, 1991. *Landbouw als mensenwerk. Arbeid en technologie in de agrarische samenleving.* Couthino. Muiderberg.

Ostrom, E., 1992. *Diseño de instituciones para sistemas de riego auto-gestionarios.* ICS Press, Institute for Contemporary Studies. San Francisco.

Uphoff, N.,1986. *Getting the process right: improving irrigation water management with farmer organization and participation.* Studies in Water Policy and Management, no.11, Westview Press. Boulder and London.

9

The Technocratic Vision of Equity in Water Distribution: a Matter of Context

Geert Diemer

The notion of equity refers to people´s ideas about what is fair and unfair in a given situation. These ideas are not absolute but concern the interests of the parties involved. This applies also to distribution of irrigation water. The social context in which engineers usually design irrigation systems structures their criteria for correct water use and their ideas about equity in water distribution. I will develop this train of thought by comparing common elements of agency-led irrigation development with those elements which are common in farmer-led irrigation development[1].

Notions of equity in water distribution on agency built schemes

Design engineers often work under the following conditions (Nijman 1993). The agency that employs or commissions them receives both its operational and investment funds from the central government. The latter uses loans from national or international development banks to finance irrigation investments. Interest and repayment are covered by the national treasury, not by the agency, so the agency has little financial incentive to push for organisationally viable schemes. The agency is tempted to favour a technically sophisticated but costly design that allows for fine-tuning of water levels to satisfy crop water requirements (automation, downstream control, lining etc.) and to simply suppose that the social arrangements needed to operate the scheme will be generated either spontaneously or through training programs and the proper design of institutions. The agency may select a site with recognised physical potential for irrigation (fertile soils near untapped waters) even when the farming population is primarily subsistence-oriented, has not pushed for irrigation and, consequently, is not organised in any way that would enable them to talk with the designer (Dia *et al.* 1996). Development banks are usually interested in a rate of return that they define as healthy and are satisfied if the agency and designers can present them with calculations that meet their standards.

In this context of development bankers and agency officials, engineers are rewarded if they define the design assignment as a technical and economic exercise. Efficiency quickly becomes a central design criterion, both for transporting water from the intake to the fields and for application of water to the crops. Water is to be allocated in such a way that, on each plot, an additional m^3 gives the same additional yield.

This practice both minimises construction costs and maximises water use efficiency. It is called 'equalising marginal returns' by economists. Although many engineers are unfamiliar with this term, they do tend to follow this routine because, within the framework of defining the design assignment as a technical and economic exercise, it provides a rational solution to the problem of how to design the canal network and distribute water. Alternative designs, varying the layout, length, width and depth of the main and secondary canals and/or the shape of plots, are drawn to find the most cost-effective layout in terms of the ratio between construction, maintenance and management costs, on the one hand, and micro and macro economic benefits, on the other. Large farmers and agribusinesses also follow this approach to install irrigation facilities.

Many design manuals for smallholder schemes implicitly adopt this approach. (For recent examples, see FAO's irrigation and drainage papers 44 and 45.) Manuals almost exclusively address relationships among soils, crops, climate, topography, hydrology, and hydraulics. They put all social relationships between brackets, those between the agency and farmers, those among farmers, those between farmers and markets, and those between designer and agency. When they do mention social relationships, it is suggested that they usually affect management and operation rather than the physical infrastructure of the system. Instead, design engineers' and or agency officials' views of desirable relationships among farmers, agency and markets enter the design, usually implicitly. An example: reports and designs may assume that farmers in upstream blocks will co-operate with farmers in downstream blocks to implement the rotation schedule and that farmers inside blocks will (re)organise themselves to make the most efficient use of water entering the block (and refrain from distributing the water on the basis of other criteria, e.g. debt relationships between large and small farmers, etc.).

In short, the designer's view of equity in water allocation and distribution:
• is defined by a particular context dominated by the development bank and the agency;
• approaches equity from the angle of optimising water use at the scheme level;
• assumes that social relationships among farmers, between farmers and officials, and between them and other parties, will revolve around implementation of the technically derived allocation schedule.

In this summary sketch of the designer view of equity, farmers are hardly recognised as knowledgeable, capable individuals who have their own ideas about social justice and about how to use the scheme. Farmer views of equity may be based on different criteria, as can be shown with an example from the Senegal river valley in West Africa. The example concerns one of the hundreds of 20 ha schemes designed by agency engineers and built in part by, on the average, 80 farmers who each invested labour to clear 1/80th of the land and dig 1/80th of the canal lengths. The plots were assigned by lottery. Farmers on these schemes developed a system of water allocation and water distribution. Two main principles were that farmers were to follow a rotation and that farmers could take as much as they wanted once they had their turn. This applied to all farmers, whether they had sandy or clayey plots. A technical extension worker sent by the agency felt that this allocation principle was inequitable because water on the sandy plots would percolate and be unavailable to the root zone of the crop whereas water on the clayey plots would be stored in the soil and benefit the crop. The extension worker proposed that farmers with sandy plots receive additional turns. His proposition was quickly dismissed because, in the words of the scheme chairman, it created more problems than it solved. It may be supposed that the proposition ran counter to the fact that farmers related the volume of water received to the volume of the investment made. As each person made the same investment, each should receive the same amount of water.

Farmers may also wish to put the intake and canals to uses that are not agricultural. Farmers on the Mwea scheme in Kenya campaigned for decades to have pipes convey water from the main canals to their compounds for easy washing of clothes and personal hygiene. Similarly, farmers on the Pithuwa scheme in Nepal have diverted some branch canals through their villages to ease access to domestic water (Pradhan, 1996).

For all its emphasis on the efficiency of water use, the conventional approach to designing canal networks generates rather limited water savings. Water is needed not only to satisfy crop requirements but also to facilitate fair, simple water distribution. This additional operational requirement (AOR) may be defined as the difference between the peak requirement and water requirements during other parts of the growing season. Meijer (1992) shows that the AOR in these schemes will be 5% to 14% of total flow. Furthermore, those schemes equipped with gates that can be set to match the changing crop water requirement may be difficult to manage. Wrong settings may easily reverse the efficiency gains, and even cause losses. And in these cases, staff must be numerous and well trained. Personnel costs will therefore be high (Horst 1987). And, last but not least, water distribution practices that create near-scarcity situations to 'gain water efficiency' may incite farmers to secure their harvests by offering bribes to water bailiffs and scheme engineers, which makes water use suboptimal at both their own and other fields.

Notions of equity in water distribution on farmer-built schemes

Notions of equity on farmer-built schemes also arise from social relationships, but are quite different. People hold rights to water that they can enforce. They may have a right to water because they belong to a certain community or because they themselves or their forefathers invested labour in the construction and maintenance of dams and canals. Examples will abound in other parts of this book. The point is that, on such schemes, the farmers *own* the irrigation infrastructure and therefore have a *right* to water (Coward 1986a and 1986b).

Here, the English-language notion of 'equity' is more pertinent than in the discussion of the conventional design approach. First, because it refers to the notion of owner-ship of shares of a company's capital stock. Second, because it also refers to rules that people apply although they are outside formal law. In farmer-managed irrigation systems, people hold rights to irrigation water because they co-own a piece of capital stock, the hydraulic infrastructure. As co-owners they develop and change, quite outside formal law, a set of rules and by-laws to settle the differences and disputes that arise as command areas expand, watersheds erode, wages rise or fall, the popu-lations grow or grey and markets expand or shrink.

The differences between the notions of equity held by farmers on farmer-managed systems and by engineers on agency-managed systems can be expressed as follows: on farmer-managed systems, water is distributed *among rightholders* and in the design reports for agency-managed systems it is planned to be distributed *among plots* or groups of plots (blocks). Also, on many farmer-built schemes, water use is primarily *optimised at the level of the individual water right* and on many agency-managed schemes primarily *at the system level*. These differences correspond to dif-ferences in design approaches and in infrastructure. On farmer-managed systems, the layout and dimensions of the canal network are chosen primarily to allow imple-mentation of the rights of co-owners, on agency-built schemes primarily to reach the most favourable cost-benefit ratio. These differences are summarised in Table 9.1.

	Farmer-built schemes	Agency-built schemes
Distribution of water	Among rightholders	Among plots
Optimisation	At the level of the individual's water right	At the scheme level.

Table 9.1: Notions of equity in water distribution on farmer- and agency-built schemes.

Concluding remarks

The designer's notion of equity in water distribution is attractive to many develop-ment agents because it seems tantamount to social justice, especially when all farm-ers have plots of the same size. This combination seems to fulfil all major conditions for social equality because each plotholder is supposed to receive the volume of water needed to harvest as much as all fellow farmers.

Real-life relationships on agency managed-schemes are not so rosy, however[2]. Farmers are not co-owners and officials are employed by an agency that is public, not private. No blueprint allocation principles apply and the allocation and distribution of water can only be the ever-changing results of negotiations and conflicts among the parties: poor, rich and middle-class farmers downstream, poor, rich and middle class farmers upstream, water bailiffs, block managers, scheme managers, general managers, politicians, traders and so on, all using different notions of equity to defend their interests.

Notes

1   The editors asked me to contribute a chapter on 'the technocratic vision of equity in water distribution'. I have taken that phrasing to refer to the equity notion that engineers tend to adhere to until they must link to other parameters. Because of this interpretation, I allude little to the ways in which engineers have materialized their notion of equity in concrete systems. Inequities in water distribution are often related to inequities in land ownership. I will not discuss these, limiting myself to technocratic notions of equity in water distribution.
2   They are not any rosier on farmer managed systems.

References

Coward, E. Walter Jr, 1986a. 'State and Locality in Asian Irrigation Development: The Property Factor', in: K.C. Nobe and R.K. Sampath (eds), *Irrigation Management in Developing Countries: Current Issues and Approaches*, Proceedings of an Invited Seminar Series Sponsored by the International School for Agricultural and Resource Development (ISARD), Studies in Water Policy and Management, No. 8, pp. 491-508.

Coward, E. Walter Jr, 1986b. 'Direct or Indirect Alternatives for Irrigation Investment and the Creation of Property', in: K.W. Easter, *Irrigation Investment, technology and Management Strategies for Development*, Studies in Water Policy and Management, No. 9, pp. 225-244.

Dia, I, G. Diemer, W.F. van Driel and F. P. Huibers, 1996. 'Designing for Farmer Management in the Senegal River Valley.' In: G. Diemer and F.P. Huibers (eds), *Crops, People and Irrigation, Water allocation practices of farmers and engineers.* London: Intermediate Technology.

FAO, 1988. 'Design and Optimization of Irrigation Distribution Networks' FAO *Irrigation and Drainage paper 44.*

FAO, 1989. 'Guidelines for Designing and Evaluating Surface Irrigation Systems'. FAO *Irrigation and Drainage Paper 45.*

Horst, L., 1987. 'Choice of Irrigation Structures: the Paradox of Operational Flexibility'. In: *Proceedings of Asian Regional Symposium Irrigation Design for Management* February 16-18, pp. 45-60.

Meijer, T.K.E.,1992. 'Three Pitfalls in Irrigation Design'. In: G. Diemer and J. Slabbers (eds) *Irrigators and Engineers*, Amsterdam; Thesis Publishers

Nijman, Ch.,1993. *A management perspective on the performance of the irrigation subsector.* Wageningen Agricultural University.

Pradhan, T.M.S., 1996. *Gated or Ungated Water Control in Government-built Irrigation Systems. Comparative Research in Nepal.* Wageningen, The Netherlands: PhD thesis, Wageningen Agricultural University.

10

Equity Considerations in System Design and in the Allocation and Distribution of Water[1]

Gilbert Levine

Irrigation system designs typically include the specification of:
- the amount and timing of water to be delivered to individual farmers or groups of farmers;
- the physical infrastructure to permit the implementation of the water delivery plan;
- a maintenance program;
- a plan for obtaining the resources for operation and maintenance;
- an organizational structure to carry out the various plans.

Each of these components of design has equity implications, as well as agricultural productivity and resource-use-efficiency implications. There are effects of the design on resulting equity, and effects of perceptions of equity on the specific design's potential success. However, while the implications of various design alternatives on productivity and efficiency are usually based upon evaluations of the local physical and economic environments, those for equity are rarely evaluated. Instead, the design almost always results in an equity that basically is defined by pre-conceived views of the designers, with little explicit consideration of the local social and cultural environments, or of farmers' views.

Amount and timing of water delivery

The amount and timing of water delivery, in essence, determines the water rights of the users: who has the right to receive water, in what amounts and when. In the design of *modern* or *modernizing* irrigation systems, especially those in which governments and/or international donors are involved, equity in water rights is defined *de facto* as *equality in meeting crop water needs*. This is usually conditioned by an anticipated crop or cropping pattern.

But in many countries there are basic rules that underlie people's perceptions of their rights to water. Generally, there are two basic types of rights, those that are attached to the land that is *riparian to a water course* (and in many countries, overlying ground water) and those that are obtained by *appropriation*. Riparian rights often are defined as a right to 'the full flow of the stream, undiminished in quality or quantity'.

Obviously, this type of right is designed for non-consumptive use activities, e.g. transportation, water power generation, fishing. In practice, the 'full flow' requirement is modified to accommodate domestic consumptive uses, including home gardens and cattle watering. Where irrigation, a decidedly consumptive use, is practiced in riparian rights situations, it usually is tolerated as long as it does not seriously adversely affect downstream users[2]. Where water is used consumptively, it must be used on riparian land. In relatively unusual situations the rights can be sold[3]. In Asia, there are customarily open access rights for domestic uses, but riparian use for other purposes, including irrigation, may not be recognized by the governments of many countries.

Appropriation rights may be derived by traditional precedent or by allocation from an authoritative source. Typically, the rights are associated with the holder of the right and they are not necessarily linked to specific land parcels. In many situations they can be leased or sold. Appropriation rights may be accorded for a variety of reasons and can take one of many forms. Priority may be given for those uses considered 'beneficial', with domestic use generally having the highest priority, but usually including irrigation as a beneficial use. Priority may be based upon early use; it may be given to meet social needs. The nature of the allocation rules associated with these rights may be relatively fixed over time, often codified in legal structures, or they may be more flexible, responding to changing conditions[4].

The rules defining water rights may be relatively simple or relatively complex. In many parts of the world, the allocation rule is one of *proportional sharing of the water*. This generally does not specify *quantity* or *quality*, and either or both may vary over time. The most common basis for proportionality is the proportion of area farmed in the command area by the water user[5]. A modification in some farmer-constructed systems is based on the degree of contribution to the construction of the system, either in kind[6] or through the purchase of shares[7]. In a few situations, proportional sharing may be based upon family size[8]. Proportional sharing of the supply does not consider climate, topography, soils or crops, and thus is not designed to optimize either economic or resource use efficiency, but reflects a specific perception of equity.

While systems that are based on proportional sharing do not customarily consider the production factors, there are examples where recognition of the implications of this lack of consideration are addressed. In Taiwan[9], for example, a sharing rule based on prior rights and size of holding exists for the various sub-systems within larger irrigation associations. When the available supply is reduced to the level (approximately 30%) where there is significant impact on those with lower priority, the customary rules are abrogated (with consent of those holding priority rights) and 'technical' rules are instituted. These rules are designed to share the *impact* of the water shortage equally among the users. When the water emergency is over, the original rules are reinstituted. Even systems with very simple resource sharing rules often have mechanisms for responding to water stress conditions that impose special hardships, based upon the differentials in production environment[10]. In these systems, the adjustments may be through arrangements among individual farmers, or through the delegation to respected village elders of the authority to make adjustments.

Many systems, however, *are* organized to consider production factors in modifying the area-based proportionality. Here, the definition of equity is changed to one of sharing the *utility of the water*, rather than the flow volume, itself. This is the underlying equity rule associated with modern design procedure, where climate, soil and crop information are used to determine an 'irrigation requirement'. In this procedure, both the amount and timing of delivery are specified[11], and vary with the cropping environment.

A further modification of the equity rule attempts to include not only the production utility of the water, but also the *economic potential of the water*. In this case, water deliveries are based upon a consideration of the differences in economic opportunity[12], as well as the physical differences in the various parts of the systems. For example, in some systems in Indonesia a mandated fraction of village agricultural land must be planted to crops specified by the government. These crops yield lower net returns than the customary paddy rice. Village decisions about who receives guaranteed water for paddy rice includes consideration of the cropping history of the individual farmers, with special consideration given to those who most recently grew the mandated crops[13].

The foregoing illustrates a wide range of possible perceptions about what constitutes equity in irrigation. While the water allocation rule for the design of new systems, or the modernization of existing ones may appropriately differ from that existing in the region or system, failure to consider the implications of the change and to mobilize acceptance for the change is likely to result in major problems in system operation.

Physical infrastructure

Three aspects of the physical infrastructure for irrigation have implications for the system equity:
• the density of the delivery system;
• the type of control structures;
• measurement capability.

Density of delivery system

In most modern and modernizing systems there is an attempt to serve each farming unit directly from an irrigation channel. For non-flooded crops, the advantages are clear; they are less obvious for flooded rice where field to field irrigation can be as efficient and effective as directly delivered water[14]. In systems where delivery to downstream users passes over others' fields, the downstream users usually have worked out arrangements with the upstream farmers to permit reasonable deliveries. Increasing the density of the channel network reduces the number of farmers in this dependent situation and may significantly affect the social fabric of the irrigation community. In addition, while increasing the density of the distribution network permits more holdings to be served directly, it also increases the length of channels that must be maintained. Usually, these tertiary or field channels must be maintained directly by the farmers, and often this responsibility falls disproportionally on the downstream and tail-end users. Moreover, the potential benefits of being served directly from the channels - more timely and more accurate water deliveries - can only be realized if there is a corresponding level of control of the flows into and along the channels. That the theoretical benefits are not always realized is clearly evident in a comment by a Thai farmer: 'They built the ditches to make us argue'.

Type of control structure

Generally, farmers in customary systems use control structures that are simple and effective in implementing the basic operating rules. Where the equity operating rule is proportionality, fixed proportional dividers (sometimes with simple on-off capability) typically are used. These often are rectangular, with the widths proportional to the relative shares of the flow. These types of proportional *weirs* can be large, dividing flows among relatively large areas, or very small at the individual farmer level. An alternative to proportional weirs, used when deliveries are made to individuals served from group channels, is a fixed opening at a specified height below the design elevation of the water surface. In those cases where the full flow in the channel is made available to the users, as in the *Warabandi*[15] type system, only on-off control at the head of the delivery channel is necessary. When accommodation to site-specific physical conditions is part of the traditional pattern, the different flow needs frequently are established by providing openings with different sizes. But, in almost all cases the outlet has *fixed* dimensions. Thus, in many traditional systems, the equity rules are embedded in the basic infrastructure of the system.

In modern designs, *variable* opening outlet structures frequently are specified. This permits the modification of deliveries to match changes in 'irrigation requirements' reflecting seasonal and plant growth changes. However, as suggested earlier, this implies an equity rule based upon utility of the water for production, rather than a proportional sharing. When this change is not arrived at through mutual agreement with the farmers, many of the gates become non-functional in a short period of time through damage by the farmers.

Measurement capability

Measurement capability encompasses the process by which the necessary measurements are obtained with instruments and techniques appropriate for the required accuracy and precision, and transmitted to the appropriate users in a suitable form for relevant decision-making. In principle, the proportional sharing equity rule does not require any measurement capability. Once the physical infrastructure is in place, the system functions according to the equity rule. However, generally, there is some need to be able to measure or estimate the flow in the channel *prior* to division, to identify problems in acquisition of the water - problems at the intake or in the leading channel.

In some situations, the proportional sharing is accomplished by specifying a *time share* of the flow, rather than a continuous division of the flow. This type of *rotation* is frequently utilized in sharing among systems using a common water source, but is also used in sharing among individuals. In relatively large systems, additional measurements may be necessary. This is exemplified by the Warabandi system, in which the time for an individual's allocation is proportional to the area to be irrigated, adjusted for losses in the channel. The timing of the individual allotments often is specified to the minute. But, in addition to measuring time (a responsibility of the individual users) two other measurements are necessary - the depth at the head of the channel (to ensure the flow is within the range of reasonable performance of the individual outlets) and the depth at the tail of the channel (to ensure that hydraulic conditions within the channel are adequate). However, both measurements are easy to carry out - though often they are not made.

In modern systems, in addition to attempting to accommodate to changes in climatic or crop growth, there often is an attempt to provide maximum opportunity for individual farmer decision-making by providing deliveries on 'demand'. The demand system requires a relatively high degree of control and measurement capability[16]. Depending upon the type of rights associated with system there will be greater or lesser need for measurement information. If there is an appropriation right of a specified quantity (e.g. hectare-meters) there must be a capability to measure the flow volumes. If the right is for sufficient water for a specified area and crop, there may be a need for measurement of appropriate meteorological and field information, to permit estimation of the water requirement. In many traditional systems with a utility equity rule, the adjustment to seasonal and crop variation often is estimated at the beginning of the season, e.g. in 10 day intervals, with readjustment only when farmer complaints suggest that the original schedule is inadequate. As can be noted, the establishment of a specific water delivery equity rule brings with it the need for a corresponding implementation mechanism.

Maintenance program

In many customary systems with relatively simple equity rules for water allocation, and with fixed physical infrastructure for implementation of the rules, system *operation* is relatively simple. However, *maintenance* of these systems often requires a mix of activities, some of which can be anticipated and others which occur in response to special circumstances. In many, with intake structures that invariably are destroyed during heavy rains, a routine reconstruction effort is required prior to the irrigating season. However, on occasion, there are dam or canal breaches that require unplanned, relatively immediate response measures. The allocation of these responsibilities illustrates another form of irrigation system equity.

A common form of sharing maintenance responsibilities follows the same proportional rule used for water delivery - in proportion to area served. However, other
forms exist. In some situations, the downstream users provide proportionately more
resources for maintenance, often as the *quid pro quo* for receiving reasonable water
deliveries. In other cases, the labor and other resources required for maintenance of
intake structures and leading canals is such that the head-end users are dependent
upon the assistance of the tail-end users. In this situation, a more equal sharing of
the burden may be the norm.

The introduction of factors that influence maintenance can materially change these
equity patterns. For example, a government program in Thailand provided concrete
to permit the construction of relatively permanent concrete intake structures in a
number of farmer-managed systems. The rationale for this action was to reduce the
annual need for bamboo and timber to repair or replace the traditional structure,
with its resultant impact on adjacent forests. However, the installation of permanent
structures eliminated the mutual maintenance dependency of the head and tail-end
users, with consequent implications for adequacy of water delivery to the tail-enders.

Resource mobilization

Implicit in the operation of almost all irrigation systems is the need to mobilize
resources - for operation, maintenance, and for periodic rehabilitation. As suggested
earlier, in customary farmer-managed systems, resource mobilization usually follows
the same equity pattern associated with the water allocation. Water fees, in cash, in
kind, and/or in labor are based upon the share of the water received. Almost always,
in government-managed systems the fee is based upon the area served, irrespective
of whether a proportional sharing or utility equity rule is used for the water allocation. In some, there may be an adjustment relating to the nature of the crops irrigated, and in a limited number of situations the fee will reflect the economic potential
of the water - an 'ability to pay' principle. In the case of the farmer-managed irrigation associations of Taiwan, a combination of principles are used. This combination
includes both *the cost of providing irrigation service* to the user and the *potential
benefit* from the water. The irrigation fee consists of two parts - a relatively low *regular
fee* and an *engineering fee*; this latter being the cost of providing water to each sub-
system of users, including the cost of providing the specific length of channel. Those
users provided with ground water find the cost of pumping included in their fees.
The fee is lower, however, for those farmers whose physical environment does not
permit two crops of rice. In the Taiwan case, resource mobilization does not match
the equity rule used for water allocation. However, notwithstanding the relative
independence of the farmer-managed irrigation associations and the lack of a national
irrigation agency, there is sufficient governmental influence and irrigator discipline
that resource mobilization generally has been successful[17].

While the rules relating to resource mobilization usually are clear, implementation
often is problematic. In farmer-managed systems, the sanctions for non-contribution

are enforced by the associated social rules, as well as by more formal measures. In Taiwan, for example, a local meeting is held prior to submitting fees to the association; at this meeting, the names of those who have not paid the fee are announced. The shame attached to this public exposure was, in earlier days, sufficient to result in very high payment rates. In many countries, however, the more powerful flout the rules, and to survive over time the systems have had to develop accommodations to this situation.

Resource mobilization from the users in government-managed systems often is weak, and a source of substantial concern in many countries, as well as to the major lending agencies. This is a significant element of the current emphasis on the turnover of government-managed systems to the users.

Organization

To carry out the multiple activities associated with irrigation systems, *organized behavior* is required. When the system is too large for the informal relations among the users to be adequate for managing this behavior, a more formal *organization* is required. Water user organizations exist with a variety of structures, rules and degrees of control. In customary systems, these organizations have evolved over time and reflect the social and cultural norms of the locality. In some, these are part of the village structure[18], in others, they are special-purpose institutions. At the present time, there are major efforts to form water-user organizations, accelerated by the emphasis on transferring irrigation systems to the users. However, the methods by which these groups are formed can markedly affect the resulting allocation of water and maintenance responsibilities[19]. Depending upon the procedure, existing inequities may be strengthened or reduced. When imposed from above, with a standard form, there is a high probability that the existing power structure will be reinforced. Experience also suggests that organizations with a relatively high degree of inequity are not likely to be effective in carrying out their responsibilities. Relatively equitable water user organizations can be established, however, where there are major differences in the relative power of different groups of users, the development of equitable, functional user organizations usually requires significant, special efforts that are not without cost - both financial and political.

Conclusions

Concern for the performance of the irrigation sectors in many countries has caused many governments to search for ways to improve the situation. Among the methods used are the rehabilitation and modernization of existing systems, and the transfer of system management to the users. Both sets of activities influence the resulting equity, and are affected by the perceptions of equity that exist in the systems. Notwithstanding evidence indicating that a failure to adequately recognize the implications of equity has serious consequences for the irrigation system operation, very few efforts explicitly address equity issues. Where there is an attempt to include equity considerations in the process of system improvement, it usually is reflected in rules governing the establishment of user organizations. For example, in the 'transfer' program in Mexico there is an explicit recognition that the communal small farmers (*ejidatarios*) are at an economic and political disadvantage in comparison to the private farmers (*pequeños propietarios*) and, therefore, membership on the board of directors ensures that the ejidatarios are numerically well-represented.

However, in very few cases are the equity implications inherent in the *technical* decisions about water allocation rules and physical infrastructure recognized, and in even fewer are they factored into the decision-making process about these elements of irrigation system design. Yet, experience shows that systems designed on the basis of productivity and efficiency, but considered unfair by many of the users, are likely to be less productive and less efficient than equitable systems with nominally lower productivity and efficiency potential.

Notes

1 Much of this material was presented previously in: Levine, G. & E.W. Coward, Jr., 1989. *Equity considerations in the modernization of irrigation systems*. ODI/IIMI Irrigation Management Network Paper 89/2b. London.
2 When ground water is used consumptively, as in irrigation, it is relatively difficult to specifically trace the impact of that use on the adverse effects experienced by other users. Thus, both legal and social controls are less effective in controlling such use than in the case of surface water.
3 For example, many years ago New York City purchased the riparian rights for much of the watershed from which it derives its public water supply. This purchase gives the city substantial control of activities in the watershed, not only to preserve the quantity of the water, but also the quality.
4 For an example of a system with a mechanism for change, see: Levine, G. 'Irrigation Association Response to Severe Water Shortage: The Case of the Yun Lin Irrigation Association, Taiwan', in *Rural Development and Local Organization in Asia*, Vol. 2 East Asia. N. Uphoff, ed. MacMillan, N.Delhi 1983.
5 Examples of farmer-managed systems with this allocation rule are described in: Tanabe, S. 1981. *Peasant Farming Systems in Thailand: A Comparative Study of Rice Cultivation and Agricultural Technology in Chiengmai and Ayutthaya*. Ph.D. dissertation, The School of Oriental and African Studies, Univ. of London; Martin. E. And Yoder, R. 1983. *Water Allocation and Resource Mobilization in Irrigation: a Comparison of Two Systems in Nepal*. Paper presented at the Annual Meeting, Nepal Studies Association, Twelfth Annual Conference on South Asia, Univ. Of Wisconsin, Madison.
6 An interesting example is described in Leach, E.R., 1961. *Pul Eliya: A Village in Ceylon*. Cambridge University Press.
7 Martin, E. and Yoder, R. 1983. Op. cit.
8 The *Pani Panchayat* systems in Southern India allocate water to serve one-half hectare per family member, to a maximum of 2.5 hectares.
9 Levine, G. op. cit.
10 See, for example, Tanabe, S. op. Cit.
11 In some systems in Mexico, the amount and timing are specified for different crops, but the area sanctioned for water is varied to provide essentially the same total water to each water user. For example, the area allocated for cotton is approximately twice that for vegetables. Thus, this is a proportional sharing of the water supply, with modification to reflect the utility of the water for specific crops.

12 See, for example, Oad. R., 1982. *Water Management and Relative Water Supply in Irrigation Systems in Indonesia*. Ph.D. dissertation, Cornell University. Ithaca, NY.

13 See, Duewel, J., 1982. 'Central Java's Dharma Tirta WUA 'Model': Peasant Organizations Under Conditions of Population Pressure'. *Agricultural Administration* (17) 4. London.

14 See, Wickham, G. and Wickham, T., 1974. *An Evaluation of Two Alternatives of Water-sharing Among Farmers*. Unpublished report of consultancy to the National Irrigation Administration, Upper Pampanga River Project. Quezon City, Philippines.

15 Warabandi is a form of timed rotation of irrigation practiced in the Punjabs of India and Pakistan. For a more complete description, see Malhotra, S.P., 1982. *The Warabandi System and Its Infrastructure*. Central Board of Irrigation and Power Publication No.157. New Delhi.

16 A 'demand' system was introduced into the Dez Pilot Irrigation Project in Iran without adequate managerial controls to constrain requests for water. As a result, water use efficiency declined from approximately 30 percent under the traditional rules to about 11 percent. (Personal Communication, Chief Engineer, Dez Pilot Project)

17 During the period from 1950 into the 1970s, the Taiwan irrigation associations had enviable fee collection records, with some associations achieving fee payments approaching 100%. Subsequent to that period, the rates of collection dropped and the irrigation associations (and most other farmer associations) accumulated substantial debts due to low collections of fees. A variety of causal factors have been identified as contributing to the problem, including the development of unfavorable terms of trade for agriculture, the loss of labor from the agricultural sector, and association corruption. After experimenting with various organizational changes, the central government assumed the association debt burden, modified the organizational structure, and has improved the agricultural profit situation.

18 See Oad, R., 1982. Ibid.

19 See Uphoff, N., 1986. *Improving International Irrigation Management with Farmer Participation: Getting the Process Right*. Westview Press. Boulder, Colorado.

11

Commodity and Community Water Values. Experiences from the U.S. Southwest

Helen Ingram and F. Lee Brown

For the last decade at least, policies and institutions in many nations have increasingly focused upon water as a commodity. Reforms in both developed and developing countries have been directed toward securing private property rights to water, the creation of water markets and facilitation of the movement of water from what is regarded as 'lower-valued' uses in agriculture to 'higher-valued' uses in urban areas. And, indeed, substantial quantities of water have moved from rural to urban uses as reflected in our study area in the arid southwestern United States, in which massive urbanization has occurred, as well as in many other areas around the globe. From a purely monetary point of view, if rural owners of water rights are paid a fair price for water, they as well as urban dwellers are made better off by the transfer. However, our work[1] studying the impacts of a rising commodity value for water upon poor communities in this region, principally Native American and Hispanic, convinces us that a narrow monetary or commodity point of view is much too limited. Water has a cultural and social value that transcends its strictly economic, i.e., scarcity, value.

Before amplifying on this theme in the context of Native American and Hispanic communities in our region of study, it is important to note that this transcendency of social and cultural values is not antithetical to an economic or scarcity value for water. Certainly, civilizations and individual communities in arid regions would not have long survived had they ignored their water scarcity problems. Nor is it impossible to construct water management institutions and policies which effectively merge these distinct values in coherent, practical ways. However, as the relative scarcity of water increases throughout the world and the commodity perspective it engenders rises in policy popularity, it becomes important to revisit the community value dimension of water lest it be crushed in a policy rush to resolve scarcity problems by treating water not only as an economic good but as strictly a commodity devoid of other values.[2]

The literature which treats water as an economic resource centers upon the individual as a participant in market exchanges. Without denying the importance of this perspective, another appropriate unit of analysis is the collective group of inhabitants of a particular place. In cultures with long histories imbedded in particular lands, the individual water user may not be regarded as the owner but as a temporary caretaker of a resource that has been handed down by past generations and should be passed along to future generations undegraded and undiminished. Water is tied not just to peoples but also to places which may take on mythical and symbolic meaning to those who inhabit them.[3] Understanding the community value of water requires a different kind of analysis.

Community-based analysis

Community-based analysis recognizes the group as the basis of interest. This conception is especially relevant to cultures and places where irrigation is longstanding. As Maass and Anderson observe, within rural communities there have evolved strong traditions of community control over water resources stemming from the desire to maintain the integrity of the social and economic community.[4] In some of these communities, these traditions may resemble market systems; in others not. Above all, however, these communities have sought to protect the group from inordinate injury resulting from the actions of individuals, to promote values that pertain specifically to the community proper, and to prevent alienation of water resources from the community as a whole. This last point is seen clearly in attitudes articulated in interviews and expressed in action by the Tohono O'Odham[5] community of Native Americans in Arizona and Hispanic communities in northern New Mexico.[6] The nature of the interest in the collective mode of analysis is emotional and symbolic rather than simply material. It becomes clear in the stories of these communities that water is valued not primarily for its economic return but for what it means for security and community self-determination.

Implicit within the community perspective on water management is the notion that rationality is a social and political process of collective evaluation and consent. This process may vary considerably from one community to another, ranging from the informal village councils of the Tohono O'Odham to the *acequia* associations (community irrigation ditch associations) whose members rotate the role of majordomo or ditch leader that exist in northern New Mexico. Whatever their form, however, these collective procedures essentially serve to varying degrees to harness individual interests to those of the community. Important community-sustaining values are reinforced in the process as well as the potential for innovation and adaptation by the community as a body.[7]

The basis of decision making in community-oriented analysis emphasizes reciprocity, sharing and cooperation. In contrast to competitive market procedures, which reward individualistic pursuit of one's own interest with the hope, and often promise, of community gain, such altruistic values tend to reinforce community bonds first as well as provide security to the individual. Such attitudes were reflected in our study of water practices in both the Hispanic communities of the Upper Rio Grande as well as the Tohono O'Odham. Systems of mutual cooperation, like the northern New Mexico *acequias* or O'Odham village councils, when they work well, encourage individual participation and responsibility, mutual trust and nurture a sense of security and equity within the community. These values tend to diminish conflict and increase social cohesion.

Participation is not viewed simply as a cost to the individual but also an opportunity for the simultaneous development of the individual and the strengthening of social bonds. The solidarity which is fostered by participation in reciprocal, cooperative relations is what Gaventa termed 'empowerment.'[8] In concert, the people within these communities have the strength to hang on to their water resources and to distribute them in ways that serve social as well as economic goals. Maass and Anderson have observed successful irrigation communities behaving in just this way. In order to control their own destinies, farmers in the five communities they studied were willing to go to great lengths to support local cooperative organizations that have sufficient strength and coherence to fend off outside domination. 'The strength and coherence of local irrigation organizations in developed regions appears to be correlated with an irrigation community's success in limiting or stabilizing growth, thereby gaining security for its members.'[9]

Northern New Mexico Hispanic acequias

European (Spanish) settlements in the mountainous, northern reaches of the Rio Grande date from 1598. During different periods, the region has been under the flags of Spain, Mexico and the United States. People of Hispanic origin are a numerical majority in many counties of the Upper Rio Grande in the State of New Mexico, and the region has maintained a distinctive, picturesque and rural character. But, amid the scenic beauty, incomes frequently fall below governmentally set poverty levels. Feelings of lack of power over community conditions are present, sometimes pervasively so.[10]

The *acequias* of northern New Mexico are both a technological and organizational institution. Technologically, irrigation was necessary to supplement rainfall, and so the colonists established their communities in the river valleys. The ditches which bring the streamflow by gravity to the fields commonly begin at a diversion two to four miles upstream from use. Organizationally, the acequias originated as associations of all persons served by the ditch.[11]

Once under the flag of the United States, New Mexico experienced migration from other parts of the country, particularly in the twentieth century, and along with demographic and economic growth came the need for additional supplies of water. One such water supply project, the San Juan-Chama Project[12], diverts roundly 100,000 acre-feet of water from the Colorado River basin in northwest New Mexico and southwest Colorado through the Continental Divide into the Rio Grande basin. Originally intended to serve irrigation districts throughout the latter basin as well as the City of Albuquerque, San Juan-Chama became a major source of conflict for the *acequias*. Originally intended to be beneficiaries of San Juan-Chama, the *acequias* ultimately opposed development of the irrigation works and the conservancy

districts which would be the organizational vehicle for repaying the federal investment. After initially supporting the San Juan-Chama legislation, the northern New
Mexico Hispanic farmers became adamant opponents of it for a number of reasons,
a major one being the realization that the conservancy districts would jurisdiction-
ally supersede the *acequia* organizations themselves. They would lose their direct
control over the community water management and see their participation decline
in the decision-making process with respect to their own livelihood strategies. This
would threaten seriously the basic security of the communities. The irrigation works
have never been constructed.

Having given up the additional irrigation water that San Juan-Chama would have
provided, the *acequias* might have thought that they were simply finished with the
project, but they were mistaken. In order to make certain that the water from San
Juan-Chama, indistinguishable from native Rio Grande water after entering its
riverbed, was carefully accounted for, the State of New Mexico went to court to
establish ownership of all rights to the native Rio Grande water itself. One of the
leading cases in what is known as a stream adjudication suit is the Aamodt case, filed
in 1966 but yet to be finally determined thirty-one years later. Under the western
U.S. water law doctrine of *prior appropriation*, the Aamodt case effectively pitted
users of Rio Grande water in the pertinent geographic region against one another, in
that each user had to establish the historical date at which beneficial use of water had
begun. Although *acequia* use is clearly senior to the rights of recent urban immigrants, records establishing the extent of their historical use are frequently inadequate or missing altogether. More importantly, however, the desire for legal certainty of ownership has forced the court system to decide between *acequia* rights to water
and the rights of Native Americans who preceded them in use of water for irrigation
and domestic purposes. The friction created by the adjudication suits has continued
to wax and wane in severity over three decades and at times has bordered upon violence.[13]

The Tohono O'Odham

Today, about 14,000 Tohono O'Odham live in the Sonoran Desert west of Tucson,
Arizona on a reservation which, approaching three million acres, is one of the largest
in the United States. By most conventional standards, the Tohono O'Odham are poor
people, yet they have learned over centuries to survive in one of the hottest and
driest deserts in the Americas. Relying heavily on ceremonies intended to ensure
adequate rainfall, whenever the wide range of gathered and cultivated crops did fail
for lack of rainfall, they moved to the refuge of still flowing rivers.

In the twentieth century, major technological efforts were made to overcome the
uncertainties of rainfall. The Bureau of Indian Affairs had dug wells drawing upon
what was thought to be an abundance of ground water. Nearby Tucson, however, had
also been relying upon this same source of water as its population grew and grew,
particularly in the latter half of the century. In 1975, when the water table on the San

Xavier portion of the Tohono O'Odham reservation closest to Tucson had been 'sucked so low that new wells hit dry bedrock,' the federal government filed suit on behalf of the tribe against the City of Tucson, mining companies and agricultural interests.[14]

The negotiations leading to the 1982 Southern Arizona Water Rights Settlement Act (SAWRSA), which resolved the dispute, stood western U.S. water practice on its head. Rather than ignoring Indian claims, or trying to settle them with money, the Indian Community received commitments for both wastewater from Tucson - which could be exchanged or used for irrigation - and an allocation of Central Arizona Project water intended to lessen groundwater overdraft in the Tucson area. As of 1996, however, the Tohono O'Odham Nation has yet to put a single drop of settlement water to use. Disagreements as to whether to lease settlement-acquired water rights to Tucson in exchange for money has torn the Native American community asunder. The San Xavier District wishes to restore and expand irrigation on allotment lands while the central tribal government claims that, under the Indian Nation's constitution, all waters are communally owned, and the overall tribal government, on which the San Xavier District has only minority representation, has final rights to decision. Further, the kind of water acquired by the tribe makes direct use by Indians in irrigation difficult. The settlement sharply limited Indian use of groundwater, and substituted what might be termed 'high technology' water. That is, both wastewater and Central Arizona Project Water require expensive engineering treatment and distribution systems that involve long-range planning. Water uses cannot simply evolve as the Native American communities experience economic development and engage in deliberative processes.

The sad reality is that participation in legislative settlement through SAWRSA linked the Tohono O'Odham to the interest-group politics and market-driven exchanges that dominate U. S. water management at the end of the 20th century. The community of interest among the Tohono O'odham has dissolved to the extent that the San Xavier District voted to secede from the union with other districts. This plebescite was an empty threat, however, since the main tribal government will not concur. The main tribal government is dominated by districts with ranching rather than farming traditions and are far more willing to bargain away water rights that promise troublesome to manage. Instead of reinforcing community feeling through securing water through legislative settlement, the sense of community has eroded.

Community value of water

The water sagas of northern New Mexico Hispanics and the Tohono O'Odham are revealing not only for the evidence they provide about the community value of water to those groups themselves. They also demonstrate a similar substrate of values within the larger population itself, even though it is a substrate that is increasingly receptive to a strictly commodity perspective. Water is not only an important kind of resource, it is regarded differently from most other resources by community members. Community-based analysis, particularly of the northern New Mexico Hispanics and the Tohono O'Odham reveals that water, in an arid region at least, is associated with the following community aspirations:

Opportunity

In an arid region, water has the midas touch. If a community has an ample, secure supply of water, it has the potential to prosper. Without water, a community simply does not have a chance. It is not only that water is an essential ingredient in most production processes (without water neither agriculture nor many industries can survive or thrive), but also because control over water signals social organization.[15] A community that cannot hold securely on to its water resources probably cannot do very much else. Weak communities become victims to the better organized and more powerful. Water in an arid region is a tracer element that marks who has economic and political power and who has skill at the game of water politics. The objective of the game has been to use political and economic resources to push off the risks associated with water to marginal communities less able to protect their interests. Further, there has been a tendency to oversubscribe available water supplies and to ignore ecological limits. Thus, the burden of increased risk is placed on the future and on the disadvantaged. Water tends to flow away from the poor and powerless toward those better endowed politically and economically.

Security

The flip side of opportunity is security. Wealthy and powerful interests and areas have hedged themselves against insecurity and risk by laying claim to all of the water they could conceivably use, even if this implies shortage to others. This pattern has meant that the areas of origin in water transfers, often poor communities with an agricultural base, are subjected to high levels of jeopardy. Community resources are then invested in defending their water rights against 'maverick' members of the community who may be willing to sell out their water rights. Time, effort and money are invested in defending against outside interests who manipulate political and legal processes to their own advantage in overruling community objections to water transfers. Preoccupation with the potential loss of water resources may discourage investment in the community and encourage emigration.

Control and Participation

Water is widely perceived as too important for small communities to leave in the hands of others. The strength of indigenous systems is that they involve the farmers directly in allocation of water, maintenance of the system and the establishment of rules for resolving disputes. The staying power of the *acequia* system in northern New Mexico lies to a large extent in local autonomy of management, according to local customs and traditions. Individuals are bound to the community through their participation in water matters and through that bond work to preserve its overall cultural character. Participation builds the social capital which enables the community to have resilience in the face of challenges and disasters and the strength to forge consensus for the solution of common problems.

Conclusion

In recent years, the northern New Mexico *acequia* associations, the Tohono O'Odham and other southwestern tribes have achieved a degree of respect for their tenacity of community purpose in water affairs. Most public water officials now recognize, sometimes grudgingly so, that water issues cannot be effectively addressed without inclusion of *acequia* or tribal interests at the discussion table. Yet, the eventual outcome of current struggles for control over water resources remains uncertain, and unless community values in water are recognized and satisfied, debilitating attitudes of hopelessness will persist, fostered by loss of opportunity and self determination. Moreover, recognition that these groups must be at the discussion table does not necessarily require an *understanding* of the values at stake. Strict adherence to a narrow commodity perspective on water, though, does necessarily reveal a *misunderstanding* of the importance of community values, and that misunderstanding will have consequences.

Notes

1   F. Lee Brown and Helen M. Ingram. *Water and Poverty in the Southwest.* University of Arizona Press, Tucson, 1987.
2   F. Lee Brown. 'Water Markets and Traditional Water Values: Merging Commodity and Community Perspectives.' *Water International*, Volume 22, No. 1 (March 1997).
3   Keith Basso. *Sits in Places: Landscape and Language Among the U.S. Apache.* University of New Mexico Press, Albuquerque, 1996.
4   Arthur Maass and Raymond Anderson '.... *And the Desert Shall Rejoice: Conflict, Growth, and Justice in Arid Environments'.* The MIT Press, Cambridge, 1978.
5   This tribe of Native Americans changed their name from 'Papago' to the more traditional Tohono O'Odham in the course of our study.
6   Brown and Ingram, Chapters 5-6 and 11-12.
7   Stephen Mumme and Helen Ingram. 'Empowerment and the Papago Tribe: Water Politics in Southern Arizona,' unpublished paper prepared for delivery at the 1984 Annual Meeting of the American Political Science Association, August 30-September 2, 1984. Copyright by the American Political Science Association.
8   John Gaventa. *Power and Powerlessness.* University of Illinois Press, Urbana, 1980.
9   Maass and Anderson, p.368.
10 Brown and Ingram, pp.46-48.
11 Ibid., p.49.
12 Federally approved on June 13, 1962.
13 Brown and Ingram, Chapters 5-8.
14 Ibid., Chapters 9-11.
15 Ibid., p.36.

12

Notes about Irrigation Projects, Equity and the Actor-Oriented Approach

Alberto Arce

Introduction

This chapter briefly addresses some conceptual elements for analysing equity issues raised by irrigation projects in rural development. The actor-oriented approach is presented as a means to examine the social aspects of irrigation. As the examples used below illustrate, there is a tendency for irrigation projects to widen social inequalities rather than generating equity. The contribution of the actor-oriented approach to irrigation studies stresses the need to explicitly view producers' organisational capacities, strategic actions and social practices. Each of these concepts is essential to assess the implications of irrigation projects for producers, and to ultimately attain more equitable relations in project implementation and development.

The actor-oriented approach started in the sociology of rural development during the 1970s, firstly, as a reaction to more conventional approaches in development policy formulation and implementation that led to extremely centralised State policies, and secondly, in an effort to reassess the orientation of experts' knowledge in planning programs and their implementation (see Long, 1977).

Some existing approaches aimed for highlighting the polarisation of rich and poor farmers. They were mainly concerned with the nature of the class structure in Third-World countries and with the capitalist process of capital accumulation. Others decided to examine the process of incorporating the rural population into the nation-state, mainly through the impact of urban centers, the spread of communications and government bureaucracy, and the organisation and expansion of the market.

Mainly, existing approaches were focused on the forms of economic organisation and political control. As such, they contributed significantly to understanding the central tendencies of rural transformations. Nevertheless, these analyses often neglected the local knowledge and capacities of participants to make choices and question the situations of rural transformation in which they were involved. More specifically, existing approaches paid little attention to differential responses and variations in organisational patterns of local rural producers. The actor-oriented approach answered some of these more evident deficiencies in the more conventional analyses.

It shows how local producers were able to generate interactions, negotiations, and social and cognitive struggles with those 'others', and in these interactions they were able to influence processes of rural change, thus affecting actions and outcomes.

Hence specific patterns and transitions of agrarian social change are to be studied, within an actor-oriented approach, by the way in which interacting individuals and social groups influence each other. 'This leads to the consideration of what we may call 'intermediate' level structures, such as social networks, household confederations, farmers' organisations, systems of production tying the farmer into his institutional environment, and organised 'interface' structures that constitute the regular modes of interaction between farmers and public authorities' (Long, 1989:121).

In the actor-oriented approach, specific patterns of agrarian change can be explained by the interaction among many persons, farmers and representatives of institutions and not just by 'describing' the nature of class structure or the logic of modernisation processes. To study the notion of choice among different courses of action, it is necessary to identify different actors' conception of equity in processes of rural change (for a discussion of justice versus equity, see Boelens & Doornbos, 1996: 82-84).

It may be necessary to recognise that, while the concept of equity may be embodied in the diverse actions of individuals, single actors are not the only entities that reach decisions and act according to a notion of justice. In this sense, to analyse the notion of equity means to collect a series of local actors' statements about equity in order to compare these with what is 'right' according to the existing construction of juridical sovereignty in a given society. This research exercise can provide us with an understanding of how different actors exert authority over others and organise the implementation of power relations in particular rural development contexts. Here, often an important issue is the way these actors interact and react with respect to the form, content and implementation of national law (i.e. the privatisation of water) in local realities.

In the past few decades intervention policies formally intended to achieve higher degrees of development and equity. Irrigation policies and projects are mainly associated with *improvement*-type policies rather than aiming at the *transformation* of social structures and relations. Technology transfer, and especially the construction of irrigation systems, was perceived as politically less radical than major interventions into people's lives, such as enforced resettlement projects (e.g. the villagisation program in Tanzania, or the implementation of agrarian reform in Latin America). The technical and physical focus of irrigation provided the idea that it was possible to achieve development without conflict. Although there were some pre-existing experiences before the 1970s that deny this assumption, these were ignored or had a minimal influence in the planning of new irrigation schemes. One may argue that if these cases had been taken more seriously, they could have generated insights which might have helped to avoid some of the experiences of failure and could have helped to change the expert's disregard for local knowledge that arose in 'new' irrigation projects in the 1970s.

Actors and irrigation. A Mexican illustration

An analysis of Mexican irrigation planning from the 1940s onwards may contribute new insights into the irrigation planning process, considering the lessons to be learned from previous - negative - experiences in irrigation development. Since this period, irrigation policy has been heavily biased towards commercial agriculture. It has favoured only ten percent of Mexican rural families and concentrated huge amounts of public resources in the North-West of the country (see Hewitt de Alcantara, 1978). These irrigation policies opened new areas to agricultural production, generating regional differences as well as differential allocation of public resources, biased towards the export-oriented commercial sector. In countries like Mexico, water engineers are traditionally criticised for assessing irrigation systems only according to technical and economic criteria and for lacking any explicit conception of rural development upon which to base their interventions. By the 1960s, experiences such as these irrigation policies in the North-West of Mexico ended up concentrating property in the hands of a small group of commercial farmers and establishing land-use patterns according to market demands of individuals rather than stimulating development in relation to national needs or ecological constraints. This sort of experiences have reinforced the need to critically analyse irrigation project development in order to explore the issue of equity from water users' point of view.

Let us first look at some important features of irrigated agriculture. Recent contributions to the field of irrigation studies have stressed the need to correlate the technical aspects of irrigation with processes of social organisation (see Coward, 1985). Here, a point of particular interest is the existence of many 'indigenous social mechanisms for water allocation', which show the intimate relations between local irrigation technology and its social organisation. Others have emphasised the need to understand the nature of 'human networks' surrounding the organisation and management of irrigation systems. They have found a particular need to analyse the co-ordination of irrigation practices (Freeman and Lowdermilk, 1985). Hunt and Hunt (1974) further investigated the social dimensions of irrigation systems. Their work, while looking at conflict situations within irrigation systems, concentrates on the role played by centralised authorities in managing irrigation systems. These studies, and various others, show that changes in irrigation development processes not only result from formal intervention objectives and planning/implementation activities, but also depend heavily on social actors' specific interactions, negotiations and struggles.

Therefore, locating key persons for social change is as important as analysing the power configurations in irrigation systems themselves. The one cannot be done without the other. Actors are embedded in various sets of social relationships that give insights into the logic and rationality of their actions and in the functioning of power structures (Long, 1989). This sort of study was attempted by e.g. Van der Zaag (1992) in his analysis of 'El Operado' in Western Mexico. He used an actor-oriented approach to analyse the importance of irrigation practices (water distribution, canal maintenance and irrigation planning). In doing this he identified the water guard (canalero) as the main actor delivering water to a diversity of local people who demanded irrigation. The 'canalero' knows how to operate the water distribution and is aware of the technical and administrative contexts of the irrigation system. He makes institutional arrangements possible in an environment of constant competition where grassroots associations and water users constantly try to shift power in order to further their interests. The canalero has also an important role with respect to discussing and negotiating the 'equity issues', responding to the various claims that people and institutions made.

In this area, a major theme of inequitable distribution in irrigation is expressed in the relation between those producers who have access to irrigated land and those who depend on rain-fed cultivation (Arce, 1989). In my own research in the zone, we found that the characteristics of rain-fed producers are low productivity, little incentive to invest in agriculture, constant pressure to reduce maize production costs, and capacity to work during only a short agricultural season. These limitations are made apparent to producers by the presence of nearby irrigated agriculture and subsequent inequalities. As a consequence of this feeling of injustice, producers who depend on rain-fed agriculture were constantly trying to gain access to some irrigation modality (i.e. to extend the canals of the irrigation system, to drill wells, to have access to irrigation pumps). In other words, the need to have access to water has been transformed by rain-fed producers into an important ideological device. This device provides the producer with a conceptual option which makes it possible for him to dream about extending his control over a previously-restricted reality (one limited by the rainy season). This control, based on access to water, projects an image to the rain-fed agriculture farmers of being able to solve all their economic and productive problems. In this sense, to achieve equitable access to irrigation constitutes an important springboard for mobilising these local producers. It is possible to say that the actual operation and implementation of irrigation schemes generates a local ideology regarding access to water as a central element in the economic life of agriculture producers. Basically this means that the experience of producers who have water is seen by rain-fed producers as the 'solution' for closing the inequality gap between them. In this vein, irrigation techniques have penetrated the social construction of agrarian development at local level, redefining their perspectives and visions of equity and their production objectives. In this case, access to irrigation has become a symbol for local political organisation, often generating conflicts between irrigation experts (who 'denied' this access), local people (who claimed access) and State representatives (who 'promised' access despite the lack of possibilities).

An Andean illustration*: the case of the Bella Vista Irrigation Unit in Cochabamba, Bolivia

Bella Vista is a new irrigation system linked to the river Chocaya. It was designed by a local irrigation agency. The initial impetus for the project is now unclear; it was approved in 1988 and the primary aim was to build infrastructure to transport water from the river to agricultural plots. Irrigation is important, because agriculture is the main occupation, commercial crops being produced for the regional market. Before the intervention, the farmers used to make improvements to the existing system without external financial assistance. The system mainly depended on natural reservoirs in the highlands of the region. The attraction of the proposed project for local farmers, in the words of one user:

> the engineers ... came to the community and they promised to help us improve our reservoirs, they offered to help us obtaining financing and then to line our existing canals with concrete in order to improve the water flow efficiency. That was why we finally said yes to the project (Simón Cervantes).

The people who participated in the project can be divided into four groups: one group (Bella Vista 'A') lived close to the reservoirs, which implies that they have decision-making power over what to do with the water. These people were peasants who had previously lived on a hacienda and today they are the best organised group in the area. The second group (Marquina) lived in an area composed of traditional small-holder farming settlements, and during the project period they were constantly fighting with the first group over the right to use the water. The third group (Sanja Pampa, Illataco and Pucarpata) were people who didn't belong to the political jurisdiction of the 'canton' (administrative division), but because they are living in the same watershed they had to interact with the first and second groups of people. The last group (Bella Vista 'B') has a traditional right to water from the Bella Vista community, access to a constant 25% of the river water.

From the beginning, there was an inherent conflict in the project between the people who lived close to the reservoir (Bella Vista 'A' and 'B'), and by implication could control the water, and those who lived downstream. The irrigation project generated expectations, especially amongst those people living in the downstream communities, particularly for the communities of Sanja Pampa, Illataco and Pucarpata, who did not form part of the political jurisdiction of the 'canton'. The main problem, before the project started, was that the downstream communities did not receive enough water due to water absorption en route, which compounded shortages created through water theft by the upstream communities. The idea of lining the canal was first to improve water use efficiency, and second to stop the theft of water, because it would be possible then to build metal sluices which could be locked.

After the project had started, the difficulties began. The amount of money approved by the institution was found to insufficient to line the six kilometres of canal which had been promised to local people. The actual amount of money was enough for only three kilometres. As a result, the engineer gave priority to the section close to the reservoir in order to improve the head-end of the water system. This generated further conflicts with the southern communities who had wanted the canal in order to gain better control over the system. As a consequence, this meant that those people, who realised that they would not receive any benefits, refused to participate in the project. The local project committee, under the control of the Bella Vista community, penalised them for this refusal. In the end, larger numbers of people started to withdraw from the project, tempers ran high, and Bella Vista was accused of misusing resources. After five years of canal lining, the downstream communities have increased their water conflicts with Bella Vista and the upstream communities. Water theft has proliferated in the area and a large number of peasants have been increasingly excluded from irrigation.

In this illustration, we can see that the institution's technical irrigation criteria prevailed over more important social conditions shaped by the context of a historical conflict between different communities. Furthermore, the project co-ordinators were not able to match the local people's expectations that had been generated by the project. Once restrictions were placed on the canal length that could be lined with concrete, conflict started to emerge. One may argue that if the planners had based their decision-making on social considerations - namely how people are organised along the watershed and develop their water access strategies - perhaps they would have started to build the canal downstream working upwards, rather than following narrow technical criteria that work must begin at the head-end of the system. In this illustration, the producers' organisational capacity, strategic action and social practices were largely ignored in the technical considerations. Rather than solve existing problems, old conflicts were reinforced and new tensions generated.

Some final remarks

In rural development, irrigation projects are typically dominated by technicist approaches. Although this has been widely criticised in research on irrigation, this emphasis still tends to predominate in project formulation, planning and implementation. In this respect, the actor-oriented approach can provide us with a different point of entry into both the technical and social aspects of rural development. It can help to critically analyse the ideas and concepts widely used to plan development interventions, focusing not only on structures and models, but also on the views of producers and other local people in their different interactions with each other and with other social actors such as the State, local landlords, donor agencies, etc. An actor-oriented approach can contribute to the field of irrigation studies, by highlighting:

Strategic action: An exploration of strategic action implies that we consider seriously the way in which people make choices, organise and consequently interact with the State and other planning agencies. The role of the central State authority or project planning agencies in capacity building for development is critical in establishing individuals' scope and scale of action.

Organisational capacities: The social action of actors in their way of organising their everyday lives around water and irrigation.

Social practices: In irrigation studies we need to pay attention to how a system is designed, how people are enrolled to participate in irrigation projects, and which are people's expectations. These processes are usually organised through interaction between irrigation experts and local populations. The way these interactions take place - how meetings are organised, and water-user associations are constituted - will affect how a system's operational functions will be internalised by local people. In water distribution it is important to understand how to mediate between technical operational activities and local demands on water resources.

Finally, the approach can contribute to analysing different notions of equity. Social research on irrigation needs to identify how local notions of equity are distributed among actors and how they are externalised in a range of social practices. These local notions of equity need to be compared with the form, content and implementation of the national law regulating irrigation activities in order to explore how some actors exercise power over others, how they are able to organise and legitimise local power relations, and which ways exist to recover forms of endogenous control.

Note

* Source: *Intervención en Sistemas de Riego Existentes en el Río Chocaya, Cantón - El Paso - Quillacollo: un Estudio desde la Perspectiva del Actor Social*, by Marina Arratia Jimenez (1994).

References

Arce, A. (1989) 'The Social Construction of Agrarian Development: A Case Study of Producer-Bureaucrat Relations in an Irrigation Unit in Western Mexico'. In: Long, N. (ed.) *Encounters at the Interface: a Perspective on Social Discontinuities in Rural Development*. Wageningen: Wageningen Agricultural University.

Arce, A. (1990) 'The Local Effects of Export Agriculture: a Case Study from Western Mexico', *Hull Papers in Developing Area Studies*. Hull: University of Hull Press.

Arce, A. (1993) *Negotiating Agricultural Development: Entanglements of Bureaucrats and Rural Producers in Western Mexico*. Wageningen: Agricultural University of Wageningen.

Boelens, R. & Doornbos, B. (1996). '*Derecho consuetudinario campesino e intervención en el riego. Visiones divergentes sobre agua y derecho en los Andes*'. SNV - CESA, Quito, Ecuador.

Coward, E.W. (1985) 'Planning Technical and Social Change in Irrigated Areas', in Cernea, M.M., *Putting People First*. Oxford: Oxford University Press (World Bank Publications).

Freeman, D.M., Lowdermilk, M.K. (1985) 'Middle-level Farmer Organisations as Links between Farms and Central Irrigation Systems', in Cernea, M.M., *Putting People First*. Oxford: Oxford University Press (World Bank Publications).

Hewitt de Alcantara, C. (1978), 'La Modernización de la Agricultura Mexicana (1940-1970). Siglo XXI, Mexico City.

Hunt, E. & Hunt, R.C. (1974), 'Irrigation, Conflict, and Politics: a Mexican Case', in: Irrigation's Impact on Society, Downing, T.E., Gibson, M. (Eds.) Tucson, Arizona: The University of Arizona Press.

Long, N. (1977), An Introduction to the Sociology of Rural Development. London & New York: Tavistock Publications.

Long, N. (1989), Encounters at the interface. A perspective on social discontinuities in rural development. Wageningse Sociologische Studies 27, Wageningen Agricultural University.

Jiménez, M.A. (1994), Intervención en Sistemas de Riego Existentes en el Río Chocaya, Cantón -El Paso - Quillacollo: un Estudio desde la Perspectiva del Actor Social. Universidad Mayor de San Simón, Cochabamba, Bolivia.

Van der Zaag, P. (1992) Chicanery at the Canal: Changing Practice in Irrigation Management in Western Mexico. Amsterdam: CEDLA.

PART IV

EQUITY CONSIDERATIONS IN PEASANT IRRIGATION: CASE STUDIES AROUND THE WORLD

Introduction

... there can be no doubt that where there is irrigated agriculture there is social stratification and that the stratification is importantly linked to differential decision-making power over the tasks of the irrigation system. (Robert Hunt & Eva Hunt, 1976, 'Canal irrigation and local social organization'. In: *Current Anthropology,* vol. 17, no. 3, pp. 389 - 398).

Notwithstanding the fact that it is common to consider irrigation as one of the rural development issues 'most worthy of backing and giving assistance', thanks to its great potential for increasing agrarian production and its projections about being a powerful mechanism for improving living conditions, in practice it is not uncommon that these dreams turn into nightmares. Nightmares, not of the haves but of the have-nots.

Frequently, the dreams of more control over their own destiny make place for a reality in which the *external* control over the production and decision-making process increases. This commonly happens, although there are many peasant irrigation systems that have demonstrated the possibility to foster a different, more equitable type of development. Brown & Ingram take up Maass & Anderson's conclusions (... *And the desert shall rejoice*) stating that

Fairness, like water, is fundamentally important to social arrangements, and so it is not at all surprising that communities have been preoccupied with the fairness of water distribution [...] As a rule, irrigators are more concerned with fairness in process than equality in results. The fairness of procedures is judged according to whether or not the procedures prevent control from being imposed from outside the community, or arbitrary actions from the community's officers. Above all, community members must be satisfied by their own participation in determining procedures. [...] Although there is no guarantee that agricultural strategies that build upon community desires and values will succeed, strategies that ignore these values are certainly doomed. (F. Lee Brown & Helen Ingram, 1987, *Water and poverty in the Southwest.* University of Arizona Press, Tucson).

This stresses the need to understand the particular peasants' visions and logic with respect to their irrigation management. Without considering these as the 'correct' perceptions or the final conclusions, they should form the starting point for any analysis, policy or collaboration related to irrigation development.

Apart from being anchored in the local environment, the peasant irrigation system is rooted in local and extra-local social structures that are wider than the scope of irrigation. Water distribution norms and practices are profoundly embedded in a wider normative system at and above the community level, which regulates not just the water allocation and management practices but structures other rights as well.

Therefore, the analysis of equitable irrigation water distribution in development processes *cannot* limit itself exclusively to the allocation and distribution of the water resources. Its relationship with other benefits, duties, functions and tasks assigned to families should be analysed, be it within the irrigation system itself or at community management level. Sometimes this connection relativizes or levels an apparent differentiation in water distribution. On the other hand, it is also common to find a strong correlation between differentiated access to water and differentiated, unequal control over other productive resources. In the latter cases, irrigation constitutes an extra mechanism reinforcing unequal power structures and perpetuating social differentiation.

The following chapters describe diverse experiences of peasant irrigation, encountered in different regions of the world, and provide a variety of analyses and points of view. In spite of the different circumstances in which these systems have developed and the diverse characteristics of the users involved, they have in common the fact that all users develop their own vision with respect to system management and the distribution of benefits and burdens. A vision that is often not shared or understood by the actors 'external' to the peasant communities.

A historical analysis of the social and technological norms and framework of the irrigation system and its people proves to be fundamental in explaining the existence of both injustice and local perceptions of equity. The following articles focus on the generation and conservation of peasant rights, the accountability relations between sectors of opposing interests, the consequences of increased peasant self-management, and the influence of opposed ideologies on irrigation development, all related to the central theme of equity.

13

Water Rights and Equity Issues. A Case from Nepal

Robert Yoder and Edward Martin[1]

The institutions - rules that individuals use to order specific relationships with one another - that govern operation and maintenance of irrigation systems are greatly influenced by the physical and social environment. We will use the story of irrigation development in Chherlung to describe how community values of fairness determine equity principles. The Chherlung example illustrates the evolution of rights to water through construction of stream diversions and canals.

Irrigators with identical physical and environmental settings in Nepal, even in neighboring communities, often craft their institutions differently. While the Chherlung example is not unique, many communities in Nepal have developed quite different rules and relationships for governing their irrigation affairs. Some communities with less social cohesion have not managed to install rules that safeguard the rights of all irrigators.[2]

The Setting

In the southern foothills of the Himalayan Mountains, deeply incised rivers drain the snowmelt from the higher mountains. Because of the hilly terrain, this immense water resource is virtually inaccessible for irrigation by gravity delivery to fields. Smaller side streams, fed only by rainfall and springs, are tapped to irrigate fields carved into hillsides in Nepal. Canals must often be cut into steep slopes in order to deliver water from a stream to fields. Fortunate farmers have fields a few hundred meters from a stream, but others, as in Chherlung, require a conveyance canal more than five kilometers long. Long canals greatly increase maintenance problems.

An important factor in developing and operating irrigation in this environment is the ability to mobilize sufficient labor, first to construct a diversion and canal and then to continually maintain it. Floods in the steep-sloped stream regularly destroy the diversion structure, and landslides repeatedly block the canal. A successful irrigation organization has the ability to respond quickly to emergencies. In addition, regular maintenance is required to clean and reshape the earthen canals that deteriorate rapidly. The need for maintenance labor requires unity within the irrigator community. Rules that embody acceptable equity for sharing the maintenance work and distributing the irrigation benefits to each participant's land are necessary. Effective governance requires means to enforce the rules as well.

Irrigation Systems using the Brangdhi Stream

The Brangdhi stream has a steep catchment of perhaps 20 km^2 in Palpa District of central Nepal. It drains northward into the Kali Gandaki river at Rani Ghat. In the dry season springs provide a base flow of about 100 l/sec making the water supply a limiting factor in irrigation decisions. In the rainy season there is generally adequate supply in the stream, but heavy rains cause high flood discharge that makes it diffi-cult to maintain diversion structures in the Brangdhi stream.

The Taplek Kulo

According to oral history, a grant of land from a local king was given to a family in 1792. The land was located at Taplek not far from the Brangdhi stream (see Figure 13.1). The father with his five sons began developing rice fields. They hired Agris, persons with rock cutting and tunneling skills acquired in nearby mines, to help cut a small canal for irrigation from the Brangdhi stream along rock cliffs to their fields. Because their fields were on a steep hillslope only two hectares are cultivated and irrigated.

Unfortunately, supernatural beings were reported at Taplek, and when the father died his sons sold the land. After several transactions, the fields were purchased by a Magar (an ethnic group in Nepal) family who lived in Gumha on the hill high above the Taplek fields. Nine related households, all descendants of the original Magar owner, were cultivating these fields in 1990 (Pradhan 1990). Water is plentiful for these fields, and, thus, few rules were developed for allocation of water among families.

The Thulo Kulo

In 1925 about fifty families lived in the Chherlung area. Their rainfed agriculture production was not keeping pace with the growing population. Two individuals encouraged others to join them in constructing a canal to bring water from Brangdhi stream - about 6 km away - to irrigate their fields. Without irrigation to increase pro-ductivity, some families would have been forced to leave the community in search of more land. Twenty-seven families agreed to assist with the expensive and risky ven-ture of building a canal. The other half remained skeptical about the feasibility of bringing water so far through steep, rocky terrain and declined to invest. So, in response to food shortages, the Thulo Kulo (Large canal) irrigation system was built by the cooperation of some, but not all, Chherlung residents (Yoder 1986).

The Chherlung farmers hired Agris to lay out the alignment and construct the canal through difficult sections. Under customary rights, backed by the civil code of Nepal

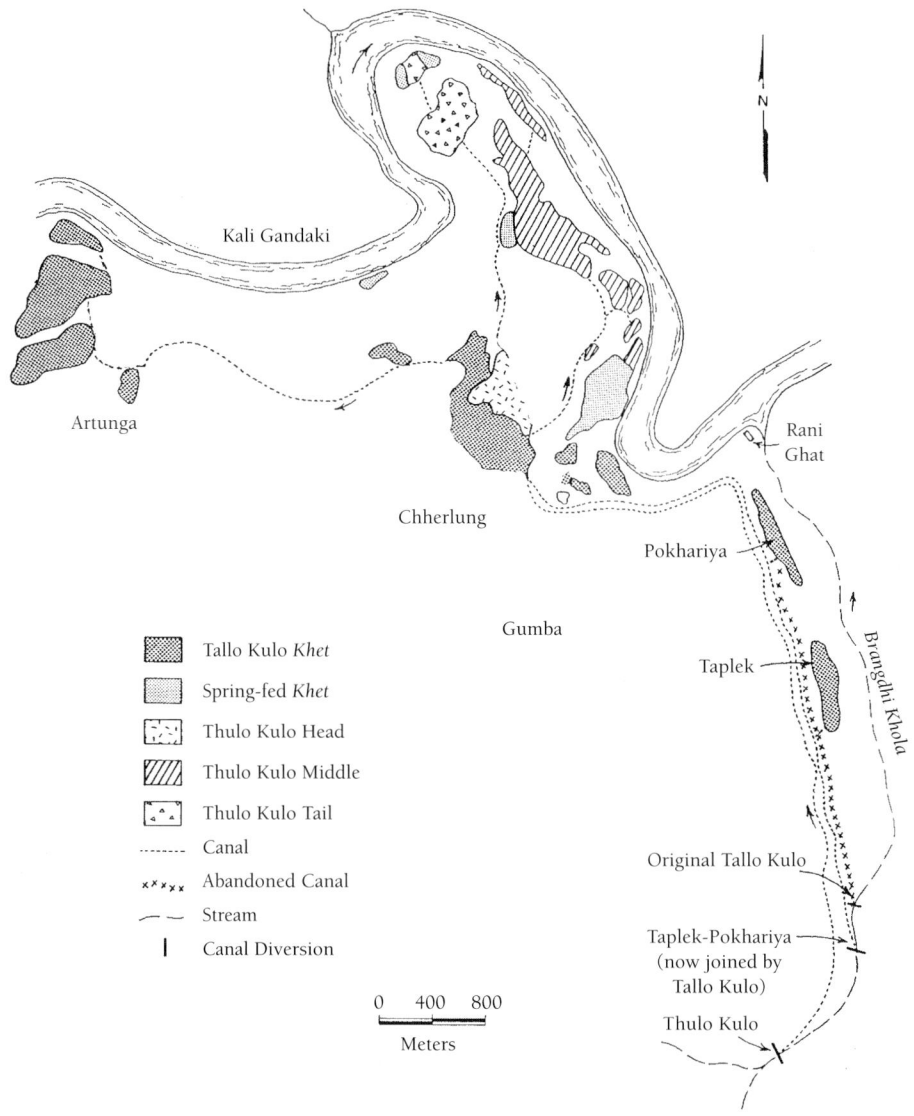

Figure 13.1: Irrigation canals in the area

at the time, an irrigation intake from a stream had to be at least 100 yards above any pre-existing diversions (Martin 1986). The Agris designed an alignment that established the diversion from the Brangdhi stream about 300 m above the Taplek Kulo diversion.

Without financial assistance from outside the community, the Chherlung farmers contributed their own labor over a four-year period to complete a small canal. They reportedly sold jewelry and some land to pay for the Agris expertise. The successful delivery of a small trickle of water after four years of work confirmed the alignment and proved to skeptics in the community that irrigation was possible. By gradual improvement of the canal and expansion of the command area the Thulo Kulo was irrigating about 35 ha of rice in 1981 (Yoder 1986).

In the process of carrying out the construction the group discovered that they needed a leader with skills in organizing the work. The leader needed to be someone all members trusted to distribute the workload fairly and to keep accurate records of each household's contribution. They found that they needed to hold frequent planning meetings to discuss and eventually agree on the details of the different tasks to be done and to determine who among them was best able to do the job. Because of the enormous amount of work that needed to be done, cooperation from all members was essential. They learned by experience that a working agreement was necessary before proceeding with an activity or else some members would not participate. Disagreements and misunderstanding over discussions resulted in assigning one person to write a record of the decisions at meetings and have all participants sign the record to attest their agreement. Because many of the farmers were illiterate they initiated the practice of reading the minutes aloud at the end of each meeting before asking those attending to sign.

Before starting construction, the Chherlung farmers agreed that the irrigation supply would be shared in proportion to the investment made by contributors. By the time the first water was delivered the investment totaled NRs 5000. This was divided into 50 shares with a value of NRs 100 each, which remains the par value of a share. Initially the capacity of the canal limited water delivery and only a small area could be irrigated by each household. After continuing to improve the canal for a few years, some families had more than sufficient water to grow rice in all their fields but others with fewer shares still required more water. Those in the community who had not contributed to the construction were now keen to purchase shares of water.

This led to the establishment of a water market which is still in operation today. A committee, elected by those who own shares, meets to establish and suggest a fair price based on the cost of initial construction and subsequent canal maintenance and improvement expenditure. Individuals interested in purchasing a share make private arrangements with a person willing to sell excess shares. They negotiate a price that reflects inflation and market opportunity. The price actually paid is not always disclosed. Because of the high cost, most transactions are for a fraction of a share. A treasurer was elected by the shareholders to record changes in share ownership for both the buyers and sellers in order to arrange irrigation distribution. The two founders of the system, who had contributed most of the initial funds by borrowing money, were able to sell their excess shares and recover much of their investment (Martin 1986).

The Tallo Kulo

Most of the original investors of the Thulo Kulo were of the Brahman caste and had their land and settlement in the lower areas of Chherlung village. They agreed to sell water as compensation for right-of-way through the upper Chherlung village populated primarily by Magars. However, the size and condition of the Thulo Kulo limited the amount of water that could be delivered. There was not nearly enough water available for sale to meet the needs of the upper Chherlung area (Pradhan 1990).

Under the leadership of two Magar men, a second canal was proposed. Initially, they requested Taplek irrigators for permission to extend the Taplek canal to the upper part of the Chherlung village. However, neighbors of the Taplek farmers from Gumha who owned land in nearby Pokhariya objected. They demanded that since their land was nearer to Taplek, they should have the first right to extend the canal to their fields. So the Chherlung farmers from the upper area started construction of a new canal from the Brangdhi stream in 1932. In the same year the Pokhariya farmers extended the Taplek Kulo to their fields. The total area for growing irrigated rice in Pokhariya is about 6 ha (Pradhan 1990).

Because of Thulo and Taplek Kulos' prior rights to the Brangdhi stream for irrigation, the new canal diversion for Chherlung had to be placed below theirs. This new canal became known as the Tallo (lower) Kulo. Since there was a good spring near the stream immediately below the Taplek diversion, the Tallo Kulo farmers concluded there would be enough water for their fields.

Construction began in 1932 but was interrupted several times by conflicts with the Tansen municipality. Tansen residents expected leakage from the canal to spoil the trail to their cremation site on the bank of the Kali Gandaki. Taplek farmers also requested compensation for allowing the Tallo Kulo a right-of-way through their fields. Water finally flowed in the Tallo Kulo in 1938.

The Tallo Kulo was financed by mobilizing the personal funds of the upper Chherlung farmers. Some of them took loans from businessmen in Tansen to raise cash. The Tallo Kulo farmers used the same procedure as the Thulo Kulo in allocating the right to irrigation by shares in proportion to each family's investment. By 1982 the Tallo Kulo was irrigating about 16 ha of rice in the upper Chherlung village.

The Joining of the Taplek/Pokhariya and Tallo Kulos

A flood in 1970 destroyed the Tallo Kulo diversion structure, and in the same year there was a landslide near the diversion. The flood also caused a spring, the Tallo Kulo's main water source in the dry season, to shift making it unavailable to the canal. This was a difficult period for the farmers. They tried building an aqueduct across the landslide, but it did not have sufficient capacity and was soon destroyed by a landslide. At times the Thulo Kulo farmers were willing to share excess water, but for several years the Tallo Kulo crops suffered from lack of adequate water despite their best efforts which included stealing water from the other canals.

The Tallo Kulo irrigators realized that the obvious solution was for them to join with the Taplek/Pokhariya canal. They tried to negotiate access rights with the Gumha farmers who owned the canal, but their offer was repeatedly rejected. They tried to get the village government to intervene, but the Taplek/Pokhariya farmers insisted that this was a matter that could only be settled among farmers and they would not tolerate external intervention. The Tallo Kulo farmers revised their offer and hosted a lavish feast for the Gumha farmers. Ultimately an agreement was concluded. Taplek/Pokhariya irrigators accepted the agreement partly because they got a good deal but also because they were afraid that the government would intervene and they would lose control of their water rights.

The agreement was signed between Tallo Kulo and Taplek/Pokhariya irrigators in 1977 allowing Tallo Kulo irrigators to become shareholders of the Taplek/Pokhariya system. The Tallo Kulo irrigators agreed to repair and improve the Taplek/Pokhariya diversion from the Brangdhi stream and to enlarge the canal. As continuing compensation for access to the canal, the Tallo Kulo irrigators agreed to take full responsibility for maintaining the diversion and canal. The Taplek/Pokhariya irrigators were exempt from maintenance except during emergencies when all members were to work equally. In return the agreement specified that half of the irrigation supply would be delivered to Taplek/Pokhariya irrigators and half would flow on to Chherlung.

Initially this sharing was done by rotating the irrigation supply among the three areas with the Tallo Kulo irrigators getting their 12 hour share only at night. As the canal was enlarged, continuous flow to each of the three areas was possible. The farmers divided the water by installing wooden proportioning structures. Openings in the proportioning weirs are adjusted to give eight shares to Taplek, twelve to Pokhariya, and twenty Chherlung. The Taplek/Pokhariya/Tallo Kulo is now generally referred to only as the Tallo Kulo. However, first rights to the water are firmly claimed by the Taplek irrigators.

Extension to Artunga

The village of Artunga is several kilometers beyond Chherlung. Farmers in Artunga have about 20 ha of land suitable for irrigation but only an unreliable water source. Seeing the success of irrigated agriculture in Chherlung, Artunga farmers requested that the Tallo Kulo be extended to their fields. This request was initially rejected by the Tallo Kulo irrigators because they had not yet converted all of the Upper Chherlung land into terraces for cultivating rice. They were unwilling to give up water rights until they were certain they had all they needed.

The Artunga villagers were able to use political channels to attract government funds to improve and extend the Tallo Kulo. They argued that the improvements would make sufficient water available for all irrigators. The district government office responsible for the funds called a meeting inviting Tallo Kulo shareholders of Chherlung, future Artunga irrigators, two persons from the village government, members from the district government, and the engineer who had surveyed the possible canal extension. The irrigators from Taplek and Pokhariya were not invited to the meeting. These key shareholders of the Tallo Kulo were ignored because neither the district government officials nor the engineer who had investigated the canal extension had any knowledge of the history of irrigation development in Chherlung. The strong tradition of water rights was not understood by the officials or the engineer.

Government officials ran the meeting. The outcome was the formation of a 'Chherlung-Artunga Irrigation Reconstruction Canal Committee'. The vice chairman of the village government was appointed chairman of the committee. This person was not a present or future user of the irrigation system. Others who were not potential irrigators were also appointed to the construction committee.

The meeting proposed that Artunga villagers be responsible to build the extension from Chherlung. Irrigators from Artunga and Chherlung were to contribute equal labor for improvements from Brangdhi diversion to Chherlung. In addition to assigning responsibility for the work, they discussed how to allocate the water among the different areas after completion of the extension and improvements. When a conclusion could not be reached, it was proposed that the District government be asked for the 'proper and just allocation' of water taking into consideration the land areas of the respective places (Pradhan 1990). Since money had already been budgeted by the district government, it was urgent to start work so the money would not lapse.

The Tallo Kulo from the Brangdhi stream to Chherlung was enlarged, and in strategic locations masonry lining was constructed. Work was completed in 1981. At this time Artunga was allocated water for irrigating wheat in the winter season because there was excess water in the winter. However, Artunga was not able to irrigate rice during the rainy season, the main irrigated crop, until after agreement was reached on the water allocation in 1983. In order to avoid giving them claim to water rights, Artunga farmers were prohibited from assisting with the maintenance of the Tallo Kulo until a formal agreement was reached.

Negotiation over allocation of water to Artunga

After work on the improvement and extension of the Tallo Kulo was completed, the Artunga farmers requested that half of the water arriving in Chherlung be passed on to Artunga as a 'proper and just water allocation'. The basis of their claim was that Artunga has about the same land area suitable for conversion to terraces for growing rice as do the Tallo Kulo shareholders in Chherlung. Chherlung irrigators interpreted 'proper and just water allocation' to mean that the total water demand of Chherlung's irrigated land was to be met first and the remaining water allocated to Artunga.

Artunga farmers tried to break the stalemate over water allocation by involving the District government. The Taplek and Pokhariya irrigators refused to get involved in the discussion. They were able to show a written and signed agreement affirming their right to half of the water diverted from the Brangdhi stream that included details of their reduced maintenance responsibility. The District government officials realized that they could not force a settlement without a court battle and were reluctant to involve themselves in the details of negotiation.

With failure to win strong support from government officials, the Artunga farmers returned to more serious negotiation. They reduced their demand in a series of offers from half of the water to one-forth. However, Chherlung irrigators maintained that their investment in constructing the original system and subsequently upgrading the Taplek/Pokhariya canal far exceeded the investment of the Artunga farmers. They agreed to allow Artunga farmers to become shareholders by purchasing shares at the market rate from Chherlung farmers willing to sell.

The agreement reached in 1983 was a compromise by all. In acknowledgement of Artunga's effort in obtaining government funds to improve the canal, Chherlung irrigators agreed to give Artunga 4 out of 59 shares of water as measured in Chherlung. Any additional shares would need to be purchased. In addition to the right to water shares, Artunga farmers could attend meetings and participate in decisions about managing the system. They were also charged with the responsibility to help maintain the system. They agreed to provide 4 person-days of labor for canal maintenance for each share of water, four times the maintenance labor rate of Chherlung shareholders.

Irrigation equity issues

Prior rights

The agreements among the different parties using the Tallo Kulo reflect the junior and senior rights and the power of the senior rights holders. Nepal civil code upholds the prior rights of investors in irrigation. However, government officials often do not collect information about prior rights during investigations of potential irrigation expansion projects. The Tallo Kulo case is interesting because, over time, the various parties reached amicable agreement. The Artunga farmers did not have a strong enough political connection to force a different outcome. However, this has often not been the case in Nepal when system improvements were imposed by the government to benefit farmers who previously did not have access to the system. The outcome in such cases has been an overall decline in system maintenance. All parties must find acceptable incentives to participate in the agreement or conflict will ensue that can cause the system to fail.

Construction and maintenance cost

The irrigators' perception of equity reflects not only the prior rights of those who first developed the water source but also the level of investment. For the Chherlung farmers the investment was more than the cash and labor that they risked to construct the canal. There is also risk of life and limb. Sections of their system had to be constructed by hanging from ropes to chisel a ledge into the rock cliff. During maintenance, accidents were not uncommon and several have died while working on the canal. The incredible risks undertaken by the Tallo Kulo irrigators was one of the arguments for raising the maintenance labor requirement for new Artunga shareholders.

Maintenance responsibility and irrigation distribution

While the level of annual routine and emergency maintenance is costly for the Tallo Kulo farmers, it cannot be neglected or deferred or the system will fail. Maintenance requirements are a driving force in the evolution of the institutions that govern the Tallo Kulo. Maintenance responsibility is coupled to the shares owned and thereby to the amount of water to which each farmer is entitled. Fairness in water distribution is ensured, even for farmers in the tail-end of the system, because the headenders are dependent on assistance from everyone for system maintenance. If water is not delivered according to the prescribed shares, shareholders could refuse to contribute their share of maintenance and the system would fail.

Transferable shares

The irrigation allocation rule for the Tallo Kulo is based on investment rather than land area. There are important concerns about equity when the irrigation resource can be separated from land. Speculation is one. This is a situation where water rights are bought not to use but to sell at a profit. Since a market for short-term allocation has not developed, speculation in irrigation shares is less profitable than in other investments, such as land in the Tallo Kulo command area. There is also fear that wealthy persons may purchase a disproportionate share of the water rights reducing water availability for others. The Tallo Kulo system avoids this problem by requiring the maintenance responsibility to be in proportion to ownership of water shares. Since maintenance cost in this system increases more rapidly than benefits from acquiring irrigation shares above some minimum level, there is financial incentive to divest all but the minimum shares necessary for adequate irrigation by labor-intensive methods.

In the Tallo Kulo there was rapid expansion in the number of members and in the area irrigated after the Tallo Kulo was first constructed. As the canal was improved to deliver more water per share, individuals found they had more water than necessary and could sell the excess for cash. Even more important, reducing shareholding reduced the shareholders' maintenance responsibility.

Notes

1   We wish to acknowledge the contribution made to this paper by our colleague Dr. Ujjwal Pradhan who is a Program Officer for the Ford Foundation, New Delhi, India.
2   For examples from other systems in Nepal and other countries see Yoder (1994).

References

Martin, E. D. 1986. *Resource mobilization, water allocation, and farmer organization in hill irrigations systems in Nepal.* Unpublished Ph.D. dissertation, Cornell University, Ithaca, NY.

Pradhan, Ujjwal. 1990. *Property structure and resource mobilization in hill irrigation systems.* Unpublished Ph.D. dissertation, Cornell University, Ithaca, NY.

Yoder, Robert. 1986. *The performance of farmer-managed irrigation systems in the hills of Nepal.* Unpublished Ph.D. dissertation, Cornell University, Ithaca, NY.

Yoder, Robert. 1994. *Locally managed irrigation systems: Essential tasks and implications for assistance, management transfer, and turnover programs.* IIMI Monograph No. 3. Colombo, Sri Lanka.

14

Equity and Accountability. Water Distribution in a South Indian Canal Irrigation System[1]

Peter P. Mollinga

Water distribution in jointly-managed, large-scale canal irrigation is notoriously inequitable (*cf.* Chambers, 1988). This is also the case in the South Indian irrigation system discussed in this paper, which I will call the Karnap system. Accountability relationships, among water users and between waters users and government managers, are a crucial factor in the management performance of irrigation systems. Being held accountable means the need to justify one's conduct and being answerable for one's actions. This paper investigates how accountability relations should be understood and affect the (in)equity of water distribution. It is argued that accountability is basically about the social relations of power among the different stakeholders in irrigation management. The example of the Karnap system shows that in the accountability relationship of water users and their leaders the characteristics of the *agrarian structure* are important. In the accountability relationship between irrigators and the irrigation bureaucracy the inter-linkage of the *political system and the administration* is crucial. An understanding of accountability relations helps to explain why some water users accept inequitable distribution, even when this contradicts existing and commonly agreed distribution rules.

In the first section I discuss the concept of accountability. After that, collective action in water distribution in the Karnap irrigation system is discussed at two levels to illustrate the relationship between accountability and equity in distribution. In section 2 the pipe outlet or tertiary level is the subject, in section 3 the distributary or secondary level. Section 4 briefly presents some conclusions.

The concept of accountability

The increasing interest in the theme of accountability in irrigation studies is the result of the realisation that efficient and productive irrigation requires effective collective action arrangements among water users, between water users and the state, and within the state. Accountability is a term that refers to the quality of these relationships. The general assumption is that good or high accountability is a prerequisite for good performance, including equitable water distribution, of the irrigation systems concerned. Problems are often identified as being caused by lack of account-ability (see for example Merrey, 1994). This normative understanding of account-ability has two elements, that of *representation and delegation* and that of *rationality*.

Inherent to the idea of good or high accountability are concepts of representative democracy and delegated leadership. Communities/groups of people appoint a limited number of persons to represent them in other domains or to perform partic-ular tasks for them. This makes life easier because in this way the whole communi-ty/group does not have to be busy with ruling and performing practical and man-agerial tasks all the time. It is a division of labour collectively controlled by the group/community, because it is the group/community's prerogative to elect and appoint. When the group/community is not satisfied with the performance of those elected or appointed, the possibility exists to replace them by other people. Officials and professionals are thus accountable to the community/group.

The second normative element is that of rationality. Those involved are expected and assumed to come to collective action arrangements on the basis of agreement, rather than, for example, violence and other forms of force. Relations of accountability can only exist when people are reasonable: when they are prepared to listen to other peo-ple's arguments and take them serious, when they are prepared to acknowledge that balancing of different people's interests is preferable to pushing their own at the cost of others. The source of this reason is a different matter, and something on which fundamental disagreement is possible, but reason is a requirement.[2]

What is clear from this discussion is that underlying accountability are social rela-tions of power. Social power can be defined as the ability to influence the behaviour of others. Accountability is exactly about who controls whom, about who has a say over the behaviour of others and in which manner. Accountability is basically the institutional regulation of authority. Such power is not only internal to the irrigation process, but also expresses and reproduces wider social relationships. This can be clarified with the following example. In his paper on accountability Merrey argues for reform of institutional arrangements in irrigation towards single-system autonomous irrigation organisations with high accountability as their characteristic feature (Merrey, 1994). He observes that this will not be easy to achieve.

> Such reforms will be successful only if governments are willing to provide a sup-portive and enabling institutional and policy framework, positive incentives for local users to take full responsibility and authority for their systems, and suffi-cient training and technical support.(p.114)

> A strong government role is necessary in most countries, not only to avoid 'cap-ture' by an influential minority, but also because the authority inherent in the government is necessary for enforcing rules to manage and conserve a common resource. (p.113-114)

Accountability at the local level thus requires accountability (representation, delegation and rationality) at higher levels. Here we enter the realm of a society's political
economy. In a different context -the provision of welfare services by the USA
government- Lipsky (1980) makes the following point about the relation between
officials who provide a service (he calls them street-level bureaucrats) and the public.

> (...) street-level bureaucrats have considerable impact on people's lives. (...) They
> socialize citizens to expectations of government services and a place in the polit-
> ical community. They determine the eligibility of citizens for government bene-
> fits and sanctions. They oversee the treatment (the service) citizens receive in
> those programs. Thus, in a sense street-level bureaucrats implicitly mediate
> aspects of the constitutional relationship of citizens to the state. In short, they
> hold the keys to a dimension of citizenship. (p.4)

The canal-level bureaucrats in South India have less hold on their clients than
Lipsky's street-level bureaucrats, but the general point he makes remains valid: in
day-to-day practices wider social relationships are reproduced.

Unequal water distribution at pipe outlet level

India's large scale irrigation systems are formally jointly managed systems. This
means that the Irrigation Department has exclusive authority in the management of
the main system 'above the outlet', and that farmers manage the local irrigation units
'below the outlet' among themselves. For the outlet level this formal situation is also
real practice. Irrigation Department officials do not move downstream of the pipe
outlet structure that leads the distributary canal water into these 50-200 acre size
local units.

One of the pipe outlet command areas that I investigated during a one-year field
work period in 1991-92 measured 60 acres and was located at the tail end of a subdistributary.[3] I call this outlet the Niiru outlet. In the early days (1950s and 1960s)
of the irrigation system's existence all farmers in the Niiru outlet could grow water-
intensive rice and sugarcane. Water was abundant because not all distributary canals
were opened for irrigation yet, and making farm land suitable for irrigation took time
as well. As a result of increasing land development in the upstream region of the distributary and cultivation of rice and sugarcane in these areas, water became scarce in
the subdistributary and in the outlet in the 1970s and 1980s.

Water users responded to this increasing scarcity in several technical and institutional ways (for more information, see Mollinga, 1995). One institutional response
was the design of detailed schedules for rotational water distribution.

Unequal water distribution and crop choice

An elaborate rotation system is in operation in the Niiru pipe outlet. When exactly it was designed is uncertain, but farmers reported that it had been in use for many years. The features of the rotation are described in figure 14.1. The rotation is on a time per acre basis, and divided the outlet command into not fully contiguous but equally sized blocks. The rotation time is a week (6 days of irrigation, one day subdistributary canal closure). Arrangements for the alternation of night and day irrigation, and which section starts at the beginning of the week are included in the schedule.

The area-based rotation is in principle reasonably equitable. Every acre in the command should receive water for the same period of time. This does not imply that each plot receives the same quantity of water, because the travel time plus the related seepage losses are not compensated for. But because this is a small outlet and the soil is a heavy clay, the ensuing differences would not be dramatic.

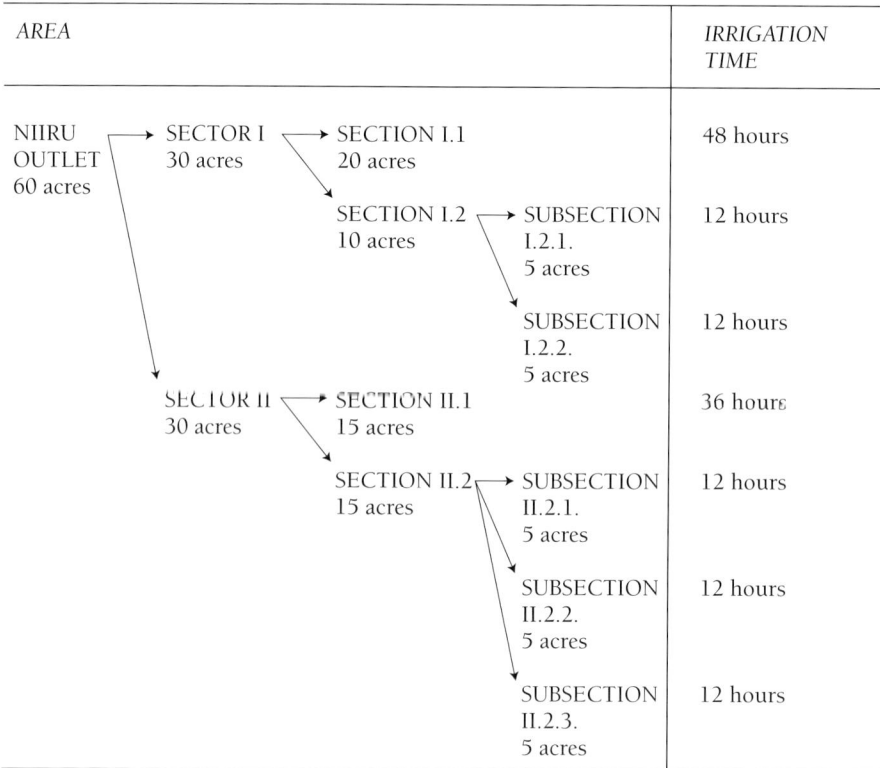

AREA				IRRIGATION TIME
NIIRU OUTLET 60 acres	SECTOR I 30 acres	SECTION I.1 20 acres		48 hours
		SECTION I.2 10 acres	SUBSECTION I.2.1. 5 acres	12 hours
			SUBSECTION I.2.2. 5 acres	12 hours
	SECTOR II 30 acres	SECTION II.1 15 acres		36 hours
		SECTION II.2 15 acres	SUBSECTION II.2.1. 5 acres	12 hours
			SUBSECTION II.2.2. 5 acres	12 hours
			SUBSECTION II.2.3. 5 acres	12 hours

Rules:
- Sectors I and II irrigate every other day; every week a different sector starts.
- The irrigation of Section I.1 should not always be on the same days of the week; Section I.2 should be allowed to irrigate on weekdays with good water supply as well.
- In Section II.1 the order of irrigation of plots is alternated after every sequence (head/tail, tail/head).
- In Subsections II.2.1, II.2.2 and II.2.3 day and night irrigation are alternated.

Figure 14.1: Rotation schedule Niiru outlet

In practice, water distribution in the outlet is highly unequal. Water is concentrated in the head end of the outlet, where rice and sugarcane are grown. The crop grown is a good indicator for water availability and over-appropriation in this case, because without exception farmers desire to grow the water intensive crops rice and sugarcane. These are commercially the most remunerative crops. Most of the rice and sugarcane land belongs to two big farmers, owning between 20 and 30 acres each (inside and outside this outlet).

The rules for equitable distribution co-exist with an actual pattern of unequal distribution without leading to public conflicts over water distribution. When one realises the ferocity and public-ness of the struggle over water at higher levels of the system (see below), the lack of daily conflicts over unequal water distribution at outlet level is, in first instance, somewhat surprising. The rotation schedule obviously does not work as an institutional resource for outlet tailenders to claim their time share. Notwithstanding the elaborate set of agreements tailenders cannot hold head-end farmers accountable for taking an excess share of available water. Why is this so?

Farmers anticipate unequal distribution by their choice of crop. By growing 'dry' crops that require little water, tail-end farmers prevent conflicts over water distribution that would emerge when they would grow thirstier crops. They anticipate they would lose such conflicts, and suffer yield reduction or crop failure. Because of the choice of crops by tailenders, the head end farmers can get away with taking additional water in large parts of the season, because the need in the tail is actually less than in the head. Another effect of cultivating 'dry' crops is that tailenders' crop cycle ends a few months before the end of the irrigation year. In the hot months of March, April and May all canal water can be used for the sugarcane and rice, because other crops have been harvested.

But still, there is a lack of water in some periods, even for the 'dry' crops that are grown. It is in these periods that the rotation schedule is implemented and operates as an institutional resource in water distribution. In these periods tailenders do make claims, and headenders keep to the rotation schedule.[4] The point thus is to find an answer to the question why tailenders anticipate and accept unequal water distribution by their choice of crop. The answer lies in the social relations between different types of farmers. The relevant relations here are land ownership, credit relations and employment relations.

Land ownership

In the Karnap system there is a reasonably regular pattern of holdings of larger farmers being located in the head reaches, and those of smaller farmers in the tail. This is not self-evident. Before the irrigation system was constructed the distribution of land holdings was -obviously- not based on this principle. In the almost 40 years that the system has been in operation this pattern emerged through a number of mechanisms.

The Karnap system was constructed in a very dry and poor district, frequently struck by famine. Socially, the region was dominated by feudal-type landlords, owning/controlling large holdings of in some parts of the district, hundreds or thousands of acres. These landlords sold part of their land to migrant farmers from the coastal areas of a neighbouring state. Smaller farmers made sales to migrant farmers because selling land was a means to clear debts, and/or because they lacked the financial means to invest in the development of their land for irrigation. The migrant farmers had a lot of experience in irrigated farming, and sold their small holdings in their home area dearly to buy cheaply in the new irrigation system, sometimes even before the canals were actually constructed (Anjaneya Swamy, 1988). Most land sold by local farmers was located in the higher parts of the landscape, far away from the village. Little rainwater infiltrated and accumulated in these lands, which were considered as 'jungle'. These were however exactly the (future) head end reaches of the canal system. Irrigation canals are built on the ridges in the landscape. The migrant farmers were eager to buy these lands. Within a few years a dramatic change in the landholding structure took place, that put a group of ambitious and experienced irrigation entrepreneurs in the head end reaches.

After settlement, migrant farmers -increasingly joined by entrepreneurial local farmers- continued to acquire land in the head end reaches. Sometimes farmers acquired land through straightforward purchases, sometimes through dowries, and sometimes through lending money to smaller farmers -eventually combined with leasing their land- and buying the land when they defaulted on the loan. In the location discussed here the large/small-head/tail pattern had crystallised strongly. In a different part of the canal system I investigated, with a much shorter history the pattern was less evident.

Credit and employment

Differences in landholding with regularity in their pattern of distribution do not in themselves explain unequal water distribution (anticipated through crop choice). Size of land holding and a water intensive highly commoditised farming system are a basis for wielding social power, but the exact mechanisms for exerting that power still need to be identified. In the case studied, the most prominent mechanism was credit relations, and secondly employment relations.

The two large farmers in the Niiru pipe outlet command supply several inputs to other farmers on credit. Fertiliser is the major one, but one of the two large farmers also sells pesticides and cotton seeds on credit, and hires out his tractor, also on credit. The other, apart from supplying inputs on credit himself, serves as a gatekeeper for credit from one of the fertiliser traders: he can recommend small farmers to the trader, who will then give them inputs on credit. At least 6 farmers in the command had such relations with the two big farmers in 1991-92.[5] The plots of these 'clients' are located in the head and middle reach of the canal. Two of them are able to grow rice (on part of their land). At least another three farmers have credit and employment relations with similar big farmers outside the command area.

The two big farmers are also employers of some small farmers in the outlet. More importantly, big farmers like the two in this outlet are the employers of the wives and daughters of small farmers, who go out to work as wage labourers to add to the household income.

The credit and employment relations are relations of dependency because farmers prefer to take credit from fertiliser traders and banks, and only make use of local suppliers/moneylenders when they have no access to the other sources. There is an over-supply of wage labour except in some of the peak periods like harvesting and transplanting. Indirect evidence that credit and employment function as mechanisms of control comes from general accounts of small farmers of their position, and on the use of these mechanisms in other situations (for example in acquiring land). In water distribution, the overall picture was one of anticipation of, consent to and no conflicts on unequal distribution.

But even consent to unequal access to a resource is a two-sided relation. What do the small farmers get in return, and to what extent do the headenders depend on them? The headenders depend -to some extent- on the possibility to exploit small farmers and their families in economic terms. However, the tailenders seem to be pretty well locked into these relations, and can derive little bargaining strength from this dependency (as expressed in low agricultural wages for example). The fact that the head end farmers do keep to the rotation schedule when it is really necessary does indicate that there is a trade off. But this lies in the realm of social capital rather than economic capital. This is discussed in the next section.

Politicians in distributary management

How to get extra water

At the level of the distributary canal the issue in water distribution is how much water goes through each pipe outlet structure. Also at this level water distribution is highly unequal. Over-appropriation, that is appropriation above the official allowance based on the design cropping pattern, can be achieved by different means. Though often described as 'chaotic' or 'anarchic', the social interactions in water distribution at distributary level have a clear pattern and structure. Perhaps they are not forms of collective action in the strong sense, but they are forms of institutionalised behaviour.

Unequal water distribution over outlets starts with the technical characteristics of the outlet structure. The design principle of the pipe outlet structure is to adapt the diameter of the pipe to the size of the command area behind it, so that -with a given water depth in the distributary canal- the pipe outlet structure exactly releases the discharge following from the design cropping pattern (on a continuous flow basis). This implies that virtually no flow regulation is necessary in the system, and that the sliding gate that is part of the outlet structure is used for full opening and closure of the structure only. However, in practice too large standard pipe sizes were used in the design and construction of the outlet structures. This means that with full opening the discharge is larger than follows from the design cropping pattern -at least in the head reach of the canal where there is still sufficient water. When land development progressed and water became scarce, the Irrigation Department started to use the sliding gates for the regulation of the discharge through the pipe by partially closing it.[6] This created the possibility for negotiation between water users and Irrigation Department officials on the size of the gate opening. This bargaining has become partly institutionalised through a set of informally agreed gate openings and conditions under which digressions are possible, which Irrigation Department gate operators use as the basis for their daily checking routines.

In the larger distributaries, rotation schedules over outlets also exist. The details of the schedules vary from distributary to distributary. The distributary rotation schedules have emerged as locally specific responses to increasing water scarcity.[7] They are stable institutions, even when their exact implementation is negotiated continuously. In periods with sufficient supply, implementation is relatively easy, and digressions can be easily allowed. In periods of scarcity, implementation is more difficult, and digressions lead to conflicts. In such periods farmers may increase discharge through their pipe outlet structures by damaging the structure in such a way that the gate opening is increased, and by raising the water level on the upstream side in the distributary canal (higher pressure pushes more water through). The latter can be done by putting obstacles in the canal, like stones, mud, straw, and bullock (cart)s. Other practices are blocking upstream gates and guarding the canal, particularly at night, to check other outlets' gate openings. Farmers also make representations to the Irrigation Department to keep up supply.

The practices of water users at the head end outlet to take extra water, those of water users at the tail end outlet to prevent this by guarding the canal and putting pressure on the Irrigation Department to keep to the formal schedule, and the Irrigation Department's need to try to implement an equitable pattern of water distribution at least to some degree (forced by policy based instructions, farmers' pressure, and the desire to survive), leads to a great number of conflicts. These can escalate into tractor expeditions of tailenders to block head end outlets, road and railway blocks, surrounding Irrigation Department officials in their offices and houses, threats to put Irrigation Department jeeps on fire -with officers in them-, and farmers threatening to kill themselves by drinking bottles of pesticides. Here I focus on the role of politicians in the mediation of conflicts between farmers and Irrigation Department officials, and the accountability relations inherent in this.

Politicians as resource brokers

India has a constituency based parliamentary system. Each member of parliament thus has a clearly defined base area. Some of these are part of irrigation systems, covering head end areas, tail end areas, or parts of both. A basic point about Indian MLAs (Members of the Legislative Assembly, the state parliament), is that they are resource brokers.

A description of MLAs as resource brokers is neither a new insight nor a recent phenomenon. Potter, describing how MLAs were perceived in the 1950s in Orissa, states that in the eyes of many people 'a successful MLA is a 'fixer' (...), someone who can get a man a job, divert development moneys into the constituency, help secure a contract, find a place in a school or a hospital' (Potter, 1986:152). The logic of this behaviour lies in the need to secure votes, that is secure re-election. Manor describes MLA activities to 'channel goods and services' to slum dwellers in India's cities and 'work hard as their advocates in dealings with state institutions' as informed by this consideration (Manor, 1993:143-144). Elsewhere Manor speaks of 'spoils distribution' politics and the 'game of patronage politics', in which 'in exchange for electoral support' groups 'gained access to resources' (Manor, 1989:337, 352, 348). Frankel characterises the phenomenon as 'competitive populism, with its attendant corruption in the disbursement of social development funds' (Frankel, 1989:511). From this perspective, it is not surprising that MLAs involve themselves in irrigation water distribution, when irrigation water is a 'most influence resource' (Brass, 1990:122) in their constituency.

Though irrigation water is a resource provided by the state with development objectives, it is not a development programme in the same way as for example a government housing scheme. Its benefits cannot be handed out at special occasions where the good deeds of the MLA and his/her political party can be commemorated, as for example can be done at the public distribution of sites for houses to former untouchables. The distribution of irrigation water is a continuous and spatially dispersed activity, for which a functional organisation, the Irrigation Department, bears day-to-day responsibility. MLAs can -thus- influence water distribution only by influencing the behaviour of Irrigation Department officials.

The mechanism that enables an MLA to do this, is his/her influence on the transfer of government officials. Chief Ministers and Ministers 'delegate' their legal decision making power with regard to transfers of members of the government administration to MLAs in exchange for support of these MLAs of the Cabinet in the Assembly (de Zwart, 1992). Wade summarises the importance of transfer determination by MLAs by stating that 'transfer is the politician's basic weapon of control over the bureaucracy, and thus the lever of surplus extraction from the clients of the bureaucracy' (1982:319). De Zwart adds to this monetary objective the argument that frequent transfers are a method for politicians to avoid competition in 'resource brooking' by government officials, who are also (potential) 'gatekeepers' for state resources (de Zwart, 1992:5-6). There is difference of opinion on the degree to which political determination of transfers is systemic and institutionalised, and involves monetary transactions, but there seems very little doubt that it exists in most places at least in some degree.

From the perspective of the farmer/water user, influencing water supply through the MLA or another politician is a deviation. Putting pressure on the Irrigation Department directly is a shorter institutional route. This is indeed very commonly done, and different methods are used for it, as indicated above.[8] These methods come into existence because there are virtually no formal accountability mechanisms between water users and Irrigation Department managers. The irrigation bureaucracy is designed on a 'management by prescription' model.[9] The absence of such accountability mechanisms makes the exertion of direct pressure a cumbersome affair. One reason is that it has to be repeated continuously. Farmers therefore regularly resort to an indirect method to influence Irrigation Department behaviour: they lobby their MLA to secure water supply. Farmers explained to me that this method gave a bigger chance of longer lasting success, and was cheaper. There is an accountability feed-back loop in political lobby in which the initiative lies on the farmers' side: the threat of an MLA not being re-elected.

Summarising, the Indian administrative system provides few possibilities for water users to hold Irrigation Department canal officials directly accountable for the performance of their duties towards them. Using the avenue of political lobby is one of the few ways in which farmers can attempt to institutionalise such an accountability relationship. Farmers exchange their electoral support for the MLA's influence on Irrigation Department officials, and in this relation the possibility to default lies on the farmers' side. The exertion of this influence allows the MLA to reproduce his/her base for re-election. (S)he can exert influence on the bureaucracy through the transfer system. Irrigation Department canal managers have very few resources to act as equal partners in this triangle, though they are not as helpless, or as innocent, as they often portray themselves to be.[10]

Three examples

I give three examples of interactions that occurred on one distributary in the Karnap system. These examples show the role an MLA can play in water management, and how accountability works in practice. They are ordered in a sequence of increasing complexity of the interaction. The distributary, with a command area of 17,000 hectares, is located in the most upstream division. There is a lot of rice and sugarcane cultivation, and the area has many ricemills and a sugar factory.

Example No.1

One good morning we passed a pipe outlet where there was a lot of commotion. Some gangmen[11] and a large group of farmers were fiercely arguing. We heard that the farmers had refused to allow the Irrigation Department gangman on duty to close the gate of the pipe outlet. As it was Wednesday, this pipe outlet had to be closed, according to the distributary rotation system. Furthermore, the farmers had raised the sill level of the distributary canal drop immediately downstream of the pipe outlet to increase the discharge through the pipe. They claimed the sill of the drop was damaged and at too low a level. One of the gangmen had already phoned the Section Officer[12] and told him to come immediately, as there was a crisis situation. This was exactly what had been the farmers' intention. They had already prepared a place to sit in the shade of a tree, and had instructed the local tea-shop owner to brew extra good quality tea. When the Section Officer came, a written petition, prepared and signed by all farmers the previous evening was presented to him. The farmers' problem was that insufficient water was flowing into the pipe outlet. They argued that the pipe level of the pipe outlet was too high relative to the bed level of the canal. The Section Officer argued back that they were cultivating rice instead of the authorised sugarcane, and that they therefore were in perpetual need of more water. After a long discussion the Section Officer agreed to leave the pipe outlet gate open this Wednesday under the condition that they would remove the stones in the drop. He told the farmers to bring the petition to his office the following day. He guessed that farmers would be satisfied with one extra day of water, and would not actually come to his office the next day. He was right.

That the Section Officer came to the field so quickly is unusual. Usually farmers have to travel to the Division office first and present their case there. In this case however it was different. Most of the land in this pipe outlet was owned by a former well known MLA and MP (member of parliament at union level), who had leased out part of his land to a number of smaller farmers. The manager of the rest of his land was the person who spoke on behalf of the farmers in the discussion with the Section Officer. As one gangman said: 'the Section Officer should take care with this pipe outlet'. The role of the politician in this case was one in the background, but still clearly felt. To summarise:

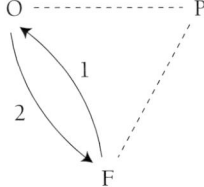

1 = pressure and request   O = Irrigation Department Officers
2 = water   P = politicians
    F = Farmers

Example No.2

The second example is the standard type of interaction that took place. In one of the tail end subdistributaries the usual pattern of water supply was that three days in a week there would be 'good water' and three days 'poor water', while the subdistributary was closed one day per week as part of the distributary rotation system. In the course of the dry *rabi* season the water levels on the good days, Monday to

Wednesday, were going down. Farmers of five pipe outlets at the tail end of the sub-distributary organised a tail end association many years back. The leaders of this association went to the Irrigation Department office to talk to the Section Officer. Also small amounts were paid to the gangmen of the subdistributary, for which money had been collected on a per acre basis. Several visits were made to the Division office, but the situation did not improve. The farmers decided to go to their MLA and one good morning a tractor full of farmers, plus the leaders on motorbikes, travelled to the MLA's house in the local town, where they explained their case. They also took the opportunity to complain about the irregularity of the bus service to the village. The MLA settled this on the spot by summoning the depot manager of the bus corporation to his verandah, and instructing him to be more punctual. The farmers also requested for a field inspection. A few days later the MLA plus Irrigation Department officials appeared on the canal to inspect the site. The Executive Engineer, head of the Division, had also come. A long discussion of the three parties followed and finally the MLA instructed the officials to release the water as per schedule. The Executive Engineer was courageous enough to protest. He said: 'but Sir, how can I release water to tailenders when at the same time you send me slips with instructions to release water to headenders?' To this the MLA replied: 'only work according to the approved schedule, ignore the slips, even if they come from me.' For some time the water situation improved. To summarise:

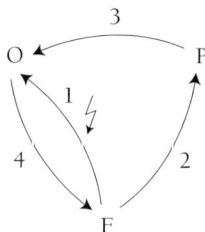

1 = request and pressure (fails)
2 = complaint
3 = instruction
4 = water

Example No.3

One of the head end subdistributaries was designed for the irrigation of light crops. However, a lot of rice was grown in the head end of this subdistributary, and a considerable tail end problem therefore existed in the subdistributary. Furthermore, the gate of the subdistributary was situated in a bend of the canal in a very unfavourable position. The drop downstream of the gate had been destroyed by farmers from lower reaches, which further reduced the discharge into the subdistributary offtake. One good night the tail end farmers of this head end subdistributary destroyed the subdistributary gate to get more water. The Irrigation Department booked a case against them, but the police took no action. The Irrigation Department tried to close the gate partially to reduce the flow, but farmers guarding the gate chased the officials away by throwing stones. The Section Officer realised he would not be able to change the situation on his own. He decided to approach the leaders of the distributary tail end farmers, who were suffering because of the lower supplies, and to ask them to go to the MLA to complain about lack of water, and ask the MLA to put pressure on the head end farmers. 'When the Irrigation Department calls a meeting farmers won't listen, but when the MLA calls it, it is different', is how he explained his strategy. The tail end farmers went to the MLA, who realised the seriousness of the situation, also after having collected additional information. The MLA took immediate action. A number of people were arrested by the police and put behind bars. The MLA left on other business for two days. The families of the arrested people got very nervous, and on the return of the MLA prayed him to release their kin. The MLA consequently organised a meeting in the village. Apart from MLA he was also the owner of a ricemill and a fertiliser shop. The farmers of this village took fertiliser on credit and also borrowed money from his fertiliser shop. In the meeting the MLA promised to release the people, if the village promised to allow the Irrigation Department to repair the gate and reduce the inflow into the subdistributary. The villagers accepted this. The MLA then instructed the Irrigation Department officials to do the work and release water to the tail end subdistributaries. To summarise:

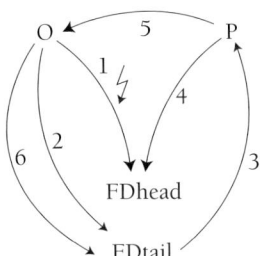

1 = ID official tries to reduce discharge (fails)
2 = ID official goes to distributary tailenders
3 = complaint and request of distributary tailenders
4 = pressure
5 = instruction
6 = water

FDhead = Farmers at the head-end of the distributary
FDtail = Farmers at the tail-end of the distributary

Some observations

First, the examples show the power of the MLA. He rules his constituency almost like a *maharaja*. Administrative officers are at his call and at his command. He receives people on the verandah of his house as if holding a *durbar*. He engages, if necessary, in the day-to-day problems of water distribution in the distributaries in his constituency. The third example suggests the close relationship between his politico-administrative and his economic power. In the third example the MLA uses his economic power directly as a resource in his operation as a politician.[13]

Second, the examples show some of the linkages between the administration and the political system. There is evidently no separation of powers. Irrigation Department officials speak of politicians mostly as being terrible nuisances coming from a different sphere, making 'scientific water management' impossible. In practice their relationship may be more complex. The Section Officer in example No.3 has good relations with the MLA, built up over a period of 10 years, working in this region in different capacities. He uses this relation to his advantage in his water management work. He has to be very careful with this. In the department he can easily be accused by others, particularly superior officers, of partialism. He has to be very careful with his relationship with the MLA because he plays the game of resource brooking himself, and may be seen by the MLA as a competitor.

Third, the tail end subdistributary discussed in the second example is an interesting case. Historically, land development in the distributary command started in the tail end section. This was because this was the land where the designed crops were rice and sugarcane. In the course of 30 years of irrigation history more and more land was developed upstream, and areas that received sufficient water first, started to experience shortages. This tail end subdistributary was a case where the fathers of the present farmers had developed strong political networks in the past, and present farmers take care to reproduce these relations. As a result they have succeeded so far to keep most of the subdistributary under rice and sugarcane cultivation. Neighbouring subdistributaries without such connections were much less well off.

Accountability and equity

These events and observations can now be related to those described in the previous section at the outlet level. MLAs are not the only persons that need to build up and reproduce social capital in the form of political support. Local leaders face the same situation, whether they are formally elected members of village and *mandal* (a group of villages) councils, or perform leadership roles in other local institutions. The two big farmers in the Niiru outlet both play such roles. One of them is the treasurer of the association of five outlets; they are called for when local conflicts arise and have to be mediated, like disputes on land and labour contracts; they are involved in and/or give money to maintaining the local school and bringing a dairy co-operative to their village. With regard to irrigation they represent their outlet in dealings with the irrigation bureaucracy and politicians. From the perspective of the MLA they act as brokers of local electoral support, from the perspective of the Irrigation Department they make bargaining with water users on water distribution easier, from the perspective of outlet water users they are the avenue for access to the political system and thereby to irrigation water, and from their own perspective these political activities function to secure local leaders' economic interests, and may be part of the pursuit of a political career as such.

My argument is that many of the smaller farmers in this outlet have direct economic relations of dependence with the two big farmers in the outlet, and more generally live in a socio-economic system where such relations are very important. Because of this, the smaller farmers avoid conflict and cultivate less remunerative 'dry' crops when they expect water will be scarce and getting more would involve confronting their patrons. The double bind is that these patrons are important for securing the water supply to the outlet. At the same time, this configuration of relations in which economic dominance is reproduced implies that the two big farmers cannot totally ignore the interests of their fellow outlet water users. That they don't is clear from the fact that they keep to the rotation schedule when scarcity is most severe and extensify their land use (and from the existence of the outlet rotation schedule in the first place). To remain local leaders in the wider sense, they must be seen to do something for tailenders as well. This also explains why there are so few conflicts at outlet level, while conflicts at distributary can be intense to the point of violent. The fights at higher levels of the system are much more open and outspoken because they are fought between patrons so to speak.

A schematic, and simplified outline of this exchange system is given in figure 14.2. The local expression that only those who are 'economically and politically sound' can be assured of a reliable and sufficient water supply succinctly summarises the nature of the system. The relations through which that 'soundness' is reproduced however imply, at the same time, inequitable water distribution and the possibility to claim some degree of equity.

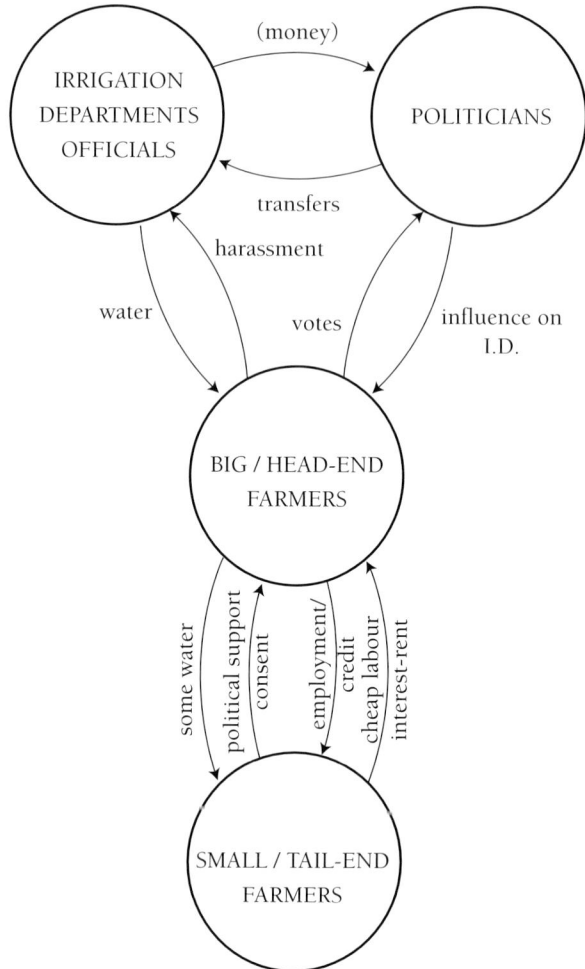

Figure 14.2: Resource negotiation in relation to water distribution

Conclusion

The discussion of unequal water distribution at outlet and at distributary level shows that accountability relations in irrigation water management, among water users and between water users and irrigation officials, are embedded in wider economic and political relations. These accountability relations form the basis for understanding the inequitable pattern of water distribution than can be observed, and how that is reproduced. Whether and how accountability exists depends on the relations of economic and political dependency in the agrarian community, as well as on the types of relations between farmers (citizens), government officials and politicians in the Indian constituency based politico-administrative system. The implication is that when inequitable distribution and the absence or quality of accountability relations is seen as an important cause for the low performance of large canal irrigation systems, changing these relations implies addressing rather fundamental political and economic issues, and not only supposedly internal administration and management issues.

Notes

1   This paper is a slightly revised version of a paper entitled *The political economy of accountability. A case from South India*, presented at a seminar at the Department of Irrigation and Soil and Water Conservation, Wageningen Agricultural University, the Netherlands, 27 October 1995. I thank Douglas Merrey and other participants for their comments. The research on which this paper is based was funded by WOTRO (Netherlands Foundation for the Advancement of Tropical Research). The support is gratefully acknowledged.

2   In neo-institutional economics, which is very influential in present thinking about institutional issues in irrigation, collective action is the outcome of everyone's individual cost/benefit considerations in decision making. When incentives and constraints are in the right place, collective action occurs automatically. The *process* of coming to mutual agreement (rule making) is not itself the subject of analysis, nor is the *process* of rule implementation and negotiation. Rules 'emerge' when the conditions are right. I disagree with the methodological individualism of neo-institutional economics as well as the cost/benefit model of human choice making. This is not the place to elaborate however. For a critique see Callinicos, 1989.

3   Distributary canals take water from the main canal (that starts from the reservoir or weir) to the outlets. When they are long they branch out into subdistributaries.

4   Interestingly, the big farmers take the initiative to seriously implement the rotation, and set/propose a starting time and date. They do this in response to problems and discussions in the outlet. This order of events nicely reflects the relationship between the bigger and smaller farmers as described below. One of the two big farmers has planted part of his land with eucalyptus and coconut trees, extensifying his land and water use. This is indication that some balance has been struck between the interests of the larger and the smaller farmers.

5   As small farmers I regard those farmers that have 10 acres or less of irrigated land, most of which have less than five. These number 20 farmers in the outlet, on a total of 30 farmers.

6   At the same time locking arrangements for the gate were introduced to increase the control capacity. See Mollinga and Bolding (1996) for discussion of how the design of the outlet structures is itself the subject of negotiation between water users and the Irrigation Department.

7   Formally they are Irrigation Department designed and implemented schedules, but their characteristics are the result of water users-ID interactions. They express the balance of forces between different groups of users and officials within the distributary command. This becomes clear when the ID one-sidedly tries to implement changes, for example in times of extreme water scarcity.

8   More systematically these methods can be summarised as 1) putting direct pressure on the ID by demonstrations, representations, etc, 2) bribing ID officials, 3) taking over operation of the canal system. See Mollinga (1995) for more detailed discussion.

9   There is a possibility for water users to take legal action against the Irrigation Department for the insufficient or non-provision of irrigation water. Several factors make this a very problematic option. The status of the water rights of farmers in a command area is not very clear, legal procedures are expensive and take a lot of time, and, legal procedures themselves are politically influenced. It is outside the scope of this paper to discuss this in more detail.

10 I do not claim that this set of relationships exists in all parts of all irrigation systems. Its occurrence depends one a number of factors, including the importance of 'irrigated voters' for the MLA, the geographical intersection of constituencies and commands, and the political history of the command area. Detailed discussion is outside the scope of this paper.

11 The gangman is the lowest category of Irrigation Department canal personnel. The gangman's duty is to monitor the gate settings of the outlets in a particular section of the canal, and adjust them if necessary to the correct level. Gangmen often have a background of having been an agricultural labourer, and have low social status. They generally are 'locals' and live in the villages along the canal.

12 The Section Officer is the engineer in charge of the management of a distributary, or part of a distributary when it is a large one, such as the one discussed here. He is often an Assistant Engineer. He is generally not a 'local', and lives in government quarters in the Irrigation Department compound at the Division office, at some distance from the distributary. He has no office -his quarters are his office- because he is supposed to spend most of his time on the canal.

13 It is in the nature of the job of MLA to have to please as many voters as possible. Because of this the MLA may be caught in contradictions. The example of the slips that he issues for water releases, illustrate this. But he can get away with the Kafka-esque answer 'ignore the slips even if they come from me'. As a gangman later observed privately, 'he never said he would stop writing slips'.

References

Anjaneya Swamy, G. (1988) *Agricultural entrepreneurship in India*. Chugh, Allahabad.

Brass, Paul R. (1990) *The politics of India since Independence*, The New Cambridge History of India IV.1, Cambridge University Press/Orient Longman, New Delhi.

Callinicos, Alex (1989) *Making history*. Polity Press, Cambridge.

Chambers, Robert (1988) *Managing canal irrigation. Practical analysis from South Asia*. Oxford and IBH, New Delhi.

Frankel, Francine R. (1989) 'Conclusion. Decline of a social order', In: Francine R. Frankel and M.S.A. Rao (eds.) *Dominance and state power in modern India. Decline of a social order. Volume II*, Oxford, Delhi.

Lipsky, Michael (1980) *Street-level bureaucracy. Dilemmas of the individual in public services*. Russell Sage Foundation, New York.

Manor, James (1989) 'Karnataka: caste, class, dominance and politics in a cohesive society', In: Francine R. Frankel and M.S.A. Rao (eds.) *Dominance and state power in modern India. Decline of a social order. Volume I*, Oxford, Delhi, pp.322-361.

Manor, James (1993) *Power, poverty and poison. Disaster and response in an Indian city*, Sage, New Delhi.

Merrey, Douglas J. (1994) 'Institutional design principles for accountability on large irrigation systems'. In: *International Conference on Irrigation Management Transfer. Wuhan, China, September 20-24, 1994. Draft Conference Papers Volume 1*. Pp.107-116.

Mollinga, Peter P. (1995) 'Constituencies and commands. The role of politicians in water control in a South Indian large scale canal irrigation system'. In: *Conference papers. Volume 1* of The Political Economy of water in South Asia: Rural and Urban Action and Interaction conference, Madras, January 5-8, 1995, pp.226-240.

Mollinga, Peter P. and Alex Bolding (1996) 'Signposts of struggle. Pipe outlets as the material interface between water users and the state in a South Indian large scale irrigation system'. In: Geert Diemer and Frans P. Huibers (eds.) *Crops, water and people. Water allocation practices of farmers and engineers*. Intermediate Technology Publications, London, pp.11-33.

Potter, David C. (1986) *India's political administrators 1919-1983*, Clarendon Press, Oxford.

Wade, Robert (1982) 'The system of administrative and political corruption: canal irrigation in South India', *Journal of Development Studies*, Vol18, No.3, pp.287-327.

Wade, Robert (1985) 'The market for public office: why the Indian state is not better at development', *World Development*, Vol.13, No.4, pp.467-497.

Zwart, Frank de (1992) *Mobiele bureaucratie. Manipulaties met overplaatsingen van ambtenaren in India*, (Mobile bureaucracy. Manipulations with transfers of civil servants in India) Amsterdam (Ph.D. thesis, in Dutch).

15

The Irrigation Scheme in Sabié: a Case Study from Mozambique

Bart Pijnenburg and Salomão Simbine

This chapter describes the history and current situation of an irrigation system in the south of Mozambique, mainly to elicit farmers' opinions. The scheme started to function only in 1995, and has many institutional problems. Currently a development aid project supports the management unit which operates and maintains the scheme. Furthermore, the project supports farmers in many ways. However, the scheme is not being used efficiently and the management unit suffers from a bad image among farmers.

Different categories of farmers, with a wide range of areas cultivated, are found within the same system and have to coordinate their activities. The scheme revived an existing association of (semi-)commercial farmers. The increased interdependence among different actors has created conflicts and it is expected that many more conflicts will arise in the future.

Irrigation in Mozambique

In colonial times, different forms of irrigation could be found in Mozambique. Individual Portuguese 'colonos', settlers, especially in the river valleys in the drier south of the country, used to irrigate with their own diesel-driven pumps. Besides there were large scale, in some cases multi-national, companies who used irrigation, for example the sugar cane estates. In order to attract more Portuguese farmers to establish themselves in Mozambique, the colonial administration built large irrigation infrastructures. At the end of the colonial era an estimated 100,000 ha were being irrigated (Gomes, 1988).

After independence (1975) most colonos left the country and most companies were nationalised. The FRELIMO[1] government inherited a focus on large-scale projects. Furthermore it was the era of 'socialization' of rural areas. Farmers had move to 'communal villages' and were told to form cooperatives. In many cases the land and infrastructure of Portuguese colonos' abandoned farms was given to such cooperatives.

In 1982, the FRELIMO congress criticized policies of socializing the rural areas and concentrating investments in large-scale state-owned farms (*machambas estatais*).

Rural development policies were to be reformulated; it was proposed to give more attention to the family sector and part of the state farms should be restructured and handed over to the family sector. However, it was also a period in which the party and the administration started diverging. Political decisions were reformulated or even blocked by the ones who were supposed to implement them (Abrahamson & Nilson, 1994). So in reality, the agricultural policy of supporting modernization and mechanizing state farms continued.

The construction of new irrigation schemes continued after independence, mostly with development aid. 1986 estimates indicate 125,000 ha with irrigation infrastructure. For various reasons, such as civil war, lack of maintenance, the failure of the policies of agricultural cooperatives, salinization, construction faults etc., only 45,000 ha were actually under cultivation (Gomes, 1988).

The irrigation scheme in Sabié

Sabié village lies on the fertile river banks where the Sabié and Incomati rivers come together. In the sixties, several Portuguese colonists obtained concessions to cultivate the area. They arrived with land titles the colonial administration and the local farmers' holdings were expropriated. The colonial government encouraged dairy farming and cotton production. The colonos also grew cultivated crops such as wheat, potatoes, tobacco and vegetables to supply the Maputo market. Irrigation was practised with individual diesel-driven pumps. Soon after independence (1975) most colonos left Sabié; by 1987 only four Portuguese colonos remained (Adam, 1994).

Construction of the irrigation scheme in Sabié was part of an integrated rural development project. The master plan for this project was written in 1982. The initial objectives of this project were very ambitious and emphasized infrastructural development. For example, the original plan envisaged 31,000 ha under irrigation. In 1985 the Mozambican government signed a contract with an Italian company to implement the project. The irrigation scheme, only one element in the project, started in 1988, to bring 1,700 ha under irrigation. At the moment (1996) 572 ha (two blocks, block 5 and block 48) can be irrigated with the existing infrastructure. The project cost 42 million US Dollars, financed by the Italian government.

The master plan of 1982 envisaged irrigation for large-scale agriculture (state-owned farms). When construction started in 1988, the layout was still based on the 1982 masterplan, for large-scale, mechanized agriculture. In 1991, as a result of political pressures from both the Italian and the Mozambican governments, it was decided that the Sabié irrigation scheme should be accessible to local farmers. This meant the land would be distributed among medium-scale and small-scale (local) farmers. In 1992, local farmers, still cultivating in block 5, were asked to leave their land for six months for the final construction work and for final levelling of the land. In April 1993, when the infrastructure was almost completed, the contractor, as a result of a conflict, suddenly stopped working and left Sabié. Canals were finished, electric pumps were installed but not connected. In the meantime, project funds were running low. There was only money for security[2] and minimal maintenance.

In March 1994, two years after they were asked to leave for 6 months, the farmers were still waiting and uncertain whether the land would be distributed. As a result of this situation, farmers re-activated their Farmers Association and took the initiative. They wrote a letter to the project coordinator, demanding immediate occupation and negotiated with the electricity company to connect the pumps and deliver energy.

In May 1994, the management unit (UGA, Unidade de Gestão e Administração) had received new Italian donor money to manage the system and to support the farmers in the irrigation system. They also started to pay the electricity bills. The scheme started operating in early 1995. In March 1996 the Sabié river overflowed, flooding large parts of the scheme.

At the moment (1996) two blocks are in use; block 5 where both 'Privados' (middle- and large-scale (semi-)commercial farmers) and 'Sector Familiar', (small-scale, family farming) are found and block 48, which was distributed to small scale farmers. In total, 572 ha can be irrigated. The following table shows how this land is divided:

Category	Farm size (ha)	Number of beneficiaries	Area in block 48 (ha)	Area in block 5 (ha)	Total area (ha)
Sector Familiar	0.5 - 3	173	106	66	172
Sector Privado medium	3 - 7	41	-		
Sector Privado large	7 - 15	15	-	400	400
Totals		229	106	466	572

Table 15.1: Actual land division in the irrigation scheme

This table, showing the large range of land holdings, is based on the three categories defined by the management unit. In fact the range of land holdings is even wider, because many farmers own plots of merely tens of square meters, the biggest being a farmer with 34 ha. Although all land is divided, not all land is being used. At the moment, only 44 % of the 572 ha is actually cultivated. Especially in the Sector Privado, land is not being utilized efficiently.

Farmers in the Sector Familiar are mainly growing staple crops such as maize and beans. Among the Privados, horticultural crops are popular, such as tomatoes, cabbage, potatoes, onions, garlic, beans, peppers, etc. Some farmers produce maize seed for a seed company. Some of the Privados own a truck and transport their products about 120 km to the Maputo market.

The scheme is operated by a management unit, the so-called UGA. This unit consists of a director and 3 managers. It is supported by a project funded by Italian aid, that provides different services and pays all costs for water. This means that farmers have not yet paid for water. The intention is to start charging for water from May 1996 onwards. Ploughing, grading and making furrows is done free of cost for the Sector Familiar. The 'privados' can, if available, rent a tractor at a fixed rate per hour.
UGA also provides inputs on credit: seeds, fertilizers and pesticides. Farmers do not pay interest but have to return the value of the inputs after 6 months. To obtain this credit, medium-scale privados (3 - 7 ha) pay an own contribution of 15 % of the value, large-scale Privados can get these inputs at a payment of 25 %, while for small-scale farmers no down payment is requested. UGA operates and maintains the scheme. Technicians are employed to open and close canal gates. Besides, UGA provides extension services; a total of 10 extension workers assist 229 farmers.

Privados work with hired labour, either full-time or per task, for example, weeding a number of beds. Workers from outside the area are often paid in cash, but the workers 'from within' are in general paid in the form of a piece of land. The landlord concedes them some beds or allows the labourers to work on the edges and along the canals of the farm.

Farmer categories

People in Sabié speak of being inside or outside (*estar dentro* or *estar fora*) the irrigation scheme. There is also a distinction (in Portuguese) between 'agricultores' or 'privados' (farmers) and 'camponeses' (peasants). Normally in Mozambique this distinction is related to size of the enterprise, the destination of production and the use of machinery, in the sense that 'agricultores/privados' have larger areas, produce for the market and use tractors. In Sabié, people add another element to the distinction between campones and agricultor: whether the producer irrigates or not. One farmer (agricultor) explained it as follows:

'A 'campones' waits for the rain, is from the dry land, but an 'agricultor' never stops working and knows how to irrigate'.

These two dimensions, dentro / fora and agricultor / campones, result in four categories:

- agricultor dentro;
- agricultor fora;
- campones dentro;
- campones fora.

Below the different groups of farmers are defined and one typical farmer of each category is presented.

Agricultor dentro

There is a group of 56 farmers who have fields in the irrigation scheme. They occupy 400 ha, an average of about 7 ha per farmer, but actually ranging from 3 to 34 hectares. They grow mostly cash crops, such as maize, tomatoes, beans, etc. and they employ paid labour.

João, Agricultor dentro

In colonial times João used to work for a Portuguese colono, Sr. Torres, who used to irrigate with a diesel pump. Working for Torres, João learned how to irrigate. After independence, the colono left and João took over part of the area left behind by his former boss. He started working in 1980 with his own diesel pump, drawing water from the Incomati river. This way he cultivated his land for eight years. During the civil war, João lost all his cattle and his pumps were destroyed by RENAMO soldiers. Besides, the Incomati river ran dry, so he stopped cultivating. At the time of the division of the fields in the irrigation scheme, he managed to get 4.5 ha. He cultivates only part of this area. The problem he faces, he says, is lack of capital to invest. With the cattle he lost his capital. Moreover the floods of this year destroyed his crop and left him further decapitalized. The project provides inputs but demands a 15 % down payment. João says he is not able to raise this money. The project will soon start charging water costs. He says: 'how will I manage: as a result of the floods I did not harvest anything and I have not ploughed yet'. Furthermore he comments: 'This irrigation scheme will have no benefit for the Mozambican. Mozambicans want to work but they do not have money to invest'. Later, it appears that João has started cleaning the canals of his fields he cultivated in the early eighties. Since it seems that the water in the river Incomati will keep on running for some time to come, he has decided to start irrigating with his own pump.

Agricultor fora

These are farmers who have large areas (above 5 hectares), produce for the market with the help of hired labour, have (access to) a tractor but do not have a field in the scheme. This, however, does not mean that they do not irrigate. These farmers have often their own diesel-driven pumps with which they draw water from the river (either the Incomati or the Sabié river) and irrigate their fields.

Fabião, Agricultor fora

Fabião bought a small, one-piston diesel pump in 1971. His father had already obtained land titles for 10 ha. Copying what they had seen while working on the colonos' fields, they started to construct canals. In 1973 he started to irrigate with water from the Incomati river.

Between 1983 and 1986 Fabião was the president of the Farmers Association. By the end of the eighties the river Incomati dried up and in 1989 Fabião decided to move and to open a field just under the Corrumane dam, along the Sabié river. He took his pump to irrigate there.

In February 1996, with the river Incomati running again, he decided to go back to his father's field. He installed his pump again, repaired the canals and five months later he had 1.7 ha of tomatoes, six hectares of maize and several smaller plots with cabbage, onion and garlic. He is married to 4 wives. He owns a tractor and a truck. His one and only constraint is access to labour.

About the irrigation scheme Fabião is very decisive; he does not want to get involved. He says: 'Há barulho alí dentro' ('there is trouble in there'). 'The people inside complain a lot: there was project money, but nobody knows where it is. It is not worth it. Besides I would need at least 10 ha.'

He also refers to the fact that working in a scheme would mean giving up independence: 'You have to coordinate your activities with others, which means that sometimes you have to wait for others before you can plough your field. No, it is not worth it.'

Campones dentro

There are 173 farmers who belong to this group and they occupy 172 ha in the scheme. They have fields ranging from 0.5 to 3 ha. This group is mainly growing crops for subsistence. These farmers do not depend only on their plot in the scheme; in general they also practice rain-fed agriculture in fields outside the scheme.

Lucas, Campones dentro

Lucas is from Inhambane. He arrived in Sabié during the eighties when fleeing from the civil war. He was given a piece of land by a family which left for South Africa. This plot lies on a location which is now part of the scheme. Therefore he was also eligible to receive a plot when the land in the scheme was distributed and he received 0,5 ha. If the family who conceded the plot will return from South Africa; 'I will have to return to the dry land'.

He did not have any experience with irrigation and he is learning from extensionists. Since the scheme only started to function in 1995, he has produced only one crop with irrigation.

He is now waiting for UGA to prepare the land. Lucas complains that, since the area was flooded, they are waiting for months to start cultivating again. Lucas says they are not allowed to enter with hoes or with oxen to prepare their own land.

'Everything depends on them (UGA)'. When asked why UGA delays, he answers: 'São os segredos de ali', ('Those are the secrets from over there' (UGA)).
But Lucas did not wait for UGA. He started cultivating a piece of 'u tsaka', an area along the river which was inundated during the rainy season. He planted maize, beans and horticultural crops. The residual moisture of this land will guarantee a good crop. He says: 'You cannot wait, we have to eat'.

Campones fora

This is the largest group, and includes thousands of farmers who practice rain-fed agriculture in the area. Within this category there is however a considerable group which does have access to the scheme one way or another. The hired labourers of the 'agricultores dentro' are recruited from among this group. In exchange for their labour, they are not only paid in money or goods, but a substantial number of them is also allowed to cultivate a small area of the employer's. People from outside the area are often paid in money but the workers from the area are paid by a concession of a small plot. In this way many people have access to the scheme. This can also be deduced from farmers' remarks such as: 'Everybody here in Sabié is working in the scheme.' and 'The scheme brings benefits to the whole population.'
Apart from cropping smaller areas within farms, these labourers exploit each square meter which is not being cultivated in the scheme, for example banks of canals and roadsides. These fields are called 'Mafia Mafia'. This practice is officially forbidden, as it causes erosion, but unofficially allowed by the management unit.

Manuel, Campones fora

Manuel is native to the area but used to work outside the district as a cook and a shop attendant during colonial times. Later he came back to work in the dairy station of Sabié. At the moment, he has a field along the Sabié river. Besides he was given three 'talhões', about 0.25 ha, in the scheme by a farmer who is currently in South Africa. This land is not being ploughed by UGA. So what he does is cultivate the so-called 'mafia mafia'. Manuel did not have any experience with irrigation. He would like to have a bigger plot in the scheme. He says it is better than dry land; 'in the scheme at least you manage to produce something to survive'. He is however aware that water should be paid for.
Manuel is a typical example of a farmer who 'officially' is not in the scheme but has access to land there. In his case, even in two ways; via sub-contracting from an absent farmer with land in the scheme and via the so-called 'mafia mafia'.

The Farmers Association

In the seventies, FRELIMO ideology prescribed that Mozambican farmers should form cooperatives and later associations. In Sabié the 'Associação dos Agricultores do Sabié-Incomati' was formed. In the eighties, several projects supported this organization. Because of the civil war, many members left and the Association seemed to

have died slowly. However, between 1992 and 1994, with the uncertain land distribution situation in the irrigation scheme, the Association is being revived.

In 1992, farmers who had been removed from block 5 were given land temporarily
in block 48. This block was provisionally pumped with some old diesel-driven
pumps from the project. When it appeared that the capacity of these pumps was not
sufficient, the privados installed some of their own pumps next to the project's
pumps. In March 1994, the Association wrote a letter to the project coordinator
demanding immediate occupation of the land in block 5. In following months, the
Association divided the land. The Association also negotiated successfully with the
electricity corporation to connect the pumps to the power grid.

The Association's objectives are to:
• defend member's interests in terms of land and water rights;
• defend economic interests of its members;
• allow technological progress by supporting members technically;
• generate funds.

Association membership qualifications remain vague. There is a strong notion that
the Association is only for 'Privados'. None of the farmers in the Sector Familiar
interviewed said they were member. They say: 'the Association, that is for the
Privados'. However, according to the chairman, anyone who is in the scheme area is
automatically a member. Apparently the Association wants to be seen as representing all farmers in the zone. This can be explained because the leaders of the
Association intend to play a future management role.

But here another problem emerges. Since the Association was formed before the irrigation scheme was constructed, it also has members who are not in the scheme. This
fact prevents the management unit from handing over more responsibilities to the
Association. The project only wants to support farmers in the scheme and is afraid
that project means might be used by one of the members outside the scheme, for
example, in case the Association would control one of the tractors.

In the meantime, small farmers have their own leader, Mr. Mondlovu. He was
appointed by consensus by all farmers in the Sector Familiar. On some occasions, he
links up with the Association's chairman, Ngomane, but on other occasions he has
direct contact with the management unit.

When farmers in the Sector Familiar were asked why they would want to organize
or establish their own organisation, they mentioned two reasons:
• to defend land and water rights;
• to generate funds.

Access to the scheme

According to the policies of the project, land in the scheme was supposed to be distributed to residents, 'deslocados' (persons internally displaced as a result of the war) and demobilized soldiers. Furthermore, land could be distributed to workers who came to Sabié to build the system. No farmer has official title to their land. Apparently there were no clear criteria. First of all, it appeared to be very difficult to assess who was a resident, a 'deslocado' or a demobilized soldier. For example, many people, originating from Sabié, but living elsewhere, came to Sabié to sign up for a plot.

In the 'Sector Familiar', people were supposed to receive 0.5 ha each. Nowadays there are people with areas up to 3 ha. In most cases they managed to arrange sufficient family members (including some living in Maputo and Ressano Garcia) to sign up and later they joined the plots.

In the 'Sector Privado' one finds greater inequalities in terms of access to land. Here plots range from 3 to 34 ha. Again criteria are not clear. The basic criterion was the area the farmer used to irrigate before the construction of the scheme. The owner of the largest plot (34 ha), Sr. Zita, used to have 30 ha under irrigation (with his own diesel pumps) in the system area. So he sees no reason why he should do with less than what he surrendered at the time of construction. Also the privados who were removed from areas where the project was supposed to construct more canals but never finished (block 50) got plots in the Sector Privado of block 5.

There are plans to re-distribute the land in the scheme. The project is concerned since the scheme is not being used efficiently. Especially in the Sector Privado, many farmers do not manage to cultivate all the land they have. Again, it is not clear who will be responsible for re-distribution and on what criteria it will be based.
According to the chairman of the Association:

> 'We have to hold title to the land. We cannot accept that the state might tell us: leave here. Some people think that we cannot manage what is ours. But we can, we have people among us who have knowledge of management. We will not let someone appear from out of the blue to manage what is ours'.

However, the project says that the state, as system owner, should be responsible for land re-distribution. But they also admit that they alone do not have power to implement:

> 'The one who is supposed to re-distribute land is the state, as owner of the scheme, but the problem in this land is that power is somehow diluted. The police do not function, the courts do not function. In Mozambique there is no power, there is no discipline. The only way I can see to work with the Association is with goodwill'.

Farmers are afraid that they may lose their land. As mentioned before, in early 1992 the farmers occupying the land where block 5 is located were asked to leave the area for final works. They were promised this work would end by November 1992. However, by 1994, the land was not yet in use. In a March 1994 letter from the Farmers Association to the project coordinator, the Association complains that the land in block 5 is not being distributed. One of the allegations is that there is a 'secret plan to sell the land to foreigners or large national landowners'.

Such allegations are not completely strange, considering the fact that other parts of the once planned but never constructed or partly constructed irrigation scheme have been sold to South African Boers. We should also not forget that it is not long ago that farmers in the area were expropriated when Portuguese Colonos came to the area.

Opinions of farmers on land use

Some farmers, especially the privados, do have experience with (furrow) irrigation. They already learned it working for the Portuguese colonos or later working for local Privados. But irrigating your own field by pumping with your own diesel pump is a very independent form of irrigation. The Sabié scheme has a strict 7 day water distribution schedule. This involved a major shift in their work. Besides, working in the same tertiary block means coordinating many activities with your neighbours. There seems to be no lack of water in the 2 blocks under irrigation. Cases of water robbery seem to be scarce.

Especially in the Sector Familiar, there is the opinion that nothing can be done without the consent of project technicians. The project prepares the land free of charge and there is the common belief that one is not allowed to enter with one's own hoe or with oxen and plough. So, all farmers wait until the project has prepared the land by tractor before any activity can be undertaken. This often leads to delays. In March 1996, floods of the Sabié river destroyed part of block 5. Although parts of the land could still be used, all farmers had to wait till all infrastructure was repaired before the land could be ploughed and prepared for the new season. It took until June before farmers could start planting.

The project management says they do not prohibit farmers from preparing their land with oxen or by hand. But farmers have stated that they are not allowed to do so. The leader of farmers in the Sector Familiar says:

> 'The management unit will not let people plant just anyhow without ploughing the land. It would embarrass them! Government visitors may come anytime and when they will see that the land is prepared by hand or by oxen, it will mean there is no irrigation scheme.'

During interviews a group of farmers was found in the scheme area who had been waiting all morning for tractors to come and plough their fields. They were promised the day before, but they waited in vain. These farmers complained a lot:

'Here we are waiting, doing nothing, while we are starving from hunger. The season for beans is passing but we have not even started cultivating.'

Besides, the project designs rigid plans for the Sector Familiar stipulating what kind of crops to grow. Farmers in this sector say: 'we depend on their plan' and: 'we have to stick to their programme'. Little effort is made by the project to involve users in the planning.

Farmers opinions on the UGA

It may be clear that farmers, especially farmers in the Sector Familiar, are extremely dependent on the management unit. They are not only dependent on the maintenance and functioning of the irrigation system. The unit also provides all kinds of other services (land preparation, extension) and inputs. It pays the electricity bills and even provides transport for farmers from and to the fields. In spite of all this support, the management unit suffers from a bad image among the farmers. There are different reasons which have contributed to this bad name. At the time of construction, several errors have been made.

The farmers who used to have their own field in block 50, for example, were asked to leave the area temporarily for construction of the irrigation infrastructure. After completion, these farmers would return to their 'own' area. All constructions, houses, canals, made and used by the farmers, but also fruit trees, etc. were destroyed. Block 50 was never finished. On several occasions, promises have been made to farmers which apparently have created high expectations. Several Privados, for example, claim that the project had offered supply credit in cash funds instead of inputs. That way they could buy their own inputs and have money to pay labour. Farmers believe that funds meant for farmers are being embezzled. Furthermore they claim that prices of the inputs provided are far too high and they consider this as 'theft from the farmers'.

The project does not allow farmers to use their own seed. The seed which was distributed in 1995 by the UGA, however, was of very poor quality. Maize seed was attacked by mildew and most of the groundnut seed proved to be empty pods. Other farmers claim that the UGA does not deliver the right inputs; they want seed for potatoes and beans while UGA provides only seed for tomatoes and cabbage. These latter crops are more difficult to market while beans and potatoes can be stored better and allow farmers to choose the right moment to sell.

Many project properties have been stolen over the years. For example, two huge pumps, each weighing several tons, were stolen. Since it was not a matter of just loading it on a pick-up, there are allegations that project staff were involved. An even more serious allegation is that the UGA tries to create friction among farmers and so divide them. 'This way they are destroying us, so that we are not united'. Some farmers say the UGA is trying to prevent the Association from being a strong organisation. They do not expect support from their own chairman because he is allegedly bribed by UGA. Some farmers believe the UGA is doing everything it can to prove that local farmers are not able to use the scheme efficiently, so that they can hand over the scheme to South African Boers; 'the UGA does not want us to work well'

What do representatives of the UGA say?

Project representatives consider that errors were made during land distribution. 'Land was distributed according to a traditional system which is not suitable for an irrigation system.' The land is not being used accordingly and that is why UGA representatives want to re-distribute the land. Who has the power to re-distribute? According to the project, the state will become the owner of the scheme. A new body is to be established, with a representative of the state as director. This body should manage the scheme and have power to re-distribute land.

There are UGA staff members who believe they have created a white elephant. They feel it was a mistake for part of the scheme to be handed over to small-scale farmers, because the system is too expensive and too sophisticated: 'We are taking away the plough they had and instead we are giving them a Boeing.' Although donors imposed that land should be distributed to the small-scale sector, the management does not believe in it. They say:

> 'Farmers do not know how to irrigate, except for 5 or 6 individuals. But Sector Familiar is worse; they do not know how to irrigate. They cannot even read and write, or count, they do not know what 25 litres per second means. Besides, they consume 60% of what they produce, how are they going to pay the costs? At the moment, the Italians are financing, but when they leave, it will stop. Why did the government allow these people be part of the scheme? It is not helping them, it is only harming them.'

They agree that the scheme will only be able to function if subsidies continue.

The project wants to keep control and is reluctant to hand over responsibilities, for example, to the Association. In 1994, the Association took the initiative and managed to get a contract with the electricity company. According to the project coordinator: 'The contract should have been in the name of the Italian Embassy and not in the name of the Association'. The main problem, according to the project, is that the current Association has members outside the scheme. For farmer representation, the project envisages three future associations in accordance with the project division: Sector Familiar, Privado Medio and Privado Grande.

The project staff admits that errors have been made and are aware that they suffer from a bad image among farmers. The project coordinator says: 'This UGA has never worked well. What is needed is communication, a dialogue'.

Conclusions

The hardware of the scheme was not constructed for the current users. Although built for large-scale use, political forces determined that the land should be distributed to medium-scale 'privados' and small-scale farmers. The system is too expensive and productivity levels of the family sector will probably never allow cost recovery.

The fact that only a few farmers make efficient use of the land makes the scheme as a whole inefficient. Only some farmers have experience with irrigation. But the ones with knowledge of irrigation have experience in working individually and very independently. Farmers are not used to working in a synchronized system in which one depends on its neighbours and on a management unit.

Some farmers have alternatives for irrigated land in the scheme; privados who have a pump and irrigate (outside the scheme) by pumping water from the river, the so-called 'u tsaka', using residual moisture in a season after the river has flooded, and the so-called 'mafia mafia', the plots along the canals and the roads in the scheme. These alternatives, although limited, lead farmers to pay less attention to their plots in the system and thus to less efficient land use, but it does give them more independence.

There are privados who claim that the down payment for credit is still prohibitive, which makes lack of capital another reason why the land in the scheme is not used fully. Considering high maintenance and operation costs (e.g. electrical energy), the irrigation scheme will only be able to function in future with subsidies; one can question its sustainability. The project is still putting in considerable resources. All farmers are highly dependent for all kinds of services, especially the family sector. What will happen when funding stops?

Notwithstanding the support given by the UGA to farmers, the management unit has a bad image among farmers because of many errors made in the past. There is a situation of uncertainty, nearly anarchy. Neither the UGA nor the Association are legal entities and they do not function on the basis of approved by-laws or rules. None of the parties has legally to obey any regulations, and there is no means of enforcement. Land rights, payments, membership of the Association, nobody has any idea what the future will bring. The project will finish at the end of 1998. Will there be a re-distribution of land? Who will implement this?

There is an apparent lack of communication and transparency. There are allegations of corruption and embezzlement of funds. Every actor seems to have his own hidden agenda and to play hide-and-seek. For example, the Association chairman says it is for all farmers in the scheme, while farmers in the sector familiar say it is only for privados. Probably the underlying reason is that the Association wants to represent all farmers in the scheme to have more management responsibilities. It is, however, questionable to what extent the Association would be interested and capable. Probably only as long as there will be outside financial support since they also realize that the system is too expensive.

The allegation by farmers that the UGA wants to divide the Association is not surprising, since indeed the project coordinator foresees three different associations. Farmer allegations that the UGA wants to prove that farmers are not able to succeed and wants to sell land to Boers is understandable as well: 1) indeed UGA representatives have the opinion that the system is too expensive and sophisticated for local farmers and 2) (unfinished) parts of the scheme have already been sold to white South Africans.

There has been hardly any involvement of users in the planning and construction phase. Farmers, especially in the sector familiar, simply wait to be told what to do. For example, in the case of land preparation there is the strong belief that farmers are not allowed to use oxen or hoe for land preparation while the management says they can. The project admits to many problems and a lack of dialogue with users but nothing is done to improve the situation. This situation of uncertainty, confusion and lack of transparency is a breeding ground for conflicts. There are already serious allegations of corruption and embezzlement of project funds.

Different factors have played a role in land division (changes in government and donor agency policies, local power structures, etc.) resulting in a wide range in land holding size. It is difficult to assess whether this unequal land distribution will be a source of future conflict and the issue needs further investigation.

Differences between the various categories (campones vs. agricultor or sector familiar vs. privado) are gradual and artificial. There are, for example, privados with resources such as a tractor and others without. They have different problems. Farmers with resources lack labour while others need capital. A study on styles of farming could shed light on the different objectives farmers have and the strategies they follow.

Notes

1   Frente de Libertação de Moçambique, the ruling socialist party.
2   During the civil war a barbed-wire fence was erected and soldiers were employed to protect the scheme from guerrilla attacks.

References

Abrahamson, H and A. Nilsson, 1994, *Moçambique em Transição, um estudo da história de desenvolvimento durante o período 1974-1992*, Padigru, Gothenburg University and CEEI-ISRI, Maputo.

Adam, Y, 1994, *From Chinhamali and Chinhahomu to 'Patroes'; the combined effect of development, destabilization and foreign aid in Sabié*, chapter 10 of PhD thesis, Maputo.

Gomes, 1988, *Algumas notas sobre agricultura irrigada em Moçambique*, INIA, Maputo.

Simbine, S. et al, 1995, *Resultados dum estudo de reconhecimento sobre as principais limitações no funcionamento do regadio de Sabié ao nivel institucional e dos produtores, Relatório das atividades de Julho 1995*, FAEF, Universidade Eduardo Mondlane, Maputo.

16

Equity and Water Distribution in the Context of Irrigation Management Transfer: the Case of the Alto Río Lerma Irrigation District, Mexico

Wim H. Kloezen and Carlos Garcés-Restrepo

Introduction

The Mexican government decided to face the economic crisis of the 1980s with drastic changes in, among others, its agricultural and irrigation policies. One of the strategies followed was developing a public-private partnership between the National Water Commission (CNA) and newly established Water User Associations (WUAs). In this partnership the CNA remains responsible for the head works and the main canals and the WUAs become financially and managerially responsible for operating the secondary system and below. The Mexican Irrigation Management Transfer (IMT) program mainly aimed to reduce public expenditures on O&M. The IMT program also provided for mechanisms that help to facilitate a more efficient use of natural resources (CNA, 1994). A secondary objective was to restore economic growth by using a system of pricing water based on international prices, marginal costs or scarcity value (Gorriz *et al*, 1995).

The Mexican IMT process can be viewed as a political process of re-negotiating the roles and responsibilities of the CNA and the water users. In this process old revolutionary ideologies and paternalistic state-client relationships are considered to be replaced by modern market ideologies and new modes of exerting economic and political control over the water users. In IMT, subjects of negotiation are the level and kind of O&M responsibilities, to whom these responsibilities are given, the O&M fee to be paid to the CNA and the WUAs, water concessions and the wider service-oriented mandates of the CNA and the WUAs. In this 'game' of negotiations the principles and practices of 'distribution of equity' are continuously redefined.

This contribution focuses on only one of the many equity impacts of IMT on Mexican agrarian production: equitable water distribution[1]. It shows how old and new actors have (or have not) modified the rules and practices of water distribution as a consequence of IMT. It describes three mechanisms that constitute the way equitable (or inequitable) access to water is defined and how different actors perceive these mechanisms. Examples are drawn from the research done by IIMI in the Alto Río Lerma Irrigation District, with emphasis on the Cortazar and Salvatierra modules. In this irrigation district transfer occurred in November 1992 under the country's general IMT program as described below.

The Mexican irrigation management transfer program

Economic and political context

The Mexican IMT program should be viewed in the context of other constitutional, political and institutional 'modernization' reforms of the early 1990s. One of the major reforms that greatly affected peasant production in the irrigation systems was the revision of Article 27 of the Constitution, which put an end to the land reforms which were a result of the Mexican revolution in the early part of the 20th century. This revision created the legal foundation for the privatization of the land reform communities (*ejidos*). In addition, a policy of dismantling the system of guaranteed crop prices and distribution of subsidized credit in exchange for market policies and compensatory programs was introduced (De Vries, 1995; Foley, 1995; Alcalá *et al*, 1996; Ibarra Mendívil, 1996).

These and other reforms have largely influenced the strategies of the new WUAs. They stimulated the discussion within the WUA on whether or not associations should expand their O&M oriented mandate toward the provision of wider agricultural support services, which until recently were provided mainly by the public sector. This, in turn, raised the question whether all water users would have equal access to the new services that are provided by the WUAs. Finally, in 1992 a new National Water Law was introduced, which allows the CNA and private parties -such as WUAs- to sign a tradable water concession agreement. This gives WUAs the possibility of buying and selling water within the agricultural sector or even with other sectors in the economy (Roemer, 1997; Rosegrant and Gazmuri, 1996).

In general, these neoliberal reforms were designed to eliminate obstacles for national and international private investment and agricultural economic growth. In the context of neoliberal ideologies, regarding water as a tradable economic good and market competition between water users as the mechanism to equitable allocation and higher productivity of water are considered to be supportive means to accomplish these reforms. Currently, the government is in the process of: (a) establishing federations of individual WUAs that would further take over responsibilities;
(b) decentralizing CNA offices to the States and away from federal control; and
(c) modifying the new National Water Law.

The strategy

Internationally, the Mexican IMT program has become 'a model', especially because of the relatively high speed of implementing IMT. By December 1996, 2.92 million hectares had been transferred to 372 WUA, which represents 90% of the area served by the 80 irrigation districts in the country (CNA, 1996). IMT has been a top-down process implemented by the government, in which government officials visited the *ejidos* to inform them to select their delegates to the newly-to-be-established WUAs. In addition to the *ejido* delegates, private growers were also asked to select their delegates to the WUAs. Subsequently, these delegates were asked to elect their leaders (president, treasurer and secretary) to the WUAs. CNA machinery and equipment to clean the canals were handed over to the WUAs and the leaders of the WUAs received training on O&M and administration. The strategy followed by the CNA was to first transfer the larger irrigation districts in the north of Mexico, where many big private producers would support IMT, in order to show that the IMT was workable.

Old and new actors

Prior to transfer, the irrigation districts were entirely managed by the CNA. The CNA employed heads of Units[2] and ditch tenders who were responsible for daily O&M. Farmers had to go to the CNA unit offices to pay their fees. After transfer, these units or modules were transferred to the WUAs. The WUAs employ their own managers, ditch tenders and administrative staff, paid out of the fees which the WUAs collect from their members. Also, hydraulic committees at the levels of the watershed and the irrigation districts were introduced to help establish annual and seasonal water allocations. In the latter, representatives of the CNA as well as of each WUA participate.

The conventional view is that IMT has led to Mexican government withdrawal from regulating water distribution. Although officially the role of the CNA below the main canals has ceased to exist, observations and press reports show that CNA continues to play an informal (but important) role in setting the O&M fee and planned seasonal water allocation within the modules, as well as conflict resolution within the WUAs. Yet, the traditional CNA-users patron-client relationships are weakened. These are being replaced by new networks of leaders of WUAs, users, private international seed and agro-chemical companies and local and state politicians. These actors play a role in setting the market prices for agricultural inputs, electricity and crop produce and it has become clear that many WUAs want to increase their stake in these networks.

WUAs have become both powerful means and actors in the political and the economic arenas of negotiation. At the risk of over-generalizing and simplifying, WUAs can be classified by two types of WUAs. The first type is the heavily politicized WUA, in which local party and *ejido* politics determine decision making processes and resource distribution, including water distribution. The second type of WUA is the more market oriented WUA, in which decision making and resource distribution are determined by cost efficiency and the aim to commercialize agriculture. One way to accomplish this is through networking in order to gain access to the market and higher-level politicians and as a result obtain better prices. As these are relatively recent developments within the new WUAs, it is still too early to answer the question whether indeed all users have equal access to these benefits. But it is an important question that needs to be raised by anyone who is interested in issues related to equity and WUAs.

The research district

The Alto Río Lerma Irrigation District, with a command area of 112,772 ha, is located in the State of Guanajuato in the agricultural heart of central Mexico. There are roughly 24,000 water users in the irrigation district, with 55% corresponding to members of ejidos (*ejidatarios*); and 45% classified as small private growers[3]. The average land holding in the irrigation district is 5 ha.

The climate has been classified as moderate sub-humid with an average yearly precipitation of 730 mm and an average temperature of 19° C. Yearly evaporation is approximately 1,900 mm and relative humidity is about 60 %.

Surface water for the district is provided by four earthen dams with a combined storage capacity of 2.14 million cubic meters. In addition, there are a total of 1,714 deep wells; thus the district relies both on surface and groundwater, with their conjunctive use playing a vital role in system operation. The irrigation network comprises 475 kilometers of main canals and 1,658 kilometers of secondary and tertiary canals. Likewise, there is a network of approximately 1,031 kilometers of drainage canals. Main crops are dependent on whether the water source is surface or groundwater, with the former used mainly for wheat, sorghum, maize and beans; and under the latter mostly wheat, vegetables and alfalfa.

The system is operated under controlled demand as follows: at the beginning of the season and according to the water available in the dams, the area to be covered and the number of irrigations to be delivered are established after negotiations between CNA and WUAs, under the umbrella of the hydraulic committee. The user can then request irrigation at any time during the season, keeping in mind the number of irrigations to which he is entitled. Presently the irrigation district is divided into 11 modules (see Table 16.1[4]), each of which is managed by an individual WUA.

Impact on equity as a result of management transfer

In the following sections we describe three mechanisms that have had an impact on an equitable water distribution in the system as a result of the transfer of management from the irrigation agency into the hands of Water Users Associations: water concessions, water allocation principles and paying of water fees.

Water concessions to the modules

The principle
The IMT program was accompanied by the introduction of the new National Water Law, so that water rights were clarified and the possibility for trading water was established. By law, each WUA within an irrigation district is granted a concession, which entitles them to a proportional share of the water available for each season, rather than to a specified volumetric water right. Although concessions are granted for periods of up to 50 years, CNA continues to have broad discretionary power over the concessional right to use water and over virtually all water transactions (sales or rental).

The practice
These concessions do not differ much from the pre-IMT system, in which water was also distributed among the modules proportionally to the area that they occupy within the irrigation district. One of the major differences, in practices under the old and new system is that, under the new water law, water can be sold, for instance between two WUAs. These sales need the approval of the CNA, as well as of a majority of the general assembly of the WUAs involved. For example, during the period 1995 to 1997 nine cases in Alto Río Lerma were observed in which WUAs bought water from other WUAs. The prices paid were negotiated by the WUAs under the umbrella of the hydraulic committee and ranged from US$0.40 /1,000 m^3 in 1995 to US$3.50 / 1,000 m^3 in 1997. In 1995, this price was approximately 10 percent of what the WUAs charged their individual users. In 1997, this price equaled the price paid by individual users.

The impact on equity
Before IMT water allocation to the modules was executed and controlled by CNA. After IMT, concessions are signed by both CNA and the WUAs. The equity definition and concern of both the CNA and the hydraulic committee is whether or not water is proportionally allocated to the modules. As the principle between the old system of water allocations and the new system of water concession proportional to the service area has not changed, we can compare this equity criterion of water distribution before and after IMT. An analysis of Table 16.1 indicates that after IMT and establishment of the hydraulic committee, actual allocations have come closer to concessions, and hence water is allocated more equally among the modules.

Under the new law, water concessions can also be given to individual water users. There appears to be a strong preference on the part of the CNA to make concessions to WUAs (Rosegrant *et al*, 1995). The idea is that WUAs develop internal rules and regulations to equally grant subsidiary water rights to their members. Yet, in the case of Alto Río Lerma none of the WUAs has established these rules and regulations. Water sales and rental arrangements (especially of well water) among farmers was and is common practice, with or without CNA approval. As a result, in practice the

Table16.1: The difference between concessioned allocation and actual supply, before (average of 1982-1991) and after (average of 1992-1997) IMT.

Module	a Canal Water Service Area (ha)	b Concession (share of available storage) (%)	c Actual Supply, Before IMT (share of total supply of the district) (%)	d Actual Supply, After IMT (share of total supply to the district) (%)	e Difference Before IMT 1-(c/b) (%)	f Difference After IMT 1-(d/b) (%)
Acambaro	6.070	8,35	7,7	6,7	-8	-20
Salvatiera	11.929	16,4	18,2	17,7	11	8
Jaral	4.529	6,23	8,4	6,4	34	2
Valle	9.297	12,78	10,5	11,0	-18	-14
Cortazar	12.712	17,48	18,0	17,2	3	-1
Salamanca	10.885	14,97	15,6	14,6	4	-3
Irapuato	4.296	5,97	5,4	5,5	-9	-7
Abasolo and Corraljo	10.318	14,18	13,4	16,8	-6	18
Huanimaro	2.700	3,71	2,9	4,1	-22	11
Totaal Sta.dev.	72.736	100	100	100	16	11

Source: own computation of modules and CNA data, Alto Rio Lerma Irrigation District

new National Water Law has not contributed much to more equal access to water among the users within the modules.

In addition to not actually granting a volumetric right, the water law is also unclear on priority in case of shortage. In case of extreme scarcity or over-exploitation of water, domestic use shall have priority. This formulation leaves plenty of room for wide interpretations, political manipulation and negotiation of water concessions by actors involved in sectors other than agriculture. Johnson (1996) reports a case in the state of Nuevo Leon where the city of Monterrey has diverted irrigation water to another dam to serve the needs of city's powerful industrialists. Yet, the WUAs have legal concessions, as well as a 1952 agreement signed by the President stating that this water belongs to the irrigation district.

These examples bring us to question the impact of the new water law, not only on implementing equitable access to water among agricultural users within the irrigation sector, but among that sector and the industrial and domestic water sectors as well.

Water allocation within the modules

The principle

Generally, the water allocation principle itself did not change after IMT. Based on the volume that has been assigned for a particular year, the WUAs decide what percentage of their fields a farmer can irrigate. Farmers request for the number of hectares that they need to irrigate. With the area and the planned water depth the weekly volume to be delivered by CNA is established and an irrigation schedule is prepared. Although the water law does not exclude well owners from access to canal water in Alto Río Lerma, it has become customary that they are excluded from such right, unless declining well discharges would jeopardize their crops.

The CNA's and the hydraulic committee's equity concern is that water is strictly distributed proportional to the service areas with rights to canal water that each of the modules within the district has. WUAs' main equity concern is that a farmer receives irrigation water and does not plant more than the planned area, irrespective of the crop he grows, the soil type of his farm, or how much water is actually supplied to his plot. The equity concern of farmers without wells is that they receive the water they have requested and paid for and that farmers who have not paid and have no 'rights' (private well owners) do not take canal water. Finally, the equity perception of farmers with private wells is that every farmer with fields within the total (canal and wells) service area of the module should have access to canal water also.

The practices

Although water allocation principles have not changed, water allocation practices and actors have changed. Before IMT, CNA employed ditch tenders responsible for distributing the water to individual farmers. Ditch tenders had close contacts with water users and functioned as the 'middleman' or interface between these users and the irrigation bureaucracy (see for instance Van der Zaag, 1992). The agency found it difficult to control ditch tenders, often resulting in a lack of accountability. As a consequence, there was opportunity for rent-seeking and other negotiations over water supply between ditch tenders and users. Farmers reported that it was common practice that ditch tenders also 'sold' canal water to owners of private wells.

After IMT, WUAs now hire technical staff responsible for administration and O&M of the system below the main system level. Generally, the manager of the module is responsible for daily O&M. He receives guidelines from the board of delegates. However, often it has been observed that the manager has to follow the direct instructions of the president of the WUA. Especially in the more politicized WUAs, this kind of close president-manager 'loyalty' has created unrest among other technical staff and farmers.

Most WUAs did not want to hire the CNA ditch tenders, basically for four reasons: 1) they wanted to reduce their numbers in order to become more cost-effective; 2) some CNA ditch tenders proved to be sensitive to rent-seeking attitudes or otherwise performed poorly; 3) they wanted to hire their 'own people', which in some cases lead to hiring relatives, who were well trained but lacked experience; 4) they wanted to eliminate union involvement in the management of the irrigation system.

With respect to water distribution, in practice the number of hours allowed to irrigate one hectare is not necessarily fixed beforehand, but rather depends on the ditch tender's experience with the complexity of the fields and his relationship with the water user.

The impacts on equity
As the number of ditch tenders was reduced, each one was forced to be responsible for more area and users. Ditch tenders are now directly accountable to the professional manager and the leaders of the modules. Observations indicate that in some modules ditch tenders, as well as other technical staff, who do not perform well have been made redundant by the users. However, in more politicized WUAs it appears as if ditch tenders can stay on if they remain politically loyal to the leaders of the WUA.

In practice, the modules do not always check whether CNA actually delivers the volumes requested. Also, ditch tenders only report roughly the time farmers receive water. Using the planned water depth they calculate the theoretical discharge (m^3/s). Instead of the actual discharge supplied to each field, ditch tenders generally record the calculated discharge in the daily irrigation reports. As a consequence of these two practices, there are large differences between the volumes planned, reported and what the authors actually measured in the system. As an example, Figure 16.1 shows the differences in the planned, the reported and the measured volumes in one of the selected secondary canals within the research area. In this example, the measured volumes are on the average 178% higher than the reported volumes. However, ditch tenders consistently report volumes that are close to the planned volumes: reported volumes are 87% of the planned volumes. The system of accountability based on making daily reports rather than actual performance explains why ditch tenders tend to *administer* rather than *manage* water distribution. These and similar observations in other modules suggest that planned equitable water allocation among secondary canals within the modules is normally not enforced.

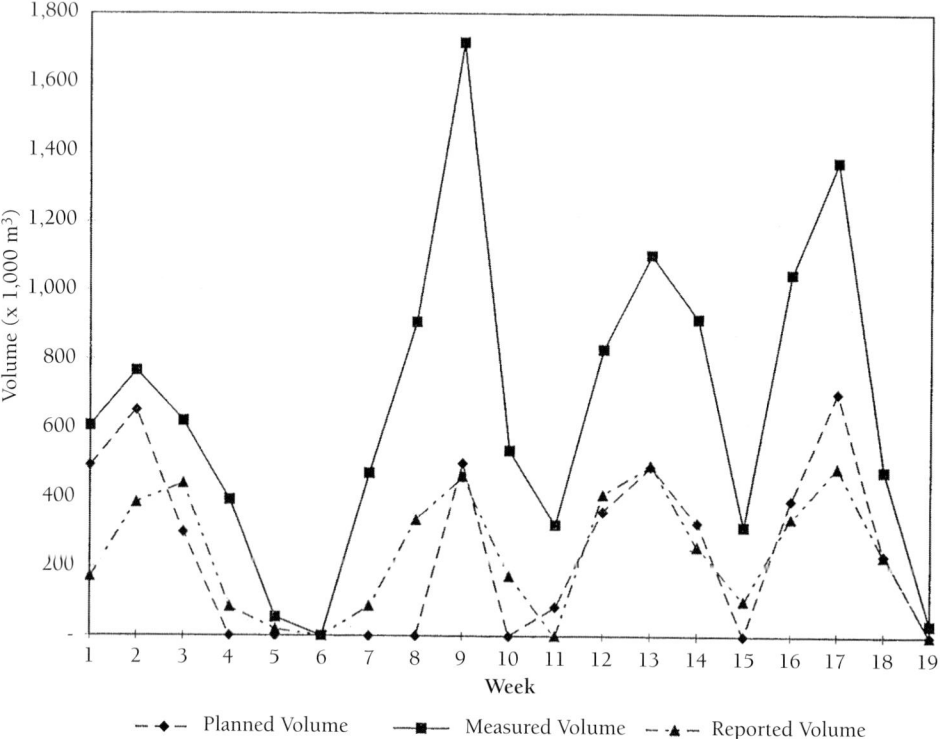

Figure 16.1: Planned Measured and Reported Volumes Canal 'A' Cortazar Module, Fall-Winter season 1995-96

As water flow measurements show that all farmers receive sufficient water to meet the theoretical crop demand, the equity issue does not seem as pressing as one would find in the more water scarce environments of the country. Nevertheless, the actual amounts delivered at different levels of the system vary widely. Measured relative water supplies (RWS[5]) range from 1.2 to 5.5 at the level of the (sub-) laterals and from 1.2 to 2.4 at the level of individual plots. There was not a significant bias in water delivery between head and tail end areas. Daily observations of ditch tenders, as well as interviews with farmers suggest that unequal water distribution along the canals can be explained in terms of changing roles and practices of the ditch tenders (Kloezen and Garcés, 1998).

With respect to equity, results from a farmer survey done by IIMI (n=125) show that 35% of the *ejidatarios* and 29% of the private growers perceive that water distribution is more fair after transfer, while 15% of both categories feel that it has become less fair. The remaining farmers see no difference in fairness of water distribution as a result of transfer. Similarly, 30% of the head-end farmers, 35% of the middle reach farmers and 34% of the tail-end farmers report an improvement in water distribution. Answers to questions on adequacy and timeliness of water delivery provided similar responses.

Both *ejidatarios* and private growers report that unauthorized appropriation of canal water by private well owners has dramatically decreased (but continues to exist) as a result of more severe control by the WUAs. Most ditch tenders report that taking of water by private well owners is the main problem that they are facing in their daily work. Observations suggest clear differences in the way ditch tenders deal with these practices: some record these allocations and appeal to the user to pay for the module, while others do not report these practices and allow the well owners to take as much water as they want. There are cases in which *ejidatarios* with private wells rely up to 75% on canal water, nevertheless ditch tenders justify their generous gesture by arguing that the canal water is only to supplement the well water.

Paying O&M fees

As WUAs are financially totally dependent on O&M fee collection, IMT forced WUAs to increase the collection rate. Before IMT, farmers also had to pay fees to the CNA, but the ratio of fees paid by farmers as a percentage of the actual O&M costs declined from 85% in the early 1960s to 15% in the late 1980s, basically due to deteriorating infrastructure and maintenance services, coupled with the declining financial contribution by users (Palacios, 1994).

The principle
Before IMT, O&M fees were paid to CNA. Now, farmers pay directly to the WUAs, who have full autonomy over the revenue. In both cases, payment was made prior to the service, where receipts had to be presented to the ditch tenders. As a condition of IMT, a percentage of the fees goes to CNA as payment for O&M of the main system and the head works. Every season the fees are established by the WUA and reviewed and concurred to by CNA.

The practice
In general, the principle is being followed. Most WUAs in the Alto Río Lerma succeeded in increasing fee collection to over 100% of the targets as a result of enhanced service, mainly in the fields of maintenance, administration and the provision of non-O&M related services (Kloezen *et al*, 1998). Individual WUAs are now negotiating the share of the fees going to CNA, based on the complexity and the level of the service provided. Service fees have remained constant (in Mexican pesos) in the

first three years after IMT as a result of the economic crisis of 1995-96 and, in some cases due to users' dissatisfaction with the service. In the latter, occasionally users do not have the political power to replace leaders, but refrain from approving higher fees as a way to signal their displeasure.

The recent economic crisis notwithstanding, not only has there been an increase in the overall fee collection rate, but also an increase in the fee level from roughly US$30 per hectare per year in 1989 to US$60 in 1996 (in 1994 constant US dollar prices).

The impact on equity
IMT has clearly reinforced the principle of 'he who pays his fees, gets the water he is entitled to', and hence has stimulated equity in water distribution according to the concept of both modules and individual users. Direct payment of O&M fees has also reduced (but not eliminated) the appropriation of water by private well owners and private growers, as it has given farmers a means to make ditch tenders more account-able. In general, it has also forced the module management and leadership to become more accountable to their users. With still one more irrigation turn to go, one of the selected modules for the study had used its entire water concession for the 1995-1996 agricultural year. As a consequence it found itself forced to buy water from private well owners in order to be able to fulfill its commitments to users who had already paid the module for their water service. Although it was not the first time in the history of the irrigation district that assigned volumes were used before the end of the season, it was the first time that users could force system managers (in this case a WUA) to deliver the service that farmers had paid for.

We have not found clear indications that the paying of O&M fees has also become a very powerful incentive to distribute water more efficiently. One of the main reasons for this is that the service is priced per hectare, rather than by crop or volume. The ditch tender only checks whether a user is not irrigating more hectares than the user has paid for, irrespective of how much water the user takes. A second reason is that cost of the service relative to other costs of production is low (more or less 5%); this, coupled with the relatively higher water availability in Alto Río Lerma, tends to diminish the importance of realizing the planned equitable water distribution *vis a vis* water pricing.

Conclusions

Preliminary results indicate that the notion of equity varies from actor to actor and often the concepts run counter to one another. For example, CNA is concerned with an equity allocation based strictly on proportionality between the physical area of each module and total water availability. Individual modules regard equity as being able to satisfy the water demand that is a result of the combination of planned service and the crops chosen, but they are less concerned about how much water the farmers actually take. Finally, for the individual farmer, the concept of equity is to make sure that his neighbor does not irrigate more than the area established for each user, regardless of the efficiency with which he manages his water allocation. One of the end-results of the different perceptions of equity among actors is inefficient management of the water resource, which is demonstrated by the relatively high values of RWS.

The above does not mean that IMT has not had an impact on water allocation and distribution. Although IMT has hardly changed the allocation and water pricing principles, it has influenced the implementation of system O&M. At the level of the irrigation district, water is allocated more closely to the proportional concession to each module. At the level of the modules users can make the technical staff more accountable and make sure that each farmer who paid his fees at least receives sufficient water to meet crop demand. Paying a service fee also provides another avenue to show their (dis)satisfaction, especially with their leaders.

The new National Water Law still allows for wide interpretations and does not guarantee individual water rights to users. One of the major drawbacks of the new law is that it does not define equity in terms of exclusion and priority of water use.

Although WUAs have been established to introduce a more cost-effective and efficient use of O&M resources, many WUAs decided to expand their mandate by taking up non-O&M related activities, which in their view are as pertinent as O&M. Future evaluations of 'equity' as a result of IMT should not only focus on equitable access to water, but also on equitable access to other services that are provided by the WUAs.

Notes

1   Other impacts of the IMT program in the Alto Río Lerma irrigation district are discussed in Kloezen *et al* (1998).
2   Before IMT irrigation districts were divided into so called Units (*Unidades*, which were more or less independent water management blocks, with sizes ranging from 3,000 ha to 20,000 ha. After IMT the Units were converted into Modules (*Módulos*).
3   The 'small private grower' concept (*pequeño propietario*) is a misnomer because in Mexico such a user category could allow ownership of up to a hundred hectares for an individual owner.
4   One of the 11 modules has its own reservoir and hence is excluded from Table 16.1. As the CNA flow data do not distinguish between the supplies to Abasolo and Corralejo we have combined these two.
5   The RWS is defined as the non-dimensional ratio of the total water supply (irrigation and total rainfall) to the crop water requirement. Values less than 1 indicate that crop water requirements are not being met. As the RWS values increase, water delivery efficiencies decrease.

References

Alcalá, Elio, Luz Ma. Del Carmen Brunt Rivera, Ma.de la Luz Parcero López and Teófilo Reyes Couturier. 1996. *Campesinos, artículo 27 y estado mexicano*. Mexico City: Plaza y Valdés and Instituto Nacional de Antropología e Historia.

CNA (Comisión Nacional del Agua). 1994. *Transferencia de los Distritos de Riego en México*. Ciudad de México, Mexico.

CNA (Comisión Nacional del Agua). 1996. *Programa de transferencia de distritos de riego: avance*. Ciudad de México, Mexico.

De Vries, Pieter. 1995. The local redefinition of the agrarian question in Mexico: transformations of practices, projects and identities in the age of globalization. Paper presented at the International Congress on Agrarian Questions-The Politics of Farming Anno 1995, May 22-24, 1995. Wageningen: Wageningen Agricultural University.

Foley, Michael W. 1995. Privatizing the countryside: The Mexican peasant movement and neoliberal reform. *Latin American Perspectives*, 84, Vol. 22 (1995), No.1, pp 59-76.

Gorriz, Cecilia M., Ashok Subramanian and Jose Simas. 1995. Irrigation management transfer in Mexico: Process and progress. *World Bank Technical Paper* Number 292. Washington, D.C.: The World Bank

Ibarra Mendívil, Jose Luis. 1996. Recent changes in the Mexican constitution and their impact on the agrarian reform. In: Randall, Laura (ed). *Reforming Mexico's agrarian reform*. New York and London: M.E. Sharp, pp 49-60.

Johnson III, Sam H. 1996. *Irrigation Management Transfer in Mexico: Moving toward sustainability*. Paper prepared for the Internal Program Review 1996. Colombo: International Irrigation Management Institute.

Kloezen, W. H. and C. Garcés-Restrepo. 1998. Assessing irrigation performance with external indicators: the case of the Alto Río Lerma irrigation district, Mexico. *Research Report 22*. Colombo, Sri Lanka: International Irrigation Management Institute

Kloezen, Wim H., Carlos Garcés-Restrepo and Sam H. Johnson III. 1998. Impact assessment of irrigation management transfer in the Alto Río Lerma Irrigation District, Mexico. *Research Report 15*. Colombo, Sri Lanka: International Irrigation Management Institute.

Palacios-Vélez, E. 1994. El desempeño de las asociaciones de usuarios en la operación y mantenimiento de los Distritos de Riego. In: *Memorias del Seminario Internacional sobre Transferencia de Sistemas de Riego*, Ciudad Obregón, Mexico, May 4-7: Colegio de Postgraduados, pp 113-118.

Roemer, Andrés. 1997. *Derecho y economia: políticas públicas del agua*. Mexico City, Mexico: Centro de Investigación y Docencia Económicas and Sociedad Mexicana de Geografía y Estadística.

Rosegrant, Mark W., Renato Gazmuri Schleyer and Satya N. Yadav. 1995. Water policy for efficient agricultural diversification: market-based approaches. *Food Policy*, Vol. 20 (1995), No. 3, pp. 202-223.

Rosegrant, M.W. and R. Gazmuri Schleyer. 1996. Establishing tradable water rights: implementation of the Mexican water law. *Irrigation and Drainage Systems* 10, pp 263-279.

Van der Zaag, Pieter. 1992. *Chicanery at the canal. Changing practices in irrigation management in Western Mexico*. Amsterdam: Centro de Estudios y Documentación Latinoamericanos.

17

Values, Ideologies, and Equity in Water Distribution. Historical Perspectives from Coastal California, United States

Kate Berry

Introduction

Black's Law Dictionary defines equity, in a general or natural sense, as 'that which strikes the ordinary conscience and sense of justice as being fair, right, and equitable' (Black 1990). Questions about equity in the distribution of water have generated discussion about how to distribute water between various users in an equitable manner. In the distribution of irrigation water in Nepal, for example, Maskey, Weber and Loof (1994) have observed horizontal and vertical dimensions to equity, based upon the distribution of water relative to the location of farmland and productivity differences between farmlands. Bishop and Long (1983) similarly interpret equity in irrigation as resulting from water delivery systems that are efficient from the perspective of engineering design, the regulatory environment, and record-keeping.

Water equity has also been interpreted in terms of the relationship between the distribution of water and the distribution of wealth. Chambers (1981) has suggested addressing questions of who will benefit from any proposed redistribution of water, with attention directed to water management reforms that achieve benefits for poorer people. Sampath has advocated applying Rawl's theory of justice to measure relative equity and has argued that government policies for water redistribution can be a means to reduce inequalities in the distribution of income (Sampath 1984, 1991).

A third approach turns the economic logic implicit in the previous approach in an entirely different direction. Capitalistic markets, as free and unfettered as possible, have been another solution proposed to provide equitable solutions to water distribution. This neoliberal approach, as proposed by Anderson (1983), Winpenny (1994) and many others, treats water strictly as an economic resource or commodity available for competition in the free market. The concept is that if appropriately priced, competition for water in the market will allow water to flow to users who value it most highly, thus promoting conservation and creating an equitable distribution of water.

It is not my intent in this chapter to debate the relative merits of these three approaches to defining and measuring equity in water distribution, beyond observing that in and of themselves they are insufficient measures. Efficiency and economic criteria do not measure equity; rather they reflect, sometimes rather obscurely, the normative dimension implicit in equitable water distribution. Equity, in water distribution as in other things, is ultimately defined in human dimensions, bounded by the norms of the community(ies) involved.

Take as an example the commonly used phrase, 'water resource'. Water as a resource derives normative import from its economic utility. The ubiquitous usage of the term throughout much of the world today underscores the strength of the value system based on economics. As a result, the utilitarian norm operationalized within the term itself influences the interpretation of equity in water distribution.

Water, however, can be valued for being more than simply a resource. Water may have cultural, symbolic, and perhaps even emotional significance in contributing to a sense of community well-being (Brown and Ingram 1987). Values, thus, reflect a normative dimension to the issue of equity and provide part of the foundation necessary to interpret and adjudicate water equities.

Similarly, ideologies underlie one's notion of what is fair, just, and equitable in the distribution of water. Ideologies, in the sense used here, do not refer to political or economic persuasions, but rather are broader matrices of interconnected values, or value systems, that guide actions in particular aspects of life. In this light, the system of values outlined by Wilkinson (1990) can be seen as the basis for many contemporary ideologies that surround water in the western United States:

*   water as a source of sustenance;
*   water as an instrument of agriculture;
*   water as a community good;
*   water as a means of transportation;
*   water as an industrial commodity;
*   water as a clean and pure resource;
*   water as beauty;
*   water as a destructive force to be controlled;
*   water as fuel for urban development;
*   water as a place for recreation and wildlife habitat.

While norms, in the form of values and ideologies, shape determinations about equity in the distribution of water, norms are not the same everywhere. Both time and technology are influential in shaping the norms related to water equity. Of greater relevance in this chapter, however, are the effects of cultural differences and inter-cultural contacts on the heterogeneity of norms. The values and ideologies that support decisions about what is equitable in water distribution clearly vary from culture to culture, and even between subcultures. Where cultures come into contact and conflict ensues, values and ideologies related to water equity can also clash. This chapter focuses on a region, which is today known as coastal California, to examine the normative dimensions involved in the distribution of water for irrigation between American Indians and the Spanish during the colonial period, 1769-1821.

Physical setting

Coastal California stretches from the San Francisco Bay southward to the present-day U.S.-Mexican border and is located in western central North America at 32.5 ° to 38 ° north latitude. The region has a mediterranean climate in which irrigation can supplement incident precipitation to provide for better crop growth. Mild temperatures prevail throughout the year, with monthly averages ranging from 7 ° to 24 ° C. Topography influences the siting of agricultural lands as relief varies throughout the region. Elevations range from sea level along the coastline to over 2,500 meters along the summit of the highest mountains which form the eastern border of the region and separate it from the adjacent Central and Imperial Valleys.

Precipitation ranges from a high in the northern region to a low in the south, for example, San Francisco averages 720 mm and San Diego averages 250 mm of precipitation each year. Precipitation is generally greater on high elevation, west-facing slopes which can receive more than 1,400 per year as compared to lower elevation, east-facing slopes which are drier (NOAA 1994). Throughout the region most precipitation occurs as rain which falls primarily during the winter months (November through April) and is followed by a drier summer period (May through October), the principal growing season for crops. Water is instrumental in the success of agriculture. By controlling the availability and timing of water applied, irrigation influences the type of crop grown and its yield. Because water is unevenly distributed, both in a temporal and spatial sense, irrigation can provide a measure of security that is unattainable with rainfall agriculture.

Indians and irrigation prior to contact with Europeans

In the Americas prior to European contact, Indians had adapted to limited water supplies in a variety of ways. Perhaps the best known examples of North American cultures that practiced irrigated agriculture are the ancient Anasazi and Hohokam of the southwestern United States and, more recently, the Pueblo tribes of northern New Mexico.

Until the mid-1960s, scholars commonly assumed that native Californians did not engage in irrigated agriculture before their contact with the Spanish. Ressler (1968) summed up the common perception that Indians were well versed in irrigated agriculture in Arizona and New Mexico but not in California: 'in the Californias there was no agriculture, let alone irrigation until the arrival of the Spanish' (p.13). More recent scholarship suggests that this assumption was incorrect, as there is a growing body of evidence that Californians developed crop irrigation as well as domestic water supplies prior to the Spanish arrival.

The Paiutes of Owens Valley, for example, as well as the Quechan, Mohave, Hachihoma, and Kamia along the lower Colorado River practiced irrigated agriculture (Hundley 1987). The Cahuilla of southern California modified their water regimes by utilizing natural artesian springs, small depression reservoirs, and digging wells (Malki Museum 1965; Bean 1972). Toward the coast, the San Luiseños most likely timed their seasonal migrations based on the availability of water supplies (True and Waugh 1982). Neighbors to the south, the Kumeyaay (Diegueños), applied simple irrigation technology by strategically aligning rocks in small waterways in order to reduce flow velocity and encourage infiltration into surrounding areas (Shipek 1996).

Irrigation at the time of contact with the Spanish

Irrigation practices and, more generally, the values and ideologies of water underwent dramatic changes with the arrival of the Spanish. After naming their newly claimed lands, Alta California, the Spanish almost immediately sought out sources of reliable water. Early exploration maps and texts of California often describe minute water features including not only perennial rivers, lakes, and streams but also noting tiny ponds, dry arroyos, muddy watering holes, and minuscule springs (Meyer 1984).

The near-obsessive concern of the Spanish over the availability of water for irrigation in Alta California had been shaped by their experiences in colonizing Baja California; they had learned from harsh experiences to locate their settlements in proximity to water sources for irrigation. Father Johann Baegert, a German Jesuit, painted a bleak water picture in Baja California and attempts of the Spanish missionary to rectify it:

> 'There is not sufficient water. Consequently, water was taken wherever and however it was found. The site for a new mission was determined, if possible, by the availability of at least some water which could be used to irrigate the land, either at the mission or in a place several miles away. No effort was spared. In some places water was brought half an hour's distance over irregular terrain through narrow channels or troughs carved out of the rock. At other locations, water was collected from six or twelve places - a handful from each source - and conducted into a single basin... Nearly everywhere it was necessary to surround the water as well as the soil with retaining walls or bulwarks, and to erect dams, partly to keep the soil from being washed away by the torrents of rain. Even so, all the work was often useless. At best one had to patch and to repair every year, and sometimes it is necessary to start all over again' (quoted in Ressler 1968, 14-15).

Normative conflict and access to irrigation water

The Spanish were not impressed with Indians they encountered in coastal California. The Spanish considered the Indians to be lacking in industry, ingenuity, mental capacity, and spiritual development - in a word, uncivilized. The need to civilize and to christianize Indians, thus, became the rationale for many actions taken by the Spanish. Institutions and rules were imposed upon the native peoples under a dualistic, and from the Spanish perspective more palatable, set of justifications: they were promoting civilization where they saw none and, at the same time, could take advantage of the opportunities for power and wealth that had drawn them to the Americas initially.

Even before setting foot in the Americas, Spain had institutionalized its vision of discovery and conquest. Codified in 1265, Las Siete Partidas set forth a mandate for human dominion over Nature and over one another: 'Man has power to do as he sees fit with those things that belong to him according to the laws of God and man' (quoted in Hundley 1992, 26). Medieval era conflicts between the Spanish and Germanic groups and Moors, as well as the encounters during the crusades, had left their mark on the Spanish legal and political systems and extended a notion of conquest and social stratification into many aspects of Spanish law, including their policies toward the water and land rights of the Indian cultures they encountered (Williams, 1990).

Once situated in the Americas, Spanish law evolved to meet the different conditions, yet it maintained as an intrinsic characteristic the hierarchy of public ownership and individual property rights. The underlying premise in New Spain was that the Spanish Crown owned everything it 'discovered' or conquered. Thus all property titles, including land and water, stemmed from the Crown because everything belonged to the Sovereign as discoverer. New World Spanish law, Las Leyes de las Indias, included a provision that water was to be used for the 'common good.' The Spanish, however, were to interpret the meaning of the common good; their determination of what constituted the best use of water was confined to Eurocentric, rather than Indian, notions of appropriate water use (Berry 1998).

The Spanish instituted a system of land and water grants made by the Crown, or its designate, to those who were looked upon favorably. Property holdings were then consolidated through purchase, plunder, inheritance, marriage, and donation. The control and management of water was linked to the potential for political and economic dominance because water affected the productive capacity of the land (Whitten 1981). The Spanish laws, for example, that governed the colonization of new land during the period that California was settled, required construction of irrigation ditches within one year and, very soon thereafter, required other water infrastructure, such as reservoirs and drains, to be constructed and maintained (Avina 1976). Typically, the work to construct and maintain this infrastructure was done by Indians who were not paid or were very poorly paid.

Another institutionalized system of favor-giving, encomiendas, were grants of the labor of Indians to favored Europeans. Landless and waterless Indians were given access to their original resources in exchange for the labor of the entire family working for the hacienda, with the obligation sometimes extending for generations (Ebright 1987). The outcome of this system of land and labor was that the hacienda owner (*hacendado*) had access to virtually free labor for agricultural activities and domestic service; the productive processes were organized in such a way that the surplus was concentrated almost exclusively in the hands of *hacendados* and their intermediaries. The land grant system in coastal California evolved more fully under Mexican rule.

Church and State relationships were closely bound together during Spanish rule. The Catholic Church was largely responsible for the more paternalistic objectives of bringing civilization to the Indians and, more particularly, providing spiritual guidance and creating the motivation to be industrious. The Catholic Church was granted vast tracts of land in coastal California to create the mission system to achieve these objectives. The missionaries established agriculture wherever possible and extended control over other resources needed for agriculture including water and the labor of Indians to irrigate crops.

Pablo Tac, a baptized Indian or neophyte, describes the work required to bring water to the San Luis Rey Mission in coastal California:

> 'We said that the Mission was placed on a hillock. Below this hillock there is an ever-flowing spring from which the neophytes and missionary bring water to drink. They made two fountains before the gate of the garden and between them a stairway to go up and down which is made all of bricks. The entering gateway has three thick timbers in the middle. One of them, driven into the earth, reaches high above the wall, with the other two more or less fastened on it, making a cross of all parts, if you would like to see it, and the water carrier wishing to pass pushes a timber, and the two turn, and in this way he passes with ease, raising the pitcher above his burdened shoulders stronger than those of asses themselves. The stairway is so very high that one cannot ascend by it in a single trip, and it is necessary to rest in the middle. It happens many times that they get tired in vain (as is said), because when they arrive at the gate and wish to pass through it with haste, the pitcher is broken, and they return to the house without water or pitcher, dripping with water' (Tac 1835, 16).

Neophytes became the source of labor to build the Church's irrigation infrastructure but also in the more sustained effort needed to maintain the infrastructure and in the actual work of irrigating crops and providing a domestic water supply.

Access to water: from the colonial and republican eras to the present-day situation

This case study illustrates the complexity involved in assessing equity in water distribution. Values and ideologies of the Spaniards regarding water represented a radical departure from those of the Indians. Unlike other regions in the Americas that the Spanish colonized, when they arrived in coastal California they immediately sought out supplies of usable water and generally ignored the extant agricultural and irrigation knowledge and norms of the resident Indians. Control of water for irrigation became essential for economic security in Spanish America. As a result, a desire to control water influenced the relationships that developed between the Spanish and Indians and the manner in which political power was exerted. Three dimensions of the control over water were fundamental to the intercultural conflict and its implications for equity in water use:

- irrigation water provided security for agriculture - the productive basis of many of the Spanish haciendas, missions, and *pueblos;*
- Indians, and in particular the neophytes, were more easily governed by controlling distribution of the products of agriculture, the foods and fibers that irrigation supported;
- labor in irrigation, as well as agricultural work more generally, was used by the missionaries and haciendados to prevent 'laziness' and to civilize and christianize the neophytes.

The colonial era ended in coastal California during the early nineteenth century. Arguably the two most significant changes during the Mexican era came with the demise of missionary-Indian relationships as missions secularized, and with the proliferation of land grants made by the government to Mexican, European, and United States citizens as well as to a few Indian communities. With increasing competition for scarce water, supplies for irrigation in Indian communities were not infrequently expropriated for use by other settlers. In many cases land was also taken from coastal Californian Indian communities, particularly if it was fertile or had a reliable source of water (Shipek 1988).

Similar direct expropriation of water and land would continue to occur after 1848 when the United States claimed California's lands and waters, but significant changes were to occur in the exertion of State power over water: While the Spanish system of water law was based on principles of equitable apportionment between competing water users, the system that developed throughout most of the western United States allocated water based upon priority in time. In California a second allocation system based upon ownership of riparian lands developed concurrently. A third doctrine, the 'Winters doctrine' or Indians' reserved water rights, was established at the beginning of the twentieth century. These rights were based upon the execution of a treaty or agreement between an Indian tribe and the federal government which explicitly or implicitly reserved rights for the use of water. The exertion of State power became further complicated with the termination of federal recognition for Californian tribes during the mid-twentieth century and the concurrent increase in the significance of the government of the state of California. Currently there are twenty-four federally recognized Indian tribes with reservation lands in coastal California, all of them in southern California[1]. The themes of water rights, the fundamental basis for water allocation and various specific legal cases are heavily debated nowadays, because of ever increasing demands and the limited availability.

It is not my intent to present coastal California as representative of regions in the Americas that were colonized by the Spanish, or even more broadly, other Europeans. While the region is distinctive, the historic nature of the case study does not diminish its relevancy. Inter-cultural conflict is present today throughout many regions in the Americas and continues to pose thorny issues of equity in water distribution that bring together economics, politics, and culture. As the case study illustrates, defining equitable solutions to water distribution hinges upon cultural norms and on the context of the relationship between cultures. The normative dimensions of water distribution, the values and ideologies that surround the use and very definition of water, are critical to evaluate in any assessment of equity in water distribution.

Note

1   The current Indian reservations, called *rancherias* in coastal California, include: Santa Ynez, Soboba, Ramona, Santa Rosa, Cahuilla, Pechanga, Pala, Pauma, Rincon, La Jolla, Los Coyotes, Santa Ysabel, Mesa Grande, San Pasqual, Inaja-Cosmit, Barona, Capitan Grande, Viejas, Cuyapaipe, Jamul, Sycuan, Manzanita, Campo, and La Posta.

References

Anderson, T.L. 1983. Water Rights: *Scarce Resource Allocation, Bureaucracy, and the Environment.* San Francisco: Pacific Institute for Public Policy Research.

Avina, R. 1976. *Spanish and Mexican Land Grants in California.* New York: Arno Press.

Bean, L. 1972. *Mukat's People: The Cahuilla Indians of Southern California.* Berkeley: University of California Press.

Berry, K.A., 1988. 'Race for Water? American Indians, Eurocentrism and Western Water', In: *Environmental Injustices, Political struggles: Race, Class and the Environment.* Edited by D. Camacho, Duke University Press.

Bishop, A.A. and A.K. Long. 1983. 'Irrigation Water Delivery for Equity between Users' *Journal of Irrigation and Drainage Engineering* 109(4): 349-356.

Black, H.C. 1990. *Black's Law Dictionary,* Sixth Edition. St. Paul: West Publishing Co.

Brown, F.L. and H.M. Ingram. 1987. *Water and Poverty in the Southwest,* Tucson: University of Arizona Press.

Chambers, R. 1981. 'In Search of a Water Revolution: Questions for Canal Irrigation Management in the 1980s' *Water Supply and Management* 5(1): 5-18.

Ebright, M. 1987. 'New Mexican Land Grants: Their Legal Background,' in *Land, Water, and Culture,* edited by C.L. Briggs and J. Van Ness. Albuquerque: University of New Mexico Press.

Hundley, N. 1987. 'California's Original Waterscape: Harmony and Manipulation'. *California History* 66(1):2-11, 69-70.

Hundley, N. 1992. *The Great Thirst: Californians and Water,* 1770s-1990s. Berkeley: University of California Press.

Malki Musuem. 1965. *The Cahuilla Indians of Southern California: Their History and Culture.* Banning: Malki Museum.

Maskey, R.K., Weber, K.E. and R. Loof. 1994. 'Equity Aspects of Irrigation Development: Evidence from Two Systems in the Hills of Nepal'. *Water Resources Development* 10(4): 431-443.

Meyer, M.C. 1984. *Water in the Hispanic Southwest: A Social and Legal History,* 1550-1850. Tucson: University of Arizona Press.

NOAA. 1994. *Climatic Summary for California - 1994.* Washington: National Oceanic Atmospheric Agency.

Ressler, J.Q. 1968. 'Indian and Spanish Water-Control on New Spain's Northwest Frontier' *Journal of the West* 7: 10-17.

Sampath, R.K. 1984. 'Income Distribution Impacts of Irrigation Water Distribution Policy' *Water Resources Research* 20(6): 647-654.

Sampath, R.K. 1991. 'A Rawlsian Evaluation of Irrigation Distribution in India' Water *Resources Bulletin* 27(5): 745-751.

Shipek, F. 1988. Pushed in the Rocks: Southern California Indian Land Tenure. Lincoln: University of Nebraska Press.

Shipek, F. 1996. 'What the Spanish and U.S. Army Saw' Paper presented at the Southern California Environment and History Conference - Southern California Before 1900: Landscape, Climate and Ecology, September 20, 1996, California State University at Northridge.

Tac, P. 1835. *Indian Life and Customs at Mission San Luis Rey.* Old Mission San Luis Rey.

True, D.L. and G. Waugh. 1982. 'Proposed Settlement Shifts during San Luis Rey Times: Northern San Diego County, California' *Journal of California and Great Basin Anthropology* 4(2): 34-54.

Whitten, N.E. Jr. 1981. 'Introduction,' in *Cultural Transformations and Ethnicity in Modern Ecuador,* edited by N.E. Whitten Jr. Urbana: University of Illinois Press.

Wilkinson, C.F. 1990. *Values and Western Water: A History of Dominant Ideas,* Western Water Policy Project Discussion Series Paper No. 1. Boulder: Natural Resources Law Center, University of Colorado.

Williams, R.A. Jr. 1990. *The American Indian in Western Legal Thought: The Discourses of Conquest.* New York: Oxford University Press.

Winpenny, J. 1994. *Managing Water as an Economic Resource.* London: Routledge.

PART V

IRRIGATION IN THE ANDES

ment of nature, democratising access to fundamental resources for production
and the State's obligation to oversee the country's food-supply security. We invite
all the grassroots sectors to join in this project to defend this resource that is fundamental for the very lives of indigenous people, peasants and other social sectors in this country. [...] First it must be used to meet people's basic needs and
help develop the poorest people's economy. That is why we speak of water's social
function [...]

Why is it important to support 'peasant economies'? We peasants are the basis of
the nation's production and development. We have provided most of the food that
is consumed in the countryside and in the city. Therefore, it is necessary to
strengthen the peasant economies, in order to conceive of a future in which basic
needs will be covered. We have to recognise the culture and value of these small-
scale economies [...]
Participation by everyone in conducting those agencies that manage water
resources is a principle of true democracy for our people. Similarly, both water
management and development must be based on the decisions and ways of seeing and acting of grassroots users organizations. [...] We, indigenous communities, peasants and Afro-Ecuadorians, all users, must have control over water
management and distribution, recognising our norms and customs. It is our
responsibility to resolve internal conflicts, according to our own norms, and
decide about the fairest way to distribute, manage and supervise water use.
(Confederation of Indigenous Nationalities of Ecuador, 1996, *Proposed Water
Law*, brochure. CONAIE, Quito).

As we can gather from peasant and indigenous claims, understanding the issues of
equity in Andean rural irrigation calls for a profound analysis, going beyond just the
local system in its current status. It is also necessary to focus on linkages with
broader social structures, the history of these peoples and communities, their culture, their environment and their peasant economy, within the wide variety of
visions, reasons and perceptions characterising the Andes. The following chapters
attempt to outline the framework and background of irrigation in the Andes, placing
peasant irrigation within its historical, social and environmental context.

18

Andean Social Construction of Identity and Political Direction

José Almeida Vinueza

Defining 'Andean' is a complex and difficult task. Apparently, it would be enough to assign such an adjective to places, people and countries touched by the mountain range that crosses the immense South American platform, but it's not so simple: although eight countries of this subcontinent are touched by its 7000-kilometre length, not all are commonly recognised as 'Andean'. In fact, within the international context, only three countries are appreciated as 'typically' Andean: Ecuador, Peru and Bolivia. Within this imagery, the indigenous presence is considered as the fundamental criterion in order to assign them this adjective.

Therefore, the Andean World is often viewed as a 'cultural area' or as a civilisation principle, considered to have reached its highest expression in the Peruvian and Bolivian 'nuclear Andes'. According to most experts on the topic[1], an original mode of human life developed there over an extensive period, along the immense mountain range and its adjacent areas. This local way of life, based on socio-economic principles of reciprocity, redistribution and ecological complementarity, was politically incorporated to and linked by the Inca empire under a common cultural horizon, a societal order coherently integrated in the cosmic vision of the four '*suyos*' (*Tawantinsuyu*). The strength and degree of this civilisation's social imprint are so deep that, in spite of the colonial dismembering of the Inca political axis and the subsequent implementation of New-World republics, various indigenous cultural features are still present in these societies, thus safeguarding a common - although heterogeneous and modified - identity in the descendants of those peoples.

Now the problem is that, coincidentally, these countries are also seen as those of lesser economic and socio-political development. Everyone knows that in the 'Andean subregion' the level of poverty reaches an appalling 70% of their population, the indigenous zones being the most affected. And the causes are evident: plundered since colonial times and exploited by the republicans, indigenous societies of these countries subsist amidst poverty, unemployment, political exclusion and socio-cultural marginalisation. Though so-called modern and democratic, the States that rule their destiny still neglect them. Their existence as peoples is not recognised; rights are not granted to them as such, nor spaces of participation in public life. The only socio-economic duties demanded of them tend to reproduce a mode of national accumulation based on super-exploitation of their work and squandering of their resources.

That is why, from this perspective, the 'Andean world' is seen as poor, degraded Indian people, subjected and inferiorised, a fact that, on the other hand, often is the basis to explain or justify the 'backwardness' or 'under-development' of countries that still have these population groups within their borders. The 'glorious' past of these people, while appreciated in the official vision of the history as a fact worthy of praise, is not reason enough to respect their descendants in contemporary life. They are definitely 'conquered cultures' that one must revere but not follow.[2] The reader will not fail to realise the aftermath of this appraisal: in order to achieve development, the only way out is to 'get rid' of this population and 'de-Indianise' society.

Although this not the place to analyse the true causes of these countries' so-called 'backwardness' or their present socio-economic, political and moral crisis, blaming it on the 'indigenous handicap' is far from a historic aberration. Actually, it is the ideological background of a mode of exploitation that, since colonial times, has continued sustaining much of certain social sectors' income in these countries. The indigenous peasants' productive and labour surplus is tapped by rural and urban economic groups who maintain not only economic but also extra-economic exploitation mechanisms to subject, degrade and devaluate indigenous people as an effective method to make the powerful wealthier. Although this mode is being classified as obsolescent and dysfunctional for the forces currently driving modern economic activity, it continues to be a vector of doubtless influence in the social life of these countries.

Therefore, official insistence on considering backwardness as a result of 'natives' unwillingness to adopt civilisation' is pathetic. In this sense, in the international context, the 'Andean world' is held within an unjust vision that equates under-development with Indianness, with the evident intention of attributing such situation to the supposed 'inferiority' of original peoples, in a definite attempt to ignore their efforts to build dignified life.

But, what then, is the real situation of these scorned, inferiorised societies? What is, at least, the appraisal these peoples have about themselves, and about their traditions and culture? What is the 'Andean world' for their leaders? Is it already over for them? Or, on the contrary, is it still a point of reference for their contemporary doubts and demands?

Doubtlessly, this has given rise to an internal re-birth of what several authors have called the 'Andean utopia'.[3] This has made it necessary to re-define 'Andean' (*Lo Andino*) and, more importantly, to re-direct the identification and political participation processes of indigenous peoples within their national societies.

In the face of the evident crisis of the economically dependent role played by these countries, and the perverse attitude of disciplining and punishing the Indians as if they were to blame for such failure, these peoples have been left with no other option than, paradoxically, to withdraw to their local traditions. There, within a niche of mutual socio-economic collaboration and affirmation of their identity, they are able to survive within systems that despise and exploit them. Now, although this has been more or less a common reaction of subjected peoples, the really novel thing of the Andean peoples is precisely the fitting of their micro-regional aspirations into macro-social imagery deeply rooted in time.

Indeed, forced by present national political contingencies, within an international context in which 'world-wide globalisation' has ironically unleashed an awakening of local identities, indigenous movements in the Andean countries have unearthed an old myth that not only remained in the memory of their people, but that has also been restructured, little by little, with the participation of indigenous and non-indigenous intellectuals. Their programme basis lies in reconstruction of the old order, in the preparation for the advent of the 'Second Tawantinsuyu'.

This 'collective creation of the future'[4] has been produced from a radical and deep criticism of what, from this viewpoint, is the 'Western and Christian civilisation'. Opposed to their dauntless 'individualism' and predatory zeal, the 'communal' spirit and 'cosmogonic' sense of the Andean mind are brought to the fore, which have to result in a way of being and living, deeply sympathising towards fellow men and women and respectful of Nature.[5]

The really important feature of this vision is that it is conceived of not only as an aspiration but as a living reality that has remained present and 'under-cover' since the Inca empire. That empire, as a political system would have been the perfect realisation of the Andean ideal, which fully matches true human nature, something that not even the contemporary 'socialist utopia' has been able to achieve, with all their knowledge and accumulated technology.[6]

Interestingly, for these ideologists of 'Indianity', 'utopia is here and now'.[7] It is only waiting to be acknowledged as the key stone to re-organise society and set up a fairer, reciprocal new order. The mythical backdrop lends a novel nuance to the political perspective of indigenous Andean peoples.

These peoples still clearly remember the Christian myth of the 'three ages', but enriched by the Andean belief in the cyclic return of past times. According to the Christian notion, the succession of ages is linear, beginning with a Golden stage, followed by a Degeneration phase. Next, Christ's first coming, paves the way to future Salvation, in this or in the 'other world', subsequently concretised in Christ's second coming. From the Andean Indians' perspective, this mythical scheme fits into their current traditions and political ambitions: the Incan empire would be the Golden Age, the zenith of solidarity, justice and material and spiritual satisfaction. Upon being destroyed by a *'Pachakutik'* ('revolution', turn) during the Spanish

Conquest, it became a fragmented society, exposed to deprivation, suffering and injustice, a situation that remains until the present time. The survival of certain communal Andean values, however, is the foundation for another *Pachakutik* which is waiting for the re-birth of a 'leader' for Andean liberation.[8]

Therefore, the recovery of Andean societies would lie in 're-Indianisation', not so much a return to a 'pure blood' as the establishment of a 'new Indian identity' (*la indianidad*). In Peru, it was expressed in such a way that

> 'Indians are all people identified with the telluric imperative... those who let themselves be inspired by the socialist, brotherly collectivism of their ancestors, projecting it towards the future destiny of Peru: Social Justice that is not an idealised utopia as in other continents, but rather a historical reality in Peru under the Incas'.[9]

Thus, this set of ideas is a crystal-clear referent towards which the new Andean indigenous organisations drive their contemporary vindications. For them, agrarian struggles led by the Left, especially during the last three decades of the present century, although they have played a historic role in the defence and/or recovery of land as an economic factor, were no more than one phase of a movement that, little by little, is regaining its scope as a Pan-Andean civilisation. This is expressed precisely in the formulation of this thesis that challenges national society and the unitarian, homogenising State format that does not allow either these peoples' particular characteristics or their collective rights, and much less their Andean sense of civilisation.

But, how did these ideas take shape among peoples who feature enormous internal variety, belonging to different countries and relating to their national societies in varying ways?

Certainly, the Andean world's different geographical characteristics have not only their economic repercussions but also impact the political-organisational level. Several authors have segmented the Andean world into at least three subunits: a) the *páramo* Andes; b) the *puna* Andes; and c) the southern Andes.[10] In the first segment, the mountain range begins to gather in the Colombo-Venezuelan plains, and then spreads southward as a narrow chain that, in Ecuador, configures wet, fertile highland valleys; through their water sources on the eastern and western slopes, these readily connect with lowlands in the coast and the Amazon. In the second segment, the mountain range gets considerably wider, in Peru and Bolivia, forming extensive dry massifs and immense mountains and highland plateaux, that configure the classical high altitude world we have become accustomed to envisioning; of course, this authentic 'roof', due to its colossal transversal extension, prevents any immediate contact between lowlands and high areas, and much less any communication between the coast and the Amazon, as in the northern Andes. Lastly, the southern segment, before vanishing into Patagonia, configures in Chile and Argentina a lengthy, narrow rocky barrier that is scarcely populated except in the plains that spread from their eastern and western slopes.

According to Ramón,[11] the first segment favoured the formation of societies open to regional exchange, politically expressed as 'ethnic dominions', which are very flexible in their contact and relationships with their intra- and extra-regional neighbours; the second, by contrast, favoured a centralised imperial system, impelled precisely by their inhabitants' need to master the broad highland expanse by creating huge infrastructural works. Through its expansion, this segment spread to include in its system the northern lands, wealthy in both material and symbolic resources. Despite their ideological and cultural coherence, this union was not fully established, judging from the ensuing dispute between Huáscar and Atahualpa. According to Ramón's interpretation, these historical figures actually expressed two contradictory tendencies within the Tawantinsuyu: the first representing the nuclear centralisation in Cuzco and the second a de-centralising drive, respectful of regional diversity. The Spanish invasion cut off these vectors, supplanting them guidelines that were foreign to these original impulses, with an alien direction which was non-redistributive, vertical, oppressive and intolerant of cultural diversity: the Colonial regime.

Ramón sees these 'historical accumulations' remaining in current Indian people's memories. They continue to guide the differences in contemporary political behaviour. Whereas in Ecuador and Colombia indigenous movements are more open to inter-regional and inter-cultural integration, those of Peru and Bolivia are more prone to rebuild the imperial system, to radically return to native roots.

Although this interesting discussion is intriguing, there is no doubt that continent-wide contact and inter-relationships among indigenous organisations has compelled a re-thinking of radical theses and a search for adaptations to national realities and the international order's characteristics.

In any event, the Inca civilisation referent continues to be welcomed as a central component of the Pan-Andean discourse. However, at the same time, political movements as a whole have opened to the thesis of plurality and respect for diversity, discarding both the restoration of totalitarian centrality and the segmentation of the remainder of national society. They all also clearly see the origin of their situation of exclusion and marginality: lack of access to material conditions for existence. Hence, their attitude of radical, constant demands and protest.

Thereby, the indigenous movements of Ecuador and Colombia, and of Peru and Bolivia, agree about the characterisation and contradictions deriving from their demographic composition, which is multi-cultural and multi-ethnic. The solution lies not only in the defence and recovery of material conditions to favour their lives, but also the right to enjoy and manage them according to their ancestral values and aspirations as contemporary citizens with different cultural profiles. Their goal is not in any sense a self-segregation or a separation from their respective national societies. Rather, they hope to design and realise a broadly democratic, participatory, inter-cultural national regimen that will respect differences.

Summing up, in this indigenous Andean movement and its political project, the idea of gathering around the 'Andean' concept shines through, both as a need to do this beyond regional varieties and domestic discrepancies, and as a need to build a Pan-Andean nation's identity to withstand the official culture's homogenisation that basically denies their existence as peoples. So, the goal would be to construct a socio-political system that will welcome the social and cultural plurality of civil society within a pluralistic, de-centralised State format, where the procedures adopted by each administrative level are based on both local traditions and internationally-accepted general principles that govern the entire national society.

This view questions the unitarian State because the latter does not have or create institutional openings for civil society's dynamic socio-cultural diversity. The maturing of political movements founded on the basis of socio-cultural diversity makes it mandatory to re-design the State, to adopt an adequate policy of multi-cultural recognition. The approach of unilateral economic integration, vertical political-administrative centralisation and cultural homogenisation can no longer be defended. It is necessary to open the Andean countries to national heterogeneity, decentralisation and interculturality.[12]

After all, this is the goal of current Andean indigenous movements and this is the teaching they leave for their fellow countrymen and women. While struggling for their resources and rights as peoples, they have driven us to re-think our countries as referents of identity and shared destiny, where there is room to respect people with different features of culture and personality.

Notes

1   See Espinosa Soriano, Waldemar (Comp.). *Los Modos de Producción en el Imperio de los Incas*, Amaru Editores, Lima, 1981.
2   This connotation summarised ingeniously in a recent Lima graffiti: 'Incas yes, Indians no!' (Pedro Roel, personal communication).
3   See Flores Galindo, Alberto. *Buscando un Inca: Identidad y Utopía en los Andes*, Casa de las Américas, La Habana, 1986.
4   See Mires, Fernando. *El Discurso de la Indianidad. La Cuestión Indígena en América Latina*, Editorial DEI, Costa Rica, 1991, p. 81.
5   See Sarkisyanz, Manuel. *Temblor en los Andes. Profetas del Resurgimiento Indio en el Perú*, Abya-Yala, Quito, 1992.
6   The most elaborate expression of this can be found in Wankar. *Tawantinsuyu. Cinco Siglos de Guerra Queshuaymara contra España*, Editorial Nueva Imagen, Mexico City, 1981.
7   It is important to distinguish between 'indianism' and mere 'indigenism'. While the latter is represented by non-native intellectuals, the first is a political thought by members of their own people, even if they have had to adopt several elements developed by the latter. See Bonfil Batalla, Guillermo (Comp.). *Utopía y Revolución. El Pensamiento Político Contemporáneo de los Indios en América Latina*, Editorial Nueva Imagen, México City, 1981.
8   This aspect, in its turn, is fed by the Andean myth of the *Inkarri*: during the Conquest, the Spaniards cut the Inca's body into pieces and buried them in different sites. This way they symbolised the destruction of the Incario. But, when the Inca will be re-integrated, a new and final return of the Tawantinsuyu will take place. Several parts have already been gathered, only the

head is missing. Following the analogy, Indians' thinking would be in its climax and the re-birth of the power of the *queshuaymaras* is imminent. On the *inkarri* myth, see ARGUEDAS, José María. *Formación de una Cultura Nacional Indoamericana*, Siglo XXI Editores, Mexico City, 1977.

9   Sivirichi, Atilio. cited by Sarkisyanz, Manuel. *Temblor en los Andes. Profetas del Resurgimiento Indio en el Perú*, Abya-Yala, Quito, 1992. p. 242.

10 See Dollfus, Olivier. *El Reto del Espacio Andino*, IEP, Lima, 1981.

11 See Ramon, Galo. *El Regreso de los Runas. La Potencialidad del Proyecto Indio en el Ecuador*, Comunidec, Quito, 1993.

12 See Taylor, Charles. *El Muticulturalismo y 'la política del Reconocimiento'*, FCE, Mexico City, 1993

19

Andean Irrigation in History

Jeanette E. Sherbondy

With the aid of irrigation technology, the ancient Andean peoples transformed the arid desert and semi-arid highlands of the Andes into fertile croplands[1]. Both eco-zones depended primarily on waters originating in the highlands and therefore these irrigation systems operated on the same agricultural calendar. Artificial irrigation on the coast enabled acreage to be extended beyond the natural floodplains of the rivers and, in the highlands, for the agricultural season to begin a few months earlier, rather than waiting for the short, irregular rainy season.

Irrigation is old in the Andes, almost as old as agriculture itself. The ancient peoples developed many varied techniques for irrigation. Most of these techniques were based on gravity-fed systems that brought water to crops, with the exception of two techniques that brought the fields to the sources of water: (1) the coastal terraces 'irrigated by fog' that were watered by cloud banks that rested on the terraces during the winter months (May-November) and (2) the 'excavated fields' that were dug down to the water table. However, most Andean irrigation systems, were networks constructed of canals and ditches with dams and reservoirs, or were mazes of ridged fields.

The greatest extent of irrigated land in the Andes was achieved during the Middle Horizon, about 1000 years ago. Maize (*Zea mays*) cultivation was the catalyst for creating extensive irrigation systems and for constructing agricultural terraces to take the best advantage of irrigation water. These large networks are more than tech-nological adaptations to geographical environments. They are also social systems that built and maintained them and that continue to use them. These systems are so fundamental to Andean agriculture that they have been the focus of cultural values and symbolisms that express the core of beliefs about life itself in the Andes.

Irrigation in the Andes is basically a communal matter, even though very large irri-gation systems certainly existed. Some interconnected several coastal valleys, but even they were composed of many smaller community-size systems, used and regu-lated by the local communities with overall coordination. A good example is the north coast of Peru, which in the Middle Horizon had large networks of many reser-voirs with canals that corresponded to local community-sized areas. These systems efficiently irrigated the same area now serviced by a recently constructed system dependent on one large reservoir. Inca Cuzco is another example of irrigation organized on a large scale. The subdivisions of this large city were communities that functioned as irrigation districts, organized the recruitment of group labor, and fulfilled their obligations to ritual maintenance of the state calendar. Presently throughout the Andes, large-scale communal work is always broken down into sections and assigned to local communal groups wherever communities control their communal lives.

These local communities are *ayllus*. This term includes a sense of kinship, of sharing common ancestors, and of originating from the same local water sources. It is the unit that gives an Andean individual his/her primary ethnic identity. The *ayllu* is a spiritual community that shares rituals and traditions (Salomon 1991). It is an economic unit that cultivates its own crops, raises its own herds and is fundamentally self-sufficient for its basic needs. It shares work obligations and redistributes a surplus among its constituent families according to an ideology of reciprocity (*ayni*). It also is a legal unit that owns its lands and waters. In brief, the *ayllu* is a microcosmos. The center of the universe is located in its midst and its life revolves around that center.

An Andean community views the world from its center, *chaupi*, where the vertical and horizontal axes of its cosmos meet. This was dramatically expressed in large population centers, such as Inca Cuzco where the water sources were especially marked with carved stones as the basis for a map (the *ceque* system) of the entire valley that organized the relationships of all lands, waters, and peoples to the Inca Emperor. Essential to this spatial organization of resources was the relationship of water sources to the center (*chaupi*). This organizational principle was the basis for how small communities as well as large population centers thought about themselves and their space. Each Andean community maintained a mental map of the water sources that were vital to them in which imaginary lines (*ceque*) connect them to their *chaupi*. Rituals that involved offerings and pilgrimages marked and commemorated these water sources keeping them ever-present in the minds of the community. As a result, the spatial extent of this ritual 'map' defined the community's sphere of social, economic, and political interaction.

This map often had another function as well, the internal distribution of the *ayllu*'s rights to waters and lands. Large socio-political units in the pre-hispanic Andes incorporated many communities or *ayllus*, but they also imitated the *ayllu* in form and in ideology. The imperial city of Cuzco, for example, was not only an organization of *ayllu* and *panaca* (royal Inca *ayllu*), but thought of itself as being one gigantic *ayllu*. Officially the Inca state presented itself as if it were a most benevolent, just, reciprocal community, although in reality it was a large redistributive state.

Although there is and was a good deal of cultural variety in the Andes, there are some common concepts about the cosmos, the *ayllu*, and water that were widespread and have persisted. These concepts are often at the heart of conflicts with national cultures, based on European (or Western) ideas and beliefs. The Andean cosmos is a finite, enclosed, curved universe in which waters circulate under, around and through the earth (Earls and Silverblatt 1979). It is not a universe of infinite possibilities for exploitation and expansion. Horizontal space is based on the four cardinal directions as measured by the movement of the sun and vertical space is distributed along a central axis that distinguishes above from below. The point at which these dimensions intersect is the center, *chaupi*, which is the point of view of all Andean communities. It is the viewpoint for contemplating the universe's hydrology because they can observe a continuously curved horizon. Waters flow down on all sides and disappear in a cosmic sea. The sun appears and disappears from the horizon in regularly recurring cycles.

Waters flow up from the within the earth to replenish those that flow out and away. These are the community's water sources, the springs, lakes, and rivers that feed their irrigation systems. These waters come from the sea that surrounds and underlies the earth and penetrates the earth. Waters flow over the surface of the earth down to this sea and then they rise again and circulate throughout the interior of the earth to reappear at openings in the earth. For Andean peoples then, 'down' also implies 'within'. Waters within the earth flow up to the surface where they provide water for their crops. A hydrological balance in the cosmos is also achieved by the constellation of the Llama within the celestial river, *Mayu* (the Milky Way), and the rainbow, because both regularly suck up the lower waters of the primordial sea to form the clouds in the skies from which water as rain returns to the earth (Zuidema and Urton 1978, Urton 1981).

Water is the most important element of the Andean cosmos. It is the dynamic principle that explains movement, circulation and the forces for change. Water is considered the essence of life itself. As one campesino says, '*Manan unu kaqtinqa manaya kawsay kanmanchu*' (If there were no water there would be no life). This ideology is the background for understanding the logic of Andean thought about the origins of peoples and communities and their rights and obligations.

The original ancestors of Andean farming peoples were created in water, as were the major bodies of the cosmos: the sun, the moon, the stars and the earth itself. For the Incas (and probably for the Tiahuanaco peoples before them), all peoples were created in Lake Titicaca where the deity Viracocha endowed them with the symbols of their ethnicity: their own language, their distinct hair style, and the particular textile designs for their clothing. The deity Viracocha submerged these created ancestors in the Lake and sent them along underground rivers to the points where they emerged to the surface of the Earth. These interior rivers were, and are, conceptualized as the blood veins of Mama Pacha, Mother Earth. Throughout the Andes other large high lakes were the origins of other communities, and on the coast the Sea played a similar role in coastal peoples' ideologies.

The ancestors emerged at points where there were springs, lake, rivers, caves, mountains or large trees. All of these features were considered sources of water and points of communication with the interior waterways of the earth. Springs, lakes, and rivers are obviously sources of water, but mountains, caves, and trees are also considered sources. Mountains have snowcaps that form streams and rivers, but there are also many mountains that are considered water sources that show no empirical evidence of being water sources. It is a widespread belief that large subterranean lakes lie under mountains and that these lakes are the sources of waters that flow from the general direction of these mountains. A large mountain is revered as a powerful lord, *apu*, who can control the supply of water. Caves are also considered sources, whether they be wet or dry, because these openings in the earth are places where communities can plead with the Earth to send forth water for the community. The dead (ancestors) are often buried in caves where they too can intercede with the Earth. Very large trees depend for their growth on water sources and so are rare in semi-arid environments. Some trees may owe their extraordinary growth to their location beside canals. Initially, these trees may have been cultivated and irrigated (Sherbondy 1986). As *mallqui* they are considered to be ancestors also. It is essential to an understanding of Andean cultures to realize that all of these places where peoples first saw the light of the Sun on Earth (*pacarina*), the lakes, springs, lakes, caves, mountains, and trees, were also sources of water. For these intertwined reasons, they are sacred to each community.

The rights of a community to those waters are based on the knowledge that their ancestors had emerged from them and that they hold them and the land that they irrigate as a kind of sacred trust for their use as long as they fulfill their obligations to them (Spalding 1984). This is *ayni*, or reciprocity, the dynamic force of all social and cosmic life in the Andes. Community after community recounts their mythohistories of how their original ancestors established claims to the lands and waters of that geographical site for the use of their descendants and heirs. Rights to specific canals were based on this original principle and on the claim that they, the community, built the canals, maintain them, and perform the rituals for their care. This fundamental concept continues to define water rights throughout the Andes.

A conflict between communal Andean and national legal concepts can be seen when a canal is constructed with government hired labor. A national government agency tends to expect a local community to take over responsibility for the canal, but the expectations of the community are the opposite: they expect the government to maintain it. The reasoning of the community is based on the bundle of rights and obligations of whoever builds irrigation systems. If the members of the community as a community build it and use it, they are obliged to maintain it; but if a government builds it with contract labor, then it is assumed that the government should continue to provide the labor for its maintenance.

Family rights to water for irrigation are contingent upon performing one's duties to the community in general and to maintenance of irrigation canals and reservoirs in particular. Failure to help with the communal cleaning of canals may entail punishment of uncooperative campesinos by giving them water last or by imposing a fine. A community is unwilling to completely deny water to the fields of the delinquent farmer because of a sense that the water basically belongs to the Earth, not to human beings. 'There is no reason to punish Mother Earth for the failings of the human beings,' was the way one campesino expressed his community's philosophy.

This relationship of *ayni* to water is personal and social, as one living being to another, but with the consciousness that human beings depend for their lives on the waters and the Earth. People think of water as the blood of Mother Earth, who sustains them. Subterranean rivers are conceptualized as blood veins; surface rivers may be associated with another vital fluid, semen. Rain is considered tears from the Sky. All of these metaphors, blood, semen and tears, demonstrate how much water is a vital part of the cosmological body. This way of thinking about water resources conflicts with the concept of water as a commodity in a mercantile or capitalist economy. The buying and selling of water provokes a profound contradiction, one that has disrupted Andean communities from the Spanish colonial period until the present. Current initiatives to privatize water will undoubtedly exacerbate this conflict between thinking of water as a vital fluid of the living body of the cosmos and thinking of it as an economic resource to be exploited rationally.

Note

1   Most of the ideas in this article are syntheses of earlier work, in particular Sherbondy 1982b and 1987. The region described refers specifically to the Andes in Peru.

References

Earls, John & Irene Silverblatt, 1978. 'La realidad física y social en la cosmología andina', *Actes du XLII Congrès International des Américanistes*, Paris, 1976, 4, 299-325.
Salomon, Frank, 1991. 'Introductory Essay: The Huarochirí Manuscript', *The Huarochirí Manuscript: A Testament of Ancient and Colonial Andean Religion*. Austin: University of Texas Press.
Sherbondy, Jeanette E., 1982a. 'El regadío, los lagos y los mitos de origen', *Allpanchis* 20:3-32.
~ 1982b. *The Canal Systems of Hanan Cuzco*. Ph.D. thesis, University of Illinois. Ann Arbor: University Microfilms International # 8218563.
~ 1986. *Mallki: Ancestros y cultivo de árboles en los Andes*. Lima: Proyecto FAO- Holanda/INFOR GCP/PER/027/NET Apoyo a las plantaciones forestales con fines energéticos y para el desarrollo de comunidades rurales de la Sierra Peruana, Documento de trabajo, 5.
~ 1987. 'Organización hidráulica y poder en el Cuzco de los Incas', *Revista Española de Antropología Americana* 17: 117-153.
~ 1995. 'El agua: Ideología y poder de los incas', in: *El Agua. Mitos, ritos y realidades*, ed. José A. González Alcantud and Antonio Malpica Cuello, Barcelona Diputación Provincial de Granada, Centro de Investigaciones Etnológicas Angel Ganivet, y Anthropos, Editorial del Hombre, 87-102.
Spalding Karen, 1984. *Huarochirí: An Andean Society Under Inca and Spanish Rule*. Stanford: Stanford University Press.
Urton, Gary, 1981. *At the Crossroads of the Earth and the Sky*. Austin: University of Texas Press.
Zuidema, R. Tom, and Gary Urton, 1978. 'La constelación de la llama en los Andes peruanos', *Allpanchis* 9: 59-119.

20

Irrigation in the Andean Environment

Linden Vincent

The Andes as a distinctive region of irrigation analysis

The Andes is one of the most important mountain chains in the world, and has an enormous diversity of agro-ecological zones within its borders. The Andean cordillera stretches from eastern Venezuela to Tierra del Fuego in the far south of Chile and is rarely less than 300 kilometres wide over a length of over 7000 kilometres. Much of the range is over 3000 metres in height and towers to over 6000-metre peaks in Ecuador, Peru, Bolivia and northern Chile. The countries of the region also have diverse histories. The Andean region not only has institutions, irrigation canals and terraces dating from Pre-Columbian times. It also has countries which have experimented with varying degrees of land reform, leaving some regions with a complex agrarian structure which can retain antagonistic and competing elements within it.

Why then is the Andean region seen as such a distinctive and specialised region? One primary reason is a considerable unity of culture and society, embodying powerful concepts of community, despite a history of conquest and colonialism. It is the interplay of past and present in land and water rights, and the evolution of social networks, which is also a distinctive dimension of Andean political economy in general, and irrigation in particular. Tradition can be a tool for very opportunistic change as well as a means for communities to defend themselves. Agrarian reforms may have shattered old social relations, but these communities have nevertheless evolved as significant political entities in the local administration of most Andean countries. Communities have used the strength of their social networks both to retain their rights and to gain new opportunities, depending on the political and economic conditions they face. Despite multiple colonisations, much Andean culture also retains a special affiliation between people and their environment, giving special social and ritual dimensions to water use and land use practices.

Secondly, the montane environment gives both specific challenges and opportunities to Andean farmers, who have shown immense skill in both innovation and adaptation of technologies to gain livelihoods in often difficult environments. Jodha (1991) emphasised the need to understand the diverse *specificities* of mountain locations, to understand production options and appropriate technical interventions. To understand the agricultural production systems and the process of technological change in the Andes, one needs to use a broad definition of technology which includes not only material objects but also the organisations, institutions and skills in their operation and use. Social networks frequently underpin the technical adaptation of Andean agriculture - and this is especially true in irrigation.

Systems of Andean irrigation reflect these sociotechnical characteristics of general Andean livelihood strategies. Thus the analysis of Andean irrigation requires not only an understanding of the diversity of irrigation environments. It also requires understanding of the power of social networks to act in order to defend or expand their resources, and their adaptive and innovative capacity in an environment which is complex, diverse and risk-prone. Thus no study of Andean irrigation can take place without a review of the environmental diversity and technological adaptation it is embedded within. This chapter therefore sets out to summarise some key aspects of the agro-ecology of Andean irrigation. Several detailed studies of Andean irrigation already exist for specific countries in the region (Mitchell and Guillet, 1994; Ruf et al, 1991; Tecnología Intermedia, 1990). A number of books are also available on engineering issues in hill irrigation (Yoder, 1995; Jacobs, 1995). However, this chapter provides a brief summary of engineering challenges and their social dimensions, as a background for the contexts of struggle discussed in this book. It also introduces a typology of irrigation systems to help portray the diversity of systems and their operational and management needs, within which equity must be negotiated or fought for.

Irrigation also merits special attention in the Andean region because of its strategic importance to the production systems of different agro-ecological zones. As Guillet and Mitchell (1994) point out, irrigation water is vital in highland and high altitudes, despite seasonal climates which often bring heavy rain at certain times of the year. Irrigation is not simply used to supply deficits in crop water requirements. It is also used to provide frost protection, and to assist in crop scheduling so that farmers avoid periods of adverse weather. Irrigation is thus a major area of economic activity often used explicitly to reaffirm or test social relations. It is also an arena of struggle for economic survival. Peasants' equity concerns frequently underpin the communal water management arrangements of irrigation (Gelles, 1994; Cornick, 1983). Nevertheless, these criteria of equity are nearly always under threat from external or internal social dynamics. It is the study of these social relationships in irrigation and struggles for water which underpin most of this book.

Key aspects of adaptation in Andean irrigated agriculture and irrigation technology can be understood from definitions of mountain environments. Messerli (1983) defines a mountain region as a land mass experiencing an altitudinal range sufficient to cause vertical differentiation in climate, and thus in vegetation and farming options. This vertical diversity, or vertical zonation as it is sometimes called in bio-geography, is often incorporated into Andean farming systems. Indeed, adaptation to time and space is a key distinctive feature of Andean farming systems, and the irrigated agriculture within it. Andean agricultural practices not only reflect the physical environment but also institutional arrangements necessary to enable use of the environment. The two should not be separated, especially in irrigation.

The incidence of steep slopes and dissected terrain are also recognised as characteristic of many mountain regions, although mountain regions also incorporate plateaux, basins and wide river valleys. These provide engineering challenges to develop canals and fields, and shape the incidence and nature of collective action in irrigation. However, in Andean irrigation, most older community schemes do not have complex engineering works. As elsewhere in the world, farmers work with the environment and avoid high-risk locations requiring extensive maintenance. However, the shortage of good water resources in some regions, as well as the difficulties in tapping streams and conveying water across slopes, will restrict the volume of water that can be transported. Thus water will be limited even before any incidence of drought or hydrological change affects water supply. Thus the critical influence of the Andean environment on irrigation management is that of water scarcity, as stressed by Mitchell and Guillet (1994). This issue of scarcity and competition for water is common across Andean irrigation, and helps to explain why the issue of equity can be studied as an overall concern within the equally distinct field of 'Andean irrigation'.

The nature of engineering and maintenance challenges faced in farmer-constructed systems also shapes the nature of irrigation management institutions, but they do not have the same prominence as in hill irrigation in other regions such as Nepal, Pakistan or Indonesia. Instead, it is the indigenous technological solutions in local land and water management which are more distinctive. This is especially true for hillside-field level water management, in the forms of terracing and field canals, raised beds and special slope cultivation practices which are more easily controlled by farmers. These field-level adaptations should be seen as part of preferred techniques of production and not simply as methods of soil conservation (although they do stabilise slopes). They can and do change both as production choices change and as the labour environment and institutional management environment change (Guillet, 1987, 1991). Some locally distinct hydraulic structures may also be found in conveyance and division structures.

Terrain, climate and hydrology of Andean watersheds

Three macro divisions of Andean physiography can be distinguished in which irrigated land is developed:
- high altitude plateaux and basins, notably the Altiplano;
- highland slopes found on valley sides;
- valley bottom lands.

However, these terrain units sit within very distinctive types of watersheds across which water must be allocated or regulated. The Andean mountain range is dissected by deep valleys resulting from both earth movements and river erosion, which broaden into substantial areas of terrain at middle altitudes. The terrain of these major river valleys are referred to as '*intervalles*' or inter-Andean valleys in Bolivia and Peru. These river systems of these larger-scale valleys often cross tremendous altitude range as well as distance. However, a general scarcity of water has given rise to immense social dependencies in the sharing of water between communities along river valleys as well as within communities. The struggle for equity is frequently reflected in struggles between irrigation communities to obtain and retain water rights, as well as within communities (Bolin, 1990). Also there are many irrigation systems for which water is mobilised from multiple sources, including points outside the local natural watershed. It is often very difficult to model the water balance of such systems. There may also be major struggles over access to water sources where the terrain of the water source is no longer under the control of a particular irrigation community. So the study of social action in Andean irrigation must integrate perspectives on water transfer at local-system and watershed-system level.

Streams and rivers form the main sources for Andean irrigation. However, the complex terrain and geology also creates groundwater sources for irrigation, either as springs, or as aquifers that can be tapped by wells. Sometimes water may be derived directly from glacial meltwater. The type of source, as well as the location of the source, may shape the nature of water rights and water use practices.

Rainfall is not the only element of latitudinal variation across the Andes. The nature of temperature variation - whether diurnal or seasonal - is also a critical influence on irrigated production. Cold night temperatures in the tropical regions of the Andes (Peru, Ecuador) are primarily linked to radiative cooling and not to the movement of cold air-masses. This cooling can induce temporary drought and the wilting of plants, as well as cold-air damage. Farmers have utilised irrigation to overcome these effects (Morlon, 1979).

There is a very strong diurnal temperature regime in the higher altitudes of the central Andes, whereas the southern Andes can have a very marked seasonal temperature regime together with a diurnal range at certain times of the year. In the central Andes, night frost seldom occurs at elevations below 2500 metres, whereas at 4000 metres at least 80 per cent of nights will have frost. Thus although micro-climates create local variations, 4000 metres is an approximate upper limit for most cultivated crops, although some grasses, tubers (e.g. oca, mashira, ollucos) and chenopods (e.g. quinoa, kanina) survive at higher altitudes.

In the central Andes, permanent settlement is possible at much higher altitudes (sometimes directly below the snow line) close to high pasture areas, although settlements at lower altitudes may also practise transhumance to use these pastures. This means that irrigable lands may also be closer to water sources, so that long conveyance canals in farmer-constructed systems are less common than in other mountain regions. However, the incidence of frost and cold night temperatures at high altitudes requires specially adapted crops and animals, and can make food storage difficult (which is why drying of foods is practised). This is quite different from parts of the southern Andes, where much attention is directed to storage for surviving the winter season.

In the central Andes, it is the incidence of cold night temperatures, in locations which otherwise have adequate sunshine and moisture, which have the biggest influence on crop options and thus irrigation. Crop planning depends on the interplay of sunshine, water and temperature, and irrigation plays a role in cold reduction and not only moisture provision. Crops in general may be rated both for general cold tolerance and for their ability to recover after low temperatures and frost. Barley is the best known commodity crop that has cold tolerance, although some wheats are also useful. Many tuber crops have good cold tolerance. Generally, the higher the altitude, the more self-consumption crops are grown. The lower, warmer areas are usually more incorporated into a market system.

The wide variation in climate gives a wide variation in the altitudes at which irrigation is found. Unfortunately, this brings some confusion in the use of terms like 'high altitude' and 'highland', and these need local interpretation. A height of 2500 metres is taken as the general start of high altitude conditions, where oxygen levels decline and create physiological difficulties (*hypoxia*) for visitors without acclimatisation. Although there is very considerable local adaptation to altitude, most humans suffer difficulties beyond heights of 4500 metres. Altitudes of 1500 or 1000 metres have been used respectively to differentiate highland areas at tropical and sub-tropical latitudes. In the tropical latitudes of the Andes, these higher elevations often have more favourable rainfall and insolation conditions, as in the highlands of Peru. In the southern Andes, highlands climates are more adverse.

Irrigation, crop production and Andean agro-ecosystems

Winterhalder (1993) specified four ways in which irrigation changes the climate for agriculture:
- *Timing*, to extend the rainy season and allow early planting to avoid adverse conditions at harvest. This is especially important for production of the subsistence maize crop in many parts of the central Andes;
- *Quantity*, to augment overall precipitation, and thus allow experimentation with different crops;
- *Predictability* of rainfall and temperature conditions. Irrigation may reduce drought risks, when special allocation arrangements may also come into force (Cornick, 1983). Irrigation can also be used on short notice to mitigate sudden night frosts or low temperatures;
- *Quality*, to improve the combinations of soil temperature and water supply at times when sunshine and air temperature are good for crop production.

However, although irrigation is regarded as a strategic resource, irrigated crops may only be grown in one season of the year in many locations. Mixed farming, integrating irrigated and rainfed cropping are prominent across the Andes. At higher altitudes, livestock are an important part of farming systems, and indeed irrigation may be used to support livestock and dairying as well as subsistence or commodity crops. The balance of rain and cold across the year may also make rainfed cropping a feasible option in many locations. Finally, the restricted production options of higher altitudes in combination with a process of deteriorating exchange conditions drive many farmers into multiple livelihood strategies, including seasonal and long-term migration to industrial or agricultural work elsewhere. Thus irrigated agriculture is again only part of a set of dynamic livelihood strategies where periods of off-farm employment are common. The land and water rights of absent migrant farmers often come into play in equity concerns. Perennial crops (such as fruit trees in the highland valleys) are also favoured in what is often a labour-scarce environment, and where reciprocal labour relations between altitudes may be present. Farmers value the development of irrigation sources, but they may not be that interested in mono-cropping strategies which feature so prominently in conventional irrigation development. The complex histories of land development and land reform have also created very strong dualisms in agriculture, where large landowners and even multinationals co-exist alongside groups of small 'peasant' farmers and ethnic Indian groups. This social differentiation is often reflected in very different cropping strategies for irrigation, and helps to fuel many struggles over access to water. These differential historical claims on water rights, and different interests in crop choices bring special challenges in water development and irrigation design in the region.

One distinctive dimension of the central Andes in particular is a range of agro-ecological zones both in a cross-section of a valley and along a valley. Murra (1975) debated the influence of this zonation on the evolution of farming systems. He identified three forms of vertical control in land use in the Peruvian Andes. The first is the *compact model* typical of small valleys with different agro-ecological environments within short distances, over which local communities had overall contiguous control. The second is the *archipelago model* where particular groups used a dispersed range of lands at various altitudes, utilised and controlled through various social relations. The third is the *extended model* found along the major Andean river valleys. In this model, populations unable to survive on localised subsistence production instead evolved local specialisation and extensive organised trading and exchange of goods (and migratory labour).

Economic change in the Andean region has broken up many of these farming patterns, although vestiges of them survive. However, the historical legacy can also be seen in patterns of land use and water use. These affect irrigation development in various ways. Irrigation may now be promoted as a new means of agricultural production for communities forced to survive in a smaller number of agro-ecological zones, or which have lost older trading ties. Thus, it is important to understand how water sources can be allocated to lands at different altitudes, where irrigated crop options may now be quite different, as old institutions for land management and production have declined (Gelles, 1993; Mayer, 1979).

Engineering challenges in Andean irrigation design and their social dimensions

Irrigation design challenges can be summarised in relation to three macro divisions of Andean physiography already mentioned: the high altitude plateaux and basins, notably the Altiplano; the highland slopes found on valley sides; and the valley bottom lands.

Key differences in engineering challenges between the three lie in the severity and complexity of hydraulic gradients to be incorporated in canal design, the need for special structures designs for gully crossings or unstable hill sections, and the need for special field layout and irrigation practices. These are greatest in the systems on the highland slopes, and least in the high altitude plateaux: however the high altitude plateaux face challenges in climatic adaptation and specialised cultivation practices. Complex hydraulic structures are usually confined to systems developed under external intervention where engineering cadres are present - as in both old Inca canals and modern agency designs.

There are naturally great variations in the hydrological characteristics of specific Andean rivers. However, most are characterised by a high seasonal fluctuation, very high flows at certain times of the year and high sediment loads. Thus construction of headworks and management of siltation are common problems for Andean irrigation systems. Most systems developed by farmers build offtakes that are designed to fail at high flows, so minimal damage occurs. Equally, it is easier to de-silt canals periodically than to design functional silt traps in river off-takes.

Systems developed by farmers are kept as simple as possible, and much of their maintenance work can be concentrated into short spells of time. These conditions help underpin the community festivals and special religious days when irrigation maintenance is done. Reconstruction of headworks, cleaning of canals and minor local repair can often be done in a few days. The ease with which such activities can be undertaken both allows a community to maintain its responsibilities and reinforces the identity which farmers have with their community and their system. It also helps to reinforce the concepts of hydraulic property prominent in Andean systems, where water rights are gained through the investments in construction and maintenance of systems.

The special slope-cultivation techniques found in the Andes can be seen as a response by farmers to their agricultural advantages, and not simply to conservation needs. Cultivation can take place on slopes without terraces, but terracing increases soil depths and assists moisture control. Both terracing and raised beds have important influences on micro-climate, helping to protect against radiative cooling and provide drainage. In wetter climates, block terraces are built with good internal drainage to maintain sub-surface soil stability as well as reduce surface runoff.

While irrigation in sloping terrain is usually linked with level terraces, this is not true everywhere. In Bolivia, Peru and Ecuador, zig-zag furrows around raised beds lying on the contour are found crossing lower gradients. The *prodero* system is used in Peru to irrigate steeper slopes without terracing with diagonal canals taken across slopes to irrigate plots of alfalfa or filed crops. Within fields, small basins may also be excavated, with small amounts of water moved across the plot in a zig-zag fashion. However, sprinklers are now increasingly used for irrigation of sloping lands. Rugged terrain can also yield water-logged and wetland sites. Specialised raised beds are used in such locations to provide drainage and temperature protection.

Bench terraces for rainfed crops are found on slopes as steep as 60 per cent, but most irrigation will be on terraces with slopes under 35 degrees. Nevertheless, locations with irrigated terraces on steeper slopes are found in Peru. The construction and maintenance of terraces also promote conditions of reciprocal labour exchange. Estimates from Peru suggest that the rebuilding of stone-walled terraces requires 1200-1400 labour days per hectare. Stone-walled terraces are difficult and expensive to build and usually have internal drainage systems.

There are several typologies in use for differentiating types of irrigation systems and their design and management challenges, which have different utility for studying Andean irrigation. The most common classification is based on hydraulic and engineering characteristics, with primary divisions distinguishing *lift, gravity, diversion or water harvesting* systems. Systems can also be described in relation to the presence of division structures, and the ordering of networks or branches of canals. This tells the reader about the kind of structures in place, the level of control possible over water delivery and the kind of managerial needs to operate a system. However, it does not tell the reader that much about the nature of institutions present and the risks to equity of access for irrigators. It also gives very little scope for the study of indigenous technologies in irrigation, which frequently defy conventional Western engineering ideals (Sengupta, 1993).

Another classification of hill irrigation systems is based on water source and mobilisation technology (Vincent 1995). This eight-fold division is the one used here to review the main types of Andean irrigation systems, and discuss the management challenges within which struggles for equity can emerge.

Offtake systems divert flows from water sources over sustained periods of time. While water is usually diverted from rivers, some systems may take water from springs, lakes or glacial meltwater. In a study in Sumatra, Indonesia, Ambler (1989) developed a four-fold classification of systems based on technical ease/difficulty of water conveyance, and adequacy/scarcity of water supply. As scarcity conditions increase, irrigation management will evolve more rules for access to water, controls over markets and auctions of water, and may involve the presence of a water guard to ensure irrigators get water allocations at times of great competition. These management tasks figure prominently in many Andean systems, and their failure often precedes equity struggles over water. Vincent (1995) also distinguished between *river-valley offtakes* and *slope offtakes*. The former has the entire irrigated area in the same valley in which the river flows and involve fewer engineering challenges in canal design, although the headworks may operate in difficult river regimes with high sediment. Slope offtakes take water from streams to springs across hillsides to land some distance away on montane benches, on footslopes or even different valleys. These often tap streams with smaller flows, but face many more challenges in water conveyance, including unstable slopes, long canal distances and problematic changes in hydraulic gradient along the canal. In these conditions, farmers may walk their canals regularly to check their stability, and have special arrangements for emergency repairs. Scarcity of water is more common in such systems, where local demand may be much greater than the volume that can be transferred.

Underground canal systems tap groundwater through gently sloping horizontal canals. These are commonly located in foothill zones. Some pre-Colombian systems can be found in Peru.

Spate systems make use of occasional flood flows in ephemeral streams, and only operate intermittently at certain times of the year. They may be found in Bolivia and northern Chile. Spate systems have quite distinctive technical, institutional and operational challenges. Since water is only available intermittently, it cannot be applied in a pre-ordained schedule, nor is water automatically available to maximise yields. Construction and maintenance are challenging since structures have to cope with high flows and heavy sediments. Uncertainty of supply makes it difficult to define a reliable area for irrigation, and it can be challenging to link rights and duties effectively. Water rights can also be extremely complex, both within a community and along a valley. Systems which have evolved locally often work well, but they are extremely difficult to improve by external intervention.

Collection systems store flows from springs into small cisterns which are emptied at regular intervals (commonly daily). They are usually small in scale and have minimal operational requirements. However, institutional arrangements for water use may be complex. They may be found in Peru and Ecuador. Excavation of a spring to improve supplies is a risky enterprise, and typical improvements involve lining of cisterns and canals, or enlargement of the cistern.

Storage systems rely on water which is stored seasonally or annually behind a dam. In the Andes, storage systems are found most prominently in foothill zones or highland valleys in Ecuador, Peru, Chile and Bolivia. In the Cochabamba region of

Bolivia, special high altitude storage dams play an important roles in *combination systems* developed by communities. Construction of a dam requires major mobilisation of resources, and contribution to construction works often helps to shape subsequent water rights. However, once constructed, institutional, technical and production activities must be shaped against the known volume of water in the tank. Competition for water is often endemic to such systems. In some cases, good community relations may support special water allocation arrangements for drought periods, for example prioritisation of subsistence crops, or a reduction in area which rotates annually to different parts of the system. However, more commonly water-saving technologies such as sprinklers have been introduced in attempt to reduce water shortages. Small dams also often have siltation problems, so the regular cleaning of the sluice gates and canals is important in the operation of the system and maintenance of water rights.

Lift systems can be divided into open channel systems that pump river water, and groundwater-based systems that utilise wells. Groundwater development is increasing throughout the Andean region as means for both new irrigation systems and augmenting existing systems supplied from rivers or dams. Lift systems often have lower capital costs than offtake or storage systems, but their operating costs are often much higher because of fuel costs of pumping and repairs to equipment. The spread of pump technology has also led to a fall of the water table in many areas. As discussed earlier, one aspect of Andean agriculture is the strong emphasis on collective action, a commitment to defend rights and an ability to contest actions which threaten livelihoods. Some hope that this consciousness will allow irrigators to find an effective answer to groundwater management. However, the commonest response to falling water tables is still just to drill deeper, even thought this threatens the profitability of irrigation and may even bankrupt farmers who have borrowed to drill wells.

Combination systems incorporate flows from a variety of sources, including small springs, wells, streams and small dams. Often combination systems are found in more open valley terrain in drier climates, and often combine natural river flows and canalised sections. Sources may be tapped which lie outside the natural catchment, so it may be very difficult to model the water balance of the region. Different sources may be used at different times of the year. Superficially, combination systems appear similar to offtake systems, and indeed diversions from local rivers may form the bulk of water. However, institutionally they can be very complex. Different communities may have different rights to different sources. The form of rights may also change across the year depending on the source of water.

The close inter-connection of water systems along a drainage system means that sometimes the entire river system of a valley has to be seen as a combination system which also serves various communities at different locations. Superficially, the release of water by one community to supply another downstream may seem rather wasteful and giving high losses. However, evidence from highland Ecuador suggested that such systems are extremely efficient on a catchment basis (Ruf *et al*, 1991; Mothes, 1987).

In other cases, it is one community which has several sources, as described in the Colca and Ayacucho valleys of Peru (Guillet, 1991), and in the Cochabamba region of Bolivia (Gandarillas *et al*, 1992). Frequently there is a strong multi-purpose element to water provided, where it can supply drinking water and generate electricity as well as supply irrigation.

Intervention to create or renovate combination systems is often a challenge. Linking up of individual systems and sources may allow water supply to be enlarged and more people supplied, ending long-term conflict. However, a great deal of negotiation will be needed to get communities to work together that were once in dispute. Nevertheless, the biggest challenges may be to get engineers to utilise realistic design criteria that ensure farmers get the water agreed. The PRIV system in Cochabamba linked up nine highland water sources to improve water to several communities. The designs made a number of assumptions about water efficiencies, land use intensities and the proportion of flow to be utilised or released at different points in the system. Protests from farmers resulted in the engineers making a number of technical and institutional amendments to the system (Gandarillas *et al*, 1992).

Wetland systems are a form of hydro-agriculture which is distinct from conventional irrigation. Wetland systems rely on local soil moisture and water-table control, while water is transferred in space and time in conventional irrigation. Three types of wetlands are identified internationally - flooded depressions, raised beds and recession agriculture. However, raised beds are the main form of hydro-agriculture found in the Andean region, occurring especially in the Lake Titicaca basin, or in high-altitude sites in Bolivia and Peru (Erickson and Candler, 1989; Immerzeel and Oosterbaan, 1989; Zimmerer, 1991). Design and construction concerns focus heavily on appropriate dimensions and spacing of beds and the lay-out of canals for drainage and water supply. Drains must not only manage flowing water, but help control problems of capillary rise and natural upward seepage of groundwater. Negotiation with farmers over both bed lay-out and water control has been vital for the success of schemes. Sound on-farm research with farmers to adapt water application techniques and cultivation methods has also been important in assuring the sustainability of livelihoods for farmers involved.

The preceding paragraphs have focused heavily on the physical and hydrological challenges of irrigation, emphasising the need to look at the local site in integration with the watershed, for land development, system engineering and water allocation. However, cultural preferences are also a major influence on technology choice and system layout. In many places, we see the continuing impact of pre-Colombian religion and lineage. Schemes are laid out in relation to the lands of kinship groups or *moieties*, and the location of hydraulic structures may have a religious dimension (Gelles, 1994; Sherbondy, 1993). Farmers may have preferences for simpler technologies with low operational requirements. These cultural preferences may also be reinforced by irrigation scheduling arrangements, with schedules organised by moiety arrangements, or incorporating special irrigation events at certain times of cultivation with religious significance. Groups may have irrigation schedules that are determined by agreed priorities of crops at times of drought. Attempts to make infrastructure and water delivery more 'efficient' by eliminating such practices is likely to be problematic.

Water scarcity, difficult terrain and risk-prone climates are all incentives to collective action in Andean irrigation, in canal system development, in development of hillslopes for cultivation, and above all in water allocation arrangements. They all help shape both distinctive environmental adaptations and communal institutions for water management. This is not to say, however, that all is harmony and change is easily achieved. Behind the apparent romance of the Andean lifeworld can lie many vicious struggles to gain control of water. Equally, claims of specialised Andean practices can provide a means to political struggle over water management, where they may or may not exist in reality.

Conclusions: understanding irrigation options in Andean agriculture

Access to irrigation is an important economic determinant for Andean farmers at virtually all altitudes, but it does entail a number of risks which farmers adapt to. If irrigation assistance programmes are to yield equitable results, then they need to pay attention to the risks in the Andean environment and farmers' preferences in coping with them.

The distinctiveness of Andean irrigation is shaped not only by its environment, but also by its history of indigenous and colonial occupation and its often radical politics and economic reforms. All link back intimately into local ecology, to shape and be shaped by it. Thus the study of Andean irrigation not only involves understanding of adaptation to the Andean environment and the niche production advantages there. It also involves an explicit study of continuity in institutions in combination with radical struggle and negotiation. These come together in formidable and exciting action in irrigation management, as will be shown in subsequent chapters. This chapter has focused on the environmental and engineering aspects of Andean irrigation. However, in reality no study can really separate the physical from the social in understanding irrigation outcomes.

From Andean experience, Dourojeanni and Molina (1983) have suggested a framework for resource management with direct relevance for Andean irrigation. They suggested that pre-Hispanic institutions looked to integrate land and water management across territorial units with three objectives: the organisation and co-ordinated participation of the community in the work; the use of technologies and working practices adapted to the zone; and control of sufficiently large vertical and horizontal area to allow various ecological levels to be managed simultaneously for adequate livelihoods. They recognised the increasing role of external agencies in water resource allocation, in practical irrigation operations and in agricultural production.

However, they felt that these older principles could still provide a model for joint State-community initiatives.

The call for 'people-centred' planning of assistance, and equity in Andean irrigation not only involves the delivery of hardware such as irrigation infrastructure. These concerns also involve support for the institutions and processes through which people manage their environment and make a living. The Andes may be described first and foremost as a mountain region, but it is also a region of distinctive cultural and social dynamics. The real challenge for technical support to Andean irrigation is to understand the dynamism of the Andean lifeworld, and its sociotechnical character, not just the perceived physical challenges of mountainous terrain.

References

Ambler, J. (1989) *Adat and aid: management of small scale irrigation in West Sumatra, Indonesia.* Unpublished Ph.D. dissertation, Cornell University, Itaca, New York.

Bolin, I. (1990) 'Upsetting the power balance: Cooperation, competition and conflict in an Andean irrigation system', *Human Organization* 49(2): 140-148.

Cornick, T. (1983) *The social organization of production in Quimiag, Ecuador: A case study of small farmer production systems in the highland Andes.* Unpublished Ph.D. Dissertation, Cornell University, Ithaca, New York.

Dourojeanni, A. & M. Molina (1983) 'The Andean peasant, water and the role of the State'. *CEPAL Review* April, pp.145 - 166.

Erickson, C.L. and Candler, K.L. (1989) 'Raised fields and sustainable agriculture in the Lake Titicaca basin of Peru', pp. 230-248 in Browder, O, (ed). *Fragile lands of Latin America.* Westview Press, Boulder, Colorado, USA.

Gandarillas, H., Salazar, L., Sánchez, L.C., Sánchez L., and De Zutter, P. (1992) *Dios da el agua: Qué hacen los proyectos?* Hisbol, Cochabamba, Bolivia.

Gelles, P. (1994) 'Channels of power, fields of contention: The politics of irrigation and land recoverer in an Andean peasant community', pp. 233-274, in Mitchell, W.P. and Guillet, D. *op. cit.*

Guillet, D. (1987) 'Terracing and irrigation in the Peruvian highlands'. *Current Anthropology,* 28(4):409-430

Guillet, D. (1991) 'Agricultural intensification and de-intensification in Lari, Colca Valley, Peru', *Research in Economic Anthropology* 8:201-224.

Immerzeel, W. van and Oosterbaan, R.J. (1990) 'Irrigation and flood control at high altitude in the Andes'. *ILRI Annual Report* 1989, International Land Reclamation Institute, The Netherlands. pp. 8-24.

Jacobs, B. (ed) (1995) *Hill irrigation engineering.* The Ford Foundation, Delhi.

Jodha, N.S. (1991) 'Sustainable mountain agriculture: Limited options and uncertain prospects'. *Appropriate Technology* 17(4): 9-11.

Lehmann, D. (ed) (1982) *Ecology and exchange in the Andes.* Cambridge University Press, London, UK.

Mayer, E. (1979) *Land use in the Andes: Ecology and agriculture in the Mantaro valley of Peru, with special reference to potatoes.* Centro Internacional de la Papa, Peru.

Messerli, B. (1983) 'Stability and instability of mountain ecosystems: introduction to a workshop sponsored by the United Nations University', *Mountain Research and Development* 3(2): 81-94.

Mitchell, W.P. and Guillet, D. (1994) *Irrigation at high altitudes: The social organization of water control systems in the Andes.* Vol 12, Society for Latin American Anthropology.

Morlon, P. (1979) *Apuntes sobre el problema agronómico relacionado con los aspectos meteorológicos. Estudio Agroclimatológico de la Cuenca del Lago Titicaca 2,* Convenio Peru-Canada, Puno, Peru.

Mothes, P. (1987) 'La acequia del pueblo de Pímampiro: Riego tradicional en el norte de Ecuador'. *Ecuador Debate* 14: 60-86.

Murra, J. (1975) *Formaciones económicas y políticas del mundo Andino*. IEP, Lima, Peru.

Ruf, T., Le Goulven, P. and Ribadeneira, H. (1991) 'Riego tradicional andino en el Ecuador'. *Ruralter* 9:177-198.

Sengupta, N. (1993) *User friendly irrigation designs*. Sage, London and New Delhi.

Sherbondy, J. (1993) 'Water and power: the role of irrigation districts in the transition from Inca to Spanish Cuzco', pp.69-98 in Mitchell, W.P. and Guillet, D, *op. cit.*

Tecnología Intermedia (1990) *Manejo de agua y adecuación de tecnología en la región andina*. CON-CYTEC/ITDG. Peru.

Vincent, L. (1995) *Hill irrigation: Water and development in mountain agriculture*. Intermediate Technology Publications, London.

Winterhalder, B. (1993) 'The ecological basis of water management in the central Andes: Rainfall and temperature in southern Peru', pp. 21-68 in Mitchell W.P. and Guillet, D. *op. cit.*

Yoder, R. (1995) *Designing irrigation structures for mountainous environments: A handbook of experience*. International Irrigation Management Institute, Sri Lanka.

Zimmerer, K. (1991) 'Wetland production and smallholder persistence: Agricultural change in a highland Peruvian region', *Annals of the Association of American Geographers*, 6(1):29-40.

21

Peasant Economy and Andean Irrigation

Rutgerd Boelens

Introduction: irrigation and vertical economies

Irrigation water often has functioned as a central factor bonding different communities and diverse ecological altitudinal zones in the Andes, both historically and at present. Communities and their families try to build their canal in such a way that it passes through both high and low zones in order to have irrigated plots in different agro-climatic areas. This vertical ecological zoning has allowed them to incorporate in several agricultural sub-sectors, to diversify their crops, to better control droughts and freeze periods, and thus distribute the risks associated with production. Irrigation in these different zones ('*pisos ecológicos*') further increases the potential for agricultural diversification. Moreover, as Golte (1980) states: 'managing several agrarian production cycles in several altitudinal, ecological zones is a basic strategy of peasants to employ their labour during a maximum number of days in the agricultural year'. The irrigation canal is often a central axis in the management of a combination of these altitudinal zones, making up an inter-zonal production and exchange system. These systems, the so called 'vertical economies', are based on integrated management of water, land and biodiversity, with inter- and intra-communal exchange of labour.

Since the irrigation system connects altitudinal zones and the corresponding families and communities along the canal, it often can be considered as an organisational fundament around which specific socio-productive relationships have developed. Links between 'high and low' through feasts, rites, family bonds, *compadrazgo* relationships, bartering, communal work, etc., have always constituted the backbone of vertical economies in which not only agricultural products are exchanged but also labour, services, people (e.g. through marriages), materials, knowledge, and ideas. Thus, irrigation has played, and often still plays, a very important dynamic and bonding role in peasant strategies, in the generation of inter- and intra-community organisations, and in the formation of local hydraulic identities.

The post-Columbian era caused a radical rupture in the great majority of vertical economies, as a result of the immense genocide, the expropriation of indigenous lands by the haciendas, and the incorporation of the productive low lands into the capitalist production process. The accumulation of land and water in a few hands reflected the new power structures. In many places, the introduction of monoculture, agro-exports and the logic of market laws have replaced the Andean social and productive relationships. It is impossible to deny the process which has spread over the whole Sierra, whereby peasants have a decreasing amount of power to make their own decisions concerning production and reproduction in their homesteads and communities. De-zoning most affects high-altitude small landowners and indigenous peasants, who have entered into a vicious circle of resource scarcity, overexploitation of their plots, degeneration of natural resources, decline in production, debt, etc. Permanent or seasonal migration and external exploitation of labour is now becoming a common phenomenon in the Andes. Furthermore, during the last decades, growing conflicts among communities have led to the loss of intercommunity and inter-zone co-operation and the disarticulation of a shared normative system in irrigation management (Alfaro et al. 1991). It appears that in this process of disintegration of irrigation practices, small communal systems have suffered less than intercomunal systems.

The above mentioned disarticulation process does not imply that the logic of vertical production has disappeared. Especially at the micro level (communities and small inter-communal systems), ecological altitudinal zones and inter-zone exchanges retain their basic importance. Besides, many communities have resisted the complete domination of external norms and structures. Irrigation schemes have often functioned as a mechanism for defence of peasants' own forms of organisation, socio-productive exchanges, and local normative systems. In spite of the fact that, since colonial times, powerful groups have tried to standardise water distribution,[1] the combination of multiple water uses and different 'kinds' and sources of water in different ecological zones, together with diverse organisational forms and levels, still produces a great diversity of water distribution modes in Andean communities. Moreover, although dominant groups have often appropriated Andean labour relationships and compelled them to serve their own goals, since the agrarian reforms many communities have managed to regain some of the real contents of reciprocal relationships.

Nowadays, communities are encountered that display a high level of internal coherence, as well as communities which are broken or disintegrating. The same can be seen in relation to indigenous and peasant irrigation systems. Generally, commercial enterprises and the State - unlike the former haciendas - have little economic interest in intervening directly in 'mountain economies', except in areas with a higher productive potential. Then their influence is generally fairly global and indirect (through the market, migrants, mass media, laws, agrarian policies, etc.) or through usurers, intermediate trade and development organisations. The presence - or absence - of social cohesion, a respected authority and a consensual normativity in irrigation communities and systems have proved to be essential for the self-governing of irrigation systems in these years of crisis.

Andean peasant economy

When considering Andean peasant irrigation systems it is essential to avoid simple and strict separations between irrigation and the integrated socio-productive system in which irrigation is practised, as if it were a 'component'. Figure 21.1 illustrates that irrigation, just as the peasant family itself, is interwoven in social relationships at the local and global levels. The peasant family's interactions with various management levels, the environmental and agro-productive conditions and the family's location in a framework of local and general social structures shape its space for decision-making regarding the production process. Each peasant family and community makes use of and extends these spaces in a different way. Against this background, the logic of production and the achievements that arise depend on the family's socio-economic starting point, practical opportunities, as well as its vision and capacities.

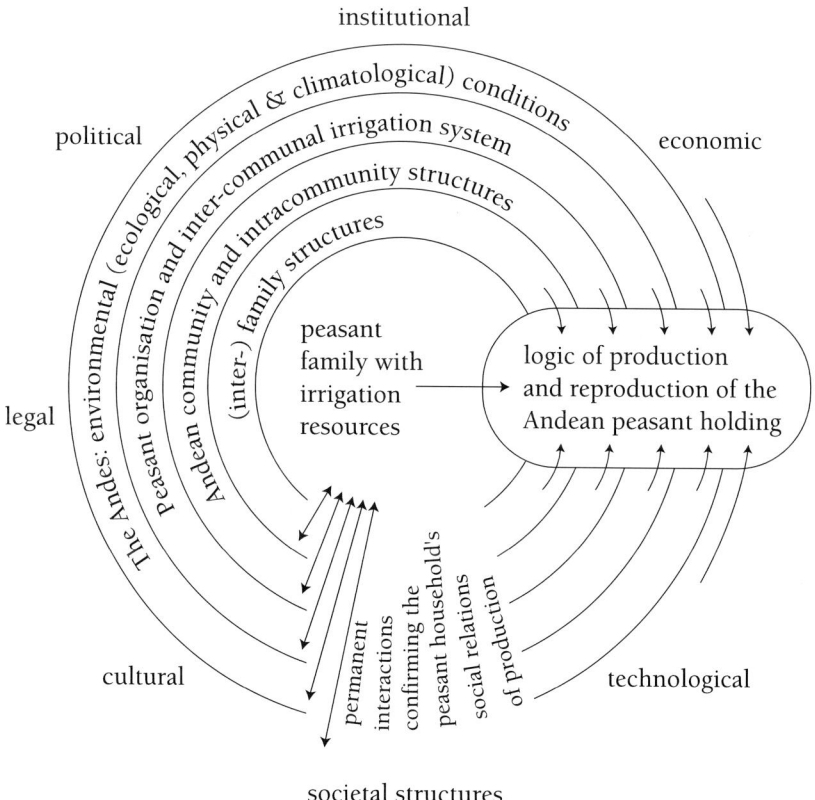

Figure 21.1: Social framework of peasant family with access to irrigation.

Only by means of an integrated analysis of the Andean peasant economy it is possible to understand local organisation forms and the variety of irrigation practices. In this peasant economy the rationalities, potentials and obstacles for irrigation are situated within a framework of family, community, inter-community, and inter-institutional management. Irrigation analysis focussing on Andean peasant economy logic will show, for example, that the outcomes of organisational processes in peasant irrigation are not simply the sum of the economic interests of individual irrigators, who 'rationally' calculate costs and benefits of collective actions, as if they were operating in a 'free market'. On the other hand, irrigation analysis based on an understanding of Andean peasant economy forces a deeper scrutiny of peasant rationality in its concrete practice which also de-mystifies certain romantic visions that emphasise a supposed harmony in the Andean and indigenous world. Further, it demonstrates the inadequacies and dogmatisms of many macro approaches of radical-universal explanation.

Here we mention only a few of the fundamental features that structure the peasant economy in irrigation communities (see Heynig 1982; Bolhuis & Van der Ploeg 1985; Dourojeanni & Molina 1982; Gianotten & De Wit 1987; Greslou & Ney 1986; Plaza 1987; Kervyn 1988; CESA 1991; Boelens 1994, 1995).

a. *Insertion in the global economy*
    The Andean peasant economy in a given area expresses itself in relation to specific interactions and relations of exploitation between peasants and social groups in the wider society. It is characterised by a variety of mechanisms of unequal exchange. The Andean peasant economy and the irrigation system are neither autarchic nor self-sufficient, but interwoven in the commoditised/mercantile and community/non-mercantile spheres of production and consumption.

b. *Heterogeneity of the peasantry and its production strategies*
    The presence of social differentiation among peasant families, communities and regions, the variety of ecological and geographical situations, the diverse histories and cultures, the varied interactions and relations of exploitation, etc., have led to a marked heterogeneity among peasants. This is evident in their diverging interests and in a great diversity of organisation forms and productive and reproductive strategies. As a result, the analyses or strategies that simplify reality (assuming that groups are homogeneous: 'all are poor', 'all are irrigators', 'all genders have the same interests', or presenting only dualistic contradictions) may lead to major mistakes and often to self-defeating results.

c. *Reproduction of the household and the community*
    The Andean peasant economy is not about maximising monetary income but ensuring stability at certain minimal levels of subsistence in the long run. It looks for a balance between efforts invested (financial, labour, materials, etc.) and the satisfaction of the household's needs. The generation and reproduction of the irrigation system and of the political and cultural organisation has to be analysed from this perspective. This challenge to continuity is not expressed as conservative resistance to change but as a dynamic force and a critical attitude facing 'progress' and 'modernisation', to be able to survive in changing and adverse situations (see also Berger 1992).[2] In other words, peasants - and most of all peasant women - always try to bring together a) the need for household and commu-

nity *reproduction* with b) the *transformation* of those social relationships that threaten this reproduction.

d. *The unit of labour and production is also the unit of consumption*
Contrary to a capitalist entrepreneur, peasants see their household both as the production unit and their home and consumption unit. This means that resources and production do not only have an exchange value but also a very important use value. The market logic of decreasing marginal benefits cannot be applied as in a commercial enterprise, because peasants face the need to satisfy household necessities. In times of crisis, (low prices, low rewards to labour), the peasant family increases its labour efforts instead of decreasing them as would the capitalist enterprise. It also means that peasant irrigation systems always try to find a balance between production for self-consumption and for the market, and that the water user organisation cannot and should not be structured in a similar way to purely mercantile organisations.

e. *Diversification of activities and products within the household and the community*
Contrary to the assumptions made in plans and intervention strategies of many irrigation projects, peasants are neither only farmers nor only irrigators. With respect to income generation or the allotment of family time and work, the role of agriculture is not even always primordial (Kervyn 1988). Peasants always seek to be employed in a variety of productive activities since it is impossible within subsistence agriculture to guarantee survival when engaging in only a few activities of marginal output. Diversification is sought both within farming itself (agriculture, animal husbandry, forestry, market and domestic consumption, irrigated and non-irrigated crops, crops at several ecological altitudinal zones, associated crops, paid labour in the hacienda's irrigation and non-paid labour in the community's system) and in non-farming activities (marketing, handicrafts, temporary migration, etc.). In the domestic unit the available work force is divided among the diverse activities. Furthermore, diversification also relates to space and time: the household activities are not necessarily carried out in the same space (this is, the peasant holding), nor at the same time (because of the strategic distribution over the agricultural season and its migration periods).

f. *Interdependence of productive activities*
The several agricultural and non-agricultural sectors, activities and products of the household economy are not isolated elements, but combine and interact to form a logical matrix. Interdependence and complementarity between, for example, agriculture, animal husbandry, handicrafts, and migration employment, make it impossible to judge the cost-effectiveness or merits of one certain activity in isolation. Often, the promotion of a technological or organisational change by an external institution can have a positive effect on one specific activity but a negative effect on many others, or it might require changing the whole production rationality, thereby producing an unstable situation. Further, it is common for peasants to accept losses in one of their activities while not abandoning it as it may constitute a basic element in their production system. It is also necessary to understand that the main objective of a certain activity does not always refer only to the final product (sometimes not cost-effective) but also to the intermediate products, and to the importance of the activity for the whole production process (e.g. in the case of crop rotation). The coherence of the *whole* set of activities and their relationships (Kervyn, 1988), within and outside the field of irrigation, should be analysed.

g. *Risk avoidance and distribution*
    The practice of risk avoidance and spreading is closely connected to the objective of the
    domestic unit's reproduction, and to the reproduction of the community (which is the
    social structure that guarantees survival). In situations of greater stability and security,
    peasants do take great risks. Thus, risk aversive behaviour is not conservative, but simply
    a necessity, the result of a survival economy. Social relationships (although sometimes
    exploitative), organisational alliances, crop patterns, livestock, complementary irrigation,
    diversification of activities, etc., all reflect social insurance systems that do not eliminate
    but seek to control risks (Dourojeanni & Molina 1982; Kervyn 1988). This is one of the
    central reasons why an eventual accompaniment to irrigation oriented towards the
    strengthening of water user organisations should take as a *point of departure* the already
    existing social security systems, such as self-sustainment strategies and peasants' local
    organisational forms.

h. *Dialectic relationship among organisation levels and between collective and individual property
    rights*
    Contrary to suppositions of both collectivist and individualist ideologies, Andean peasants
    do not always work or reason from a collective point of view, nor just from an individual
    or family perspective. In their production strategies they combine different formal and
    informal organisation levels dialectically, according to the practical and concrete requirements
    of the domestic unit, the community and the irrigation system. Peasant property rights
    may be institutionalised both at the family and at the collective level. In most irrigation
    systems, individual rights to usage of water and infrastructure are derived from the fulfilment
    of obligations and conditions related to the collective property and management of the
    irrigation system. Collective rights refer, among others, to participation in system management
    and decision-making.

i. *Interaction between rites and productive practices*
    Although differing in degree according to region and ethnic and social structure, rituals
    are found in many Andean economies. These are based on Andean 'cosmovisions', and
    reinforce economic activities and social relationships. Rites also reflect common owner-
    ship and collective rights related to the territory and the irrigation system. They guaran-
    tee the family's production and reproduction as well as that of the community and the
    irrigation system, by establishing and maintaining a relationship between the past, the
    present and the future. The local history of Andean communities is not transferred to new
    generations in writing but through oral stories and myths. On the one hand, they relate
    community members to their collective history and, on the other, they interact with the
    present, thus contributing to the construction of the future. Especially in more traditional
    indigenous communities the role of rites and myths in irrigation and the daily economy
    is strong. They both reflect and may produce a rationality of production.

j. *Labour strategies based on a 'collective, contractual reciprocity'*
    In Andean irrigation systems as well as in the communities themselves, families apply
    several reciprocal social relationships of labour exchange which provide the labour force
    and other scarce resources needed for production, without having to buy them in the mar-
    ket, which would lead to the accumulation of corresponding financial debts. Each one of
    these relationships, such as the *ayni*, the *maquimañachi*, the *minga*, the *faena*, *trabajar en
    compañía* ('work together'), etc., has different contents and names throughout the Andean

Sierra. They are all relationships that, to a certain point, can counter social differentiation and, above all, make available the necessary resources to the less well-off, without denying the fact that this reciprocity is sometimes asymmetric. In many irrigation systems Andean labour relationships play an important role in structuring informal organisations, networks and practices. The peasant and/or indigenous community is one of the central organisational forms by means of which Andean peasants have institutionalised this 'collective contractual reciprocity' to ensure the subsistence of the community and its components.

This set of features is not exhaustive and some might be more important in a certain region than others. They can be considered as the basic materials that combine to form various matrices. From the understanding of peasant economies in specific localities it may follow sometimes that certain equities or inequities, which seem 'apparent' to the external analyst, are different in both appearance and content when analysed more deeply.[3] The analysis of both 'internal' and 'external' equities and inequities in Andean irrigation, as well as any proposals for assistance or alternative agricultural policies, require an approach which goes beyond superficial and/or universal models.

> Often it is believed that the Andean alternative would be the adoption or construction of a more adequate model to be applied in the region. 'Adequate' would mean: to take into account certain regional particularities. However, it is symptomatic to see that the proposals made for the Andes often correspond to worldwide tendencies that defend similar postulates. This seems to happen with eco-development, ethno-development, endo-development, etc.... The procedure used is generally that of starting to observe the Andean reality in the light of a new theory with universalising vocation and, when discovering in the region a great potential for the application and development of such a theory, to 'Andeanise' it... Very seldom we really get nearer in order to understand how the Andes are, to understand how the Andeans look at themselves, how they look at us, and how they look at, suppose or wish their relationships with national society (Zutter 1988).

An understanding of the diverse visions of the Andean peasants is of central importance, not in order to accept them as unquestionable facts, but to consider them as starting-points, to understand their struggle for *both* reproduction and resistance *and* transformation.

Peasant economy: the interaction between community and market spheres

A basic phenomenon of peasant economies is their co-determination by exchanges in both the mercantile and non-mercantile spheres. In peasant societies,

> 'both spheres compete for the same space and for the same social actors. While the result of this struggle seems resolved historically, this is not the case for those

who interact within this dilemma, searching for their physical maintenance. They have to structure their labour and their behaviour to be able to assure their food supplies and the general conditions of their existence. Therefore, the household optimises its intervention in the social process of production looking both at income generation through the general market, and at what can be obtained through the non-mercantile sphere. Thus the households' strategies are doubly determined... The researcher, when trying to understand the dynamics of the organisation of production and exchange in the Andean field, has to start from this double determination and has to analyse it as a whole, meanwhile separating both spheres since we are dealing with two different, overlapping and sometimes opposing rationalities. This is the key of the problem: to separate the inseparable. . .' (Golte & De la Cadena 1983).

In practice these different and unequal, though inseparable, spheres interact continuously. In a given Andean locality, it is not uncommon that the *same* products and services sometimes circulate through the market and sometimes remain in the communal, non-commoditised sphere[4], according to the respective family's or community's vision and conditions, the agricultural season, and the incentives or disincentives offered by community and market junctures. Examples of this can be found in every family, community, and irrigation system. For example, it is very common that in one and the same system, some families contract labour commercially to work for them in the construction and maintenance of infrastructure, while other families carry out *mingas* and *faenas* with their own labour efforts or, in case of absence, fulfil their duties through *ayni*. Another example: in one and the same family, regarding the sexual division of labour, it is not uncommon to find that a women fulfils irrigation duties though community *mingas* while her husband works for a salary selling his labour through temporary migration activities. A third example: from one and the same irrigated plot, even with the same crop, say alfalfa or vegetables, a (variable) part is taken to the market and the rest is for domestic consumption, according to current incentives and necessities. The list is infinite.

In spite of the capitalist market's penetration in the Andean community, non-mercantile sphere exchanges and interactions have resisted - and will resist in the future - substitution for purely commoditised relationships. The principal reason is that neither peasant families and communities nor their irrigation systems will be able to reproduce themselves amidst exclusively mercantile relationships, and they are well aware of this fact. A community, with its collective power, its internal forms of organisation and its external alliances, forms a central axis for the adequate individual and collective use of the communities' productive resources. Non-commodity Andean relationships ensure long-term reproduction and offer a protective framework against the vicious circles of poverty, debts and exploitation.

Moreover, many exchanges, incentives and activities in Andean livelihood strategies and irrigation systems - often key elements of the peasant economy's community sphere - simply *cannot* be reduced to just market economy issues. For example, the social function of water, rituals, agricultural and irrigation feasts, etc., are all important features and exchanges considered not additional to but necessary *for* reproduction.

Instead, mercantile relationships - which apart from unjust exchanges certainly do offer important short-term solutions and opportunities - cannot guarantee stability within an economy of producers with scarce subsistence resources. Due to the disadvantageous features of Andean peasant agriculture (generally small and fragmented plots in fragile and steep hill terrain) and to the unequal exchange relationship in the market place, peasants do not receive sufficient value for their products and labour in order to subsist in a pure commodity economy. In other words, they need to maintain the non-mercantile community economy while, at the same time, they face the need to incorporate themselves into the commodity economy.

Based on this and other interpretations, some authors have created their theories of how peasant economies are functional to the capitalist system (see e.g. De Janvry 1981). The latter appropriates the surplus values of peasant production and labour.[5] Some consider peasants as a transitory class, condemned to capitalist exploitation until total proletarisation causes the disappearance of peasants: 'de-peasantisation'. Others compare peasant economy to the entrepreneurial model and forecast its disappearance due to its 'backwardness', incapable of competitive participation in the capitalist market. However, besides the fact that these approaches deny peasant resistance and logic of survival (see Berger 1992), it is also necessary to focus on the peasant rationale in functionalising, in turn, the market to sustain important elements of peasant economies. For example, at certain times of the year, the Andean peasant works mainly within a non-commodity economy, at others he or she 'takes advantage' of temporary migration (capitalist employment), not as surplus and proletarian labour but as a result of the relative, seasonal unemployment *inherent* to peasant economies. Furthermore, the community may commercialise certain goods (mercantile sphere) to reinvest the money in rehabilitating the self-managed irrigation system, which guarantees a major part of the collective reproduction (non-mercantile sphere). Examples abound. In other words, the capitalist system uses and exploits the peasant, and the peasant somehow uses the capitalist system to guarantee part of the production and reproduction of his/her household and community. *The functionality is mutual but not equivalent* since it is based on unequal powers and on a continuous extraction of the resources that are possessed or generated by peasants.

The situation is different and worse for those poor families and communities who, due to their total surrender to the capitalist rationality, their debts and market dependence, and their broken links with collective reciprocity and protection, are losing not only the value peasants generate but also the productive resources themselves and their *logic* of production. This logic or rationality is externalised: the fundamental decisions concerning productive processes and technologies to be applied are not taken by the family or community anymore but by market forces and institutions. In these cases, it is not the family itself who deliberately decides whether or not to incorporate certain mercantile elements, it is the exogenous logic of commodity relations which controls and dominates the process and defines the production norms. Generally in this situation, which is *also* present in the Andes, there is a limited number of individuals and groups that 'succeed' and many others that get transformed into the so called 'disposable' persons or families ('*los desechables*') or communities considered as 'factories of poverty' ('*las fábricas de pobreza*'), deeply distressing terms for deeply inhuman situations.

In the field of irrigation, why is it so important to have a profound understanding of the interaction between 'commodity' and 'community' in peasant economy, and the consequences this has for a sustainable reproduction? Currently, 'peasant self-management of irrigation systems' is pursued by many, from radical to neo-liberal visions and policies, although the intentions and objectives differ. However, at the same time, most projects plan an almost radical transformation towards commodity-based (re)production, not just in their economic documents but also and especially in their technical designs. (Something that in no way is undone by the social and participatory 'components' of the same irrigation projects). The irrigation technology to be applied, the planned rotation system, the crops to be planted, pesticides, fertilisers, labour organisation, etc., all tend to be aimed at future commodity production, with respect to both inputs and outputs.

Moreover, due to the internal logic of public policy and development programmes, many institutions *must* design this total transformation towards market rationality, simply because only profitable projects are to receive funds, i.e. projects with high commercial output (to recuperate both O&M and investment costs). Therefore, in the practice of project planning and presentation, whenever possible *costs* are charged to the non-mercantile, community sphere (e.g. 'free' provision of collective peasant labour and productive resources and *results* are projected towards the mercantile sphere. And when planning these results, 'there is a structural deceit in relation to the presentation of irrigation projects' possibilities and potentials' (SNV-UNL 1994): the *over-estimation* of commercial results - to make these projects viable and bankable - means that the project practical objectives and activities are directed completely towards 'achievements' in the mercantile sphere. This approach ignores the community sphere which, however, is the *base* of a guaranteed reproduction, and also ignores the benefits of a social character (considered to be 'important but secondary'). These projects are bound to fail, because they do not fulfil the expected achievements in the mercantile sphere and, on the other hand, they do not establish a sustainable base because of having omitted the community sphere. In this way, neither sustainable peasant management nor a more balanced interaction between the two spheres is achieved. The culprits are easily found: the 'backward' peasants who do not want to change their maize, beans and broad bean crops and so refuse to fulfil in this way the project's expectations. A technician on an irrigation project in Tungurahua, Ecuador, excused himself by stating:

'You can't get rid of the culture of maize in only a few days. It is difficult, but in the end we'll manage to make these peasants understand' (in Boelens & Doornbos 1996).

This is the irony of irrigation development: under the flag of 'self-management' many interventions externalise the knowledge and means available and needed for irrigated agriculture, thus increasing the peasants' dependence on products and services of commercial institutions and on the very development institutions themselves, and leaving the control of the productive process in the hands of actors outside the community.

It is often inevitable, but not necessarily problematic, that the introduction or improvement of peasant irrigation means 'more market'. It is not a question of either embracing or denying this market. As stated, in contemporary Andean society peasants also *require* some aspects of the mercantile sphere to be able to obtain some complementary resources needed for the reproduction of their families and community. Therefore, the strategies should be based on a) the strengthening of *endogenous control* over decision-making with respect to the questions of why, where, how and when to relate to the market; b) ensuring access to markets in a collective, equitable and organised manner; c) finding the required balance in the interaction between the commodity and the community spheres, considering that the latter constitutes the fundamental basis both for the reproduction of the collectivity and its parts, and for access to the market without losing the capacity for self-management.

Thus, peasant irrigation development and the subsequent incorporation of commodities and market relations do not necessarily imply 'the total loss of peasant production logic and styles'. On the contrary, as argued above, peasant irrigation development *can* also play a fundamental role as the backbone of an *endogenous peasant economy* and the strengthening of the 'community domain'. In that case, the challenge is to defend peasant irrigation rationality - in a future which is based on 'commodity-community' interaction - by maintaining its roots in the collectivity, the accumulated experience and the peasant-control of decisions.

Notes

1   'Let us not forget that the rotation system was the common allocation modality in medieval Spain, imposed since 1557 by Toledo (through the so called 'Ordenanzas de Toledo'). Since then, in continuing negation of the contributions made by Andean irrigation, State instances of the republican and contemporary periods have promulgated laws... that all aimed at the same goal, trying only to turn the rotation modality into something even more efficient for their objectives of national integration and production, by means of a centralised State water administration. In spite of this standardising initiative, the degree of convergence or opposition among the Andean, Hispanic and modern or 'bureaucratic' traditions relating to the society-water relationship, has determined the great diversity of irrigation water allocation situations and modalities that nowadays exist in Andean communities. Each Andean community whose agriculture was based on irrigation had to adopt this foreign rotation system, but they all did it "their own way"' (Greslou 1989).
2   As Berger (1992) states, for the peasantry the historical process of 'agricultural modernisation' has always meant a project of eliminating these same peasants, since the dominant and non peasant sectors consider that peasants are caught in a vicious circle of inefficiency, conservatism, and technological backwardness.
3   For example: the apparent injustice of a peasant considered poor (with little water and a small irrigation area in the system) who nevertheless possesses other plots scattered over various irrigation canals in the area or who has other important non-agricultural incomes. On the other hand, the apparent justice of reciprocal relationships that in certain cases, however, show much asymmetry. Or, the rationality of continuing the exploitative relations in certain cases of *compadrazgo* (godfathership), etc. Presuppositions and conclusions on equity and justice should not be generalised but investigated in specific, concrete cases.
4   In this text we refer to this non-commodity domain as the 'community sphere' (esfera comunal/ comunitaria). It is used as a conceptual tool and does not literally refer to the Andean community as such (in which both commodity and community spheres interact).
5   This happens by means of unequal exchange in the market (under-valuation of peasant products) and exploitation of contracted peasant labour (salaries lower than those necessary to survive). This is possible because the peasants' subsistence is already 'subsidised' by the peasant economy and, besides, peasant's labour supply is abundant and not organised in trade unions. Thus its functionality to the capitalist system.

References

Alfaro, J., F. Guardia, J. Golte, L. Masson & M.T. Oré, 1991. *La organización social del riego.* Ruralter 9, CICDA, Lima.

Berger, J., 1992. *Into their labours (Pig earth, Once in Europe, Lilac and Flag).* Pantheon Books, New York.

Boelens, R., 1994. *Irrigatieprojekten en behoud van natuurlijke hulpbronnen in de ecuadoraanse minifundiolandbouw. Macht en milieubeheer.* SNV. Cusco.

Boelens, R., 1995. *El promotor campesino: Capacitador u organizador?* IIRR-ADRAI-FUDECOOP. Riobamba/Quito.

Boelens, R. & B. Doornbos, 1996. *Derecho consuetudinario campesino e intervención en el riego andino.* SNV-CESA, Quito.

Bolhuis, E. & J.D. Van der Ploeg, 1985. *Boerenarbeid en stijlen van landbouwbeoefening.* PhD thesis, Leiden Development Studies 8, Leiden University, Leiden.

CESA, 1991. *Campesinado y entorno ecosocial.* CESA, Quito.

Dourojeanni, A. & M. Molina, 1982. *El poblador rural, el manejo del agua en las cuencas alto andinas y el rol del Estado.* CEPAL, Quito / Santiago de Chile.

Gianotten, V. & T. De Wit, 1987. *Organización campesina: el objetivo político de la Educación Popular y la Investigación Participativa.* TAREA, Lima & CEDLA, Ámsterdam.

Golte, J., 1980. *La racionalidad de la organización andina.* IEP, Lima.

Golte, J. & M. De la Cadena, 1983. *La codeterminación de la organización social andina.* Allpanchis no.22, vol 19, Instituto de Pastoral Andina, Cusco.

Greslou, F. & B. Ney, 1986. *Un sistema de producción andino.* Debates Andinos 10, Instituto Francés de Estudios Andinos & Bartolomé de las Casas. Cusco.

Greslou, F., 1989. *Visión andina y usos campesinos del agua.* PRATEC, Lima.

Heynig, K., 1982. *Principales enfoques sobre la economía campesina.* CEPAL, Quito / Santiago de Chile.

Janvry, A. De, 1981. *The agrarian question and reformism in Latin America.* Johns Hopkins University, Baltimore.

Kervyn, B., 1988. *La economía campesina en el Perú. Teorías y políticas.* Debates Andinos no.14. Bartolomé de las Casas, Cusco.

Plaza, O. (ed.), 1987. *Economía Campesina.* DESCO, Lima.

SNV-UNL, 1994. *Riego comunitario andino y organización de usuarios.* SNV- Universidad Nacional de Loja, Loja.

Zutter, P. De, 1988. Mitos del desarrollo rural andino. Grupo Tinkuy. Editorial Horizonte, Lima.

22

Water Distribution, Social Organisation and Equity in the Andean Vision

Zulema Gutiérrez & Gerben Gerbrandy

Introduction

Andean irrigation systems and water management awed the first European settlers with their high technological achievements. They bear witness to the people's significant level of organisation at that time. During the colonial intervention process, many of these systems and much of the knowledge that made their construction and operation possible were lost. Nevertheless, current Andean irrigation systems show that not all the ancient water distribution capacity was destroyed. The different ways communities distribute water show a wealth of organisational ability, criteria of justice and equity, and a sense of balance between natural conditions and human inhabitants. However, water distribution arrangements are rooted in each irrigation systems' local conditions and historical background. Thus, to understand the equity criteria underlying water distribution, these irrigation systems must be analysed within their local, cultural, and historical context.

In Andean irrigation systems, equity concepts involve not only basic water distribution norms but also the creativity of irrigation system management. Irrigators live with their irrigation systems, watching over equitable access to water at all distribution levels. Distribution modes are intertwined with the communal organisation and the relationships between people and their environment. There are no blue prints for equity criteria in irrigation management. These norms depend on historical development of distribution rules and local systems' conditions.

A review of opinions on equity in irrigation water distribution

It is difficult to grasp a concept such as equity because we define it according to our perception of the phenomenon we want to describe. Equity is related to equality but they are not the same. According to the dictionary, equity means 'equanimity' and equality means the condition of one thing being equal to another. Equity is also associated with 'justice'. One dictionary definition of equity is 'natural justice, as compared to legal justice'. This definition puts equity in a local context, what is considered just or legitimate in a local society. However, what is just for someone is not necessarily just for another person.

Bleumink and Sijbrandij (1990), saw 'equity' in Andean irrigation as a social or normative concept: the agreement among members of a society about what is just. Equity involves equality, too, but it is a broader concept. Equity is like a feeling. The way equity is expressed depends on the culture. These authors also indicate that equity comprises three important factors:
- participation by all members and mutual supervision;
- transparency in all members' understanding of operational decisions;
- equality: even sharing of benefits and burdens among members of a society.

According to Levine & Coward (1989) irrigators perceive a pattern of water sharing as equitable if all claims for water are based on principles that are accepted as just or correct by the group of irrigators. After an analysis of several irrigation systems in different parts of the world, they found differences in the definition of equity. The variety of water allocation rules shows that the perception of equity is different for different social groups and different irrigation systems. These authors feel that the least equitable of these systems are rules that allocate the resource on a time basis: first come, first served. A second definition of equity allocates water flow or time in proportion to the irrigator's land area. A third type of water allocation that these authors found is proportional division based on each irrigator's contribution towards the construction of irrigation infrastructure. This individual contribution often correlates with landholding, but can be independent, i.e., irrigators may irrigate the amount of land they are able to cultivate.

These authors point out that irrigation projects[1] frequently try to recognise these factors. Still, while the irrigators' criteria of equity normally refer to equity among persons or families and their *chacras* (plots), projects employ criteria related to productivity. That is why many projects, when designing water distribution, also consider rules of proportionality between the area of plots to be irrigated and the plot owners' labour contribution. However, projects give these equity criteria a technocratic meaning and tend to differentiate among soil types, climates and crops' consumptive use to determine irrigation requirements. Under this different definition of equity, water utility and not only water volume is shared.

We also find these different conceptions about water distribution equity in Andean irrigation systems. There is a striking difference between irrigation systems managed by the irrigators (the first three definitions found by Levine & Coward) and irrigation systems managed by external (State) institutions. This also shows how community members' perception differs from irrigation projects employee views. Projects very seldom consider the criteria irrigators use, to decide about agricultural production and irrigation water distribution.

We find several references to equity in papers written by other authors who have discussed distribution norms. According to Valderrama (1989), in reference to irrigation systems in the Colca Valley of southern Peru, equity is perceived when the amount of water allocated is based on the amount of work contributed to building and maintaining the system.

Equity can also appear at different levels. Gerbrandy (1991) describes criteria of equity to define water-volume shares in systems with multiple water sources: everyone earns a water share proportional in time to the shareholder's contribution to the water system. Thus, shares are not equal for different families, since there can be shares of, for example, a couple of minutes and 60-minute ones, but this is considered fair because it depends on someone's efforts to acquire a share. In daily practice, however, water is distributed equitably when each irrigator has access to water according to his rights. Equity in water distribution is actually expressed through each family's right to use water, and their actual use of such rights.

This brief outline of equity concepts demonstrates that water rights equity can have different contents according to the context of the irrigation systems considered. In the Sullcayana *allyu* in the Bolivian *Altiplano* and in Chilijchi in the inter-Andean valleys of Cochabamba, water rights are assigned to all community members and to all irrigable land (see ch. 28 and ch. 29). In the case of Punata, Bolivia this right is directly proportional to a family's time working on infrastructure (see ch. 30). This creates rights that are independent of the amount of land each family owns. However, only those members recognised by the communal organisation and by the irrigation association can be granted water rights.

Water in the Andean vision: equity, equivalence and reciprocity

To better understand the concepts of equity in Andean irrigation, it is indispensable to analyse the Andean vision about water. What follows is an interpretation of Andean thinking by several authors.

In Andean irrigation, it is important for all irrigators to participate in defining equity and for all to enforce and control the practice of this equity. Equitable distribution results from negotiations and relationships among people with their own perceptions of equity.

Perceptions of water distribution equity involve relationships among people and between people and their environment. These relationships are part of cultural norms and values and, conversely, cultural norms and values largely determine how people and nature are considered. Therefore, to understand irrigation's roots in culture and society, we must understand how Andean people contemplate and organise their world.

The Andean worldview is an agrocentric vision built around farming activities in the Andes. It contains three communities of living beings: the community of nature (*sallqa*), the community of deities (*las huacas*) and the human community (*runa*). These communities are made up of living beings that communicate with each other.

Moreover, this is a world of peers with no hierarchies based on origin or biological composition. The Andean world is not a biologically evolving world in which a monkey is more evolved than a fish and people occupy the highest rank of all.

Relationships among these three communities are complementary and reciprocal to foster life and maintain an equilibrium among the three communities. Balance among elements and respect for nature and gods are also important for Andean technology. This technology has two dimensions, empirical and symbolical, that always go together. An Andean community member never starts to farm or built without having asked for the consent of *Pachamama* (Mother Earth), the *Apu* (the main mountain, guardian of the community), or other deities. Andean technology is collective, without the universal knowledge of Western technology. Instead, reproduction of knowledge and abilities depends on the environment and takes place in communal activities.

Like everything in the Andean world, water is also a living being, a 'person' who inhabits the landscape or *pacha*. Moreover, water also bestows life and fecundity. Without water, life would not be possible. Therefore, it is linked to rituals and beliefs. The importance of water is especially demonstrated in several myths in which water appears as a *huaca* (deity). In the Andean vision there are several kinds of water (rain, hail, snow, rivers, springs and reservoirs). Each water type has its own odours, flavours and consistencies. The relationship with each of them is embodied in dialogue and conversation among living beings, because all nature is a living being.

The two dimensions of Andean technology are also found in the ways Andean people manage water and how they relate to water. Salazar (1995) describes how

> irrigation is seen as a re-creation of water, a way to rear water like a child. Each source of water changes its flow from year to year and rural folk create and re-create norms for equitable use to suit circumstances. Varying weather and water flows at each source result in constant renewal of norms and agreements.

> Irrigation organisation, infrastructure, irrigation system management, production decisions, and criteria and goals, reflect this culture of contingency and conversation with variable circumstances. The fundamental goal is always to guarantee foods supply for family survival and to guarantee the reproduction of conditions required to go on producing. On this basis, practical rural experiences of reciprocity and mutual duties have been developed that make irrigation system management sustainable: conflict control and management, decision-making, distribution methods and mechanisms, rights validation, water source ownership and property of irrigation system facilities.

> The ways in which the groups of users interrelate with territory, sources of water, soil, infrastructure, agriculture - how they manage these components and how

these components make up an ecosystem and condition users to organise with rules and norms - this is the socio-cultural context of each irrigation system, where water management is the particular lifestyle of each unit.

Water distribution and its organisation in Andean irrigation

To understand criteria of equity, equality and equivalence in irrigation we must observe water distribution activities, to see who irrigates, when they irrigate, how long they irrigate, how much water they use and, especially, we must listen to irrigators.

These daily activities can be summarised as 'water distribution': all management of physical infrastructure to operate an irrigation system. Distribution also refers to all social activities organised by irrigators to distribute water such as delegating responsibility and monitoring distribution. Finally, distribution also includes norms, mechanisms and regulations governing water distribution: how water-use rights, irrigation scheduling and so on are organised.

Water distribution, sometimes also called 'water delivery', is a crucial activity in an irrigation system. However, a literature review about irrigation systems reveals that very little importance has been given to this aspect. The issue is fundamental, not only as a starting point for a social analysis of irrigation in Andean regions, but to cope with the enormous challenges of adjusting traditional irrigation systems to new demands for enlargement and improvement, or the creation of new systems. It is important to know what rural concepts and criteria constitute the base to determine one form or another of distribution in different Andean irrigation systems.

Andean region social organisation is tightly linked to resource management, within which water organisation is very important. Water distribution is linked to the communal and inter-communal organisation. There are many Andean organisation principles governing water distribution:

Existence of several distribution authorities in a single region or community

Organisations linked to water are based on the reciprocity relationships established among different types of water according to their source or their quality, and the organisational levels within the community (users organisations or inter-family groups, kinship groups). Each community member may belong to various water-delivery organisations which are not fixed or constant. Some can disappear, new ones can appear according to the available types of water and according to needs and group composition. For example, in the irrigation systems that handle basic river flows (in the valleys of Cochabamba, Bolivia, called *'mitas'*) apparently there are no distribution organisations. All communities know their turns and within the communities, customs have been established regarding the distribution schedules, also known by everyone. However, when a conflict appears, the organisation becomes apparent.

Dialogue among irrigators and waters

For water distribution, decisions are discussed and made by everyone, on different occasions. In many Andean systems, the intake becomes the place for negotiation and agreement at the moment of irrigation. In other systems, the moment of dialogue is the meeting of the users organisation or, in case of conflicts between canals or irrigation groups, the meeting at the site of conflict. There are also systems in which irrigators meet every morning with the water judge and others in charge, to organise irrigation for the day.

Water distribution organisations are part of communal organisation

Irrigation organisation is intertwined with the communal organisation. Water rights are collective rights: the prerequisite to obtain access to irrigation water is to belong to the communal organisation and to obey all related obligations. Although there are specific water delivery organisations, these are generally placed under the communal or inter-communal organisation.

Everyone is knowledgeable about irrigation

There is no water distribution related specialisation since everyone has access to irrigation system knowledge. For water control and surveillance, everybody has to observe their rotating duties (gate keepers, ditch tenders, time keepers, assistants, guards, water judges, etc.).

Andean water distribution criteria

Irrigation system management in the Andes is based on reciprocity and dialogue among users. Over time, this organisation has established agreements that guide equitable distribution among community members. Since there is an ongoing dialogue among users about these agreements, distribution is dynamic and rules are subject to constant renovation. This reflects the changes in the community itself (each generation of families is different) and environmental changes (river patterns, changes in land ownership and type of agricultural production, etc.). Irrigation systems have to react in a flexible way to this dynamic setting. Therefore, agreements must be clear to and controllable by all members. Transparency in distribution also means that systems must not be complicated; each group of users must have some autonomy. These characteristics are evident through different distribution mechanisms that users apply in irrigation systems. Behind these ways of water allotment we can recognise transparent, flexible, autonomous criteria that see to the equitable resource distribution to the community members and their *chacras*. First, we will see how we can understand these criteria.

Transparency

Gandarillas *et al.* (1992) demonstrate that transparency is shown in the norms and rules of distribution: a system is transparent when 'the norms and rules of distribution are visible to all users and they can recognise any modification introduced in the system.'

A first sign of transparent distribution is that in practically all irrigation systems in Bolivia's inter-Andean valleys water is distributed by rotating one water flow from one user to the next. The whole cycle back to the first user, lasts a reasonable time to satisfy all crop requirements. If the number of users is too large to allow irrigation one by one, shifts are usually assigned to groups which will define the water sharing among them (turns or fractions of water volume).

In compound irrigation systems, with different types of water (from different sources), each system with its own rights, the single flow system guarantees that users will not mix different types of water. In the case of Punata, for example, different types of water arrive simultaneously to the main intake (see ch. 30). Here, waters are separated and each water has its own turn, preventing two types of water from running at the same time in the same area. A system is transparent when, at a given time in the area, a single source is operating with a single flow, and users know which source this flow belongs to, which group of users it corresponds to, and what the unit of measure is.

Flexibility

Bleumink & Sijbrandij (1990) say that flexibility in Andean irrigation systems is the possibility to change or diversify the operating system in response to regional/national changes and/or individual objectives. They distinguish two levels of flexibility: 'system flexibility', user's possibilities to choose when, how much and where to apply water; and 'general flexibility', the system's capacity to adapt to changes in the social climate and productive conditions. The irrigation system should make it possible to change agricultural production, to crops with different water requirements. Since members of certain communities can use water from different systems arriving on different schedules, they have access to water at different times, and can satisfy different requirements for different crops. An irrigation system's flexibility also allows selling, buying, or exchanging water turns. This fact, together with the existence of different systems, enables users to arrange their access to water to satisfy their crop's requirements. Single flows rotation systems also make flexibility possible in where water ends up, and thus also allows for changing the areas under irrigation.

Autonomy

Unlike centralised operating systems, water management in Andean peasant systems is characterised by a high degree of autonomy at the community level. This means that there are conditions for a high degree of participation by users.

There is autonomy when systems are operated and administered by the users them-selves. The community has autonomy regarding scheduling in relation to other communities and control and decisions over how to distribute water within the community. Distribution is carried out by the community itself, as is system maintenance from the intake to the community.

Communal autonomy in irrigation systems is also reflected in few operating levels (at most, one higher level and one lower level in the community structure). Therefore, system operation is characterised by a high degree of routine, with decen-tralised operating responsibility.

Note

1   It is common for technicians to use the concepts of irrigation system and irrigation project interchangeably. However, by 'irrigation projects' we mean a situation in which there is an external institution outside the irrigators' institutions, which intervenes in the irrigation sys-tem, influences, and sometimes defines, water distribution.

References

Bleumink, Hans & Sijbrandij, Piet,1990. *De monoflujo a multiflujo, organización de riego en el valle alto de Cochabamba*, Cochabamba: unpublished.

Gandarillas, H., *et al.*, 1994. *Dios da el agua ¿Qué hacen los proyectos? Maneja de agua y organización campesina*. La Paz: Hisbol, PRIV.

Gerbrandy, Gerben, 1991. *Concepción Campesina de Gestión de agua*. GTZ, unpublished.

Greslou, Francisco, 1990. *Visión andina y usos campesinos del agua, visión andina y usos campesinos*, La Paz: Hisbol.

Grillo, Eduardo, 1993.'La cosmovisión andina de siempre y la cosmología occidental moderna'. in:*¿Desarrollo o descolonización en los Andes?* Lima: PRATEC.

Gutiérrez, Zulema & Claure Washington, 1995. *El proceso social en la definición de la distribución del agua de la represa de Totora Khocha en la zona de Riego Punata*. MSc-Thesis, Wageningen Agricultural University.

Kessel, Juan Van & Dionisio Condori Cruz, 1992. *Criar la vida*, Vivarium, Santiago de Chile, 178 pp.

Levine, Gilbert & Coward, Walter, 1989.'Equity considerations in the modernization of irrigation systems'. In: *ODI, Irrigation Management Network*, ODI, London.

Salazar Luis, 1995. *Curso de Postgrado 'Gestión Campesina de Riego'*, PRIV-PEIRAV-CESU, Cochabamba.

Valderrama, R., 1989. *Sistemas de riego y organización social en el valle de Colca. El caso de Yaque*. Centro de Estudios y Promoción de Desarrollo, Lima, Perú.

PART VI

**ANDEAN IRRIGATION:
POLICY AND LEGISLATION**

Introduction

Does not the contradiction between a discourse on social justice and the persistent poverty reflect the domination of political regulation by the logic of production? (UNESCO, Discussion document for the Equity Workshop, Brighton, September 1978).

The social relations of production, based on the existing power structures and expressed by the unequal distribution of means of production and generated wealth, have a decisive influence on the formulation of policies and legislation related both to water resources in general and to peasant irrigation in particular. Even in those cases where specific peasant interests formally have been recognised for the elaboration of intervention policies and legislation, this is not translated automatically into social practice.

In the analysis of the relationship between peasants and State or dominant groups, and its role in the formulation and implementation of national policies and laws, it is necessary to consider another implicit aspect. This is the relationship and tension between generality and particularity (See Part 1). This is manifested in a tension between formal equality and actual differences; imposed uniformity and diverse identities; positivist law and people's customary law; official justice and local equities. In irrigation practice, it displays itself as a permanent contradiction between the uniform treatment given to very diverse irrigation systems (according to a universalising model of 'the modern') and the great diversity of needs, potentials and livelihood styles and strategies found in the present Andean reality, which require a diversified treatment.

This tendency towards uniformity, on the one hand, and the existing power structures that reinforce an unequal influence on the making of law and policy on the other, are two faces of the same coin: uniformity as a result of imposed norms facilitates the exogenous control of powerful groups. In the past decades, this process was carried out through State regulations and policy. Presently it is increasingly realised through 'free market' regulations, that need to privatise water resources and standardise its values according to the rationality of commodities. The banner has changed but, wittingly or unwittingly, the same objective is to be achieved. Both State power and market power require an individualisation and a standardisation of values and rules to increase their control over peasant irrigation.

With respect to the current emphasis on neoliberal market logic, a common criticism is the fact that a pure market lacks morals, that it is not capable of taking care of the social and cultural functions of water. It does not change but rather accentuates the long history of water accumulation in hands of the few. But would a free market for water also be anti-economic and anti-productive, or in its own words, 'irrational'?

> With respect to the issue of water, the economic optimum is obtained essentially through the collaboration and participation of different users and not through competition. It is not reasonable to compete between reservoirs or between canals, nor between intakes of the same river. On the contrary, shared and multiple use of water should be encouraged (Axel Dourojeanni, interview Agronoticias, April 1993, Lima).

So, instead of centralising control, rules, rights and obligations related to irrigation *and* instead of completely 'de-centralising' them to the miracles of private mercantile regulation, the State should (taking into account the State's inherent characteristic of 'generality') guarantee the *provision according to justice* of water to all social sectors and communities. These sectors, in turn, due to their 'particularity', can and should organise *demand according to equity*, making use of and establishing or re-establishing the diversity of collective local rules. Besides, the State would be the referee in those conflicts that extend beyond the local capacity for establishing consensus.

However, in most Andean countries the legislation fails to adequately recognise local peasant law systems. Frequently, local conceptions of equity and corresponding social practices and forms of organisation are not taken into consideration in the formulation of laws,

> [...] many of which result from copying foreign legal systems [...] In spite of the diverse character of society, laws have been made uniformly, considering the whole society as a homogeneous reality where there is no place for diverse types of law and rights. (Ana Maria Vidal, 1990. 'Derecho oficial y derecho campesino en el mundo andino'. In: *Entre la ley y la costumbre,* Stavenhagen & Iturralde (eds.), I.I.I. & I.I.D.H., Mexico).

Peasants often show a strong resistance to accepting imposed external laws and regulations concerning irrigation, while, at the same time, they take advantage of certain elements of these laws if considered opportune. So, State law and peasant law in irrigation are normative systems that interact permanently, but have a very different, sometimes contradictory character. They reflect different control and management rationales.

Incorporating customary law and peasant conceptions of equity in irrigation into State law is impossible due to their tremendous diversity, nor would it be desirable because of the disastrous impact it would have: peasant rules would be made uniform, institutionalised and, consequently, suffocated and annihilated. Besides, peasant law would lose its identity and function when applied in a different context.

> It is absurd to try to reproduce in the Law, in an explicit and substantive manner, a system of customary law, and *a fortiori* fragments of it that only make sense within the system where they come from [...] Considering that such rules are continuously renewed social products, what must be recognised to minority groups whose customary rights are to be respected, *are not the specific rules but the authority to create them*. (Manuela Carneiro da Cunha, 1990. 'El concepto de derecho consuetudinario y los derechos indígenas en la nueva constitución de Brasil'. In: *Ibid.*)

The following chapters focus on law and policies in three Andean countries that have undergone strong (centralising and/or privatising) State influence with respect to regulation of water resource issues: Peru, Ecuador, and Chile. They show how and why the formulation and implementation of law and policies on irrigation are subject to confrontations between diverse interests and powers.

In these confrontations and negotiations, so important for the definition of the rules of the game and dividing up the cake, change towards a more just water distribution and respect for specific forms of peasant-controlled equity, are central claims of peasant and indigenous peoples.

23

Competing Cultural Logics: State and 'Indigenous' Models in Conflict

Paul H. Gelles

Introduction

This chapter provides an historical and interpretive analysis of an Andean irrigation system. It argues that to understand a given social group's relationship with the environment requires us, among other things, to understand their perception of that environment. To invoke Geertz, 'irrigation systems are texts to be read.' However, the reading of these systems should enable us to understand not only the cultural models that they embody, but the power relationships that underwrite the use of these models.

My previous research has revealed that there is conflict between State and Local Models of irrigation in the community of Cabanaconde (Caylloma, Arequipa, Peru) and in many other Andean communities.[1] Organization of water distribution, and the mapping of these different cultural models and sets of social relations onto the fields and canal system of Cabanaconde, are dynamic and contested. Local and State Models of water distribution embody fundamentally different historical processes, as well as different cultural rationales concerning power, authority, resource management, and ethnic identity.

A concept that has grown out of my own reading of irrigation systems, one that I have found useful for understanding the conflict between the two models, is that of 'ethnohydrology' (Sherbondy 1982b), shorthand for the cultural construction of water, hydraulic processes, and irrigation systems as found in different societies. In Cabaneño ethnohydrology there are two basic elements: one, technical expertise about water flows, terrace and canal construction, and the changing chemical properties of water at different times of the year; and two, a set of religious beliefs and ritual practices associated with irrigation water, mountains, and the earth.

This chapter seeks to bring an understanding to the cultural rationale for attaining an abundance of water, and fertility for the fields of Cabanaconde. I am interested here in explicating the logic behind irrigation ritual and the ways in which this constitutes a medium for transmitting and reproducing collective representations about fertility, disease, power, ethnic identity, and the cosmos in general. This ideology is viewed not as a form of 'misrecognition' or 'false consciousness' masking the 'true' relations of power, but as something which has 'social efficacy' and which can 'actively produce practices and policies that constitute social reality' (Tambiah 1990: 2).

Elucidation of these collective representations is crucial, I will argue, if we wish to understand the resistance of the Local Model to the State Model of irrigation. It is also key to an understanding of the ritual, spiritual, and social dimensions of water management, and of the elements the Cabaneños feel are required in these different senses to set a successful agricultural cycle in motion.

The community of Cabanaconde

Located at 3270 meters above sea level (m.a.s.l.) on the semi-arid west slope of the southern Peruvian Andes, Cabanaconde was established as a nucleated settlement (*reducción*) in the 1570s. It was made a district capital in the early 19th century, and became an officially recognized Peasant Community with corporate legal status in 1979. It has two annexes, Pinchullo and Acpi. The people of Cabanaconde today are bilingual Quechua and Spanish speakers.

The population of Cabanaconde has more than doubled over the last century, rising from 1,796 inhabitants in 1876 and 2,960 in 1940, to 3,421 in 1981 and 4,000 in 1987 (Cook 1982: 41, 84; Denevan 1987: 17; Ministry of Agriculture 1987). Though it is difficult to get a precise figure for this shifting population, there were at least 600 households in the community as of 1988.[2] Today, there are large migrant colonies of Cabaneños in Arequipa and Lima, as well as a smaller colony in Washington, D.C. Cabanaconde has been tied into larger political and economic systems since time immemorial. Archeological and ethnohistorical studies reveal that Cabanaconde was the seat of an important prehispanic polity, was incorporated into at least two pan Andean empires (Wari and Inka), and was an important centre of production and administration during the Inka empire and during the Spanish colonial period. Cabanaconde, never a static entity, has experienced especially rapid social change since 1965, when the road finally reached the community.

The territory of Cabanaconde is environmentally diverse, and there are 'production zones' (Mayer 1985) ranging from 2000 to 4500 m.a.s.l. These zones are all within a day's walk of the community, constituting a classic case of 'compressed verticality' (Brush 1977). In the Colca canyon at 2000 m.a.s.l., the farmers cultivate fruit, alfalfa, maize, and prickly pear cactus. The latter produces a delicious fruit and serves as a habitat for cochinilla (small insects which contain a red colorant that is sold commercially as dye). In the high pastures, located at between 3800-4500 m.a.s.l., there are a number of alpaca, llama, sheep, and cattle herds. The bulk of agricultural production takes place between approximately 3000 and 3350 m.a.s.l., where the famous Cabanita maize grows. There are over 1200 hectares of irrigated fields, approximately three quarters of which are planted in maize. Peasants from many parts of the southern Andes come to barter for this product.

<u>One hundred percent of Cabanaconde's agriculture is irrigated;</u> this water comes from the Majes Canal and the snow melt of Hualca-Hualca, a 6000 meter peak. Twenty-four hours a day for nine to ten months out of the year, irrigation water descends the Hualca-Hualca river, and then passes directly through a series of canals to the more than 1,200 hectares of terraced fields which are presently cultivated in Cabanaconde.

A conceptual dual grid overlays these fields and guides the ritualized alternation of the irrigation specialists, known as Water Mayors (*yaku alcalde*), who deliver Hualca-Hualca's life-giving fluid to the parched plots of land. Hualca-Hualca is a very striking mountain, its snow-covered base peaking in a jagged rocky crest. People are very proud of this feature, and it appears in stories, childrens' drawings, and every-day conversation. Together with the 'Earthmother', Hualca-Hualca mountain is a principal deity for the people of Cabanaconde. She is the object of much worship by the general populace, and receives special offerings from the Water Mayors. Obviously, the belief and practice of dualism and telluric worship constitute only one of several ideologies that influence the religious, political, social, and cultural life of the Cabaneños. Nevertheless, the beliefs associated with Hualca-Hualca mountain and the Water Mayors are an important structuring force in community life.

The Local Model of irrigation: dual organization

During most of the yearly distribution cycle in Cabanaconde, water management is in the hands of the Water Mayors, who carry snake-headed staffs of authority and who often have flowers adorning their hats. There are two Water Mayors at any one time, one of whom is responsible for providing water to the fields classified as *anansaya* (upper moiety), and the other for those classified as *urinsaya* (lower moiety). With the help of his wife and other family members, each Water Mayor works a shift of four consecutive days and nights, after which he is relieved by the other Water Mayor. The Water Mayor is one of many rotating political offices known as *cargo* that townspeople assume as a form of community service. This *cargo* contrasts with the more formally religious *cargos* of the community, which today are voluntary and sometimes have long waiting lists. The *cargo* of Water Mayor lasts an entire round of water distribution (at present 45-50 days), and is considered to be the most onerous of *cargos*. The dangers of nocturnal irrigation, the diversion of almost two months of labor from personal agricultural and pastoral activities, and the responsibility of managing a politically and spiritually charged resource are some of the reasons why people try to avoid being named to this office.

There is an established order for the distribution of water: by canal, by the different sectors along each canal, and by the plots of land within each sector. The irrigators, by watching the course of the water during the day or through word of mouth, anticipate what time of day or night the water will reach their particular fields. They usually arrive a few hours beforehand and prepare their plots of land and feeder canals; they then await the commands of the Water Mayor. He makes sure that water follows the established order, that intakes are opened and closed correctly, and mediates any conflicts that arise. The irrigators give him coca, alcohol, and occasionally food and small amounts of money.

The Water Mayors also guard against water theft. Water robbery is chronic. Though officially condemned, it is a socially accepted practice. However, there are 'correct' and 'incorrect' ways to steal water. The latter are wasteful, cause the Water Mayor to suffer, and are detectable. People generally steal water at night in the upper reaches of the fields. For this reason the Water Mayor is usually accompanied by his son or son-in law at night. One of them oversees distribution, while the other patrols the length of the canals.

Historical evidence suggests that an earlier system of distribution by socially and spatially localized moieties has been transformed into one in which the only remaining expression of moiety affiliation is through the Water Mayors themselves. The only individuals who today are designated as belonging to *anan* or *urin saya* are the Water Mayors and these only during their *cargo*. This is because almost every individual possesses lands in both *anansaya* and *urinsaya*. Water is distributed according to whether or not land is defined as *anansaya* or *urinsaya*, but unlike elsewhere in the Andes, these divisions are not geographically exclusive. There is, however, a fairly clear axis that denotes where a stricter division probably was made in the past. This has largely disintegrated as evidenced in the scattered nature of each *saya*'s fields. Though most *anansaya* fields are geographically contiguous, a few *urinsaya* fields are scattered among them. The opposite is also true: the areas which are predominately *urinsaya* contain pockets of *anansaya* fields. Hence, along any one canal some of the fields are *anansaya*, and others *urinsaya*.

The *anan/urin* system of dual organization gives the Local Model of water management its general form, and is semantically related to a wider set of dualisms which are a fundamental part of the Cabaneño world view. The dual system of distribution also encompasses a set of religious ideas and practices associated with irrigation water, mountains, and the earth which are important cosmological referents of this model. Because the sacred water from Hualca-Hualca mountain not only nurtures fields and people but can also bewitch and kill, the Water Mayors must perform the proper rituals to guarantee abundance of water, fertility, and the personal safety of their families.

Cosmological referents of the Local Model

On the first day of his 45 to 50 day round each Water Mayor assisted by a ritual specialist (*paqo*) must make offerings (*q'apa*) to the mountain Hualca-Hualca and to the irrigation water itself. These offerings, part of a larger ritual known as *yakutinkay*, assure that water is abundant and runs swiftly, and that no accidents befall the Water Mayor or his family. This is an elaborate ritual; coca, alcohol, and cigarettes are consumed and the fetus of a llama, alpaca, or vicuña is offered to the mountain Hualca-

Hualca. The Water Mayors continue to make offerings, or at least pray with incense, at the beginning of each four day period, or at the intake of each major canal. These and other periodic rituals are viewed as necessary for the proper completion of a round of water (see Gelles 1990 for detail).

The general ritual complex associated with Hualca-Hualca mountain is quite ancient. In 1586, Juan de Ulloa Mogollón (a Spanish Crown official) found that 'according to tradition, those of the province of the Cavanas came to the town of Cavanas. The water of the town comes from the snow of a mountain that is in front of it, snow-capped and crowned, which is called Gualcagualca... they take advantage of the water from its snow-melt for their irrigated fields' (Ulloa Mogollón 1965 [1586]). The same document reveals that Hualca-Hualca was worshipped by the Cavana people. Beliefs about origins in, and worship of, mountains and other sources of water is an ancient and widespread characteristic of many ethnic groups in the Andes (Sherbondy 1982, Reinhard 1985). Today in Cabanaconde, mountains are gendered, and it is generally female mountains that provide irrigation water. Hualca-Hualca is considered to be the most important mountain of the community, and the irrigation water she provides is likened to mother's milk.

Thus the offerings by the two Water Mayors not only reproduce an ancient cosmology and ethnic identity, but communicate many meanings that are of transcendental importance to the lives of the Cabaneños. Furthermore, the crucial importance of assuring an abundant supply of water is evident by the elaboration and redundancy found in each ritual and over each cycle. As Tambiah states, 'the longer a rite is staged and the grander the scale of the ritual's outlay and adornment, the more important, the more efficacious the ceremony is deemed to be' (1985: 153). No other ritual arena receives such elaboration as that over which the Water Mayors preside.

Assuring fertility, health and prosperity, and avoiding disease, accidents, and envy are fairly universal concerns. The rituals found in Cabanaconde, as well as the cosmology that is embedded in them, provides an idiosyncratic representation of these two polar extremes of existence. The mountain gods, the Earthmother, the Watering Holes, and the Watermother herself have the potential to harm or help, to provide or to deprive, to give life or cause death.

In the case of the orchards, as in other areas of the Andes (Gelles 1984), a central notion of Andean 'ethnohydrology' concerns 'filtration' (filtraciones). Indeed, the notion of filtration allows us to understand how for Andean peoples ecological and technical knowledge of this process is fused with mountain cults, and the particular concept of power and connection with power that each orchard, field, mountain, and community possesses. Thus, the cult to Hualca-Hualca, and irrigation practices of the main fields, are part of a much larger hydraulic space and cosmology. This applies not only to the regional cult which functions in relation to certain mother mountains, but also within the micro-hydrology of different ecological floors of the community itself.

In the orchards, one performs rituals to the mountains and lakes which are seen as providing the water for the small springs (*puquios*), which emerge from the steep cliffsides of the Colca canyon. For example, in the case of Ayun, Hualca-Hualca is worshipped, whereas in Awaliwa and Aqpi (orchard and annex respectively), towards the western end of Cabanaconde's territory, Mukurka lake and Ampato mountain are worshipped. There appears to be a general division between the upper and lower orchards, with the Hualca-Hualca river serving as the dividing line. The people who have orchards on either side of this divide worship the perceived source of water for each place as well as the spring itself. Almost invariably, however, Hualca-Hualca mountain finds her way into these different offerings and libations, no matter where they occur on the communal territory.

The salience of Hualca-Hualca is not only evident in the myriad prayers made to her in the community based activities of agriculture, pastoralism, health care, and irrigation but also extends beyond the community's borders. Cabanaconde's most commercially successful musical group, Los Laureles de Cabanaconde, named their first record *Nevadito Hualca-Hualca*, and a migrant from the community won an international hairstyling contest with the Hualca-Hualca haircut, a multitiered three layered cut modeled on the form of the mountain.

Tinkachus and competition: social correlates of the Local Model

The rituals of the first morning described above are followed in the afternoon by a large social event called *tinkachu,* which is sponsored by the Water Mayor and his family. Family members, neighbors, and irrigators gather here to drink, eat, and pledge support to the Water Mayor, his wife, and other family members who help him during this important and hazardous *cargo*. Here the power of the Water Mayors is manifest: not only family and friends attend, but also other community members who want to assure that their fields receive plenty of water.

I would argue that all of these different events, ritual offerings and large social event, are just different facets of the *yakutinkay* taken as a whole: the correct fulfilment of the social event complements the ritual events of the morning, setting the tone for the successful completion of duties as Water Mayor, insuring the safety of the participants, and a good flow of water. It also mobilizes a large group of friends and family, who will be supportive in the arduous job ahead. According to several people the principal reason that friends and family gather to honor the Water Mayor and his wife – and that the latter sponsor the *fiesta* – is 'so that the water advances.'

There is competition between the two Water Mayors. The townspeople comment on the quality of the *tinkachus* noting the number of family members and friends (*munaqkuna*) each Water Mayor is able to mobilize. They also compete in water distribution: to finish one's 45-50 day round first brings a limited amount of prestige to the winner. The Water Mayors employ many techniques, including magic, to hurry their water along and to slow down that of their competition. Ritual offerings during the rounds are used to not only secure safety for the Water Mayor and his family, then, but to also create greater volume of water.

Historical roots of the Dual Model

Though the present system of dual organization encompasses many domains such as competition and spirituality, and is also related to a wide range of conceptual and social dualisms within the community, its origins exhibit an entirely different dynamic. Maria Benavides has recently argued that dual organization in the communities of the Colca valley was linked to colonial structures of power, as well as to local elites during the early part of the present century (Benavides 1988). This is certainly the case for Cabanaconde, where dual organization served the interests of the Inca empire, Spanish colonists, and later local elites (Gelles 1990, 1995). Dual organization, one of many pre-Inca social and symbolic forms the Inca empire expanded upon, assumed a strongly defined political character under Inca hegemony. Two ethnic lords (*kurakas*) were appointed to each conquered group, the leader of *anansaya* superior in command to that of *urinsaya*. Dual organization was the conduit through which great revenues and surpluses were extracted from peasants by the state.

This dual administrative system – like other Inca institutions such as labor service (*mit'a*) – was appropriated and redirected by the Spaniards to serve the ends of the Spanish Crown and *encomienda* system. The latter were grants of Indian labor given to certain Spaniards during the 16th century for their service to the Crown; there are references to the *encomiendas* of Cabana *anansaya* and Cabana *urinsaya* as early as 1549 (Cook 1982: 4). Labor and tribute to the *encomienda* owners were extracted through this renovated form of dual organization. When Cabanaconde was established as a nucleated settlement (*reducción*) later in the century, these endogamous moieties became spatially localized within the town. After the *encomiendas* faded, dual organization continued to serve Crown interests as well as the large number of Spaniards who settled in the town.

As Benavides has noted, the social division into moieties (often called *parcialidades*) in the 19th and 20th centuries has been 'a mechanism of control exercised by the local authorities in the province of Caylloma and in other regions of the Andes' (Benavides 1988: 51). In Cabanaconde the moiety division continued to serve an administrative purpose even after independence: there were tribute collectors for each *saya* or *parcialidad* well into the mid-19th century. Though the principle of endogamy appears to have faded before the turn of the century, the moieties continued to be used as a means for organizing varied activities, such as the sponsorship of *fiestas* and 'public works' well into the 1930s. In fact these public works often provided private benefits for the local priests, and for the descendents of the powerful Spaniards who used to rule over the community. Clearly, then, the present division of plots of land into *anan* and *urin*, each with a corresponding Water Mayor, was at one time part of an all-encompassing moiety system used for extractive purposes by the Inca and Spanish states, one that had social and spatial correlates within the community itself.

Thus, the physically demanding, time consuming, and dangerous job of Water Mayor is a carry-over of an exploitive system which required poor peasants, formerly illiterate 'Indians,' to oversee the physical distribution of water. The colonial nature of this *cargo* is all the more apparent if we consider that before the 1970s, this service was for an entire year, not seven weeks as is the case today. Today, the Water Mayors are sometimes jokingly referred to as the 'ragged mayors' (*saqsa alcaldes*). This is partly because of their tattered appearance after several consecutive days and nights on the job. It is also an ironic comparison to the figure of the much more powerful town mayor found in Cabanaconde and in other Andean communities. Until the 1960's, there was a fairly rigid social and economic divide between the principal authority figures and the peasants who undertook the office of Water Mayor. Even today powerful individuals often manage to evade this duty by occupying the more prestigious and powerful offices, or by paying poor peasants to take their place.

However, one of the paradoxes of the traditional system is that the people who assume or who are forced to assume the office of Water Mayor, and who are obliged to divert tremendous amounts of time and energy from their normal agricultural and pastoral duties, become spiritually, socially, and materially empowered during their tenure. This is indicated by the important rituals they are entrusted with carrying out, by the social events they sponsor, and by their ability to provide additional water to the fields of family and friends. Though this power is restricted to the irrigation activities themselves, ends with the Water Mayor's tenure, and is ultimately small compared to the power of many other communal authorities, the staffbearing Water Mayors are deferred to as important ritual actors and as water managers during their *cargo*.

The State Model

For a brief, but important, period in the annual irrigation cycle there is a different type of 'repartitioner', or person in charge of distribution. These individuals, who are community members like the Water Mayors, implement the State Model of distribution. They are called Controlers (*controladores*), and distribute water to the fields sequentially from 'one end to the other' (*de canto*), ignoring the dual classification of the plots. They are not fulfilling a major *cargo* as are the Water Mayors, but rather a minor civic duty. Rather than receive coca and alcohol, they are paid a monetary wage by the irrigators. They neither perform elaborate rituals nor sponsor large social events as do the Water Mayors. Today and over the last fifty years, there have been attempts to completely supplant the Local Model of distribution for that of the State Model. Though the State Model, part of what Lynch (1988) has called the 'bureaucratic transition,' has gained ground over the years, the Local Model remains firmly entrenched (Gelles 1990).

Like their divergent cultural rationales, the historical roots of the State Model differ from those of the Local Model. The State Model of water management has its roots in both Spanish and more contemporary 'bureaucratic' traditions. The Irrigators Commission, the <u>local manifestation of the state's irrigation bureaucracy,</u> is operative throughout the year in that it oversees and has <u>legal authority over the Water Mayors and the traditional *anan/urin* system</u>. Yet it is only during part of the rainy season that the State Model, based on the General Water Laws (*Ley General de Aguas*), is used to distribute water.

Rationality and ritual assurance

The Water Mayors and the *anan/urin* model of dual organization embody a fundamentally different cultural rationale concerning power and authority than that of the Controllers and the *de canto* model of water management. The State Model legitimates its authority and attempts to control irrigation primarily through the written word, which until the 1960s was the province of a small elite. Today the seals of authority and the Minutes of the Irrigators Commission are treated as powerful objects; the written word is still a symbol of power. However, this symbolism yields to the ultimately more powerful authority represented by the snake-headed staffs and offerings of the Water Mayors. This is largely because the Irrigators Commission is made up of community members who fully participate in the religious ideas and practices embodied in the Local Model.

cf. underore
ritual

Adherence to the Local Model must also be seen as resistance to the <u>hegemonic ideology implicit in the State Model itself.</u> This involves the cultural politics of the coast and the highlands in Peru, in which the relationship between the two areas is completely infused with a colonial mindset that views the human and natural resources of the Andean highlands as inferior to the Hispanic coast. This is expressed in a Ministry of Agriculture document elaborated in 1980 which states that the problems of the Colca valley villages (which most surely applies to the highlands as a whole) are due to 'the low cultural level of the irrigators...[and] a certain resistance to rational work methods' (ORDEA 1980). This prejudiced view completely ignores the State's own shortcomings in helping to improve and expand the hydraulic resources of the community. It also ignores the cultural rationales of the indigenous knowledge systems concerning irrigation.

This lack of understanding is exhibited in the state's attempt to 'rationalize' the distribution process itself. As previously noted, during the rainy season the Controllers do <u>not</u> follow the *anan/urin* system, but rather irrigate continuously from one field to the next adjacent field (*de canto*). For many years the State has attempted to institute the *de canto* system for the entire yearly cycle, which would do away completely with the *anan/urin* model of distribution. The *de canto* model is supposedly more rational and efficient since it saves a considerable amount of water that is lost when one Water Mayor has to return to a few plots of land along a canal in which the majority of plots have already been irrigated by the other Water Mayor.

Though townspeople are well aware of this water loss, they say that the State Model is even less efficient: paying hourly wages provides no incentives to hurry the water along, and Controllers slow down to collect more money on each plot. Moreover, the dual model provides a cognitive map and fixed sequence of distribution not found in the State Model. Under the State Model, as evidenced in previous attempts by local elites to use the *de canto* system to irrigate unauthorized fields, decisions regarding distribution can be more capricious and subject to manipulation by powerful individuals. The nature of the offices of Controller and Water Mayor differs significantly, and there is also greater pressure in the Local Model for the Water Mayor to be conscientious and fair in distribution.

Conclusions

The Local and State Models embody different conceptions of power, authority, efficiency, and availability. During the time of year when assuring the fertility of the fields is especially important, well prepared ritual offerings made by each Water Mayor are carried out to secure an abundance of water; a well performed ritual is believed to actually *increase* the flow of water. The notion of abundance is part of the larger semantic domain of fertility and ritual action which figures so importantly within Cabanaconde's religious tradition.

Taken together, the actions of the two Water Mayors constitute another ritual level, that of dual organization (Maybury-Lewis 1989), which seeks equilibrium through the alternation of complementary opposites, and which is related to many other conceptual and social dualisms. Indeed, dualism is a fundamental feature of Andean culture. As Sallnow (1987:239) has put it, 'dualism is the cultural mechanism by which the random power of the wild is channelled into the domain of human society.' In this sense, the Local Model of dual organization not only establishes a pace of distribution along a set path, but also provides the gameboard for the Water Mayors. The ritual competition between them, in which their social and spiritual selves are publicly displayed, advances the water quickly. The entire community observes and participates in this other ritual level.

In this chapter I have attempted to shed light on the culturally plural nature of Peruvian society and irrigation management, as well as on the ways that irrigation models serve extractive purposes and are transformed over time. The Water Mayors, a legacy of Inca and Spanish hegemony, today embody and implement the local 'indigenous' form of irrigation management, one used, among other things, to ritually attain abundant water, fertility, and safety, as well as to resist State interference in local affairs. Cabaneño ethnohydrology and the Local Model of irrigation, then, have their own 'communicative rationality,' one which suggests designs for living and which structures social practice. Unfortunately, the irrigation bureaucracies of the Peruvian State and non-governmental organizations rarely take Andean models of irrigation and community into account. Rather they ignore and denigrate these very models, and this explains to some degree local resistance to, and resentment of, foreign-imposed 'development.'

Notes

1. For detail on the data presented here, gathered in the years 1987-1988, see Gelles (1984, 1990, 1993a, 1993b, 1994, 1995).
2. Population growth has placed more and more pressure on land, water, and the other productive resources of the community. The demographic expansion, combined with a bilateral inheritance pattern, creates rampant partitioning of land holdings (*minifundismo*). Because of this and because Cabanaconde is an economically differentiated community (though not as much as many other communities in the region), many farmers must often rely on sharecropping arrangements and land rental to make ends meet.

References

Benavides, María, 1988. 'La división social y geográfica Hanansaya/Hurinsaya en el valle de Colca y la provincia de Caylloma'. *Boletín de Lima* 60: 49-53.

Brush, Stephen, 1977. *Mountain, Field, and Family.* Philadelphia: University of Pennsylvania Press.

Cabanaconde: Books of the Irrigators Commission (BIC); Books of the Municipal Council (BMC); Books of the Peasant Community (BPC).

Cook, David N., 1982. *The People of the Colca Valley: A Population Study.* Boulder: Westview Press.

De la Vera Cruz, Pablo, 1987. *Cambios en los patrones de asentamiento y el uso y abandono de los andenes en Cabanaconde, Valle del Colca, Perú.* Oxford: B.A.R. International Series. Denevan, William (ed.).

~ 1987. *Terrace Abandonment in the Colca Valley, Peru.* Oxford: B.A.R. International Series.

~ 1988 (ed.). *The Cultural Ecology, Archeology, and History of Terracing and Terrace Abandonment in the Colca Valley of Southern Peru.* Technical Report, Volume 2, University of Wisconsin at Madison.

Geertz, Clifford, 1980. *Negara.* New Jersey: Princeton University Press.

Gelles, Paul H., 1984. *Agua, faenas, y organización comunal en los Andes: el caso de San Pedro de Casta.* M.A. thesis. Universidad Católica, Lima.

~ 1990. *Channels of Power, Fields of Contention: The Politics and Ideology of Irrigation in an Andean Peasant Community.* Ph.D. Dissertation. Harvard University.

~ 1993a. 'Irrigation as a Cultural System: Introductory remarks.' *Proceedings of the 24th Chacmool Conference*, pp. 329-332. Alberta: University of Calgary Archeological Association.

~ 1993b. 'Cabaneño Ethnohydrology: The Cosmological Referents and Historical Roots of an Andean Irrigation System.' *Proceedings of the 24th Chacmool Conference*, pp. 353-361. Alberta: University of Calgary Archeological Association.

~ 1994. 'Channels of Power, Fields of Contention: The Politics of Irrigation and Land Recovery in an Andean Peasant Community.' In *Irrigation at High Altitudes: The Social Organization of Water Control Systems in the Andes.* William Mitchell and David Guillet (editors), pp.233-273. Society for Latin American Anthropology Publication Series, Vol.12, American Anthropological Association, Washington D.C.

~ 1995. 'Equilibrium and Extraction: Dual Organization in the Andes.' *American Ethnologist* 22 (4): 710-742.

Lynch, Barbara, 1988. *The Bureaucratic Transition: Peruvian Government Intervention in Sierra Small Scale Irrigation.* Ph.D. Dissertation. Cornell University.

Maybury-Lewis, David (ed.), 1989. 'The Quest for Harmony'. In: *The Attraction of Opposites:*

Thought and Society in the Dualistic Mode. D. Maybury-Lewis and U. Almagor, eds. Ann Arbor: University of Michigan Press.

Mayer, Enrique, 1985. 'Production Zones', In: *Andean Ecology and Civilization*. Masuda, Shozo, et al. pp.45-84 Tokyo: University of Tokyo Press.

ORDEA, 1980. Diagnóstico del distrito de riego no. 49: Colca. Arequipa: Sub-dirección nacional de aguas y suelo.

Rasnake, Roger, 1988. *Domination and Cultural Resistance. Authority and Power among an Andean People*. Durham and London: Duke University Press.

Reinhard, Joseph, 1985. 'Chavin and Tiahuanaco: A New Look at Two Andean Ceremonial Centers.' *National Geographic Research Reports*. 1 (3): 395-422.

Sallnow, Michael J.,1987. *Pilgrims of the Andes*. Smithsonian, Washington D. C.

Sherbondy, Jeanette, 1982a. *The Canal Systems of Hanan Cuzco*. Ph.D. Dissertation. University of Illinois, Urbana.

~ 1982b. 'El regadío, los lagos y los mitos de origen'. *Allpanchis* (Cuzco) 17 (20).

Tambiah, Stanley J., 1985. *Culture, Thought, and Social Practice*.

~ 1990. *Magic, Science, Religion, and the Scope of Rationality*. Cambridge: Cambridge University Press.

Treacy, John, 1989. *Canal Irrigation in Corporaque. The Fields of Coporaque: Agricultural Terracing and Water Management in the Colca Valley, Arequipa, Peru*. Ph.D. Dissertation. University of Wisconsin, Madison.

~ 1994. *Las Chacras de Coporaque: Andenería y Riego en el Valle de Colca*. Lima: I.E.P.

Ulloa Mogollón, Juan de, 1965 [1586]. 'Relación de la Provincia de los Collaguas para la discrepción de las Indias que su majestad manda hacer'. In *Relaciones Geográficas de Indias*. Vol.1. Marcos Jiménez de la Espada, Madrid.

Valderrama, Ricardo and Escalante, Carmen, 1988. *Del Tata Mallku a la MamaPacha: Riego, sociedad y ritos en los Andes peruanos*. Lima.

24

From Agrarian Reform to Privatisation of Land and Water: the Case of the Peruvian Coast

María Teresa Oré

Introduction

This chapter covers the period from 1969 to the present (1997), during which two successive processes - contradictory in many ways - have restructured agrarian legislation and policy in Peru. On the one hand, the government took over control of land and water through agrarian reform. On the other, the reverse process of privatising these same resources began in the 1980s, and has been institutionalised and legalised over the last six years. During both processes, the agrarian sector has followed the overall economic policy implemented by the respective governments.

Our topic centres mainly on social organisation of irrigation on the Peruvian coast, since other chapters covered the issues of Andean systems in Peru[1]. These two systems have evolved in different processes. Nevertheless, it is very useful to compare and analyse them together, because national agrarian and water legislation, formulated on the basis of the coastal situation, is often in effect for the entire country, sometimes with powerful consequences in the Andes. For example, in a previous paper we have already pointed out how, under agrarian reform, the Law on Users Organisations overrode any other form of organisation. 'This new irrigation organisation set up by the government imposed a single organisational model for all irrigators in the highlands and on the coast, ignoring their geographical and ecological differences, and their productive, social and cultural differences'.[2] This chapter seeks to show some of the background for these laws and policies, and their relationship with the reality on the coast.

It is on the Peruvian coast where, since the turn of the century, the largest irrigation systems have been developed. Agriculture in this area is fundamentally irrigated farming. This is where our country's main export cash crops have been grown, including sugar and cotton. Moreover, during this century, the coast has been decisively affected by State intervention in irrigation organisation, whereas such intervention has generally been much less in Andean irrigation systems where, on the contrary, the community has played a major role.

Our interest is to show the changes that have occurred in social organisation of irrigation and the process of governmental transfer of irrigation systems to be controlled by the users: what has State intervention meant in irrigation systems, how have State irrigation systems been transferred to the users, how has the debate evolved regarding water privatisation, what is the role of users' associations? These are some of the questions that we will attempt to address below.

Agrarian reform[3]

The agrarian reform process began in 1969, under the government of General Velasco-Alvarado, converting large haciendas on the coast into agrarian production co-operatives (CAPs) and, in the highlands, into 'agrarian societies of social interest' (SAISs). Both were initially under State control. However, smallholdings and coastal farm towns, as well as village communities (mostly in the highlands) kept their prior organisation and continued working the land traditionally.

That same year, the new Water Code came into effect, in place of the 1902 code. The new code established, for the first time, that the State was the sole owner of both surface and underground water, which would hereafter be considered a public good rather than private property. Agencies such as the Water Bureau and the Technical Irrigation Administration wielded the Ministry of Agriculture's control and regulation of irrigation. This eliminated the previous organisation, controlled by hacienda owners. Governmental agencies and officials were the promoters of the new agricultural development model. The tasks involving irrigation, which had been handled by technical commissions and the farmers themselves, were now to be administered and directed exclusively by the new governmental irrigation agencies, run by engineers and technicians.

Ten years later, in 1979, a new organisation was created for irrigation users. This involved two entities: the Users' Association, gathering the beneficiaries from an entire irrigation district, and the Irrigators' Commission, including the beneficiaries of a single sector. Both agencies were autonomous, although they were to work together. In practice, the irrigators' involvement was formal, limited to paying fees for the right to use water. The role of governmental officials was fundamental for water administration and distribution.

Water was considered to be a natural resource, the use and management of which required no social organisation. Similarly, the concept of agricultural development was grounded in technified, mechanised farming, geared toward growing high-profit export crops. This concept took form in the new irrigation organisation structure.

So, co-operatives were favoured, for obvious political reasons and because they are open to technology and to production for export. This cast a shadow over small peasant plots, used mainly for day-to-day subsistence, and supported medium-sized landholdings (mainly the former hacienda owners, whom the agrarian reform law left with a limited 'unaffectable minimum' amount of land). The amount of water was determined according to the average need for each crop, according to annual scheduling.

Finally, activities ranging from building new infrastructure to upkeep and cleaning were handled by specialised technical personnel, using modern machinery. This pushed aside the users, who had been responsible for these tasks. As for small users and peasants, their right to water resulting from collective work contributions, according to their own norms, was eliminated. Rather, the right to water depended on payment in money. Consequently, their organisations were deactivated. The new Water Code did not recognise them anyway. However, this also cut off the transmission of traditional lore which till then had been passed down from generation to generation.

This broke up a long-standing tradition of community practices and organisation, and contributed to worsening disorganisation and scattering of villagers, which is still a problem to this day. The relationship between the State and peasants had always been tense and conflict-ridden, but this disorganisation resulting from the new institutional arrangement prevented them from presenting their demands or proposals coherently.

As the co-operatives went through increasingly serious problems with administration, medium-sized landowners began assuming greater power in irrigators' commissions and gaining greater privileges in irrigation. They also had access to underground water, which was out of peasants' reach. Conflicts among different types of irrigators regarding irrigation were ongoing, and the agencies charged with the new administration were swamped with conflicts to be resolved. They became merely formal entities, with little possibility of efficiently administering irrigation.

It is curious to see now that this complex situation did not, at the time, arouse much interest or provoke significant action from agrarian scholars, nation-wide rural organisations, or political parties. During those years, the perception of the agrarian problem hinged on land, and the political forces related to the Military Government and the leftist parties agreed that land was the issue. Mottoes such as 'Land is for the people working on it', or 'Peasant: the boss will have to stop feeding on your poverty' were as far as agrarian discussion went in regard to land distribution.

By contrast, the water problem was ignored, left out of all social or political demands, and remained circumscribed to technical issues. The new 1969 Water Code was welcomed by the government and by the Left: finally, hacienda owners' death-grip on water had been broken, along with the hacienda-oriented concepts of the 1902 code. The role of the State in the new irrigation organisation raised no eyebrows, and no one paid much attention to the elimination of the irrigation organisation that haciendas had controlled. Much less attention was paid to the implications of all this for peasant organisation and reproduction of the rural sociocultural world.

The situation after agrarian reform

During the early 1980s, in coastal co-operatives and agrarian societies of social interest in the highlands, certain isolated attempts were made, at the initiative of the members involved, to divide the water themselves. Production and management-related problems were becoming serious. The governmental model of co-operative agricultural enterprises entered a phase of crisis, and redivision of water and land became generalised during the eighties. This began the post-agrarian reform process, which concluded at the end of the eighties with the liquidation of the co-operative enterprises.

Redivision of co-operatives made government administration of irrigation more complicated, because of increasing demands by former co-operative members regarding available water. The Technical Irrigation Administration for each valley, and the users' associations, were not prepared to meet the new irrigators' demands, and these smallholders - the *parceleros* - were growing in number rapidly.

Concurrently, tremendous political violence broke out, driven by such armed groups as the Shining Path and the Túpac Amaru Revolutionary Movement. After beginning in rural zones of the highlands, they spread gradually almost everywhere throughout the country. Favoured targets were precisely the water intakes and dams, as well as other water infrastructure. Therefore, maintaining these facilities was risky, dangerous work, and mainly ground to a halt. Consequently, irrigation infrastructure was abandoned.

By the late eighties, the internal situation within users' associations was complex. Former co-operatives, which were the irrigation users in 1969, were followed by the smallholders, who were the new users, along with others who had not been co-operative members, and owners of larger plots as well. The latter, by the end of the eighties, had diversified their production and were prospering with new export crops. As the most successful farmers, they took the lead in water user associations. Co-ordinating closely with government officials, they oversaw and administered irrigation water for all users, but ensured that they got the lion's share for themselves. This entailed generalised discontent among peasants, and anarchy and disorganisation spread. There were no clear norms or regulations, or any authority that was actually respected - a situation of chaos and disorder.

The new role of irrigation water users

By the early 1990s, amidst the profoundest national economic crisis, along with an unprecedented upward spiral of violence, the worst of the century, the State abandoned its previous functions and services that it had been performing to oversee and administer irrigation. This began a new stage in agrarian policy, in which the market was expected to be the ruling force.

By late 1989, as Alan García-Pérez' term of office drew to a close, Supreme Decree No. 037-89AG transferred all control over and administration of irrigation to users' associations, as the State pulled out of this area. Some months later, in 1990, new water use fee regulations were issued, empowering users' organisations to collect fees for agricultural water use and to operate and maintain irrigation systems. This granted a new series of duties to these organisations, which the Government had been performing before.[4] This began a transformation process (still underway) whereby users' associations are undertaking water management. Overall, this coincided with the election of Alberto Fujimori's government in July 1990.

The users' associations faced a difficult situation in the early nineties. With precarious budgets, obsolete machinery, insufficient technical or administrative capacity to adequately perform their work, their most serious problem was the lack of any internal organisation among users, where intense conflicts and lack of authority were the order of the day. Associations were led by users' groups who did not represent the entire constituency, and moreover lacked any initiative. This was the result of the dependent relationship that they had developed with government institutions for years.

Things also looked very difficult for the governmental agencies that had previously administered irrigation: the Ministry of Agriculture was soon dismantled and the General Directorate of Waters was severely downsized and incorporated (in 1992) into the National Institute of Natural Resources (INRENA). This closed the cycle that had begun early this century, in regard to government intervention in irrigation administration.

This situation of State devolution happened during times when the intense process of violence scourged the entire country, especially in rural areas. This all became worse yet with a drought affecting extensive agricultural zones. Water problems became more acute, conflicts heightened, and users' associations found themselves powerless to solve such problems. The water infrastructure broke down, funds were in short supply, and fees were hardly collected, water was scarce and associations' organisational problems completed the outlook at the beginning of the process to 'transfer' government irrigation systems to irrigators' own control.

Proposed water laws and discussion: privatisation of water and land

By early 1993, the first drafts of a new Water Law began making the rounds. Its most noteworthy features were the government's extremely liberal position, emphasising *privatisation of water* and its interest in creating and promoting a water market. This meant that water was not a State-owned resource for the public interest, but a private resource, after all. The model to be applied was the Chilean one, since water had been privatised in Chile. These draft proposals caused profound debates; critical discussions were realised at the regional and national level with active participation by users' associations, which stopped the enactment of this law.

In 1994 a decree was issued (D.S. O27-PRES) that regulated concession to the private sector of major irrigation infrastructure operation and maintenance. In that same year, another Water Law was announced as imminent. However, opposition again arose and, in view of the upcoming elections, the law was again put off.

In July 1995, amidst great opposition, the majority in parliament passed the new Land Law (No. 26505), which legally created a land market, especially on the coast. Meanwhile, because of the opposition among users and the different institutions related to agriculture, and even within the government itself, the draft water law remained pending.

In 1996 a new version of the Water Law was circulated. It differed from its predecessors because it no longer referred to privatising water resources; it underscored the need for autonomous authority in watersheds, and reconfirmed the idea that water is State property - but with the variation that water could be granted to private users on a concession basis. This arrangement would be registered along with real estate records, and could be sold or mortgaged independently from land.

This new version continued to focus on coastal valleys as the main element of agrarian policy, ignoring the needs and differences of Andean irrigation systems. The main consequence of passing this version of the law would be to form water monopolies, either by individual users or private companies related to agriculture or not, but with strong economic power in each zone. Consequently, small farmers would basically be cut off from access to water. At this writing (October 1997), the Water Law has not yet been passed. Various political problems have brought the Fujimori government to its lowest popularity rating since he took office. This has intensified political tension over the last few months and has meant that the proposed law, now before Congress in a new version, is still being postponed.

Users' associations, challenged by liberal policy

The question arising now is: who are the current users of irrigation water, and what is the outlook for irrigators' associations after water management is 'transferred'?

Users' new profile

The most significant change in the last few years has been the increase in the number of users, those on associations' records and informal users as well, for whom no accurate information is available. Similarly, the number of users has also broadened in terms of location: water users are no longer just farmers, but non-farmers are included by the new laws as users. These include industries, mining, and even urban waterworks, although their participation on users' associations has not yet been defined.

Agrarian users are currently divided into very small farmers (up to three hectares), small farmers (3-10 ha), medium landowners (10-50 ha) and agribusiness (over 50 ha). According to the 1993 census, most irrigators are in the 1-10 ha range, involving the first two categories, who are basically producing staple foodstuffs (grains, legumes and vegetables) for cities' growing and insistent demand, as well as fundamentally traditional export commodities such as cotton. The medium and agribusiness users are mainly producing for export, especially non-traditional products such as asparagus, mangoes, and so on.

Many of these new users are city folk, who rent land from small landowners and farmers to grow vegetables and legumes, especially in the valleys near large cities. They are known as 'renters', and are highly varied in origin, but many are basically business persons.

> 'Here there are people that have been farming here since their ancestors, and we don't have any trouble with them; they know their obligations, and you don't have to tell them to go clean out their canals, because they already know. The problem is with these new renters. They cause problems and disorder, because they have the land, but they are not farmers, and they think that because they are new, there is nothing they have to respect: they don't respect the canals, they don't respect the work obligations, they don't respect anything. Right now, what are we becoming? Labourers for the renters, and after all the land is ours. We rent them our land and then we have to work on it for them'. (Ezequiel Ramos, *parcelero* from Chillón valley).

Then there are the informal irrigation users. Since they are not on the books, no one knows how many of them there are, but they have become an important component. Most come from the highlands provinces alongside the coastal valleys, who were affected in the last few years by the violence. These new users have set up on previously uncultivated land, and their location and production are very precarious, but they demand more and more irrigation water.

Other informal irrigation users include new population settlements that have sprung up in the different coastal valleys, at the borderline between the rural and urban sectors. This has happened in the Santa, Chillón and Ica valleys. These settlements are located near irrigation systems and the residents use water in various ways. One of the greatest problems entailed by these precarious settlements that have grown up in the last few years is the water pollution that they cause in irrigation systems, which are causing problems for nearby people and farming.

Finally, there has recently been a marked increase in women's involvement as irrigation users, within the various social groups mentioned above. Traditionally, female irrigators were the exception in rural areas, the only ones being widows and single women. However, as migration - especially male - to cities on the coast and in the jungle has increased, women have been left in charge of family plots. They have been dealing with obligations regarding irrigation on the farm, and their dedication and care in the work of daytime surveillance (and even at night, in extreme cases, to prevent water robbery) is widely acknowledged.

> 'When it's my turn, we get a certain day, say Wednesday for instance, and we have the water in the morning, and we begin irrigating, so then we walk the canal because other folks would like to take away our water. . . yes, yes, we keep watch over the part that is ours, of course, because we have to defend our day, until our time is up for irrigating; sometimes when one does not watch out, other people take away our water. . .' (Mrs. Adela de Ramírez, Huarangal, Chillón Valley.)

Major changes have happened in Users' Associations over the last six years, because of the duties that they have taken over according to the new orientation of agrarian policy and transfer of irrigation management. Who are the users taking part in assemblies, and occupying positions of leadership on the associations?

On a formal level, all users are entitled to participate in meetings and be elected as leaders. However, in reality things are different. Association facilities are mostly located in cities, and meeting notices are not always well disseminated, so relatively few users regularly attend meetings. This means that decisions are made by a small group of irrigators. Association positions are generally medium landowners, with a few smaller farmers.

Although the number of users has diversified and increased, and the organisation's functions have expanded, in practice these changes have not been reflected in new organisational or participatory forms. Women, for example, are not represented, because they are involved in the irrigation work itself, but left out of formal irrigation organisation.

Consequently, these days, users are significantly increasing in number, and they are extremely heterogeneous in terms of land ownership, production, social diversity, and even gender. This expands the diversity of demands and needs regarding limited water resources. This complex panorama characterises irrigation users nowadays, and poses the need to reformulate organisational arrangements.

The current setting for water associations

Given the diverse conditions under which users' associations operate in the coastal valleys, their new functions are also diversified. The State has a very limited role, through the Technical Administration, but does wield some control over users' associations.

At the leadership level, most associations have had some turnover and, in general, they are becoming more dynamic and taking more initiative than when they were led directly by government agencies. Local, regional and national debates about the new proposed water law and recent legal provisions have contributed to reactivating and stimulating their organisations. However, most users are still poorly informed about changes in legal provisions regarding irrigators' organisations and the new land law.

The outlook for users' associations in technical terms is as follows: with the exception of certain valleys (e.g. Chancay-Lambayeque, where the irrigation system is well maintained) most have serious maintenance problems at river intakes and distributary structures, with obsolete, rustic, and even ruined facilities, gates that will not operate, and no measurement devices, among other serious deficiencies. This all causes major difficulties in controlling and administering water efficiently[5].

Water distribution has become a burning issue among users and a tinderbox of tension during meetings. The lack of security about having irrigation water available leads to ongoing conflicts among users, who demand efficient, equitable administration and distribution of irrigation water among everyone. This insecurity promotes water theft; to prevent robbery, each user must have guards to watch over the area when it is their turn to irrigate; in other cases, the board hires guards.

Legally, irrigators' organisations face a contradiction because the law says they are autonomous decision-makers, but in practice the Technical Irrigation Administration (which continues to operate on a limited basis) still retains the final word regarding decisions that are really only the associations' business. This results in conflicts between associations and the Administration. Setting the price for water fees is just one example of the running battle between these authorities.

Socially and organisationally, associations still have serious problems. In addition to irrigators' heterogeneity, the only revenues that associations have are the water fees they charge users. This is not enough to cover the manifold needs of maintaining the irrigation infrastructure, including payment of service personnel, among other items. The greatest problem here for associations is the delay in users' payment of these fees. Users' generalised discontent regarding deficient system management makes them reluctant to pay the fees.

As for internal organisational issues, association leaders have little legitimacy in the eyes of users. They do not have, or know how to achieve, an ongoing relationship with different irrigation users, and fail to keep them informed about their activities. Generally, users reproach their leaders for not undertaking projects or providing information about how they use the money collected; mistrust of leaders is common. Regarding logistics and infrastructure, although services have actually improved and modernised over the last couple of years, association offices have little current information on their users or system operation. This prevents them from efficiently managing system maintenance.

And in terms of management, associations stand before a new arena created by recent legislation: they can become companies and enter directly into international agreements with technical co-operation agencies. However, their current situation is extremely difficult: underfunded, understaffed, without people trained to prepare studies or projects or in management skills. These shortcomings prevent them from efficiently managing water resources.

Concluding remarks

The proposed Water Law promoting privatisation of water resources caught the eye of users and politicians in all sectors as early as 1993. So far, that new law has not been passed, and it is expected to remain in limbo. However, internal organisational changes affecting users' organisations in Peru have not received the same degree of attention. These bodies have assumed new functions, as irrigation systems have been transferred to users. Associations are undergoing serious technical, legal and management problems, which are forcing them to consider the need to create new organisational forms in order to efficiently manage water resources.

The use of irrigation water for political purposes has been clearly present throughout Peru's agrarian history. Initially, there were campaign promises of implementing new irrigation projects every time a presidential election came around. Nowadays, the government is utilising the 'El Niño' phenomenon to bolster its public image: cleaning out irrigation canals and building up levies on riverbanks have become the government's best-publicised activities. However, users, irrigators' commissions, and users' associations have not been included in these actions, which paradoxically are precisely what they were created to oversee. Users' organisations have been left out of all these actions.

Over the last three decades, Peruvian agriculture has undergone major structural changes in regard to land and water, but this is now occurring in a context in which agriculture is seen separately from the central issues of the government's economic policy in regard to its importance in terms of production and in regard to farmers themselves. At the same time, users, the government, analysts and promoters seem to have lost any perspective on how to handle the current situation. This is going on amidst increasing heterogeneity among irrigation users.

We may also conclude that, in regard to water resources, the inter-relationships between cities and the countryside are increasing as cities grow and new users demand more and more water. The countryside is become relatively urbanised, both on the coast and in the Andean region.

According to the new orientation of agrarian policy, hinging upon the marketplace, the government has postponed regionalisation, reinforcing centralisation and governmental control over resources and decision-making. Transfer of governmental irrigation systems to users, rather than the outgrowth of a well-planned policy, is a de facto situation unrelated to any clear strategy.

Finally in regard to equity, social organisation of irrigation is currently far from equitable for all users. Achieving truly equitable management will be the task to be achieved over the coming years.

Notes

1   Observation added by the editors.
2   In: J. Alfaro, F. Guardia, J. Golte, L. Masson & M.T. Oré, 1991. 'La organización social del riego'. *Ruralter no. 9*, CICDA, Lima.
3   This first part has been prepared on the basis of the book entitled *Riego y Organización. Evolución Histórica y Experiencias Actuales en el Perú*, (Lima, 1989), by the same author.
4   In 1991, Decree D.S. O48-91 AG was issued, ratifying the Technical Irrigation Administrator as the water authority, and creating the autonomous watershed authority, closely co-ordinating with users' associations and irrigators' commissions.
5   In summary, the nation's irrigation infrastructure is precarious everywhere, with serious maintenance problems, which became painfully evident during the 1994 flooding, and which will cause further problems in the upcoming months for the 1997-1998 'El Niño'-Phenomenon.

25

The Ecuadorian Water Legislation and Policy Analysed from the Indigenous-Peasant Point of View

Nina Pacari

The crisis now affecting Ecuador, and most other Latin American countries, is as global as the economic structure. Neoliberal globalisation necessarily calls for structural adjustments and legal-economic reordering. Serving the interests of small, financially powerful groups, governments have had to encourage privatisation, labelling it lately as 'modernisation'. Agriculture has not escaped this trend. In 1994, they imposed a Law of Agrarian Development on us, the main objective of which was the 'land market' as a new possibility for peasants and indigenous people to overcome their poverty. However, it was obviously designed to re-concentrate land by those who have economic power to buy it. This meant deepening social inequity, which would have caused problems even more serious than those we are facing now.

The Law of Agrarian Development, in such terms, was viewed as a threat to the life of indigenous peoples. Therefore, the National Confederation of Indigenous Nationalities of Ecuador (CONAIE) produced a counter-proposal that was rejected by the National Congress. So, CONAIE reacted by developing a national mobilisation, which led to official discussion of some amendments. One amendment involved the chapter on water, to stop the privatisation and monopolisation of water resources. We all know that water is a basic resource for survival. In the indigenous world, water is a 'source of life', like 'blood inside our bodies'. The indigenous vision of water revolves around three features: water as a source of life; water as a living being, and water as part of a whole.

For an indigenous society, water scarcity and irrigation have been, and still are, one of the most dramatic problems. Indigenous communities own land for agriculture - often relatively small pieces - but only a minimal part of it counts with irrigation water.

These circumstances, and not only processes of modernisation and State down sizing in productive and socio-economic activities in general, make it essential to include this historically conflictive element, water, in the agrarian debate.

Currently, a series of proposals are waiting to be discussed by the National Congress that reflect the interests of diverse sectors. CONAIE has presented them from its point of view. Some essential points are summarised in the final part of this analysis.

The State and agribusiness proposal

The State proposal about 'irrigation and water' is very limited and prioritises only the *transfer of management, operation and maintenance of irrigation systems built and oper-ated by the state, to the users,* fundamentally to private companies and non govern-mental entities that, according to the State view, 'are in a position to manage them'. For agricultural entrepreneurs, on the other hand, its importance also lies in the pri-vatisation of water itself and not only in the privatisation of existing infrastructure. Thus, once the State has bowed out of these responsibilities, business will be able to get back the 'investments' they never made by charging high fees and prices.

In fact, such 'solutions' will intensify peasant poverty and will cause conflicts due to water monopolisation, abuse and unfairness, just as in colonial times. We believe that neither privatisation nor transfer *per se* will solve the fundamental irrigation problems of bad distribution, system operation, and use of water. Therefore, the debate about the Water Law and access to water must also take indigenous popula-tion groups into account, to achieve a broader, deeper, complementary, integrated understanding of these problems.

Community conceptions and regulations related to water resources

In the indigenous world, water - like stones, mountains, trees, etc. - is conceived of as a living being who feels, speaks, watches and protects. It is 'just like us'. This con-cept is based on the harmonious relationship between human beings and Nature, a relationship not based on domination, for men and women are not the only beings with souls. Animals, plants, rocks, water sources, rivers, the sun, the moon, that is, *everything that exists*, holds a spirit and maintains relationships similar to the social relations that human beings have. They also get married, have children, make a fam-ily, get divorced, cry. Sometimes they are happy, sometimes angry. So, for example, water is a being that can behave nicely one day and break hearts the next. This liv-ing expression of Andean conceptions permeating daily indigenous life, is indicative of the need to establish a dialogue, respect, trust and reciprocity with Nature to be able to understand ourselves and to learn to live together, building between humans and Nature a relationship of harmony and, above all, complementarity. We need them, they need our care. Our religious feeling worships not only water but life itself, since water is the source of life.

But we are now witnessing the irreparable loss of Nature. Many analysts, including those from the Inter-American Development Bank, simply point out that 'there is water scarcity due to excessive deforestation' or that 'charging low rates or nothing for irrigation water is the main reason for production deficiency and lack of profitability'. There is no integrated approach to resource management. The indigenous world understands water as *a part of the whole*. It is not possible to consider water separately from its environment, i.e. from the other resources that make up what we call an 'ecosystem' or 'biodiversity'. Neither can people be imagined separately from communities. Human beings, Nature and society walk together. This integrated view is realised on the *chacra* (the peasant's piece of agricultural land), where reciprocity, religious and life relationships are established. During irrigation activities, sowing times and harvests, singing is still there. The songs are weak these days, but they have not vanished. However, the modern conception is that 'water is a mere production factor, a resource possessed by human beings to be used 'rationally', in order to give the crops the amount of moisture they require, at the appropriate time'.

With respect to the water management and/or access to the water in our country, it is necessary to observe that, despite several institutional changes, the poor and unequal distribution of the resource still lingers on. It is well known that the former Ecuadorian Institute of Water Resources (INERHI) granted water unequally, slighting indigenous communities and favouring large private farm owners: the *hacendados*. Now, to take the place of this unjust reality, does a community based irrigation water regulation exist? Indeed it does: peasant and indigenous communities have and apply normative principles that orient irrigation water distribution. Let us analyse them:

- In the first place, *equity* is the egalitarian, just enjoyment of water among all irrigators. If there is enough water, it is distributed in relation to the area to be irrigated: more land, more water. But when water is scarce, all community members decide in assembly to get the same amount of water. Even if one member has more land to irrigate, he will get the same amount of water as others who have less irrigable land. In several workshops on the topic, neighbours have pointed out that 'water gets distributed so the amount available will go around for all, according to the agreement reached by all members'. This example reflects two circumstances:
  - decisions are debated and agreed upon by everybody, in different meetings, and
  - the *availability* of water is taken into consideration. Therefore, the equity principle is a guiding factor in their irrigation systems.

- This first principle leads us immediately to another involving *flexibility* in irrigation water use and allocation. The distribution system does not obey a strict irrigation schedule. According to the reality of social dynamics, crop pattern diversity, and community members' needs, turns can be exchanged. In other words, the irrigation turn is subject to agreements among community members. For example, one irrigator could exchange his turn of water for a certain number of fallow days. So one might think that water distribution would be chaotic, with no centralised administration, no irrigation specialists, and haphazard use that makes problems worse.

- But *collective management and social action* in distribution, use and control of water demonstrates that there is organised community participation as well as norms regulating water use. Leaders, canal operators, intake wardens and irrigators in general have functions and have to obey certain norms that they themselves have adopted. In this context, water and irrigation management is an intricate process in which many elements converge that tend to be ignored by agricultural sciences, which grant them only quantitative interest regarding water scarcity; and by social sciences, such as Law, which have never incorporated the normative dynamics of indigenous peoples; and by the State's own actions. Therefore, irrigation should be analysed in an integrated, inter-disciplinary manner to avoid biased interpretations that will result in incomplete, insufficient measures leading to failure.

The modern concept of irrigation reduces it to a water-plant relationship ('to increase production and productivity'), omitting the social and technological situation. This is why, in Ecuador, transfer of ownership by the State does not solve the problems, especially since almost 80% of the irrigated area in the country is not State-owned, but largely irrigated by the indigenous and peasant sector without any support. Indigenous communities have not benefitted especially from State irrigation systems.

Thus, the need arises of rehabilitating peasant irrigation systems as an alternative, raising a question: what is the role of the State and what do we understand by privatisation of irrigation systems?

Several institutions have pointed out that privately-owned irrigation also includes peasant systems, which generally use small-flow independent canals (*acequias*). According to some experts' calculations, in the highlands of Ecuador (*Sierra*) there are more than 2000 such canals that make up a network of small systems with intricate operation and dire problems with efficiency. This type of irrigation has problems related to water conduction and distribution, both due to deficient infrastructure and poor operation of what little there is, and schedule- and equity-related problems and conflicts due to turns granted by INERHI (now called the National Council of Water Resources - CNRH), that have quite frequently clashed with systems adopted by indigenous communities.

Therefore, it is necessary for the government, along with community organisations, to share the responsibility for undertaking a just redistribution of water, and a process to rehabilitate both physical facilities and respect for traditional ways of organising, using and managing water. The form of organisation to administer irrigation, currently proposed by the State, destructs the traditional forms of organisation, generating conflicts and weakening decision-making.

There is no doubt that indigenous and peasants' irrigation organisations and systems have the following advantages to manage irrigation systems:

- Their strong organisational and participatory process makes it possible to have democratic management and more equitable access to water. Further, several forms of operation, maintenance and management are already consolidated.
- They foster the development of efficient, viable agriculture, from the indigenous and peasant communities' point of view and also in terms of general economics, because they are based on integrated natural resources management.
- Collective water management generates or maintains social stability since its operation is based on group capacity and establishing agreements.
- Community participation lowers rehabilitation, operation, supervisory and managing costs (in both private systems and State systems transferred to organisations), thanks to the beneficiaries' contributions (e.g. in labour, a considerable but underestimated economic resource). The State should contribute financially to facilitate these peasant activities and works.

In conclusion, *water must obligatorily perform a social function.*

Water policy issues are part of the agrarian policy debate. In analysing the diverse proposals it is necessary to know what they want to support and who is to benefit. In our proposal, which was not taken into account but remains valid, we developed among others the following about agro-productive resources:

'Erosion - the cancer of soil -, and forest logging are incredibly wide spread in Ecuador. This deforestation has endangered ecosystem stability and threatens us with total desertification and agricultural non-sustainability, although agriculture is Ecuador's main activity. During the last few years, between 200 and 340 thousand hectares of forest per year have been cut down, which means that in 60 years all natural forest will be gone if this trend continues, sooner if it accelerates. We are ashamed to have the highest deforestation rate in the Americas'. (CONAIE, Agrarian Law proposal, 1993)

According to a study by Whitaker, resources such as water are highly subsidised: only 4% of the total costs are recovered; water is inefficiently used because the actually irrigated land area is only one-third of the installed capacity, and it is excessively concentrated among a few large landowners, since 6% of the irrigators, the hacienda-owners, get 41% of the benefits, while 60%, indigenous and peasant farmers, receive only 13%. (Whitaker, M.D. 1990. El rol de la agricultura en el desarrollo económico del Ecuador'. PP. 242-243).

Soil and resources mismanagement, social injustice, migration and conflicts generate an unsuitable environment for production, an issue requiring urgent efforts. In order to guarantee domestic peace it is necessary to decrease and eliminate poverty and the enormous social differences, i.e. to distribute land, water and irrigation, credit and technical support, etc., equitably.

In brief, we proposed that land, water and forest protection and recovery should be fostered; that new non-polluting sciences and technologies that are appropriate for the Andean conditions should be developed; that biodiversity should be protected.

Basic principles for the Water Law: the CONAIE proposal

Regarding the Water Law, the below points summarise the main questions posed by the indigenous peoples, collected by CONAIE in several meetings and assemblies:

1   In the first place is to *defend against water privatisation*. Authority over water and its property are State affairs, and water is a common good for public use.

2   Indigenous peoples envision integrated resource management; everything is interrelated and performs a balanced function, making integrated development necessary and possible. Since *water is one part of the whole*, to separate land and water management is unacceptable, and water cannot be viewed as a mere resource to produce only economic enrichment; for indigenous people water means life, as explained earlier.

3   *Sacred places, such as pucyos* (water springs) should be exclusively managed by indigenous peoples. The indigenous definition would be an understanding like this: 'Sacred Water: all waters born or running through sacred sites such as *pucyos, pacchas*, springs, falls and lakes where members of indigenous, peasant and Afro-Ecuadorian communities practice their rituals and religiosity to strengthen and preserve their cultures... will be preserved, managed and overseen by the indigenous, peasant and Afro-Ecuadorian communities territorially or culturally linked to them' (CONAIE Water Law proposal, 1996).

4   Beyond transferring the management of State irrigation systems to the users (this is, the private sector), our proposal considers it more important to prioritise *equitable water distribution and profitting, and fundamentally water conservation and quality*, as well as the rehabilitation of peasant irrigation systems and the construction of these systems in arid areas. This is an emergent, national priority, also in order to recover soil quality.

5   This proposal also addresses community and inter-institutional watershed management. We should not forget that our farms and fields are not isolated units, but form part of a watershed. Each basin has three parts: an upper part with grassland; a middle part, the space for reforestation, and the lower part with crops. This implies that we should not think only about 'my individual *chacra*' (field) but about the whole; we should not think about partial basin management and one single irrigation canal but rather integrated resource management. This means also that we must include mythical, sacred and cultural issues and the direct, active participation of indigenous communities in irrigation management. Sustainable farming will be achieved only this way, including and integrating

agriculture, animal husbandry, forestry and water management. One reason State rural development models have failed is because they have not incorporated community participation among their strategies. Thus it is necessary to find integrated solutions to these problems.

6   The Law must include support for the recovery and rehabilitation of indigenous irrigation systems for the following reasons: a) besides what has been pointed out previously, water is a strategic resource for agricultural production to develop indigenous and peasant economies, improving and intensifying production and income. When we talk about the *social function* we recognise the potential of water to increase output as well as the fact that it must serve the underprivileged sectors. Therefore, water is obliged to fulfil it social function. b) Indigenous and peasant irrigation systems have very evident *economic and social potential*; economic because they require low implementation and management cost, and there are solid management organisations; social because there is social stability in the agricultural sector. Social action in irrigation - at the same time a State interest - is basically a contribution of indigenous 'hydraulic cultures', and it consolidates the latter.

7   Whereas other proposals are based on merely business criteria about water management, we believe that it cannot be managed individually, which is why water requires *collective management* all over the world. It is necessary to consider *the existing peasant and indigenous organisations* for irrigation management. With respect to this, our communities are very important.

8   According to our proposal, access by communities to water must be ensured, which implies guaranteed collective access to irrigation. We know that communities establish allocation and distribution rules. They organise irrigation operation and maintenance by assigning responsibilities for managing water use, schedules, cleaning, distribution, construction and reparation work, etc. This collective management is rooted in the social, economic and political structures of our people, and reflects their *decision-making power*. Our proposal incorporates and respects internal indigenous community norms regarding water issues, highlighting active community participation (CONAIE Water Law proposal, 1996).

In conclusion, we believe that we need an integrated vision of development, an integrated vision of social, economic, political and cultural processes if we want to solve problems and to achieve full recognition of the rights held by the multiple, heterogeneous stakeholders in irrigation, especially those who have been systematically ignored: Ecuador's indigenous peoples and peasants.

Nina Pacari Vega

new social, economic and political conditions and to the new institutional structure in the 1990s. In this process of institutional re-structuring, the establishment of Regional Development Corporations and the creation of the National Council of Water Resources (CNRH), which replaced INERHI, have been important actions. There are multiple social and productive sectors involved directly in benefitting from water resources: irrigation, water for human consumption, industry, energy and tourism, among other uses. Thus, we find actors with varied and sometimes opposing interests. Among the users of irrigation water we find State and private systems; large, medium-sized and small farmers; peasants who practise subsistence agriculture; high-profit agriculture; Provincial Councils and Municipalities, etc.

Processes of change and economic and political tendencies affecting the country at large favour revision of the irrigation sector's legal framework. This situation also fosters the elaboration of proposals to adapt the sector to current circumstances and to those that might arise in the future, to achieve efficient, equitable, sustainable use of water.

General analysis of the legal framework's precepts

It is important to understand the general context of the point in time at which the Water Law was enacted. This Law was the first and the only one, and has not undergone any substantial modification in 25 years.

Irrigation beneficiaries

Apparently, the Law and its Regulations were written and published to regulate an agricultural sector with supposedly more or less homogeneous characteristics, with determined levels of education, training, organisation, and capacity for financial, legal, social and technical management. However, these are not the conditions under which irrigators operate at present: the diversity in practice is enormous.

Ecuador shows extreme differentiations in land tenure structure and in the socio-economic characteristics of irrigators, perhaps more than any other country. Furthermore, the irrigation sector is divided into State and privately managed irrigation systems. Both of them can be found in the three geographic zones (*Costa* [the coastal region], *Sierra* [the Andean region] and *Oriente* [the Amazon region]). Each zone has very different characteristics. For example, irrigation systems for over 40.000 hectares that benefit producers of rice, sugar cane and other exportation crops, coexist with Andean irrigation systems as small as 200 hectares or less that serve indigenous communities producing for self-support. Notwithstanding the tremendously diverse irrigation sector, legal regulations are basically the same for all and do not differentiate among diverse series of problems within this great variety.

The legal precepts regarding obligations and attributions of water right beneficiaries,

Water Directorates and Irrigation Boards implicitly assume a capacity for 'sophisticated' self-management. We will analyse below some of these legal requirements, attributions and suppositions.

To acquire a water-use right, a petition must contain the following: names and detailed location of the source; flow and place of intake; names and addresses of known users; purpose for which water is going to be used; structures and installations required to be able to use the water; time frame to implement works, and studies and technical plans to justify and explain the request (Art. 84 of the Law). Those interested in obtaining a water right concession for irrigation systems between 10 and 500 hectares need more detailed documentation, including a financial analysis of the project (Art. 111 of the Regulations).

On the other hand, irrigation beneficiaries are obliged to construct all hydraulic structures of the system (Art. 15 of the Law). Furthermore, they must elaborate internal rules; make and update the List of Users, which includes the name, date of the concession and flow awarded, irrigation plots and locations, type of measurement structure, capacity of the intakes, total area to be irrigated, name of the source, number of intakes, area occupied by each crop and sowing periods, cropping area in the following agricultural year, etc. They must also establish the irrigation schedule, plan operation and maintenance, require control of the corresponding flows, approve budgets and oversee investments, apply legal sanctions, obtain reports, and send an annual report to the INERHI (Art.36 of the Regulations).

According to Art. 43 b. of the Regulations, users must 'proportionally to their rights of use, pay for the construction of the structures needed to be able to practise the individual or collective right of profit to satisfy the operation, maintenance and improvement expenses'; something that small farmers and marginalised cultivators cannot afford.

With respect to the self-managed administration of irrigation (in charge of the users themselves), the Regulations (Title IV) foresees the creation of Irrigation and Drainage Commissions that would be responsible for planning, designing, financing, constructing and managing their own irrigation systems. In this process, the responsibility of the INERHI is limited to the role of specific technical advisor and to approve plans, rules, budgets, studies and layouts.

With respect to the State irrigation systems, INERHI does have major responsibilities[1]. It is in charge of the implementation and administration of the main intake and conveyance structures, as well as the execution of studies and complementary structures and the annual update of the list of irrigators. In these systems, irrigators have the responsibility of construction and maintenance of secondary, tertiary and field distributary canals, and of irrigation fee payment to INERHI.

Who were or are the users able to assume these responsibilities? In some cases these users did not exist, as is the case with the Irrigation and Drainage Commissions, for they were either never formed or their reach was very limited. Further, the benefits from irrigation in the country correspond to an extremely inequitable distribution. According to Whitaker (1990), farmers with less than one hectare, who represent 60% of all farmers, receive only 13% of the benefits of State spending in the irrigation sector. Large owners, who make up 6% of all farmers, receive 41% of the profits generated by irrigation investments. So, especially the large owners managed to benefit from the national irrigation policy and practice.

We cannot conclude that the Law itself has generated this injustice, but it could be said that the Law has not succeeded in reducing this concentration in the hands of few. The class of 'water-holders' has greater access to legal and practical benefits. Other effects of the Law and its Regulations are best analysed regarding private and State irrigation separately.

Private irrigation can refer generally to one farmer or a small group of farmers, to a Water Directorate of medium-sized, small or subsistence farmers, rural and indigenous communities, or to a Directorate of several of these types of users.

Among the most common situations that have occurred, the following stand out:
• Users with greater economic power, overall management capacity and with political influence get their water rights sooner and are more successful in legal conflicts over irrigation, at the expense of third parties who could potentially use the same water source but have less influence or 'modern' management capacity. This has produced unequal distribution of water, as well as complicated legal and technical conflicts over the distribution of scarce water, which can take several years to resolve.
• Directorates that do not have the economic capacity to fulfil stipulated legal responsibilities regarding the irrigation system must request support from INERHI and other agencies, especially to construct part of the infrastructure. In these cases remains the problem of lack of distribution, control and measurement structures. There is also a lack of training and support programmes for farmers in order to achieve efficient agricultural development, including the basic chapters of social organisation and appropriate irrigation administration. In the great majority of cases, the State does not have or does not allocate enough funds for these activities, especially among indigenous sectors.

In *State irrigation*, INERHI, the institution responsible for the irrigation sector at the country level, was established during the boom years of petroleum exploitation. Due to the 'need for investment', it was biased towards investment in large irrigation systems. Its structure was set up to meet that end and was devoted basically to the design, construction, operation and maintenance of main irrigation structures.
• INERHI did not implement most of the systems in an integrated, adequate way, because these responsibilities were not specified in its legal and institutional framework.

- Exclusion of future users from decision-making bodies and processes and users' minimal or non-existent participation in the study, design, funding and construction of irrigation systems has had an impact in many cases: they do not play their part in the responsibilities outlined in the Law, such as construction at the distribution and farm levels, the management counterpart (including operation and maintenance), or payment of irrigation fees.
- Users are aware that State funding mostly assisted those who have larger extensions of land, because ultimately nobody made proportional payment for investments (via the 'basic fee').
- While giving priority to infrastructure there has been a disregard of complementary activities and structures at the distributary and plot levels. This disregard has also affected training and technical and management support for efficient agricultural exploitation. Therefore, the declared objectives of increasing productivity, diversifying production and improving rural people's standard of living have not been achieved; these objectives are fundamental for the economic reactivating of the sector and the country.

With respect to non-equitable water distribution within State systems, the basic idea behind distribution according to the Law states the obligation to irrigate all suitable land under the State canals (Art. 51), and it also provides that water distribution will be done based on technical guidelines according to the area of each property (Art. 40 of the Regulations). Therefore, when irrigators have a large acreage, according to the Law they *must* receive a major investment of the project, and afterwards - obligatorily - they *must* receive more water. This differentiation is legally institutionalised and there is no opportunity for more equitable local concepts to distribute water in case of scarcity in the irrigation system (Boelens and Doornbos 1996).

For both systems, State and private, another perceived problem involves user organisation regulations that 'impose a rigid structure to which irrigators have to adapt, creating new, artificial forms of leadership and parallel organisational structures. These are inadequate since they lack a democratic base, which generally threatens the existing structure of communal organisations in many Andean communities. In this respect, laws and rules must be germane for the specific circumstances of the social groups of irrigators in each zone, reflecting their needs, capacities and forms of communal and inter-communal organisation' (Boelens 1995).

Moreover, neither State nor private irrigation have fostered or set priorities for allocation of economic resources so that INERHI can fulfil those activities explicitly stipulated in its charter and in the Water Law and its Regulations. These activities have to do with strengthening user organisations, training irrigators in administration and integrated irrigation management and agricultural development, management of watersheds and environmental protection.

Generally, many injustices in the treatment of different users have occurred because user organisations are not well represented in decision-making entities that relate to the highest-level State authority for this sector.

Irrigation service costs

Not only in Ecuador but in many countries, farmers at various economic levels are inclined to pay the costs - calculated differentially and based on equity criteria - corresponding to a service of timely, sufficient and reliable irrigation. In our case, irrigation costs and fees must be analysed separately for State and private irrigation systems.

Concession fees for water-use rights. Private irrigation
For private irrigation, INERHI was in charge of granting rights over irrigation water and collecting the corresponding concession fees. It was users' obligation to build, operate and maintain the necessary regulation, control and measurement structures, with INERHI's supervision and technical assistance. The Law mentions that the minimum term of concession will be ten years, and the total irrigation fee will be established initially for a 5-year period, after which it may be revised at INERHI's request. The low, 'symbolic' fees must be paid annually.

Irrigation service fees and collection. State irrigation
In State irrigation systems, according to Art.17 of the Law, the value of investments in hydraulic infrastructure and operation and maintenance expenses paid for with State funds will be recovered. To compute fees, INERHI has been applying a single method for all State systems and all users, with a Basic Fee to recover the investment and a Volumetric Fee to finance operation and maintenance expenditures. To recover investment costs 'no distinction is made between costly and inexpensive projects nor between different projects and regions regarding the potential for increased productivity. Furthermore, there is no differentiation in relation to users' economic conditions, or between systems mainly aimed at self-consumption agriculture and systems for export/high-profit agriculture' (Boelens 1995).

These uniform fees applied nation-wide are levied in Districts and are sent to the 'Single Treasury Account' from where they are arbitrarily reallocated to other investments or objectives, not necessarily for irrigation. Consequently, contributions and O & M investments are not proportional. General dissatisfaction with this fee system has fostered resistance to payment and the consequently impossibility of levying fees in acceptable proportions, especially the basic fee part (to recover the cost of infrastructure). Thus, the circle begins: the lack of funding prevents the State and users from adequately managing the irrigation systems, and users do not pay because the systems do not function well.

The same Art.17 of the Law, regarding recovers of investments and O & M costs, provides possibilities for differential treatment: 'investments made for reasons of social service and that do not influence the economic output of the work, will not be considered when deciding the value of the fees levied'. However, this option has not been applied, not even in the case of marginalised peasants producing for self-support with any surplus used for the necessary subsistence items. Thus, in applying the Law, an important possibility to generate greater justice and to accomplish more equitable distribution of users' contributions has been lost.

Due to pressure from peasants and to objections to this uniform fee system, in 1993, after the substantial increase in fees (to cover increased, real costs), INERHI was compelled to apply differentiated fees depending on the size of the irrigated land area: the smaller the plot, the lower the fees per hectare. This was accepted by user organisations,[2] although the actual implementation of this more equitable idea was never realised sufficiently. Differentiated fees are applied successfully in some non-State systems where payments are related to the users of these systems: small land owners, medium-sized farms, *hacienda* owners, flower or fruit growers.

On the actuality of the legal framework

The Law is indeed based on certain just principles - e.g. that water is a national heritage for public use, excluding private property, and that it is controlled and allocated according to social priorities (resp. human consumption, agriculture, use for industry and energy). However, in many aspects it is too detailed and rigid, particularly in relation to irrigation system management. In fact, it forces the development and adoption of certain forms of organisation that do not correspond to existing organisations and rationalities of the peasant and indigenous communities. In institutional re-structuring and legal modification these points should be discussed. There is a need to make the standards more flexible, more general and more based on fundamental principles than on particular details that limit or exclude indigenous and peasant irrigators and organisations. Recognition and authorisation of local indigenous norms, procedures and customs in coexistence with official Law is an important step, polishing them if necessary, without denying or omitting them. What is needed is the recognition of the authority and faculty to establish and refine their norms and to propitiate and sustain their own regulations through participatory negotiation processes.

Moreover, it is very important to consider new concepts and strategies for water resource management principles. These principles have been clearly affirmed,[3] placing particular emphasis on treating water as both an economic and a social factor, and on realising the commitment of all interested parties at all management levels. This means that users must participate in every step of the process, including equitable financing, since the essence of effective arrangements is that interested parties decide how much they wish to spend to obtain the irrigation service and that available resources are allocated to those investments that produce the most socially just and environmentally sound benefits.

Current and proposed trends

In Ecuador, the institutional framework of the irrigation sector was re-structured in 1994 with the disappearance of INERHI and the creation of the National Council of

Water Resources as the legal norm-setting institution to co-ordinate and define water-use policies. Regional Development Corporations were established to replace the former Irrigation Districts. This institutional re-structuring process followed general policies of modernisation with developmentalist tendencies for agrarian change, based on economic transformation by re-structuring rural society.

Because of the problems encountered in State irrigation, a process has been initiated in which the main objectives are institutional strengthening, training of users in irrigation management, and management transfer to irrigators organisations. In this respect, the current legal framework is not conducive to adequate transfer of irrigation management. Therefore, several support and peasant entities have taken the initiative of analysing and discussing various options that are socially more fair and acceptable.[4]

The criteria and reflections found in this chapter do not aim to deal in depth with all major legal problems regarding water resources in Ecuador. Rather, we are attempting to analyse and review relevant aspects of the Water Law and Regulations that evidently produce, or have produced, unjust treatment for different irrigation users. This analysis and review are based on the experiences in many irrigation projects with assorted characteristics. It is essential to avoid or to correct these injustices in the future. As a result of this analysis and review, we would like to make the following summary of recommendations:

- Marginalised farmers and peasant and indigenous irrigators must have genuine representation on decision-making bodies, not only at the local level, but also at a regional and national level.
- Considering the extreme differences among the various groups of users and irrigation systems, the legal framework must envisage and recognise different situations, bearing in mind social policies targeting marginalised farmers. In this sense, it is necessary to maintain and further elaborate differentiated irrigation policies (e.g. providing subsidies to develop and implement irrigation for poorer sectors).
- Rules must be clear and flexible enough to adapt to a changing reality, considering and respecting the existence of local normative systems established according to the varied, specific conditions throughout Ecuador.
- In water resource concessions, a space must be granted for communal rights of water, and in the Law collective allocations must override individual ones, for irrigation asks for a collective and social management. Water must be able to fulfil its social role as well as its economic function.
- In allocating economic resources, the training activities and technical and organisational support must take priority in order to even out socio-economic differentiation among irrigation users and to strengthen local capacity to sustain their systems.
- As demonstrated in practice, often the Law's socially-oriented provisions are not applied. On the contrary, several other inequitable rulings are applied, such as the uniform fees, that are not expressly established in the Law. Therefore, it is imperative

that the Law be modified, including solid and integrated stipulations about the institutional and financial structure to guarantee effective enforcement with greater justice for marginalised communities and families.

- To implement or improve irrigation systems, users must decide and commit themselves to contribute equitably the quantities required to obtain and manage the irrigation service. The farmer's contributions in labour, transport of materials (mingas), care of canals, local materials, management and other items must be duly valued.

- The Law must contain mechanisms and standards to guarantee more equitable access to water resources and specifically increase access to water for marginalised farmers. This refers for example to a change in the rigid standards regulating water rights in proportion to land tenure for every farmer, proposing more equitable alternatives; as well as to fairer rules for fee contribution and for regulations over rights and obligations; and to a change in the 'water tenure structure' in Ecuador.

It is amazing that in Ecuador, as in the rest of Latin America, so much has been discussed about Agrarian Reform, but so little has been argued about the very necessary - although neglected - equitable re-distribution of water rights through a Water Reform.

Notes

1   Regulations, and Regulations for the Management of INERHI Irrigation Systems, 06-1992.
2   However, in reality the differences between the fees per hectare paid by large landowners and by small farmers have been minimal.
3   E.g. at the United Nations World Conference on Environment and Development held in Rio de Janeiro in 1992.
4   These institutions formulated, among others, a 'Methodology for Responsible Transfer of Irrigation Systems'. Further, in 1996, these institutions created a national Interinstitutional Irrigation Forum (FIR), to debate irrigation policies, exchange experiences, and co-ordinate efforts to improve irrigation interventions in Ecuador. Peasant and indigenous organizations, State institutions, universities, NGOs and international co-operation agencies participate in FIR and will have to give body to the debates in the near future.

References

Boelens, R., 1995. 'La nueva política del riego en el Ecuador'. In: *Ecuador Debate,* vol. 36, CAAP, Quito.

Boelens, R., & B. Doornbos, 1996. *Derecho consuetudinario campesino e intervención en el riego. Visiones divergentes sobre derecho y agua en los Andes.* SNV-CESA, Quito.

Briscoe, J., & M. Garn, 1994. *Financiando la Agenda 21: Agua Dulce.* World Bank, Washington D.C.

Camacho, C., 1993. *Proyecto de Asistencia Técnica para el Subsector Riego en el Ecuador.* MAG-BIRF-IDEA, Quito.

Castanier, H., 1992. Ponencias sobre el Programa de Capacitación en Riego del PRONADER. Workshop paper, Quito.

Castanier, H., 1993. Accounts of the Workshop 'Administración y Transferencia a los Usuarios de Sistemas de Riego'. Colombia. PRONADER. Quito.

Castanier, H., 1994. *Políticas de Riego desde la Perspectiva del Estado.* Seminar Irrigation, CESA, Riobamba.

Cisneros, I., 1995. *Riego Campesino y Modernización.* IEDECA-CICDA, Cayambe.

CNRH-COTESU-DGIS-PRICA-SNV-CESA, 1996. *Metodología para una Transferencia Responsable de Sistemas de Riego.* International Seminar, Riobamba-1995, Quito.

MAG, 1972/1973. Ley de Aguas (1972) y Reglamento (1973), Quito.

MAG/INERHI, 1992. Reglamento para la Administración de Sistemas de Riego del INERHI, Quito.

ITDG-SNV, 1993. *Gestión del Agua y Crisis Institucional. Un Análisis Multidisciplinario del Riego en el Perú.* Lima.

Vincent, L., 1994. *Issues in Irrigation.* IHE, Delft.

Whitaker, M.D. (ed.), 1990. *El rol de la agricultura en el desarrollo económico del Ecuador.* IDEA, Quito.

27

Water as Private Property. Notes on the Case of Chile

Jan Hendriks

Prologue

This chapter brings together information and appraisals regarding the theme of water policy and regulation, obtained by the author during his two and a half years' contact with northern Chile's reality. It is important to mention that it is an empirical contribution, not based on explicit research. In spite of the importance water has in several economic sectors and for life itself, this text has been written from the perspective of its agricultural use, specifically in irrigation systems.

Any analysis of the theme of water tends to involve a great diversity of physical, economic, social, cultural and, therefore, ideological factors. The ensuing debate has delicate hues that, in the last few years, have centered on legislature trends toward privatising water rights, following the Chilean example.[1]

The Chilean context

The territory of Chile spreads over 757,000 square kilometres, from parallel 17°30' southern latitude, in the warm desert, to parallel 56°30' in the Chilean Antarctic. This latitudinal distance translates into more than 4,000 kilometres between north and south, and a mean width of barely 190 kilometres. When crossing this width in the north, one ascends from sea level to the highland plateaux above 4,300 meters altitude.

While half of this territory is classified as arid, with 0 mm of rainfall per year in some parts of the Atacama desert, there are other regions with a rainfall of around 2000 mm/year. It is not surprising that, out of the total area under cultivation, approximately 5,000,000 hectares, around 1,800,000 are irrigated.

Over this varied geography, human cultures have settled for more than 12,000 years. In certain parts of the country some indigenous cultures are still present: Mapuches in the south, and Atacameños and Ayamaras in the north. However, most of the territory is occupied by descendants of immigrants who came during colonial times and more recently.

The use of land and natural resources has evolved markedly in many parts of the country. In the south, the Mapuches originally gathered what nature offered. Afterwards, in a process that was anything but peaceful, farmers settled, whose main activities were related to the cultivation of wheat. Nowadays, this crop has been replaced by large-scale forestry activities. In the more central areas (center and north-center) of the country, high-tech fruit and wine production has acquired great importance for the country's economy.

In the north, mining activities have traditional importance, from exploitation of guano in the past century, passing through saltpetre extraction, to large-scale copper production during the last few decades. In comparison with mining activities, agricultural production in the desert oases of the north can be considered marginal in economic terms. However, from the social point of view and in relation to territorial occupation, this marginal agriculture in small valleys, gulches, plains and oases is basic for the existence of many small desert villages.

This compact summary of Chile's geographical, human and economic diversity leads to the supposition that it has been difficult to harmonise different interests and thoughts with regard to territorial occupation, natural resources use and development of economic activities. In this sense, also in relation to the topic of water, several recurrent alternatives are introduced, as will be seen below.

The Chilean Water Code

Under the previous Chilean water legislation, effective until 1981, water regulations had the following characteristics:
- water use rights, understood as State concessions, were linked to land rights;
- water concessions were not considered as rights that could be 'moved' from one place to another;
- as a concession, water was not an item to be 'negotiated' between natural or juridical persons;
- concessions were granted for actual water use, not accumulable as private reserves.

The previous legislation may reflect a historic period comparatively free of water-related conflicts: a country with incipient industrial development, with extensive agriculture on less irrigated area, with less population density and less per capita water consumption, and a greater State presence in the economy (for example, in the sectors of drinking water, mining and hydro-power). All these were factors that diminished private competition for access to water.

The current Chilean Water Code was enacted in 1981 via Decree with Force of Law No.1122. According to Article 5 of that Code, 'water is a national good for public use, granting private persons the right to use them...'. Following is Article 6: 'Usage right is a real right concerning water resources and consisting in their use and enjoyment...

and... is under the control of its holder, who will be able to use, enjoy and dispose of it...'. The right is expressed in water volume per time unit.

To grant real usage rights, once on record with the Registry of Waters, water could be considered in practice as negotiable private property that can be mortgaged, leased or sold, under market conditions. Usage rights may refer to consumptive use (for example, irrigation) or to non-consumptive use with return to the river bed (for example, in the case of hydropower). Usage rights are usually permanent, but can also be granted as occasional, discontinuous or alternating rights.

The Water Code does not establish priorities for the several uses of water, be it drinking water, or for mining, agriculture, industry, tourism or other uses. If water is freely available at the source, there will be no problem in granting usage rights to a new user. However, if any kind of opposition appears, the Code establishes an auction procedure to give the rights to the highest bidder. When water sources are declared as depleted, no more usage rights can be granted. Then, the only way to get water is to buy it from other users, either the usage rights, with the respective Water Registry transfer, or specific access to water, without transferring rights.

When two or more rightholders share a common intake or natural canal or riverbed, the Water Code provides for the following water user associations: Water Community, Association of Canal Users, or Board of Surveillance. Each holder's relative weight in decision-making within the organisation depends on the quantity of water-use rights, expressed in water shares, totally comparable to shareholders in a company.

In the last years there have been several legislative attempts to amend the current Water Code. The main topic of debate is that, in its current form, the Law theoretically allows hoarding, monopolisation and speculation with water use rights, without effective, short-term utilisation.

State intervention

The General Water Directorate of the Ministry of Public Works is the organisation in charge of granting usage rights, planning natural water sources, researching and measuring water resources, protecting natural river beds of public use, and supervising the operation of the Boards of Surveillance at the level of individual waterways.

Budgetary and legal restrictions limit certain functions of the General Water Directorate and its regional offices. For example, in the Pica community oasis, supposedly depleted, there are still applications for usage rights, which the GWD is obliged to process: there is no money to carry out the formal study that would declare Pica oasis as a Restriction or Prohibition Zone. With such study the Authority could refuse the applications. Meanwhile, it is estimated that in Pica there are already nearly 600 wells, almost all without water rights entitlement.

Understandably, under the current Water Code's approach of private rights and investments, the Chilean State has not invested much in public water development as has, for example, Peru. There is the Program of Medium-Sized and Small Works, and a program to subsidise up to 75% of investment for private improvement in irrigation and drainage, realised by means of competitive bidding organised by the National Water Commission (Decree Law 18,450).

With regard to the planning function, the same spirit as in the Water Code is reflected in the assumption that the market is the best allocator and, hence, the best planner of scarce resources. However, the subject of natural resource planning is becoming sensitive in Chile, because of the need to confront certain problems more globally (for example, at the watershed level) and not only by playing the 'Russian roulette' of rights, powers and interests among private users. This possible conceptual readjustment could be reinforced by the water supply problems suffered by metropolitan Santiago. Here, the General Water Directorate had to intervene in the allocation of water from the Mapocho and Maipú rivers in order to reassign momentary flow to the different drinking-water companies.

The State does not intervene in user organisations' internal administration, except as indicated by Law. Neither does it apply any development policy for their operation. In practice, the rational or irrational, equitable or inequitable use of water resources in the environment of Water Communities, Canal User Associations, Boards of Surveillance, or other local organisations entrusted *de facto* with their functions, depends almost exclusively on these organisations' managing capacity.

Water market performance

Since publication of the Water Code in 1981, the long process of regulating existing uses of water - often based on local practices and customs - and granting rights to new applications, has led to a situation in which today much water in Chile is in private hands. There are water owners, but there is no consensus as whether an actual water market has been created in Chile. In any event, the performance of this 'market' is rather strange.

Considering the universe of water shares and the number of users, the quantity of buying-and-selling transactions is quite reduced. It is a static market. This can explained by various reasons. In the first place, water is so vital for a user's economic activity (farmer, mining company, water company, etc.), that none will readily sell his or her rights, except in case of completely abandoning the productive activities of that site. Besides, holding surplus rights unused bears no cost for the user. If there were such costs, these would encourage the sale of the surplus waters. Instead, it is currently advisable to speculate by holding 'surplus usage rights'.

Secondly, water is relatively immobile and difficult to reallocate, it requires infrastructure to carry it to its place of use. To use a metaphor: 'when you purchase the merchandise, it forces you to acquire not only the truck but even to build the road to be able to transport it'. Only large companies are willing and able to carry out the investment package involved in the effective use of acquired water rights.

In the third place, especially in agriculture, water buying and selling is often related to other transactions, such as land purchase.

In brief, these and other reasons generated a conditioned, static water market because of particular, water-related factors that normally do not form part of other types of transactions.

In the dry north of Chile, water rights applications, grants and transactions entail a high degree of public sensitivity. This is due not only to fear of affecting social or economic sectors, but also because of the spectacular amounts involved. For example, in 1995 a chemical company bought water use rights from two farmers in the Community of Quillagua (Antofagasta Region). Rights to 885,600 m³/year (equivalent to 28 l/s) were sold for approximately US$280,000, and other rights to 238,568 m³/year (equivalent to 8 l/s) were settled at US$235,000. It is easy to understand that, in view of the relative marginality of agriculture compared to the economic power of other productive sectors, and considering the temptations to sell for such figures, these transactions caused a serious stir in the town of Quillagua. Their concern was to be expected: a fragile green habitat in the middle of the desert and the quality of life of the families living there, in danger of disappearing after water rights are reallocated to activities outside agriculture.

Not only water rights transactions involve high amounts of money and high public sensitivity. The water itself has also a high cost (financial, political, etc.) in the north of Chile. Thus, for example, treated waste water sold by a treatment company to horticulture farmers of the La Chimba sector, in the outskirts of the city of Antofagasta, costs approximately US$0.70 per m³, resulting in a cost of water of about US$3,000 per hectare per growing season. This has produced public protests on more than one opportunity, pointing out, among other objections, that the selling company holds quite a monopoly in a supposedly free market.[2]

The topic of water rights transactions (and of the water itself) is under the regional authorities' jurisdiction, although the Water Code leaves little room to apply policy to regulate, adapt or guide certain change processes that involve social impacts of water problems. Supported by the Indigenous Law (Law 19,253), the National Corporation for Indigenous Development (CONADI) organises campaigns to convince and provide legal assistance among indigenous people, so that they will convert their individual water rights into communal rights, as an Indigenous Community. In this public institution's defence of cultural heritage, communal water use rights would paralyse water rights transactions, since they would require approval by a majority of the community. In places where this policy is successful

Map 27.1: Region I and II in Chile

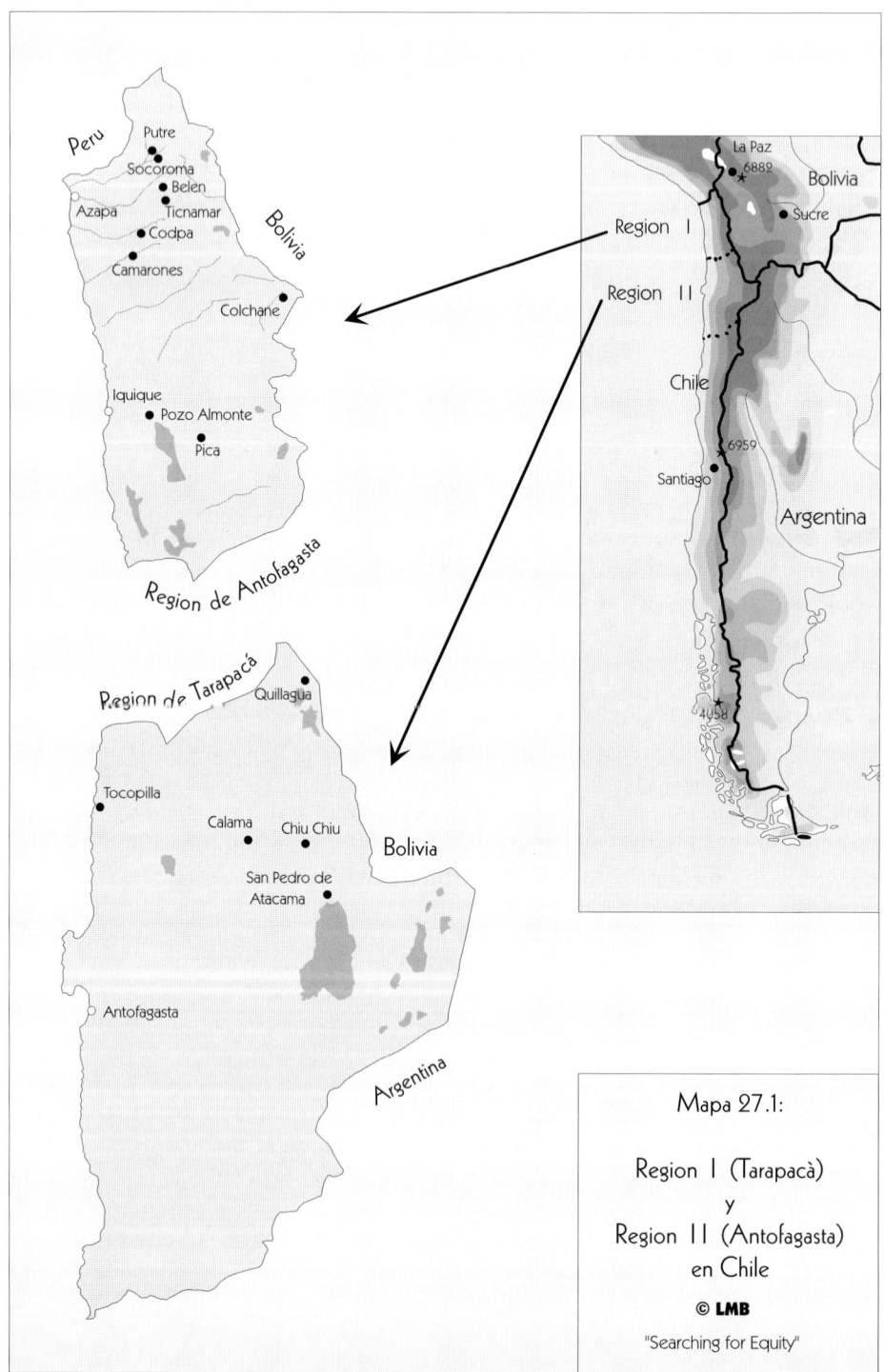

Mapa 27.1:

Region I (Tarapacà)
y
Region II (Antofagasta)
en Chile

© **LMB**

"Searching for Equity"

(especially in the Region of Antofagasta), communities have greater possibilities of keeping and even developing their habitat, avoiding losses of their 'liquid heritage' due to individual decisions to sell rights to other sectors outside their communities.

When agricultural activities in dry locations are endangered by the threat of selling water use rights to outside economic sectors, this also questions the appropriateness of continuing to invest in improving local irrigation systems when one is not sure that 'tomorrow' the same amount of water will be circulating. These possible doubts about investment policies are part of the vicious circle degrading some local habitats that survive in the desert.

Individual water rights and collective rationality in irrigation water distribution systems[3]

Clearly, adequate irrigation application frequency is crucial to maintain perspectives for developing desert agriculture that has traditionally been quite marginal. Timely access to water determines whether the farmer will succeed in sowing some alfalfa, rudimentary but resistant to drought, or if he can try more innovative agricultural technology such as horticulture or other intensive crops. The dry regions of Chile feature an enormous variability of production systems, from subsistence agriculture to high-tech, highly commercial plots, even among producers at the same social level.

Very coincidentally, there is a very close relationship between irrigation frequency and the degree of agricultural development. Irrigation frequency ranges from every 25 days (San Pedro de Atacama) to every 180 days (Ticnamar) in the inhabited villages of marginal agricultural development or of agricultural subsistence, respectively. Of course, not all dynamics in agricultural activity depend on irrigation frequency; on the contrary, this frequency mirrors a people's agricultural dynamics, in terms of their insertion into the market, migratory rhythm,[4] etc.

In environments of relative prosperity (Valle Azapa, Chiu-Chiu, Río Grande, La Chimba, etc.) farmers can receive irrigation water at 7-day or shorter intervals. It shows that the problems for agriculture are not always related to quantity or (chemical) quality of available water, but especially to timely access to water for crops.

Limited absolute availability is actually relative, as shown in the following example. The Valley of Azapa, in the vicinity of the city of Arica, irrigates with only about 0.30 l/s/ha (both surface and underground water) but has developed very intensive agriculture (the valley is well-known because it supplies large quantities of tomatoes to the city of Santiago). On the other hand, just a few dozen kilometres further, the farmers of Precordillera have almost double the water availability per hectare, but with only every 30 to 90-days' turns they get low yields of alfalfa and oregano and they have little possibility to diversify crops under current scheduling arrangements.

These limitations are due not just to differences in climate when comparing to the Valley of Azapa.

The following observations should be understood within the framework of the above agricultural development considerations and prospects.

Notwithstanding the fact that the Chilean Water Code is a fairly precise and extensive legal text with all 'of its respective regulations, enforcement and daily control of water flows expose a series of problems. In general, much time, effort and money are spent resolving legal questions, but, once the formal legal part is resolved, there is little verification as to whether the volume and flow are distributed among users accordingly. Only extreme cases are administratively or judicially processed and punished.

Water users' lack of organisation and actual quantified control limits the rationality of their distribution systems; in the North of Chile, extremely scarce water is wasted. It seems that the Water Code favours the hypothesis of market rationality for possible business transactions, however, without paying much attention to the relative (ir)rationality in using water once it has been assigned to a user.

Within a water distribution system, institutionalised via a Water Community, Association of Canal Users or Board of Surveillance, the water use rights are defined as water shares (for example, quantified in hours of individual assignment within a schedule among users). There is often unnecessary confusion between the concepts of 'shares' and 'turns'. However, water shares are fixed, granted by resolution of the General Water Directorate, while any water user association may change their schedule (turns, irrigation frequency), only if such a fractionation or adjustment maintains the proportionality of shares originally granted. This conceptual confusion between 'shares' and 'hours of water turn' hinders the implementation or modification of irrigation frequencies to adjust better to crop water demand. For example, in the Valley of Codpa (Tarapacá Region), in times of *mitación* a 63- day list is required to cover the shares of all farmers. Within this schedule, each farmer receives his turn according to his quantity of shares. Only recently, through promotional work by external agents, farmers began to understand that they could receive two or more individual turns within the same 63-day period, without affecting the sum of their water share rights.

Another mismatch between individuals and the system involves territorial ordering of individual irrigation turns. In some locations, water is distributed in the order in which the irrigators are listed, perhaps by chronological order, taking the successive location of farms along the distribution canals only partially into account. Likewise, when a farmer receives his 'water share', he often uses the water where there is an immediate need for irrigation, whatever its location within the irrigated area.

In other words, in these cases the distribution canals are soaked several times, intermittently and with no rational order, by a share list, or by the farmer's choice of using his water shares in certain plots. Of course, excessive, repeated soaking and infiltration in the canals produces considerable conduction losses. Time is also wasted by moving water around within the system, further delaying the irrigation rounds. On the average, as a system, the time intervals between successive irrigations of a given plot are unnecessarily prolonged.

These repeated losses in the canals also happen when, within the system, some farmers try to arrange with each other ('*pasar agüita*', sharing and exchanging turns) in order to irrigate each's holding more often, as an individual and partial solution within a system which is highly inflexible. For example, in Saxamar and Lupica, within a traditional agricultural system, several farmers are modernising and need to irrigate more frequently to fill their ponds. Sooner or later, this innovation process will spread, leading to an overall redefinition of water distribution among the users there.

The Chilean Water Code has no relationship between water use rights for agricultural uses and land ownership. They are considered as commercial goods that are totally independent from each other. Within this context, it is not surprising to find quite a disproportional relationship between farmers' water share property and the agricultural area he owns. A recent study in the Valley of Codpa shows that water rights range from 200 to 10,000 m^3 per hectare per turn. Farmers at the low end of the range suffer from serious water shortage, while their neighbours enjoy plentiful irrigation water with no need to use it carefully.

This over-entitlement for some holders reflects relative irrationality at the system's level in handling and distributing this scarcity. While these disparities are somewhat ameliorated by water transfers among neighbours, there is no explicit water market ('water rentals') in the zone, except maybe in the valley of Azapa.

When some own abundant water shares within systems that require careful handling of scarce water, this has also repercussions on decision-making within the irrigators' organisations. This is because the relative weight of a user's vote is proportionate to their shares owned. This means that users with abundant water and less need for careful use of available water have more weight in decision-making, which often affects the rationality of the system's operation.

The following example, taken from the community of Pica, illustrates the decision-making problems in an irrigators' organisation, most of whose votes are cast by the farmers with more water. The Miraflores sector's schedule is strictly a 14-day period. By contrast, the Resbaladero sector irrigates each field 'until finished',[5] which prolongs the period to 28-30 days. A farmer who has land in both sectors states that with the same quantity of irrigation water he grows 4000 m^2 of fruit trees in Miraflores and just 2,000 m^2 of fruit trees in the sector Resbaladero. Asked why they do not change the regulations in Resbaladero to encourage efficiency and increase the system's coverage, he states that such a decision is prevented by the minority group that possesses the majority of water shares.

Similarly in Belén (Precordillera Comuna de Putre), the administration of an irrigation improvement project called for certain changes in the allocation of irrigation
turns. The great majority of farmers there, living by their agriculture, totally agreed
with the project, ratifying their decision in several assemblies, but then the following 'external' problem appeared. In Belén, a majority of water shares is owned by a
group of farmers who keep their plots, but reside in the city of Arica because they
work at other economic activities. They go to the precordillera only when there are
important (productive, cultural) activities to carry out there, such as, to be present
during their water turns. Obviously, this group has no interest in increasing irrigation frequency, for it would mean more time and travel costs to and from the city
when, as a matter of fact, this agricultural activity is only a part of their family
economy.

Unfortunately, this group's voting weight of water shares still prevents smaller
farmers who are more dependent on agriculture, who spend most of their time in
Belén, from changing the schedule in order to intensify their agriculture. This
problem of resistance to change, by people who migrate to the city and own a relatively heavy weight of water shares, is recurrent in many remote locations in the
north of Chile. This prevents the people who actually live there from developing
their productivity.

The general trend in problems involving irrigation water within Chilean systems is
highly legalistic, especially in conflict resolution, but does not necessarily reflect
logical rationality regarding actual system operation.

The last topic of this chapter deals with a delicate aspect, not easily substantiated
objectively: the possible effect of individualisation of water rights on the notion of
overall system appropriation. The hypothesis is: 'the more individual owners of
water, the fewer owners of the system'. Here are a couple of impressions.

Currently, the weak operation and even the non-existence of organisations of users
is noticeable in many locations, valleys, oases, etc. of the desert, precisely when the
scarcity of water could, in principle, be expected to induce a well-organised and
quite solid administration. Each farmer busily receives the water, but there is not
much communal activity with regard to the irrigation system shared by all users. It
is difficult to achieve a quorum for an assembly, even on very important topics. There
is little local contribution to maintenance or improvement of the canal network.
Little is sanctioned or corrected in relation to undue water extraction ('robbery') of
water, because the local agency to complain to is not effective. The social pressure by
the other users, when an individual is opposed to certain measures, is ineffective.

Investigating the property of the hydraulic infrastructure in a location, one finds
answers that are not very clear. Only in communities with longer cultural tradition
and less external intervention, canals are seen as property of the community, as
'ours'. In other cases, the notion of property varies according to the distributary or

subcanal, depending especially on who made construction investments or improvements: the State, different support institutions, some group of farmers who bought a couple of cement bags, etc. Thus, one and the same canal or system can have several owners at the same time, via legal definitions and/or via perceptions.

In brief, it is still not very clear if individual owners of water rights also are or feel like co-owners of the irrigation system they share. Evidently, this means that there is not much responsibility shared by users in regard to system operation, maintenance and improvement. It also means that users appeal and complain more to outside agencies (State institutions) to resolve problems, to take responsibility for the maintenance, to invest in improvements, etc. Apparently, 'the individual water owners are searching to find a system's owner who is disposed to be responsible for the whole system'.

Equity

There are multiple definitions and interpretations of the concept of 'equity'. In general, it is not understood as 'the same for all', but as an approximation towards equality in the opportunities to access goods, services, and rights: capital, technology, education and, in this case of course, water use rights and outside support to improve water use.

Since the Water Code was enacted in 1981, it has been expensive to regularise and be granted new water rights, both institutionally and legally. Part of these costs must be paid by the applicant: presentation of technical antecedents (geographical co-ordinates, flow, etc.), publication in the official gazette, public registration and lawyers' fees, travel, lodging, etc., to arrange this paperwork. For low-income people, these costs could be limiting or prohibitive if they want to legally guarantee their rights. At certain moments and in some territories, the General Water Directorate has supported the regularisation of water use rights by means of specific projects. In 1995, the Chilean State began to subsidise the regularisation of water use rights, and only for native people or organisations. This support is channelled through the National Indigenous Development Corporation.

Apart from the subject of legal access to water use rights, problems of equity have arisen with regard to State subsidies for improvements in irrigation and drainage, under Law 18,450 (operated through the National Irrigation Commission). This Law specifies a 75% refund of private investments in projects that have earned this allowance by competitive selection. To be able to enter the competition, applicants must deliver a thick technical and legal dossier, following precise norms and formats. Evidently, it is quite costly to elaborate the study, affordable for a medium-size agricultural business, but too expensive for small (groups of) farmers. As a reference, one recent example: a small study project to improve an irrigation sector in the community of Pica, to be presented to the National Irrigation Commission, cost US$20,000.

It is not surprising that, with the procedures and costs involved, out of a universe of 951 projects granted between 1986 and 1990, only 61 (6.4% of the total) benefitted the rural sector, receiving 4.6% of the allowances. Obviously, there has been a problem of access to State subsidies for relatively needier groups in society. In the last few years, the National Irrigation Commission has taken measures to remedy this problem.

The previous chapter introduced some examples of the effects of concentrating water shares in a few users of an irrigation system, who do not necessarily make very productive use of the resource. Especially in locations where a strong communal tradition is maintained, the legal procedure calculating the weight of individual votes in relation to the water shares owned, is seen as an inequitable way to make decisions. As with the example in Belén, this creates a conflict between traditional communal democratic procedures and the legally specified system.

Neither does owning water use rights finally resolve a problem that is almost universal in all irrigation systems in the world: less water in the 'tail' than in the head-end canals, due to an inherent loss of water in the system. In other words, the tail-end user receives less water than the head-end user, even if they have exactly the same amount of water use rights (since rights are usually specified at the point of intake from the main canal). Here, inequalities will be corrected only through 'good neighbour' arrangements among users at the local level, without appeal to higher authorities. For example, in the Valley of Codpa, in times of *mitación*, the lower-part users in the system receive their water allotments with an extra 20% on top of the times legally assigned.

However, the topic of equity regarding investments and water rights in irrigation systems is overshadowed by the national debate about private management of scarce water. The 'big' discussion, driven by a great, nation-wide drought during the last few years, revolves around the concentration of water use rights in the hands of a small universe of companies. Some examples from the hydro-power sector: the three major generating companies accumulate 78% (1324 m³/s) of the water used for this purpose; they have rights to 73% (8162 m³/s) of the currently unused water; and they have applied for 69% (26,753 m³/s) of the total volume pending grants. It is estimated that at the total, nation-wide level a flow exists of 30,000 cubic metres per second usable for electric generation. The same tendency of concentrating water rights is repeated in mining activity in the dry northern region.

In view of all these antecedents, the debate about equity in access to water ultimately becomes a transcendent issue, since water is so vital for all economic sectors, for all citizens and for the entire environment, flora and fauna.

Notes

1 The author wishes to be as objective as possible; in any case, the text has been written in a strictly personal way.
2 The tariffs of companies selling drinking-water are governed by a regulatory system controlled by the Superintendency of Sanitation Services. In practice, apparently, this system does not function in an optimal way in the case of raw or treated waste waters.
3 This section mainly refers to irrigation water distribution systems and the problems among irrigators.
4 As will be seen later, the phenomenon of (temporary) rural-urban migration is an important reason for 'farmers' to resist shortening of the interval between irrigation turns (that is, intensifying the irrigation frequency).
5 This criterion, i.e. disregarding the length of turn granted, means a regular discrepancy between the practice of delivery of water volumes and the legal possession of water use rights.

References

Comisión Nacional de Riego, 1991. 'Ley 18.450 de Fomento al Riego y Drenaje'. Santiago de Chile.
Corporación Nacional de Desarrollo Indígena, 1995. 'Ley Indígena (Ley No. 19.253 D. of. 05-10-1993)'. Temuco.
Guerrero Cossio, Victor, 1991. 'Recursos Hídricos y Conflictos Sociales en Tarapacá'. In *Cuaderno de Investigación Social*, No. 31. Centro de Investigación de la Realidad del Norte (CREAR). Iquique.
Instituto de Agronomía, 1995. *Identificación de la demanda de inversión en infraestructura de riego, parcelas demostrativas y potencial asociativo*. Consultancy for Programa Chile Norte. Arica, 1995.
Legislación estatal: 'Código de Aguas'. Editora Jurídica Manuel Montt S.A., Santiago de Chile, (1993).
ONU, 1991. *América Latina y el Caribe: El Manejo de la Escasez de Agua*. Estudios e Informes de la CEPAL, No. 82. Publication of the United Nations. Santiago de Chile.
ORCAL, 1992. *Cultura Hídrica: un Caso en Chile*. Oficina Regional de Cultura para América Latina y el Caribe (ORCAL). Havana.
Romero, Hugo I. & Andrés Rivera, 1992. *Los Efectos de los Cambios Climáticos sobre las Alternativas de Desarrollo Socio-Económico del Norte de Chile*. Universidad de Chile. Proyecto FONDECYT. Santiago de Chile.

PART VII

CONCEPTIONS OF EQUITY
IN ANDEAN IRRIGATION: EXPERIENCES

Introduction

Rather than starting with axioms of social justice, it appears necessary to explore better the cultural diversity of conceptions of social justice that characterise the various societies. At all events, the fact must be borne in mind that these conceptions are not necessarily homogeneous according to the position occupied in the social structure (UNESCO, Working document for the meeting on Equity, Brighton, September 1978).

The cases examined in the following chapters gather experiences from several Andean countries. They show that conceptions of equity vary enormously according to the irrigation systems themselves, the approaches of governmental and non governmental organisations assisting the projects and the kind of peasant organisation making use of the system. In view of such a diverse panorama, entities in charge of legislating and intervening in irrigation management often relativize the possibility of taking into account those peasant norms on irrigation management that are based on principles of a more fair distribution. This is expressed in often heard statements defending the following position: 'The validity of the peasant point of view is very relative since it varies from place to place. We cannot formulate laws or intervention strategies that are founded on peasant visions and conceptions, for they are too diverse and often in contradiction with each other.'

However, while it is possible to discover certain common features in the Andean peasants' conceptions of irrigation equity, it is even more important to consider that these diverse, particular visions of equity constitute the *central fundaments* - the rationality of functioning and maintenance - of *each particular* peasant system.

From this perspective, the notion of equity upon which a certain irrigation system is built (as well as any inequity perceived by its users) is one of the basic criteria for understanding peasant irrigation in each particular case. Understanding the equity notions makes it possible to approach both the negative aspects of a certain system (e.g. users' disillusion, disorganisation and malfunctioning of the system) and its positive ones (e.g. its potentials, successes and own dynamics).

> [...] the conception of equity that emerges from the concept of a development achieved by man and for man cannot be measured solely in terms of the consumption of resources. To the contrary, it implies an active intervention by man in the modelling of his own future (UNESCO, *Ibid.*).

28

River Water Distribution in a Community of the Bolivian *Altiplano*.

The Case of Sullcayana: Equivalence between Plots and People

Gerben Gerbrandy

Sullcayana, its plots and its people

Sullcayana is an *ayllu* (traditional community) with 116 families in the Department of Oruro, at an altitude of 3900 metres above sea level. Its landscape is made up of medium to high mountain ranges and a topography of moderate to gentle slopes, in general, rather uniform. It is one of six *ayllus* that make up the Canton of San Pedro de Condo. *Ayllu* Sullcayana shares the water of the Azanaques River with *ayllu* Collapa and four smaller *ayllus*. Sullcayana is the head *ayllu* and Collapa Grande is the *ayllu* below. Two smaller *ayllus* have border on Collapa Grande and the other two small ones are like islands within Collapa.

The Azanaques River has a flow of 35-40 l/s during the dry season. Due to mining activities, the river is contaminated with *copajira*, which restricts irrigating with its water. Sullcayana does not depend solely on this river but has good quality water from the Sallawi River (10 l/s) and several springs. However, these sources provide less water than the Azanaques river. All sources come from the Azanaques mountain, an important *Apu* in the region (see ch. 19 and 22). Irrigation infrastructure consists of several canals with direct river intakes.

In ancient times, Sullcayana *ayllu* was divided into 10 vertical *mantas*.[1] The irrigation sectors are perpendicular to these strips of land, just above the river, i.e. at the bottom part of the *mantas*. Probably *manta* rotation previously was practised in the irrigated sectors too, and *manta* land was communal. According to the peasants, all members now own *chacras* (plots) in all irrigation sectors. This is due to the land privatisation process where each family has obtained a piece of irrigated land in each *manta*. In other words, there used to be an annual rotation of the ten *mantas*, and in each *manta* each family would cultivate their *chacra*. But *chacras* that were previously cultivated by each family in the irrigated sector have become private plots that, moreover, are now cultivated annually.

Communal production is for self-supply and subsistence; they can sell some to obtain other agricultural products that are not produced locally.

Water rights

Sullcayana is entitled to use Azanaques River water during daytime hours; the other *ayllus* share the water, taking turns during the night over a four-day cycle. The other sources can be utilised on a full-time basis. Commune members indicate that irrigation has always been as it is nowadays. They recall that their great-great-grandfathers already held water rights. Water is a communal resource, a gift from Nature and nobody should be excluded from access to it. There are no individual rights. To go on having water rights, families must comply both with irrigation-related duties (cleaning, construction) and with communal obligations (accepting positions, participating in ceremonies and feasts).

Each male member of an *ayllu* who has a family has the right to be a water user, as long as he complies with its inherent duties and functions. Irrigation is organised around families. *Chacras* belong to the family and are inherited from fathers to sons; in extraordinary cases they can be inherited by daughters. Water rights are related to both the *chacra* and the family, the latter represented by the head of the household, usually the father. This does not mean that women are excluded from access to water. It is rather for the family to decide who irrigates: the father, the mother, both parents or someone else within the family. In practice, both men and women irrigate, more or less equally. The man could be working on one *chacra* while the woman is irrigating another one.

Offspring can automatically receive water rights when they establish a family. If the family happens to have only daughters, the right can go to the son-in-law, who is afterwards treated as a son. Youngsters who do not yet have land of their own often sharecrop on land of people from outside the community. They get water rights as if they had their own lands.

Communal organisation determines whether someone is fulfilling his duties and functions in order to grant him water rights. To keep one's water rights, it is mandatory to participate in cleaning and other activities related to the irrigation canal. It is also obligatory to participate in activities not directly related to actual practice of irrigation, such as joining in ceremonies and accepting communal posts (Cacique, judge, *Jarreador*, *Kamayoj*, etc.). It used to be mandatory to sponsor the celebration corresponding to each position; now this is voluntary.

When an irrigator does not fulfill his canal-cleaning duties or make up for that day's work, or obey the judge's admonitions, he can be punished by withdrawal of his water rights, but this is never permanent. People who have been unable to fulfill their duties because, for example, they were away, can make up for their day's work next time. Penalty enforcement is not rigid and there is much tolerance among members, and little non-compliance. For example, if someone cannot comply with his day's work or cannot send a labourer in his place he can always be authorised to compensate for his day's work by paying 12 Bolivianos (equivalent to US$3). We overheard in a conversation: 'If you don't come to work, you've got to leave your contribution'.

If someone does not wish to accept a position entrusted to him, he can sometimes reach an agreement with the community in which he has to pay, for instance, half the expenses of his proxy. If he does not do this either, his water rights could be withdrawn, something that has happened only once in the past few years.

Water distribution positions

The organisation in charge of irrigation is the basic *ayllu* organisation itself. In each *ayllu* the most important post or *cargo* related to water distribution is the water judge or water mayor. Each *ayllu* has only one water mayor. Besides the water mayor, each canal may have its own judge who performs duties related only to the distribution within that particular canal (there are three such judges in Sullcayana). Water mayors are in charge of water distribution within the *ayllus*. To do this, they set up a list of scheduled turns. The election of water mayors is carried out during the first cleaning of the canal.

The water mayor of Sullcayana is also the inter-*ayllu* water mayor, called the canton judge. He is in charge of watching over the proper distribution of water from the Azanaques River among the five *ayllus*. His duty is to control the closing of intakes at Sullcayana *Ayllu* and to open at the same time the other ayllu's intakes. The canton judge is elected by the five *ayllus* but always belongs to Sullcayana. Elections take place in July or August, when the river flow begins to diminish. The new judge is sworn in by the *Cacique Mayor* (Main Chief).

A water judge is supported by a *Jarreador* in his water distribution duties. The *Jarreador* is his direct collaborator in the *ayllu* and verifies whether the crops of people who have asked for water actually need irrigation, to list turns for farmers who need water for their crops.

The highest *ayllu* authority, the *Cacique* (Chief), oversees the *ayllu's* general interests. He organises ritual activities, such as water-exchange rites and religious services to pray for rain. He arranges meetings in order to discuss communal problems and penalise community members who have not fulfilled their communal duties. He also authorises the actions of water judges. The *Cacique* is elected annually, during the temptation festivities (*fiesta de tentaciones*), the same day that *mantas* rotate. The new *Cacique* appoints the new *Kamayoj*, a youngster who serves the *ayllu* for the first time. He is in charge of protecting that *manta's chacras* from animals that could damage the crops.

There is a high degree of respect for traditional authorities, and it is an honour to be elected. Positions rotate at Sullcayana and each member must accept the election for one of these positions. It is a duty to serve the *ayllu*.

Water distribution at the inter-community level

Since Sullcayana is the *ayllu* at the head-end of the irrigation system, it is the only *ayllu* that irrigates during the daytime only (5 a.m. to 5 p.m.). The four *ayllus* down-stream irrigate during the night (5 p.m. to 5 a.m.). The sixth *ayllu*, Cagualli Mago, does not irrigate at all because it is too far. *Ayllu* Cagualli Araya has not been able to irrigate for the last few years either, because water does not reach them. However, they hope to solve this problem by improving the canal.

When one of the four *ayllus* has its turn to irrigate at night, in the evening the *ayllu's* water mayor meets with all the farmers who will irrigate during the coming night. This gathering takes place at the canal intake. The intakes for the four *ayllus* down-stream are located in Sullcayana. After deciding who will irrigate and in what order, the first person to irrigate closes the intake at 5 p.m. and walks in the direction of the flowing water, closing all the other Sullcayana intakes; accompanying the water until it reaches his *ayllu* and irrigates his plot.

If someone steals water in Sullcayana during the night, the bordering *ayllus* complain to the Canton Judge, who is also the judge for the Sullcayana River. He punishes the thieves by cancelling their next turn to irrigate.

Water distribution at the community level

The irrigation turn in Sullcayana must be applied for, from the water mayor or judge. The *Jarreador* evaluates the status of the plot and informs the judge about how urgent irrigation is needed. So to speak, the *Jarreador* evaluates the land's irrigation needs while the judge evaluates people's irrigation needs. The judge decides who is to irrigate during the next day. The irrigation schedule also considers the efficient use of canals to avoid wasting water by watering *chacras* belonging to different sectors.

Each morning at 6 a.m., users who need to irrigate that day gather at a sacred hill near Sullcayana called Paraj Huilque to ask the judge for water, telling him that their broad bean crops are drying up. To know how urgent this is, and the proper order, the judge gathers data from his *Jarreador*. The latter goes to applicants' cultivated fields and checks on who needs irrigation and who can wait for a while. The water judge, based on the *Jarreador's* report, determines who will irrigate first in the morning and who next. Some will have to wait for one or two more days.

To define water distribution priorities, the judge uses the parameter of the broad bean field that is nearest to its permanent wilting point. Broad beans are the top priority crop for irrigation and are restricted; a family is entitled to sow and irrigate broad beans only every two years. The judge rules on order of turns, not their duration. Families are entitled to finish irrigating their plots. Only when one user has finished irrigating can the next one begin. The first turns are assigned to those *chacras* that most urgently need irrigation. Users whose crops are not so dry have to wait until the users who urgently need water have finished. Water distribution sequence in the canals can be top-down, bottom-up or middle-out, depending on the location of the first plot to be irrigated.

In the rainy season or when scattered rains occur, the judge suspends the water distribution system and irrigation is free.

System maintenance and improvement

Users gather for system maintenance. The first meeting, in August, is attended by all users who will sow that year. To clean the system, only those users who will be planting clean their canals. They also clean the main canal and repair their traditional intake when rains have clogged canals with earth washed down from neighbouring hills.

One canal was recently rehabilitated. Users from Sullcayana organised construction work groups on the basis of their perception of equity. They realised that the job was considerable. They reasoned that since some had large acreages while others had less, it would be unfair for them all to have the same amount of work. The users decided to weight each user's contribution according to the number of *arrobas* (a measure equal to 11.5 kg) of seed they plant. Thus, eight working groups were organised into categories. The first group comprised those families who sow the most, and the last group those who sow the least. Each group had a specific task, of a different magnitude, in relation to their category. These groups were made up of only those users who already had *chacras* and, therefore, water rights.

No new rights were created; there was no philosophy of creating individual property through individual labour investment. Each group kept track of days worked, about which everyone was promptly informed. Anyone who lagged behind could catch up by hiring labourers or by receiving *ayni*[2] from a neighbour.

Irrigation-related rituals

We have already mentioned that participation in rituals is mandatory for everyone. These rituals reproduce relationships among families, Nature and deities. Rituals are necessary to keep them all in equilibrium. One of the most important rituals is water exchange. The *Kamayoj* plays an important role in this ritual, since he is in charge of organising it. Everything starts when rains do not begin when expected. The *Kamayoj* agrees with the *Ayllu Cacique*, and both agree with the *Caciques* and *Kamayojs* of the other *ayllus* so the whole population participates mandatory in this ritual.

First, all community members gather at a place known as Paraj Huilque (a chapel with an Andean cross). This meeting takes place the night before the 'water exchange'. During the meeting everyone dances with their pennants around the chapel, accompanied by their *ayahuayas* (native musical instruments), *pijchan* (chewing) coca and *ch'allan (blessing)*. Afterwards they prepare 12 dishes (*mesas, mysteries, sullu* medicines to *Qhowar*[3]). The number of dishes may vary, eight or ten according to the *Kamayoj's* financial possibilities, because he has to pay for the ritual expenses. The previous *Kamayoj* helps him prepare the ritual and dishes.

All dishes are prepared by a *C'amili* (sorcerer, fortune-teller) and are brought the next day to the Azanaques (the main regional *Apu*) by a commission of community members. They are elected at random or they themselves volunteer, as in an *ayni*-reciprocal relationship. The *Kamayoj* provides the commission with coca, cigars and drinks. In former days, all commune members used to carry twelve dishes.

Commission members climb the mountain to *ch'allar* and *Qhowar* these dishes and to collect spring water (male waters that flow from the *Apu*, the mountain deity). The water exchange takes place at Paraj Huilque with neighbours from other *ayllus*, who also bring water in pails from Lake Poopoo (female waters from Mother Earth / *Pacha Mama*), at the foothills of the Azanaques. Finally, the exchanged waters are taken back to where they came from, and poured in the lake and the Azanaques springs.

An evaluation of equity concepts

In Sullcayana, agriculture retains many features of communal agriculture. Sowing and irrigation activities are planned collectively. The site for sowing is also defined by the *ayllu* organisation, rotating by the *manta* pattern. However, *chacras* with access to water are not rotated or left fallow anymore, but are cultivated annually. A remaining phenomenon from the *manta* system and its irrigated areas is the fact that all families have different *chacras* in all irrigation sectors of the *ayllu*.

An equilibrium is sought in water distribution decisions, both among families and among *chacras*. The *Jarreador* evaluates the land's irrigation needs and the judge evaluates family needs. Decisions on water scheduling are made at a sacred place, to confer with the deities. By balancing these three elements (land, people and deities), decisions are made regarding distribution. Once a year before sowing, special rituals are celebrated to reproduce an equilibrium among land, people, water and gods, and the most important positions are appointed, i.e., those responsible for maintaining equilibrium in the *ayllu* during the coming year. Equity in the distribution of positions (organisational and cultural contributions) is expressed by rotating these positions.

The mechanism of equitable water distribution among families and *chacras* is grounded in restrictive sowing rules: the priority crop, which always gets irrigation water, is broad beans. A family is allowed to plant this crop only every two years.

However, equity does not mean that everyone is equal. Community members recognise that some families plant more than others. This inequality is taken into account in the distribution, proportional to future benefits, of the inputs that different families have to deliver for the construction of new irrigation infrastructures in the system.

Notes

1   An ancient form of agricultural production in the Andes involved rotation of land sections called *mantas* or *aynocas*. *Ayllus* were divided into vertical land strips that were worked communally. Each year, work was moved up one strip in sequential rotation. Decisions regarding sowing were made communally and each family was assigned several *chacras*; they were responsible for their production.
2   *Ayni* is a type of reciprocal work between families. A family that helps another will receive help from the latter at another time. This type of reciprocal support need not involve the same kind of work and does not have fixed rules; instead, *ayni* is just for the 'pleasure of giving' ('el *gusto de dar*').
3   *Qhowa* is an offering in which frankincense is burned (incensing), in the form of figures of the elements to be blessed, with coca and alcohol.

29

River Water Distribution in the Inter-Andean Valleys: the Case of Chilijchi, Bolivia[1]

Gerben Gerbrandy

The context

In this section, we present a case of water distribution in the community of Chilijchi, in one of the inter-Andean valleys with a temperate climate in Cochabamba. We do not want to detail the community's history and organisation but to emphasise key features that have led to the current arrangements for water distribution and that show the inherent notion of equity. Chilijchi's case can be considered typical among Bolivian inter-Andean valleys.

Chilijchi is one of the eight communities that share water from the Machajmarka River, which originates in the nearby mountains. Chilijchi is located approximately in the mid-course of this river, with other communities lying both upstream and downstream. The river meanders and has a wide and rocky bed. Except in the rainy season, when the river can be turbulent, the flow is ca. 200 l/s. The communities build stone and sod intakes that must be rebuilt every year after the rainy season. No canal is capturing all available water, mainly because of the river's and intakes' physical features. Down-river from the intakes, water not diverted is joined by underground flows and further watershed runoff.

Contrary to what happened to the *altiplano* ayllu described in the previous chapter, with no direct influence from large holdings, the history of Chilijchi was primarily determined by the haciendas that were divided and distributed during the 1953 Agrarian Reform. Nevertheless, not all of Chilijchi belonged to a hacienda. About one third of the community belonged to *piqueros*.[2] Today the community has 70 families, almost all with access to water.

Increased water scarcity after the 1953 Agrarian Reform

Before the Agrarian Reform, most canals were owned by the haciendas. At that time *hacendados* (hacienda owners) decided which plots should be irrigated. According to the tradition of those days, complicated distribution systems were not yet needed;

each hacienda could take the river water they needed and even so there was water enough left for the *piquero* communities downstream. This situation has changed over time. After land distribution among *arrenderos* (see note 2) and with increased population, land use became more dispersed and intensive, increasing demand for water. Moreover, it is probable that the water flow during the dry season has diminished over the years due to changes in rainfall patterns and increasing watershed erosion.

The growing demand for water, however, has mainly been caused by the construction of new irrigation canals, upstream from the existing ones. Besides, some old canals have been lengthened. Water scarcity caused by interventions in almost all communities has led to the formulation of stricter rules for water distribution, especially for the driest period (September to November). These rules have developed especially within communities. Inter-community agreements on the amount of river water for each community are unusual. The main reason for this may be that it is more difficult to enforce such agreements between faraway communities, than within a community. This is the case in Chilijchi. It has four canals available, of which one is the old hacienda canal (*canal viejo*). The second canal (*canal nuevo*) was built after the Agrarian Reform and has its intake upstream from the old canal. The other two are less important and are not discussed here.

Current conditions for access to water

Water distribution rules have been adjusted to increasing water scarcity, as have the conditions for obtaining water rights. In Chilijchi all members of a syndicate[3] with irrigable land inside the community are entitled to water for irrigation. This right, however, entails certain obligations: to participate in maintaining the irrigation system, to pay syndicate fees and to attend syndicate meetings. Those who do not fulfil these obligations first must pay a fine and then fulfil them anyway. In cases of continued failure to comply, water rights may be suspended. Rules and sanctions are made by the syndicate. The syndicate also collects fines, to cover general syndicate expenses.

Water rights: an individual claim according to collective determinations

Notwithstanding the fact that water rights in a community are individual, they involve many collective determinations, i.e. individual families claim water and use it for their own good, but in no sense is it their property. The amount of water a family can claim is not quantified. Their water rights change according to the time of the year and depend on how water is distributed along the canal. Generally, if there is enough water in the canal, water is used freely, but when it begins to run short, this 'disorganised' use must become stricter.

Water rights mean a claim to part of the water, but the whole community determines, according to the canal and time of year, what that claim means in practice, regarding water distribution in terms of volume and time. This collective control means that water cannot be sold or officially bartered either. In practice, the water distribution mode makes it almost impossible to sell water rights. Water is linked to the time of the year when the irrigators' group has its turn in a specific section of a specific canal. All that can happen is exchanging or lending turns (more details below).

Flexibility in the application of requirements

Although the above requirements for water use are recognised by everyone, in practice there are some exceptions to the rules, if the syndicate has approved them and if they do not cause conflicts. There are, for example, six households outside the syndicate that have water access rights anyhow. These families belong to a different community but have land in Chilijchi. In another case, it is the son of a syndicate leader who got land from his father but has not yet been accepted in the syndicate. In Chilijchi there are four syndicated irrigators who do not have irrigable land but possess water rights. They rent irrigable land to make use of their rights. When they begin to cultivate a piece of irrigable land, they are automatically classified in the irrigator's group that is in charge of that sector. These families who do not meet all the requirements, but in practice have access to water, must comply with the participation and fee requirements that apply for other syndicate members. Only ill or elderly syndicate members are exempted from these obligations without losing their water rights.

Water distribution systems

Over time, increasing water scarcity forced Chilijchi to introduce changes in water distribution to make it go around for all users all the way down to the last users of the canals. The most important change was the introduction of a distribution system for the driest times. This system is known as the *mita*, with two different periods in the irrigation cycle, each with its own rules. The period before the *mita* is called the 'free irrigation' period.

Free irrigation

This is the irrigation mode during and after the rainy season[4]. Free irrigation means, in principle, that one can use the appropriate amount of water during the time needed without having to wait a turn. Free irrigation is in effect until water begins to run short and problems arise; then the *mita* begins.

However, free irrigation does not mean that there are no rules. For example, the canal cannot be completely closed during irrigation, so there will always be some water for other users and for domestic consumption. Furthermore, just a limited number of users can irrigate at once, to avoid exceeding the canal's capacity. Control of the number of simultaneous users varies according to the canal. For larger-volume canals, users are divided into groups. These groups have internal agreements to ensure that an appropriate number of people are irrigating simultaneously, to have enough water for everyone, while more than one group member irrigates.

Another rule is that people who want to use water upstream have to discuss this with people who are already irrigating; they redistribute the water, agreeing as they go along. Generally during free irrigation users agree on water use. During this period, the limiting factor is usually the canal capacity and not the amount of river water. Therefore, no agreements between canals or between different communities are needed.

Distribution systems by scheduled turns: The mita[5]

During August and September, crops planted after the winter begin to fully develop and the need of water increases. This happens exactly when water is increasingly scarce. The first consequence is an increasing number of conflicts among canal users; especially those whose plots are along the lower portion of the canals suffer from water shortage. Generally they are the ones who suggest the change towards a scheduled system, i.e. the mita. To do this, these users mention the water shortage to the ditch tender or water judge. He, in turn, summons all the irrigators to jointly decide the date when the mita will start. With larger-capacity canals, this happens during the syndicate meeting.

Montón

However, before starting the mita, most canals allow users at the end of the system to irrigate freely one last time. This period is known as the montón and lasts from 24 hours to three days. The meeting determines who can make use of the montón; anyway, it is always the tail-end groups and families.

Mita

Once the montón is over, the true mita goes into effect. In daily practice, peasants use this concept both for the distribution system and for the turns themselves. About the system they say 'it's in mita', meaning that the system of water distribution scheduling has come into operation. But the turn itself is called mita too, e.g. 'a 24-hour mita', or 'I have the mita.'

Mita begins by assigning turns canal by canal, to use the total flow in 12-hour or 24-hour units. However, each canal has its own system to distribute water during the mita. The basic mechanisms and criteria for this scheduled allocation are outlined below:

Broadly, there are two *mita* systems: land-based and people-based allocation. These systems reflect the ways people think about water rights within their communities. Everybody has rights to use water, but all plots also have this right, since no human being and no plot can thrive without water. However, when water is short, it is not possible to supply water to everybody and to all plots, for excessive water dispersion could lead to unreasonably long intervals between turns to irrigate.

Some communities have people-based systems during dry times while others based theirs on land. On the old Chilijchi canal these criteria are combined - primary allocations are related to land, secondary to people. There are also differences between major and minor canals since distribution in a canal with much arable land and many users is more complicated than in canals with less capacity and fewer irrigators. In the latter case, rules are generally simpler and users reach agreements on their own.

The mita on Chilijchi's old canal

Along Chilijchi's old canal the *land* to be irrigated has been divided into *sectors* considered to have, more or less, the same area (in practice, however this area varies considerably). Water is distributed among sectors by equal time units; within each sector water is distributed among families with land. In principle, one family might have land in different sectors, and several turns.

Chilijchi's old canal has 66 irrigators and is divided into seven sectors, each receiving water for 24 hours. Sector 1 always receives water on a Monday, sector 2 on a Tuesday, and so on. While the flow allows, all irrigators in one sector irrigate at the same time, i.e. the flow is divided into equal parts for everyone. First the sector canal is filled and then irrigation starts. When the flow is not sufficient, irrigators in one sector are divided into groups, each group receiving an equal amount of water from the 24-hour turn. Within the group there is an equal division, i.e. everyone gets the same amount of water regardless of the amount of land held. As water supply dries up groups are increasingly reduced until a point is reached where groups disappear and water has to be shifted among individual users. The time allocated to the sector is then divided equitably among the individual sector members.

The Mita on Chilijchi's New Canal: fixed groups

Another solution for the scheduling on canals with many users is to divide the *irrigators* into *fixed groups*. This is the case with Chilijchi's New canal. A user of this canal can have only the right to one irrigation turn, within one single group. The turn's duration for the group is fixed. Along Chilijchi's New Canal, the 31 users are divided into two fixed groups, each irrigating during four days so that users get to irrigate at 8-day intervals.

If the flow allows, irrigation within fixed groups is free. When flow decreases, the fixed groups are divided into subgroups and then into individuals, who get an equal share of the time assigned to the group. Users who have several plots along the canal must distribute the time they are entitled to among these plots.

Mitas on other canals

To show other distribution options we will now mention the canals in a community downstream from Chilijchi. In this community, Conda, another system of irrigation turns is applied. Users are divided into groups, but the group size is variable. The principle is that each group can irrigate for 12 hours and, within the group, each irrigates until finishing. When the flow diminishes and the *mita* is introduced, users are divided into groups of three or four people. When the flow diminishes further and users within groups cannot finish irrigating, the size of groups begins to decrease. However, the turn duration per group remains 12 hours. The lower the flow, the more groups and the longer the irrigation interval for individual users.

Wayqueo

In the canals of Chilijchi, scheduling always goes downstream, the turns are distributed from the head-end down to the tail-end of the canals. The advantage is that there is no waiting time when changing turns (when the last group finishes and the first group irrigates again). The time needed to fill the canal is distributed among all groups or users. An important additional aspect of this system is that when a new cycle starts, i.e. when people at the head-end irrigate again, there is surplus water called *wayqueo*. Officially, the last groups or users on the Chilijchi canals have the right to use *wayqueo*. This is to compensate for these users' losses due to canal leakage, which leaves them less water than users at the head-end.

Equity in the redistribution of rights

In the previous section we have seen that water distribution criteria are based on equity criteria for both land and families. These criteria can vary within a single community on two different canals that, moreover, are partially used by the same families. This section will analyse conditions that have led to these differences.

As mentioned above, after Agrarian Reform there was a rapid increase in water scarcity due to land distribution and expanding irrigated agriculture. Consequently, the free irrigation principle caused more and more water distribution conflicts. When the *mita* was introduced on the old Chilijchi canal, the new one was unfinished and still under construction.

Introduction of the *mita* along the old canal was a gradual process. Initially, individual users tried to solve problems by mutual agreements. Then the canal was subdivided into sections, each with its turn. Totally free water use was gradually supplanted by increasingly systematic irrigation, i.e. by sectors along the canal. We can see from the minutes of meetings at the time, that this still did not lead toward unequivocal agreements or co-ordinated water distribution. Water distribution was the main subject of syndicate meetings.

To put an end to the lack of clarity and conflicts, it was finally the local judge, who was also an irrigator and knew about all the conflicts and ad-hoc rules along the canal, who produced an adequate proposal. Indeed, he tried to formalise existing practice, i.e. irrigation in sectors along the canal. He used the criterion that each sector had to be more or less of equal area and that it should get water for the same time. To define sector limits, however, land area was not measured; instead they observed the time needed by groups to finish irrigation under normal conditions at different points along the canal. The sector size was figured out by the irrigable land area in a 24-hour period. This automatically compensates for flow loss over distance due to infiltration losses. In other words, sectors are smaller downstream. In practice, all plots must have the opportunity to irrigate with the same amount of water.

It seems to have been unimportant in those days that people with land in more than one sector had access to more water. When the *mita* was first introduced, it was possible to irrigate all cultivated plots. Everyone could get the water they needed. The main difference from free irrigation was that the systematic turn assignment prevented water waste from irrigating non-adjacent sites. Besides, use of irrigation time was optimised. In the previous situation there were frequent quarrels for water, but no one irrigated at night. After the *mita* started, water began to be short on a daily basis, due to a constant decrease in water supply (upstream from Chilijchi, people were using more water, too) and a constant increase in water demand.

The introduction of the *mita* along the old canal actually consolidated the prevailing situation in 1960. Until then, any farmer could irrigate all land on that canal, no matter its area. The scarcity that had begun to be felt in this system over time, has been spread out, so to speak, among sectors. Moreover, the consequence is that families who have relatively large amounts of land in certain sectors cannot irrigate their entire plots anymore, while families with relatively small amounts of land in several sectors can go on irrigating them completely. This is because, in each sector, each irrigator has water rights for an equal amount of time, whatever the land area. This is why, only in recent years, it has become an advantage to have plots in different sectors. However, rules have not changed (yet).

The *mita* along the new canal has another history, which makes it different. First, there are restrictions on this canal since its intake is upriver from the old canal's intake, which was already short on water. Actually, this did not cause many conflicts since it involved mainly the same people who were irrigating with the old canal; they had no interest in decreasing its flow. Due to water shortages and the prohibition of taking water from the old canal, the *mita* was needed along the new canal from the beginning.

However, this canal did not have to preserve an irrigation tradition. Therefore, a new criterion was applied regarding turn assignment: each family should be able to use the same amount of water from this canal. Thus, it is not the amount of land that determines the turn duration, since everyone with land along the new canal had contributed the same amount of labour during its construction and everyone should therefore get the same benefits from the canal. Not land but irrigators were divided into two groups, so the members of each could irrigate during the same time span. The group located upstream included more families than the group downstream to compensate for water losses along the canal. However, the amount of water received by the second group, both in terms of families and land area, has decreased because the canal has been increasingly extended.

So, each canal has its history and each has a historical reason and logic within irrigator's relationships that have led towards the current distribution system. However, a central theme in this philosophy is that the starting point always lies in an equitable distribution formulated by everybody. Nevertheless, it seems difficult to change a 'historical' key to water distribution. This is why we saw that people with abundant land along the old canal could irrigate abundantly in past times. Conflicts arose due to the scarcity of water and then a new system was established, preserving previous principles of access related to land possession. However, these negotiations took place under new relationships among people. Customs along the old canal developed when *hacendados* dictated the rules. When the *mita* was introduced, Agrarian Reform had been applied and each community member had one vote. This has favoured people with less land in the sectors. However, the new relationships were further expressed after the introduction of new water distribution rules along the new canal. The new canal had no old customs and a new type of water distribution was introduced, based on equitable labour contribution and equitable rights among users.

All this does not mean that there are no conflicts. In Chilijchi, for example, one of the sons of the *hacendado* has been trying for years to change the norm of group-based division along the new canal in favour of a sector-based division. Until he gets his way, he increases his water access indirectly through sharecropping-type rental agreements, in which he supplies the land while a partner supplies the water. Such contradictions between large landowners and people with less land will probably continue. Generally, people with much land will prefer to link water rights with land, while people with less land will prefer proportional distribution among users.

However, we have found a common criterion in all communities, that is, the collective character of water. All communities feel that everyone has a right to use water as long as they fulfil their obligations. Nevertheless, rulings over water distribution frequently favour the rich and powerful in town. These people wield influence through *compadrazgo* (godfather-) relationships. A godson will not be prone to oppose his godfather. One example is the violation of the rule that sons still living in their parents' households cannot independently have a *mita*. However, this happens in two cases in Chilijchi: in one case it is the son of a leader and in the other a member of the ex-*hacendado* family. In spite of the protests of many syndicate members, these cases are not penalised.

A reflection on equity in Chilijchi

In Chilijchi the sense of equity means that all community members have the right to use water as a collective resource. Families can use their rights according to community regulations.

There is the belief that equity is related to water rights both for land and for families. Families have water rights and plots have the right to be irrigated. This link of equity with land or people is influenced by historical customs: in the old canal water turns are assigned at the overall canal level to land sectors, while at the sector level turns are assigned to families with land within the sector. However, in the new canal rights are directly linked to the investment that families have made in building the canal.

The criterion of equity means, above all, that there is a· consensus that something must be equitable or equal. For example, all users think that the division of irrigable land into sectors is based on equal areas (actually there are differences of up to 50%). The perception of equity is also expressed in compensation for disadvantageous positions along the canals. Users who get to irrigate last are entitled to an extra turn before the *mita* starts (*montón*) and to use surplus water in the canal when a new cycle begins (*wayqueo*).

From a family standpoint, *within sectors* equity among families increased as water availability worsened: families with less land within a sector would finish irrigating while families with much land could not completely irrigate their plots. However, this system also creates inequity between families with plots in several sectors and families with their plots in a single sector. Someone with plots in different sectors can irrigate each of them while families with plots in only one sector can irrigate only once. Families with large areas spread along several sectors irrigate them all, while families with large areas in one sector cannot irrigate completely.

Notes

1   In this chapter we have used data from research on water management carried out in 1984 by Maarten van Bentum and Maarten Bredero, advised by the author of this chapter. The study, published in Dutch, was entitled: 'Kommunaal Waterbeheer in Bolivia.'
2   In previous critical periods, hacienda owners often used to sell sections of the hacienda to free peasants. These sections were called *piquerías* and the people who bought them, *piqueros*. In other instances, menial peasants bought their liberty from their *hacendado* and got from him a piece of land (*pegujal*); these were the *pegujaleros*. Menial households that lived inside a hacienda and who had to serve the *hacendado* were named *arrenderos*.
3   A syndicate is the basic formal organisation of rural communities. The Bolivian Law of Agrarian Reform (1953) provides that all rural communities must be organised into syndicates
4   The only exception is the *Kollpa* canal, where *mita* irrigation occurs along the year round.
5   During pre-Columbian times, the *mita* was a rendering of services to the Inca Emperor. Spaniards incorporated the concept into their power structure to require mandatory work in mines. In rural areas, *hacendados* used the concept to divide the contribution by each hacienda during construction of irrigation canals. With these contributions, each hacienda would earn its turn for irrigation.

30
Multiple-Source Irrigation Systems and Transparency: the Case of Punata, Bolivia

Zulema Gutiérrez & Gerben Gerbrandy

Introduction

The Punata irrigation area is located in the Andean valley of Cochabamba, 50 km away from the regional capital of the same name. Several water sources serve an area of around 4.000 hectares at an altitude of approximately 2.700 metres above sea level, divided into 55 communities. These communities are both the administrative and legal units of rural organisations. Their main agricultural disadvantages are the irregular rainfall pattern during the rainy season and water scarcity at the beginning of the growing season. Average annual rainfall is 450 mm, of which 85% occurs during the summer months (December through March). Night-time frost occurs only during the winter months (July through August). So, Punata is suitable for agriculture almost year-round. The main factor preventing intensive production is the lack of water between June and November. Punata's principal crops are maize and alfalfa (rainfed) and vegetables and potatoes (irrigated). Punata uses several water sources: the river, reservoirs and springs.[1] The discharges of these sources are lowest at the beginning of the growing season (August to December). During the rainy season, all communities have access to Pucara River water, but in the dry season the number drops to almost half and a time-based distribution of the flow is instated.

Twenty-two communities built two reservoirs (*lagunas*) on the nearby slopes and two reservoir committees were organised to manage their use. The first reservoir, Laguna Robada, was built during the first decade of this century and irrigates the land of ten communities. Twelve communities use the reservoir known as Llushka Khocha, built in the 1960s. The rest (23 communities) had no reservoir water until a new reservoir was inaugurated in 1990. This one, Totora Khocha, is shared by 31 communities in the adjacent province of Tiraque, where all these *lagunas* are located. All Punata communities have access to water from this reservoir, including those that already irrigate from Laguna Robada and Llushka Khocha.

During the dry season, water from these reservoirs is conducted downriver to the system's main intake. The water from all sources goes through the same grid to reach groups of water right holders. This means that, simultaneously, water from two or more sources can flow through the same river and canals, to be separated again at the irrigation area. A stone marks the original flow level just below the division point, before water from another source is incorporated. When the additional water reaches the irrigation area, enough water is taken from the full flow to make it return to the original level, prior to incorporating the second flow.

Each source has its specific families with rights, a water share. These shares are expressed in time units, i.e. the minutes each user can use the source during each *largada*.[2] The *largada* time is based on the contribution in days of work and fees invested by each member to build the reservoirs. In other words, members earn a share by reservoir-building work.

Once the flows from different sources are separated, each 'water' follows its own course along the plots of users with water rights. During the *largada* each rightholder gets the total flow (up to 200 l/s) during his or her rotation turn. Only for Totora Khocha, with a flow of up to 1000-1200 l/s at the intake, it is not possible to irrigate with such a flow. To maintain the principle applied for other sources, here the flow is divided into eight equal flows. Each one-eighth has its own users in almost equal numbers. To even out differences in numbers of users, a system of grading the closure of the reservoir is applied at the end of the *largada* (the reservoir outlet flow is regulated in three stages). With this method, more numerous groups go on irrigating when others have already finished. To eliminate the last differences, the flow from finished groups passes on to groups that go on irrigating to 'help finish out the irrigation'. Here, these groups handle two simultaneous flows in their zone.

With the introduction of the Totora Khocha system it was no longer possible to separate water just by marking stones. Therefore, nowadays all division points rely on regulation gates and measurement structures that indicate the flow in litres per second. With this method, water from Totora Khocha is split into equal flows. However, division and measurement structures are not utilised to separate water from different reservoirs.

Equity in water distribution among the communities

We will consider two levels of equity: distribution among communities at the system level and distribution within communities. At the system level, we will refer mainly to the mechanisms, criteria and norms that have made it possible to start operating a new system, as happens with Totora Khocha. At the community level, we will also mention these mechanisms and look at how distribution organisation principles achieve a high degree of equity.

As explained in the introduction, Totora Khocha is a new system that began operating in 1991.[3] The distribution criteria in existing reservoirs were used as a basis for Totora Khocha system operation. All agreements to operate Totora Khocha were designed to maintain equity in water distribution.

Independent operation by sub-systems

The decision to bring water *largada* after *largada*, reservoir by reservoir, is a result of the firmly rooted criterion of transparency in irrigation system management. Transparency is reflected in independence and maintains equity. Initially, the project placed division structures to distribute water with an utility criterion, according to the sizes of irrigated areas, without regarding the water sources. This criterion was incompatible with user's feelings about equity. Currently, division structures are employed to separate water from a single source into equal flows, but they cannot be used to distinguish among waters from different sources. For the irrigators, the introduction of structures for the measurement of water flows does not help maintain transparency in distinguishing among several sources:

> 'There would be problems at the intake and I don't think rules would help distribute waters from two reservoirs ... I think we would never be able to get equal distribution. If one reservoir is opened, we have to wait until it is drained to open the second one. We would NOT allow two flows to come together'. (R. Gutiérrez, leader of Wañakahua Grande)

Thus, to maintain transparency in operating two reservoirs, they are opened sequentially to avoid confusing 'waters from different reservoirs'. Water *separation* is applied only between reservoirs and *other* river water (as in the *mita*). Exceptionally, in cases of drastic demand, Laguna Robada and Llushka Khocha are opened together', but Totora Khocha 'always comes alone'.

Division into comparable groups of irrigators, bi-partition

Water distribution experience in existing systems (Laguna Robada and Llushka Khocha) was based on rotation, one community after the other. Since there are more communities for Totora Khocha and a larger flow to be operated, this system was no longer appropriate and an arrangement for division among irrigating groups was introduced.

Division calls for other mechanisms and instruments to achieve equality. The condition is for only one irrigation system to be operating. With Totora Khocha, division into eight irrigating groups was easily decided, because all groups get the same flow. The decision that all groups irrigate with the same amount of water avoids specialisation (the control is not by volume) and there is also no centralisation of decision-making, since all users can monitor equity (just by looking at the scales). Equity means sharing the advantages and disadvantages through mutual acceptance. We can perceive this when users state that water must be distributed at the main intake using the scales of the measurement structures.

The Laguna Robada system, after the one-year experience with Totora Khocha, changed from their inter-community rotation distribution (single flow expressed in units of time) to division into groups (in this case two groups). Water is shared by halving: halves or quarters, etc., a criterion that makes it possible to ensure equity.

Tolerance time for filling the canals

When the Totora Khocha system began to operate, users proposed that, since communities are not at an equal distance from the intake, differences in 'tolerance time' should be considered to compensate for the time needed to fill the canals, a time known as *descorredura*,[4] as is done in Laguna Robada and Llushka Khocha. The main argument was to compensate losses that would affect remote communities. Communities close to the intake suggested this compensation for the more distant ones. In the words of an irrigator from the Pucara community, situated just a few metres away from the intake that receives water from Llushka Khocha:

> 'We want to distribute water at the intake at 30-minute intervals for each member; since some of us have to take it a long way, we can arrange internally to grant them a few extra minutes. Fellow leaders, we must analyse to solve the case of faraway communities a bit. I reckon we must concede three or four[5] extra minutes; this is reasonable because water is lost for those who live downstream, not so for those who live upstream. At the time of the first *largada* we will see how much is lost; we don't know how long it will take to reach the plots. Only by experimenting will we be able to appreciate losses; since we don't know yet, we cannot know how much we should compensate'.

On the basis of this suggestion, they decided that for the first *largada* a two-hour tolerance time should be given for filling the canals. They agreed to make necessary adjustments after this first experience. During the tolerance time they compensate for community irrigation turns. Otherwise, differences among communities would arise due to their location and position in relation to the intake. This mechanism maintains a high degree of equity during water distribution. Tolerance times are established through practice and mutual control among communities; once established, they become fixed. Don Damián Waranka, leader of Wasamayu, explains how these times have been instituted in the Laguna Robada system:

> '... I was going along the far shore of the river, there, to Tambillo Centro. Another neighbouring syndicate leader came along. From Khochi to Wañakahua, from Tacko they come to Wañakahua Chico and so on. At the meeting they said 'in so many hours it has reached this community and in so many that one'. This way, some communities take three hours, four hours, according to how the water arrives. Therefore, there was an advantage of four hours supposed to be given by people upstream'.

To solve the problem of communities' location in relation to the intake, each system has generated its own solution by managing des*corredurias*. For example, in Laguna Robada each community has two to four hours of free time depending on their distance from the intake; this is what they call 'time for the canal'. Only after this time has transpired, they count scheduled irrigation time for the community.

Management of tail water

The reservoirs are located an average of 30 km from the irrigation area. Therefore, when the water first reaches the irrigation area, it does so through a smaller flow called 'the head' that stabilises and finally drops away again when the reservoir is closed; this last flow is known as 'tail water'. It is normal to have tail water after all the communities have had their turn. The management of tail water in the Totora Khocha system is also an equity mechanism since it guarantees that all users irrigate. Although the flow decreases at the end, they compensate by increasing irrigation time. To be able to calculate time for closing the reservoir, irrigators make many experimenting efforts to maintain a more or less equal flow for several hours before finishing the turn. They assume that with these hours (with the same volume) they can compensate for some difficulties that might arise in the scheduled cycle.

Equity in water distribution within communities

Within communities there has been an active participation by the people in defining how to distribute waters from Totora Khocha. Every resolution was taken in community meetings by consensus. New communities, although lacking experience in using the reservoir, were skilled in water management with other systems. The distribution criteria from those systems served as a foundation for reservoir-based distribution; therefore it was easy to maintain and enhance existing distribution criteria. By monitoring *largadas* and interviews, we have found that the most important thing in water distribution at the community level is maintaining 'equity', something which is much more evident at this level than at the inter-system or intra-system levels. Equity in water distribution within communities means: all members should have the same opportunity to get their water entitlement if they have fulfilled all their obligations. Within a community, according to the agreements, they have developed a series of mechanisms to achieve equity. We present below some mechanisms we have identified in Totora Khocha water distribution.

Group establishment and size

The 'size' factor affects overall communal organisation. When the number of members becomes unmanageable, the community tends to divide and new ones are formed. The same applies to water distribution: if communities are numerous, they are prone to divide and establish smaller groups. Since water distribution during a *largada* is very intensive work, users are divided into groups to secure a reciprocal social obligation so everyone collaborates during the *largada*. Within these large communities, there are irrigation groups with their own irrigation organisation. Each group has its own water judge and time-keepers. In practice, each group manages its water independently but outside the community there is still only one representative. Subdivision of communities into smaller groups makes it necessary for the sub-communities to negotiate with each other and new social relationships are thus established. This is what happened with Paracaya I, a large community and 'new' to reservoir water:

> 'In the first *largada* we all had to irrigate together; all of us had to walk, all 120 members had to walk for 64 hours. After that, for the second *largada* that same year, in order not to stay up late and get sick, we divided it into hours. We had to think and we divided up. Since the second *largada* the Pabellón group goes alone, the middle group goes alone, and people don't have to stay up late. We monitor each other, we respect each other's hours [...] Each checks in his own group, each judge has its group, and time-keepers too'. (B Gutiérrez, Secretary of Conflicts, Paracaya I)

The same phenomenon occurred in the Chillcar Grande community, not so much to solve the problem of monitoring reciprocal work but to make each person's work proportional to the amount of water they were entitled to. This community already got water from Llushka Khocha. With the building of Totora Khocha and the water rights adjustment, several irrigation times and types of water rights related to Totora Khocha appeared. Consequently, not everyone had to work equally to oversee and monitor equitable distribution during the *largada*. According to the secretary recording, during the first *largada* everybody participated with the same amount of work. Afterwards, people with less irrigation time realised that it was unfair for them to work as much as people with more shares. They found a way inside the community to balance this situation to avoid conflict. They formed five working groups to monitor according to the duration of their irrigation turns.

> 'There were three groups before 1991, not five. They divided our community into groups when they realised that the ones with 15 minutes were doing the same amount of work as those with 30 minutes. They walked the same, they kept guard the same, they watched over the intake the same. For the second *largada*, we have been planning: we are going to make groups according to the number of minutes of water. Those with 15 minutes will have to walk just ten hours. Those with 24 minutes will have to walk 12 hours. Those who have 30 minutes will have to walk 18 hours. Those who have 42 minutes will have to walk one round together with those who have 15 minutes and one round with those who have 30 minutes. Those who have a double share have to walk two 18-hour rounds. This is how it is calculated, each group in its schedule, that's the way we all walk'. (J. Espinosa, Secretary of Records, Chillcar Grande).

Within the community of Wañakawa Chico, with a smaller number of members, there are two irrigation groups. Very large communities are subdivided to better monitor the performance of duties. In this smaller community, Wañakawa Chico, groups were established mainly based on family kinship. Each group has its own water judge, time keepers and *khawadores*,[6] but the intake keepers are the same for

both groups. This smaller group size enhances processes of negotiation about irrigation management performance and stimulates *ayni*[7] among the irrigators. *Ayni* allows
someone who has not been able to do his or her work for one reason or another, to
get water anyway. As we have mentioned, the number of members and the amount
of variation in water rights are determining factors in establishing groups; this mechanism is an important way to maintain equity in water distribution.

Rotation of the schedule order (head-tail)

Schedule order rotation is a mechanism used to preserve distribution equity.
Rotation within a community works like this: groups within a community rotate so
that every group has its chance to irrigate first. When there are no groups, in one
largada users start irrigating from the top down and in the next one from the bottom
up.

Schedule order rotation is also the result of agreements among users. All must suffer
the consequences of being first (smaller flow) and the advantages of being last (to be
able to buy the community's ' tail water'). Tambillo Grande community's tail water is
sold when the cycle ends. In case one group does not want to use tail water, it nego-
tiates its tail position with another group. Doña Elena Crespo, community cashier,
tells us how groups rotate in Tambillo Grande because of their interest in the 'tail
water':

> '... people complain that we have finished irrigating just on one end, and that we
> should finish on the other end too; here neither the leader nor the one in charge
> of public relations get involved. It is only the people who decide at which end irri-
> gation should finish. We say 'all right, take it', but we warn them: 'if there is sur-
> plus water you'll have to buy it'. They say that it is okay, that is why we want it
> to finish at our end'.

Rotation also guarantees that the same people do not get to irrigate always during
the daytime or at night. Don Roberto Gutiérrez, leader of Wañakahua Grande, talks
about rotation in his community:

> 'When we start with the first *largada*, for example if we start by the corner sector,
> then we go to the middle part of the canal where water also goes. Later we go to
> the canal by the road, and then we take water down there, where it ends. In the
> other *largada*, where we ended is where we start. We do it like this because some
> people can irrigate during the daytime, others during the night; next *largada*,
> those who got the night can irrigate by day and the others work at night. This is
> why we rotate, because we know, after so many years of water distribution'.

Rotation, in all these forms, guarantees that all have the same advantages and
handicaps during irrigation, which reflects rural people's idea of irrigation equity.

Single-flow and halving

Many peasant irrigation systems have single-flow (full-volume) water delivery, as one factor guaranteeing transparency which is why irrigators favour this form of delivery (Gerbrandy 1991; Gutiérrez and Claure 1995). Nevertheless, water distribution *within* groups does not necessarily have to be like that. In several Punata communities, members reveal that they divide water, when it is permitted by the infrastructure of canals. Halving the flow does not make transparency disappear. In other communities, the flow is not divided, due to a larger flow required for the type of land preparation (tractor or bullock-team ploughing) and crops they have.

Defining whether distribution in a community will be through single-flow or halving is also the result of agreements among users. They consider the types of soil, the season and crops in the community. Next, we present two quotes that show why some communities distribute on a single-flow basis while others tend to use halving:

> '... we think that we have to divide water within the syndicate. Since Totora Khocha gives plenty of water and it's difficult to irrigate with so much, we've always said at the syndicate that we have to divide it. Always, until right now, we have divided Laguna Robada'. (F. Paredes, irrigator from Barrientos Grande)

> 'We irrigate our land with the whole flow. With only a little water it's not possible to irrigate everything, but when a lot of water comes one can irrigate all over the land immediately. If just a little comes, it gets lost because the earth sucks it up. With a lot of water, one can irrigate at once, that's why we do it this way' (F Crespo, cashier of Tambillo Grande)

Irrigating with a single-flow or with flows divided into halves ensures equity in distribution because everyone will get a quantity proportional to the water rights held by each. Logically, this happens only after one has fulfilled all obligations pertaining such rights. Project officers, considering that the flows from Totora Khocha were too large to be managed as a single-flow, initially suggested that it should be divided into fractions proportional to the number of shares per area. In this way, assorted flows would have been created for each zone. This was rejected fiercely by the peasants. They themselves applied halving later, since it fits better with the logic behind transparency and allows a finer control of equity.

Shared 'descorreduras'

Another equity mechanism is distribution of *descorreduras* within the community. The sharing of the time needed for the *descorreduras* allows everyone to irrigate and no member comes up short. This mechanism socialises distribution losses within the community. Since some plots inside a community are located close and others far from the head zone, there is a reduction in irrigation times for all. This way, they avoid people with faraway plots having to irrigate less, for everyone irrigates their plots during the same time interval, regardless of plot location. In those communities with water that comes only from Totora Khocha, all members have a discount of three minutes:

'... we have told people that we are not going to get 30 minutes, that we are going to miss some water. Since we are getting water for the first time, we'll get 28 minutes, all of us. This way people have come to understand and everybody is happy now' (N. Borda, Secretary of Relations of Tambillo Centro)

Distribution control and community organisation

The community water distribution organisation is in charge of maintaining equilibrium to have every member receive water equitably. This organisation consists of a number of authorities and everyone can and must be an authority at some time; from an early age everybody learns to occupy a position. Being an authority does not mean having power, because people watch each other. Being an authority means serving the community:

'I am obliged, I am serving my community, therefore I have taken oath and I have to obey because people have chosen me. Here they elect an honest person as a water judge and they see him as a father and we take oath so we will be neutral'. (C. Gutiérrez, water judge of the community of Wañakahua Chico, 1995)

To be able to make use of the water right it is necessary to be recognised as a member of the community; this is accomplished only by attending all meetings and activities summoned by the community (not only those related to maintenance and water distribution). In practice, it is not forbidden for someone who has not totally complied with his/her obligations to use water, but the community isolates this person by hindering irrigation. During *largadas* it was observed that one person who has land in the community and has a right to the water registered for the community, cannot use it for he has not been recognised as a community member, since he has not participated in the community activities. Don David Gutiérrez (time keeper of the community of Wañakahua during the second *largada* from Totora Khocha) says:

'These guys don't feel like working in the community, they don't even attend the meetings. When we attend them, we lose almost half a working day. There are some who have land here but live in other communities, such as don Daniel from Rumi Rumi, but he does attend the meetings and sends a labourer to work. We have decided then that those who do not come do not get any water. Sometimes they act pushy and want to irrigate because they have money but the decision has been taken'.

Claims by people not considered members of the community, although they have water rights, are not analysed or considered. Although they can make some kinds of decisions about their land, they cannot decide about water, because irrigation is a communal exercise. A consensus-based agreement is indispensable to be able to use such right. To be considered as a member of the community, one has to participate equitably in all communal obligations.

Next we cite the common features we have found in the organisations of different communities in Punata. They express the peasant notion of equity both in water distribution and in duty assignment. In community organisation each function or position has its own features. During the *largada*, a water judge is the top authority and this role is honoured:

> 'We first have a meeting where all appointments are made. The chief water judge knows where irrigation is to start and gives instructions to everyone for the *largada*. At this meeting the gate keepers (*tomeros*), wardens (*controles*) and time keepers (*relojeros*) are appointed, and the schedule for their tasks is decided. Also the height wardens (*controles de las alturas*) are designated, they know their turns. They see the day of their turn and go where they have been appointed to go. All this is done by the chief water judge and the leader only watches and doesn't get involved. The water route is also specified. The meeting decides upon the sequence of water turns in the schedule, downwards or upwards. Since it goes upwards once and downwards the next time, once the sequence has been decided no one can change it. Everything has to follow the rules'. (T. Claros, President of the community of Pucara)

Contrary to the custom in outside organisations, in these communities the authorities are not appointed through elections but by identifying the most appropriate member. We can see how an authority is selected, in this case a water judge, in the following quotation:

> 'I have been water judge for almost three years, since my father died some time ago. I have learned thanks to the fact that my father sent me to school and also because sometimes I replaced him in his functions. That's why the syndicate has appointed me. You have to be it, they told me, since your father worked for so long at this. Then you, as chief water judge, will have to help us, that's why I am chief water judge'. (V. Alcocer, water judge of Pucara)

Another characteristic is that authorities emerge according to the circumstances. In the case of the *largada*, there are many authorities (gate keepers, time keepers, wardens, etc.), and the number increases or decreases according to tension over water in the zone. Moreover, appointments rotate to make everybody knows the distribution, to ensure transparency and equity in water distribution. This also prevents bribing of persons, which might happen if they hold the same position too long.

> 'We send the intake keepers according to a list of all members. We begin at the head and we also begin at the end. That way everybody does it, men and women'. (R. García, Vice-president of Paracaya I)

'Time keepers work by turns. They know they have to watch until the time is over. They cannot leave their post, since if they do who is going to get the water to the members? Also if it is a woman, she has to do it anyway. She might be a widow and if she can't go, she must send her son. Not just a few should know about distributing water, everybody should know if there is enough water or not. Inside the syndicate, everybody should know how to help. We cannot decide that only one is going to be a time keeper, all of us have decided that everybody should learn how to distribute water'. (V. Alcocer, water judge of Pucara)

It has been observed that during a *largada*, nobody has absolute power. There is mutual monitoring, a warden watches the time keepers, but they also keep an eye on the warden.

'When they don't find the gate keeper at his post, they cut off his water because he has not performed his duty. I don't go anywhere, I have everything with me, including food and *chicha*. When I am on watch, I do the same. I go up and then come back. This way, a warden registers the hours when someone wasn't there. The warden has to tell at the meeting that such and such people weren't there at such time. Right now, wardens have already done four rounds. They reach the intake and we have to watch them, too. We count how many rounds they have done'. We must watch them and they must watch us'. (L. Tapia, intake keeper interviewed in the community of Tacko)

If, during a *largada*, there are attitudes that disturb the smooth operation, penalties are established to make water available for everyone.

'During the last *largada*, don Nicola and don Renato went on patrol and caught five who had come back to the intake. Now they have a punishment of ten minutes less water. They came back at 4 p.m. and they should have stayed until 8 p.m. They came back and were seized by the leaders, now there is no excuse for this and we are not going to pardon them. If we pardon them, they are going to get used to it and they are going to ask not to be punished. That's the way punishments are'. (E. Crespo, cashier of Tambillo Grande)

In summary, we have perceived that the community is always looking to strike a balance to avoid inequalities. The authority responsible for maintaining this equilibrium during a *largada*, the water judge, needs special charisma. Don Valentín says that a water judge must fulfil the following requisites:

'Legally it means that you have to walk the straight and narrow path. A man acting as water judge must not be selfish ever. He has to be a sensible man, he has to do the distribution honestly. He has to act as if he had a piece of bread that he has to divide equally. Like a father or mother, a water judge has to distribute equally'. (V. Rojas, President of the Llushka Khocha Committee)

To get water to the plots there is much participatory work within the community. This is what we have called distribution control organisation. During distribution there are authorities such as the water judge and his collaborators (time keepers, gate keepers, wardens, etc.) who get water to the plots and ensure correct allotment. Performing these functions in monitoring and distributing is seen as a responsibility given by the community. Since efforts are shared, then all should be able to use the water without any gender- or age-related consideration. To reach this goal everyone plays a part; so that power will not corrupt they rotate positions. Besides, during every *largada* there is a constant societal oversight to guarantee equitable distribution. The community establishes agreements and mechanisms to secure equity: rotation, shared *descorreduras* and so on.

Conclusions: transparency within a variety of rights

Equity is expressed in a direct ratio between relative volumes of water-use rights, amount of labour, and economic contributions by each entitled family. Rights are distributed in the form of water shares. People differentiate clearly between sources since the sense of justice bonds water rights and specific sources of water, to irrigate autonomously and independently.

Since the Punata irrigation system is large and complex, equitable control during water distribution has been emphasised: there is no mixing of water from different sources, water is distributed in halves and halves of halves, and the utmost effort is made to keep a full, single-flow at least until water reaches the community. That means that one can assess water features by looking at its flow. People say: ' Laguna Robada is in the community of Huaña Khawa and it has plenty of water [200 l/s] while this water here is *mita* water, it is just a little bit [30-50 l/s]'. For equity in water distribution, irrigation must be transparent for every user. In Punata, there is a great transparency in water distribution for there is not much to be administered: each irrigation group is in charge of distributing and controlling water from their source. The group with its scheduled in turn takes water from the intake, walks with the water toward the community and, when the turn is over, the next group comes to take it. It is prohibited to combine an individual turn with that of another community. The unit of measure is known and fixed. The system is transparent because they know when to start and when to end a turn. Users know what they are allowed to use.

Strong decentralisation of the system through deliveries at the communal level allows a high degree of participation. Since distribution begins at the community level, equity is achieved through social control mechanisms.

Behind these there is a series of mechanisms to divide distribution labour and maintenance in proportion to the users' rights. As in the case of Chilijchi (ch. 29) there are compensation measures for faraway users in a disadvantageous situation.

However the mechanisms are different (time compensations during *descorredura*). Here they use the tail water to compensate those users who have not been able to irrigate completely during their allotted time. To compensate for flow fluctuations in the *largadas* the order of scheduled turns is rotated.

Notes

1   Tubular wells were drilled in a small portion of Punata to cover 200 ha scattered over the whole Punata area.
2   Reservoirs are opened for long enough to allow each user to irrigate during his turn. The time between opening and closure is known as the *largada*.
3   The reservoir was inaugurated one year earlier. A rainy season was needed to accumulate water in order for the whole system to work.
4   *Descorredura* is the time for water to fill the canals, and normally this time is charged to the irrigating community; some minutes are taken from every user to compensate for *descorredura* losses. When this time is charged to the system, it is called tolerance time. Here, the irrigation time-counting of the community begins only when the *descorredura* has passed, so, when the canal has been filled and its flow has stabilised. In this case, the *descorredura* is the time between the arrival of water (from the reservoir via the river) to the intake at the head of the irrigation area, until the beginning of time-counting on the irrigation schedule.
5   This irrigator refers to the compensation minutes for each member, dividing total *descorredura* loss (which can be nearly two hours) by the total number of members.
6   Khawador comes from the quechua name *khaway* that means 'to watch'. A *khawador* is 'the one who watches', keeping guard against theft by third persons.
7   Reciprocal work among families in the Andean zone.

References

Gerbrandy, Gerben, 1991. *Concepción Campesina de Gestión de agua. Sistemas de riego en las provincias de Punata y Tiraque.* (unpublished), GTZ, Cochabamba.
Gutiérrez, Zulema & Claure Washington, 1995. *El proceso social en la definición de la distribución del agua de la represa de Totora Khocha en la zona de Riego Punata.* MSc thesis, Wageningen Agricultural University, Wageningen.

31

Irrigation, Guarani Territory and Conceptions of Equity

Nico van Dixhoorn and José Luis Gareca Arias

The Bolivian Guarani Chaco: a brief history

Thousands of Guarani were concentrated on the pampas of Kuruyuki. *Mburuvichas* from all the mountains conducted the assembly, haranguing the warriors, whipping up their courage. They were convinced that death would be better than oppression. The *Tüpa Hapiaoeki*[1] assured them that the gods would make the *karai* rifles spit only water. It was January 1892. The Republican army not only defeated the Guarani warriors but for several weeks, persecuted all men, leaving a balance of approximately 15,000 Guaranis killed.

The Guarani communities of Bolivia are one of the ethnic minorities that have succeeded in surviving in spite of the more than 500 years of constant domination in all facets of life during colonial and republican periods. Nowadays, although the State recognises communities' legal status, they have not been able to overcome their poverty or rid themselves of large landowners and stockbreeders who subject peasants and entire communities to a situation of permanent confinement and submission. Many laws enacted since the early days of the Republic until this day have simply consolidated pillaging of land and enslavement of these indigenous communities.

Unlike most cases considered in the book, the geographical location of the Guarani communities is not the Andes, but the base of the mountain range of what is properly known as the Chaco.

The economic basis of the Guarani people is maize, and around its production are their life, their culture, their religion, their festivities, etc. are based on maize growing. Land is owned communally and their concept of territory is the *ivi* (soil, water, flora, fauna and human beings). Here, humans are a part of Nature and not vice versa. This in important since, for example, irrigation means managing a watershed with the active participation of all stakeholders in the geographical-ecological unit.

Present-day Guarani communities have substantial differences among each other and distinctive features, depending on the degree of contact with 'civilisation', on the characteristics of oppression to which they have been subjected and on the influence of religious and other types of institutions that have contacted them.

In communities where the *mburuvicha* (traditional patriarchal authority) has been converted into an Indian chief and used as a functional token within the oppressors' system, there is a vertical power structure where the Captain (Indian chief) has inherited the mechanisms of subjection used by large landowners. In many cases, these persons prey on *Indian problems*, turning them into a gold mine yielding strictly personal benefits. Frequently, development institutions and the State itself support these organisations and prefer to overlook this despotic reality.

Communities that have had contact with religious missions - besides the cultural and religious symbiosis this has meant - often have abandoned the core communal features of Christian inspiration: equality and fraternity among brothers. Their deadliest feature is the creation of paternalistic bonds that have the community members waiting for everything to fall from heaven.

In present-day communities, rebuilt in zones where landowners and haciendas are still strong, a great cultural vacuum is apparent and people have difficulties overcoming the mental structure of the enslaved (a perceived need to have a boss). Even those who become free due to resettlements of Guarani families on purchased properties, have the boss (*patrón*) deeply embedded in their soul. As they obtain palpable results from their production, and direct benefits from individual and communal plots (*chacos*), they can rediscover their traditional power and banish new bosses and chiefs from their lives.

There are also traditional communities that have had little or no contact with civilisation, becoming a mirror and a symbol of communal traditional organisation. This, for example, is the case of the people of the Tenta Yapi community who to this day keep rejecting white men's religion and schools. They are pestered by researchers and all sorts of curious people who, in most cases, see the natives as wildlife in an ecological park, 'worth studying'.

The Assembly of the Guarani People (APG), an organisation that hopes to bring together all the Guaranis of Bolivia, is working to overcome 'chieftainism' and 'clientelism' structures in their organisational pyramid in order to respect a community structure where it is the assembly that decides, rather than a leadership elite.

There is a strong twofold pressure on indigenous organisations, as in the case of CIDOB (Indigenous Confederation of Oriente, Chaco and Bolivian Amazonia). (Inter)national support institutions require organisations to be of a grass-roots and non-political nature. Under this flag, CIDOB has received major funding on behalf of the people they represent. But their leaders are increasingly isolated from their roots, becoming clever politicians, perhaps as a new form of chieftanism? 'It seems they are with the big ones, with the internationals, while we are working at the grass-root levels', says a leader of a zonal APG. A group of zonal leaders called an assembly of local and communal Guarani leaders. By majority vote they appointed a new Board of Directors in order to improve fund management and work on priorities agreed upon by the general assembly.

Irrigation and concepts of equity in Guarani communities

The concepts of equity within the Guarani community are closely linked to traditional values about nature and how to use it:

- The land and other natural resources, water, flora and fauna are communal property. Although there is strong pressure to somehow allow outsiders to use their land, when community members have wanted to rent their *chacos* to an outsider the community has forbidden it in many cases. In some of such cases, members have been expelled from the community by the communal assembly.
- Natural resources are used according to each family's needs: for example, if the family is larger or stays in the community more than others, they have more access.
- The one who has more, as the consequence of a good harvest, shares with the rest.
- Everyone should have their *oka* (house and garden) and access to the community's *koorenda* (communal production area) where their *chaco* is located.
- Beyond the communal land there is the *guatarenda*, which includes all the forests, with their vegetation, animals and gullies. In the *guatarenda*, there is no concept of people's property.

On the whole, the *guatarenda*, the *koorenda* and the *oka* are the *ivi*. For the Guarani, there is no strict separation of its components; for them, the concept of land is actually a concept of territory, of ecological unity. In this sense, water is just another element. However, it is not possible to generalise this situation to all communities. The colonial and republican influences, as mentioned above, have left strong differences among communities and among their members.

Irrigation and other forms of water management are generally governed by this territory concept, and by what the Guarani consider fair. For example, access to irrigation water depends on peoples' need and mutual agreements and is related to the work they have done:

> 'To do the cleaning everyone gathers. When the cleaning is done they decide who needs the water more and they decide how to irrigate: someone says 'you go first, you second, and then me ... ' Also, for example, if some people's corn can hold on a bit more, they give the water to those who need it most, to those who are really hurting for water'. (Guarani from an irrigating community)

In irrigation projects, the elements of *ivi* are separated and there is no integrated concept about natural resource management. These interventions involve a type of management foreign to Guarani life and a separation from their communal equity concepts. Few outside efforts make any attempt to manage the watershed, which encompasses an ecological unit with all four categories of (renewable) natural resources. Therefore, these projects have had very diverse results, depending on their approach. Let us see two examples:

For Guaranis, equity (i.e. rights, duties and the respective rules) is both related internally to the community and externally to others. For example, in the Tiguipa resettlement, when a drinking water system was installed, the overall worry was to give water to everyone and to make sure the white *karai* got theirs too, since they also had the right to receive water. Nobody was going to deny their water right, but they would have to take on their duties in the work of installing the system. The shared rule was the community member's and the *karai's* commitment to use the water strictly for human consumption and not for irrigation or cattle.

In the Pipi community, constituents and leaders have opposed the implementation of an irrigation project. In the name of Participación Popular[2] and with municipal funding, the project's real benefit for the community was to be only 10 irrigated hectares, while the hacienda owner, who was also the mayor, was going to irrigate 80 hectares of his property. The community did not accept this situation since it would have meant strengthening the *patrón* and condemn the whole community to permanent *empatronamiento* (subjugation to the *patrón*). Also, recovering land would have become impossible since, due to the irrigation facilities, the zone would have been classified as 'improved lands', which the State cannot expropriate. Moreover, land would become more expensive.

Irrigation and institutional conceptions of equity in development proposals for Guarani communities

Guarani conceptions strongly interact with those of outside institutions, often with a decisive impact which does not follow Guarani norms and way of thinking. Both the State, looking for 'a nation in which everyone benefits from progress and economic and social growth'[3], and the NGOs and PDIs[4] pursue a concept of justice and equity in their organisational programmes and field activities. Both always state that they will 'respect native culture and identity', which means recognising communal practices related to equity, according to the corporate culture of their organisation. [5] In agricultural and livestock projects under implementation in Guarani communities though, the main objective is to boost farmers' production levels and income, so in spite the discourse, the community's traditional practices and wisdom are not always taken into account.

This situation means that initial goals are out of phase with daily practice and equitable distribution. Sometimes only a few benefit. Furthermore, 'development' always implies a change in certain cultural aspects. For instance, an irrigation project has to consider its impact on the market since one cannot produce just to produce. This notably alters social production relationships. E.g., Guaranis are not used to micro-irrigation or other 'technified' ways of irrigating. When they do incorporate these methods, they have to produce for the market. At present, there are no Guarani market fairs but, with the production diversification, even women will have to join in the production-marketing cycle, which is now male-dominated.

Equity considerations clearly appear in everyday life, especially if production is for self-supply since this production is frequently shared. The real challenge in the defence of equity comes with market-oriented production, e.g. after introducing modern technology or irrigation.[6] Some influences of institutional co-operation with respect to communal management practices are briefly analysed below.

Support institutions: NGOs and PDIs

Most NGOs working in the area have idealised the community, keeping some traditional concepts rather than accepting that they have changed and that there has been assimilation with other cultures. Many have reinforced the power of community chieftains who favour the interests of haciendas, sugar cane harvesting and political *pongueaje,* 'in the name of tradition'. Ignoring these changes and differences among communities has often strengthened internal power groups. Family X has a leader, so his children will all benefit from all training projects: the wife leads the women's group and the trained children get jobs with the institutions and not within the community. Many NGOs want to maintain a paternalistic handout approach, especially those institutions linked with the church that still think like missionaries.

PDIs are betting that the future of the communities lies in market-oriented production. But their belief in an ideal community has not given them time to think that, when it comes to sharing benefits, there are differences that interfere with equitable benefits for all. This model deepens these differences and becomes an essential role for the outside agent. This prevents the community from reflecting independently, under pressure from interests such as credit, work groups, etc. However, in the area of Kaaguasu several communities have preferred to let their production rot, and even to hunger, rather than let unclear distribution mechanisms benefit just a handful of leaders. It is not enough for everyone to work; also, those who work must benefit proportionally from their labour.

In the Kapiguasuti community a work group ('those from below') was installed by a support institution. The people wished to irrigate their *chacos* in the lower zone. 'Those from above' had originally taken the initiative, but there were very few of them and, according to the institution, they could build a canal on their own to irrigate a family *chaco* close to the water source. The institutional concept of equity was based on the principle of supporting the majority and preventing a small favoured group from receiving greater benefits than the others. Twenty 'below' members dug 1500 metres of irrigation canal, but had to stop because of internal problems. After all that work, they were unable to irrigate any land. Half a year later, when just about ten members lengthened the canal 700 metres, they reached a community *chaco* and were able to cultivate and irrigate onions, carrots and maize. Production was very good but income distribution became a problem:

> 'People are complaining! They want their work at the canal, the farming and the fencing to be recognised. Ms. F. said that Mr. C. had spent 150 pesos from the communal onion income and that Mr. M. was waiting for him to repay that money in order to be able to pay the rest. She said the community president wants the ten members to stop all work on the canal since it can't be that just ten are taking advantage of the benefits. It would be better if nobody worked!'. (member of the Kapiguasuti irrigation group)

The 'work group' and 'work community' model was introduced by CIPCA (Centre for Research and Promotion of Peasants) during the 1970s. This model was based on the communal spirit of the Guarani, idealising its characteristics of equity. It is true that CIPCA was thus able to reach marginalised groups since those who were well-off, within the community or not, were not interested in working (and sharing) in a group. The basic concept in the 'work community' model is equality, which in practice does not necessarily mean a more equitable, fairer situation. The model's weakness is precisely the fact that it is a *model*, with a pre-defined framework to be applied according to supposedly objective rules. The sizable socio-cultural and economic differences among zones and Guarani communities, and local specific variations are incompatible with such a uniform approach. Guarani community members organise to produce as a group only under special conditions, such as building and maintaining an irrigation system or a shared infrastructure for cattle.

In Taperillas, an irrigation scheme had been installed with the participation of the whole community and with families' own contributions. But there was a family group that was taking over all surplus and benefits, and this has condemned the irrigation system to non-feasibility. The community felt that the project divided them, produced fights among families and gave power to only a few. This all ended when the community completely abandoned the project and the entire infrastructure is now unused.

The above clearly shows that institutions' projects without equity criteria can have dreadful results. People like the Guaranis have the custom of not blaming a brother. For example, they feel that the culprit is not the one who accepts money or favours but the one who offers them. Taperillos fiasco was not the fault of the unscrupulous neighbour who wanted to take advantage of the situation, but of the irrigation infrastructure, seen as a devilish intruder in the community.

Nevertheless, there are some communities, such as those resettled in Tenta Piau, Iguasurenda, that are thriving and successful and have been able to attain positions of power in municipalities through their economic strength. But, what is these communities' secret? They have managed to develop a system of rights, duties and, above all, of equitable benefit distribution that guarantees the success of any project.

If these communities, perhaps with institutional support, can vigourously guarantee everyone's rights, with a fair distribution of benefits, their undertakings will be viable. Support institutions should consider, besides their technical and scientific resources, communal participation while planning the equity approach.

At the municipal and national levels

Generally, municipal and governmental proposal for the Guaranis cause problems requiring Guarani natives to stop being community members and start being citizens, with citizenship rights and duties. The municipal scope homogenises everybody and, rhetorically, the most humble community member is as much a citizen as the most powerful landowner. And even so, the lack of equity criteria and of a recognition of diversity in municipal and national irrigation projects favours local powers and consolidates social differences.

On the other hand, the whole country is going through a major de-centralisation process called *Participación Popular*. All resources that had been allocated to national departments and assigned until 1994 for rural infrastructure, have been transferred to municipalities and programmes implemented at the municipal level. This means that municipalities are no longer concerned only with taking care of the small elites of their urban centre, in order to focus on their rural communities. Mayors are no longer only famous *karai* (non-indigenous) since, in many Guarani municipalities, APG leaders have been elected as city council members and mayors. Participation by community members in municipal politics has increased considerably. For example, APG's zonal strategies are now integrated into municipal plans. A *karai* mayor, backed by the APG, states: 'sometimes in the communities I say one thing but the community members propose something else and this is good. Of course I would like to develop my own political ideas but I can't do it because of the Participación Popular Law. And this is good because everyone should have the chance to be heard'.

Conclusion

In a transition time, indigenous organisations call for greater attention to the problems shared by all Native Peoples and, at the same time, they are trying to have their leaders continue to respect the voice of communities, where equity is a daily and more common practice. Outside projects, technicians and agents, and communities' own leaders, must not disregard this practice. When discussing irrigation and its management, the Guarani concept of equity within their *ivi* should be taken into account. What will the varied 'institutional fauna' present in the Guarani Chaco do with this concept? How will they manage to have the Guaranis themselves find a common direction for all development proposals? An integrated concept of irrigation, located within the *ivi*, has much to teach us about the way Guaranis think about their daily subsistence and about equity in the production process. Taking the dynamic, structural changes into account, how can *ivi* be vindicated as a special and vibrant value, rather than an attraction within an ecological or tourism park?

Notes

1   *Tüpa* (Man-God), Hapiaoeki, a great Guarani leader.
2   The Law of Popular Participation, enacted in early 1994, has decentralised powers and funds with the aim of giving citizens responsibility for their municipal government.
3   *Plan general de desarrollo económico y social de la República. El cambio para todos. Ministerio de Desarrollo Sostenible y Medio Ambiente* - La Paz, 1994.
4   During the past few years there has been a boom of NGOs in Bolivia. It is estimated that thousands of companies have their own NGOs in order to avoid taxes. This situation has led a group of major Bolivian NGOs to break away from this tendency and call themselves 'Private Development Institutes'.
5   Corporate culture is a pattern of basic assumptions - invented, discovered, or developed by a group as it learns to cope with its problems of external adaptation and internal integration - that has worked well enough to be considered valid and, therefore, to be taught to new members as the correct way to perceive, think and feel in relation to those problems (Schein 1985:9 in Marrewijk 1995:1).
6   Changes towards market-oriented production are not always evident for the families involved. In 1995 only some ten families were left in a zone since all others had left to work elsewhere. However, when these ten families got a loan and developed a semi-mechanised agricultural project, all their relatives came back to share in the abundant harvest. By the next year, the project was abandoned and the community deserted.

References

Most of this article is based on the authors' field work and experiences.
Literature used:
Dixhoorn, Nico van, 1996. *Manejo de agua en el Chaco Guaraní*, CIPCA-SNV, Santa Cruz.
Marrewijk, Alfons van, 1994. *Quien tiene la plata manda?*, CIPCA- Leiden University, La Paz - Leiden

32

Peasants, Andean Irrigation and Equity. The Experience in Chingazo-Pungales, Ecuador

Nelson Martínez B.

The reality

Many years ago, the low demographic pressure in the zone of Chingazo-Pungales enabled small settlements to make a decent living. As a local peasant told: 'Our great-grandparents used to plant their fields - they had about 10 hectares each - and the climate was good, with enough rain, nice and warm. In Guanando they could grow sugar cane'.

Later, as population pressure on the land increased, the rural folk began cutting down the native tree species in the forests and 'the rain began to go away, the climate got worse, and temperatures got colder'. As population continued to expand, landowners kept dividing their land into smaller and smaller plots as inheritance for their children, and agriculture began to be more intensive, with overgrazing becoming ever more common. This started a process of (semi) desertification in the zone.

As the peasants tell, over about 60 years' time, the topsoil was gradually lost, and people were left with almost unproductive land. Therefore, in 1978 the main cash crop was the sisal plant (American agave). The severe erosion kept natural vegetation limited to scattered brush, such as *chilca* and *retama* (broom) bushes. Agricultural production was very low. Maize was producing 3 or 4 units of harvest for each unit sown. Alfalfa was planted without irrigation and used just to harvest seed again. They would get some 6 to 8 pounds per hectare, cutting the alfalfa only twice a year, although the plants could last 5 to 10 years. The soil was sandy and of poor quality, the climate and small, parcelled holdings kept families from prospering, so the youth, especially males, were forced to migrate to the city on an intermittent basis to look for work. The women, elderly and children stayed behind to take care of what little they could grow, and to work with the agave, cutting the leaves to extract the sisal fiber.

This situation, especially the temporary migration of people from almost every family and much of their skilled manpower, even wore down the communities' socio-organisational capacity in the area. 'Poverty and despair when we looked to the future', explained a villager, 'made us think that there were other areas, especially the large hacienda plantations, that looked green and produced well, because they had irrigation. They also told us that, around Riobamba, people were growing good alfal-fa and vegetables, because they were irrigating with water taken from the Chambo river'.

The search for solutions

The presence and influence of good leaders, plus the extreme poverty affecting families in these communities, led them to the conclusion that their only chance was to work decidedly and build an irrigation canal. In Pungales, irrigation water became a top priority, and the peasant families felt it was vital for their socioeconomic self-development: 'This whole situation made us think that the solution for our area was irrigation, and some of the folks who think a bit more began to discuss this, first within the communities and then among the communities. We gathered representatives of Santa Marianita, Pungal Grande and La Providencia. A group of us went to the government office (INERHI) in Riobamba, and asked for help with the studies and building of an irrigation canal. They offered to proceed with this project, but we waited for years and they never concretised the things they had offered'.

The peasant families of the communities of the Chingazo-Pungales region presented a number of applications to authorities, but all in vain. The commitment initially established with the Provincial Council did not result in concrete support to construct an irrigation system. So, their relations with public institutions were not so good. As one of the local residents put it, 'they have never kept their word to us'. This same disappointment occurred when political candidates campaigned through their communities. 'They would offer to help us with the canal, but whenever they got into office they would forget all about us'.

The communities had seen the need to get together on a zonal level, because the attempts that they had made as individual communities, without support from other neighbouring communities, had not wielded enough weight. The projects carried out until then - on a community level, such as schools and roadways - had never joined the communities because not all were interested. However, when they spoke of *irrigation water*, they discovered that this was a mobilising, unifying issue for most people and organisations. They also discovered that, in addition to some contributions from outside institutions, inter-community participation and community contributions were indispensable. 'Since nobody will do it for us, we have to contribute and move forward on our own. We have to chip in the communities' own "two bits" and the institutions have to put in their "two bits", too'.

Despite the difficulties and disappointments, the communities - now united - continued seeking genuine support and finally contacted CESA (Ecuadorian Agricultural Service Office). This NGO made the commitment with the communities of Chingazo-Pungales to jointly build an irrigation system, and a project was designed, along with the villagers, to obtain the respective financing. The project covered about 600 hectares net, belonging to 635 peasant families, with some 1300 plots. INERHI allocated a flow of 700 litres per second, for which they would have to build a canal 26 kilometres long, with 33 secondary canals and a hundred tertiary canals.

Peasant organisation and assistance provided

The NGO gave priority to the following major issues in supporting the peasants:
- The need to strengthen their organisation, which was incipient and, before the project initiative, operated only at the community level;
- Lack of experience for many peasants regarding many of the technical issues that are indispensable to construct, operate and maintain the irrigation facilities;
- Lack of economic resources, since goodwill alone is not enough.

A feeling of mutual trust surrounded their joint undertaking of the job of strengthening peasant organisation on two levels: community and inter-community. The latter achieved legal status and can at present make any kind of representation effort that will benefit the sector.

Negotiation with the contractor, who was engaged to implement the facilities requiring engineering, made it mandatory for this engineer to hire local labour from the Chingazo-Pungales communities. This was subsequently very beneficial for the villagers, because they were trained and manpower remained in the zone with experience in surveying, masonry and carpentry. In the future, they were very useful to the organisation, because - under their own responsibility, rather than with outside oversight - they had the capacity to sign contracts with funding agencies to improve the irrigation infrastructure. This was successful, both because of the quality of the work and the profits generated for the organisation's benefit. They gradually accumulated capital resources for emergency work on the canal.

The peasants and CESA had negotiated with INERHI for the fore-mentioned allocation of water and to receive support in regard to certain technical criteria. The search for economic backing was difficult, so they applied to other public institutions jointly. Finally, the Swiss Agency for Development and Co-operation (COSUDE) provided the necessary support to carry out this project.

Rural folk in this area are generally mistrustful, due to the weight of a history of exploitation and injustice, but when they give an institution or person a try and have a good experience, then they are highly motivated to co-ordinate work toward a better future. Thus, in Pungales the leaders exercised true leadership. They took the initiative to contact institutions and held community and inter-community meetings to encourage collective decision-making about the need to undertake actions to get the irrigation water.

When communities have good leaders, their social fabric and rural economy can be completely revitalised. Good leaders guide, encourage and motivate them, both to examine the problem and solutions, and to implement the corresponding actions.

The organisation did not arise 'out of custom' or because of a 'historic need', as certain theoretical discourses would have it, but because the rural families themselves saw the organisation as indispensable for negotiating and obtaining support, planning, design and construction of the infrastructure and management of the irrigation system. Such organisation, with grassroots recognition, has and will continue to have lasting strength.

After the first inter-community sessions, the peasants of Chingazo-Pungales elected their board of directors, which has representatives from all communities. This representative board prepared policies and activities. Important decisions were made in a general assembly, and such decisions are considered 'sacred' in terms of the obligation to follow up on their implementation. A mainstay of the organisation during the first years was to build the irrigation canal, which had to benefit the Chingazos sector (three zones) and five communities and two parishes of the Pungales sector. They made commitments to CESA to provide unskilled labour, with an average of one community workday (*minga*) per week and also to pay all necessary dues. From 1979 through 1992, they recorded 700 '*rayas*' (*minga* days) per family.

Alternatives to distribute the water

The peasant organisation and the NGO developed a lengthy process of discussion about alternatives for irrigation water distribution, and they reached the point of having to decide among the following proposals:

- *Technical distribution*: On the basis of essential data such as temperature, precipitation, crop types and coefficients, relative humidity, evapotranspiration, wind speed, soil texture, surface area of crops, etc., the volumes and frequencies of irrigation would be calculated that would be appropriate for each irrigation zone and type of crops. The peasants considered this alternative difficult, because it was necessary to 'apply lots of technology'. Also, some of the necessary data were not available, and the diversity of crops made it difficult to establish a cropping pattern or fixed, pre-established planting seasons for all zones in the irrigation system.

- *Equal distribution*: Since they all contributed equally to building the infrastructure, they felt it would be fair to distribute the water equally. That is, everyone should receive the same amount of water for the same amount of time. Later, after analysing the proposal with the peasants, some problems were noted, such as difficulties involving landholding, in which the small-plot owners would create a water market, selling part of their (excess) water to people with more land, or to non-members without water rights. Also, peasants with larger and smaller land areas would have to continue paying the same water fees, regardless of the land area irrigated.

*   *Distribution in proportion to the land area*: For this distribution, the proposal was to provide the flow for a given amount of time, according to the land area owned by each beneficiary in each sector (dividing up the total available flow among the hectares in the system). The peasants, after analysing this proposal, considered it the best because it provided them with a fixed patter or distribution arrangement. Moreover, from then on they could pay for the use of water according to the amount of land irrigated, so those having more land would receive more water, but this was compensated for because they would also pay more.

Irrigation and equity

Although everyone worked equally, they did not receive the same amount of water. Nevertheless, the people in Pungales proposed this equal contribution to construction -although not for fee payment - as necessary for everyone to have the same right to participate in managing the system. What is fundamental for them is to have participated on an equal basis, so everyone can have equal decision-making rights.

One possibility that the peasant organisation did not take advantage of was to set up a differentiated fee schedule: higher fees per hectare in case of irrigating larger land areas. The income would benefit everyone, but the payments would be higher for those who received the greatest benefits from the irrigation system and collective work. This proposal was not accepted by the peasants.

After some observations and field calculations, they reached the conclusion that they should provide a flow rate of 10 l/s for 10 hours and 45 minutes per hectare, which is what they are currently entitled to and receive. According to their plot's conditions (soil, slope) and the crop (growing phase, type of crop), an irrigator applies these 10 litres per second differently. Sometimes, they subdivide the flow among a number of straight furrows or *canteros* (zig-zag furrows). Generally, irrigation is applied more technically to more profitable crops, such as alfalfa, peas, and fruits, for which they make furrows and canteros. For maize 'we just irrigate any way one prefers, without making furrows'.

To increase social justice in the system, the peasant organisation and the NGO had prepared a number of activities:
*   One of the things that communities considered most unfair was to exclude one sector of the community of San Miguel from irrigation. This sector, which had worked hard during system construction, is located above the canal elevation, which made it impossible for them to receive irrigation water. All the families felt that those families were, however, entitled to water rights. So, as a solution, they installed a turbopumping system. With the energy of the water as it falls, three

turbines are driven, which lifts a flow of 3 x 10 l/s to heights of 80, 120 and 150 m above the canal, making it possible to irrigate another 30 hectares in the higher sector.

- Another important activity was to create a 'land bank' managed by the peasant organisation. With a loan from a public institution (FODERUMA), the project purchased certain pieces of land - which were for sale prior to the arrival of the water - to redistribute it to those who had less land, at reasonable prices. This was an effort to reduce the speculation that often accompanies the development of irrigation in a region and, to a certain degree, this made it possible for the poorer people to participate in the irrigation system. A total of 14 hectares were purchased.

- Not all families in the irrigated zone are members. Unlike members, the non-members have not worked on building the system, either out of scepticism or because of unwillingness to make the sacrifice. Some peasants did not believe that the irrigation system would become a reality, and did not join the organisation. A few said that 'if the water ever gets here, we will straighten things out with a little money'. However, because they did not participate, they have no rights to irrigation water at present. In order to not close the door to them altogether, to leave them the possibility of gaining access to the irrigation, and thus reinforce peasant unity, the irrigators' organisation prepared regulations regarding the entry of non-members, upon payment of an entry fee.

At present, the reality in the Chingazo-Pungales region has changed. The initial situation called for true commitment, which is difficult but not impossible to achieve. On the one hand, the peasants, aware of their decision and well-organised, have sought to appropriate the irrigation system, and on the other, the promoters and technicians, understanding the social problems, realised, through a long learning process, that it would be necessary to provide support for the peasants' own management efforts. Bit by bit, the NGO has withdrawn from this support role, and the peasants now have all the capacity and experience they need to handle their system unaided.

33

Andean Irrigation and the Education of Professionals in Agrarian Sciences: an Ecuadorian Experience

Félix Hernández C. and Ketty Vivanco C.

Introduction

The Andean region is very diverse. Men and women from this region have gone through a process of historical adaptation to a wide range bio-physical features. Factors such as topography and climate act on the living beings - human beings, fauna and flora - that inhabit the region, generating incredible genetic variability. People have tended to concentrate in the Andes, in spite of limiting factors such as rainfall and river water scarcity. Imbalances brought about by faulty rainfall distribution over time and space have not been absolute obstacles but rather have led to the creation of a water-use culture adapted to this situation. The vertical management of several altitudinal zones with varied potential is one of the survival strategies used in the past. Later it was modified, basically as a consequence of the Conquest, Colonisation and, afterwards due to the application of certain development policies that have transformed the agrarian structure, preventing the use of ecological zones with diverse opportunities.

Accordingly, the peasant strategy to produce agricultural goods and thus achieve social reproduction has also changed. Strategies are oriented especially towards diversification of production activities (agriculture, animal husbandry, handicrafts, etc.), food production for self-supply and for market, sale of labour capacity, migration to cities to reduce land-fractioning and achieve higher recognition for work capacities, and maintenance of traditions and customs of solidarity and reciprocity. These strategies, among others, have helped to reduce subsistence risks and to re-create the Andean culture.

Technological transfer has generally influenced the Andean region in such a way that the agrarian producers, in many cases, have adopted foreign realities and exigencies. However, large farm machinery built for flat land and introduced in the Andes could never prepare hilly land without accelerating erosion processes. Agrochemicals used to decrease losses from parasites and diseases have not done well in the Andes, where a great variety of associated and companion crops are planted and rotated.

Relationships between human beings and communities, in the production and reproduction process, have made this a dynamic region and created alternative life forms
in it. In spite of the inattention to rural matters, a large percentage of the population
is still devoted to agriculture and animal husbandry, providing food and helping
guarantee food security for the population in general. Agriculture is still one of the
main sectors for the region's socio-economic development, since it also guarantees
employment for much of the active population and contributes significantly to the
GDP. Therefore, the Ecuadorian State, trying to guide and promote agrarian development, designs rural development policies, projects, and programmes in which
agrarian professionals intervene, although often not very creatively.

This is made clear when these professionals get to work and find diverse activities
for which they were not trained: agrarian research, rural extension, plant health services, project design, implementation and assessment, agrarian credit, social organisation, agro-economic studies, etc. Without integrated understanding of rural ways
of life, the necessary creativity and sufficient experience, they find it difficult to
become engaged in the search for possible solutions to problems faced by Andean
peasant communities. The lack of attention to or understanding of problems and
alternatives related to Andean irrigation is an exemplary case. This leads us directly
to a critical analysis of the processes of education of professionals.

Agrarian education in the Ecuadorian Andes

Development models and policies established in Ecuador, with a neo-liberal
approach, have affected professional training in agrarian sciences in such a way that
institutes, universities, and polytechnic schools especially train technical engineers
to work with and support agribusiness activities. Agricultural curricula have been
structured on the basis of advances in western technology and science. Approaches,
elements and factors from outside Ecuador are preferred. Generally, proposals are
inadequate and/or technologies are inaccessible for small farmers in the region.

During the 1960s and 1970s professional specialist training was one of the trends
geared to meeting agribusiness demands. This situation has deeply influenced university curricula; the number of specialties and programmes increased substantially,
and ever more courses were specialised rather than general. Also, it was and still is
believed essential to only train excellent techno-scientific professionals, even if they
lack any training in social approaches or rural sociology. The goal was to turn out
efficient, successful professionals, without considering how excluding this professional practice would be when widespread.

Professional practice assessments show how little communication capacity these
professionals and graduate students have when dealing with peasants. They often are
conceited, bossy, and impose 'standard' solutions without understanding local
functioning and rationale. We must recognise the deep gap that exists between university training contents and methods, and the activities these professionals will have

to carry out in their professional practice. The professionals' technocratic attitude is a result of the overly academic approach of university curricula and their imbalance with the diverse ecological, socio-economic, and cultural conditions in which Ecuadorian Andean peasants live.

Within this context, there are several issues that have to be considered regarding the training process:
- eminently theoretical agricultural learning keeps professionals from contributing in a creative way the technological innovations demanded by Andean agricultural activities;
- few teachers have experience and knowledge regarding the problems of peasant and indigenous farmers who supply food for domestic, national consumption.
- national society and politics pay little attention to peasant agriculture, so policies and strategies to boost small producers' production are lacking;
- results from research used to develop training processes have been generated in countries with very different biophysical and socio-economic conditions from those of the Andean region;
- major up-to-date publications are in foreign languages that most students do not understand;
- universities' financial limitations mean they lack laboratory equipment and infrastructure to do applied research;
- libraries are under-used and lack up-to-date material;
- agrarian training has not yet been included seriously in development plans and university reform does not respond to society's real needs;
- universities and faculties have not established adequate inter institutional coordination; they do not share their efforts with governmental and non-governmental agencies.

These cloistered practices make it impossible to focus the totality of integrated production processes, especially within Andean communities; the production systems' peculiarities are not studied or understood. These factors also explain why relevant contents have not been introduced into agrarian sciences' curricula to comprehend Andean irrigation schemes, built and managed by peasants and indigenous peoples within the context of their production processes and communal coexistence.

The teaching of irrigated agriculture

Temporal, spatial and social differences when managing and using water for agriculture in this region have fostered an extraordinary variety of irrigated production systems in the Andes. Nevertheless, professionals who are going to intervene in irrigated agriculture are trained to understand how these systems function in other regions and under other conditions. Hendriks (1994) states to this respect that professionals have a large background of guidelines and prescriptions to calculate the different elements that make up an hydraulic system, however, the irrigation project's or system's reality, as part of a development perspective, demands knowledge of problems related to production and exchange processes, an understanding of how other dimensions - social, economic, ecological, cultural and political - affect irrigation schemes.

The *technocentric concepts* which irrigation professionals learn to apply are oriented only towards satisfying water requirements according to crop planning, area to be irrigated, water volumes to be managed, flows to be delivered to plots, and irrigation methods. This approach goes against *peasant concepts and conceptions* of storing water in the soil and delivering flows according to collective rights, norms, and decisions. These opposing visions, i.e. professional training vs. peasant reality, is fundamentally due to their little or no contact between peasants and students during schooling. Also, in social relationships between professionals and peasants, agronomists want to increase production through authoritarian, paternalistic attitudes that ignore peasant knowledge and create deep estrangement between professionals and peasants.

The Andean region has a wide range of water supply systems, among others related to the variety and uncertainty of precipitation, and has generated very diverse communal organisation forms that are not analysed during professional training. If they are studied in university curricula, then they are dealt with only as theoretical knowledge rather than a theoretical-practical reflection. For example, future professionals don't know that, in rural sectors, when water availability decreases, the need to manage and regulate water distribution is different than when there is more water.

Often professionals don't have the sensitivity to try to strategically modify programming and are unable to understand that Andean irrigation organisations function according to a changing reality. They don't know that there is only an organisation when they need it, and that it follows the rhythm of communal daily life. This problem is rooted in the way students approach this reality during their university years: through a 'scientific observation trip', a 'field day' or 'practice'. Such events are too superficial for them to understand peasants' daily life.

In general, this situation is due to a *traditional discipline-bound curriculum* that has been implemented in Andean and especially Ecuadorian universities, with an encyclopaedic, theoretical approach, remote from social issues. Even when a technician does acquire social knowledge, it often remains isolated from technical knowledge and, therefore s/he is not able to join the two aspects in her/his work. A communal irrigation system requires integrated management of socio-organisational, hydraulic and agronomic aspects. It relatively easy to add one subject to a curriculum when a gap has been detected. But it is much more difficult to get professionals to assimilate all subjects together, as one tool, for their work in the integrated communal reality. This is the main challenge for our universities.

Future challenges

The United Nations Food and Agriculture Organisation (FAO), through its Latin American and Caribbean regional office, is disseminating the document entitled *Higher Agricultural Education*. It presents the following challenges for Latin America and the Caribbean:

- to understand that humanity must not complacently ignore the existing profound injustices or social inequities, not only among rich and poor countries, but especially among rich and poor people within each country;
- to study and to face the recent challenge of promoting sustainable agricultural development, to adopt technological alternatives that maintain or recover the soil's productive capacity and preserve natural resources and the environment;
- to face and to resolve the challenge of reorienting agriculture's' technological matrix so it can be more efficient, in the sense of producing more per person, per unit of land, energy, capital and time;
- to pose viable, possible strategies to realise the immense new challenge of meeting these challenges in spite of the neoliberal trend, which reduces fiscal resources for agricultural development, privatises operational structures in agricultural support services, and eliminates subsidies;
- to link these principles with conceptual and methodological processes of alternative teaching, to achieve better results than the current ones, which aim at human resource training for the primary agro-exporting sector only.

However, the FAO document states that 'professional who would drive these pro posals and implement them have not yet been trained' (FAO 1993). Several postsecondary educational institutions in the country have attempted to improve the education of professionals, especially those in the agrarian field; however, results are not much different from previous decades.

Moreover, nowadays factors such as trans-nationalisation of the communication media and economic globalisation policies explicitly or implicitly propitiate the homogenisation of cultural and spiritual patterns, particularly among youngsters. This has generated a kind of anti-value rejecting local models and interests including those from the rural environment. Therefore, it is necessary to redefine the higher education system and generate deep changes in professional training. It is fundamental for agricultural development assistance to be realised by professionals who have a high standard of scientific and technical expertise but also know about rural reality and are committed to achieving social equity and justice through their work.

Any processes of limited university reform have partially attempted to redefine the 'new type' of professional profile. Some pioneering initiatives have critically revised this type of professionals' education. For example, the National University of Loja (UNL) has been engaged in university reform since 1990.

University reform at UNL

The National University of Loja educational reform has attempted to leave aside its academic structure by disciplines (subjects). Its goal is for students to achieve significant learning by integrating social and technical knowledge with real-life problems. This new approach to professional education in general and the agricultural area specifically, is based on a new proposed curriculum: *modular education system by transformation objects*. This system pursues a new type of linkage between the university and society in general and the rural sector in particular. Its dynamic, participatory learning process is based on modular research as the methodological and cognitive foundation of the educational processes.

The goal is for both professors and students to get together within academic and social work where reflection leads to questioning academic knowledge, criticising and making proposals, enhancing creativity and stimulating initiative. It is a curricular structure that joins agricultural students and professors with rural communities and peasants, in a process of effective communication and respect for each sector's cultures. Professors and students also address their Transformation Objects (professional problems) directly, de-coding them, studying them, analysing them, and structuring them in order to understand their logic and interactions. By means of this knowledge they try to contribute to solving concrete rural problems. Only inasmuch as future professionals get into direct contact with all dimensions of rural problems they will be able to support viable, workable proposals to help solve them.

It is hoped that these academic reforms will continually narrow the distance between what is taught and what needs to be learned. This model seeks to train professionals with greater capacity to find integrated solutions based on producing knowledge and the recovering traditional, day-to-day wisdom. With respect to irrigation, one programme is the Andean Community Irrigation Postgraduate Programme (PRICA). Its modules focus integratedly on agricultural, economic, environmental, hydraulic, organisational, politico-legal, socio-economic and institutional aspects, to train professionals who will be able to support peasant irrigation development processes.

Alternative teaching and the learning process

A traditional curriculum, organised by disciplines, encyclopaedic, and far from the problems of its environment, has direct implications for the teaching practice: lectures by professors to passive students who listen, memorise, and do what they are ordered to do, varied educational technologies do not make any real difference.

If we conceive of a curriculum as a scientific, political-academic proposal to carry out the process of training professional human resources, then other factors beyond the contents of certain specialisations and ensuing activities must be considered. It is also necessary to integrate social, economic, cultural, political and ideological dimensions into the curriculum. This proposal calls for *alternative teaching,*

Map 34.1: The Morasloma Irrigation System

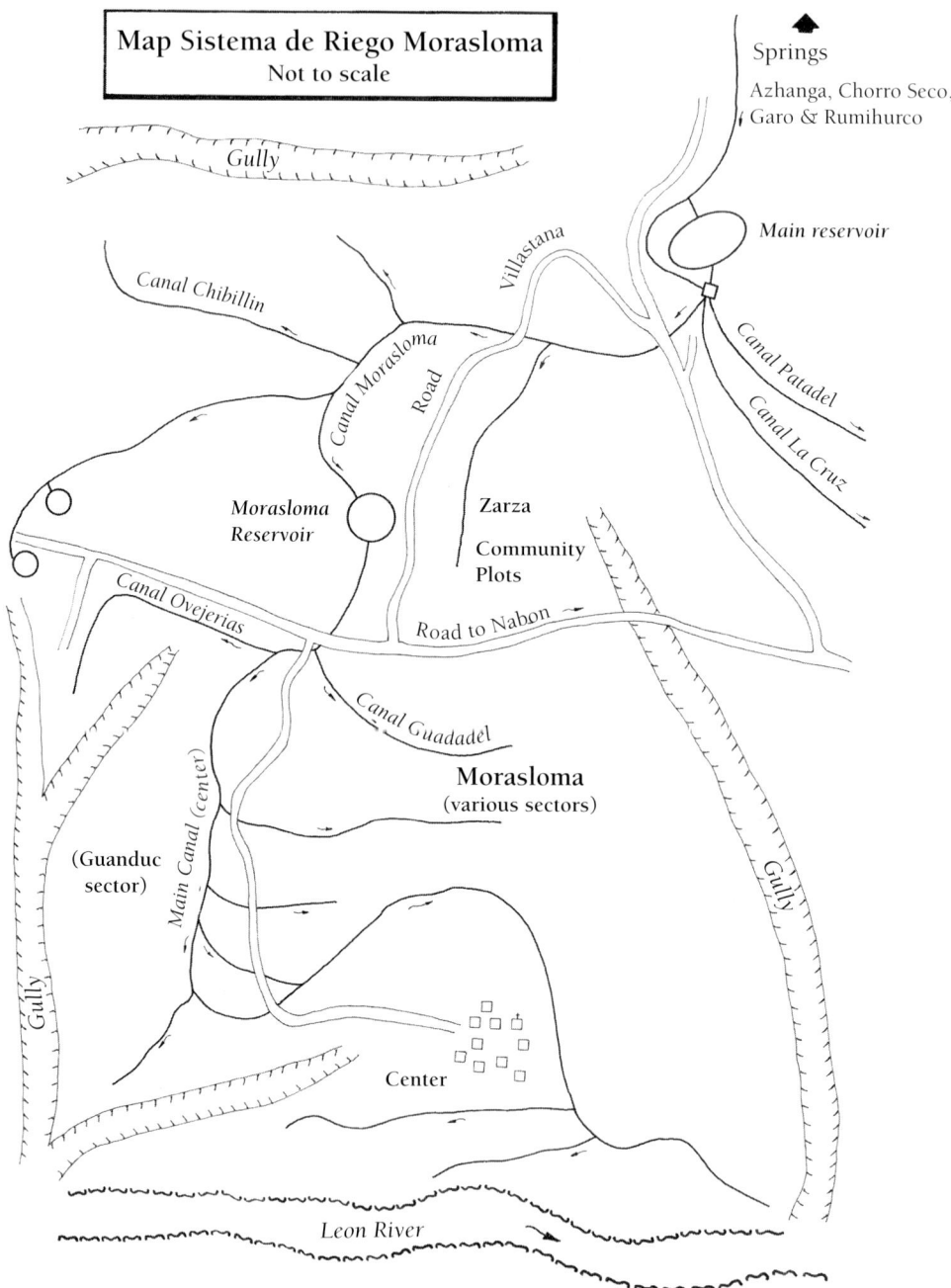

deforestation and intense natural resource use, due mainly to population growth. In interaction with conjunctural processes, this has driven the zone into critical poverty through a vicious circle of impoverishment and overexploitation.

Under these conditions 'pendulum-type' migration, since the mid-1900s but more intensely since the 1970s, has developed as the principal subsistence strategy. This migration process currently includes 85% of the men and around 50% of the young women. Agricultural production has become a complementary source of subsistence. Maize, barley, wheat, *melloco* (an Andean tuber), potatoes and some garden vegetables are cultivated, in addition to pasture and alfalfa.

An increasingly tight labour market leaves few alternatives to the peasants and inspires them with conviction and interest to improve their own agricultural production system. This would give them some control over their migration frequency and, above all, improve subsistence conditions for people remaining in the community. Holdings are very small (*minifundios*) and irrigation water and other natural resources that are the foundation of the peasant family economy are scarce, limiting this 're-peasantisation' process.

Social organisation of irrigation water rights

Evolution of the water rights

In the early 1970s, water resources were nationalised in Ecuador. In 1975, the town of Nabón tried to take advantage of the new legal situation and take over the water from these four springs. So, the Morasloma community and the sectors of Patadel and La Cruz took action; both their historical use and geographic location made them the natural water beneficiaries.

In 1975, a Water Directorate was appointed by the three communities to conduct the negotiations in order to obtain the legal water rights from the former state agency, INERHI (Ecuadorian Institute of Water Resources). This process concluded with the Allocation Agreement conferred to the Morasloma, Patadel and La Cruz group. With this official ruling, INERHI allocated 200 litres per second to 255 users holding a total of 200 hectares.

In addition to the official water rights, in previous years inhabitants had invested much labour in construction and rehabilitation of the canal. This earned them the right to use the canal and the water and to participate in decision-making. By carrying out cleaning and canal maintenance *mingas* (communal work) the users have kept their rights up to the present time.

However, even when their rights were officially awarded, users did not manage to organise the water distribution in a way that suited every family. Irrigation practice was very disorganised, taking water from the mean intake and guiding it to each field without any consensus on the arrangement of turns. This situation generated frequent conflicts among the three sectors and among dwellers in the same sector, especially in dry-season months. This is why efforts were made to improve the conduction network and clarify system operation norms.

Peasant families have improved canal infrastructure through *mingas* and lobbied at CREA (Centre for the Economic Restructuring of Azuay Province) for the construction of storage reservoirs. In 1984, with great physical and financial effort by community members to complement the institutional support, four reservoirs were completed; a main one and smaller ones for each of the three sectors, altogether storing around 100,000 cubic metres.

These new physical conditions facilitated water redistribution, which was based on the number of users and the land area registered with the State agency: 40% for La Cruz, 30% for Patadel and 30% for Morasloma. However, although this water distribution procedure is considered fair by the respective peasant families, the users of Morasloma cheated themselves by declaring smaller land areas than the actual ones, fearing that this declaration might be utilised for State tax collection. This 'self deceit', very common in the Andean world and evident in many irrigation projects, is the consequence of a long history of deprivation and abuse of indigenous populations by the authorities.

To materialise water distribution among the three communities, a structure was built that divides the flow into the above proportions. Downstream from this division structure, each community manages the system with relative autonomy.

Characterisation of water distribution

The creation of water rights, briefly outlined above, was linked to the investment made by the users in the construction of the canals and reservoirs. Equitable investment, in this case, means equal obligations for all. Therefore, according to the peasant conception, water allocation and distribution rules must also be based on criteria of equity. As we will see, this does not necessarily mean a strictly equal distribution.

According to the inter-community agreement, Morasloma is entitled to a flow of 60 l/s. However, when water is scarce, this can decrease considerably and is regulated by using the reservoirs. The irrigation area is 150 hectares, divided among 64 families. Land tenure, i.e. the *irrigable* area, differs much from one family to the next. However, families do *not* irrigate their whole irrigable land area. In spite of water scarcity, absence of fixed schedules or regulations defining exact areas to be irrigated by each family, and notwithstanding the fact that certain families have the potential to irrigate much more than the area currently irrigated by them, there are almost no conflicts in the community. To better understand this situation, let us analyse in more detail the water distribution norms that have developed.

Regarding the *characteristics* of the local water rights, it can be stated that water is linked to the plot, i.e. the user has no right to re-direct the flow to any other plot than the assigned one. Therefore, the turn that corresponds to a user is utilised until the irrigation of that plot is finished. Thus, there is no fixed time for the turn, which implies that the schedule (the timing) is also variable. Once the irrigation of a plot is finished, the turn is passed on to the neighbour. The basic field distribution principle could be called: 'fill the sown plot' (the user has the right to 'fill' that part of his plot that has been sown with irrigation-dependent crops).

This modality immediately suggests some questions. For example: How long do turns last? The answer is between 6 and 20 hours... The reflection that directly emerges is about equity and justice in irrigation. In the same way, a question that immediately comes to the fore is: so every user tries to sow as much as he or she can, in order to have more water usage rights? However, dear reader, the system is not as unjust as you might be thinking.

Firstly, there is no great range in the areas irrigated by each family that could privilege those who have more land; rather, according to an unwritten rule, peasants say that they only irrigate a relatively standard, limited area 'so as not to harm others'. Secondly, some farmers in the lower part have flat plots with granular characteristics of high infiltration.They do not subdivide their fieldflow over many furrows, but irrigate one after another with a larger part of their flow. However, because of the losses, they need longer turns to 'fill their fields'. Peasants permit this and explain the situation by saying: 'It is not that our neighbour is wicked, it is a question of Nature'. Furthermore, lands with steep slopes and erodible soils or low water absorption properties require the application of only very small flows to the plots. These users often take a smaller share of the canal flow, and need more time to irrigate than those users with regular fields.
What's more, the families at the tail-end of the canal, generally the least favoured in irrigation systems, also benefit from this approach. They get smaller flows due to water seepage and infiltration along the canal, but with this flexible scheduling they can enjoy their right to sufficient water, using longer turns to finish irrigation. For all these reasons, there is a substantial difference in the number of hours used by different users.

On the basis of the above sketch, general differences with the common, Western understanding of a just and proper water allocation might be highlighted. Regarding this theme, we asked white-mestizo farmers from an area neighbouring Morasloma, 'how do your water rights and irrigation schedules work?'. The answer of one of the farmers is illustrative, telling that his turn lasts between three and four days (so obviously he was using the water for much more time than the other system users), but he felt that such a situation was fair, because he was paying a higher annual fee. This anecdote may illustrate the differing conceptions about what is 'just' among different population groups.

Does this practice not lead to unacceptable long turns and so to irrigation intervals that are too large? Not (yet) in present-day Morasloma. Another Morasloma practice is that irrigators do not water all the fields they possess. On average, each farmer has some six little plots along an irregular topography and only irrigates the two or three that have better soil, because they take into consideration the scanty volume of water available for the community. This attitude, in Morasloma peasants' words, is: '*To give everyone advantages*'. This also explains the relative homogeneity in the area irrigated by each farmer.

We could offer many conceptual explanations for this principle of respect for neighbours, which we might call an 'ethical principle'. However, we think that it is not justifiable to idealise it under the diffuse concept of 'Andean solidarity'. Such a concept does focus on collective interests and common objectives within the Andean community, but easily disregards the (sometimes opposing) interests of individual families in these communities. The collectivity does not construct its force and sustainability on the basis of solidarity-without-personal-interests, but formulates - consciously or unconsciously - the rules of a *collective contractual reciprocity*. Reciprocity has a compulsory nature, so collective and mutual interests can defeat individual and separating interests.

This is one of the main reasons why Morasloma's irrigators decide to limit their irrigated area in times of water scarcity, despite the fact that nobody restricts them through a formal schedule or area limitation rules. Respect for neighbours is institutionalised through strong social control that enforces the informal collective contract. The ethical principle, then, does not refer to philanthropic values in Andean communities but to the communal prescription of a reciprocal norm. This norm demands respect for common interests so the community and irrigation system will survive as collective management institutions.

As for spatial features of turn organisation, distribution order is organised according to altitudinal criteria, but interestingly the turns start from the tail-end up and from the lateral canals. So, irrigation begins at the last plot, which, in this case, is the first to get water. Thus, shifts to neighbours are transferred upwards to avoid, according to the peasants, 'the temptation of head-end irrigators to harm tail-end ones'.

The function of the storage reservoirs is not so much to expand the irrigated area, as to help get them through dry periods. Then, the reservoirs serve to regulate the irrigation flow. Three modes of distribution ('turns') are used in Morasloma. They are implemented according to climate and rainfall conditions in particular periods of the agricultural season:

- The *Annual Turn* is kept practically all year round as a complement to rainfall. For the annual turn, water from the reservoirs' spillway is used; reserve water itself is not used for irrigation. During this phase, peasants have much liberty to take the water they need, but they must respect the ascending order and the day that water is assigned to their sector. Normally, four to eight users irrigate each day simultaneously, and not all families necessarily use the turn. Water distribution extends from Monday to Saturday, and water is distributed for two days per 'sector'. The several sectors in the community have been grouped into three irrigation sectors. On Sundays, flowing water is freely available, if the need arises.

• The *General Turn* becomes necessary during dry times. After several rainless days, when crops begin to be affected, verbal petitions are made to the president of the Water Board, who summons a General Assembly of the three communities. At this Assembly they decide the date when the general turn will begin. A general turn can last from a few days to several weeks. In this distribution mode, present in dry periods, there is no more reservoir overflow. Therefore, the irrigation representative opens the pond valves and turns are organised in such a way that water is distributed to 18 or 19 irrigators per day. Five users irrigate from the tail-end of the 'Ovejerías' branch canal and five from the tail-end of the main canal, coming together at the Guanduc sector (see map). Meanwhile, in the Zarza sector, where families have communal lands, and in the Villastana sector, 8 or 9 users irrigate daily. The longer a general turn lasts, the less flow is let out of the main reservoir, for the pond must not run out during dry times. Night irrigation is not practised since the pond is filled from the springs at night. There is no irrigation on Sundays either because the main reservoir valves are closed to store water: 'On Sundays, the water needs to rest'.

The community has forbidden irrigation of pastures during a general turn. During an annual turn, it is possible to irrigate cultivated range, though not natural grassland. This also limits and regulates the area's livestock activities.

Since turn schedules are not fixed, irrigation intervals also vary. The irrigation frequency is every week in the rainy season (winter, annual turn, three sectors) and lengthens to between 15 and 30 days in dry times (general turn).

• A *Complementary Turn*, as implied in the name, is an extra watering especially for potato and sometimes vegetable crops, which cannot wait more than one week without irrigation. The irrigation representative gives families who are in this critical situation an extra turn, because in the normal cycle the family gets its turn only after 15 to 30 days.

These three distribution or 'turn' regimes, in combination with irrigated area self-limitation, are the materialisation of peasant families' collective concept of relatively equitable water distribution.

A final consideration

The 'ethical principle', defined as a reciprocal contractual and collective norm, is very important, but it is not the only reason why Morasloma families limit their irrigated areas. Other reasons include: restriction due to lack of time (*mingas*, agricultural labour, migration, etc.); restriction due to lack of financial means (e.g. seed potato is expensive); restriction due to lack of modern technology that would enable them to cultivate a larger area with less labour; no priority given to agriculture by the few families that have achieved a good income from migration; restriction due to lack of irrigable lands in the case of some of the poorest families.

It would be too simple and also inaccurate to state that only climatic and technical production-related factors define the water requirements and scarcity in this irrigation system. Ultimately, it is within the system's collective management where social rules determine a *collective water demand.* This collective demand - one of the operational keys to the system - is possible because, under strong social control, the system has struck a balance between the interests of individual families *and* those of the collectivity.

However, this current (and relatively recent) equilibrium must not be seen as a fixed, static balance. The equilibrium can be destroyed, as a result of some families' individual initiative, or under the impact of external interventions, the market and other processes that influence the communal production system. Under these circumstances individual interests may become intensified and override collective ones.

For example, the introduction and generalisation of new potato and vegetable varieties would modify water requirements and could increase individual demand for irrigation water. Similarly, a programme to intensify livestock raising in the zone could encourage individual interests to ignore the common rule of 'no pasture irrigation'. In the same way, there are various other factors than can *individualise water demand* and by doing so, generate a serious water shortage.[2] It is not crops but human beings who define the social demand for irrigation water. Water scarcity is not absolute but relative, and related directly to the balance or imbalance among social interests.

If such an imbalance is caused in the future under the influence of external interventions or internal changes, and irrigation water becomes increasingly scarce, the only solution to maintain the collective management in Morasloma would seem to be the communal re-definition of water allocation and distribution rules, such as more strictly scheduled turns, fixed volumes, or pre-established irrigation areas for every family. Would rural development intervention generate its own jobs?

Notes

1   Document based on a research by CESA (Ecuadorian Agricultural Services Centre) assisted by SNV and SDC/COSUDE (resp. Dutch and Swiss development cooperation).
2   So, serious research related to the analysis of possibilities for irrigation system support should not only answer the question: 'What could we do to improve irrigation?' but it should especially look for answers to the frequently omitted challenge: 'What must we *not* do?'.

35

The Historical Development of Equity in Irrigation: Changes in Water Distribution in Urcuquí, Ecuador

Frédéric Apollin, Pablo Núñez & Thierry Ruf

Urcuquí: An ancient hydraulic territory in northern Ecuador

In Ecuador, the inter-Andean valley between the western and eastern cordilleras is made up of a series of large river basins. Over this whole mountainous area a complex hydraulic system of hundreds of canals has developed since time immemorial. Nowadays, it provides irrigation water for some 400,000 ha of land in the Andes.

The basin of the Mira river, in the northern part of the Ecuadorian Andes, is the location of one of the main groups of traditional canals. The history of water management here goes back to pre-Hispanic times, when irrigation was carried out by means of *camellones* (raised beds between water furrows) in the humid zones near to the numerous small lakes of the provinces of Imbabura and Carchi. The native populations, belonging to the Cara culture, lived in communities (*ayllus*) in an area around the volcanoes Imbabura, Cayambe, Cotacachi and Piñán. In 1646, the census of the town of Urcuquí, located on the western bank of the Andean valley on the slopes of the Yanahurco de Piñán volcano, refers to two *ayllus*: Urcuquiango and Yacelga. These correspond mainly to an area defined by the ridges of the Piñán hill, the river Cariyacu to the south, the river Ambi to the east, and the Pigunchuela gorge to the north.

Nowadays this area contains twenty canals that capture over four cubic metres per second from the rivers Cariyacu, Huarmiyacu, Ambi and Pigunchuela. These canals irrigate approximately 5,000 ha in the temperate and warm zones located between 1,500 and 2,800 metres above sea level.

One of these canals, which was probably constructed in 1582, is called 'Acequia Grande' (Grand Canal) or 'Acequia de Caciques' (Chieftains' Canal, see Figure 35.1). It irrigates approximately 320 ha between the altitudes of 2,000 and 2,500 metres a.s.l., benefitting 435 users. The canal is still an earth canal, 19 kilometres long, with a capacity of 200 litres/second. At present it is managed by a group of rural associations from two parishes, Urcuquí and San Blas, while the other canals still give irrigation service to large or medium-sized owners. Only one of twenty canals is state-owned, the Salinas canal, but it serves primarily the haciendas of the neighbouring zone of Tumbabiro and Salinas, with a few beneficiaries in the warm area of Urcuquí.

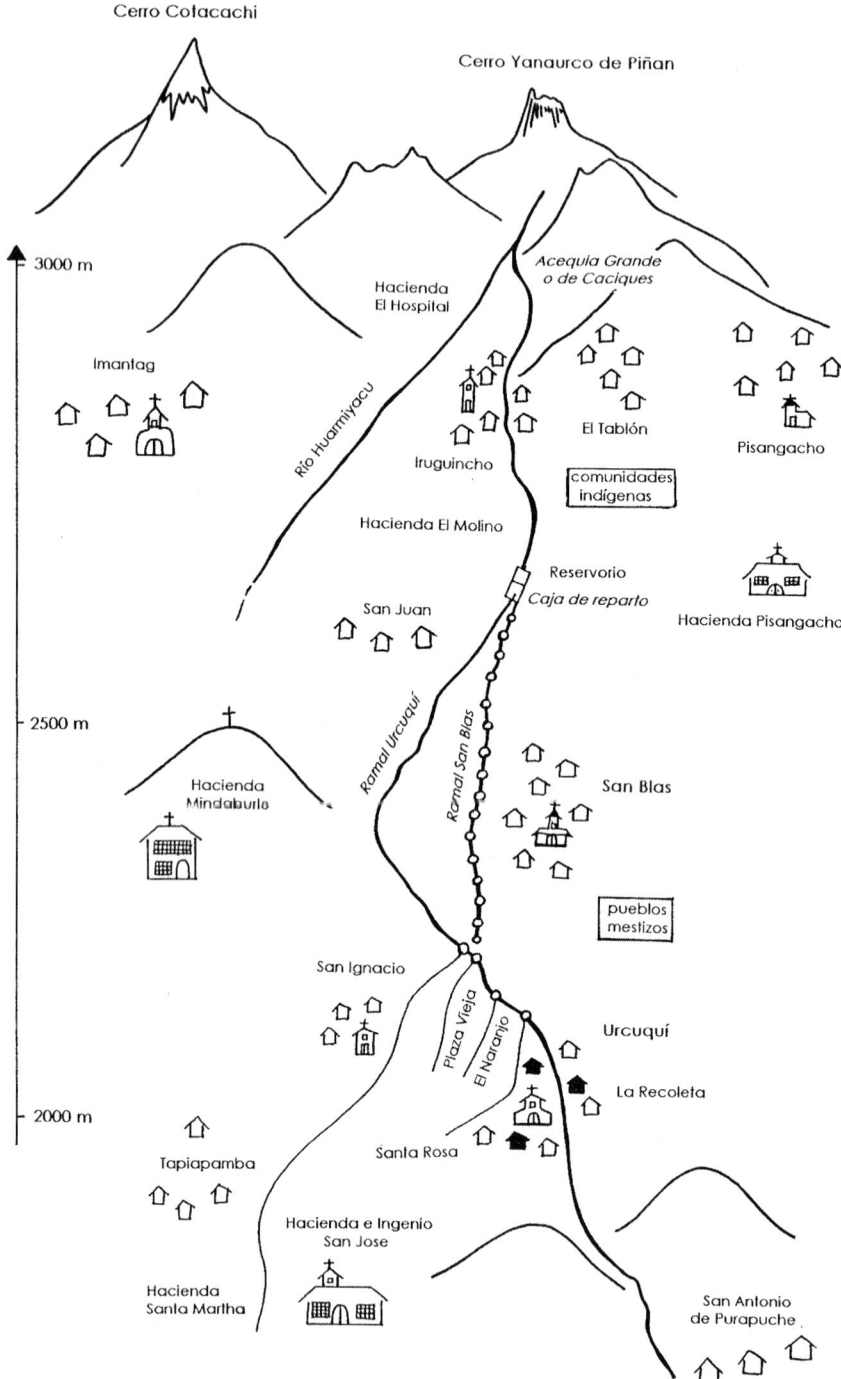

Figure 35.1: The Acequia Grande or Acequia de Caciques. Source: CICDA

How was this network of canals established historically? What historical agreements have permitted access to and distribution of the water resources? How was the current severe inequity of water distribution among hacienda-owners, small private owners and communities finally established?

History and equity: the shaping of an inequitable water distribution, 1500 - 1945

The history of irrigation in colonial times was linked from the start to explicit notions of equity concerning the distribution of water. In the text of the *Leyes de las Indias,* King Carlos V already refers in 1536 to distribution of water between natives and Spaniards. For example, Law xj states that the lands, now distributed among Europeans, should be irrigated according to the order established by the indigenous people and that the latter themselves should be in charge of doing it. If someone disobeyed this order, water would be withdrawn from this person, until all the irrigators in the lower part had finished watering their lands.[1]

This legal document does not specifically refer to the situation of Urcuquí, nor even to the current area that now forms Ecuador. But historical research on Urcuquí, based on a fundamental source of information, the water trials[2], demonstrates the repeated attempts by all local and regional, royal and later republican authorities, throughout the four centuries to put forward and to implement regulations and agreements among the different actors concerning the allocation of water. We try here to summarise the facts and analyses already published about the history of the foundation of these twenty canals from the 16th to the 20th century.[3] Specific to the area of Urcuquí is the fact that the indigenous *caciques* (chieftains, the original authorities, local power owners) retained power over the water during the whole of the 16th century in spite of rivalries among themselves and in the face of the arrival of the Spanish *hacendados*.

At the beginning of the colonial period, the indigenous groups of Urcuquí, Tumbabiro and Cahuasquí typically employed a form of vertical control from the heights of Yanahurco de Piñán, at over 4,500 metres, to the lowest part of the basin. The plain of Coambo takes up most of this hotter stratum, which lies between 1,600 and 1,800 metres a.s.l. According to the first trials in the years 1550-1580, these warm lands have two main uses: the highlands received irrigation water from ten derivations from the Pigunchuela gorge, and were used for the cultivation of coca and cotton; the lands below received extra salt water (Cachiyacu) and were used for salt extraction. A sign of times past, this sector is still called Salinas ('salt mines' in Spanish) today.

There was not enough water for the agricultural requirements of the Coambo plain. The summer flow was not sufficient to allow equitable distribution of water among the ten derivations and intakes. From 1550, conflicts escalated between various actors such as the chieftains of Urcuquí, who cultivated the lands on the right (south) bank of the gorge, and the other chieftains of Tumbabiro, who were on the left (north) bank.

In addition to these conflicts between chieftains, the Spaniards also demanded water from both the chieftains and the colonial authorities. It is worth mentioning that people called 'Spaniards' actually constituted a very heterogeneous group: certain people have a Spanish last name but may be the sons or daughters of Spanish fathers and indigenous mothers of chieftain-level families. This issue of the origin of the families of future landowners is very important: in the following centuries, for both hacienda owners and peasants, having indigenous blood could be used to justify privileged access to natural resources, while 'being white' had an immediate social and political function. *Throughout history, the concept of equity in the distribution of water resources has been managed this way, at times privileging the access to water by historic (and in this case indigenous) rights, and at other times through the power of appropriation of and priority accorded to the 'whites'.*

In the 1580s the chieftains of Urcuquí adopted a totally new strategy to deal with the problems of water scarcity. They constructed a new canal which diverted the water of the Huarmiyacu at the 2,700-metre line. The water was conducted to the 2,600 metre line above the settlement located in the temperate zone, and the principal objective of the new irrigation works was the irrigation of the plain of Coambo below the 2,000-metre line. The canal which today is called 'Grande de Caciques' or 'Grand Canal of the Chieftains' has been functioning since 1586, the year of the first conflict concerning water distribution.

In this period the allocation of water was ruled by 12 founder caciques, the chieftains belonging to the two *ayllus* of Urcuquí. Each chieftain had a one-day right over half of the diverted flow. This right began at midday and ended at midday of the next day, which meant that the 12 rights were distributed every week. Each seventh day of the week corresponded to the right of the priest's farm, someone who undoubtedly had a mediatory role in this new hydraulic organisation. Furthermore, every day the two chieftains who were each in charge of the management of half the flow of the canal, divided the flow into 12 subdivisions for internal distribution. Right from the beginning the Grand Canal had sufficient capacity to divert all the base-flow from the micro-watershed area of 17 square kilometres, i.e. 200 l/s. This meant that the basic irrigation field supply for the system corresponded to half the base-flow divided by 12, i.e. 8.25 l/s. For a complete day of 24 hours every week, this corresponded to a water endowment of 713 cubic metres per turn. This system of distribution and organisation found at the end of the 16th century reflects a basic notion of equity that is still employed to this day.

However, a few years after its creation, a series of conflicts surrounding access to water from the Grand Canal and the other water sources arose. In the 17th century, indigenous chieftains were confronted with orders from the Spanish demanding that 'indigenous waters should be handed over to them', arguing that the natives did not manage the water well and that 'they needed the water for their very dry haciendas'. Several lawsuits concluded with a kind of agreement of cession of a chieftain's complete right consisting of a whole day of half flow, in exchange for general maintenance of the main canal by the hacienda. This process represented the beginning of the loss of water control by the chieftains. It is important to note that the farmers in Urcuquí that still retain chieftain's rights today reject the idea of sharing the work of maintenance with non-chieftain farmers as a result of this ancient agreement.

Some families lost their historically acquired right as a result of purchase-sale processes despite the fact that most chieftains were against the cession of rights. As the society became increasingly mestizo during the course of the 18th century, two hacienda-owners became the major land and water-right owners, also managing and controlling an important part of the population, consisting of workers, peons or sharecroppers.

In the 18th and 19th centuries the management of all the basins of this territory was under the control of the haciendas. Nevertheless, this did not prevent the eruption of periodical conflicts concerning the construction of new canals throughout the process which resulted in the establishment of the present network of twenty canals. At the beginning of the 20th century the large canals were established (e.g. Salinas) that take water from the Ambi river canyon, and are characterised by their extensive hydraulic constructions (intakes, aqueducts, siphons and long platforms).

The indigenous chieftains who wielded authority over water and land at the beginning of the Spanish colonisation lost their power gradually. However, they did maintain one particular right throughout the whole process. This consisted, until the mid 19th century, of the right to one day of irrigation every week (from Saturday noon to the same hour on Sunday). This historically constituted right remains operative even today as a sign of the continuity of the history of the canal and of its conflicts and agreements.

Nevertheless, conflicts also arose in within the town between the chieftains and the mestizo peasants, who preferred to be called 'white'. The chieftains were obliged to share by alternating with the whites the only day of the week which remained under their control. Thus, under an agreement from 1855 a pattern was established of a fortnight for the chieftains and a fortnight for the whites.

Later, in the 20th century, a peasant struggle started in Urcuquí to recover the waters of the Grand Canal. After twenty years of tension, partial agreements and repression, the Urcuquireños achieved their goal in 1945 with the expropriation of waters from the San José hacienda.

Evidence from the water trials held in Quito, Ibarra and Urcuquí provides a means to understanding how the irrigation infrastructure in the zone has become established in a progressive though highly conflictive manner. Once the canal was finished, rivalries, disagreements and fights, the purchase and sale of rights, and inheritances and quarrels among the inheritors all contributed to the broad current scenario: an area divided into tens of small and medium-sized irrigation perimeters with very different water allocations and a extreme inequity regarding the distribution of the resource. While the available water is monopolised by some, other families have very little or no water. Due to the increasing competition for water, the conflicts over access among land owners and communities continue to be manifold, and there is no doubt that, in the coming years, more cases will be added to the lawsuits of the previous four centuries.

Reconstructing this historic process of the hydraulic and social construction of the irrigation systems of this zone contributes to an understanding of the current rivalries in Urcuquí between the 'chieftain' users and the other 'white' users in the town. The chieftains defend their right of priority access to water, and as owners and founders of the canal they have always refused to participate in the maintenance of the canal. The history of irrigation in Urcuquí can thus be considered an element which is indispensable to understanding contemporary rivalry and conflicts.

The Grand or Chieftains' Canal: evolution of allocation rules and water rights over the last 50 years

The expropriation of waters of the hacienda-owners

In 1944, the political conjuncture of the time led to the total return of the waters of the Grand Canal to the town of Urcuquí. The Socialist Party formed the majority of the Constituent Assembly that took over political power that year. The urcuquireños residing in Quito who were linked to the party took advantage of these circumstances and got the Assembly to decree the expropriation of waters from the conservative leader Jacinto Jijón y Caamaño, a hacienda-owner in Urcuquí. This Executive Decree, issued in December of 1944, also stated that the Board of Water Administration should be established as a legally created agency.

Water was now to be managed by a Board of Users and not by the ancient group of chieftains, who still claimed to be, up to the present day, the only co-owners of the canal. In January of 1945, under the control of the urcuquireños living in Quito, the organisation of the allocation of water called 'normal turn' or *turno comuneras* began, in order to differentiate it from the water of the 'chieftains' turn', whose specific and historic right was not affected despite being contested by some residents.

For this normal turn, the rules are laid down clearly and explicitly in the Statutes: the water quantity has to be related to the extent of land; as a defence mechanism, the haciendas in general and all properties larger than 15 ha, are not considered in this allocation. By the same reasoning, no property has a definitely acquired right to a certain quantity or time of water; this may be modified according to the needs of the population. Furthermore, the water became property of the plot listed in the Registry, and not that of the owner.

In the period from 1945 to 1948, the Colonia of Quito drew up a distribution plan. The Urcuquí Water Board was little more than a passive agent in charge of receiving the registrations and keeping an eye on temporary allocations. The intensive communication between the leaders of the Board and the Colonia of Quito surrounding any administrative, economic or political decision gives an indication of the amount of influence the Colonia had over the Board. Moreover, analysis of the distribution plan of 1948 shows that they had a thorough knowledge of what was happening in Urcuquí and it can be asserted that without their help the accomplishments would have been minimal.

This Water Distribution Plan was a project of great complexity. A study of the different rights present in the irrigation zone was carried out under the supervision of the legal representative of the Directorate. At the same time a map was made by topographers of the Military Geographic Institute, which included all irrigable plots in Urcuquí, listing their dimensions and owner. The construction of distribution boxes was introduced by a hydraulic engineer, who also drew up plans for the first water allocation. Despite several attempts to implement the latter, there was no success in that direction.

From 1948 to 1953 a new process of plot registration to obtain water was introduced. This completely invalidated the Military Geographic Institute map and went even beyond the irrigated area. In 1949 a contradictory order was issued that water be allocated to all those with irrigable land, disregarding previous registration. During the same period the Board suffered continuous economic deterioration, which was evident from the imposition of new taxes, delayed registrations and the suspension of works. In addition to these factors, the Colonia of Quito, the intellectual force behind the project, now distanced itself from the whole process and this also contributed to the lack of decision.

Attempts to achieve a technical water allocation

Between 1950 and 1956 the irrigation system underwent some changes. Until 1953 the assigned time for each hectare was two hours. In this year the Board decided to modify the rules and to distribute the flow according to the volume of water. In 1957, after several attempts to obtain a technician from Central Government who could implement this allocation, a new model for distribution was installed and three hours were assigned to each hectare. However, members of the Board found several faults in this system of allocation. The information available indicates that this attempt to establish a Technical Allocation was not successful. The 1960s saw a number of changes within the irrigation organisation. In 1961, the Directory ratified that the waters should be distributed under the system of turns. Regarding water distribution, there is evidence that, in 1963, plots smaller than one hectare were fully irrigated while those between one and three hectares in size were assigned only three hours of water. In 1965 the Directory received complaints concerning unfair water distribution. It was once again confirmed that smaller parcels were being irrigated until 'satiation'. Some users saw problems in this form of allocation and strong discussions arose about how to modify the form of distribution, especially in relation to the unlimited assignment of water to smaller plots, which appeared to be the cause of the stretching of the irrigation interval.

The intervention of INERHI and the impact of the nationalisation of water

The Ecuadorian Institute of Hydraulic Resources (INERHI) was created in 1966. However, its regulatory function did not become evident until 1973, the year in which water was nationalised. INERHI demanded that the Directorate hand over the allocation programme, together with its related co-owners, hectares, hours of irrigation and titles of ownership. In addition it demanded payment for water concessions and an annual use tax, which was only enforced a few years later.

Although INERHI did not intervene directly in the Water Board nor in its internal organisation, in many cases from this date the Board tended to lose power regarding rulings over conflicts, given the strong role assumed by the State authorities in the 'water courts'. State authority, backed by the law in settling conflicts through lawsuits, gained a position of increasing superiority over the traditional power of the Water Board.

The controversial 'Right of Chieftains'

As has been explained, the Right of Chieftains has a very ancient origin and is the product of the initial water distribution during the final years of the 16th century among the founding families of the canal. By the middle of the 19th century the only water available for the town was that obtained by this right (the other was the right accorded to the haciendas). In 1855 the Chieftains agree to rotate this right with the 'whites' of Urcuquí. Upon the return of all the waters to the town in 1945, the Chieftains' 'inheritors' became an obstacle to the implementation of the allocation as they refused to pay for their irrigation time. They considered that they had their 'own right' to the water and repeatedly refused to integrate their rights with the other villagers' water rights, which they called the *aguas comuneras*.

These rivalries were worsened by the fact that the contemporary Chieftains constituted a heterogeneous group: while some were descendants of the original families, many had acquired chieftainship by buying a plot with rights to chieftains' water. The 'chieftain' inheritance became not so much a question of lineage as a question of the history of land ownership in the area.

A similar conflict arose with the nationalisation of water: INERHI officials failed to recognise this type of right and in 1975 they sent a letter to the Directorate ordering that the Right of Chieftains be integrated with the general allocation. The response of the Board is unknown but this order remained unenforced and the chieftains reiterated that if they lost this right they should be compensated with supplementary hours. In 1977 the discussion over this right was reactivated because the users of the *comunera* water demanded payment for maintenance and use from the chieftains.

These problems with the chieftains remained latent until 1982, when INERHI pronounced judgement on the allocation of waters and established that the percentage to be paid by the chieftains for maintenance and conservation of the canal should be 7,8% of the total expenses. Ironically it was the Water Board which negotiated with INERHI in 1981 in defence of the permanency of their rights. In 1983 this body notified the Board that such rights would be maintained, thus respecting tradition and customs.

The history of the establishment of the canal plays a major role in the development the concept of equity or, more accurately the notion of 'equality' developed by some users of the normal turn of the *comunera* waters.

New regulations for water distribution: the process of insertion in the State bureaucratic framework

In the course of 1973, at a time when INERHI was carrying out the paperwork to legalise water, the Board proceeded to reform the statutes with the objective of '...providing the users with regulations that would ensure uniformity and good performance of all the shareholders'. The most significant modification in these new statutes was the establishment of three hours of irrigation per hectare, which although already in effect, only acquired a legal character in 1974 with the addition of a clause that the minimum size of plot with the right to irrigation should be 1/8 of a hectare, with a maximum period of half an hour. It was during the years 1974 and 1975 when this regulation for irrigation became implemented as discussions continued within the Board regarding the convenience of extending the irrigation times.

Under the 1973 reform, the Statutes regulated a 3-hour allocation of water per hectare; however, this ordinance was not followed and the irrigation interval period underwent a continuous expansion. While the minutes and accounts indicate the absence of additional registrations after 1973, the Allocation List was altered every year, which means that some users had a certain number of hours one year and a different amount the next year. These 'registrations' were obtained through various channels, including personal relations with successive members of the Water Boards, economic power, *viveza criolla* (local dodge) and, in a few cases, as a result of the financial needs of the same Directorate in periods of economic difficulty. The majority of these 'reassignments' or 'registrations' can therefore be regarded as irregular in relation to the Statutes of the Board. Throughout the 1980s there were continuous complaints from the users and the Inspector, but the respective Directorates did nothing to settle these problems, leaving them to accumulate.

Finally, concerning this period of organisation of the Board and definition of the user rights and obligations for access to and use of water, it is worth mentioning three important points:

- First, it seems that the canal users have never arrived at a real agreement for technical allocation in spite of numerous attempts during the last 50 years, with the professional support of various institutions. Although the 1973 INERHI intervention was an attempt to oblige the users to decide upon and to try to apply a form of allocation, to this date a consensus has not been achieved nor at least an agreement by a majority of users; many of them continue irrigating on the basis of a right which is considered higher than the one stipulated in the Statutes of the Board and in the allocation list presented to INERHI.
- There is no doubt that the lack of established rules and agreements between the users about the allocation, and the weakness of several Boards in their position as 'hydraulic authority' has led to the development of a variety of plot irrigation practices outside the official guidelines of the Statutes. It is difficult to carry out the profound changes in the water distribution which would benefit the majority, because these practices have now become customs and traditions defended by some users.
- Finally, while the chieftains' rights are considered by some users to be a privilege from a time long past, the Board and even INERHI finally recognised these historic rights that permit, partly because of their antiquity, the recovery of water retained by the haciendas. The chieftains' right and the history of the foundation of the canal have become elements of defence of the rights of the Town, even if for some people, whether users or technicians, they reflect inequity in the allocation of rights.

The implementation of a new social contract for water distribution: in favour of a concept of consensual equity[4]

A conflict-ridden water distribution

The contemporary situation in Urcuquí and San Blas provides a good example of the deterioration of the functioning of various ancient rural irrigation systems in the Sierra: while the water concession is sufficient for the 320 irrigated hectares, the water allocation among users does not cover crop requirements. The economic environment and the opening of new markets have induced farmers to intensify their crop systems by growing two cycles per year of maize-beans mixed cropping, or introducing new crops such as vegetables and fruits. In addition to the agricultural problems (loss of soil fertility, phytosanitary problems, great heterogeneity of material used), water allocation undoubtedly limits the productivity of the crops.

In Urcuquí, for example, the irrigation allocations are high (35 litres/second) but the intervals between irrigations are too long (three weeks to a month in some neighbourhoods). This situation has arisen as a result of the over-registration of the amount of water hours by users over the last 50 years: while the number of registered hours was 700 in 1945, according to present figures more than 950 hours are now allocated!

Besides the high production losses, this situation has led to intense rivalries and conflicts between different groups of users over the irrigation network as a result of robbery and neglect, illegally registered rights in the allocation lists, or merely attempts to enforce respect for specific rights, some of which are historically established as in the case of the chieftain users. There are also conflicts with the nearby haciendas and even with other towns that continue to compete for water access. In summary, these conflicts are leading towards an ever worsening degradation of the irrigation infrastructure due to a lack of standards, rules and agreements for the maintenance of the system among users or among the Water Boards. This could eventually threaten the entire agriculture of this area.

The irrigation system: rivalries and social cohesion

In spite of the above, the irrigation network is still the element that gives coherence to this agrarian space and water is still the one element that requires management and communal agreements for its exploitation. This holds for groups and people with distinct social interests and, especially now, those with distinct political and economic interests.

At the same time, the equilibrium and identity of distinct social groups and towns are still based on the conflicts, especially those related to the control of the water, whether between Urcuquí and San Blas, neighbourhoods with different histories, groups of different users, or between chieftains, etc. Both towns of Urcuquí and San Blas are thus locked into perpetual rivalry in order to demonstrate and maintain their social, historic, and political differences: while San Blas is still a parish, Urcuquí has become an administrative and political centre as the head of the Canton. Within this context, water is an element through which these rivalries and conflicts are crystallised, resulting in the avoidance of an 'equality' which nobody wants.[5]

Even though they are much criticised by the majority of the users, some chieftain descendants of the founder families of the canal, originating in specific neighbourhoods of Urcuquí, strongly oppose the disappearance of the special turn to which they have the right every fortnight and which many consider a privilege that can no longer be justified. Arguing that they are the owners of this canal due to historical facts since they or their ancestors built it or got it by means of open deals, these families reject this idea of 'equity' proposed by other people, especially the younger ones.

In the end, water becomes an element of rivalries and conflicts which are indispensable for affirmation of identity and leadership within the communities and neighbourhoods, and for obtaining political power. It is thus confirmed that in rural irrigation practice 'although irrigation water is governed by the laws of hydraulics and hydrology, when managed by peasants it obeys above all the laws and social rules of the group that uses it'.[6]

Searching for a new form of water distribution: from research to action

From the beginning of 1994, CICDA (the International Center of Co-operation for Agricultural Development, a French NGO) has been executing the project *Riegus* (Rehabilitation of the Irrigation Systems of Urcuquí and San Blas). One of the main objectives of this project is to support the Water Directorate of the Grand or Chieftains' Canal to improve water management and distribution among all the users, both in Urcuquí and San Blas to enable crop requirements to be met. As water is not only a means of production but also an element of cohesion and of social rivalry in this agrarian society, the principal objective is the implementation of a new social contract concerning water allocation in case of a conflict.

Furthermore, the project attempts to indirectly strengthen the administrative and economic capacities of the Board, especially for the maintenance and operation of the irrigation system and to strengthen its power as hydraulic authority in charge of the management and control of water distribution and conflict arbitration.

While some users or groups would like to see the disappearance of the chieftains' turn, the principal objective is the reorganisation of the normal turn. The integration of the chieftains' turn into the normal turn can only be achieved as the result of a majority decision by the users, chieftains and others, and in no way from the project's strategies and policies. Water distribution equity among all the inhabitants, without distinguishing between chieftains and non-chieftains, must be their own decision. Moreover, we should ask ourselves about the pertinence of bringing about the disappearance of an historic element that is a keystone in the defence of the water rights of the town.

The project staff and the irrigation leaders have developed several strategies and proposals to improve irrigation. Here we will focus on the proposal to change the irrigation turns. The most controversial proposal is:
- to adjust and redistribute the users' rights based on a 4-hour allocation per hectare (the present mean is 6 hours per hectare) so as to be able to return to a system of turns with 15-day intervals in Urcuquí,
- to create a sixth additional irrigation rotation unit (*regador*), thus decrease the flow by a number of litres in each of the sectors.

Some users, as a result of accumulated historical rights, had up to 24 hours per hectare while others had less than three hours, the minimum stipulated in the Statutes. This proposal should then result in the reduction of rights to some users and in the increase of water granted to others. To negotiate a new allocation is a difficult task and the key to its success is communication. Lack of communication and diffusion of information strengthens the existing conflicts, and rumours that emerge are the source of new conflicts. Therefore, information and awareness building about the problem among the users was one of the main strategies developed by the project.

To develop valid and agronomically viable proposals, it was necessary to carry out *technical studies*, as well as *social and historical research* in order to test the validity of the proposal against the norms, traditions, customs and social rationales of the different Urcuquí user groups:

- Historical analysis of the Records of the Water User Board from 1945: as we have already stressed, this analysis showed that there never was a consensual and validated technical allocation in spite of several proposals developed by technicians over the last 50 years. These proposals were always rejected. Furthermore, this investigation confirmed that the reorganisation of the rights already had been implemented in San Blas in 1965 under the authority of a President of the Board who was able to impose a return to a turn of three hours per hectare, and a cancellation of all supplementary and illegal registrations made.
- The technical study of the practices of field irrigation: to propose eventual changes in the water allocation also required knowledge, evaluation and explanation of several irrigation techniques (flooding, furrows, etc.) utilised by the users of the irrigation system of Urcuquí, in diverse economic, social and rights situations. This technical work permitted demonstration of the feasibility of the proposal to readjust rights to four hours per hectare. This adjustment figure is derived from the experience of the same users that already possessed this right or less. Also it was possible to identify some workable proposals regarding the improvement of field irrigation techniques that have to accompany the reorganisation of irrigation turns.
- Analysis of the social use of the water: while the historical analysis permitted understanding of the reason for the rejection of previous proposals of allocation, and the technical work permitted the formulation or confirmation of technical proposals that were agriculturally feasible, it was essential to develop a deeper analysis of the social aspects of irrigation. The identification of the social practices related to the use of the water (swap, loan, etc.), as well as the social and economic determinants related to irrigation, led to the understanding of those factors that may influence the process of negotiation for the implementation of a new allocation (availability of labour, social status linked to the possession of rights, economic value of the rights of water, etc.).

Given that many users insist that 'theory is one thing, practice another', or that they must 'see in order to believe', all proposals for improvement of the allocation must also be accompanied by demonstrations, trials, visits and interchanges with other farmers. Therefore, the trial phase of a new schedule became the fundamental strategy for achieving a socially accepted change, both by Urcuquí and San Blas people. This proposal and the trial results were discussed by users and leaders in several neighbourhood, community and inter-community spaces, until the new water allocation was finally approved in the General Users' Assemblies of 1996.

The activities that were implemented made that several proposals were approved by the Central Directorate and the Boards: opening of a supplementary rotation unit with a minimum though effective reduction in the flow to the old rotation units; regulation of the opening of the gate of the main reservoir so as to have the same flows for the rotation units of San Blas and Urcuquí during the morning and the afternoon; construction and placement of gates with locks in the main distribution structures, to avoid theft in particular.

Also, as the result of an initiative of the Central Directory and the Boards of Urcuquí, San Blas and Caciques, new rules of maintenance for the irrigation system have been installed, as well as rules for the 'good use of water'. This has been done to update the 1973 Statutes, to achieve better management of the irrigation system and to consolidate the hydraulic authority function of the Central Directorate. These rules were drawn up after thorough consultation with the users and ex-members of the Water Directorate. These are key elements and constitute the first achievements for the operation and maintenance of the irrigation system on a long-term basis and for a better definition of the rights and obligations of the users.

The compilation of the water distribution schedule: two distinct views of water and equity in irrigation

The basic criterion backing the development of this new allocation was that all the users must have four hours per hectare in order to achieve 'equity' for all. This is why it was decided to compile a new schedule. This task resulted in a decrease of rights for several users while others saw their rights increase. While the users of Urcuquí approved the introduction of this new schedule, the Assembly of December 1995 rejected it firmly, where the great majority of users were not even in favour of a future test. This rejection can be explained by three main factors:

- '*Water is what gives the land its value*'. The investigations of the social use of water and rights led to the conclusion that, among other factors, water is thought of by the users as an *economic good* that, although not able to be sold separately from the land, has a price and is 'capitalised'. This concept of 'water capitalisation' through rights was under-evaluated in the proposals put forward. The great majority of users considered the decrease in water rights as an economic loss (in terms if the amount of l/s and/or irrigation hours per turn), even after having been explained that this decrease would enable them to have water twice every month (since the frequency would be increased), and to improve the yield of cultivated crops. This economic criterion became still more important for the users given the current policy of the Municipality of Urcuquí, (i.e. to promote the urbanisation of the town) considering that the users with more water could sell their plots at a higher price. Furthermore, there is the example of the recent sale of a plot in a neighbourhood of Urcuquí to a rancher for a high price thanks to the many rights of water possessed.[7] This example strengthens the rejection of the decrease in their water rights (in terms of the water flow rate; the water share does not decrease). Although the project focused its action and reflection on con-sidering water as both a means of production and also a social factor, it did not pay sufficient attention during this whole first negotiation phase to the economic value that water rights represent in these mestizo towns.

• *The project's erroneous concept of equity: 'to take from the poor to give to the rich'.* The second profound reason for this rejection is that, by according a right of four hours per hectare to all the users, some plots increased their rights, especially the large ones which, paradoxically, on average have a right that is less than four hours per hectare. Now, the majority of the users that are small owners see a decrease in their rights as the result of having small plots with high average rights. For these small owners, this change of allocation is summarised as 'taking from the poor to give to the rich'.

For these small farmers this change increases even further the inequity that exists at the level of the distribution of other resources, especially land. 'Equality' and 'justice' proposed by the project and by several members of the Directorate who supported the compilation of the inventory of waters thus became contradictory to the concept of equity used by the users themselves, and led to a rejection by most of them. For the users, this form of equity does not signify an equality of rights (in terms of irrigation hours or volume per hectare). Users could not accept the removal of water rights to favour others, much less if it was going to favour the 'richest'. For the users the new allocation was supposed to avoid in particular the 'monopolisation of water' in hands of a few; but many users also utilise this concept to block a decrease in their water rights, considering themselves as the least favoured and 'poorest' regarding rights and resources. On the other hand, many could not accept the decrease after realising that their own neighbours were not affected and, what is more, that they were increasing their rights. Here, the relation with the others was a determining factor. In brief, the concept of equity, as employed in Urcuquí, has much to do with customs. To reject the new alloca-tion was to reject the modification of the collective irrigation uses and customs.

• *From a demand-driven distribution to a technical allocation.* The customs in the allo-cation and the use of water developed over the last fifty years have become the law for the users. This makes the process of change difficult. Historical stud-ies and monitoring of current irrigation practice show that the present situation approximates a demand-driven distribution where every user can irrigate the plot until finishing, without major in-plot control and management of the water, whether it is because irrigators have rights that permit this or because they have the power to negotiate a longer irrigation turn with the water inspectors. While there is a consensus over the objective of an irrigation frequency of 15 days, some users were not willing to make a complementary effort to meet this goal. The same reasoning provides a better understanding of the first rejection of the new allocation: some users were afraid that the trial would also be soon converted into a custom and finally replace 'the current law'.

The trial phase: 'Let custom become law'

In view of the users' reaction in 1996, the project, through the new Water Directorate and CICDA staff, corrected the inventory of waters. This was done respecting the decision of the users themselves to receive four hours per hectare but without increasing water rights for plots (generally the larger ones) whose rights were less than this endowment.

Throughout 1996 the new inventory was tested. At the same time, the permanent monitoring of this trial in all the irrigation quarters permitted continued updating of the schedule, thus finally enabling the step from 'technical equity' to 'social equity', which would be agreed to by a majority of users. After four months of trying the new allocation, the staff of the project and Water Directorate were able to corroborate that in the areas being tested there was already a predisposition of the users to accept the change of rights and to recognise the validity of this allocation upon effectively returning to the 15-day irrigation interval for their plots. After two years of work and negotiation, the trial phase was beginning to succeed through a change of attitudes of the users that went surprisingly fast.

In December 1996, the trial finally resulted in the approval of this new distribution schedule by the General Assembly. Today, one year later, the new schedule has been fully implemented and has been approved of by the National Council of Water Resources. This is an important recognition for a distribution schedule that is not completely 'technical' if we take into consideration some of the application inequalities according to the land-water ratio. However, it is genuinely equitable from the users' point of view and consequently socially acceptable, applicable and sustainable.

Undoubtedly, however, some questions remain regarding the future of this process: will the Board be prepared to continue in its function as hydraulic authority, so that this new allocation continues to be implemented, which would mean dealing with complaints from some powerful users, and even lawsuits? If it is approved, what impact will the new Water Law (currently in preparation) have over this process of change in Urcuquí, in the face of a possible privatisation of water rights that would recognise those who were claiming the ownership of their rights as an argument against changes?

In spite of all this, this process of permanent dialogue between the actors involved has allowed the users to begin questioning water distribution modes, the previous allocation, the current administration and has finally created space for collective debate on very controversial and previously undiscussed topics. Users have begun to discuss, debate and defend certain criteria of equity and justice both relating to access to rights and to the obligations thereof. The rules produced, the decisions already taken by the users or the Boards, and the changes in allocation are the results and achievements of this process.

Moreover, these two years have demonstrated that the execution of new water distribution modes in peasant systems cannot be limited only to establishing standards and technical calculations based on number of users, surface area irrigated, concessions granted and crop requirements. This long process requires also a deep investigation of the history of the establishment of the irrigation system and the creation of distinct types of rights, and an understanding of the history of the rules, modes, traditions and customs of water allocation and the rights in the particular society, and the criteria supporting them.

In addition, it requires investigating and understanding the meaning of water in a rural society, which is not restricted to what engineers call a production medium but is a key element of social and economic strategies, very often unrelated to agricultural production. In the case of Urcuquí, this process of investigation finally led to an understanding of the concepts of equity, justice and democracy as they are managed by the members of this society even if these do not coincide with the classical mode of thought of the project technicians. It also enabled negotiation with the users to obtain a water allocation that contradicts neither with the social and economic strategies nor with the traditions and customs.

The challenge of achieving a new, more consensual allocation in Urcuquí required the implementation of these preliminary steps in order to manage a concept of equity that had the approval of the majority of the users, in a fair balance between the historical rights and the more recent notion of equality among all.

Notes

1   Summarised from: Emperor Charles V, the empress G. in Valladolid ... November 20, 1536. Ivlian de Paredes, 1681. Compilation of the laws of the kingdoms of the Indies. Ed. Cultura Hispánica, 1973, Vol. II, folio 113.
2   85 different trials were identified and analysed between 1550 and 1995 for the Urcuquí zone, in several archives in Quito, Ibarra and Urcuquí.
3   See the 1992, 1993 and 1994 publications by Thierry Ruf and Pablo Núñez.
4   This section is further developed in the forthcoming 'Rehabilitación del Riego Campesino Particular y Participación de los Usuarios: Cuatro Años del Proyecto Riegus' by Frédéric Apollin *et al.*
5   The rehabilitation of the main division structure in Urcuquí and San Blas, carried out by the project in 1995, is a perfect example of this phenomenon: although constituting a request from both Boards and having their direct participation, this work revived their ancient rivalries. While it was possible to know that the work did not include any hydraulic failure related to the allocation of waters, the division structure became a topic of much controversy. Also, this shows that the construction of such an irrigation structure is never socially neutral.
6   Frédéric Apollin y Christophe Eberhart, *Agricultura Campesina y Función Social del Agua en Tiquipaya (Valle de Cochabamba, Bolivia)*, PEIRAV-CNEARC, Dec. 1994.
7   Besides, this intrusion of an hacienda owner in the Urcuquí irrigation system represents a danger for the future of the system, already surrounded by haciendas; historically, there has been a struggle going on against the haciendas to keep their rights. This was precisely how the town lost its waters in past centuries.

References

Alfaro, E. 1996. *El uso de las tradiciones para acceder al poder en Urcuquí y San Blas* (draft). CICDA/ORSTOM. Quito.

Apollin, F. 1994-1996. *Informes de actividades CICDA Ecuador*. CICDA. Quito.

Apollin, F. et al. 1996. *Rehabilitación del riego campesino particular y participación de los usuarios: Tres años del proyecto de rehabilitación de los sistemas de riego de Urcuquí y San Blas*. CICDA. Quito.

Bernard, S. and C. Chevignon. 1996. *Estudio de las prácticas sociales de riego en Urcuquí: Implicaciones para el proyecto*. CICDA/CNEARC. Quito.

CICDA. 1994. *Rehabilitación de los Sistemas de Riego de Urcuquí y San Blas: Project Documento*. Quito.

Eberhart, C. and F. Apollin. 1995. *Agricultura Campesina y Gestión Social del Agua en Tiquipaya (Bolivia)*. PEIRAV/CNEARC. La Paz.

Gilot, L. 1993. *Diagnóstico de un perímetro regado a partir del análisis del turno de agua: el caso de Urcuquí*. ORSTOM/INERHI. Quito.

Gilot, L. 1994. Alternativas para el mejoramiento del turno de agua en Urcuquí: Mission Report. CICDA/ORSTOM. Quito.

Núñez, P. 1995. *El manejo del agua por una organización campesina: el caso de la Junta de Aguas de Urcuquí (1921 - 1994) - Informe de la investigación histórica en los archivos de la Junta Central de la Acequia Grande o De Caciques*. CICDA. Quito.

Núñez, P. and T. Ruf. 1995 *Funcionamiento del riego particular en los Andes: Historia del riego en Urcuquí*. ORSTOM/INERHI. Quito.

Núñez, P. and T. Ruf. 1991. 'Enfoque histórico del riego tradicional en los Andes ecuatorianos'. *Revista Memoria Marka* 2 (2).

Ruf, T. 1995. Rapport de mission en Equateur - 18 octobre-4 novembre de 1995. ORSTOM.

Ruf, T. et al. 1993. *Sistemas de riego particular en la ZARI de Urcuquí*. ORSTOM/INERHI. Quito.

Ullauri, M. 1995. *Prácticas sociales de riego parcelario en Urcuquí*. CICDA. Quito.

Ullauri, M. 1995. Informe de actividades del Programa Turno de Agua: Diciembre de 1994-Octubre de 1995. CICDA. Quito.

PART VIII

ANDEAN IRRIGATION, ORGANISATION AND EQUITY

Introduction

The empowerment approach, which is fundamental to an alternative development, places the emphasis on autonomy in the decision-making of territorially organized communities, local self-reliance (but not autarchy), direct (participatory) democracy, and experiential social learning. Its starting point is the locality, because civil society is most readily mobilized around local issues. But local action is severely constrained by global economic forces, structures of unequal wealth, and hostile class alliances. Unless these are changed as well, alternative development can never be more than a holding action to keep the poor from even greater misery and to deter the further devastation of nature. If an alternative development looks for the mobilization of civil society at the grass roots ... it must also seek to transform social power into political power and to engage the struggle for emancipation on a larger - national and international - terrain. (John Friedmann, 1992, *Empowerment, the politics of an alternative development*. Blackwell Publishers. Cambridge, Massachusetts & Oxford)

The concept of 'empowerment' becomes fundamental to achieving greater concrete equity. There is no point in analysing and understanding equity, if this analysis does not materialise in peasants' daily practice in irrigation. Peasants do not start with theories and dreams, but concrete practice. They know that a strong, democratic organisation, with the power to make proposals and present claims, is indispensable if they are to achieve greater social justice in the field of irrigation.

This last part of the book focuses in greater detail on the topics related to organisation-building and empowerment of communities by analysing peasant irrigation experiences. This empowerment is related to issues of gender equity as an organisational force, a community's self-management capacity, internal justice or injustice in rural organisation, the wider social structures, etc.

Generally, public and private development institutions play a role in this process, and share responsibility towards the consolidating irrigation system. It is recognised that top-down interventions often increase social injustice and go against villagers' concepts of equity. However, with the exception of some important examples, couldn't a similar observation justifiably be made about interventions by 'enlightened' or progressive institutions as well, whether they be governmental or non-governmental?

> What is the difference between 'promotion' and 'extension' in those projects that follow this old 'developmentalist' approach, and the 'consciousness-raising' that we want to encourage? Generally, they all start with the same attitude, the same belief: there are some folks who know, and others who do not. Some see reality and are aware of it, and others do not and are not. One raises the consciousness of unconscious people, just as one builds capacity in the incapable.
> For decades we have criticised verticality, the banker's approach to traditional education. We have questioned it because of its reactionary contents and its methodological criteria and concepts. We have done this brilliantly and pro-foundly. There is no doubt about it. However, at the same time we have promoted a methodological approach that essentially commits the same original sins.
> We have spoken of consciousness-raising. Who is conscious, and who is not? We conscious intellectuals go after the unconscious who are exploited and live every day of their lives in exploitation. They live with it, but we decide about their level of 'awareness'. [...]
> Workshops (seeking to 'strengthen organisations') always begin with what Organisation means to *us*: since we cannot find the structure we want, with its functions or positions, we conclude that there is no organisation. We then go after the trainees with our group dynamics, to strengthen their organisation. We are not going to support *their* reflection about their *own* organisation, but simply plug in our own model. [...]
>
> Actually, for the peasants the important thing was not the organisational model, but rather the benefits and beneficiaries of what was being created.' (Humberto Gandarillas, Luis Salazar, Loyda Sánchez, Luis Carlos Sánchez & Pierre de Zutter, 1992. *Dios da el agua ¿Qué hacen los proyectos?* Hisbol-PRIV, Cochabamba)

In many irrigation interventions in peasant systems, it is common for the means to become ends. Proper application of participatory techniques and methods overrides people's own problem-solving capacity. In an irrigation project, greater importance is often given to carefully detailed planning than to designing educational or commu-nicational strategies oriented toward enabling peasants to take over irrigation management. This is because projects often fail to understand or to actually accept that irrigation development is a continual and reiterated process of negotiation.

It is often considered more important to set up 'more democratic' organisational models than to generate self-governing organisations through the practice of action and reflection.

Instead of considering conflict as a crucial means in the process of negotiation and irrigation development, and supporting its unfolding toward necessary consensus, avoiding conflicts is often made an overarching objective.

The Project pressured, promised, threatened, seduced, explained and explained. It did everything. [...] Until one day we finally realised several things. On the one hand, that the very presence of the project in the middle of the confrontation was negative. It distorted the fundamental discussion between the parties. It encouraged pressures and alliances that interfered with the genuine negotiation. Moreover, it was not necessary to try to avoid conflict, because conflict itself is not a bad thing. On the contrary, the villagers taught us, as they addressed contradictions in their own irrigation systems, that conflict was the point at which things were expressed without beating around the bush and that these conflicts made it possible - unavoidable - to reach agreements, to establish more lasting arrangements. (Gandarillas *et al.*, *Ibid.*)

In developing verticalist irrigation systems, designed *for* peasants, the system users are no longer the home team, with the right to build their own housing and way of life together; no, they are often 'beneficiaries' of complex projects that become gift-wrapped mechanisms for outside control. The Trojan horse wears a mask of Charity and Development.

By contrast, when peasant irrigation is developed sustainably, the peasants, rather than 'inheriting' an irrigation system that is 'transferred' to them, they themselves are the protagonists of their own production systems, sometimes with support from advisory institutions.

Despite the manifold hurdles encountered, there are also many experiences showing that peasant irrigation development in the Andes sheds significant light on empowering rural communities. Generally, the villagers themselves consider irrigation to be a mobilising pivot, able not only to enhance and boost productivity and strengthen organisation, but also to recover and/or lend a distinctive identity to the community, through which they can develop their own proposals for action in the future.

We discovered, increasingly, that we, as a project, had the good fortune of working with a very strong mobilising theme, namely irrigation; and that irrigation in turn was an element that was making communities more dynamic, giving them back their vitality and energy. Communities began to renew their own identity and revisit their role as cultural, social and territorial spheres, where peasants can make and re-create their own history. (Gandarillas *et al.*, *Ibid*)

36

Andean Irrigation and Gender Equity[1]

Aline Arroyo & Rutgerd Boelens

'Never an Indian, much less an Indian woman!'

An aunt who died recently, she told me where she really came from, why we had changed our way of dressing. It happened that my great-great-grandmother was of the community of Lluishi. She had remained unmarried, but in those times this was not permitted because the whites of the town imposed an order that an Indian woman couldn't stay single. As she did so, she had to pay a fine, a kind of tax paid by single people. But she didn't have any money, so they captured this woman called María Guayña. As she couldn't pay, she was taken out of prison by the Rivera family. The landlord or some other devil possessed her and she had a child, hence the change of our clothes. There was a *mestizaje*[2], they changed my mother's clothes, her language, everything changed. But not on my father's side, he is from the indigenous community of Tulabug and my father's family still uses *anaco*[3].

So begins the story of Rosa, now one of the women leaders in the zone of Licto, a town in the Ecuadorian Andes. Her life is characterised by the struggle to liberate marginalised families from oppression by the 'blanco-mestizos': the landlords and other power-bearing groups in the town of Licto. It has also been a search for the valuation of herself and all women as mothers, farmers, Indians and potential community leaders. Rosa shows that the topic of equity in irrigation should not only be taken seriously when analysing the position of the peasant family and organisation face to face with 'outside' actors: it is of equal importance to look *towards the 'inside'*. For the defence and realisation of equitable irrigation practices, it is not enough to acquire sufficient collective power and create an organisation that knows how to defend itself against just individualistic or outside interests; it is also of utmost importance to consider the internal equity, including gender equity. In addition to the valid reasons of social justice and fair distribution of rights and obligations in irrigation, there are other equally important arguments. Sustainability of the production system, organisational strength and, literally, people's survival, are qualities that in these peasant communities - with strong male migration - are achieved only with the co-participation of female leaders, promoters, organisers and irrigators.

Within my own family I have seen how the Indians are scorned, but without considering that we *are* Indians. I searched for my reality, to know who I really am, and through this identity I have pledged myself to a task.

Historically, as in many parts of the Andes, in the zone of Licto there has been a process of subordination of indigenous communities to the haciendas, to the mestizos and whites 'of the town'. The central town's relationships with the indigenous communities located around it have always been characterised by discrimination and processes of exploitation, through unequal exchange and expropriation of agricultural products and lands. Not only their products, but also the members of indigenous families were often 'expropriated', e.g. as labourers, servant-girls or victims of sexual violence. Forced godfathership (*compadrazgo*) and the obligation of being feast sponsors (*priostes*) further marginalised peasant and indigenous families.

The situation of the *indigena* was like this: they imposed on him a feast, for the Catholic feasts they charged him and this still happens today, he is the sponsor of San Pedro for example, and the unfortunate peasant, whether he had the money or not, had to pay for this feast. When the peasant rented the inn he was in charge of four or five casks of *chicha*, some three or four large pans of rice and potatoes to be given as food, and once this was finished he could go. Guess who enriched themselves! And this person, to be able to go from the inn to the church, had to pay a tax, so that he could talk to the priest. All this was arranged, so indigenous people became poorer every day. This way the feasts of San Pedro were held, the feasts of All Souls, the Child's feasts, the parties of the foremen. So, indigenous people were always lagging way behind.

If they caught you drunk on the street, the commissary or the town's political administrator locked you up in prison, and the following day you had to clean up the streets, do the *minga*[4], fix the water, or simply work in the lands of the governor or whoever it was. The peasant was mistreated. There was a chieftainship whereby two families had control of the whole situation in Licto town, dirty deals were made with the town's administration board, the parish priest, and the doctor. In order to celebrate a baptism you had to go to this family, so that they would speak to the priest. In order to get the doctor you had to go to this family and ask them make an arrangement with him. It was an imposition, a crushing burden, a terrible oppression.

I feel Indian, my parents are Indians, and we saw the abuse and the injustice. My father was a carpenter and was sent away to work and always the town mestizos took away his work. The town's administrator made him deliver his work to the mestizos and never paid my father. They put him in jail and they didn't pay him anything, all this, it hurt me so deeply!

Rosa has always lived in the town of Licto, not in the indigenous communities, but her commitment lies with them. In spite of the fact that she does not dress like an indigenous woman and understands but does not speak Quichua, she is not a mestizo. Sometimes, a few indigenous male peasants, who envy her for her position as a woman leader, call her 'mestizo' but all community members know that this is not fair. It is not only the blood but, more than anything, one's self-identification, struggle and commitment which determines ethnicity in rural Andean zones.

> We were not brought up with shoes. It was a question of poverty but also because they didn't allow us to use shoes. Because we didn't have a right to dress, to put on clothes as we wanted, because the mestizos tore our clothes to pieces. My mother's family was always identified as *cutos*. *Cutos* were the Indians who were brought to the service of mestizos or whites, who then changed their clothes. And to differentiate them from both indigenous and mestizo people they cut their hair, they were shorn, no matter how. They no longer use *anaco*, nor *poncho*, their hair is already shorn. They are different from the Indian, the peasant, the *indigena*, they are also different from the mestizo. They no longer identify themselves as Indians.

> We used to say, why us, why did they do to us whatever they wanted, with my grandmother, my great-grandmother, they abused them, they did with them what they pleased. But we shouldn't be embarrassed, we should feel proud of being Indians! We couldn't use braids, the mestizos could, we couldn't, because if we identified ourselves with them, they insulted us, they hit us. My brother sent me two dresses, and just because I wore a dress at school, they didn't give me my Christmas toy. The teacher didn't give me the toy and she didn't let me enter the school, just because I wore that dress and slippers. They gave us the name of *cutos*, and we had to dress as *cutos*. When they saw you with shoes they said: 'take a look at the Indian, she certainly shows off her feet', they yelled at you. All those things, one accumulates. We were already sick of their abuse, saying to us just anything. Why are they going to tear our clothes, why are they going to hit us, because they indeed mistreated us.

In spite of all being indigenous, peasants and *cutos*, in spite of all suffering under the same discrimination and economic misery, it is not equal for men and women. Even economic and ethnic oppression and suffering are not evenly distributed along gender lines.

> We were domestic maids at the Coast, where we looked for work, with my older sister. We were going to work in a house and my older sister got pregnant by the boss, and she had many problems. My sister stayed sick after the pregnancy. It hurt me very deep, I never said anything to my parents, but it remained inside me. Then I said: 'this situation must change!'.

The Church has always played a fundamental role in the life of Rosa, both in negative and positive ways. In Licto, the Church oppressed both Indians and women.

> Religion was quite oppressive, I suppose it must have been this way during the Conquest, it's the image I have. There was a process of humiliating rural people in Licto. I remember a day when the cunning priest went and came back with the Bible and he stopped amid the assembly. He said: 'who of you, illiterate Indians, Indians who don't know even what a vowel is, dares to raise voice against the second God of Earth, to God's minister'.

> How they characterised us! For example, the priest said in his sermon: 'please, don't mix with Rosa Guamán, because it is the same as getting along with sin, they are communists'. Once I quarrelled with the priest. I told him: 'I am the church and you don't come to tell me anything'.

This was the Church of the powerful, of oppression. On the other hand, with the progressive Church, especially under the direction of Monseñor Proaño, the 'Archbishop of the Indians', Rosa got to know Liberation Theology. Some priests helped the women of Licto to become both craftspeople and to develop their own critical capacity.

When she was 17, Rosa made her first steps in popular organisation. Starting with groups of youngsters and local committees, she spent an important period in the mothers' committee of the centre for women with young children. At 21 she had her first daughter.

> My daughter was just two months old or so, it was my first meeting and they had been electing the board. They elected me as president, and I began to discuss with the women about what we could do: do we only want to receive food or do we want something different. But we didn't have any preparation.

With the women of the centre they did courses on handicrafts, dressmaking and other subjects. Some husbands did not want women to become qualified labourers. In order not to give them reasons to complain, the women looked after children during the courses, and they got up very early and did not go to bed until late in order to carry out all domestic tasks.

> We were pregnant, carrying our child in our hands and in our bellies. Our husbands didn't want us to go anymore but we went anyway. We even got beaten up, because they said that women were made for the kitchen and nothing more. We sat down to talk and we said: why do our husbands say that to us, why do they treat us like this? We didn't have any trainers, we had the nuns, but they think differently. We have a different situation, we live in a different reality. The nuns don't live like us, like mothers. What I have learned, more than to do handicrafts, is to value myself somehow, that is, to see that, yes, we can! Because the town men always told us we were stupid, foolish, that we were not worth anything, they always belittled us. They don't understand that we also want to be somebody.

I always thought and said: 'I've got to be someone!'. I have achieved more than just handicraft abilities and that, more than anything, helps me to be a link in order to speak to other women, to share with other women. The main thing has been that we value ourselves.

Power groups in town realised that these women were a threat, both to their power position, the white-mestizo hegemony, and, at the same time, to their macho values which regulated social life in Licto town. Repression was intense and present at several levels: discrimination and oppression to women was applied because of being indigenous (ethnic group), peasants (class) and female (gender).

In the town a really hard fight went on. As a person I have suffered the aftermath, because I began to lead and people began to look at me. We no longer centred only on the family, no longer was the change present only at home and in the family, but in the whole town. I was pregnant with my fourth daughter when my husband arrived and said to me that they were going to set our house on fire.

The priest had denounced us, saying that we were communist agitators and what not, and they came to get us with an order for our arrest. He had warned the town people by telling them: 'Either I leave or you send Rosa Guamán and Inés Chapi away'. Well, he is a priest, he is Father God's priest, then the town's people said, no, it's better that they leave, they were going to set my home on fire, they had armed themselves with sticks. I was already eight months pregnant then, I got really scared. I went to the hospital, I was in bed, I almost died, because I was ill. It may have been because of the tension, anyway, my delivery was premature because of this situation.

The authorities and the Church of Riobamba intervened and calmed down the situation. However, perhaps more than the economic and physical repression, the psychological repression has been the hardest.

They told us: 'those mannish women that don't obey their husbands, they don't respect home nor the Cross of God'. Then they said to us that we are like men, that's what I really came under fire for, because I began to participate in something different, very different from what my mother did.

Hideous cartoons left in my husband's workshop humiliated me. They knew they were touching me in my most painful part. It hurt a lot. When I had my fourth child, then my husband showed me the cartoons. He said to me: 'this is what you have earned. Look, from now on I don't want you to go on like that, why don't you stay home'. Inés and I saw each other undercover, like two forbidden lovers. We realised that we could no longer live like that. I read Domitila Chungara's book about Bolivia and it helped me a lot in my thinking. Strengthened with her ideas, I rushed with much more force to organise woman groups. We also began a network of peasant women of different towns at the provincial level.

From the first years of the 90's, the NGO CESA[5] began its participation in the Licto-Guargualla State irrigation project. The situation was complex: the State project, already there for several years, had always been characterised by its vertical management and little user participation, so that the most powerful, with more contacts and information, would seize the water and the irrigation management. Besides, the town's white-mestizos possessed the best lands of the project area, precisely at the head-end of the system. This would enable them to steal and take all the water in times of scarcity, leaving nothing for the 16 indigenous communities downstream. This would give the wealthy even more power over the indigenous population.

A strategy was set up whereby all indigenous communities were to be organised, except the town of Licto. Once solid and strong, this organisation, with its *own* norms and capacity for negotiation and alliance, would 'invite' the town of Licto to join in the organisation, *but under equitable criteria already established by the communities*. One of the central criteria was: 'water is for those who participate in the organisation and work in the mingas established by users'. So, only paying the fees to the State would not be enough for obtaining water rights.

The strategy was successful. The communal irrigation organisation, within the peasant and indigenous organisation CODOCAL,[6] earned much respect. It gained power, to the point of constituting the major force in the entire zone of Licto. And all this even *before* the arrival of any irrigation water. The town's white-mestizos had no answer, they saw their power position affected and tried to manipulate the town's people: 'don't worry, the moment water arrives we will talk to our friends at the State irrigation agency and we are going to get all the water. It is not necessary to work in mingas. Good Heaven, how can we work with the Indians!'

However, Rosa, Inés and other women in Licto town analysed the question more seriously. They had gained respect among the poorer groups in town and summoned all the town's neighbourhoods to create a democratic organisation in Licto too.

> They didn't know how to get organised for irrigation. I suggested that it should be done by neighbourhoods, with a representative for each neighbourhood. For the central neighbourhood they appointed me; there were seven neighbourhoods. We had already worked for years in order to change the board. We had all those problems, I thought that the town really didn't see yet in me a person who could serve them, but at that time they appointed me as the central neighbourhood representative, which had more mestizos than the others, and I was surprised.

The seven delegates had to propose the internal distribution of the directorate posts. Men were afraid that they would be unable to live up to the requirements of the posts and face all the problems, and they said that representatives from the two powerful families should be asked. But the women were opposed to this.

Our male fellows said: 'no, *compañeras*, we should call Don Esteban, the co-operative manager; we are not going to be able to do anything'. He and his family were always the ones who manipulated us. Then I said: 'excuse me, my friends, if you are not worth anything, well I am, so here we are going to elect the dignitaries'.

That is how Rosa became the first president of the Licto Irrigation Committee, approved by all neighbourhoods. It is rare in Ecuador for a woman to be elected within an irrigators' organisation, except in cases where she replaces her husband. It is even rarer to elect a woman *president* of such a 'masculine' organisation. There was much protest from the priest, the town's administration board and the white-mestizo families. They tried to disqualify the new president saying that an Indian could not represent the town of Licto and that, besides, she would steal the organisation funds.

They didn't want to accept it, first because they have lived dominating us, and second because we are women. 'How can a woman be in charge of such an irrigation committee. Never an Indian, much less an Indian woman!'

A strategic step was taken when Rosa, the other women and the poorest peasants of the town decided that the Committee of Licto, just as all other surrounding communities, would have to join the indigenous organisation (CODOCAL) and their inter-communal irrigation organisation: the Water Directorate. Licto's women and poor people saw the irrigation project as a way to obtain their main objective of emancipation and equity in the town itself.

The peasant organisation accepted the application with some distrust: what interest would the town's mestizos have in joining the indigenous organisation after so many years of deceit and oppression? But they accepted. Organisational strategies were defined by both sides: Licto entered into the irrigation organisation accepting the communities' conditions and equity criteria, and Licto's women and poor people achieved a union with the indigenous communities to back up their fight against the town's internal oppression, successfully confronting the abusive power. They mobilised and organised themselves, not for an abstract, political goal but in order to realise very concrete aims and objectives related to their common future, their irrigation. In the same way, gender relations cannot be analysed in an abstract manner: they are dynamic relations which are shaped and reshaped in people's ordinary life, in concrete space and time, according to the peculiarities of each local reality. In the Andes this means, for example, that gender analysis and practice most often cannot be separated from class and ethnic analysis and reality.

From the time when we began to organise, we knew organisation was costly, and certainly, it has cost me a lot. The aim is not to achieve fame or power, it is necessary for our people. But likewise, the time I've been in the organisation has been one of great happiness in spite of the suffering, because I have met many women and I have seen how they start to speak and defend themselves. This is my happiness. With the organisation we see a different future, it means social change. Before, families were dispersed, now a unity exists that joins families, where irrigation is discussed, but also other topics. We are better human beings too. Young people, who had never participated, now develop in a conscious way: a big family is being formed.

Since then, the organisation has earned respect not only from the poor, the Indians, the institutions and the State, but also, increasingly, from the very mestizos, who 'make the best of a bad job' and even request admission to the irrigation organisation.

Once my father said to me: 'Rosa, I think that what you're doing is the best I have waited for in my family. Pity that you're a woman', said my father, 'If you'd been one of my male children I would have been even prouder. But, even being a woman, I know what you've done, and you'll never surrender. I don't want you ever to be humiliated by these horrible mestizos because they've always humiliated us'. This I kept in my mind, because I knew how we were mistreated, humiliated and marginalised. That's what my father told me. 'Rosa, don't you ever surrender. You have succeeded in breaking what we were not able to break'.

* * *

Male migration and changing social relationships

In the Andean area there are many points of view from which to analyse relationships between men and women, from external approaches that have been 'Andeanised' to locally developed approaches. Behind these various views there is a wider debate on the production mode of Andean rural society, since women's position and role and gender relationships are closely connected to power structures and production rationalities constituting the mode of production. Here, an important topic is the degree of incorporation of the Andean community and the peasant family into the capitalist system: the form and intensity of subordination to capitalist logic and the articulation with national and urban economies. Variation is large, since, apart from the widely varying Andean local situations, 'traditional' conditions and social relationships have gone through very different historical processes. And the current 'external' influences not only differ by region and family, but also face very diverse peasant answers, from gradual acceptance to firm resistance against processes of incorporation. One thing is for sure: current community norms in irrigation systems and peasant families are not products that appeared autarchically but are rather the result of interactions with other normative systems, ideologies, and production and subordination logics, many of which host inequitable gender-related norms.

In Andean gender relations analysis, the concept of 'duality' is often heard and discussed. Duality would be a central quality or property of historical and current

Andean society, a society based on complementary parts and counterparts. This duality refers to, for example, relationships between men and women, as well as to many other aspects of Andean life. Although many diverging opinions exist, accepting duality as a structuring quality of Andean relationships does not necessarily mean, however, that there is a symmetric relationship between the constituting parts. In fact, often there is no such symmetry. As in any other dualistic relationship, many important contradictions may arise and they certainly do.

It is evident that the historical processes of conquest, colonisation and current capitalism have taken possession of most (reciprocal and/or asymmetrical) Andean traditional relationships. To a varying degree, they have influenced all Andean regions and communities. As we see all over the world, the colonial system has left severe injuries among the oppressed peoples, sometimes overt and sometimes covert. One of the most hideous expressions of the colonial influence is the fight *between* oppressed peoples, *between* black peoples, *between* the exploited, etc. In colonised societies, colonial violence may become internalised and cause a society to turn inwards upon itself.[7] Violence was not only directed as a macro-process against whole peoples, but it also penetrated strongly at the community and even family level. It would not be too strange to suppose, after so many centuries of physical, psychological and economic violence and rape in the Andes during the Spanish conquest and during post-colonial times, that certain features of the oppression have been internalised, establishing new power structures at several levels, from the national level to the family and gender levels. Andean coexistence has changed through the incorporation of external structures, in spite of the dynamics and resistance of Andean reciprocal relationships. Likewise, we also know that the historical and current capitalist system by nature creates contradictions and takes advantage of existent asymmetries in order to intensify them.

One of the many important examples is the sexual division of labour in most peasant communities in Ecuador, and in other Andean countries. The historical process of change, from more autonomous decision-making over the (intra-community and intra-family) division of labour towards strong outside influence on labour division, subordinated to the labour market, presents an essential background for current developments. The sexual division of labour is a basic mechanism for legitimising and determining gender relations - or, perhaps, it is rather a clear expression of them - because we are talking about the division of roles, posts, status, rewards, resources and power, both at micro and macro levels.

A brief historical analysis beginning in colonial times shows that, after the expropriation and concentration of the best lands in the hands of large landowners that broke the duality of so-called 'vertical economies' (by including the low lands of Andean micro-regions in the mercantile economy), indigenous populations were forced to take refuge in high zones with steep slopes and fragile, unproductive soils, generally without water resources. Today, these communities are characterised by the existence of extremely small *minifundios*, with deterioration of natural resources, deep poverty and absence of employment possibilities. The commoditisation process has penetrated and its laws determine a large part of family and communal survival strategies. Symbols of Andean collective coexistence are being increasingly eroded through the imposition of foreign norms and regulating mechanisms that individualise and commoditise: disappearance of communal lands and waters; commoditisation of labour relations; incorporation of urban customs; buying and selling of land, changing its symbolic value for a merely economic one. This expropriation and commoditisation process also expresses itself through a high-impact phenomenon in many parts of the Andes: intermittent and permanent male migration from Andean communities. Most often, men leave to search for an income that, until recently, was considered additional to agricultural production; now, in many communities it is reverse: income from subsistence agriculture has become additional to that of migration. The former sexual division of labour within peasant families, with specific responsibilities for men and women, has been intensified, exaggerated or transformed due to the new capitalist economic conditions. This system has expropriated a large part of the decision-making power over the sexual division of labour, decisions that in former days were taken mainly within the communal coexistence. The appreciation of assigned tasks to men and women has also changed, giving less importance and social recognition to the latter.

The brutal and cruel rupture of the family structure has created a situation with new conditions in many Andean communities. The survival responses and strategies have changed, as well as, necessarily, labour divisions and gender relations. It is not strange anymore to see women ploughing with the yoke of oxen; they increasingly participate in posts that were exclusively reserved for males; in many communities they irrigate, and so on. Depending on the family and the community, some males return at weekends, others once a month, once a season or year, or even less. Due to this semi-permanent migration, it is common to find communities where more than 80% of the economically active population is made up of women.

> There is migration, so every day women go down to work at the neighbouring haciendas, and men migrate to the cities. In this sector of Molobog, for example, with a couple of cottages, only one man has stayed, don Juan Quishpe, the rest are only women. I believe that women are the ones in charge of most of the work here, aren't they? For example, they raise the children, take care of the animals, and more than anything, they cultivate and work the land. As men migrate to the city, women have to do all the work, right? We work on the communal lands, we go to mingas, we work to sustain the family, in the haciendas we work irrigating (Ana, Molobog, Licto).

In these situations, where families find themselves in a 'break-down position', consequences generally are different for the two genders. Certain relations are broken that in a united family might have guaranteed an equitable functioning: exchanges of capacities and labour, etc. In communities with much male migration, women must generally face all the productive, reproductive and community management tasks; the husband can only join her at certain times. However, women have not been trained for all these roles. In general, they have not had the possibility to acquire the capacities, knowledge and contacts that are considered necessary to fulfil all these new responsibilities.

So, let us briefly return to the point of the changing Andean reality outlined above. Certain theories and visions consider that the total incorporation of Andean communities into the capitalist system is already a fact, a concretised process. Some of them state that communities are functional within the national or world-wide mercantile system. Communities provide labour to enterprises, which can be extremely cheap because the community itself is in charge of offering the additional means needed to survive. So, the work of the ones who have remained in the community, especially women, 'subsidises' the capitalist system.

Other theories, on the contrary, doubt the degree of incorporation of Andean communities into the capitalist system. They state that the dynamics of the Andean peasant community structures have much elasticity and force to resist imposed, alien commodity norms and relations of production.

In any of these theories, it is crucial to recognise that, generally, the survival and the well-being of the Andean community is only possible through the disproportionate contribution of women. Many aspects of the 'duality' have been distorted in an asymmetrical way. Above all, in those many Andean regions where a process of feminisation of the communities is daily reality, peasant women carry most of the responsibilities related to family, communal and inter-communal survival. In this relatively new situation, in order to be able to cultivate reciprocal relationships and defend and revive the community, women do not need either to be trained as domesticated housewives, or theories that emphasise the supposed existence of harmonious relationships between genders. They need concrete capacities, knowledge, contacts and tools, adapted in a creative way to the specific needs of the locality. These form part of the means which are needed to (re-)build equitable relationships at the family, community and peasant organisation levels.

> Husbands go to work and come back after a year, others in three months, two weeks, one week; so, they don't know when meetings and work take place. Meanwhile, women are there, in the community, and they know which day the meeting takes place, which days are working days, and so on (María, Santa Rosa, Flores).

A conscious intervention can have an important assisting role in this field. Obviously, these are challenges that exceed the traditionally planned activities for women: it means joining in a struggle, where capable women with self-esteem can fully share the collective management of the Andean communities and (inter-)communal irrigation systems. Irrigation project interventions have not always devoted enough attention to this fundamental topic. Let us analyse this briefly.

Irrigation projects and gender relations: some notes

In spite of the great diversity we encounter in Andean gender and irrigation issues, it is strange to see that, when considering the impact on gender relations, the central *problems* found during and after irrigation interventions are largely the same. Surely this cannot be explained by a supposed relative homogeneity of social problems in Andean irrigation systems, but rather by the great uniformity of intervention methodology practised by most irrigation projects. With pre-established planning, rigid funding, prescriptive implementation and 'foreseen' achievements, many of them do not include the required dynamic strategies to investigate, in a critical and participatory way, the local reality, in order to understand social and gender relationships and to discuss and design lines of action creatively.

One of the main problems is that projects introduce non-validated, stereotyped suppositions into the localities. These are often shown to be mistaken because they are based on the intervening logic and position, with ethnocentric, class, educational and or gender biases. However, these biases are seldom unmasked. Besides, irrigation is perceived basically as a technical issue understood only by (male) engineers. The intervention strategies commonly deny the fact that irrigation in Andean communities is a social construction based on social relationships, and not only on hydraulic infrastructure. If it is common to deny the importance of social relations in irrigation in general, attention paid to irrigation-related gender issues is even less. When planning and executing irrigation projects, the differences between gender interests frequently remain hidden and are not dealt with. In intervention practice, female work and women's voices usually go unrecognised and are kept out of focus: women appear as invisible actors. The active presence, potentialities and irrigation rights of women are denied (and made invisible) not only by agencies or male farmers but also, very often, by the women themselves, i.e. through internalised ideological concepts.

> When I first entered here, to join the discussions on irrigation, I used to say: 'But what will I do, I do not know anything about irrigation'. My husband bothered me, he said: 'What are you going to do in the users organisation, you, the one who has only raised babies'. Indeed, I didn't know, I was a dumb girl, but able to learn. It is not only for men to decide: we both have to think, we both have to talk. We, the women, we ourselves at times are guilty since we give only men priority, the man is better than anybody and has to be present. Some men say that women don't know anything, so 'what can they contribute?' We like to tell them 'How come we don't know, how come we can't think? All that a man has, she has too, so women have to participate in everything' (Inés, Licto-town).

It is necessary, then, to visualise women's role in irrigation projects and tasks. The problem is not that peasant women do not 'participate', that they are not 'incorporated' into the development process. They *are* participating and *are* incorporated, but generally in a subordinate way: women's rights and potentials are not recognised and they are not given sufficient control over the intervention and production process.

In many projects' implicit approach, the man 'channels' all the irrigation project benefits in an equitable manner towards his family. Women are supposed to fulfil, above all, reproductive functions and they supposedly feel protected and safe within the family, behind big male shoulders. Therefore, these projects are usually directed mostly to men,[8] to train them, to allow them to make decisions, lead committees and users organisations and manage the irrigation system. Women do not formally represent the family and, therefore, they cannot be formal members of the irrigators' organisation. They have neither voice, vote, nor decision-making power in the management of the system. It is supposed, however, that women are available and have time to help in canal construction and water application.

> We had harvest mingas all week, and on top of it we had to do it by night. With my mom we used to go to our fields. I went down at night, carrying my baby girl in my shawl and with a load of manure. We worked in darkness, in order to be able to work next day at the community minga. We also got up very early, at five we were already cutting the maize so that at eight we could go the minga: it was tough. For us, harvesting usually begins at five. We finished at eight thirty, nine in the evening, we arrived home and then we had to go over to the community meetings (Ana, Molobog, Licto).

Both State regulations and formal project procedures often establish norms related to men only, the 'head of the household', be it when granting land titles, water rights, access to credit, attendance of courses and other work areas. Many regulations and interventions create or reinforce the inequitable gender relations that previously, in many cases, may not have had such presence and intensity in the community. It is impressive to see that in many projects the institution is 'disposed to sacrifice' and work during weekends in case males come back from migration activities, because 'during the week there is nobody in the community'. Decisions are taken in the presence of men, and women have to execute them during the week.

It is common that women's problems and specific obstacles are not dealt with when training sessions, courses, mingas, discussion meetings and projects in general are planned. These obstacles can have many causes, for example:
- Language: many Andean women do not speak Spanish very well, and - unlike men - in certain communities they are monolingual;
- Education level: generally women have had less access to formal education and (informal) professional training than men;
- Distance and lack of transport: in general, the area of action of women is much more limited than that of men because they lack the means of transport which men do have;

- Lack of authorisation to mobilise: many peasant women do not get permission to go to events relatively far from the community, and even less when these are carried out at night;
- The agricultural calendar and domestic and productive tasks: due to the sexual division of labour, many women's tasks have a different schedule from men's tasks. Furthermore, the work load differs according to the moment in the agricultural year, which at times makes it impossible to attend the scheduled events regularly.

Before, mothers used to say that only men have to go to school, they didn't let women go. Women had to herd sheep and other animals. You have to shear the sheep, to stay in the kitchen, they used to tell us. They used to keep women inside the house, therefore mothers don't know how to read and write, they don't speak Spanish but only Quichua. Nowadays we, young women, because we are younger, we speak more or less Quichua and Spanish. But the old mothers don't know how to speak or understand this (Dolores, Guanlur, Licto).

The above mentioned is reflected in most projects' irrigation training sessions: often, even when 'mixed events' are arranged, only men take part. In cases where women do participate, it is very common for them to sit on the floor and listen silently while men discuss and make decisions with the institution's technicians. Since irrigation topics institutionally are considered 'masculine', technicians also tend to be men.[9]

It is true that in the field peasant women are less, in other words, they give them less importance. They, that is, only men, are the ones who talk more, the ones who reason more. On the other hand, women do not talk, that is, they can't speak Spanish, they're afraid to speak to any engineer or in any assembly. Women often do not read or write, can't speak Spanish and don't understand some words, that is the problem. Therefore, that's why they're afraid, and ask for men's support. (María, Santa Rosa, Flores).

Generally, institutions do not recognise or worry about these 'dialogues among men', because the received wisdom is that 'it is the Andean custom that before and after any event, decisions are democratically discussed within the family, between husbands and wives, the latter as the ones in charge of the internal management of home and family'. However, this supposition is too general and is not validated in many zones and specific cases. We know of many cases where this dialogue and a common agreement between genders do happen, but also many examples where decisions have been taken only by men, sometimes directly against certain women's interests. Furthermore, as seen before, relations are changing and are not the same as thirty years ago. In migration zones, many households simply cannot rely (anymore) on men as representatives in important meetings, nor can many single mothers and widows. These families enter into a vicious circle: for not being able to express their irrigation-related problems and interests, they see their control over irrigated agriculture worsening, and lose their power and capacity to influence irrigation matters.

Not only the *problems* in irrigation projects and systems are gender specific. Also interests and needs can be differentiated according to which gender is using the system. For example, in many communities women mention that irrigation water is, or will be, important to facilitate the activities of clothes washing or bathing children, tasks that can take up many walking hours. In other communities, they expect that water will revitalise nearby bushes to ease their responsibilities regarding animal herding and firewood gathering. There are also many communities that lack drinking-water. Here, women first think of the great value of irrigation water to purify some of it and include tap water supply systems to the infrastructure design, since carrying water is generally a woman's task, with support from the children.

These interests can have important consequences for the design of the system. In some cases, women prefer a continuous water allocation during the day and tertiary or field canals that carry water very close to their homes. With this allocation they get more planning flexibility and less work load when fulfilling activities that require water for domestic use. When men are the ones in charge of irrigating, they may prefer non-permanent rotation turns in order to irrigate with a larger flow and in less time. Another common interest of women regarding irrigation design is to avoid night irrigation, which may cause danger and fear because of possible gender-violence, losses of turns due to lack of social control, practical problems in water application and soil erosion, and husbands' jealousy and repercussions. Most often, night irrigation is not compatible with other functions and tasks women already have at home, such as taking care of little children.

> When the husband is at home, in our community he is the one who takes care of irrigation tasks, but in homes where men migrate, women assume all the responsibility. For them is it is really hard. Furthermore, when women are single, they are the ones who have to take up irrigation more strongly. They have to irrigate by night in order not to lose their turns. Since taking care of the children is mama's responsibility, she has to leave the children alone when she goes to irrigate, and so many problems arise when a child wakes up, starts to cry, when children are left unattended. As we used to say, only the bravest woman leaves by night. (Clelia, Guanando, Pungales).

By contrast, we found in some cases that males prefer nocturnal irrigation for obtaining higher irrigation efficiencies ('less evapotranspiration at night') and because, during daytime, the sun burns the leaves if sprinkler irrigation is done. These and other gender-related priorities with respect to irrigation design differ strongly with location. They cannot be assumed but must be investigated empirically.

The above mentioned specific interests especially relate to the *use and purpose of water*. However, there are many other topics related to irrigation but not directly to the use of water itself, in which interests and needs can have gender differences. We may think of the selection of crops to be planted (e.g. whether for domestic consumption or for commercialisation); priorities and time dedicated to different activities in the subsistence strategies; topics that should be dealt with within the users organisation; destination of agricultural credit in the irrigation project; felt training needs; irrigation schedules; proposed irrigation techniques; work modes in infrastructure construction; system management; formulation of norms related to the creation and conservation of rights and obligations, and many others. Generally, when certain interests and needs with respect to irrigation issues are valued differently by the two genders, not only the benefits but also the costs and sacrifices are valued differently.[10] Women, when speaking of their specific problems, interests, sacrifices, limitations and obstacles, often already have ideas about how to seek and realise alternatives or solutions.

Water, just as land, is an element of great power in most Andean communities. Irrigation intervention processes in new or existing systems aim to introduce or redefine the distribution of this powerful resource and, generally, intervention also implies a new distribution of other benefits and obligations related to the 'bundle of rights' that governs peasant irrigation systems. This means that - consciously or not - social relationships necessarily will be subjected to a process of change and redefinition. Within this process of change gender relations will also be modified, in a positive or negative way. Now, if a project has this certainty and consciousness it has also the responsibility of taking care of the direction of these changes, together with the men and women involved in each community.

Equitable distribution of rights

One of the basic principles of Andean communities is the norm that says that rights to irrigation water and decision-making need to be created and earned when a community starts to build its irrigation system. The irrigation rights refer to each family's individual right to use water and infrastructure, as well as to the collective right to participate in decision-making in the management of the irrigation system. Families create their rights during the construction of the system, through their labour and sweat during the mingas, participation in meetings and payment of contributions accorded by the irrigation directorate. They know that after 'creating their own rights' they must 'conserve or re-establish' these rights through system maintenance and rehabilitation works. During the construction of the system, community members not only build up their rights and lay down the management rules but, at the same time, they build and strengthen their specific organisation according to the demands of the zone and its people. Thus, they construct infrastructure, a normative system and an organisation, adapted to the needs and problems found in the area: for them, it is at the same time a process of 'appropriation of the system'.

In the Licto project, this logic was not understood by the State agency that previously, in an isolated way, had been in charge of the construction of the system. It denied peasant participation in the design and execution of the technical, organisational and normative aspects of the system. However, water rights cannot be 'installed' externally simply by means of water-fee payments. It is even worse to try to 'install' an irrigators' organisation. As mentioned before, since the beginning of the 1990s, the project has been re-formulated. Currently, future irrigators are conscious that they are, and must be, the main managers of their system. Together with the assisting institutions they have elaborated strategies to strengthen the water users' organisation, design and implement the work through participation, and collectively generate system regulation norms. The creation of water rights is an important element to this respect. As Edith states:

> Our project is not the same as the neighbouring ancient State canal, already functioning. Here, we ourselves, all irrigators and central leaders have established the rules. Now, it is in the users' hands, that is, the Indians. It is not like in that project, to go to and pay the State, no, to get benefits here, everyone must do it through mingas, fees and assemblies. We know how many people are the beneficiaries in each community and we go with the list to the meetings, or we run the list at the mingas. This way we know who participates in the meetings, the mingas, this is the way we work in the communities, in all labours, mingas, monthly fees, everything. Each year we give a minga certificate to all who have been at the mingas, have paid the monthly fees and have been present at the assemblies. Everything is delivered at the general assemblies, also the certificate. People who did not fulfil their mingas don't get it. Those who are lacking some mingas must catch up, we give them the chance to enter too (Edith, Molobog Licto).

So, unlike the project's previous phases, now users generate their own rights to water and decision-making, under conditions of peasant co-management. However, this has not only meant that the role of peasant management has increased. Also family workloads and specifically women's workloads have increased.[11] Whereas it was possible to buy rights from the State, now you have to work and earn them.

An important question comes to the fore: *Who* are the ones to obtain these self-created water rights? Generally, in irrigation systems only men can be granted water rights, and thus be members of the organisation, because they are the 'heads of the household'. Only widows or unmarried women would have the possibility of participating as members with voice and vote. It is common to see that women cannot be direct members of the user organisations except when the formal head of the household is a woman. So, generally a woman cannot occupy a directive post. Thus, although it were women, more than anyone else, who through their work at mingas have created the family water right - i.e. the right to irrigate and to participate in system management - they have few possibilities to claim and realise this right in practice, nor can they learn to dominate the art of management and develop themselves to progress as persons and as protagonists in community and system development. This way women lose, men lose, the community loses and the peasant irrigation system loses.

This is why in the Licto project it was decided to change the standard irrigation members' list imposed by the state agency. It was modified in such a way that it does not speak anymore of a 'family chief', but of a 'family father' and a 'family mother'. There are many myths that say that men will never accept this change; others say that this change goes against the Andean logic. However, in Licto we have seen that it was often both men and women who promoted and supported changing the conventional scheduling norms for irrigation water rights. And with respect to the Andean rationality: this is based on the idea that the family, both man and woman, is the one entrusted to take care of and guarantee community's survival. If through structural changes in the prevailing conditions, such as male migration, women stay in charge of irrigation, Andean communities usually do not reason from fixed dogmas but gradually change their roles and responsibilities. The resistance to changing the communities' subsistence strategies, in the name of 'Andeanity' but in fact with a macho approach, is usually found within intervening institutions more than in the very peasant communities themselves. In Licto both women and men generate irrigation rights,[12] and women even more than men. Therefore, the organisation has decided to value their work by means of formal rights to water and to decision-making in management positions. With respect to the latter, this is a gradual change, not an abrupt one, and much still has to be done. The process of emancipation is one of successes and setbacks. However, every year there are more women in decision-making positions. Micaela, of the community of Resgualay, states in this respect:

> For me it's very important to have a rights certificate. For us, water means life. That's what we've worked for, we have done many mingas, we have helped with fees too.

Inés, a peasant woman and *promotora campesina*, is one of the organisers in charge of drawing up and explaining irrigation member lists and schedules. She knows more than anybody that this is the way to open spaces, both for men and women, to have the right to water, the right to negotiate one's own interests with State and other agencies and, above all, the right to participate as formal members in the arena of decision-making; in other words, the right to manage irrigation both at the level of the household, the community and the system. In a Directorate meeting she explained this to the leaders:

> Compañeros, we are going to make the irrigation schedule. This list carries the name of the family father and the family mother. Why the name of the family mother? Because women, family mothers, we work too. We have also the right to be in the irrigation list. So, compañero Juan. . . will join in the list with his wife Mary....

Collective, personal and 'collective personal' interests

With respect to themes related to gender in irrigation projects, urgent debates are often mystified and obstructed when erroneous contradictions are brought to the fore: so-called contradictions between *collective objectives* and *individual objectives*. In the Andes, this is mainly expressed by the following opinions: 'the specific attention to gender issues weakens the communities' social struggle against class and ethnic oppression' versus 'the attention to community's unity as a social force distracts the attention from individual, gender-related interests'. We suggest that an approach that aims at reinforcing the 'communal' or the 'collective' power and defence, has to part from the fact of heterogeneity in the community and family, recognising specific interests, at times shared, at times opposed. At the same time, in the practice of Andean peasant irrigation, approaches that search for changing gender relations without considering the interests of the collectivity, have no sense. Besides, changes should not be pursued just in individual cases, but through the collectivity, in order to be more effective and sustainable in the long term. Communal irrigation systems, which often constitute central axes of Andean communities' survival strategies, cannot be managed individually. It is not a question of solidarity among male and female community members but rather the search and necessity of a collective contractual reciprocity: individuals, men and women, must collaborate, often intensively, to sustain this collective activity so fundamental for life in the community. Thus, the 'collective approach' must necessarily imply a gender approach, and this 'gender approach' must incorporate the comprehension of community's survival by means of collective Andean irrigation.

In the end, the satisfaction of an Andean irrigation system relies on the capacity, the creativity, and the power expressed by the peasant organisation, within a reciprocal and equitable structure. The power of an irrigators' organisation that knows how to fight for more equitable inside and outside relations depends on their members: capable and committed men and women, with shared as well as specific needs and knowledge, both participating in management and decision-making. Thus, paradoxically, the recognition of differences is the key for constructing unity. And the strength of this unity is based on the equitable and reciprocal relationship between the constituting parts. In Rosa's words:

> ... We are mostly small peasants, people who don't have a lot of land, maybe some acres; we don't have land enough to be able to say, 'Okay, we are going to compete with the big landowners', but we have indeed demonstrated that we are capable, that we are united, that we know how to fight and that we know how to work to go forward, and that, united, we can achieve a lot. Among the 16 communities we are exchanging ideas, we are exchanging thoughts and, finally, we are arriving at a single conclusion: being united and maintaining solidarity among ourselves is what benefits us, because we must not only improve our organisation, no, we should also be an example for other communities.

The union of the organisation has been brought about among the water users' communities. Therefore, we have achieved true participation, not only as a working mechanism but also as a means to contribute with our ideas, our sacrifice for a project that will sustain our self-provision of products, to improve our household's nutrition.

It is also through women's participation in aspects not only related to work but through the participation in ideas, that we have discovered very worthy women that have become leaders. Thus, with the users' organisation we are going to see, to understand, how valuable and human it is to be solidary among many friends. There have been diverse ideas, diverse opinions, and in the end we have arrived at something that could be called joint conclusions. An effort where we not only do physical work but also the work of becoming more aware, work of going forward, even to be an example for other regions, for other places, and to be also a bit like a driving motor for developing a model of a new organisation, and in this way suggest alternatives so our short-term governments recognise that we too can be organised, that we too can advance by means of our own effort, and that they have to keep their word and give us the resources that belong to us. Because we are organised, and organised we are going to demand, organised we are going to construct a better world, a new society, more just, more human, where all of us have better living conditions.

We are going to carry on and we want to be like a radio, to communicate with the rest of the people, maybe not only in our country but also in others. And thus begin to get listened to and valued as human beings by our governments.

Our irrigation system, we have to defend it, we have to defend it because it is our work and it cost us much effort. So many mingas, so many meetings, so many commissions, so many problems we have faced in the Guargualla irrigation project! And we have to defend it because they cannot impose on us, not the landowners, not the State, they cannot leave us without this project that has been achieved with the organisation's effort, with the effort of all, with the effort of people that have stopped sleeping, of women who have left their duties at home, we have had to go to work in the mingas while carrying our children, all this, we have to defend it and nobody can take it away from us. We have to defend it to death because of what it cost us, of how much it hurt, and we can't let nobody take from us what has cost us so much sacrifice.

We have seen also that women have been discovered here, women who before did not have the chance to demonstrate their capacities. We have seen women who begin to lead, women who become members of directorates, besides women's participation in workdays. But we don't think that it must be participation only in the labour tasks, no, the struggle is also to become more aware of their role as women, as mothers, but more than anything, as persons, and as thinking persons!

Notes

1   This chapter is based on the authors' book: *Mujer Campesina e Intervención en el Riego Andino. Sistemas de Riego y Relaciones de Género.* ('Peasant Women and Intervention in Andean Irrigation. Irrigation Systems and Gender Relations') The book presents an analysis of central topics that combine irrigation & gender themes, on the basis of life stories of Licto women. These central topics are: social organisation of irrigation; promotion and training processes in irrigation; processes of participatory construction in irrigation; generation of irrigation rights; access to water as a strategic resource; control over irrigation benefits; consequences of women's work overload in irrigation; and self-management and formation of leaders in irrigation. We would like to thank Gloria Dávila, Magdalena Mayorca, Hugo van Drunen and Cily Keizer for their valuable comments.

2   Mixing up of indigenous and white/mestizo people. *Mestizaje* refers also to the intentional, bio-political process of assimilating indigenous people and their culture in main stream (white and mestizo) society, where they must abandon their cultural and ethnic backgrounds.

3   Indigenous woman's clothing.

4   The *minga* is a communal labour day in the Andes. However, historically, in many cases the dominating classes expropriated this reciprocal labour relation from the communities, using it for their own class interests (obligatory working days for the peasants and indigenous population). In some cases, as we will see later in this chapter, communities have 're-conquered' the communal and reciprocal contents of the minga.

5   Acronym in Spanish of the Ecuadorian Centre of Agricultural Services. This NGO received support from COSUDE (Swiss Development Co-operation) and SNV (Netherlands Development Organisation).

6   Acronym in Spanish of the Licto Peasant Organisations Corporation.

7   Frantz Fanon (*Peau noire, masques blanques* (1952); *Les damnés de la terre* (1961)) and after him various others, have analysed this process of internalising colonisation and racism in much depth. See also Peggy Reeves Sanday (1986) for an analysis of the Colonial system and its effects on gender relations.

8   A very common bias in irrigation projects is that it is presupposed that all beneficiaries live in a family consisting of a man, a woman and children, and sometimes other relatives. The reality, in many cases, is different, both due to the male migration phenomenon and other reasons (single mothers, widows, etc.). The man is considered as the 'head of the household' in all situations; it is assumed that he provides the main family income, he must make decisions and take responsibility for the execution of the project, with just the 'help' from his wife, and afterwards he is considered to distribute the benefits of all technical and social support. These benefits can be both tangible project effects, such as agricultural production, financial resources, agricultural tools, etc., and less visible ones, such as received training and knowledge, contacts, information and others.

9   It would be too easy and mistaken to refer to irrigation interventions only, when searching for the causes of injustices in irrigation-related gender relationships. Stories such as Rosa's and those of many other women show that irrigation can be *both* an instrument to generate or to intensify social injustice, and a vehicle for achieving emancipation and fighting for equity. An 'irrigation-centric' analysis to study injustices in the field of 'Irrigation & Gender' can never be complete. As mentioned before, gender relations in irrigation systems are part of the wider social relations and power structures, so, other relationships and social forces outside the direct irrigation (intervention) context have an equally important influence over gender relations. Furthermore, not only the Andean community but also the very support institutions are within this wider context of unjust gender relationships. A self-analysis is essential, not only related to *biases and blindness* but also to *institutional relationships and interests*. In Popular Education projects, a 'self-diagnostic' often is common practice. However, this almost always refers to a process in which institutional promoters facilitate a self-diagnostic process of problems and perspectives by and for peasants; it seldom refers to the crucial *internal* diagnosis of the sup-

port institution itself, 'in charge of' irrigation interventions. In fact, from this self-analysis other topics will come to the fore, even topics unrelated to irrigation, that do have a central impact on possible institutional gender strategies in irrigation development. It can be observed, for example, that the great majority of development agencies, including NGOs, produce a strong contradiction when they intervene in Andean communities: while the discourse and the ideology proclaimed are those of Popular Education and of horizontal relationships with the target-groups, institutional practice often is characterised by a rigid hierarchy and a verticality that penetrates all institutional activities. This necessarily influences the so-called 'participatory' and gender-focused planning process. Other important points to be brought to the fore in this institutional self-analysis are the resistance that often exists against really using a gender approach, and the low representation of women in high decision-making instances in the institutions and irrigation projects. Furthermore, technical labour and professions, often institutionally dominated by men, have a higher valuation than 'social' and 'gender' programmes.

Support institutions, recognising their own interests, can contribute with physical and social tools to accompany the most oppressed and subordinate people in the process of social change. Here, a profound analysis of the relative powers of negotiation is of utmost importance. In this analysis also other power relations intervene that cross gender relations, such as class, ethnic, educational, cast and age relationships. Social change that emerges from this 'political arena' with conflicting interests, is not produced without struggle, conflicts and social costs. Generally, it is not the institutions and their field teams that are the ones affected by the risks and problems of social change, but the very peasant women. Therefore, in planning strategies and objectives it is essential that women themselves identify their own problems and plan their own objectives, since they are the ones who have to engage in their own struggle. In this struggle they consider also the family and communal interests. In the end, when we talk about gender we talk about power, and power can hardly be planned with anticipation. It is a question of struggle and negotiation. Nevertheless, actions *can* be planned in such a way that they contribute to the generation or strengthening of processes that lead to changing inequitable power structures.

10 It is common that irrigation projects' activities are planned based on the supposition that 'peasant' is a synonym for 'irrigator', as if men and women work full time in irrigation. However, Andean peasant economy strategies require that a peasant family dedicates time to other rural and urban activities outside irrigation. Interventions very seldom question the work loads they provoke, the priorities for establishing schedules and the lack of co-ordination with other components of peasant subsistence strategies. This problem specially affects women.

11 In Arroyo & Boelens (1997) Licto women analyse this problem and its possible solutions.

12 When we speak of *water rights*, it has been suggested that, very often, these are extremely important for women to enable them to participate in decision-making and get irrigation water. However, in practice this right does not necessarily coincide with the actual (and equitable) *access to water*. There are several limitations that hamper the acquisition of the quantity and timing of water according to the theoretical and agreed-upon right. For an analysis see Arroyo & Boelens (1997). Another key issue dealt with is: Who has *control* (decision power) over the final *benefits of irrigation*, i.e. agricultural production? The distribution of control between men and women over agricultural production has much to do with sexual division of labour itself, which is very heterogeneous in the Andes. Carmen Diana Deere and Magdalena León de Leal (1981) write in this respect that it is influenced by the degree of household's incorporation into the capitalistic process of production, as well as the social differentiation between peasant families of a region. Family access to means of production influences, and has a narrow relation with, the sexual composition of the familial labour force. The poorer the families (less access to means of production), the more women participate in the household's agricultural production. In these cases, men migrate in larger numbers. Furthermore, these families cannot contract farm labourers, so that women have to carry out the larger part of productive tasks. In these cases, sexual division of labour is less rigid, since all family members have to fight for subsistence. Barbara Deutsch Lynch (1991) arrives at the same conclusion.

approaches are examined, in order to facilitate a more adequate analysis and to discuss some pathways that may lead to a more equitable process of peasant irrigation development.

Water users' organisations

Peasant knowledge

In the Andes setting, as in other regions of the world with unpredictable climates and unstable, complex geophysical conditions, it is important to highlight a particular, fundamental characteristic of peasant irrigation systems: more than almost any other economic activity or rural development issue, irrigation is grounded in *mutual dependence and intrinsic obligations for intensive co-operation* among users. Irrigation forces people to operate collectively, permanently, every day. It is impossible to manage a peasant system in this difficult Andean context just with individuals or small groups: intra- and inter-community collaboration and their respective collective agreements are indispensable prerequisites to ensure access to and utilisation of water. This fact, in combination with the increasing scarcity of water, can lead to the appearance of strong organisations, but also to long-lasting, intense conflicts.

The need to survive through collective action, together with the shortage of irrigation water and the rooting of irrigation practice in other social and productive spheres of peasant coexistence, all lead to Andean peasants having a specific vision of irrigation organisation, which often differs from the concepts of outside institutions:

- Whereas State agencies usually place great emphasis on the importance of formalised structures in the irrigation organisation, peasants pay more attention to the issues of why organise or why not, for which objectives and how and when. Because of this friction, very commonly, in bureaucratically or jointly managed systems formal organisational structures do not correspond to actual organisational practice.
- Whereas many support institutions stress the need to establish purely functional users' organisations that will operate and maintain the irrigation system only, those peasant systems that best succeed, in addition to having clear, functional rules for irrigation, often know how to orient their organisations toward multiple social and productive functions.
- Although several political currents see peasant and grassroots organisation as an end, for peasants - especially in the field of irrigation - organisation is a *process* and a *means* (although it does have political effect and potential for change). In the peasant world, water users do not work with an abstract definition of equity: they keep their eyes on concrete matters, on consequences in direct practice.

It is especially the peasants' own knowledge and perceptions regarding the organisation of users, rather than universal schemes and concepts, which will have to constitute the foundation and starting point for any process of organisation-strengthening and capacity-building. Both community and its individuals have their specific experiences and knowledge[4], constantly enriched during social interactions in the field of irrigation. Peasant systems which are strong and sustainable have a 'routine lore' for irrigation management under common, stable situations, which is institutionalised in management procedures. They also have a 'creative lore' to address unforeseen changes (such as landslides), conjunctural discontinuities (such as redefinitions of the water law and the product market) or unexpected situations of scarcity (such as intense droughts), and to make changes and improvements in the irrigation system. The two types of knowledge are indispensable for system sustainability.

In co-managed irrigation development processes, it is crucial to recover and incorporate these peasant lore components.[5] For example, in Ecuador's Central Highlands, a participatory research was carried out (based on previous work on peasant organisation: SNV 1992a; SNV-UNL 1994) in order to co-formulate and analyse the local key variables for a strong organisation, in a specific system (Licto, Chimborazo, Table 37.1). Not only the end results, but above all the process of discussing and selecting the variables with the water users and discovering, expressing and analysing, among peasants and technicians, the contents and indicators of the variables, proved to be an important step in the process of organisation-strengthening in a recently created system.

Category of variables	Variables
Roots in users' group	• Representativeness • Identity and Identification • Confidence / Credibility of the organisation
Internal structure and operation	• Equity • Managerial and leadership capacity • Decision-making and Internal democracy • Cohesion • Institutional knowledge and learning • Transparency and clarity of management • Solidarity • Conflict management and mastery • Continuity /Stability
Activities and outcomes	• Problem-solving capacity and Effectiveness • Independence /Autonomy • Degree of integration • Coherence
Referential factors	• Legitimacy • Alliance-building and networking capacity • Capacity for negotiation

Table 37.1: Variables[6] to discuss and characterise the strength of a users' organisation (case of Licto, Ecuador). Source: based on SNV 1992a; Van der Does 1994; SNV-UNL 1994; CESA 1994; Boelens 1995.

Exchanging experiences with other peasant systems can offer important opportunities for learning. For example, in the same region of Ecuador, in 1996, a contest was held among various peasant irrigation systems to tell their stories: 'Let's talk about justice in our irrigation system'. The discussion among peasants was spread by the peasant and indigenous radio station, to broadcast reflection on the theme to many other irrigation systems. These are just a few examples from many other possibilities, such as irrigation excursions, gatherings, festivals, etc., to promote exchanges among peasants and among peasant organisations and support institutions. They stimulate the generation of new knowledge and proposals to empower the irrigators' organisation.

This mutual hybridisation of knowledge in the field of irrigation, among peasants and between peasants and academics, also has the potential to unmask and break up the hegemony of the dominant discourse, which presumes to present 'universal scientific solutions to modernise agriculture' based on imposing outside technologies and organisational models. It is necessary to change the relations of knowledge production that ideologically underpin unjust structures (Fals Borda 1985) and break up the process of externalising peasant knowledge.

Organisational levels and characteristics

'Probably there are as many ways to allocate and distribute as there are types of water and organisational levels within Andean society (family, inter-family group, community, *ayllu*, ethnic group, etc.) ... As a result of or response to the relationship of dialogue among the types of water and different organisational levels present in society, there are various entities within a community to distribute water, and each community member may belong to several of them' (Greslou 1989). Informal forms of organisation can play a highly important role in irrigation, for example in the distribution of water. Therefore, our approach must go beyond just formal Users' Associations (the Board, the Committee, etc.) and formalised rules and practices, even though they may be a key element in peasants' organisational practice in zones with irrigation.

Regarding organisational or management levels in peasant irrigation, the most common ones are the family level (often the extended family), the inter-family or group level (e.g., irrigators on a distributary canal, or the neighbourhood irrigation committee), the communal level (the peasant community), the inter-community level (e.g. the supra-communal irrigators' organisation) and the inter-institutional level (e.g. the watershed boards, the irrigation confederations at the regional or national level, and inter-institutional consortia comprising peasant organisations and development institutions). The existence of effective networks, which achieve appropriate co-ordination and communication *among* organisational levels, characterises the strength of the organisational system overall, and is essential for irrigation system management and defence of irrigators' interests.[7]

Organisational levels interact and overlap in regard to social actors and functions. However, in general the lower levels deal mainly with water and infrastructure management (technical management, oversight of physical processes in irrigation), intermediate levels seek to control people's attitudes (organisational management of the irrigation system) and higher levels attempt to influence agricultural policies regarding water resources (control over socio-economic and political processes) (see Bolding *et al.* 1995).

Although there is social differentiation in any irrigation system, and there will be more in one than in the other, it is important to observe that several traits of irrigation organisation in the Andes (see attachment), together with the characteristics of the Andean peasant economy (see Ch. 21 and 22), have a major impact on curbing the process of unfair development, and evening out unequal powers. A few examples, among many others, include the requirement of being a community member complying with the contributions to collective tasks (even outside the domain of irrigation) in order to have access to irrigation; equal votes for each family; collective monitoring; contractual reciprocity; collective ownership of the system; rotation of management positions; inter-dependence among families; mutual accountability among leaders and members; investment of work and not (only) money to gain and maintain irrigation rights, etc. Communities also have various rules to counteract speculation regarding the prices of water and irrigated land. In general, such mechanisms control and/or suppress individual, opportunistic attitudes that go against the collective group's interests. The situation may often be more complicated in those communities that are anchored in large bureaucratic systems (see Boelens 1995), (co)managed by various institutions, a topic that falls outside this analysis.

Autonomy and assistance

It is a widespread assumption that poor peasant groups require outside assistance - with grassroots educators, social and technical promoters, change catalysts, animators, interactive designers, participatory researchers or others - to carry out a process of organisation-building and irrigation development. However, it is useful to observe that in most cases peasants do not need outside educators to become aware of their oppression and poverty, nor to critically analyse them. Moreover, most small peasant systems in the Andes have been 'catalysed' by the (leaders of the) users themselves, investigated and organised by them, and designed and constructed endogenously. Sometimes this has happened with their own resources, but in many cases the communities have raised the necessary legal, financial or technical backing to create their system according to their own vision of viability and operation, with them designing their own 'project' interactively, raising their fellow irrigators' consciousness, and forming the necessary strategic alliances[8].

Nor is it a question of denying the possible importance of a process of intervention in certain other cases. Especially when it is requested by the consensus of a peasant population and in systems with relatively complex design, construction and management requirements, assistance may be vitally important. In such situations, advisory institutions can, depending on the case, share the financial and time-related risks, conduct studies and technical constructions of great complexity, co-formulate strategies for interactive design, co-manage the system's organisation-building, support exchanges, platforms, networks and alliances, provide key information and contacts, co-systematise and analyse experiences, etc., providing the peasant population maintains the last word, and future dependence is avoided.

Design of artificial institutions

In good functioning peasant-managed irrigation systems, users have institutionalised the management of many routine, recurrent operational activities. Rules, roles, procedures, etc. have been crystallised in organisational structures in order to promote efficiency and facilitate clear day-to-day practices. This institutionalisation of peasant behaviours varies from one irrigation system to the next, reflecting the different customs and experiences and responding to the needs and institutional landscape of each locality. However, a static, uniform interpretation of this practice of endogenous institutionalisation, in combination with the existence of centralised legislation and the rigid application of 'institution-building' approaches in intervention policies, has established the illusion that it would be possible to 'design peasant irrigation organisations' according to a recipe-book, based on pre-established criteria, national regulations and universalising principles.

It is true: effective irrigation system management requires strong peasant institutions. They also play a major role in achieving a more equitable distribution of benefits and responsibilities and, in general, these institutions do not emerge 'automatically'. However, rather than accompanying users in the search to design their own specific organisation which are suited to the new challenges, 'paper organisations' have often arisen. These all to often institutionalise and reinforce existing injustices, and are frequently defined as 'project counterparts'. In practice, they have often been created for channelling the interests and messages of intervening institutions and State agencies, or for reinforcing national legal irrigation regulations. 'Many irrigation projects pay lip service to local level participation but pay little heed to existing indigenous management strategies…. Projects which impose preconceived values and organisational models are often unsuccessful, lead to conflict, and represent instruments of control rather than of enhanced production'. (Gelles 1993)

In many cases, these new artificial organisations have attempted to supplant existing peasant grassroots organisations. An intervention process that does not take as its starting-point, in a critical dialectical manner, the local logic and considerations regarding organisation, will usually destroy local capacities rather than reinforcing the collectivity's potential. It will also ignore peasant concepts regarding equitable distribution of benefits and burdens as basic inputs for building up organisational sustainability and social justice in irrigation.

Chapter 8 discussed the logic of inter-dependence, congruence and unity of the three central elements of a peasant irrigation system: from the creation of the system onwards, there is constant interaction among the *organisational* system, the *normative* system and the *infrastructural* system. 'A change in one of them entails changes in the others'; otherwise, the system loses management coherence and sustainability. How different is the logic for intervention in many irrigation projects that break up this unity and its basic congruence. They generally follow a rigid project cycle that, in practice, is often expressed as follows (Boelens & Doornbos 1996, see fig. 37.1):

1   *Planning, design and construction.* First (T1), they conduct the planning, design and construction of the *infrastructure*, generally led by civil engineers, hydrologists and planners. Peasant participation means eliciting 'social' data and obtaining unpaid labour. Designs are often 'complete, detailed and final', leaving little room for changes or discussion. The rigidity rules out any process of negotiation or adjustment with users.[9]

2   *Implementation.* In a second phase (T2), social promoters and professionals arrive, to set up the irrigators' *organisation* and 'get the system working according to the technical design', often with 'proven' organisational models, and - ironically - with participatory methods.

3   *Follow-up.* Next (T3), legal training is provided to explain the *rules* of play to the peasants: their rights (scheduling, etc.) and their obligations (fees, cleaning, etc.). Agronomists join the club to explain and train on the production logic under the new conditions of irrigated agriculture.

Figure 37.1: Dynamics of an irrigation system designed according to a process of 'social and legal engineering' (see Ch. 8)

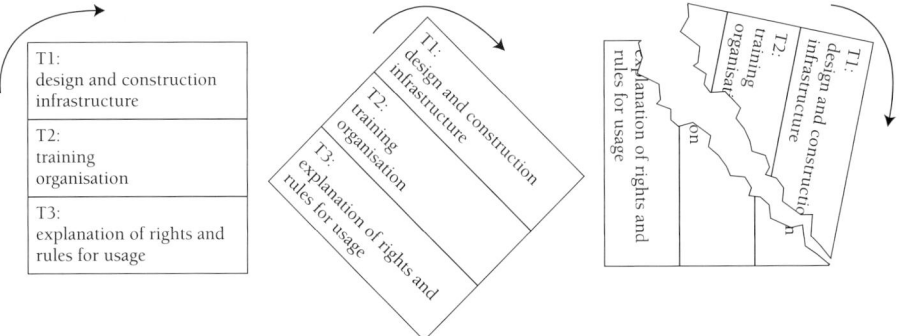

Another common problem of many irrigation projects is the separation of the technical and economic aspects from the socio-organisational and normative issues. The last project phases - to organise and train users - are sometimes characterised by application of participatory methodologies and grassroots communication techniques. However, participatory extension and formation of an irrigators' organisation as phases *after* the infrastructure has been designed and constructed means pushing peasant users and their existing relationships into a technical mould that has been pre-established by outside concepts (Apollin & Boelens 1996).

Intervention experiences in already existing peasant systems are not always more encouraging, since infrastructure rehabilitation processes often break up normative systems, because they do not consider the peasant logic of generating and conserving water rights. Users have generated their individual and collective irrigation rights by investing in the creation of irrigation infrastructure that, at the same time, has become collective property. This is normally the central axis and a strong foundation for social action in peasant irrigation. Unconscious rehabilitation activities in peasant systems often deny, disorganise and destroy these rights, thus breaking up collective social action (see also Coward 1986; Gerbrandy & Hoogendam 1996).

Peasant self-reliance and assistance

Figure 37.2a outlines endogenous irrigation development in peasant systems, with the inter-dependence and unity among the organisational, normative and infrastructural systems mentioned above. These three form a 'wheel' and peasant management, with its strategic alliances and organisational levels, makes this wheel 'go round', building and adapting property rights in the system.

In those cases where the movement of the wheel has been obstructed, or when certain resources and capacities that peasants require are lacking, an assistance process may be very useful. This process must not supplant the existing wheel, but rather give it the necessary push to continue moving in a lasting manner, in the direction decided by consensus (Fig. 37.2b).[10] This challenge of a horizontal assistance process is equally valid in co-managed systems, whether permanent co-management or temporary.[11]

Figure 37.2a: Relationship of interdependence among the infrastructure, rights and organisation in endogenous design and management processes.

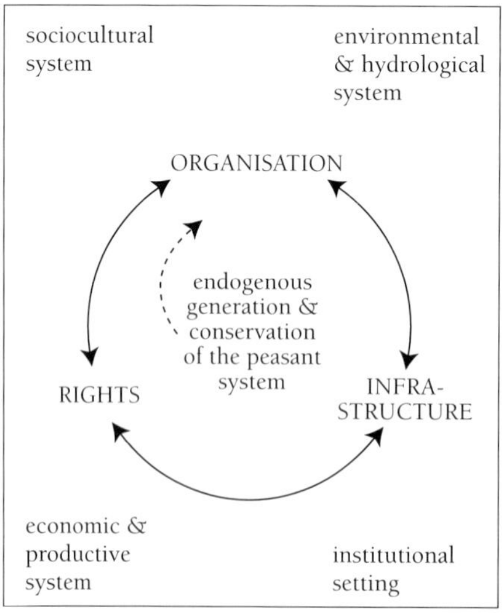

Figure 37.2b: Process of assistance for endogenous design and management.

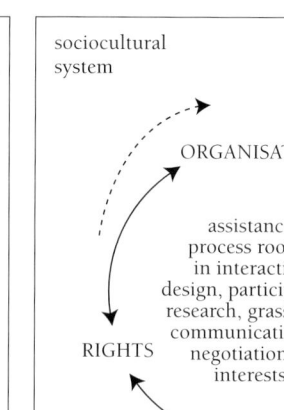

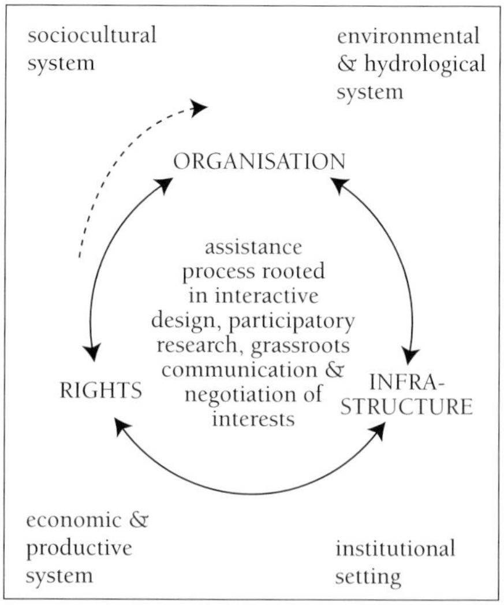

The primary criterion in peasant irrigation development must be their own rationality, their own 'wheel', in combination with critical, consensus-based self analysis by the users, amidst both diverging and shared interests. Therefore, interactive design processes[12] and assistance for peasant systems must answer the question: Who is the *protagonist* in irrigation development?

> Because of the insecurity and insufficiency of water supply from their community's old canal, the peasants of Ceceles (Chimborazo, Ecuador) had struggled to expand their water flow by participating in another system, which would bring a new secondary canal to their community. The command areas of both canals would overlap, but this new, higher canal would provide more water to the community, serving an even larger area than the old system. A long, intensive discussion ensued when participatory research was conducted, and many peasant meetings were held to establish the basic criteria for future distribution of the water. Should two separate systems be made in the same irrigation area, in order to respect the previous rights? Should the flows be mixed in order to apply a single distribution system? Should the water be mixed into a single system, but respecting the previous system's rights? How to realise these or other options technically and organisationally? and so on. Several interest groups were in opposition to each other, long before the infrastructure was built. This finally resulted in the basic criterion that was shared by most of the users: *organisational unity and strength,* with a single system, mixing the water and distributing it through a single scheduling arrangement. Existing rights should change, and everyone would be obliged to participate in the new system. The support institution agreed with this peasant decision, although it had expected a decision recognising the existing rights, since prior rights are usually highly valued and powerful in the Andes (See Boelens & Doornbos 1996).

Basically, the peasant communities themselves will have to build and conserve their irrigation rights, by investing their capacities and efforts in the irrigation system. They have to decide with whom to interact in developing their irrigation system, on the basis of their analysis of the surrounding actors and structures. Therefore, it is necessary for development professionals and institutions to realise and take seriously that they are the ones participating in the peasant reality, and not the other way round. This, however, is not the same as 'peasantism', 'populism', 'short-term-ism', etc. On the contrary, it is necessary for *both* peasant organisations and advisory institutions to discuss and explicitly define the *intervention criteria.* These are the inputs for a more open negotiation process, in which they must verify the mutual feasibility - or impossibility - of collaborating with reciprocal benefits[13].

As a result of this negotiation, the *terms of co-operation* must be clarified and made explicit, to condition contributions and set commitments, for both intervening institutions and users (see Hendriks 1994)[14]. The relationship arising in this way is dialectical and involves mutual constructive criticism. Both parties also have the chance to say 'no, except when…'. Basic rules and concepts for equitable distribution of water (rights and obligations) must be an integral part of these criteria and terms. They constitute the indispensable bases, both for franker, more fruitful subsequent negotiations, and for deliberate co-definition of intervention strategies.

At the beginning of the project to rehabilitate the old La Estrella canal in Mollepata (Cusco, Peru), the peasants and the support institution decided, after many meetings and discussions, that one of the central criteria for intervention would be equal distribution of water to all families belonging to the four participating communities. 'Each member is entitled to the equivalent of 1 l/sec.' (Flores & Olazával 1993). After the reconstruction process and during system operation, the concrete expression of this allocation (in terms of flow and turn duration per plot) was sometimes adapted, according to communities' characteristics and the irrigators' growing skill, but they firmly kept to the basic agreement on each family's share. This proved to be very important to overcome demands by wealthier farmers, conflicts between communities, and the need to hold the organisation together through the difficult stages of shared project management. The minimal levels of contributions by each member, in days of work, were adapted to this basic right. Another co-defined criterion, the peasants' self-reliant management of the system after the co-management stage, was also materialised in clear terms of co-operation, indicating the mutual responsibilities of peasants and the institution, in regard to the project's financial, technical and socio-organisational aspects (also see Hendriks 1988; Boelens & Temmink 1990).

During implementation of the irrigation system in Patococha (Cañar, Ecuador), the peasant organisation and governmental agency had never established clear criteria or agreements about the rights and obligations of future users. Only the rigid national criteria for distribution were binding (water supply according to fees paid, which goes largely unenforced in practice). When the main system was finally built, the peasant organisation asked for the water not to be delivered to the irrigation area until all families had completed the minimum of 40 workdays that, according to the organisation, would entitle them to water rights. Because of the need to obtain short-term results, the governmental institution did not back this criterion, nor were other criteria established, or sufficient support programmes for internal irrigation management. For many years, water was distributed in a disorderly, inequitable manner, and peasants' contributions and work to sustain the system were minimal, and hardly recorded.

As mentioned by Gianotten & De Wit (1987) and Hendriks (1994), it is necessary to get rid of the classic institutional attitude of promoting the project by convincing the peasants of the benefits it will provide. Instead of *convincing* them, the attitude should be one of *questioning*. Consequently, the peasant organisation is encouraged to reflect on its own capacities, project feasibility, system sustainability, internal injustice, etc. Similarly, the peasant organisation will have to question the promoting institution, and seek more viable counter-proposals. In practice, both counterparts - the institution and the peasant organisation - tend to underestimate the capacities, qualities, time and resources required to set up an irrigation system of a given complexity[15]. It is not enough for the project to be 'participatory' - it must have a sound technical, economic and socio-organisational foundation. This, in order not to be faced with the common reality, further down the road, that they have been fooling themselves with a system which fails from the moment of its implementation, causing maintenance obligations far beyond the benefits generated or demanding, for operation and maintenance, a mobilisation of peasant resources in excess of those available (see also Hendriks 1994).

A methodology based on questioning strengthens both peasants' valuation of their own inputs, their power to demand and negotiate, as well as their capacity for analysis and counter-proposals. These are important elements in order to reinforce, at the same time, the political counter-weight that peasants can wield in society at large.

Collaboration this way does not work on the basis of an assumed harmony of interests but rather will recognise and make explicit the diverging interests as a basis for establishing a more honest negotiation. This also makes it feasible for assistance to *fit into the dynamics of peasants' own irrigation development,* encouraging and reinforcing it. Peasants' own dynamics lead to building up their own normative system (including, among other issues, property rights) and their 'hydraulic identity': a local identity that is interwoven and articulated with the other identities that belong to Andean peasants, such as the indigenous, the peasant, or, in general, the Andean identity. (See Figure 37.3). It is necessary to dispose of the current linear view of 'project development' with its pre-established contents of the project phases. Instead, we should try to understand the dynamic, 'loop-structured' logic of rural change and endogenous peasant irrigation development of which, at a certain point in time and space, project intervention *may* be an element; an *element* which does or does not take into consideration the logic of existing reality.

Figure 37.3: Schematic representation of the dynamics of peasant irrigation development: a process through which management capacity is strengthened and local 'hydraulic identity' is constructed. Source: Based on Boelens & Doornbos (1996) and Mollinga (1997).

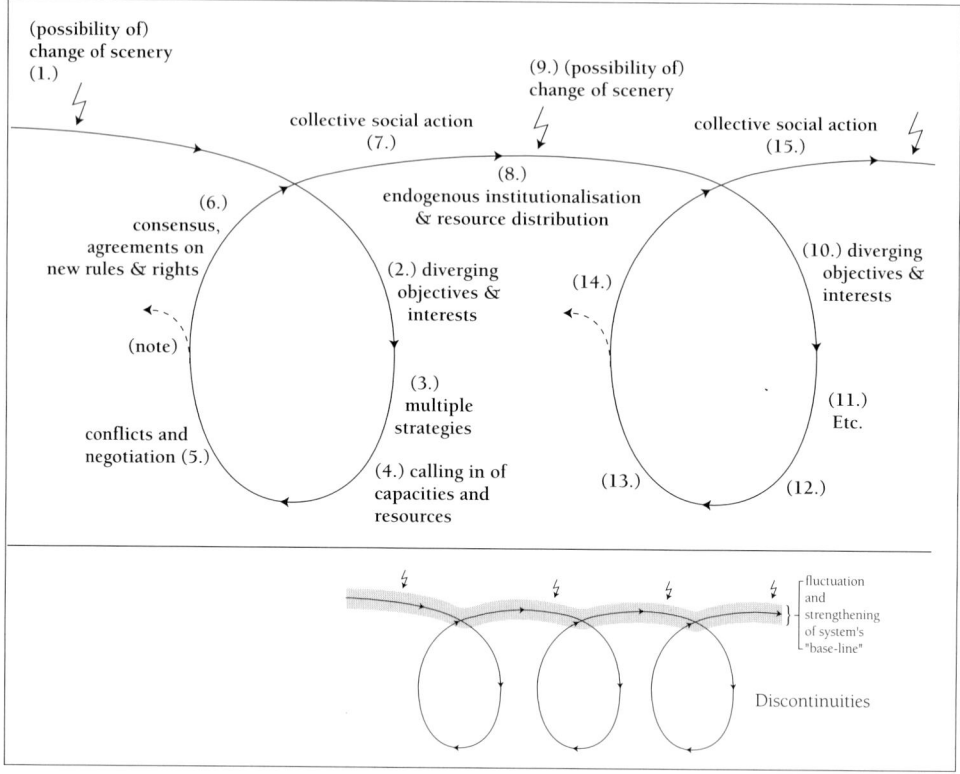

(1) **Change of scenery**: Changes or possibilities for change may have multiple sources and causes, for example, the possibility of an irrigation intervention, changes in the legal framework, a sudden situation of water shortage, strong market price fluctuations, and so on.

(2) **Diverging objectives and interests**: Differentiation of social groups happens both within the peasant population and between peasants and other actors ('internal' and 'external' to the irrigation system). Therefore, interests in irrigation development are characteristically quite divergent.

(3) **Multiple strategies**: Different interest groups formulate their strategies in different ways and create or restructure a range of networks and organisational forms, generally informal, to pursue their aims.

(4) **Calling in of capacities and resources**: Strategies become concrete through the calling in and use of specific resources. These may be mobilised from inside or outside the interest group, and the access to them generally is unequal. Important resources comprise human capacities (both individual and collective), social relations, images (e.g. authorities granted consciously or unconsciously to politicians, specialists, etc.), financial means, material and technical inputs, the spoken word (e.g. at meetings), and the written word (e.g. internal regulations, laws, project documents).

(5) **Conflicts and negotiation**: Negotiation platforms may be formal and institutionalised, or informal and everyday. In these negotiations, the processes of technological, normative and organisational change in peasant irrigation become concrete.

(6) **Agreements and consensus**: In Andean systems, commitments are often based on the majority opinion (for example, the decision of a General Assembly). This does not mean that certain individuals could not play a major role in 'moulding' this opinion. Nevertheless, the consensus is generally based on the convergence of certain collective interests. The most important one is the need to operate and sustain the irrigation system, which results in the obligation to manage it collectively. If such collective objectives are formulated, this does *not* imply that any total, permanent harmony of interests has been achieved.

* **(Note)**: In the case of imposed decisions, or failure to achieve commitments, at this point of the spiral 'the peasant dynamic breaks down'. The imposition may be 'internal' (e.g. by leaders or local elites) or 'external' (e.g. by development institutions or the State).

(7) **Collective social action**: *Collective contractual reciprocity* (mutual collaboration at the level of individual and collective properties, as a fundamental condition for subsistence), jointly with *creation and consolidation of irrigation rights* and appropriation of the system (shared property), often are the foundation for collective action in peasant irrigation. In this cohesion, social actors with specific strengths and deficiencies complement each other. Peasants know that the reproduction of their families, irrigation system and community often also depends on strategic pacts, in which stakeholders with different interests come together.

(8) **Endogenous institutionalisation and resource distribution**: Users institutionalise their new agreements, rules and procedures within their organisational framework and within their particular system management, thereby (re)generating and reinforcing their hydraulic identity.

The diagram also illustrates that fitting into this process in order to assist in endogenous development of peasant irrigation involves accepting that it is impossible to plan, in a detailed, precise manner, the results of the intervention. To achieve success and sustainability, there must be a process of open negotiation without pre-established conclusions, which may lead to unexpected outcomes. Among other aspects, this is one of the reasons why many development institutions are reluctant to take part in an endogenous development process. Often, they are concerned about losing control over their project objectives, resources, timeframes and outcomes, if they are to accept a logic that is different from their own: a logic in which much of clarity in goal-setting is not done in detail beforehand, but during project negotiations.

Nevertheless, an effective, interactive assistance effort does not mean 'starting from scratch and being willing to try anything'. On the contrary, as was mentioned before, in the first phase of the encounter it is necessary to make the existing interests and the mutual criteria for intervention as explicit as possible, in order to be able to negotiate and clarify the fundamental terms of co-operation, even before concretely defining the final collaboration. Much initial discussion and clarity, with little rigidity, form a setting in which *creativity* can flourish, which is so important for adapting irrigation systems to local, specific needs.

Institutions that do not choose a more flexible, peasant-type approach will *also* encounter unexpected outcomes and continual changes. However, unlike projects seeking to support peasants' own self-reliant efforts, the consequences of rigid planning and pre-established goals are lasting disappointment and undermining of local capacity for action, or lead to true peasant resistance. Peasant irrigation entails, in fact, the existence of conflicts and rivalries, both internal and external. However, there are different types of conflict: some can and should be avoided, whereas others may provide the basis for the negotiation that leads to peasant-controlled develop-ment. Recognising the interests and contradictions, and knowing how to handle conflicts, are pivotal issues.

Empowerment

Peasants need to have enough room for manoeuvre (Van der Ploeg, Ch. 4) or strategic space (Ruijven & Uit het Broek 1992) to be able to act in a way which will satisfy and defend their interests. This space is created by the access that families or the organisation have to strategic resources and by their power to make decisions about these resources (see SNV 1992b). The use and expansion of this strategic space is a key part of the process of peasant empowerment, at the level of individuals and family units, and collectively.

In each process of empowerment, the acquisition of power in the social, economic, psychological and political domains of people's life is central. Regarding irrigation development, the continuous interaction of collective action and reflection is an important way to approach this goal. The process begins at the local level, but effec-tive and autonomous control of irrigation cannot be achieved by just organising 'inwardly'. Organisation must expand to higher levels in order to be effective and sus-tainable enough (see Friedmann 1992). Irrigation management is interwoven in overall production relationships. Not only at the micro level but also at the level of economic, political, legal and institutional structures there are major stumbling-blocks to the process of endogenous (re) production. The role of the State, whether centralised or decentralised, often greatly influences the empowerment or disem-powerment of local systems. Generally its function is ambiguous, since, depending on the situation, its impact may mean support for local management of peasant sys-tems, or the conservation of exploiting relationships and expropriation of peasants' returns on their work[16].

So, the notions of participatory democracy and peasants' political counter-weight go beyond the internal structures of irrigators' organisations: a structural change is required in the injustices of society at large. Peasant organisation must achieve inward, vertical and horizontal strengthening and linkages in order to defend equity and their interests regarding water resources (see Esman & Uphoff 1984; Ruijven & Uit het Broek 1992). Vertical linking could mean, for example, a regional or national *peasant or indigenous confederation* to defend these people's interests regarding water, or forming democratic, *multi-sectoral committees* at the watershed level, or a region-al or national *irrigators' confederation*[17], according to the particular features and rural history of each country. Horizontal linking could involve peasant organisations' exchanges of experiences and knowledge, and the creation of strategic networks and alliances.

However, in subsistence economies, peasants often want to first assure the (re) pro-duction of their own household unit, community and irrigation system. In general, local and short-range objectives necessarily prevail over longer-term structural change objectives. In order to achieve empowerment at higher levels as well, one must go beyond just 'ideological reflections' on structural, macro changes, to work on creating the concrete conditions at the local level that must enable this process of horizontal and vertical linking[18]. Concretising a sustainable local irrigation system is thus often an important step for peasants, since a system that is well-sustained and consciously organised offers a certain degree of economic security, common rights and a good organisational framework. It is also like a nest, sheltering an internal school for capacity-building, reflection and organisation, and offering a home base for wider organisational activities. Therefore, it is precisely the collectively managed irrigation system, which has the potential, first of all, to offer the basic 'room for manoeuvre', which, secondly, can be used to expand peasants' strategic space at higher levels in society.

According to this outlook on broader organisational linkages, to be anchored in concrete socio-productive foundations (self-reliant systems), the organisation and the supporting institution must *both* overcome a) 'immediatism' and 'infrastructuralism' which lack a strategic vision and organised political action *and* b) the politicised, dogmatic discourses that deny peasants' own rationality, dynamics and their practical, concrete demands. The encountering and exchanges between the above mentioned 'hydraulic identities' in peasant irrigation systems, and interconnections among their organisations, may lead to collective discussion and expanded action. This is a process of empowerment, which makes the defence of peasant concepts regarding equity not just a theoretical, but also a very realistic and practical prospect.

Finally

Confronting local injustice and strengthening local organisations: a contradiction?

Peasant and indigenous identities are not static leftovers from the past, although they do have their roots in history and irrigation rights have often arisen through historical processes. Identities are being constructed at this very moment, in today's peasant and indigenous struggles, in irrigation development and community work, amidst internal and external structures that are both equitable and exploiting. The same goes for the above hydraulic identities. This means that we cannot romanticise today's culture, or take for granted that the equitable qualities and practices of the (idealised) culture of yesteryear have survived. It is necessary to de-mythify peasant society, in the Andes and elsewhere, since romanticising rural life weakens their capacity to wield political counter-weight and work for equity on the basis of the actual facts. Frantz Fanon wrote about the attitude of colonialists with respect to the dreadful impacts of colonialism on the local culture: 'Colonial specialists do not want to recognise that the culture has changed, and they hasten to support the traditions of native society. It is precisely the colonialists who have become the defenders and advocates of a native lifestyle'. (Fanon 1984)

An uncritical defence of irrigation traditions and the distribution of rights and benefits in peasant irrigation denies the existence of power structures that not only maintain internal injustice but also play along with unfair outside interests and production relationships in society at large.

> 'Local management of irrigation does not always ensure the egalitarian distribu-tion of water. The control over water is a key element in social stratification, and the battle over water rights is a major theme in many communities. Hacendados and powerful townspeople have often dominated the distribution of water, frequently giving water to peasants only in return for labour. Even in those sys-tems controlled by peasants, farmers often fight over water … Since only power-ful peasants are able to mobilise significant support, they are able to obtain more water for themselves and for their allies…' (Mitchell & Guillet 1994).

The idea is not to 'defend peasant traditions because they are supposedly more equi-table', but to defend the right to autonomous development of peasant irrigation, in which men and women structure their own future on the basis of a critical analysis of local and global society. Therefore, it is indispensable to combine 1) the recogni-tion that peasant irrigation development has its own logic and dynamics that can be a source of cohesion and identity, with 2) the need to develop and work from a political vision and action that will address existing injustices and that simultane-ously takes this endogenous development as point of departure. This is the paradox of creating room for endogenous development and not accepting injustice. Poor peasants themselves cannot afford to deny or accept prevailing injustices either. They know that they must find the roots of these injustices, and cut them out, when they feel that there is a good enough chance of succeeding. For them, this is not a theo-retical issue, since it is a question of life - achieving an acceptable level of survival through irrigation - or death - the conflicts, injuries, casualties that occur when building the irrigation system or when defending it.

The Andean saying that *'Blood flows along with the water'* shows that water is the object of great conflict. Like land, it is often a very necessary, extremely powerful fac-tor. In the near future, the need for water and the power associated with it will increase even more, as it becomes ever more scarce. Rivalries, conflicts and injustices will increase. Once again, it is not a question of denying local injustice, but of work-ing on it. Organisational structures often reflect and reconfirm existing relationships of power, but *organisational processes can also change them* if these relationships are deemed unfair. Irrigation, in addition to conflicts, also means organisational poten-tial, and irrigation organisation can be a means to materialise conceptions regarding equity.[19]

So, a strong organisation is one of the key means to work on the issue of existing social injustice. Outwardly, it makes people listen to and respect peasant conceptions regarding equitable irrigation and the right to self-determination. Vertical and hori-zontal linkages reinforce their voice. Inwardly, a strong organisation has the necessary capacity to discuss and formulate their own rules for equitable distribution and to enforce consensus-based agreements among all users. Furthermore, notwithstanding the fact that it is important to work on the basis of existing peasant experiences and organisational forms, this starting-point must not be dogmatised. In practice, marginalised groups are organised dynamically around the objectives they share, on the basis of their own analysis of the situation. If they feel it is necessary, and if they have some degree of strategic space, but do *not* manage to negotiate and reformulate those organisational forms they consider unfair, they will often seek to generate *another* organisation that can represent and defend their interests.

Can equity be organised?

Equity in peasant irrigation, being the people's own, local, specific perception of social justice, being the collective definition of how advantages and disadvantages are to be shared, being a mutual agreement about the distribution of rights and obligations - can *only* emerge from self-determination and participatory democracy in the process of organising irrigation. The converse is not necessarily true: self-determination does not automatically lead to equity, rather, it is a *prerequisite* for local equity.

In the Andes, the foundation for an approach to equity in peasant irrigation is grounded in existing and potential organisational practices of peasants and indigenous peoples. The Andean community - which may gather its social force rooted in *the collective action to survive and the common territorial base* - in conjunction with the peasant irrigation system - which operates on the basis of peasants' *collective hydraulic property and common irrigation rights* - generates a highly strong and undervalued potential. Besides, this joint potential also has very concrete objectives: it addresses the problems of increasing scarcity and inequitable distribution of land and water, both very powerful factors in the Andes. Together, the community and the irrigation system, the land and the water, can generate the required collective force for both transformation and reproduction, for change and resistance.

Equity cannot be institutionalised through rigid outside rules and procedures, nor can it be given to peasants as a handout.[20] In fact, equity cannot be organised by external institutions, but they *can* facilitate the necessary platforms and arenas for negotiation and realisation of equitable irrigation. Equity in irrigation can indeed be organised, through the active mobilisation of and by peasant families themselves. By linking its horizontal and vertical levels, the organisational potential can achieve greater equity both in local irrigation systems and in wider society. Apart from empowerment through peasant networks and alliances, claiming government support is generally indispensable[21] and backing by other institutions may prove important: providing there is an honest hybridisation of knowledge and capacities, and providing both counterparts recognise their specific interests, which should be negotiated in a frank manner in order to result in clear, mutual commitments and terms of co-operation. This kind of support and mutual collaboration has nothing to do with the ideological, but empty, discourses on participation. Neither is it about the opposite, a kind of philanthropic or infrastructuralist activism. It is about the down-to-earth, interactive and endogenous design of people's own technological, organisational, and normative frameworks. Peasants' strategic space to actively develop these own models must be fought for, something which they are doing right at this moment, day in day out.

Notes

1   We thank Bernita Doornbos for her constructive observations on a previous version of this document.
2   Even when dealing with exactly the same issue, the concepts and rules expressed 'for internal use' may be different from those stated 'for external use', both in nature and in form, since internal relations often have some other function beyond those of external relationships (with, for example, people without rights, the State, or intervening agencies.)
3   'Organisation' basically has two meanings: 'group' (for example, the users' organisation) and 'process' (for example, to organise an assembly or march). Peasant organisation is commonly referred to as a group. However, it should also and especially be seen as the set of strategies and actions of organising peasants. Self-reliant organisation is not only the means or group structure, but also an important *process,* to achieve greater equity.
4   On the one hand, the users' organisation already has knowledge, either inherited from collective tradition and history, or through previous experience of its members (e.g. irrigation skills) or its leaders (e.g. organisational experiences) that are incorporated into the irrigation system; on the other hand, knowledge is acquired through a process of 'learning by doing'.
5   In their eagerness to support peasants, rural development assistance often focuses especially on the people's *problems and deficiencies* rather than establishing a policy grounded in their *capacities, knowledge and strengths.* However, 'peasants are made up not only of needs, but also capacities' (Ribeiro, in Gianotten & De Wit 1987).
6   To define the variables, their indicators and location in an operational instrument, see Van der Does (1994) and CESA (1994).
7   Internally, the levels are not homogenous. Heterogeneity *within* each organisational level is rooted in contradictions such as class, gender, ethnic origin, legal status, and so on. It is crucial to recognise not only the factors of conflict and instability, but also the *organising potential of heterogeneity.* First, because heterogeneity can reinforce the forms of co-operation based on interdependence and complementation of capacities and resources. Second, because it reinforces identity (based on awareness of class, ethnic group, gender, etc.) among groups of users, and calls for their organised action.
8   That is, endogenous or autonomous development is never done in a legal, institutional, or other vacuum, and must not be confused with a (non-existent) autarchic development. For example, governmental presence is almost always a decisive factor.
9   The need to present a project that is 'viable and bankable' leads to overestimating benefits, yields and technical and social efficiency, while underestimating real social and financial costs. It is common to create an image of the ultimate outcome, which the peasants ultimately cannot and do not want to make reality.
10 Design is not considered as a particular phase in the irrigation intervention process. It is an ongoing process of proposals, alternatives, negotiation, changes and agreements in irrigation development.
11 This temporary co-management may be indispensable, for example when constructing or rehabilitating systems under situations that are too geophysically or economically complex for the peasant organisation alone.
12 During the past decade, theoretically and practically, great headway has been made in searching for interactive development of irrigation systems, to reinforce users' capacities, organisation and decision-making power (see, for example, Uphoff 1986; Hendriks 1988; Chambers *et al.*

1989; Haverkort *et al.* 1991; Ostrom 1992; Gandarillas *et al.* 1992; Ubels & Horst 1993; SNV-UNL 1994; Yoder 1994; Diemer & Huibers 1996, Scheer 1996, among others).

13 The common use of the obscuring concept of 'project beneficiaries', when referring to the peasant irrigators, masks the fact that all parts - water users, State and support institutions, with their specific interests - expect to benefit from the co-operation (otherwise, they would not enter into a co-operation relationship).

14 In SNV-UNL (1994), Chapter 9, we offer a series of practical examples of intervention criteria and the corresponding terms of co-operation.

15 Please note that, in the case of building larger or more complex systems, this does not imply that peasants must manage and understand all the *project's* technical and administrative details, which would be impossible and largely pointless. In addition to their key role in decision-making about the project's objectives, strategies and unfolding, the peasant organisation must deal with those aspects of the project, which are fundamental for its formation, so that they can management the *system* by themselves (see Hendriks 1994).

16 See the chapters in Part 6 and the last note. Furthermore, in bureaucratic systems government authority is, of course, more direct and decisive than in rural communal systems (see Boelens 1995). In the Andes, governmental presence in irrigation differs considerably from country to country. Moreover, on the Coast, the government's influence is more direct than in the Highlands. And, in the Highlands, we might argue the following: 'Cuanto más alto, menos Estado' [The higher the altitude, the less the government is around].

17 Such as, respectively, the CONAIE (indigenous) in Ecuador, certain Watershed Committees (multi-sectoral users) in Peru, or the FEDERIEGO (irrigation) in Colombia.

18 The same goes for the local level (design, construction and administration of the irrigation system): it is very important not only to work with a participatory methodology, but also to create the *practical conditions and make it possible* for women and poor families to actually participate in collective action and management (paying attention not only to rules, rights and procedures, but also to day-to-day subsistence constraints, such as workload, transport, language, lack of means, etc.).

19 In rural zones, the poor people often take advantage of the opportunity of an irrigation project to fight for their emancipation, generating their water rights and their rural organisation, and formulating usage norms (see, for instance, Chapter 36) By contrast, the more well-heeled generally seek to increase their influence and rights not through their own work, but through contacts with institutions, money or 'free' contributions to the poor, in the form of machinery, etc. We have seen several cases in which the poor firmly reject this 'aid' from the rich, to prevent the latter from appropriating rights without getting their hands dirty. In such situations, the political vision and attitude of any advisory institution may often prove decisive.

20 See also Chapter 3 and the work of Bernard Schaffer & Geoff Lamb (*Can equity be organised?* 1981, Institute of Development Studies, Sussex University, Brighton), focusing on public action in society in general.

21 Equity can and must be backed by the State, although it cannot be defined and legalised as universal, detailed principles of justice (see the chapters of Part 1). Above all, State support to equity calls for creating the necessary conditions, such as through 'enabling legislation', services, financing and indirect investment, backing of supra-local co-ordination (e.g. at watershed level), etc., apart from arbitration in conflicts going beyond local management capacity. However, peasant strategies must begin with *what the State is* in concrete cases, and not be grounded in *what it could be*, as if this already were today's reality. In this respect, the required State contribution and backing is something that is to be claimed, since State power interests often contradict peasants' interests.

Appendix
Some overall features of water users' organisations in Andean peasant irrigation
Notwithstanding the many exceptions and the wide variety of irrigation management forms in the Andes, there are certain traits shared by many water users' organisations in those peasant-

managed systems that have achieved some degree of sustainability. In addition to a number of general principles of Andean peasant economy that outline the framework for the organisation's actions (see Chapter 21), specific features such as the following may often be observed:

- **Organisational structure**: Generally, the horizontal and vertical division into operational units is interwoven in the Andean community structure, often with certain functional modifications for irrigation O&M. Because they are deep-rooted in the community, the irrigation organisations, in addition to sustaining the productive technical infrastructure, also incorporate strong cultural and political notions. Normally, they are 'horizontal organisations' with few formal hierarchical layers. The basic units of water distribution are small enough to make reciprocity possible, with direct co-ordination, flexibility and transparency. Generally, in addition to the general assembly, there is an intercommunity executive body and sometimes specific inter-community commissions, apart from assemblies or bodies at the community level.
- **Objectives**: Although water distribution and the irrigation system's reproduction are the central objectives, other important aims of the same organisation are characteristically multi-directional and cover areas outside irrigation, since irrigation management is positioned integrally within social relationships for rural coexistence. By contrast with trade-union and political organisations, the objectives of users' organisations are generally very direct and concrete.
- **Procedures**: Despite the fact that routine procedures are generally internally institutionalised to increase transparency and efficiency, the organisation has few formal procedures. Those that there are, are relatively flexible, but based on general rules known by all members. The informal procedures carry a lot of weight. For informal procedures, and the great majority of internal formal procedures, the written word commonly is not used.
- **Rights**: Rights and obligations are the foundations of operational rules, the organisational structure and collective action. Generation and conservation of rights through investments by peasants in building or rehabilitating infrastructure, constituting collective property, is an important mechanism for sustainable functioning of the system (comparable to Coward 1986). Irrigation rights are both individual (use of water and infrastructure) and collective (right to participate in management, see Ch. 8).
- **Legal basis**: Most peasant families or systems have or seek to have a legal formalisation of their rights, to defend themselves from claims by others. Legal formulas differ greatly from one Andean country to another, from detailed organisational prescriptions (such as in Ecuador) to more flexible legal frameworks (as in Bolivia). In the former case, concrete practice and actual normative relations differ greatly from the official legal framework.
- **Members**: All irrigation right-holders are members of the organisation, but there are many cases in which the peasant organisation, representing as it does whole communities, also includes families without access to water. That is, the organisation may be 'broader' than just irrigator families and irrigation affairs, despite the fact that organisations do generally attempt to incorporate all community members into the irrigation system. In such cases, there are generally specific irrigation committees or 'submeetings' within the peasant organisation. Depending on the mechanism for obtaining rights (see Ch. 8), conditions to join and reaffirm one's membership often have to do with obligations related not only to irrigation but also to other community activities.
- **Leadership**: Leaders are elected by the membership at large, in (inter) community assemblies. Lines of communication with members are short, often informal, and characterised by mutual social control. Relationships of mutual accountability are strong. Positions in irrigation organisations are usually rotated and in many cases remunerated not financially but in respect (sometimes leaders are also exempted from certain work or granted compensations in products). Internal rotation means there is little 'expertocratisation' in irrigation management, although 'natural leaders' may carry a lot of weight. Functions in irrigation management often go along with corresponding community functions (*cargos*).
- **Resources**: The most important resources, as in any organisation, are the members, their organisational experiences, capacities and knowledge, and the relationships between them. See Figure 37.3 for the other resources present. Resources mobilised are both community-owned and individual property, apart from the calling in of outside resources.

- **Management mode:** Often, the internal governance ranges from direct democracy (all members may speak and vote, at the level of their operational unit and community, and at the overall level of the general assembly) and/or representative democracy (since there are often agreements established at meetings of grassroots representatives). Some systems (especially the smaller ones) tend more toward the former mode, others toward the latter, and many systems combine both, depending on the importance of certain decisions to be made. It is not uncommon for hundreds of families to come together in order to express their opinions and vote at biannual assemblies.
- **Results:** Generally, the relationship between the organisation's actions and outcomes is very direct. Therefore, the organisation may hold greater control over its own actions, analysing the cause of problems, the solutions provided and their effectiveness and efficiency. This is in marked contrast with management in bureaucratic systems (e.g. collection of fees for the national budget and subsequent lack of transparency in 'redistribution to the irrigation sector'; bureaucratic conflict management; or the many steps that must be taken to repair a landslide, etc.).
- **Monitoring:** In many systems there are specific persons responsible for monitoring, such as ditch wardens, timekeepers, water judges, etc. However, the strongest basis for internal control and detection of problems and solutions is the informal collective monitoring (among others, social control), on a daily basis in each organisational unit, at the different levels. The conclusions of informal discussions are concentrated in formal assemblies to collectively formulate or improve objectives, goals and planning. The assembly plays the role of a periodic climax in the organisation's monitoring process.

References

Alfaro, J., F. Guardia, J. Golte, L. Masson & M.T. Oré, 1991. 'La organización social del riego'. In: *Ruralter no. 9*, CICDA, Lima.

Apollin, F. & R. Boelens, 1996. *El riego en la comunidad andina. Una construcción social.* CICDA-CESA-SNV-CAMAREN. Quito.

Boelens, R. & G.J. Temmink, 1990. 'Irrigatietechnologie en participatie in de Peruaanse Andes'. In: *Derde Wereld*, 90 1 / 2, DWC, Nijmegen.

Boelens, R., 1995. 'Transferencia del Manejo de Sistemas de Riego: la nueva política de riego en el Ecuador'. In: *Ecuador Debate,* vol.36, CAAP, Quito.

Boelens, R. & B. Doornbos, 1996. *Derecho consuetudinario campesino e intervención en el riego. Visiones divergentes sobre agua y derecho en los Andes.* SNV-CESA. Quito.

Bolding, A., P. Mollinga & K. Van Straaten (1995). 'Modules for modernisation. Colonial irrigation in India and the technological dimension of agrarian change'. *Journal of Development Studies.* Vol. 31, no.6, p. 805 - 844.

CESA, 1994. *Fortalecimiento de la organización de regantes.* Workshop proceedings. CESA, Riobamba.

Chambers, R., A. Pacey & L.A. Thrupp. Farmer First. *Farmer innovation and agricultural research.* Intermediate Technology Publications, London.

Coward, E.W.,1986. 'State and locality in Asian irrigation development. The property factor'. In: *Irrigation management in developing countries: current issues and approaches.* Eds. Nobe & Sampath. ISARD Studies in Water Policy and Management 9, pp.491-508.

Does, M. Van der, 1994. *Fortalecimiento de la organización de regantes. Una propuesta para un instrumento de medición.* CESA/SNV, Riobamba.

Diemer, G., & F.P. Huibers (eds.), 1996. *Crops, people and irrigation. Water allocation practices of farmers and engineers.* Intermediate Technology Publications, London.

Esman, M.J. & N. Uphoff, 1984. *Local organizations, intermediaries in rural development.* Cornell University Press, Ithaca & London.

Fals Borda, O., 1985. *Conocimiento y poder popular.* Punta de Lanza / Siglo Veintiuno Editores, Bogotá.

Fanon, F., 1984. *Zwarte huid, blanke maskers.* (Peau noir, masques blancs, 1954). Van Gennep, Amsterdam.

Flores, J. & H. Olazával, 1993. *Proyecto de rehabilitación del antiguo canal La Estrella, Mollepata, Perú.* CADEP 'J.M.A.', Cusco.

Friedmann, J., 1992. *Empowerment, the politics of alternative development.* Blackwell Publishers, Cambridge Massachusetts.

Gandarillas, H., et al, 1992. *Dios da el agua, Qué hacen los proyectos? Manejo de agua y organización campesina.* PRIV-Hisbol, Cochabamba.

Gelles, P., 1993. 'Irrigation as a cultural system: Introductory remarks'. In: *Culture and environment: a fragile coexistence.* R.W. Jamieson, S. Abonyi & N.A. Mirai (eds.), 1993, Archaeological Association, University of Calgary, Calgary.

Gerbrandy G. & P. Hoogendam, 1996. 'The materialization of water rights'. In: Diemer & Huibers (eds.) 1996.

Gianotten, V. & T. De Wit, 1987. *Organización campesina: el objetivo político de la Educación Popular y la Investigación Participativa.* TAREA, Lima & CEDLA, Amsterdam.

Greslou, F., 1989. *Visión andina y usos campesinos del agua.* PRATEC, Lima.

Haverkort, B., J. Van der Kamp & A. Waters-Bayer (eds), 1991. *Joining farmers' experiments. Experiences in participatory technology development.* Intermediate Technology Publications, London.

Hendriks, J., 1988. *Promoción rural y proyectos de riego.* CADEP, Cusco.

Hendriks, J., 1994. '*La intervención de la institución de apoyo referente a la organización de usuarios'.* In: SNV-UNL 1994.

Mitchell, W.P. & D. Guillet, 1994. *Irrigation at high altitudes: the social organization of water control systems in the Andes.* Society for Latin American Anthropology & American Anthropological Association, USA.

Mollinga, P., 1997. *Water control in sociotechnical systems: a conceptual framework for interdisciplinary irrigation studies.* Draft. Reader 'Intervention methodologies for irrigation reform'. Dpt. Irrigation, Wageningen Agricultural University.

Ostrom, E., 1992. *Diseño de instituciones para sistemas de riego auto-gestionarios.* Institute for Contemporary Studies, San Francisco.

Ploeg, J.D. van der, & A. Long (eds), 1994. *Born from within. Practice and perspectives of endogenous rural development.* Van Gorcum, Assen.

Ruijven, N. Van & F. Uit het Broek, 1992. *Que florezcan mil organizaciones.* SNV, The Hague.

Scheer, S., 1996. *Communication between irrigation engineers and farmers.* PhD Dissertation, Wageningen Agricultural University, Wageningen.

SNV, 1992a. *Fortalecimiento de organización de los grupos meta. Metodología y medición de resultados.* Seminar proceedings. Lima.

SNV, 1992b. *Rumbo a espacio para mujeres.* SNV, The Hague.

SNV-UNL, 1994. *Riego comunitario andino y organización de usuarios. Una guía para proyectos.* SNV / National University of Loja, Loja.

Ubels, J. & L. Horst (eds), 1993. *Irrigation design in Africa. Towards an interactive method.* Wageningen Agricultural University & CTA, Ede.

Uphoff, N., 1986. *Getting the process right: improving irrigation water management with farmer organization and participation.* Studies in Water Policy and Management, no. 11, Westview Press, Boulder and London.

Yoder, R., 1994. *Locally managed irrigation systems. Essential tasks and implications for assistance, management transfer and turnover programs.* IIMI, Colombo

REFLECTIONS

When I stopped to think

When I stopped to think about it
Reason gave me the option to choose
Between being who I am, or stepping
Into someone else's shoes.

But I said to myself: if copying
Were law, nobody would ever be born –
Because they would just repeat
What others had done before:
So, I proclaimed, from the bottom of my heart,
Oh soul of mine, be who you are!

José Martí (1853 - 1895)
(Transl. from: *José Martí. Poesía Completa*,
 Alianza Editorial, S.A., Madrid, 1995).

Cuando me puse a pensar

Cuando me puse a pensar
La razón me dio a elegir
Entre ser quien soy, o ir
El ser ajeno a emprestar,

Mas me dije: si el copiar
Fuera ley, no nacería
Hombre alguno, pues haría
Lo que antes de él se ha hecho:
Y dije, llamando al pecho,
Sé quien eres, alma mía!

(*Ibid.*)

Reflections

Rutgerd Boelens & Gloria Dávila[1]

Water is life: a basic right to be shared by everyone

In the quest to broaden and deepen the pressing debate on equity and justice in irrigation, the book's authors have presented a wealth of experiences and knowledge. The contributions to this discussion range from conceptual elaborations to empirical experience, and from academic expertise to peasant lore. Through the book's 'funnel' structure, from general to particular, concrete case studies have been set within a wider framework. In these final reflections, we will not attempt to summarise or revisit the huge volume of observations, illustrations and recommendations that have been presented. What we do intend to do is to highlight and reflect on some of the central issues.

The contributions have shown that peasant irrigation development tightly inter-weaves the technological and social realms. Irrigation water is not only a fundamental source of life, but also a factor involving great power. Within unequal power structures, different societal bodies - both 'outside' actors and different user groups - define their strategies in order to defend and materialise their own group's interests in controlling the water or the process of irrigation development. They establish their alliances, call in their capacities and resources, confront each other and negotiate. Resulting conflicts and consensus, and the norms and rules that each interest group manages to establish or impose, determine the historical and contemporary development of irrigation. Thus, social norms and interests, and the power they represent, structure the development of irrigation technology. In turn, irrigation technology embodies social norms; its use structures social practice and the way that the benefits generated will be distributed.

We have examined the Andean case in detail in this book. However, this is not in order to generalise the outcomes, as if they might form a pattern for peasant irrigation the world over. Rather, in the search for equity and justice in rural development

---

1   We would like to thank Jan Hendriks for his valuable comments on a previous version of these reflections. Of course, only the authors of this text are responsible for its contents.

and the diverse concepts and practices in this regard, we have explored peasant irrigation and water distribution as our *core field of interest*; then, to illustrate and probe this field, we have focused on the *concrete case* of the Andes. We hope that others who are convinced of the need to seek greater social justice in rural and urban development - development driven by the people themselves - will broaden this discussion and deepen this quest.[2] Rather than an attempt to discover general, universal concepts of justice and equity, it is a question of analysing their logic and operation in concrete situations, in their historical, cultural setting, in concrete fields of interest.

We cannot embrace equity or justice without analysing their social content in concrete cases. They are ideological constructs that are grounded, *inter alia*, in the ideas and interests of specific human groups regarding the distribution of resources in society. These groups attempt to influence the formulation and implementation of rules for equity and justice. In other words, key questions include:

- at the ideological level: what kind of equity are we talking about? That is, who defines its rules, with what interests in mind, from what social and political position, and with what power?
- at the social and substantive level: how is equity realised in practice? This implies answering questions about who the actual beneficiaries are, who bear the disadvantages, how equity is expressed in current social relationships, and how equity is used to legitimise these social relationships.

The fact that equity is an ideological construct, created by social groups, does not make it less real, powerful and important as a guide in practice. It may be used *both* in the hands of those in a privileged position, *and* in the hands of the less fortunate, such as oppressed peasants, indigenous people and women. The preceding chapters have sought to shed light on these two versions, their frictions and consequences in particular cases of peasant irrigation. The latter, equity from the perspective of the less powerful groups, is of central interest. It is also interesting to note that the respective conceptions of equity and its organisational forms are instruments - or weapons, if you will - both to *defend* social reality and to *change* it: defence in the case of norms which are considered to be more equitable, change in cases of great injustice. So, water is indeed life, a basic right everyone must have, but it is also power and requires organisation and social struggle.

Three fundamental issues

In analysing the issues of justice and equity in peasant irrigation, we basically encounter three fundamental, inter-related themes. These form simultaneously the

---

2   Perhaps by going more deeply into this same field of interest, peasant irrigation, maybe in some other region of the world; or perhaps by exploring other fields of social action, such as education, health, drinking-water supply, urban development, forestry, trade, communication, etc. Or perhaps through investigating other areas, such as environmental issues, gender, land tenancy and reform, and so on.

three reasons that force us to address the topic of equity in irrigation, at the level of specific irrigation systems and at the regional or (inter)national level.

First of all, in many systems and regions within the central case, i.e. the Andes, but also in other zones of the world, one is appalled by the *prevailing flagrant injustice* regarding water distribution. Generally, although not always, this is closely related to highly unequal landholding: 'water flows in the direction of power'. Peasant and indigenous communities usually lack the water resources they need, and are forced to farm the most fragile and least productive land. Meanwhile, water accumulates - often abundantly - in the hands of the few dominant sectors. Even so, in many places around the world, the peasants and indigenous farmers are the ones who provide most of the country's food. That is, the unfair distribution of water is manifested not only in terms of poverty in peasant communities, but also in terms of a serious threat to many nations' food-supply security, a breakdown of its environment, and a waste of the relative abundance of water by the 'water-lords'. For many peasants and indigenous people, it must sound quite hollow to speak of 'the conservation of natural resources' (such as land and water) because one cannot conserve what has already been taken away by others.

Secondly, it is a bitter and almost widespread fact that the development of new irrigation systems and the rehabilitation of existing ones leads to an *acceleration of social differentiation*. Existing injustices are consolidated and reinforced. This has to do with the differential power that interest groups involved wield, as well as the lack of adequate understanding of peasant irrigation and the erroneous consideration that development of irrigation systems boils down to building neutral, purely physical facilities. In general, emphasis on just building infrastructure and increasing agricultural production - emphasising solely the 'potential results of irrigation' - draws attention away from the real social and productive outcomes, which are often less encouraging and are already evident in so many other development experiences.[3]

---

3   These potential results can only be achieved in practice by fundamentally tackling the issues of management, power and distribution. However, many intervention processes actually seem to accept the 'rule' and embody the 'unfortunately insurmountable fact' that irrigation, apart from its great development potential, is also predestined to increase social injustice, further separating those who have more from those who have less. Since the wealthier have more farmland to begin with, they 'must' receive more water, more investment and more services and they 'must' necessarily enjoy a much higher boost in net production and the net value of their land, proportional to the irrigated land they own. 'They require more benefits, simply *because* from the outset they already have more'. A simple but common example: farmer A has half a hectare, B has 10 ha. With irrigation, production increases by US$1000/ha/year and the value of land by US$3000/ha. This means that A receives a productive increase in value of US$500/year, and B receives an extra US$10,000/year from the project. Moreover, the increase in land value nets A only US$1500, but the project's benefits for B amount to US$30,000. Because B is richer, it is *justified* - 'what is *just*' is an ideological construct - that B should benefit disproportionately from public spending.

However, there are more equitable ways. It is not a contradiction but a paradox that several chapters have pointed out that, *at the same time*, in many peasant irrigation systems, there is a *great diversity and wealth of equitable rules and practices*, considered as such by the users themselves. They show that it is possible to organise the distribution of irrigation benefits and burdens more equitably. These rules and practices, which receive more emphasis as water becomes scarcer, have hardly been investigated and are seldom taken into account in policies, laws or interventions. They involve both the distribution of water and the distribution of other rights and obligations, advantages and disadvantages, benefits and burdens. Of course, there are also many peasant systems without a consensus on equity reflecting most families' perceptions. In such systems, there often are ongoing conflicts and even greater disorganisation exists. If distribution of irrigation rights and obligations corresponds to equity as perceived and constructed by the peasants themselves, and if there is transparency and clarity, users will establish sustainable, effective systems with united, strong organisations. This is the third basic reason to focus on concepts of equity in irrigation.

Ignorance and denial of specific equity rules, and their replacement by supposedly universal rules and organisational arrangements, means changing and often breaking the back of peasant irrigation systems, which are the heart of rural survival and coexistence. It also means opening the floodgates to accelerating social differentiation.

The right to equality and the right to difference

As we have seen in the preceding chapters, official or legal justice is often expressed in general rules and concepts (equality and generality), whereas equity actually involves local, particular conceptions about what is socially just or fair (diversity and locality). These two approaches may be contradictory, but need not always be. With very good reason, peasant and indigenous irrigators claim both the right to equality and the right to be different. This is not contradictory: in practice, this becomes manifest in a general demand for greater justice and equality regarding distribution of water and other benefits among the different groups and sectors of society, but there is also the demand for internal distribution to be based on autonomous decisions, local peasant rights and their own organisational forms, according to their own, particular conceptions about equity in each irrigation system.

This demand, for the right to be equal and also to be different, is fundamental. It requires guaranteeing local sufficiency *and* respecting local diversity, as a foundation for equity and sustainability. It goes against legal or institutional impositions of equality according to outside models of resource distribution and irrigated production systems, or according to standardised organisational forms and imposed blueprint rights.

Peasant rights, rooted in local rationality regarding coexistence and survival

The contributions to this book show the vast heterogeneity of conceptions about equity in peasant irrigation. This equity does not necessarily imply equality. It is expressed in rules, procedures and results that vary from system to system, so it is not uncommon to come across norms that are even contradictory when a given system is compared with a neighbouring system. However, this diversity by no means belittles the importance of these conceptions about equity. On the contrary, it is an intrinsic consequence of the local process of negotiations within an irrigation system, the specific interaction with other legal frameworks, and the matching of regulatory norms, organisational forms and hydraulic infrastructure to the particular circumstances and needs of each locality. It shows that, in each system, along with certain more generalised norms, there is also a particular, own background logic, which is generally the fundamental pivot of the irrigation system[4]. To understand peasant irrigation, it is critical to understand these plural normative roots, within their historical and cultural perspective and the current constellation of powers.

However, romanticising peasant lore, peasant economy and common law fosters the perpetuation of prevailing injustice and provides a backdrop which is not just inadequate but actually counterproductive in the effort to achieve greater equity in peasant irrigation. As several chapters have pointed out, peasant rights are not necessarily always the most equitable, nor are social or gender relations within peasant families and communities. Given that peasant irrigation is interwoven in micro and macro level power structures, it is necessary to collectively analyse and critically discuss - with and within irrigating communities and families - the characteristics of current social relations[5]. Should they be continued, modified or transformed? By whom, in what direction and with what perspective?

So, prevailing norms, social relations and organisational forms in peasant irrigation are certainly starting-points, but they are not necessarily the finish line. They are, and have to be, dynamic. Peasants themselves also create and re-create their irrigation rights dynamically, in interaction with other normative systems and the formal legal framework. This is manifested, for example, in the collective meetings of those peasant systems which are based on participatory democracy, where reflection on (in)equity in irrigation and corresponding rights is generally a central, ongoing activity.

---

4   This 'peasant customary law' often embodies particular combinations of elements from various normative sources (official and non-official) interacting in the field of each specific irrigation system.
5   Moreover, in some cases, policies or institutions promote the institutionalisation and standardisation of certain so-called 'peasant customs', whether real or only fictitious, in order to make irrigation management norms uniform, and thus increase their control over this social and productive sector, under the banner of 'local community empowerment'.

Moreover, these norms and forms of organisation must be dynamic if they are to survive. It is necessary to demystify the assumption that peasant irrigation systems generally 'work well and sustainably'. For example, in the Andes, peasant systems have undergone significant structural change processes over the last few decades, due to such factors as gaps in traditional power, commoditisation of peasant coexistence, demographic growth, decreasing availability of water, economic crisis and migration with its consequences for both feminisation of peasant communities, work overload and a short-term vacuum in irrigation management. These factors are often related causally to the weakening of grassroots organisations. However, as several chapters have shown, sometimes these same factors open up new potential for local empowerment. In the changing circumstances, organisations simply *have* to find new answers.

Community dynamics are expressed, *inter alia*, in rules and rights regulating peasant irrigation management. Aside from governmental concessions and socio-territorial entitlements, it is common for the development of collective and individual rights in peasant systems to be grounded in the logic of creating and reconfirming these water rights. Rights are earned through peasant investment in the construction and rehabilitation of irrigation infrastructure. This practice also leads to collective appropriation of the system. In many traditional systems, families obtain territorial irrigation rights not only through their own contemporary investment in building the collective facilities, but also as an inheritance of the investment made by their ancestors and as a loan contracted with the deities. This is confirmed through rituals rooted in irrigation practice.

Families create and reconfirm both their right to use water and infrastructure and the right to take part in decision-making and collective irrigation management. It is also very important to realise that water rights are generally granted to families and not (only) to the irrigated area, as governmental agencies usually do. In the Andes, peasant rules often require families, in order to maintain their water rights, to be members in good standing not only in irrigation activities but also in other collective activities in general. So, irrigation rights are intimately rooted in the entire local social and production system.

Formal and informal forms of organisation to operate and maintain the peasant system are the *particular* manifestation and institutionalisation of agreed irrigation rules. In turn, this organisation oversees compliance with these rules in practice. Water distribution rules usually consider the various uses of water, which has economic and productive, but also social and cultural functions and efficiencies.

Considering their diversity, dynamics and rootedness in local social relationships, the rules of peasant law systems should not and cannot be institutionalised by official legislation, which would remove them from their context and make them useless. Above all, it is necessary for national laws to create a strategic space for their operation and strengthening. One way to achieve this may be by presenting a framework which appeals to critical awareness and grants the necessary authority for the peasant systems themselves to develop and implement the norms that foster self-reliant irrigation management.

Conceptions of equity in peasant irrigation

In general, the following analytical levels may be distinguished regarding conceptions and practices of equity in peasant irrigation systems. They involve the distribution of irrigation benefits and burdens, and not only of the water itself. In practice, there are countless illustrations of each level.[6]

- Equitable distribution of the *water*: for example, irrigating from the tail-end upwards; allocating water to families rather than awarding it to land areas owned; more time or volume for the last families or user communities; sharing scarcity through equal rights; allocating water with a top limit; allocating water according to agreed users' investment; allocating the water according to the real economic and productive utility for the users, etc.
- Equitable distribution of the *services involved in irrigation development*: such as agricultural services and training for users; subsidies for construction and reha-bilitation; production loans; support for operation and maintenance, etc.
- Equitable distribution of the added *agricultural production* under irrigation: for example, priority for irrigation on community land; reciprocal exchange and sharing of resources among families with and without access to irrigated land; setting up of 'land banks'; collective marketing, etc.
- Equitable distribution of *obligations, functions and positions*: e.g. rotating leader-ship positions; differentiated, progressive fee structures; exemption from fee pay-ment for the poorest; (personal) work obligations for everyone able; etc.
- Equity in the *balance between irrigation rights and obligations*: e.g. maintenance contributions proportional to the area each family irrigates; all contribute equal-ly to obtain equal rights; contributions proportional not to the volume of water but to its actual utility, etc.
- Equitable distribution of the *rights to participate in the decision-making process*: e.g. everyone has a right to speak and vote independently of the land they possess; anyone can be elected to leadership positions; membership status for both men and women; etc.

When these levels are investigated in practice, it is necessary to distinguish, at each level, between the *rules* (both formal and informal rules), the respective *procedures* (whether agreed upon or not), the actual *behaviours* and the *results* in practice (fore-seen or not), which do not necessarily coincide. Compliance with rules depends on

---

6   The examples must not be taken out of context; the concrete contents of these rules and prac-tices differ from one system or organisation to another. Even within a single system there can be different conceptions about equity, according to the stakeholders' interests. Furthermore, in a single system, rules on equity and distribution may vary considerably during the annual irri-gation cycle, according to the degree of water scarcity.

a number of factors including the actual interest in following them, organisational possibilities (management capacity), technical possibilities (e.g. the features of the irrigation infrastructure) and the power that the respective individuals or groups can bring to bear.

The first levels refer, above all, to conceptions about rules that lead to *equitable results*. The last level refers to another fundamental aspect of peasant and indigenous conceptions: rules that guarantee the *equity of the process*. Irrigation management must develop as an equitable process. For example, in one irrigation season, not everyone can be a water president or judge (which are indivisible functions or rights), but it is considered more important to have a process in which everyone can vote and everyone is eligible for office. Another example: even in situations of scarcity, water might be allocated 'according to landholding' rather than 'by families' (i.e. less equality if landholding is differential), however, when this decision is not imposed, but accepted collectively after a process of discussion and negotiation, families will consider it relatively equitable. Another important illustration of a process generally considered equitable is the peasant process of earning and reconfirming irrigation rights.

In general, peasant perception of equity, being a combination of the equity perceived in results and in the process, grants great importance to transparent and horizontal management, discussion and collective negotiation of the rules, and clarity in socialising these rules. This view of equity attaches importance to the use of social control to impart and reinforce compliance with collective rules.[7] The lack of these qualities - a situation that also arises in many peasant systems - is generally considered 'inequitable'.

The above rules and practices regarding more equitable irrigation refer, especially, to the irrigation system level. However, to achieve, for example, a more fundamental impact on unfair 'water-holding' at the regional or national level through a 'water reform', it will be necessary to work not only on internal changes, but also on *constitutional changes, changes in agrarian policy and in public action*. Moreover, as has been outlined in various chapters, these two levels are closely related. This process of change requires the formation of broader networks and strategic alliances, with demands and proposals transcending local irrigation management.

Project intervention in peasant irrigation

Productive, economic and social outcomes of irrigation systems depend directly on the possibility for users to materialise the principles that they consider equitable. It is therefore fundamental to have clear rules that have been discussed, accepted and socialised. They also require adequate infrastructure, appropriate organisational forms, and effective procedures to put these principles into practice. Thus, the

---

7   In practice, this usually results in organisational and technical designs, such as, for example, small, self-controllable basic irrigation units, which adapt to the community structure.

process of technical, normative and organisational design plays a key role in creating systems that will not only be more equitable, but also more sustainable and productive.

Irrigation systems are sociotechnological complexes. Decisions about technical system design have direct consequences for distribution rules and, therefore, for system equity or inequity. It is not difficult to imagine that decisions about a specific scheduling of turns and the roster of users, the type of distribution works, the layout of the canals, flow rates, canal and reservoir capacity, cropping patterns, etc., will each have major impacts on water distribution within the system. Each of these so-called 'technical' decisions will also have direct consequences for the management and organisational forms required. Conversely, each decision on water distribution rules has direct implications for the corresponding physical and organisational infrastructure.

Nevertheless, support institutions and their technicians rarely discuss and question their irrigation designs, much less try to offer several alternatives or design the irrigation system really together with the users. In practice, irrigation development through institutional interventions (governmental or non-governmental) is usually biased tremendously toward infrastructuralism and short-termism, without taking the time to analyse and understand local norms and organisational forms, without considering the importance of achieving grassroots organisation and elementary agreements about system management and the distribution of its benefits and burdens. Unfortunately, apart from the official policy- and paper-work, in general there is no explicit, in-depth collective discussion about justice and equity in irrigation during the concrete development of most systems. This necessary, collective and practical discussion is replaced by 'established' and 'proven' institutional and governmental policies and professional criteria.

Thus, the project is often grounded in implicit norms about equity *among professionals and intervening institutions*, focusing above all on 'efficiency and productivity' in the strict technical and economic sense, frequently ignoring the need for organisational consistency, local perception of equitable norms and existing rationality of conflict management. This not only reinforces existing injustices, concretely granting more resources and power to the more privileged farmers. Also, as pointed out by Levine (Ch. 10), 'experience shows that systems designed on the basis of productivity and efficiency, but considered unfair by many of the users, are likely to be less productive and less efficient than equitable systems with nominally lower productivity and efficiency potential'.

Peasant designs, such as in the Andean case, generally seek to share water among all members of their collective group, whereas intervening institutions tend to design distribution according to the 'optimal water requirements' of crops, and by doing so they maximise benefits for a limited number of users. In the former case, users often choose 'less thirsty crops', combining self-consumption crops with growing for market; in the latter case, in order to improve the cost-benefit ratio, institutions - like wealthy users - generally plan crops with high commercial value but also high water requirements.[8]

This kind of intervention practice also shows a lack of understanding about the dual determination of peasant economies: to sustain themselves, families generally operate both in the mercantile ('capitalist') sphere and in the non-mercantile ('community') sphere. The latter is based on a *sine qua non* reciprocity: an indispensable condition for survival and reproduction of the community and its parts. Forced complete commoditisation of peasant coexistence, as a result of, *inter alia*, outside planning and design of irrigation, breaks up the community organisationally and socially, and stands in the way of better balanced, more productive, more sustainable alternatives.

Notwithstanding internal heterogeneity, achieving and maintaining collective unity to guarantee reproduction is a central aim in many peasant community systems. In designing their systems, peasants usually try to avoid building canals which bisect and therefore separate existing communities or organisations, even when this entails greater investment or lesser productivity. If such a division is unavoidable, there are often local solutions available, or they are sought, to somehow include 'the neighbours above the canal' in irrigation benefits and so maintain unity. Intervening institutions must realise how important this is, and support 'local solutions' through participatory investigation and by enabling collective discussions and peasant exchanges among different systems.[9]

In public and private interventions, peasant normative systems are often misunderstood, despite their central importance for proper operation of irrigation systems. It is not rare for interventions, because of their outside investments in irrigation systems, to generate new and/or exogenous property relationships. This can paralyse or destroy the foundations of collective social action in peasant irrigation: the local rights systems based on self-generated rights and common system ownership.

Therefore it is indispensable for irrigation intervention practice to carry out an ongoing process of mutual learning and participatory, historical investigation, in order to understand the social relations of production and distribution, and the logic

---

8   This also shows that scarcity of water is most often not an absolute fact, but a relationship between availability and demand, which are defined both by physical/technical criteria and, especially, by social norms and local power structures, whether equitable or not.

9   Not only when water is in short supply, but *also* when there is enough, and water is distributed proportionally to each family's irrigable area, there are many ways to counteract injustice and compensate for unequal benefits. Examples are exemption from amortisation for those who have less than a given amount of land, setting up differentiated, progressive fees, extraordinary payments and dues or sharing of surplus-values, compensations through other services, redistribution and exchange of irrigated land, and so on. Collective reflection often generates many new, creative possibilities.

of the irrigation system's backbone: peasant rights systems, and their roots in local concepts about equity.

This also means that it is necessary to understand that constructing, rehabilitating or changing irrigation infrastructure implies *simultaneously* (and often unconsciously) changing these rights and the organisation. That is, it directly influences the equity of distribution. Therefore, it is necessary to examine and work not just on the elements of an irrigation system (technical-productive or socio-organisational and cultural) but also, especially, on the integration and interaction among the components. Further, through a process of interactive design and joint preparation of a 'strategy for indirect institutional investment', that sustains and promotes peasant investment in irrigation infrastructure, users can create, reformulate and consolidate their own water rights and collective property of the irrigation system. This can establish more sustainable, more equitable systems, better suited to local characteristics and requirements. During community investment in building and repair, the collectivity also (re-)establishes appropriate organisational forms, in order to take over responsibility to manage and ensure continuity of the system.

When peasants are considered as the protagonists of their own system, not all the outcomes of the intervention (nor all the 'peasant rules') can be planned in advance. This does not take away the great importance of establishing - through open discussion and collective negotiation - the rules of play and mutual criteria for intervention and collaboration with regard to the central issues, *from the first step* of the intervention. Irrigation design must also fit into this process approach: it is an ongoing process of negotiations, not a cut-and-dried project phase. Diverse social groups - users and intervening institutions - will attempt to realise their interests in the technical, organisational and normative design: in order to also include the interests and notions concerning equity of the neediest, the interactive design process requires a participatory communication methodology, and constant interaction between collective action and critical reflection. Moreover, focusing on the equity perspective of the least powerful groups - often characterised by their class, gender, caste and/or ethnic status - implies the need to formulate and defend a political (non-partisan) position, and accompany these groups explicitly and concretely in the 'political arena' that an irrigation intervention fundamentally constitutes.

Working jointly on equity also means that supporting institutions, along with peasant organisations, have to take a critical look 'inward'. This is a basic condition for undertaking a genuine collaboration process, to establish a horizontal relationship of 'critical and mutual questioning' among the parties involved. Moreover, in this collaborating role, advisory institutions must not only ask themselves what activities they can carry out to improve irrigation practice, but also and above all: 'What should we *not* do?'

In summary, let us forget those schemes and blueprints that pre-establish how to design for users and organise them. Let us listen to the rationality of their own organisational forms, normative systems and technical and productive foundations as a starting-point, and then co-define, if necessary, strategies for interactive technological design, organisation-strengthening and empowerment of the peasant economy.

Collaboration or competition?

We are currently witnessing an international process of privatising usage rights of water resources. This is often based on the fundamental error of believing that the market - through so-called free competition among users and among uses and applications of water - will be able to allocate and distribute water more efficiently throughout the countryside, regardless of the particular features of the regions and user families in question. However, peasant irrigation, which generally copes with a social and physical/technical setting that is adverse, complex and unpredictable, can only operate sustainably by achieving collaboration - not competition - between different user groups. This is not a question of solidarity or harmony, but a day-to-day necessity: users *must* work collectively. It is a *'collective contractual reciprocity'* to sustain the irrigation system and the community livelihood, a self-imposed mutual accountability. At the level of the watershed, this ironic paradox is also manifest: amidst diverging interests, differential powers and different uses of the same water resources, it is fundamentally important to seek mutual collaboration rather than encouraging market-based competition.

The latter usually leads not only to accumulation, monopolisation and speculation with water rights, hoarded by dominant sectors, but also tends to foster disorganisation by individualising irrigation practice. As shown by Hendriks (Ch.27) for the case of peasant systems in situations of insecurity and subsistence: 'The more individual owners of water, the fewer owners of the system'[10] And, we may add: ... the less collaboration and co-ordination at the watershed level. A paradoxical, concrete perspective of privatising and individualising water rights is the discouragement of personal and collective investment in the system and sustaining it, since each irrigator tends to figure: 'why invest today, if tomorrow my neighbours may have sold their rights to outside parties, which will disrupt the schedule, decrease my own flow or maybe even cut the water off from my land?' Also, outside rights-holders generally do not have the same commitment regarding their contribution to operating and maintaining the system, especially if they take the water elsewhere or use it for activities other than irrigation. Discouragement from investment is even stronger when, as in certain proposals or policies in the Andes, the privileged sectors or persons can buy not only water usage rights but also - and proportionately to the water purchased - decision-making rights regarding irrigation system management. In this

---

10 And, as was argued, individualising privatisation of water rights ironically generates an intrinsic contradiction: because it breaks up and individualises collective organisation, the users - individualised rights-holders and claim-makers who are incapable of managing the whole system - tend to turn to outside institutions to 'take care of things'.

way, monopolisation of decision-making power by elites and wealthy sectors, and breakdown of peasant systems is only a matter of a few years.

Water resource legislation must offer an appropriate legal framework, considering both the social and productive/ economic functions of water. A framework should accentuate not only the market value, but also the community values of water. Through public-domain and common property approaches rather than private ownership, the State would have to reorganise the 'supply' of water to all social sectors. This supply should also be provided with justice, preventing concentration of water and other resources related to irrigation development. Further, in the national setting of multiple uses for water, it is fundamental to establish social priorities, which will defend production and food-supply security for everyone, and the opportunity to live with sufficiency and dignity, also for the less privileged people.

A central, democratic supply does not, by any means, necessarily imply centralising or bureaucratising water resource *management*. On the contrary, in the case of peasant irrigation, wherever possible[11], the 'demand' must be organised autonomously and collectively, according to local irrigation conditions, people's own normative systems and critical reflections on existing equity concepts in particular cases. Therefore, instead of pushing for 'individualisation' of water rights and thus dividing users, legislation would have to promote local, collective control of water, granting authority to local administration and self-reliant management. In peasant irrigation systems, the 'particular and collective management of demand' will have to be structured so that it will guarantee both collective irrigation rights and water usage rights for individuals belonging to systems. The dilemma often presented - an 'inescapable' choice between bureaucratic centralisation of water resources or their privatisation - is quite misleading. Because of the social importance of water and the diverse features of peasant irrigation, it is necessary to do without both centralising and privatising policies. The solution will not come from regulations based on the market alone, or the State alone, but above all from the peasant organisations and watershed boards that require authority to manage irrigation, with the necessary backing from the State.

Equity, the State and peasants

Despite the importance of the above - 'users organise the demand with local equity and the State supplies it with general justice' - this cannot be the answer that excludes further discussion. We cannot start from the ending-point. We have to start from the beginning, from what there is now, rather than assuming a State and social structures that will always act benevolently towards peasants and indigenous people. There is no reason to assume, after centuries of vertical control and the correspond-

---

11 In the present book, attention has mainly been devoted to peasant-managed irrigation systems, with the exception of some large-scale State-managed systems outside the Andean region. Various aspects of the latter require a specific analysis.

ing peasant reaction, that the contradictions and diverging interests between the State and the peasantry will disappear just because 'it is possible to create a more sustainable, equitable framework to organise irrigation management'. The Andean case shows that by far the most public investment in irrigation is done to benefit the areas and stakeholders who are already quite well off. The statistics are bitterly appalling. Public action and governmental institutions are not neutral and access to resources generally reflects the interests of those groups that can influence the formulation and implementation of national rules on distribution. For an analysis of irrigation equity, it is essential to investigate not only the rationales and structures of peasant domains, but also those of development agencies and public assistance.

Irrigation systems, even when constructed and managed by the peasants themselves, always have significant interaction with governmental agencies and laws. In the Andean case, for example, governmental policies and peasant regulations frequently represent different concepts regarding irrigation equity. The former frequently establish rules which are copied from laws elsewhere and organisational arrangements that are artificial and rigid. Sometimes, the technology applied is better suited to the norms and expectations of western farmers, intervening institutions and commercial enterprises, than to local coexistence and peasant management. Consequently, in order to implement the planned management of the systems, the latter may often be faced with authoritarian administration, which also breaks with organisational forms and local usage rules. Peasants are aware that the local power groups are better informed and able to hobnob with the official administration. They often hesitate to accept the legal provisions on irrigation management, since they know that the law tends to generate more injustice in water distribution, and entails loss of local control.

Even so, the *potential* role of the State is very important and must not be denied. It has the potential to contribute to more equitable, sustainable development of irrigation through, for instance, a just national supply of water and other irrigation benefits; legal and operational backing for peasants' own management of irrigation systems; arbitration in the event of conflicts that cannot be resolved locally; public reflection on local irrigation injustices; co-financing and co-creation of peasant irrigation systems; backing for watershed boards with governmental and user representation; formulation and co-ordination of a 'strategic operating plan' for national water resources and concessions; interactive capacity-building with users; etc. Strategies must be established which regard this governmental role not as a fait accompli but as a goal for social struggle and demands. In order to implement this role in reality, it is necessary to focus peasants' capacity to demand, negotiate and influence public policy and action, and to demand a more horizontal, democratic relationship, through their formal and informal organisations.

Equity cannot be bought or given as a handout

The expression of irrigation equity conceptions through rules and concrete practices means organisation, capacity, power and social struggle. The above claim-making capacity must go hand-in-hand with creative, protagonist capacity: capacity for analysis and (counter-)proposal. Peasant demands and proposals must be concretely expressed at the level of the irrigation system, but must not be limited only to the system level. Broader alliances and networks are indispensable, in order to join complementary capacities and forces; to hybridise equity principles; to withstand imposed norms; and to influence both the rules and the results. Such user alliances do not necessarily consist of only peasants or irrigators. It is also possible to create organisational bodies at, for example, the watershed level, to defend local interests and co-ordinate activities related to multiple water uses and sectors, with a democratic foundation that will prevent economic power from taking over the hegemony.

In many rural regions, equity and justice in peasant irrigation are not requesting for some marginal change in isolated irrigation systems, but a more fundamental transformation in land and water ownership. In view of the increasing scarcity of water resources, which will be a key issue in the 21st century, working on equity and justice in irrigation calls for a *genuine, substantial commitment* to the weakest, most oppressed groups. It is not necessary to include peasants in development or in society at large, because they are already there, often facing the worst side of development and society. Charity is not required, but critical political action - by institutions, organisations, networks and individuals, whether peasants or not - combined with appropriate technical expertise, creative capacity and profound understanding of local coexistence, its logic and strategies, its problems and solutions, its equities and inequities.

Irrigation development, which is a very powerful key issue in many rural areas, causing collective mobilisation and providing new future potentials, need not unavoidably cause greater dependence and injustice. It is also an important means to empower peasant and indigenous organisations, communities and systems, both in the economic and production realm and with regard to their cultural and political force. As stated before: a principal prerequisite for the creation and re-creation of sustainable, locally-managed systems is that they be grounded in the users' criteria on equity. These criteria must be translated into rules, rights, procedures, organisational forms and technical designs, suited to each locality's particular features.

At the end of the day, the search for equity in peasant irrigation means participating in the struggle to counteract flagrant injustice and social differentiation, while contributing to the creation of strategic spaces in which peasants and indigenous peoples, men and women, develop, autonomously and critically, their own criteria. It means acknowledging that they have the right to construct their own local models and hydraulic cultures.

About the authors

José Almeida Vinueza is an Anthropologist and Lecturer of the Faculty of Social Sciences at the Pontificada Universidad Católica del Ecuador. He has worked with the national indigenous movement, the CONAIE (Confederación de Nacionalidades Indígenas del Ecuador) and has conducted several studies on discrimination and the identity of black and indigenous peoples.

Frédéric Apollin is an Agro-economist. He is Head of CICDA (Centro Internacional de Cooperación para el Desarrollo Agrícola) in Ecuador and Regional Co-ordinator for CICDA-Latin America. He currently co-ordinates the Project for Rehabilitation of the Urcuquí and San Blas System and the inter-Andean irrigation programme of CICDA.

Alberto Arce is Senior Lecturer in the Sociology of Development in the Department of Social Sciences at the Centre for Rural Development Sociology of the Wageningen Agricultural University in the Netherlands. His research interests include State - peasant relationships in Latin America and Africa, as well as globalisation processes in agriculture, the sociology of knowledge and project intervention in rural development.

Aline Arroyo is a Sociologist. She has worked as a communication and extension adviser with CESA (Central Ecuatoriana de Servicios Agrícolas) in the Licto Irrigation Project and is currently a member of the CICDA -team in the Penipe Irrigation Project, both in Ecuador.

Franz von Benda-Beckmann is Professor of Agrarian Law and Rural Development in the Department of Social Sciences of the Wageningen Agricultural University, The Netherlands. He has carried out legal anthropological research on issues of resource management, property rights and social (in)security of rural populations in Africa and Indonesia. He has published and co-edited several books and articles on problems of legal pluralism and theoretical and methodological issues in the social scientific study of law.

Keebet von Benda-Beckmann is Associate Professor in Legal Anthropology and Legal Sociology at the Faculty of Law, Erasmus University Rotterdam, The Netherlands. She has carried out legal anthropological research on issues of resource management, dispute management and social (in)security of rural populations in Indonesia. She has published and co-edited several books and articles on problems of legal pluralism and theoretical and methodological issues in the social scientific study of law.

Kate Berry is Assistant Professor of the Department of Geography at the University of Nevada, Reno, USA. She has been involved in studies and written publications on water management policies and practices of both governmental institutions and indigenous and hispanic peoples throughout the western United States.

Rutgerd Boelens has worked on the theme of International Solidarity in The Netherlands with the Netherlands Development Organisation (SNV). In Ecuador he worked as an Irrigation Engineer with SNV, CESA (Central Ecuatoriana de Servicios Agrícolas) and peasant and indigenous organisations, assisting irrigation systems and networks. He studied management practices of peasant irrigation in Ecuador and Peru. Currently he is Lecturer and Researcher at the Irrigation and Water Engineering Group at Wageningen Agricultural University, The Netherlands.

F. Lee Brown has co-ordinated several water management research programmes with indigenous and hispanic communities in the U.S. South-West. He is Professor of Economics at the University of New Mexico and Executive Director of the International Water Resources Association in Albuquerque, New Mexico, USA.

Ximena Caiza is a Cattle-farming Technician. She works for CESA (Central Ecuatoriana de Servicios Agrícolas) as an agricultural extension worker on the Rural Development Project in Nabón, Azuay, Ecuador, where she has participated in research on irrigation management practices of indigenous communities.

Homero Castanier has provided assistance to various irrigation programmes and projects in the Ecuadorian Andes. He is a Civil Engineer and currently working as an independent consultant, advising irrigation and sanitation programmes.

Gloria Dávila is a Pedagogue and Communication Adviser for the Netherlands Development Organisation (SNV) in Ecuador. She has worked with several non governmental development institutions in rural and urban *Educación Popular* programmes in Colombia and Ecuador. Currently she is assisting various activities of SNV in Ecuador, including the irrigation, health and gender programmes.

Geert Diemer is an Anthropologist. He was Senior Lecturer of the Irrigation and Water Engineering Group at Wageningen Agricultural University in the Netherlands and currently works with the Participatory Irrigation Management (PIM) Programme of the World Bank in Washington, United States. He has published, among others, studies on engineers' and farmers' conceptions of irrigation development in African countries.

Nico van Dixhoorn is an Irrigation Engineer. Since 1992 he has assisted the water programme of SNV (Netherlands Development Organisation) and CIPCA (Centro de Investigación y Promoción del Campesinado) in the Guaraní-communities in Bolivia.

Carlos Garcés-Restrepo is an Irrigation Specialist and Head of the Mexico Programme office of the International Irrigation Management Institute (IIMI). Formerly, he was Head of IIMI's Andean Regional Project in Colombia.

José Luis Gareca Arias is a Sociologist and has studied and worked on the improvement of the socio-economic conditions of the Guaraní population in Bolivia. Currently he is working as an independent consultant.

Paul H. Gelles is Assistant Professor of Anthropology at the University of California at Riverside, USA. He has conducted fieldwork in the central and southern Peruvian Andes, studying topics including indigenous narratives, transnationalism, and the way that ethnic identity and cultural politics condition water management.

Gerben Gerbrandy is an Irrigation Engineer and currently co-ordinates the irrigation programme of the Netherlands Development Organisation (SNV) in Ecuador. He has worked in Bolivian irrigation projects and programmes from 1982 to 1996, where he assisted peasant irrigation systems and carried out studies on indigenous irrigation management. He was Co-ordinator of the research and training programme of PEIRAV (Programa de Enseñanza e Investigación de Riego Andino y de los Valles Interandinos) at San Simón University in Cochabamba.

Zulema Gutiérrez is an Irrigation Engineer and Researcher with PEIRAV (Programa de Enseñanza e Investigación de Riego Andino y de los Valles Interandinos) at San Simón University in Cochabamba, Bolivia. She has made several studies of Andean irrigation management.

Jan Hendriks worked from 1983 to 1994 in the Peruvian Andes, first as co-ordinator of an NGO Community Irrigation Programme, and after that as Water Management Consultant of the Netherlands Development Organisation (SNV). Currently he works for DHV-Consultants in a regional development programme in the north of Chile, financed by the European Community.

Félix Hernandez Cueva is an Agronomist and Lecturer of the PRICA-programme (Postgrado de Riego Comunitario Andino) at the Universidad Nacional de Loja in Ecuador. Within the PRICA-programme he is conducting investigations on Andean irrigation and he teaches and supervises students' research on this issue.

Gerrit Huizer is Professor of Development Studies at the Catholic University of Nijmegen, The Netherlands. He worked for many years in various Latin American and other Third World countries as a United Nations Adviser on the themes of popular and peasant movements, development policies and indigenous resistance.

Helen Ingram is Warmington Endowed Professor of Social Ecology at the University of California, Irvine, USA. She specialises in the politics of water policy, especially as it affects equity and participation of indigenous and hispanic minorities.

Wim H. Kloezen is an expert in Irrigation Management and works with the Mexico Programme office of the International Irrigation Management Institute (IIMI). He has studied the processes and impacts of irrigation management transfer programmes in Mexico and Sri Lanka.

Pat Lauderdale is Professor of Justice Studies and Director of the PhD Programme in Justice Studies, Law and Social Sciences at Arizona State University, Tempe, USA. He is co-editor of 'Lives in the Balance: Perspectives on Global Injustice and Inequity' (Brill Publishing, 1997).

Gilbert Levine is Professor Emeritus at Cornell University, Ithaca, USA. He has conducted many studies on irrigation management by peasant organisations and State institutions, especially in Asian countries.

Edward Martin is Secretary for Central and Southern Asia with the Mennonite Central Committee, Akron, Pennsylvania, USA. He has studied and published on irrigation management practices, especially in Asian countries.

Nelson Martínez B. has been working for many years with CESA (Central Ecuatoriana de Servicios Agrícolas) as Co-ordinator of the Pungales Irrigation Project and Head of the CESA- Centro Sierra Department in Ecuador. Currently he is Head of the Rural Development Programme of the Curia de Riobamba.

Xavier Mena Vásconez is a Lawyer and works for the United Nations Mission in Guatemala (MINUGUA) as a Human Rights Officer in Guatemala City. Previously, he acted as an independent Human Rights Lawyer in Quito, Ecuador, and as a MINUGUA Legal Advisor in Petén, Guatemala.

Rigoberta Menchú Tum is one of the principal leaders of the international indigenous movement, a winner of the Nobel Peace Price, and Ambassador of Peace for UNESCO. She works with national and international indigenous and human rights organisations.

Peter P. Mollinga is an Irrigation Engineer and Senior Lecturer of the Irrigation and Water Engineering Group at Wageningen Agricultural University in the Netherlands. He studies the political economy of irrigation in South Asia, particularly in India.

Pablo Nuñez is a History Scientist, specialising in the history of traditional Andean irrigation. He participated in the research programme of CICDA (Centro Internacional de Cooperación para el Desarrollo Agrícola) and ORSTOM France (Institute of Scientific Research for Development Co-operation) on the irrigation history of Urcuquí, Ecuador.

Annamarie Oliverio is a Visiting Professor in Social and Behavioral Sciences at Arizona State University West, Phoenix, USA. She has studied the State and themes of justice (or injustice) in Italian and North American cases.

Maria Teresa Oré is a Sociologist and Researcher at the Universidad Agraria in Lima, Peru. She has worked with various irrigation and development institutions and has made studies of water legislation and irrigation management in the Andean and Coastal zone of Peru.

Nina Pacari is a Lawyer and one of the principal leaders of the CONAIE (Confederación de Nacionalidades Indígenas del Ecuador), the national indigenous organisation. She works in various national and international indigenous and human rights platforms, and currently advises the Pacha Kutik movement in the Ecuadorian Congress.

Bart Pijnenburg is a Sociologist and works as a Lecturer and Researcher at the Eduardo Mondlane University, Maputo, Mozambique, in the area of agricultural research and extension and the analysis of development interventions. He has previously worked in farming systems research and rural development programmes in Zambia.

Jan Douwe van der Ploeg is Professor of Rural Sociology at Wageningen Agricultural University. During the 1970s and 1980s he was involved in several research programmes in Latin America. Since then he has worked, among others, on African and Western European agricultural systems.

Thierry Ruf is an Agro-economist and Director of the Laboratory of Agrarian Studies of ORSTOM France (Institute of Scientific Research for Development Co-operation). In the 1987 - 1992 co-operation between ORSTOM and INERHI (Instituto Ecuatoriano de Recursos Hidráulicos) he participated in research on traditional Andean irrigation in Ecuador.

Jeanette Sherbondy is Associate Professor of Anthropology at Washington College in Chestertown, Maryland, USA. She has done various studies on Andean ethno-history and published several works on culture, irrigation and organisation in the Inca empire, especially in the region of Cusco, Perú.

Salomao Simbine is a student of Agronomy at the Eduardo Mondlane University, Maputo, Mozambique, and studied agricultural knowledge systems in the Sabie Irrigation System.

Joep Spiertz is Jurist and Senior Lecturer in Agrarian Law and Rural Development at the Wageningen Agricultural University, The Netherlands. He has carried out research on legal pluralism and the role of law in irrigated agriculture on Bali. His publications are on the significance of law for natural resource management, where the main focus is on the theoretical aspects of the study of water rights within farmer managed irrigation systems in some Asian countries.

Fernando Terán is an Agronomist. He has worked on various rural development and irrigation projects in the Ecuadorian Andes. He was recently Co-ordinator of the Patacocha Project in Cañar and currently he is Co-ordinator of the Licto project in Chimborazo, Ecuador, with CESA (Central Ecuatoriana de Servicios Agrícolas).

René Unda is a Sociologist and has worked on rural development projects in Bolivia and Ecuador. Currently he works for CESA (Central Ecuatoriana de Servicios Agrícolas) and is Co-ordinator of the Rural Development Project in Nabón, Azuay, Ecuador.

Linden Vincent is Professor and Head of the Irrigation and Water Engineering Group at Wageningen Agricultural University, The Netherlands. She was editor of the Irrigation Management Network at the Overseas Development Institute in the early 1990s, and has undertaken research and development work in irrigation and water resource management in Africa, the Middle East, Asia and Latin America.

Ketty Vivanco Criollo is a Pedagogue and teaches at the Universidad Nacional de Loja in Ecuador. She also provides assistance to the education and research programme of PRICA (Postgrado de Riego Comunitario Andino) of the Loja University.

Robert Yoder is Senior Engineer and Senior Associate with Associates in Rural Development in Burlington, Vermont, USA. He has studied and written about institutions and technologies enabling successful local management of irrigation in South and Southeast Asia. As Head of IIMI's Field Operations in Nepal from 1985 to 1990 he assisted in establishing the Farmer-Managed Irrigation Systems Network.

About the Contributing Institutions

Below, the agencies that have supported the publication of this book give a brief description of their own institution and the interest they show in the central theme of the book.

 **Swiss Agency for Development and Cooperation (SDC / COSUDE)**

Part of the Swiss Ministry of Foreign Relations (DFAE), the Swiss Agency for Development and Co-operation (SDC; in Spanish, COSUDE) is responsible for development co-operation activities and humanitarian aid in Asia, Africa and Latin America and for technical co-operation with Eastern Europe.

SDC has an annual budget of around one billion Swiss francs and some 400 employees. Both abroad and in Switzerland, SDC carries out direct action, finances national institutions for socio-economic development, supports programmes of multilateral organisations, co-finances programmes of Swiss and international NGOs or grants them financial contributions.

The aim of the development co-operation efforts is to fight poverty, helping the persons concerned to help themselves. In particular, it wishes to stimulate the economic and political autonomy of states, to help improve production conditions, provide support in solving ecological problems and to secure better access to information and basic sanitary assistance for the less privileged groups.

In South America, many of SDC's activities concentrate in the Andean zone. For the past 30 years SDC has supported diverse programmes and projects in Ecuador, many of which give priority to the agricultural sector. It has lent assistance to development projects for sustainable agriculture based on irrigated production, covering approximately 5,000 hectares belonging to small farmers - mostly indigenous peasants - in the highlands. The theme of equity is of crucial importance in these projects, both in the planning phase and in the phases of execution, follow-up and evaluation. By support for this book, SDC hopes to contribute to spreading and understanding the theme and to stimulate exchange of experiences about achievements, methodologies, instruments, benefits and limitations that have been encountered.

Netherlands Development Organisation

SNV is a Dutch international development co-operation organisation whose core activity is the exchange of know-how, skills, ideas and technology. SNV has 26 Field Offices in 28 countries in Africa, Latin America, Asia and Europe. Some 700 professionals, of which almost 300 are local staff, are currently collaborating with local population groups in order to achieve a better prospect for the future. In their activities, they work in close co-operation with the population, local governments and NGOs. Most of them work in rural areas or in provincial cities.

The activities of SNV form part of Dutch foreign policy geared to the alleviation of poverty. Because of its many years of experience working in the field, SNV has been able to develop knowledge on technical aspects and on the organisation and implementation of development projects. Because of SNV's local presence, the organisation more easily becomes aware of the nature of specific problems and their possible solutions. To an increasing extent, third parties ask SNV to advise them on the setting up of development activities. At the same time, SNV wants to contribute to the mutual exchange of know-how and skills between organisations in the southern countries themselves. Here, the infrastructure of SNV - the chain of 26 Field Offices and the large number of professionals working at community level - has proved to be important. Not just for establishing the contacts and exchanges in the southern countries themselves but also between those of the south and the north. SNV's priority is to focus on sustainable rural development and to support co-operation between local governments and grass-roots organisations.

SNV's focus on Sustainable Regional Development means that solutions for problems must be sustainable not only in an ecological sense, but also socially, economically and institutionally. These aspects are dealt with in this publication. SNV considers the themes of the present book very urgent and important and, in that sense, it can take pride in knowing that it could contribute to the realisation of this book.

Embassy of the Kingdom of the Netherlands in Quito

The Embassy of the Kingdom of the Netherlands in Quito manages the Dutch Government's programme for technical co-operation in Ecuador. The programme in Ecuador is active in the sectors of rural development, health, environmental issues and women and development. The activities of the Embassy are concentrated in the

Andean Highlands, especially in the Austro region. In the area of Rural Development it finances various projects with irrigation components.

In this context, the Embassy considers it very important to support the initiative of working out the issue and publishing the present book, which gathers the ideas and visions of so many experts involved in the theme, presenting also a great number of experiences. We think that the book may contribute in a significant way to the future of irrigation in Ecuador.

German Agro Action

- was founded in 1962 as part of an international campaign by the United Nations, to combat disaster, poverty and famine by means of private initiatives.
- is under patronage of the President of the Federal Republic of Germany.
- is a non-governmental organisation engaged in world-wide development co-operation. It is sponsored by institutions and associations of political and social importance. It is non-profit-making, has no political affiliations and is not linked to any religious community.
- orients its work on the guiding principle of self-help to enable people to achieve food security through their own efforts.
- supports development, human rights, the environment and rural development, in particular the increase of agricultural yields, with the aim of achieving freedom from hunger and freedom for people.
- fights poverty in developing countries in order to improve the living conditions of the rural population and socially weak sections of the urban population. It employs its resources directly where people are in need.
- provides emergency aid and reconstruction aid in cases of conflict and disaster.
- works with local partner organisations in developing countries in order to lay the foundations of permanent and sustainable development.
- carries out education and public relations work on development political issues in the Federal Republic of Germany. Local action groups support German Agro Action.
- finances its work from donations and public grants. It has committed itself to economical and transparent financial management, for which it received the seal of approval for donation-worthiness from the Central Institute for Social Questions (DZI).

 ICCO

The mission of ICCO, Interchurch organisation for development co-operation, based in Zeist, The Netherlands, is to work towards a world where poverty and injustice are no longer present. The co-financing organisation ICCO receives about NLG 185 million from the Dutch and European governments, to support development projects in many countries in Asia, Africa, the Middle East, Latin America and Eastern Europe. ICCO's work consists in financing activities which stimulate and enable people, in their own way, to organise dignified housing and living conditions. ICCO supports activities related to the themes of, among others, human rights, food security, water management and sanitation, income generating activities, agriculture and rural development, health, education, organisation-building, forestry and sustainable use of forests.

The promotion of a good and socially fair water management is always and in every place a first, necessary step to lay the foundation of food security and sustainable rural development. The experiences described in this publication, about the very complex and interesting water management in the Andes, offer the possibility to learn a lot about water management in general. In this sense, ICCO is convinced that this publication provides an important contribution to the deepening and broadening of the discussions about water management, which finally will result in concrete proposals that aim for realising an appropriate and fair water management, in all world's places.

Wageningen Agricultural University
Irrigation and Water Engineering Group

The Irrigation and Water Engineering Group (IWEG) is a section of the Department of Environmental Sciences at Wageningen Agricultural University, The Netherlands. This University offers programmes for International Masters Degrees and Ph.D. programmes, as well as a substantial number of study programmes for Dutch students who study to Master's level.

IWEG, headed by the Professor of Irrigation and Water Engineering has 12 staff members active in research and education. They give courses for undergraduates within the study programme 'Tropical Land Use'. An Irrigation specialisation at MSc level is offered within the International MSc programme 'Soil and Water' at the University. IWEG also supports an international Ph.D. programme with research in Latin America, Asia and Africa.

Within the group, irrigation is studied and researched as a sociotechnical system, such that the social dimensions of irrigation technology and irrigated agriculture are studied integrally with the physical behaviour of irrigation infrastructure and ecological dynamics of irrigated production. This has enabled to group to pursue current research interests related to irrigation design and implementation processes, irrigation practices of farmers, the reality of water control in irrigation, and the interrelation of irrigation technology and management institutions. Through this framework, the group also researches the dynamics of local and agency action in irrigation, under contemporary public intervention programmes of privatisation, poverty alleviation and modernisation, and also contemporary social struggles shaped by growing resource scarcity and transformation in agrarian relations. Equity is therefore a very prominent concern in these research initiatives.

IWEG seeks actively to collaborate with southern partners, through University collaboration and research programmes. It has direct Inter-University collaboration programmes for research and curriculum development with centres in Africa, Asia and Latin America and participates in various networks. It undertakes advisory work related to projects and programmes on poverty alleviation and food security through irrigation development, and on design operations and institutional development in irrigation systems. IWEG seeks to promote south-south collaboration in research and education, and attempts wherever possible to work with local counterparts in research and advisory work, including NGOs, water user organisations and staff in public water resource agencies.

Colophon

The present book was written, composed and edited on a non-profit basis. The Authors and the General Editors did not receive any payments for their work.

Figures, maps and tables have been elaborated by the articles' Authors, in some cases with support from the Publisher. The map in Chapter 27 (Chile) and the map "South America and the Andes" were made by LMB-productions. The paintings (used for cover and introductions to the Parts) were made by Humberto Latacunga especially for this book. The design of the introductions to the Parts and Figure 1 were made by Robert Keun. He also prepared the design of the book's cover. Cover design, lay-out and printing of the book was done by Van Gorcum.

Translations and technical revisions were done by Patricio A. Mena Vàsconez, Samuel Dubois, Sara van Otterloo and the General Editors, with support in the final phase from Isabel Palpieris.

SDC/COSUDE, SNV, ICCO, Royal Dutch Embassy Ecuador, German Agro Action and IWEG/Wageningen Agricultural University gave financial support to the publication. SNV and IWEG/WAU also supported the editing process.

The authors themselves are responsible for the opinions expressed in their texts. The above institutions do not bear responsibility for any of the contents of this book.